Lincoln
Rear-wheel drive
Automotive
Repair
Manual

by Mark Ryan
and John H Haynes
Member of the Guild of Motoring Writers

Models covered:

1970 through 1987 Continental,
1981 through 1996 Town Car and
1970 through 1992 Mark Series models

Does not include Versailles models, V6 or diesel engine information

(12Y3 - 59010)
(2117)

ABCDE
FGHIJ
KLMN

Haynes Publishing Group
Sparkford Nr Yeovil
Somerset BA22 7JJ England

Haynes North America, Inc
861 Lawrence Drive
Newbury Park
California 91320 USA

Acknowledgements

Technical writers who contributed to this project include Rob Maddox, Mike Stubblefield and Larry Warren.

© **Haynes North America, Inc. 1995, 1996**

With permission from J.H. Haynes & Co. Ltd.

A book in the Haynes Automotive Repair Manual Series

Printed in the U.S.A.

ISBN 1 56392 240 1

Library of Congress Catalog Card Number 96-78645

While every attempt is made to ensure that the information in this manual is correct, no liability can be accepted by the authors or publishers for loss, damage or injury caused by any errors in, or omissions from, the information given.

Contents

Haynes mechanic, author and photographer with 1988 Lincoln Town Car

About this manual

Its purpose

The purpose of this manual is to help you get the best value from your vehicle. It can do so in several ways. It can help you decide what work must be done, even if you choose to have it done by a dealer service department or a repair shop; it provides information and procedures for routine maintenance and servicing; and it offers diagnostic and repair procedures to follow when trouble occurs.

We hope you use the manual to tackle the work yourself. For many simpler jobs, doing it yourself may be quicker than arranging an appointment to get the vehicle into a shop and making the trips to leave it and pick it up. More importantly, a lot of money can be saved by avoiding the expense the shop must pass on to you to cover its labor and overhead costs. An added benefit is the sense of satisfaction and accomplishment that you feel after doing the job yourself.

Using the manual

The manual is divided into Chapters. Each Chapter is divided into numbered Sections, which are headed in bold type between horizontal lines. Each Section consists of consecutively numbered paragraphs.

At the beginning of each numbered Section you will be referred to any illustrations which apply to the procedures in that Section. The reference numbers used in illustration captions pinpoint the pertinent Section and the Step within that Section. That is, illustration 3.2 means the illustration refers to Section 3 and Step (or paragraph) 2 within that Section.

Procedures, once described in the text, are not normally repeated. When it's necessary to refer to another Chapter, the reference will be given as Chapter and Section number. Cross references given without use of the word "Chapter" apply to Sections and/or paragraphs in the same Chapter. For example, "see Section 8" means in the same Chapter.

References to the left or right side of the vehicle assume you are sitting in the driver's seat, facing forward.

Even though we have prepared this manual with extreme care, neither the publisher nor the author can accept responsibility for any errors in, or omissions from, the information given.

NOTE

A **Note** provides information necessary to properly complete a procedure or information which will make the procedure easier to understand.

CAUTION

A **Caution** provides a special procedure or special steps which must be taken while completing the procedure where the Caution is found. Not heeding a Caution can result in damage to the assembly being worked on.

WARNING

A **Warning** provides a special procedure or special steps which must be taken while completing the procedure where the Warning is found. Not heeding a Warning can result in personal injury.

Introduction to the Lincoln Continental, Town Car and Mark Series

The models covered by this manual are available in two-and four-door sedan body styles. These cars have the conventional front engine/rear-wheel drive layout. All are equipped with a carbureted or fuel-injected V8 engine.

Power from the engine is transferred through an automatic transmission to the differential mounted in the solid rear axle assembly by a tubular driveshaft incorporating universal joints. Axles inside the assembly carry power from the differential to the rear wheels.

Suspension is independent in the front, with either strut-type or upper and lower control arms used to locate the knuckle assembly at each wheel. The solid rear axle is located by three or four suspension arms, depending on model and year. The front and rear suspension features coil springs and shock absorbers. Some models are equipped with air suspension.

The steering gear unit is mounted in front of the steering arms. Both conventional and rack-and-pinion type is used, depending on model. Power assisted steering is standard.

The brakes are disc at the front and drum or disc (later models) at the rear with vacuum assist standard. Some models are equipped with an Anti-lock Braking System (ABS).

Vehicle identification numbers

Modifications are a continuing and unpublicized process in vehicle manufacturing. Since spare parts lists and manuals are compiled on a numerical basis, the individual vehicle numbers are necessary to correctly identify the component required.

Vehicle Identification Number (VIN)

This very important identification number is stamped on a plate attached to the dashboard inside the windshield on the driver's side of the vehicle (see illustration). The VIN also appears on the Vehicle Certificate of Title and Registration. It contains information such as where and when the vehicle was manufactured, the model year and the body style.

VIN engine and model year codes

Two particularly important pieces of information found in the VIN are the engine code and the model year code.

On 1980 and earlier models, counting from the left, the model year code is the first digit and the engine code is the 5th digit (see illustration).

On 1981 and later models, counting from the left, the engine code is the 8th digit and the model year code is the 10th digit (see illustration).

Engine codes:

A	460 cu in
S	400 cu in
H	351 cu in
F	302 cu in
W	4.6L OHC V8

Model year codes:

0	1970
1	1971
2	1972
3	1973
4	1974
5	1975
6	1976
7	1977
8	1978
9	1979
0	1980
B	1981
C	1982
D	1983
E	1984
F	1985
G	1986
H	1987
J	1988
K	1989
L	1990
M	1991
N	1992
P	1993
R	1994
S	1995

Vehicle Certification Label

The Vehicle Certification Label is attached to the driver's side door. Information on this label includes the name of the manufacturer, the month and year of production, the Gross Vehicle Weight Rating (GVWR), the Gross Axle Weight Rating (GAWR) and the certification statement.

Engine numbers

Labels containing the engine code, engine number and build date can be found on the valve cover. The engine number is also stamped onto a machined pad on an external surface of the engine block.

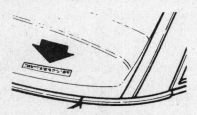

The VIN number is visible through the driver's side windshield

Example (1980 and earlier models):

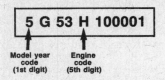

On 1980 and earlier models, the engine code is the 5th digit of the VIN number; the model year code is the first digit

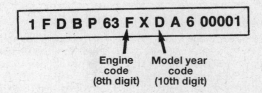

On 1981 and later models, the engine code is the 8th digit of the VIN number; the model year code is the 10th digit

Buying parts

Replacement parts are available from many sources, which generally fall into one of two categories - authorized dealer parts departments and independent retail auto parts stores. Our advice concerning these parts is as follows:

Retail auto parts stores: Good auto parts stores will stock frequently needed components which wear out relatively fast, such as clutch components, exhaust systems, brake parts, tune-up parts, etc. These stores often supply new or reconditioned parts on an exchange basis, which can save a considerable amount of money. Discount auto parts stores are often very good places to buy materials and parts needed for general vehicle maintenance such as oil, grease, filters, spark plugs, belts, touch-up paint, bulbs, etc. They also usually sell tools and general accessories, have convenient hours, charge lower prices and can often be found not far from home.

Authorized dealer parts department: This is the best source for parts which are unique to the vehicle and not generally available elsewhere (such as major engine parts, transmission parts, trim pieces, etc.).

Warranty information: If the vehicle is still covered under warranty, be sure that any replacement parts purchased - regardless of the source - do not invalidate the warranty!

To be sure of obtaining the correct parts, have engine and chassis numbers available and, if possible, take the old parts along for positive identification.

Maintenance techniques, tools and working facilities

Maintenance techniques

There are a number of techniques involved in maintenance and repair that will be referred to throughout this manual. Application of these techniques will enable the home mechanic to be more efficient, better organized and capable of performing the various tasks properly, which will ensure that the repair job is thorough and complete.

Fasteners

Fasteners are nuts, bolts, studs and screws used to hold two or more parts together. There are a few things to keep in mind when working with fasteners. Almost all of them use a locking device of some type, either a lockwasher, locknut, locking tab or thread adhesive. All threaded fasteners should be clean and straight, with undamaged threads and undamaged corners on the hex head where the wrench fits. Develop the habit of replacing all damaged nuts and bolts with new ones. Special locknuts with nylon or fiber inserts can only be used once. If they are removed, they lose their locking ability and must be replaced with new ones.

Rusted nuts and bolts should be treated with a penetrating fluid to ease removal and prevent breakage. Some mechanics use turpentine in a spout-type oil can, which works quite well. After applying the rust penetrant, let it work for a few minutes before trying to loosen the nut or bolt. Badly rusted fasteners may have to be chiseled or sawed off or removed with a special nut breaker, available at tool stores.

If a bolt or stud breaks off in an assembly, it can be drilled and removed with a special tool commonly available for this purpose. Most automotive machine shops can perform this task, as well as other repair procedures, such as the repair of threaded holes that have been stripped out.

Flat washers and lockwashers, when removed from an assembly, should always be replaced exactly as removed. Replace any damaged washers with new ones. Never use a lockwasher on any soft metal surface (such as aluminum), thin sheet metal or plastic.

Fastener sizes

For a number of reasons, automobile manufacturers are making wider and wider use of metric fasteners. Therefore, it is important to be able to tell the difference between standard (sometimes called U.S. or SAE) and metric hardware, since they cannot be interchanged.

All bolts, whether standard or metric, are sized according to diameter, thread pitch and length. For example, a standard 1/2 - 13 x 1 bolt is 1/2 inch in diameter, has 13 threads per inch and is 1 inch long. An M12 - 1.75 x 25 metric bolt is 12 mm in diameter, has a thread pitch of 1.75 mm (the distance between threads) and is 25 mm long. The two bolts are nearly identical, and easily confused, but they are not interchangeable.

In addition to the differences in diameter, thread pitch and length, metric and standard bolts can also be distinguished by examining the bolt heads. To begin with, the distance across the flats on a standard bolt head is measured in inches, while the same dimension on a metric bolt is sized in millimeters (the same is true for nuts). As a result, a standard wrench should not be used on a metric bolt and a metric wrench should not be used on a standard bolt. Also, most standard bolts have slashes radiating out from the center of the head to denote the grade or strength of the bolt, which is an indication of the amount of torque that can be applied to it. The greater the number of slashes, the greater the strength of the bolt. Grades 0 through 5 are commonly used on automobiles. Metric bolts have a property class (grade) number, rather than a slash, molded into their heads to indicate bolt strength. In this case, the higher the number, the stronger the bolt. Property class numbers 8.8, 9.8 and 10.9 are commonly used on automobiles.

Strength markings can also be used to distinguish standard hex nuts from metric hex nuts. Many standard nuts have dots stamped into one side, while metric nuts are marked with a number. The greater the number of dots, or the higher the number, the greater the strength of the nut.

Metric studs are also marked on their ends according to property class (grade). Larger studs are numbered (the same as metric bolts), while smaller studs carry a geometric code to denote grade.

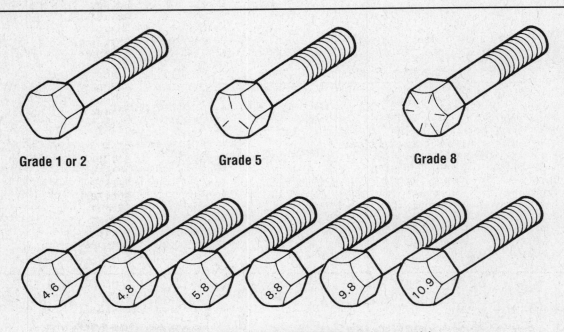

Grade 1 or 2   Grade 5   Grade 8

Bolt strength markings (top - standard/SAE/USS; bottom - metric)

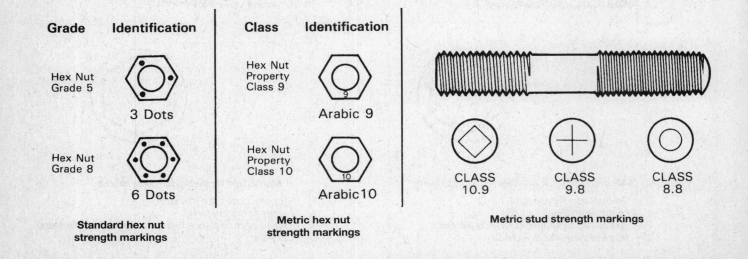

Standard hex nut strength markings

Metric hex nut strength markings

Metric stud strength markings

It should be noted that many fasteners, especially Grades 0 through 2, have no distinguishing marks on them. When such is the case, the only way to determine whether it is standard or metric is to measure the thread pitch or compare it to a known fastener of the same size.

Standard fasteners are often referred to as SAE, as opposed to metric. However, it should be noted that SAE technically refers to a non-metric fine thread fastener only. Coarse thread non-metric fasteners are referred to as USS sizes.

Since fasteners of the same size (both standard and metric) may have different strength ratings, be sure to reinstall any bolts, studs or nuts removed from your vehicle in their original locations. Also, when replacing a fastener with a new one, make sure that the new one has a strength rating equal to or greater than the original.

Tightening sequences and procedures

Most threaded fasteners should be tightened to a specific torque value (torque is the twisting force applied to a threaded component such as a nut or bolt). Overtightening the fastener can weaken it and cause it to break, while undertightening can cause it to eventually come loose. Bolts, screws and studs, depending on the material they are made of and their thread diameters, have specific torque values, many of which are noted in the Specifications at the beginning of each Chapter. Be sure to follow the torque recommendations closely. For fasteners not assigned a specific torque, a general torque value chart is presented here as a guide. These torque values are for dry (unlubricated) fasteners threaded into steel or cast iron (not aluminum). As was previously mentioned, the size and grade of a fastener determine the amount of torque that can safely be applied to it. The

Metric thread sizes	Ft-lbs	Nm
M-6	6 to 9	9 to 12
M-8	14 to 21	19 to 28
M-10	28 to 40	38 to 54
M-12	50 to 71	68 to 96
M-14	80 to 140	109 to 154
Pipe thread sizes		
1/8	5 to 8	7 to 10
1/4	12 to 18	17 to 24
3/8	22 to 33	30 to 44
1/2	25 to 35	34 to 47
U.S. thread sizes		
1/4 - 20	6 to 9	9 to 12
5/16 - 18	12 to 18	17 to 24
5/16 - 24	14 to 20	19 to 27
3/8 - 16	22 to 32	30 to 43
3/8 - 24	27 to 38	37 to 51
7/16 - 14	40 to 55	55 to 74
7/16 - 20	40 to 60	55 to 81
1/2 - 13	55 to 80	75 to 108

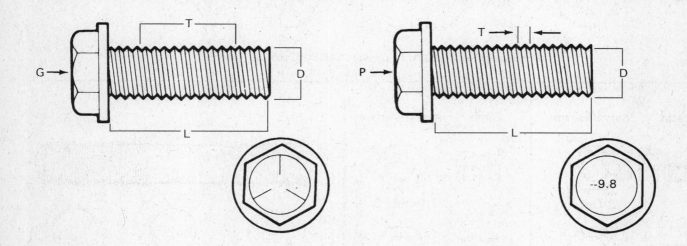

Standard (SAE and USS) bolt dimensions/grade marks

G   Grade marks (bolt length)
L   Length (in inches)
T   Thread pitch (number of threads per inch)
D   Nominal diameter (in inches)

Metric bolt dimensions/grade marks

P   Property class (bolt strength)
L   Length (in millimeters)
T   Thread pitch (distance between threads in millimeters)
D   Diameter

figures listed here are approximate for Grade 2 and Grade 3 fasteners. Higher grades can tolerate higher torque values.

Fasteners laid out in a pattern, such as cylinder head bolts, oil pan bolts, differential cover bolts, etc., must be loosened or tightened in sequence to avoid warping the component. This sequence will normally be shown in the appropriate Chapter. If a specific pattern is not given, the following procedures can be used to prevent warping.

Initially, the bolts or nuts should be assembled finger-tight only. Next, they should be tightened one full turn each, in a criss-cross or diagonal pattern. After each one has been tightened one full turn, return to the first one and tighten them all one-half turn, following the same pattern. Finally, tighten each of them one-quarter turn at a time until each fastener has been tightened to the proper torque. To loosen and remove the fasteners, the procedure would be reversed.

Component disassembly

Component disassembly should be done with care and purpose to help ensure that the parts go back together properly. Always keep track of the sequence in which parts are removed. Make note of special characteristics or marks on parts that can be installed more than one way, such as a grooved thrust washer on a shaft. It is a good idea to lay the disassembled parts out on a clean surface in the order that they were removed. It may also be helpful to make sketches or take instant photos of components before removal.

When removing fasteners from a component, keep track of their locations. Sometimes threading a bolt back in a part, or putting the washers and nut back on a stud, can prevent mix-ups later. If nuts and bolts cannot be returned to their original locations, they should be kept in a compartmented box or a series of small boxes. A cupcake or muffin tin is ideal for this purpose, since each cavity can hold the bolts and nuts from a particular area (i.e. oil pan bolts, valve cover bolts, engine mount bolts, etc.). A pan of this type is especially helpful when working on assemblies with very small parts, such as the carburetor, alternator, valve train or interior dash and trim pieces. The cavities can be marked with paint or tape to identify the contents.

Whenever wiring looms, harnesses or connectors are separated, it is a good idea to identify the two halves with numbered pieces of masking tape so they can be easily reconnected.

Gasket sealing surfaces

Throughout any vehicle, gaskets are used to seal the mating surfaces between two parts and keep lubricants, fluids, vacuum or pressure contained in an assembly.

Many times these gaskets are coated with a liquid or paste-type gasket sealing compound before assembly. Age, heat and pressure can sometimes cause the two parts to stick together so tightly that they are very difficult to separate. Often, the assembly can be loosened by striking it with a soft-face hammer near the mating surfaces. A regular hammer can be used if a block of wood is placed between the hammer and the part. Do not hammer on cast parts or parts that could be easily damaged. With any particularly stubborn part, always recheck to make sure that every fastener has been removed.

Avoid using a screwdriver or bar to pry apart an assembly, as they can easily mar the gasket sealing surfaces of the parts, which must remain smooth. If prying is absolutely necessary, use an old broom handle, but keep in mind that extra clean up will be necessary if the wood splinters.

After the parts are separated, the old gasket must be carefully scraped off and the gasket surfaces cleaned. Stubborn gasket material can be soaked with rust penetrant or treated with a special chemical to soften it so it can be easily scraped off. A scraper can be fashioned from a piece of copper tubing by flattening and sharpening one end. Copper is recommended because it is usually softer than the surfaces to be scraped, which reduces the chance of gouging the part. Some gaskets can be removed with a wire brush, but regardless of the method used, the mating surfaces must be left clean and smooth. If for some reason the gasket surface is gouged, then a gasket sealer thick enough to fill scratches will have to be used during reassembly of the components. For most applications, a non-drying (or semi-drying) gasket sealer should be used.

Hose removal tips

Warning: *If the vehicle is equipped with air conditioning, do not disconnect any of the A/C hoses without first having the system depressurized by a dealer service department or a service station.*

Hose removal precautions closely parallel gasket removal precautions. Avoid scratching or gouging the surface that the hose mates against or the connection may leak. This is especially true for radiator hoses. Because of various chemical reactions, the rubber in hoses can bond itself to the metal spigot that the hose fits over. To remove a hose, first loosen the hose clamps that secure it to the spigot. Then, with slip-joint pliers, grab the hose at the clamp and rotate it around the spigot. Work it back and forth until it is completely free, then pull it off. Silicone or other lubricants will ease removal if they can be applied between the hose and the outside of the spigot. Apply the same lubricant to the inside of the hose and the outside of the spigot to simplify installation.

As a last resort (and if the hose is to be replaced with a new one anyway), the rubber can be slit with a knife and the hose peeled from the spigot. If this must be done, be careful that the metal connection is not damaged.

If a hose clamp is broken or damaged, do not reuse it. Wire-type clamps usually weaken with age, so it is a good idea to replace them with screw-type clamps whenever a hose is removed.

Tools

A selection of good tools is a basic requirement for anyone who plans to maintain and repair his or her own vehicle. For the owner who has few tools, the initial investment might seem high, but when compared to the spiraling costs of professional auto maintenance and repair, it is a wise one.

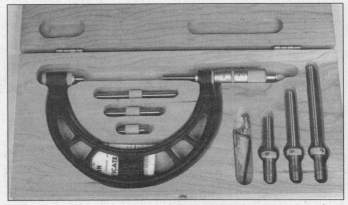

Micrometer set

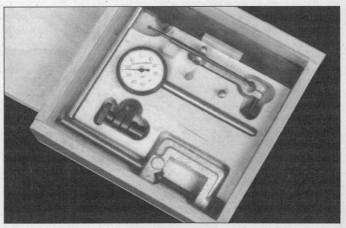

Dial indicator set

Dial caliper

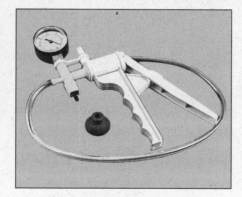

Hand-operated vacuum pump

Timing light

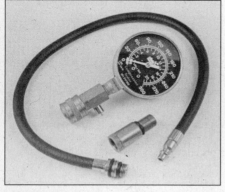

Compression gauge with spark plug hole adapter

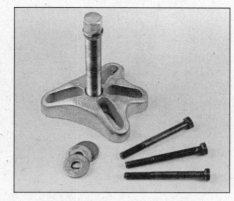

Damper/steering wheel puller

General purpose puller

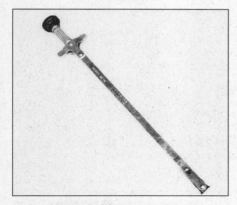

Hydraulic lifter removal tool

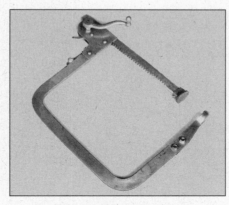

Valve spring compressor

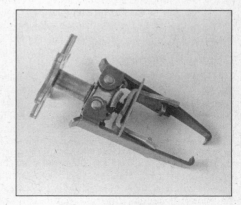

Valve spring compressor

Ridge reamer

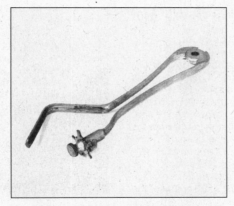

Piston ring groove cleaning tool

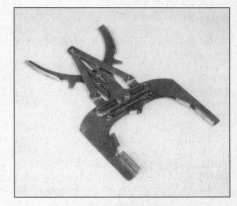

Ring removal/installation tool

Ring compressor

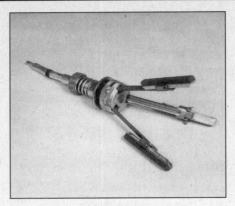

Cylinder hone

Brake hold-down spring tool

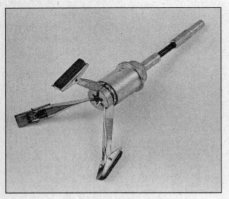

Brake cylinder hone

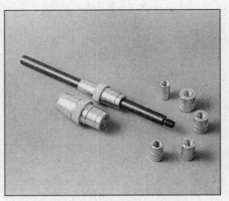

Clutch plate alignment tool

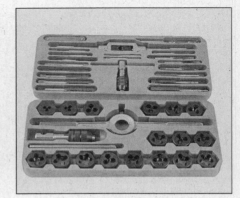

Tap and die set

To help the owner decide which tools are needed to perform the tasks detailed in this manual, the following tool lists are offered: *Maintenance and minor repair, Repair/overhaul* and *Special*.

The newcomer to practical mechanics should start off with the *maintenance and minor repair* tool kit, which is adequate for the simpler jobs performed on a vehicle. Then, as confidence and experience grow, the owner can tackle more difficult tasks, buying additional tools as they are needed. Eventually the basic kit will be expanded into the *repair and overhaul* tool set. Over a period of time, the experienced do-it-yourselfer will assemble a tool set complete enough for most repair and overhaul procedures and will add tools from the special category when it is felt that the expense is justified by the frequency of use.

Maintenance and minor repair tool kit

The tools in this list should be considered the minimum required for performance of routine maintenance, servicing and minor repair work. We recommend the purchase of combination wrenches (box-end and open-end combined in one wrench). While more expensive than open end wrenches, they offer the advantages of both types of wrench.

Combination wrench set (1/4-inch to 1 inch or 6 mm to 19 mm)
Adjustable wrench, 8 inch
Spark plug wrench with rubber insert
Spark plug gap adjusting tool
Feeler gauge set
Brake bleeder wrench
Standard screwdriver (5/16-inch x 6 inch)
Phillips screwdriver (No. 2 x 6 inch)
Combination pliers - 6 inch
Hacksaw and assortment of blades
Tire pressure gauge
Grease gun

Oil can
Fine emery cloth
Wire brush
Battery post and cable cleaning tool
Oil filter wrench
Funnel (medium size)
Safety goggles
Jackstands (2)
Drain pan

Note: *If basic tune-ups are going to be part of routine maintenance, it will be necessary to purchase a good quality stroboscopic timing light and combination tachometer/dwell meter. Although they are included in the list of special tools, it is mentioned here because they are absolutely necessary for tuning most vehicles properly.*

Repair and overhaul tool set

These tools are essential for anyone who plans to perform major repairs and are in addition to those in the maintenance and minor repair tool kit. Included is a comprehensive set of sockets which, though expensive, are invaluable because of their versatility, especially when various extensions and drives are available. We recommend the 1/2-inch drive over the 3/8-inch drive. Although the larger drive is bulky and more expensive, it has the capacity of accepting a very wide range of large sockets. Ideally, however, the mechanic should have a 3/8-inch drive set and a 1/2-inch drive set.

Socket set(s)
Reversible ratchet
Extension - 10 inch
Universal joint
Torque wrench (same size drive as sockets)
Ball peen hammer - 8 ounce
Soft-face hammer (plastic/rubber)
Standard screwdriver (1/4-inch x 6 inch)

Standard screwdriver (stubby - 5/16-inch)
Phillips screwdriver (No. 3 x 8 inch)
Phillips screwdriver (stubby - No. 2)
Pliers - vise grip
Pliers - lineman's
Pliers - needle nose
Pliers - snap-ring (internal and external)
Cold chisel - 1/2-inch
Scribe
Scraper (made from flattened copper tubing)
Centerpunch
Pin punches (1/16, 1/8, 3/16-inch)
Steel rule/straightedge - 12 inch
Allen wrench set (1/8 to 3/8-inch or 4 mm to 10 mm)
A selection of files
Wire brush (large)
Jackstands (second set)
Jack (scissor or hydraulic type)

Note: *Another tool which is often useful is an electric drill with a chuck capacity of 3/8-inch and a set of good quality drill bits.*

Special tools

The tools in this list include those which are not used regularly, are expensive to buy, or which need to be used in accordance with their manufacturer's instructions. Unless these tools will be used frequently, it is not very economical to purchase many of them. A consideration would be to split the cost and use between yourself and a friend or friends. In addition, most of these tools can be obtained from a tool rental shop on a temporary basis.

This list primarily contains only those tools and instruments widely available to the public, and not those special tools produced by the vehicle manufacturer for distribution to dealer service departments. Occasionally, references to the manufacturer's special tools are included in the text of this manual. Generally, an alternative method of doing the job without the special tool is offered. However, sometimes there is no alternative to their use. Where this is the case, and the tool cannot be purchased or borrowed, the work should be turned over to the dealer service department or an automotive repair shop.

Valve spring compressor
Piston ring groove cleaning tool
Piston ring compressor
Piston ring installation tool
Cylinder compression gauge
Cylinder ridge reamer
Cylinder surfacing hone
Cylinder bore gauge
Micrometers and/or dial calipers
Hydraulic lifter removal tool
Balljoint separator
Universal-type puller
Impact screwdriver
Dial indicator set
Stroboscopic timing light (inductive pick-up)
Hand operated vacuum/pressure pump
Tachometer/dwell meter
Universal electrical multimeter
Cable hoist
Brake spring removal and installation tools
Floor jack

Buying tools

For the do-it-yourselfer who is just starting to get involved in vehicle maintenance and repair, there are a number of options available when purchasing tools. If maintenance and minor repair is the extent of the work to be done, the purchase of individual tools is satisfactory. If, on the other hand, extensive work is planned, it would

be a good idea to purchase a modest tool set from one of the large retail chain stores. A set can usually be bought at a substantial savings over the individual tool prices, and they often come with a tool box. As additional tools are needed, add-on sets, individual tools and a larger tool box can be purchased to expand the tool selection. Building a tool set gradually allows the cost of the tools to be spread over a longer period of time and gives the mechanic the freedom to choose only those tools that will actually be used.

Tool stores will often be the only source of some of the special tools that are needed, but regardless of where tools are bought, try to avoid cheap ones, especially when buying screwdrivers and sockets, because they won't last very long. The expense involved in replacing cheap tools will eventually be greater than the initial cost of quality tools.

Care and maintenance of tools

Good tools are expensive, so it makes sense to treat them with respect. Keep them clean and in usable condition and store them properly when not in use. Always wipe off any dirt, grease or metal chips before putting them away. Never leave tools lying around in the work area. Upon completion of a job, always check closely under the hood for tools that may have been left there so they won't get lost during a test drive.

Some tools, such as screwdrivers, pliers, wrenches and sockets, can be hung on a panel mounted on the garage or workshop wall, while others should be kept in a tool box or tray. Measuring instruments, gauges, meters, etc. must be carefully stored where they cannot be damaged by weather or impact from other tools.

When tools are used with care and stored properly, they will last a very long time. Even with the best of care, though, tools will wear out if used frequently. When a tool is damaged or worn out, replace it. Subsequent jobs will be safer and more enjoyable if you do.

Working facilities

Not to be overlooked when discussing tools is the workshop. If anything more than routine maintenance is to be carried out, some sort of suitable work area is essential.

It is understood, and appreciated, that many home mechanics do not have a good workshop or garage available, and end up removing an engine or doing major repairs outside. It is recommended, however, that the overhaul or repair be completed under the cover of a roof.

A clean, flat workbench or table of comfortable working height is an absolute necessity. The workbench should be equipped with a vise that has a jaw opening of at least four inches.

As mentioned previously, some clean, dry storage space is also required for tools, as well as the lubricants, fluids, cleaning solvents, etc. which soon become necessary.

Sometimes waste oil and fluids, drained from the engine or cooling system during normal maintenance or repairs, present a disposal problem. To avoid pouring them on the ground or into a sewage system, pour the used fluids into large containers, seal them with caps and take them to an authorized disposal site or recycling center. Plastic jugs, such as old antifreeze containers, are ideal for this purpose.

Always keep a supply of old newspapers and clean rags available. Old towels are excellent for mopping up spills. Many mechanics use rolls of paper towels for most work because they are readily available and disposable. To help keep the area under the vehicle clean, a large cardboard box can be cut open and flattened to protect the garage or shop floor.

Whenever working over a painted surface, such as when leaning over a fender to service something under the hood, always cover it with an old blanket or bedspread to protect the finish. Vinyl covered pads, made especially for this purpose, are available at auto parts stores.

Jacking and towing

Jacking

Warning: *The jack supplied with the vehicle should only be used for changing a tire or placing jackstands under the frame. Never work under the vehicle or start the engine while this jack is being used as the only means of support.*

The vehicle should be located on level ground. Place the shift lever in Park. Block the wheel diagonally opposite the wheel being changed. Set the parking brake. On models equipped with air suspension, turn off the air suspension switch before raising the vehicle.

Remove the spare tire and jack from stowage. If equipped with anti-theft wheel covers, pry off the ornament and remove the bolt with the special key provided with the vehicle **(see illustration)**. Remove the wheel cover and trim ring (if so equipped) with the tapered end of the lug nut wrench by inserting and twisting the handle and then prying against the back of the wheel cover. Loosen, but do not remove, the lug nuts (one-half turn is sufficient).

1990 and earlier models

These models are equipped with a ratchet-type jack designed to lift one corner of the car from either the front or rear bumper **(see illustration)**. Assemble the jack by inserting the bottom end securely into the base. With the lever on the jack in the UP position, pull the ratchet assembly up and insert the hook into the slot in the underside of the bumper. With the base of the jack angled in slightly toward the vehicle and using the lug wrench as a handle, raise the vehicle enough to remove the wheel.

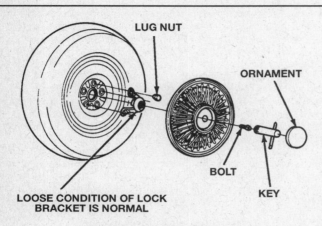

LUG NUT

ORNAMENT

BOLT

KEY

LOOSE CONDITION OF LOCK BRACKET IS NORMAL

Anti-theft wheel cover details

1991 and later models

Place the scissors-type jack under the side of the vehicle and adjust the jack height until it fits between the notches in the vertical rocker panel flange nearest the wheel being changed. There is a front and rear jacking point on each side of the vehicle **(see illustration)**.

Turn the jack handle clockwise until the tire clears the ground. Remove the lug nuts and pull the wheel off. Replace it with the spare.

Install the lug nuts with the beveled edges facing in. Tighten them

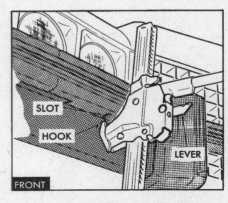

SLOT

HOOK

LEVER

FRONT

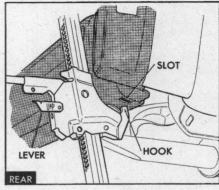

SLOT

LEVER

HOOK

REAR

On earlier models, a bumper jack is used to raise the vehicle - it either fits into a slot on the bumper, as shown here, or hooks onto the lower edge of the bumper at a specific location (see your owner's manual for the exact location)

snugly. Don't attempt to tighten them completely until the vehicle is lowered or it could slip off the jack. Lower the vehicle. Remove the jack and tighten the lug nuts in a criss-cross pattern.

Install the cover (and trim ring, if used) and be sure it's snapped into place all the way around.

Stow the tire, jack and wrench. Unblock the wheels.

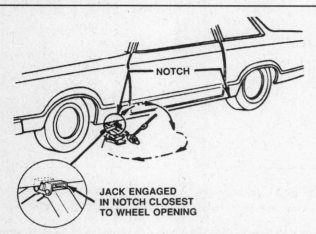

NOTCH

JACK ENGAGED
IN NOTCH CLOSEST
TO WHEEL OPENING

Place the jack so it engages in the notch in the rocker panel nearest the wheel to be raised

Towing

As a general rule, the vehicle should be towed with the rear wheels off the ground. If they can't be raised, either place them on a dolly or disconnect the driveshaft from the differential. When a vehicle is towed with the rear wheels raised, the steering wheel must be clamped in the straight ahead position with a special device designed for use during towing The ignition key must be in the OFF position, since the steering lock mechanism isn't strong enough to hold the front wheels straight while towing.

Vehicles equipped with an automatic transmission can be towed from the front only with all four wheels on the ground, provided that speeds don't exceed 35 mph and the distance is not over 50 miles. Before towing, check the transmission fluid level (see Chapter 1). If the level is below the HOT line on the dipstick, add fluid or use a towing dolly. Release the parking brake, put the transmission in Neutral and place the ignition key in the OFF position. There's no distance limitation when towing with either the rear wheels off the ground or the driveshaft disconnected, but don't exceed 50 mph.

Equipment specifically designed for towing should be used. It should be attached to the main structural members of the vehicle, not the bumpers or brackets.

Safety is a major consideration when towing and all applicable state and local laws must be obeyed. A safety chain system must be used at all times. Remember that power steering and power brakes will not work with the engine off.

Booster battery (jump) starting

Observe these precautions when using a booster battery to start a vehicle:

a) *Before connecting the booster battery, make sure the ignition switch is in the Off position.*
b) *Turn off the lights, heater and other electrical loads.*
c) *Your eyes should be shielded. Safety goggles are a good idea.*
d) *Make sure the booster battery is the same voltage as the dead one in the vehicle.*
e) *The two vehicles MUST NOT TOUCH each other!*
f) *Make sure the transaxle is in Neutral (manual) or Park (automatic).*
g) *If the booster battery is not a maintenance-free type, remove the vent caps and lay a cloth over the vent holes.*

Connect the red jumper cable to the positive (+) terminals of each battery **(see illustration)**.

Connect one end of the black jumper cable to the negative (-) terminal of the booster battery. The other end of this cable should be connected to a good ground on the vehicle to be started, such as a bolt or bracket on the body.

Start the engine using the booster battery, then, with the engine running at idle speed, disconnect the jumper cables in the reverse order of connection.

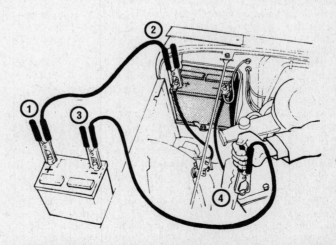

Make the booster battery cable connections in the numerical order shown (note that the negative cable of the booster battery is NOT attached the negative terminal of the dead battery)

Automotive chemicals and lubricants

A number of automotive chemicals and lubricants are available for use during vehicle maintenance and repair. They include a wide variety of products ranging from cleaning solvents and degreasers to lubricants and protective sprays for rubber, plastic and vinyl.

Cleaners

Carburetor cleaner and choke cleaner is a strong solvent for gum, varnish and carbon. Most carburetor cleaners leave a dry-type lubricant film which will not harden or gum up. Because of this film it is not recommended for use on electrical components.

Brake system cleaner is used to remove grease and brake fluid from the brake system, where clean surfaces are absolutely necessary. It leaves no residue and often eliminates brake squeal caused by contaminants.

Electrical cleaner removes oxidation, corrosion and carbon deposits from electrical contacts, restoring full current flow. It can also be used to clean spark plugs, carburetor jets, voltage regulators and other parts where an oil-free surface is desired.

Demoisturants remove water and moisture from electrical components such as alternators, voltage regulators, electrical connectors and fuse blocks. They are non-conductive, non-corrosive and non-flammable.

Degreasers are heavy-duty solvents used to remove grease from the outside of the engine and from chassis components. They can be sprayed or brushed on and, depending on the type, are rinsed off either with water or solvent.

Lubricants

Motor oil is the lubricant formulated for use in engines. It normally contains a wide variety of additives to prevent corrosion and reduce foaming and wear. Motor oil comes in various weights (viscosity ratings) from 5 to 80. The recommended weight of the oil depends on the season, temperature and the demands on the engine. Light oil is used in cold climates and under light load conditions. Heavy oil is used in hot climates and where high loads are encountered. Multi-viscosity oils are designed to have characteristics of both light and heavy oils and are available in a number of weights from 5W-20 to 20W-50.

Gear oil is designed to be used in differentials, manual transmissions and other areas where high-temperature lubrication is required.

Chassis and wheel bearing grease is a heavy grease used where increased loads and friction are encountered, such as for wheel bearings, balljoints, tie-rod ends and universal joints.

High-temperature wheel bearing grease is designed to withstand the extreme temperatures encountered by wheel bearings in disc brake equipped vehicles. It usually contains molybdenum disulfide (moly), which is a dry-type lubricant.

White grease is a heavy grease for metal-to-metal applications where water is a problem. White grease stays soft under both low and high temperatures (usually from -100 to +190-degrees F), and will not wash off or dilute in the presence of water.

Assembly lube is a special extreme pressure lubricant, usually containing moly, used to lubricate high-load parts (such as main and rod bearings and cam lobes) for initial start-up of a new engine. The assembly lube lubricates the parts without being squeezed out or washed away until the engine oiling system begins to function.

Silicone lubricants are used to protect rubber, plastic, vinyl and nylon parts.

Graphite lubricants are used where oils cannot be used due to contamination problems, such as in locks. The dry graphite will lubricate metal parts while remaining uncontaminated by dirt, water, oil or acids. It is electrically conductive and will not foul electrical contacts in locks such as the ignition switch.

Moly penetrants loosen and lubricate frozen, rusted and corroded fasteners and prevent future rusting or freezing.

Heat-sink grease is a special electrically non-conductive grease that is used for mounting electronic ignition modules where it is essential that heat is transferred away from the module.

Sealants

RTV sealant is one of the most widely used gasket compounds. Made from silicone, RTV is air curing, it seals, bonds, waterproofs, fills surface irregularities, remains flexible, doesn't shrink, is relatively easy to remove, and is used as a supplementary sealer with almost all low and medium temperature gaskets.

Anaerobic sealant is much like RTV in that it can be used either to seal gaskets or to form gaskets by itself. It remains flexible, is solvent resistant and fills surface imperfections. The difference between an anaerobic sealant and an RTV-type sealant is in the curing. RTV cures when exposed to air, while an anaerobic sealant cures only in the absence of air. This means that an anaerobic sealant cures only after the assembly of parts, sealing them together.

Thread and pipe sealant is used for sealing hydraulic and pneumatic fittings and vacuum lines. It is usually made from a Teflon compound, and comes in a spray, a paint-on liquid and as a wrap-around tape.

Chemicals

Anti-seize compound prevents seizing, galling, cold welding, rust and corrosion in fasteners. High-temperature ant-seize, usually made with copper and graphite lubricants, is used for exhaust system and exhaust manifold bolts.

Anaerobic locking compounds are used to keep fasteners from vibrating or working loose and cure only after installation, in the absence of air. Medium strength locking compound is used for small nuts, bolts and screws that may be removed later. High-strength locking compound is for large nuts, bolts and studs which aren't removed on a regular basis.

Oil additives range from viscosity index improvers to chemical treatments that claim to reduce internal engine friction. It should be noted that most oil manufacturers caution against using additives with their oils.

Gas additives perform several functions, depending on their chemical makeup. They usually contain solvents that help dissolve gum and varnish that build up on carburetor, fuel injection and intake parts. They also serve to break down carbon deposits that form on the inside surfaces of the combustion chambers. Some additives contain upper cylinder lubricants for valves and piston rings, and others contain chemicals to remove condensation from the gas tank.

Miscellaneous

Brake fluid is specially formulated hydraulic fluid that can withstand the heat and pressure encountered in brake systems. Care must be taken so this fluid does not come in contact with painted surfaces or plastics. An opened container should always be resealed to prevent contamination by water or dirt.

Weatherstrip adhesive is used to bond weatherstripping around doors, windows and trunk lids. It is sometimes used to attach trim pieces.

Undercoating is a petroleum-based, tar-like substance that is designed to protect metal surfaces on the underside of the vehicle from corrosion. It also acts as a sound-deadening agent by insulating the bottom of the vehicle.

Waxes and polishes are used to help protect painted and plated surfaces from the weather. Different types of paint may require the use of different types of wax and polish. Some polishes utilize a chemical or abrasive cleaner to help remove the top layer of oxidized (dull) paint on older vehicles. In recent years many non-wax polishes that contain a wide variety of chemicals such as polymers and silicones have been introduced. These non-wax polishes are usually easier to apply and last longer than conventional waxes and polishes.

Conversion factors

Length (distance)

Inches (in)	X	25.4	= Millimetres (mm)	X	0.0394	= Inches (in)
Feet (ft)	X	0.305	= Metres (m)	X	3.281	= Feet (ft)
Miles	X	1.609	= Kilometres (km)	X	0.621	= Miles

Volume (capacity)

Cubic inches (cu in; in³)	X	16.387	= Cubic centimetres (cc; cm³)	X	0.061	= Cubic inches (cu in; in³)
Imperial pints (Imp pt)	X	0.568	= Litres (l)	X	1.76	= Imperial pints (Imp pt)
Imperial quarts (Imp qt)	X	1.137	= Litres (l)	X	0.88	= Imperial quarts (Imp qt)
Imperial quarts (Imp qt)	X	1.201	= US quarts (US qt)	X	0.833	= Imperial quarts (Imp qt)
US quarts (US qt)	X	0.946	= Litres (l)	X	1.057	= US quarts (US qt)
Imperial gallons (Imp gal)	X	4.546	= Litres (l)	X	0.22	= Imperial gallons (Imp gal)
Imperial gallons (Imp gal)	X	1.201	= US gallons (US gal)	X	0.833	= Imperial gallons (Imp gal)
US gallons (US gal)	X	3.785	= Litres (l)	X	0.264	= US gallons (US gal)

Mass (weight)

Ounces (oz)	X	28.35	= Grams (g)	X	0.035	Ounces (oz)
Pounds (lb)	X	0.454	= Kilograms (kg)	X	2.205	= Pounds (lb)

Force

Ounces-force (ozf; oz)	X	0.278	= Newtons (N)	X	3.6	= Ounces-force (ozf; oz)
Pounds-force (lbf; lb)	X	4.448	= Newtons (N)	X	0.225	= Pounds-force (lbf; lb)
Newtons (N)	X	0.1	= Kilograms-force (kgf; kg)	X	9.81	= Newtons (N)

Pressure

Pounds-force per square inch (psi; lbf/in²; lb/in²)	X	0.070	= Kilograms-force per square centimetre (kgf/cm²; kg/cm²)	X	14.223	= Pounds-force per square inch (psi; lbf/in²; lb/in²)
Pounds-force per square inch (psi; lbf/in²; lb/in²)	X	0.068	= Atmospheres (atm)	X	14.696	= Pounds-force per square inch (psi; lbf/in²; lb/in²)
Pounds-force per square inch (psi; lbf/in²; lb/in²)	X	0.069	= Bars	X	14.5	= Pounds-force per square inch (psi; lbf/in²; lb/in²)
Pounds-force per square inch (psi; lbf/in²; lb/in²)	X	6.895	= Kilopascals (kPa)	X	0.145	= Pounds-force per square inch (psi; lbf/in²; lb/in²)
Kilopascals (kPa)	X	0.01	= Kilograms-force per square centimetre (kgf/cm²; kg/cm²)	X	98.1	= Kilopascals (kPa)

Torque (moment of force)

Pounds-force inches (lbf in; lb in)	X	1.152	= Kilograms-force centimetre (kgf cm; kg cm)	X	0.868	= Pounds-force inches (lbf in; lb in)
Pounds-force inches (lbf in; lb in)	X	0.113	= Newton metres (Nm)	X	8.85	= Pounds-force inches (lbf in; lb in)
Pounds-force inches (lbf in; lb in)	X	0.083	= Pounds-force feet (lbf ft; lb ft)	X	12	= Pounds-force inches (lbf in; lb in)
Pounds-force feet (lbf ft; lb ft)	X	0.138	= Kilograms-force metres (kgf m; kg m)	X	7.233	= Pounds-force feet (lbf ft; lb ft)
Pounds-force feet (lbf ft; lb ft)	X	1.356	= Newton metres (Nm)	X	0.738	= Pounds-force feet (lbf ft; lb ft)
Newton metres (Nm)	X	0.102	= Kilograms-force metres (kgf m; kg m)	X	9.804	= Newton metres (Nm)

Power

Horsepower (hp)	X	745.7	= Watts (W)	X	0.0013	= Horsepower (hp)

Velocity (speed)

Miles per hour (miles/hr; mph)	X	1.609	= Kilometres per hour (km/hr; kph)	X	0.621	= Miles per hour (miles/hr; mph)

Fuel consumption*

Miles per gallon, Imperial (mpg)	X	0.354	= Kilometres per litre (km/l)	X	2.825	= Miles per gallon, Imperial (mpg)
Miles per gallon, US (mpg)	X	0.425	= Kilometres per litre (km/l)	X	2.352	= Miles per gallon, US (mpg)

Temperature

Degrees Fahrenheit $= (°C \times 1.8) + 32$ Degrees Celsius (Degrees Centigrade; °C) $= (°F - 32) \times 0.56$

*It is common practice to convert from miles per gallon (mpg) to litres/100 kilometres (l/100km), where mpg (Imperial) x l/100 km = 282 and mpg (US) x l/100 km = 235

Safety first

Regardless of how enthusiastic you may be about getting on with the job at hand, take the time to ensure that your safety is not jeopardized. A moment's lack of attention can result in an accident, as can failure to observe certain simple safety precautions. The possibility of an accident will always exist, and the following points should not be considered a comprehensive list of all dangers. Rather, they are intended to make you aware of the risks and to encourage a safety conscious approach to all work you carry out on your vehicle.

Essential DOs and DON'Ts

DON'T rely on a jack when working under the vehicle. Always use approved jackstands to support the weight of the vehicle and place them under the recommended lift or support points.

DON'T attempt to loosen extremely tight fasteners (i.e. wheel lug nuts) while the vehicle is on a jack - it may fall.

DON'T start the engine without first making sure that the transmission is in Neutral (or Park where applicable) and the parking brake is set.

DON'T remove the radiator cap from a hot cooling system - let it cool or cover it with a cloth and release the pressure gradually.

DON'T attempt to drain the engine oil until you are sure it has cooled to the point that it will not burn you.

DON'T touch any part of the engine or exhaust system until it has cooled sufficiently to avoid burns.

DON'T siphon toxic liquids such as gasoline, antifreeze and brake fluid by mouth, or allow them to remain on your skin.

DON'T inhale brake lining dust - it is potentially hazardous (see *Asbestos* below).

DON'T allow spilled oil or grease to remain on the floor - wipe it up before someone slips on it.

DON'T use loose fitting wrenches or other tools which may slip and cause injury.

DON'T push on wrenches when loosening or tightening nuts or bolts. Always try to pull the wrench toward you. If the situation calls for pushing the wrench away, push with an open hand to avoid scraped knuckles if the wrench should slip.

DON'T attempt to lift a heavy component alone - get someone to help you.

DON'T rush or take unsafe shortcuts to finish a job.

DON'T allow children or animals in or around the vehicle while you are working on it.

DO wear eye protection when using power tools such as a drill, sander, bench grinder, etc. and when working under a vehicle.

DO keep loose clothing and long hair well out of the way of moving parts.

DO make sure that any hoist used has a safe working load rating adequate for the job.

DO get someone to check on you periodically when working alone on a vehicle.

DO carry out work in a logical sequence and make sure that everything is correctly assembled and tightened.

DO keep chemicals and fluids tightly capped and out of the reach of children and pets.

DO remember that your vehicle's safety affects that of yourself and others. If in doubt on any point, get professional advice.

Asbestos

Certain friction, insulating, sealing, and other products - such as brake linings, brake bands, clutch linings, torque converters, gaskets, etc. - contain asbestos. Extreme care must be taken to avoid inhalation of dust from such products, since it is hazardous to health. If in doubt, assume that they do contain asbestos.

Fire

Remember at all times that gasoline is highly flammable. Never smoke or have any kind of open flame around when working on a vehicle. But the risk does not end there. A spark caused by an electrical short circuit, by two metal surfaces contacting each other, or even by static electricity built up in your body under certain conditions, can ignite gasoline vapors, which in a confined space are highly explosive. Do not, under any circumstances, use gasoline for cleaning parts. Use an approved safety solvent.

Always disconnect the battery ground (-) cable at the battery before working on any part of the fuel system or electrical system. Never risk spilling fuel on a hot engine or exhaust component. It is strongly recommended that a fire extinguisher suitable for use on fuel and electrical fires be kept handy in the garage or workshop at all times. Never try to extinguish a fuel or electrical fire with water.

Fumes

Certain fumes are highly toxic and can quickly cause unconsciousness and even death if inhaled to any extent. Gasoline vapor falls into this category, as do the vapors from some cleaning solvents. Any draining or pouring of such volatile fluids should be done in a well ventilated area.

When using cleaning fluids and solvents, read the instructions on the container carefully. Never use materials from unmarked containers.

Never run the engine in an enclosed space, such as a garage. Exhaust fumes contain carbon monoxide, which is extremely poisonous. If you need to run the engine, always do so in the open air, or at least have the rear of the vehicle outside the work area.

If you are fortunate enough to have the use of an inspection pit, never drain or pour gasoline and never run the engine while the vehicle is over the pit. The fumes, being heavier than air, will concentrate in the pit with possibly lethal results.

The battery

Never create a spark or allow a bare light bulb near a battery. They normally give off a certain amount of hydrogen gas, which is highly explosive.

Always disconnect the battery ground (-) cable at the battery before working on the fuel or electrical systems.

If possible, loosen the filler caps or cover when charging the battery from an external source (this does not apply to sealed or maintenance-free batteries). Do not charge at an excessive rate or the battery may burst.

Take care when adding water to a non maintenance-free battery and when carrying a battery. The electrolyte, even when diluted, is very corrosive and should not be allowed to contact clothing or skin.

Always wear eye protection when cleaning the battery to prevent the caustic deposits from entering your eyes.

Household current

When using an electric power tool, inspection light, etc., which operates on household current, always make sure that the tool is correctly connected to its plug and that, where necessary, it is properly grounded. Do not use such items in damp conditions and, again, do not create a spark or apply excessive heat in the vicinity of fuel or fuel vapor.

Secondary ignition system voltage

A severe electric shock can result from touching certain parts of the ignition system (such as the spark plug wires) when the engine is running or being cranked, particularly if components are damp or the insulation is defective. In the case of an electronic ignition system, the secondary system voltage is much higher and could prove fatal.

Troubleshooting

Contents

This Section provides an easy reference guide to the more common problems that may occur during the operation of your vehicle. Various symptoms and their probable causes are grouped under headings denoting components or systems, such as Engine, Cooling system, etc. They also refer to the Chapter and/or Section that deals with the problem.

Remember that successful troubleshooting isn't a mysterious art practiced only by professional mechanics, it's simply the result of knowledge combined with an intelligent, systematic approach to a problem. Always use a process of elimination starting with the simplest solution and working through to the most complex - and never overlook the obvious. Anyone can run the gas tank dry or leave the lights on overnight, so don't assume that you're exempt from such oversights.

Finally, always establish a clear idea why a problem has occurred and take steps to ensure that it doesn't happen again. If the electrical system fails because of a poor connection, check all other connections in the system to make sure they don't fail as well. If a particular fuse continues to blow, find out why - don't just go on replacing fuses. Remember, failure of a small component can often be indicative of potential failure or incorrect functioning of a more important component or system.

Engine

1 Engine will not rotate when attempting to start

1   Battery terminal connections loose or corroded. Check the cable terminals at the battery; tighten cable clamp and/or clean off corrosion as necessary (see Chapter 1).
2   Battery discharged or faulty. If the cable ends are clean and tight on the battery posts, turn the key to the On position and switch on the headlights or windshield wipers. If they won't run, the battery is discharged.
3   Automatic transmission not engaged in park (P) or Neutral (N).
4   Broken, loose or disconnected wires in the starting circuit. Inspect all wires and connectors at the battery, starter solenoid and ignition switch (on steering column).
5   Starter motor pinion jammed in driveplate ring gear. Remove starter (Chapter 5) and inspect pinion and driveplate (Chapter 2).
6   Starter solenoid faulty (Chapter 5).
7   Starter motor faulty (Chapter 5).
8   Ignition switch faulty (Chapter 12).
9   Engine seized. Try to turn the crankshaft with a large socket and breaker bar on the pulley bolt.

2 Engine rotates but will not start

1   Fuel tank empty.
2   Battery discharged (engine rotates slowly).
3   Battery terminal connections loose or corroded.
4   Fuel not reaching carburetor or fuel injector(s). Check for clogged fuel filter or lines and defective fuel pump. Also make sure the tank vent lines aren't clogged (Chapter 4).
5   Faulty distributor components (if equipped). Check the cap and rotor (Chapter 1).
6   Low cylinder compression. Check as described in Chapter 2.
7   Water in fuel. Drain tank and fill with new fuel.
8   Defective ignition coil(s) (Chapter 5).
9   Dirty or clogged fuel injector(s) (Chapter 4B).
10   Wet or damaged ignition components (Chapters 1 and 5).
11   Worn, faulty or incorrectly gapped spark plugs (Chapter 1).
12   Broken, loose or disconnected wires in the starting circuit (see previous Section).
13   Loose distributor (if equipped). Turn the distributor body as

necessary to start the engine, then adjust the ignition timing as soon as possible (Chapter 5).
14   Broken, loose or disconnected wires at the ignition coil or faulty coil (Chapter 5).
15   Timing chain failure or wear affecting valve timing (Chapter 2).
16   Carburetor, fuel injection or engine control systems failure (Chapters 4 and 6).

3 Starter motor operates without turning engine

1   Starter pinion sticking. Remove the starter (Chapter 5) and inspect.
2   Starter pinion or driveplate teeth worn or broken. Remove the inspection cover and inspect.

4 Engine hard to start when cold

1   Battery discharged or low. Check as described in Chapter 1.
2   Fuel not reaching the carburetor or fuel injectors. Check the fuel filter, lines and fuel pump (Chapters 1 and 4).
3   Defective spark plugs (Chapter 1).
4   Defective engine coolant temperature sensor (Chapter 6).
5   Carburetor, fuel injection or engine control systems malfunction (Chapters 4 and 6).

5 Engine hard to start when hot

1   Air filter dirty (Chapter 1).
2   Fuel not reaching the carburetor or fuel injectors (see Chapter 4). Check for a vapor lock situation, brought about by clogged fuel tank vent lines.
3   Bad engine ground connection.
4   Defective pick-up coil in distributor (Chapter 5).
5   Carburetor, fuel injection or engine control systems malfunction (Chapters 4 and 6).

6 Starter motor noisy or engages roughly

1   Pinion or driveplate teeth worn or broken. Remove the inspection cover on the left side of the engine and inspect.
2   Starter motor mounting bolts loose or missing.

7 Engine starts but stops immediately

1   Loose or damaged wire harness connections at distributor, coil or alternator.
2   Intake manifold vacuum leaks. Make sure all mounting bolts/nuts are tight and all vacuum hoses connected to the manifold are attached properly and in good condition.
3   Insufficient fuel pressure (see Chapter 4).
4   Fuel injection or engine control systems malfunction (Chapters 4B and 6).
5   Defective ballast resistor wire (see Chapter 5).

8 Engine 'lopes' while idling or idles erratically

1   Vacuum leaks. Check mounting bolts at the intake manifold for tightness. Make sure that all vacuum hoses are connected and in good condition. Use a stethoscope or a length of fuel hose held against your ear to listen for vacuum leaks while the engine is running. A hissing

sound will be heard. A soapy water solution will also detect leaks. Check the intake manifold gasket surfaces.

2   Leaking EGR valve or plugged PCV valve (see Chapters 1 and 6).
3   Air filter clogged (Chapter 1).
4   Fuel pump not delivering sufficient fuel (Chapter 4).
5   Leaking head gasket. Perform a cylinder compression check (Chapter 2).
6   Timing chain(s) worn (Chapter 2).
7   Camshaft lobes worn (Chapter 2).
8   Valves burned or otherwise leaking (Chapter 2).
9   Ignition timing out of adjustment (Chapter 5).
10   Ignition system not operating properly (Chapters 1 and 5).
11   Fuel injection or engine control systems malfunction (Chapters 4B and 6).
12   Carburetor in need of adjustment or overhaul (Chapter 4A).

9   Engine misses at idle speed

1   Spark plugs faulty or not gapped properly (Chapter 1).
2   Faulty spark plug wires (Chapter 1).
3   Wet or damaged distributor components (Chapter 1).
4   Short circuits in ignition, coil or spark plug wires (Chapters 1 and 5).
5   Sticking or faulty emissions systems (see Chapter 6).
6   Clogged fuel filter and/or foreign matter in fuel. Remove the fuel filter (Chapter 1) and inspect.
7   Vacuum leaks at intake manifold or hose connections. Check as described in Section 8.
8   Incorrect idle speed (Chapter 4).
9   Low or uneven cylinder compression. Check as described in Chapter 2.
10   Fuel injection or engine control systems malfunction (Chapters 4B and 6).

10   Excessively high idle speed

1   Sticking throttle linkage (Chapter 4).
2   Vacuum leaks at intake manifold or hose connections. Check as described in Section 8.
3   Fuel injection or engine control systems malfunction (Chapters 4B and 6).
4   Carburetor in need of adjustment (Chapter 4A).

11   Battery will not hold a charge

1   Alternator drivebelt defective or not adjusted properly (Chapter 1).
2   Battery cables loose or corroded (Chapter 1).
3   Alternator not charging properly (Chapter 5).
4   Loose, broken or faulty wires in the charging circuit (Chapter 5).
5   Short circuit causing a continuous drain on the battery.
6   Battery defective internally.

12   Alternator light stays on

1   Fault in alternator or charging circuit (Chapter 5).
2   Alternator drivebelt defective or not properly adjusted (Chapter 1).

13   Alternator light fails to come on when key is turned on

1   Faulty bulb (Chapter 12).
2   Defective alternator (Chapter 5).
3   Fault in the printed circuit, dash wiring or bulb holder (Chapter 12).

14   Engine misses throughout driving speed range

1   Fuel filter clogged and/or impurities in the fuel system. Check fuel filter (Chapter 1) or clean system (Chapter 4).
2   Faulty or incorrectly gapped spark plugs (Chapter 1).
3   Incorrect ignition timing (Chapter 1).
4   Cracked distributor cap, disconnected distributor wires or damaged distributor components (Chapter 1).
5   Defective spark plug wires (Chapter 1).
6   Emissions system components faulty (Chapter 6).
7   Low or uneven cylinder compression pressures. Check as described in Chapter 2.
8   Weak or faulty ignition coil(s) (Chapter 5).
9   Weak or faulty ignition system (Chapter 5).
10   Vacuum leaks at intake manifold or vacuum hoses (see Section 8).
11   Dirty or clogged fuel injector(s) (Chapter 4B).
12   Leaky EGR valve (Chapter 6).
13   Fuel injection or engine control systems malfunction (Chapters 4B and 6).

15   Hesitation or stumble during acceleration

1   Ignition system not operating properly (Chapter 5).
2   Dirty or clogged fuel injector(s) (Chapter 4B).
3   Low fuel pressure. Check for proper operation of the fuel pump and for restrictions in the fuel filter and lines (Chapter 4).
4   Fuel injection or engine control systems malfunction (Chapters 4B and 6).
5   Accelerator pump in carburetor worn (Chapter 4A).

16   Engine stalls

1   Idle speed incorrect (Chapter 4).
2   Fuel filter clogged and/or water and impurities in the fuel system (Chapter 1).
3   Damaged or wet distributor cap and wires.
4   Emissions system components faulty (Chapter 6).
5   Faulty or incorrectly gapped spark plugs (Chapter 1). Also check the spark plug wires (Chapter 1).
6   Vacuum leak at the intake manifold or vacuum hoses. Check as described in Section 8.
7   Fuel injection or engine control systems malfunction (Chapters 4B and 6).
8   Carburetor malfunction (Chapter 4A).

17   Engine lacks power

1   Incorrect ignition timing (Chapter 1).
2   Excessive play in distributor shaft (if equipped). At the same time check for faulty distributor cap, wires, etc. (Chapter 1).
3   Faulty or incorrectly gapped spark plugs (Chapter 1).
4   Air filter dirty (Chapter 1).
5   Faulty ignition coil(s) (Chapter 5).
6   Brakes binding (Chapters 1 and 10).
7   Automatic transmission fluid level incorrect, causing slippage (Chapter 1).
8   Fuel filter clogged and/or impurities in the fuel system (Chapters 1 and 4).
9   EGR system not functioning properly (Chapter 6).
10   Use of sub-standard fuel. Fill tank with proper octane fuel.
11   Low or uneven cylinder compression pressures. Check as described in Chapter 2.
12   Vacuum leak at intake manifold or vacuum hoses (check as described in Section 8).

13 Dirty or clogged fuel injector(s) (Chapters 1 and 4).
14 Fuel injection or engine control systems malfunction (Chapters 4B and 6).
15 Carburetor in need of adjustment or overhaul (Chapter 4A).
16 Restricted exhaust system (Chapter 4).

18 Engine backfires

1 EGR system not functioning properly (Chapter 6).
2 Ignition timing incorrect (Chapter 5).
3 Vacuum leak (refer to Section 8).
4 Damaged valve springs or sticking valves (Chapter 2).
5 Vacuum leak at the intake manifold or vacuum hoses (see Section 8).
6 Carburetor in need of adjustment or overhaul (Chapter 4A).
7 Fuel injection or engine control systems malfunction (Chapters 4B and 6).

19 Engine surges while holding accelerator steady

1 Vacuum leak at the intake manifold or vacuum hoses (see Section 8).
2 Restricted air filter (Chapter 1).
3 Fuel pump or pressure regulator defective (Chapter 4).
4 Fuel injection or engine control systems malfunction (Chapters 4B and 6).

20 Pinging or knocking engine sounds when engine is under load

1 Incorrect grade of fuel. Fill tank with fuel of the proper octane rating.
2 Ignition timing incorrect (Chapter 1).
3 Carbon build-up in combustion chambers. Remove cylinder head(s) and clean combustion chambers (Chapter 2).
4 Incorrect spark plugs (Chapter 1).
5 Fuel injection or engine control systems malfunction (Chapters 4 and 6).
6 Restricted exhaust system (Chapter 4).

21 Engine diesels (continues to run) after being turned off

1 Idle speed too high (Chapter 4A).
2 Ignition timing incorrect (Chapter 5).
3 Incorrect spark plug heat range (Chapter 1).
4 Vacuum leak at the intake manifold or vacuum hoses (see Section 8).
5 Carbon build-up in combustion chambers. Remove the cylinder head(s) and clean the combustion chambers (Chapter 2).
6 Valves sticking (Chapter 2).
7 EGR system not operating properly (Chapter 6).
8 Fuel injection or engine control systems malfunction (Chapters 4 and 6).
9 Check for causes of overheating (Section 27).

22 Low oil pressure

1 Improper grade of oil.
2 Oil pump worn or damaged (Chapter 2).
3 Engine overheating (refer to Section 27).
4 Clogged oil filter (Chapter 1).
5 Clogged oil strainer (Chapter 2).
6 Oil pressure gauge not working properly (Chapter 2).

23 Excessive oil consumption

1 Loose oil drain plug.
2 Loose bolts or damaged oil pan gasket (Chapter 2).
3 Loose bolts or damaged front cover gasket (Chapter 2).
4 Front or rear crankshaft oil seal leaking (Chapter 2).
5 Loose bolts or damaged valve cover gasket (Chapter 2).
6 Loose oil filter (Chapter 1).
7 Loose or damaged oil pressure switch (Chapter 2).
8 Pistons and cylinders excessively worn (Chapter 2).
9 Piston rings not installed correctly on pistons (Chapter 2).
10 Worn or damaged piston rings (Chapter 2).
11 Intake and/or exhaust valve oil seals worn or damaged (Chapter 2).
12 Worn valve stems or guides.
13 Worn or damaged valves/guides (Chapter 2).
14 Faulty or incorrect PCV valve allowing too much crankcase airflow.

24 Excessive fuel consumption

1 Dirty or clogged air filter element (Chapter 1).
2 Incorrect ignition timing (Chapter 5).
3 Incorrect idle speed (Chapter 4).
4 Low tire pressure or incorrect tire size (Chapter 10).
5 Inspect for binding brakes.
6 Fuel leakage. Check all connections, lines and components in the fuel system (Chapter 4).
7 Dirty or clogged fuel injectors (Chapter 4B).
8 Fuel injection or engine control systems malfunction (Chapters 4B and 6).
9 Carburetor in need of adjustment or overhaul (Chapter 4B).
10 Thermostat stuck open or not installed.
11 Improperly operating transmission.

25 Fuel odor

1 Fuel leakage. Check all connections, lines and components in the fuel system (Chapter 4).
2 Fuel tank overfilled. Fill only to automatic shut-off.
3 Charcoal canister filter in Evaporative Emissions Control system clogged (Chapter 1).
4 Vapor leaks from Evaporative Emissions Control system lines (Chapter 6).

26 Miscellaneous engine noises

1 A strong dull noise that becomes more rapid as the engine accelerates indicates worn or damaged crankshaft bearings or an unevenly worn crankshaft. To pinpoint the trouble spot, remove the spark plug wire from one plug at a time and crank the engine over. If the noise stops, the cylinder with the removed plug wire indicates the problem area. Replace the bearing and/or service or replace the crankshaft (Chapter 2).
2 A similar (yet slightly higher pitched) noise to the crankshaft knocking described in the previous paragraph, that becomes more rapid as the engine accelerates, indicates worn or damaged connecting rod bearings (Chapter 2). The procedure for locating the problem cylinder is the same as described in Paragraph 1.
3 An overlapping metallic noise that increases in intensity as the engine speed increases, yet diminishes as the engine warms up indicates abnormal piston and cylinder wear (Chapter 2). To locate the problem cylinder, use the procedure described in Paragraph 1.
4 A rapid clicking noise that becomes faster as the engine

accelerates indicates a worn piston pin or piston pin hole. This sound will happen each time the piston hits the highest and lowest points in the stroke (Chapter 2). The procedure for locating the problem piston is described in Paragraph 1.

5   A metallic clicking noise coming from the water pump indicates worn or damaged water pump bearings or pump. Replace the water pump with a new one (Chapter 3).

6   A rapid tapping sound or clicking sound that becomes faster as the engine speed increases indicates "valve tapping." This can be identified by holding one end of a section of hose to your ear and placing the other end at different spots along the valve cover. The point where the sound is loudest indicates the problem valve. If the pushrod and rocker arm components are in good shape, you likely have a collapsed valve lifter. Changing the engine oil and adding a high viscosity oil treatment will sometimes cure a stuck lifter problem. If the problem persists, the lifters, pushrods and rocker arms must be removed for inspection (see Chapter 2).

7   A steady metallic rattling or rapping sound coming from the area of the timing chain cover indicates a worn, damaged or out-of-adjustment timing chain. Service or replace the chain and related components (Chapter 2).

Cooling system

27   Overheating

1   Insufficient coolant in system (Chapter 1).
2   Drivebelt defective or not adjusted properly (Chapter 1).
3   Radiator core blocked or radiator grille dirty and restricted (Chapter 3).
4   Thermostat faulty (Chapter 3).
5   Cooling fan not functioning properly (Chapter 3).
6   Radiator cap not maintaining proper pressure. Have cap pressure tested by gas station or repair shop.
7   Ignition timing incorrect (Chapter 5).
8   Defective water pump (Chapter 3).
9   Improper grade of engine oil.
10   Inaccurate temperature gauge (Chapter 12).

28   Overcooling

1   Thermostat faulty (Chapter 3).
2   Inaccurate temperature gauge (Chapter 12).

29   External coolant leakage

1   Deteriorated or damaged hoses. Loose clamps at hose connections (Chapter 1).
2   Water pump seals defective. If this is the case, water will drip from the weep hole in the water pump body (Chapter 3).
3   Leakage from radiator core or header tank. This will require the radiator to be professionally repaired (see Chapter 3 for removal procedures).
4   Leakage from the coolant expansion tank.
5   Engine drain plugs or water jacket freeze plugs leaking (see Chapters 1 and 2).
6   Leak from coolant temperature switch (Chapter 3).
7   Leak from damaged gaskets or small cracks (Chapter 2).

30   Internal coolant leakage

Note: *Internal coolant leaks can usually be detected by examining the oil. Check the dipstick and inside the rocker arm cover for water*

deposits and an oil consistency like that of a milkshake.

1   Leaking cylinder head gasket. Have the system pressure tested or remove the cylinder head (Chapter 2) and inspect.
2   Cracked cylinder bore or cylinder head. Dismantle engine and inspect (Chapter 2).
3   Loose cylinder head bolts (tighten as described in Chapter 2).

31   Abnormal coolant loss

1   Overfilling system (Chapter 1).
2   Coolant boiling away due to overheating (see causes in Section 27).
3   Internal or external leakage (see Sections 29 and 30).
4   Faulty radiator cap. Have the cap pressure tested.
5   Cooling system being pressurized by engine compression. This could be due to a cracked head or block or leaking head gasket(s).

32   Poor coolant circulation

1   Inoperative water pump. A quick test is to pinch the top radiator hose closed with your hand while the engine is idling, then release it. You should feel a surge of coolant if the pump is working properly (Chapter 3).
2   Restriction in cooling system. Drain, flush and refill the system (Chapter 1). If necessary, remove the radiator (Chapter 3) and have it reverse flushed or professionally cleaned.
3   Loose water pump drivebelt (Chapter 1).
4   Thermostat sticking (Chapter 3).
5   Insufficient coolant (Chapter 1).

33   Corrosion

1   Excessive impurities in the water. Soft, clean water is recommended. Distilled or rainwater is satisfactory.
2   Insufficient antifreeze solution (refer to Chapter 1 for the proper ratio of water to antifreeze).
3   Infrequent flushing and draining of system. Regular flushing of the cooling system should be carried out at the specified intervals as described in (Chapter 1).

Automatic transmission

Note: *Due to the complexity of the automatic transmission, it's difficult for the home mechanic to properly diagnose and service. For problems other than the following, the vehicle should be taken to a reputable mechanic.*

34   Fluid leakage

1   Automatic transmission fluid is a deep red color, and fluid leaks should not be confused with engine oil which can easily be blown by air flow to the transmission.
2   To pinpoint a leak, first remove all built-up dirt and grime from the transmission. Degreasing agents and/or steam cleaning will achieve this. With the underside clean, drive the vehicle at low speeds so the air flow will not blow the leak far from its source. Raise the vehicle and determine where the leak is located. Common areas of leakage are:

a)   *Fluid pan: tighten mounting bolts and/or replace pan gasket as necessary (Chapter 1).*
b)   *Rear extension: tighten bolts and/or replace oil seal as necessary.*
c)   *Filler pipe: replace the rubber oil seal where pipe enters transmission case.*

d) **Transmission oil lines:** tighten fittings where lines enter transmission case and/or replace lines.
e) **Vent pipe:** transmission overfilled and/or water in fluid (see checking procedures, Chapter 1).
f) **Speedometer connector:** replace the O-ring where speedometer cable enters transmission case.

35 General shift mechanism problems

Chapter 7 deals with checking and adjusting the shift linkage on automatic transmissions. Common problems which may be caused by out of adjustment linkage are:

a) Engine starting in gears other than P (park) or N (Neutral).
b) Indicator pointing to a gear other than the one actually engaged.
c) Vehicle moves with transmission in P (Park) position.

36 Transmission will not downshift with the accelerator pedal pressed to the floor

Chapter 7 deals with adjusting the throttle valve cable to enable the transmission to downshift properly.

37 Engine will start in gears other than Park or Neutral

Chapter 7 deals with adjusting the Neutral start switch installed on automatic transmissions.

38 Transmission slips, shifts rough, is noisy or has no drive in forward or Reverse gears

1   There are many probable causes for the above problems, but the home mechanic should concern himself only with one possibility; fluid level.
2   Before taking the vehicle to a shop, check the fluid level and condition as described in Chapter 1. Add fluid, if necessary, or change the fluid and filter if needed. If problems persist, have a professional diagnose the transmission.

Driveshaft
Note: Refer to Chapter 8, unless otherwise specified, for service information.

39 Leaks at front of driveshaft

Defective transmission or transfer case seal. See Chapter 7 for replacement procedure. As this is done, check the splined yoke for burrs or roughness that could damage the new seal. Remove burrs with a fine file or whetstone.

40 Knock or clunk when transmission is under initial load (just after transmission is put into gear)

1   Loose or disconnected rear suspension components. Check all mounting bolts and bushings (Chapters 7 and 10).
2   Loose driveshaft bolts. Inspect all bolts and nuts and tighten them securely.
3   Worn or damaged universal joint bearings (Chapter 8).
4   Worn sleeve yoke and mainshaft spline.

41 Metallic grating sound consistent with vehicle speed

Pronounced wear in the universal joint bearings. Replace U-joints or driveshaft, as necessary.

42 Vibration

Note: Before blaming the driveshaft, make sure the tires are perfectly balanced and perform the following test.
1   Install a tachometer inside the vehicle to monitor engine speed as the vehicle is driven. Drive the vehicle and note the engine speed at which the vibration (roughness) is most pronounced. Now shift the transmission to a different gear and bring the engine speed to the same point.
2   If the vibration occurs at the same engine speed (rpm) regardless of which gear the transmission is in, the driveshaft is NOT at fault since the driveshaft speed varies.
3   If the vibration decreases or is eliminated when the transmission is in a different gear at the same engine speed, refer to the following probable causes:

a) Bent or dented driveshaft. Inspect and replace as necessary.
b) Undercoating or built-up dirt, etc. on the driveshaft. Clean the shaft thoroughly.
c) Worn universal joint bearings. Replace the U-joints or driveshaft as necessary.
d) Driveshaft and/or companion flange out of balance. Check for missing weights on the shaft. Remove driveshaft and reinstall 180-degrees from original position, then recheck. Have the driveshaft balanced if problem persists.
e) Loose driveshaft mounting bolts/nuts.
f) Worn transmission rear bushing (Chapter 7).

43 Scraping noise

Make sure there is nothing, such as an exhaust heat shield, rubbing on the driveshaft.

Axle(s) and differential(s)
Note: For differential servicing information, refer to Chapter 8, unless otherwise specified.

44 Noise - same when in drive as when vehicle is coasting

1   Road noise. No corrective action available.
2   Tire noise. Inspect tires and check tire pressures (Chapter 1).
3   Front wheel bearings loose, worn or damaged (Chapter 1).
4   Insufficient differential oil (Chapter 1).
5   Defective differential.

45 Knocking sound when starting or shifting gears

Defective or incorrectly adjusted differential.

46 Noise when turning

Defective differential.

47   Vibration

See probable causes under Driveshaft. Proceed under the guidelines listed for the driveshaft. If the problem persists, check the rear wheel bearings by raising the rear of the vehicle and spinning the wheels by hand. Listen for evidence of rough (noisy) bearings. Remove and inspect (Chapter 8).

48   Oil leaks

1   Pinion oil seal damaged (Chapter 8).
2   Axleshaft oil seals damaged (Chapter 8).
3   Differential cover leaking. Tighten mounting bolts or replace the gasket as required.
4   Loose filler plug on differential (Chapter 1).
5   Clogged or damaged breather on differential.

Brakes

Note: *Before assuming a brake problem exists, make sure the tires are in good condition and inflated properly, the front end alignment is correct and the vehicle is not loaded with weight in an unequal manner. All service procedures for the brakes are included in Chapter 9, unless otherwise noted.*

49   Vehicle pulls to one side during braking

1   Defective, damaged or oil contaminated brake pad or lining on one side. Inspect as described in Chapter 1. Refer to Chapter 9 if replacement is required.
2   Excessive wear of brake pad or lining material, disc or drum on one side. Inspect and repair as necessary.
3   Loose or disconnected front suspension components. Inspect and tighten all bolts securely (Chapters 1 and 10).
4   Defective front brake caliper assembly. Remove caliper and inspect for stuck piston or damage.
5   Brake lining adjustment needed. Inspect automatic adjusting mechanism for proper operation.
6   Scored or out of round disc or drum.
7   Loose front brake caliper mounting bolts.
8   Incorrect wheel bearing adjustment.

50   Noise (high-pitched squeal)

1   Front brake pads worn out. This noise comes from the wear sensor rubbing against the disc. Replace pads with new ones immediately!
2   Glazed or contaminated pads.
3   Dirty or scored rotor.
4   Bent support plate.

51   Excessive brake pedal travel

1   Partial brake system failure. Inspect entire system (Chapter 1) and correct as required.
2   Insufficient fluid in master cylinder. Check (Chapter 1) and add fluid - bleed system if necessary.
3   Air in system. Bleed system.
4   Excessive lateral rotor play.
5   Brakes out of adjustment. Check the operation of the automatic adjusters.

6   Defective proportioning valve. Replace valve and bleed system.
7   Defective master cylinder.

52   Brake pedal feels spongy when depressed

1   Air in brake lines. Bleed the brake system.
2   Deteriorated rubber brake hoses. Inspect all system hoses and lines. Replace parts as necessary.
3   Master cylinder mounting nuts loose. Inspect master cylinder bolts (nuts) and tighten them securely.
4   Master cylinder faulty.
5   Incorrect shoe or pad clearance.
6   Defective check valve. Replace valve and bleed system.
7   Clogged reservoir cap vent hole.
8   Deformed rubber brake lines.
9   Soft or swollen caliper seals.
10   Poor quality brake fluid. Bleed entire system and fill with new approved fluid.

53   Excessive effort required to stop vehicle

1   Power brake booster not operating properly.
2   Excessively worn linings or pads. Check and replace if necessary.
3   One or more caliper pistons seized or sticking. Inspect and rebuild as required.
4   Brake pads or linings contaminated with oil or grease. Inspect and replace as required.
5   Worn or damaged master cylinder or caliper assemblies. Check particularly for frozen pistons.

54   Pedal travels to the floor with little resistance

Little or no fluid in the master cylinder reservoir caused by leaking caliper piston(s) or loose, damaged or disconnected brake lines. Inspect entire system and repair as necessary.

55   Brake pedal pulsates during brake application

1   Wheel bearings damaged, worn or out of adjustment (Chapter 1).
2   Caliper not sliding properly due to improper installation or obstructions. Remove and inspect.
3   Rotor not within specifications. Remove the rotor and check for excessive lateral runout and parallelism. Have the rotors resurfaced or replace them with new ones. Also make sure that all rotors are the same thickness.
4   Out of round rear brake drums. Remove the drums and have them turned or replace them with new ones.

56   Brakes drag (indicated by sluggish engine performance or wheels being very hot after driving)

1   Pushrod adjustment incorrect at the brake pedal or power booster.
2   Obstructed master cylinder compensator. Disassemble master cylinder and clean.
3   Master cylinder piston seized in bore. Overhaul master cylinder.
4   Caliper assembly in need of overhaul.
5   Brake pads or shoes worn out.
6   Piston cups in master cylinder or caliper assembly deformed. Overhaul master cylinder.
7   Rotor not within specifications.

8 Parking brake assembly will not release.
9 Clogged brake lines.
10 Wheel bearings out of adjustment (Chapter 1).
11 Brake pedal height improperly adjusted.
12 Wheel cylinder needs overhaul.
13 Improper shoe to drum clearance. Adjust as necessary.

57 Rear brakes lock up under light brake application

1 Tire pressures too high.
2 Tires excessively worn (Chapter 1).
3 Defective power brake booster.
4 Rear axle seal(s) leaking contaminating brake lining(s) with rear axle lubricant (Chapter 8).

58 Rear brakes lock up under heavy brake application

1 Tire pressures too high.
2 Tires excessively worn (Chapter 1).
3 Front brake pads contaminated with oil, mud or water. Clean or replace the pads.
4 Front brake pads excessively worn.
5 Defective master cylinder or caliper assembly.

59 Slow or incomplete brake pedal return (Hydro-Boost)

1 Binding in the pedal and/or pedal linkage.
2 Restriction in return line from booster to pump reservoir.
3 Internal restriction in the Hydro-Boost fluid return system.

60 Over-sensitive braking (Hydro-Boost)

1 Binding in the pedal and/or pedal linkage.
2 Defective Hydro-Boost unit.

Suspension and steering

Note: *All service procedures for the suspension and steering systems are included in Chapter 10, unless otherwise noted.*

61 Vehicle pulls to one side

1 Tire pressures uneven (Chapter 1).
2 Defective tire (Chapter 1).
3 Excessive wear in suspension or steering components (Chapter 1).
4 Front end alignment incorrect.
5 Front brakes dragging. Inspect as described in Section 71.
6 Wheel bearings improperly adjusted (Chapter 1).
7 Wheel lug nuts loose.

62 Shimmy, shake or vibration

1 Tire or wheel out of balance or out of round.
2 Loose, worn or out of adjustment wheel bearings (Chapter 1).
3 Shock absorbers and/or suspension components worn or damaged (see Chapter 10).

63 Excessive pitching and/or rolling around corners or during braking

1 Defective shock absorbers. Replace as a set.
2 Broken or weak leaf springs and/or suspension components.
3 Worn or damaged stabilizer bar or bushings.

64 Wandering or general instability

1 Improper tire pressures.
2 Incorrect front end alignment.
3 Worn or damaged steering linkage or suspension components.
4 Improperly adjusted steering gear.
5 Out-of-balance wheels.
6 Loose wheel lug nuts.
7 Worn rear shock absorbers.
8 Fatigued or damaged rear leaf springs.

65 Excessively stiff steering

1 Lack of fluid in the power steering fluid reservoir, where appropriate (Chapter 1).
2 Incorrect tire pressures (Chapter 1).
3 Lack of lubrication at balljoints (Chapter 1).
4 Front end out of alignment.
5 Steering gear out of adjustment or lacking lubrication.
6 Improperly adjusted wheel bearings.
7 Worn or damaged steering gear.
8 Interference of steering column with turn signal switch.
9 Low tire pressures.
10 Worn or damaged balljoints.
11 Worn or damaged steering linkage.

66 Excessive play in steering

1 Loose wheel bearings (Chapter 1).
2 Excessive wear in suspension bushings (Chapter 1).
3 Steering gear improperly adjusted.
4 Incorrect front end alignment.
5 Steering gear mounting bolts loose.
6 Worn steering linkage.

67 Lack of power assistance

1 Steering pump drivebelt faulty or not adjusted properly (Chapter 1).
2 Fluid level low (Chapter 1).
3 Hoses or pipes restricting the flow. Inspect and replace parts as necessary.
4 Air in power steering system. Bleed system.
5 Defective power steering pump.

68 Steering wheel fails to return to straight-ahead position

1 Incorrect front end alignment.
2 Tire pressures low.
3 Steering gears improperly engaged.
4 Steering column out of alignment.
5 Worn or damaged balljoint.
6 Worn or damaged steering linkage.

7   Improperly lubricated idler arm.
8   Insufficient oil in steering gear.
9   Lack of fluid in power steering pump.

69 Steering effort not the same in both directions (power system)

1   Leaks in steering gear.
2   Clogged fluid passage in steering gear.

70 Noisy power steering pump

1   Insufficient oil in pump.
2   Clogged hoses or oil filter in pump.
3   Loose pulley.
4   Improperly adjusted drivebelt (Chapter 1).
5   Defective pump.

71 Miscellaneous noises

1   Improper tire pressures.
2   Insufficiently lubricated balljoint or steering linkage.
3   Loose or worn steering gear, steering linkage or suspension components.
4   Defective shock absorber.
5   Defective wheel bearing.
6   Worn or damaged suspension bushings.
7   Damaged leaf spring.
8   Loose wheel lug nuts.
9   Worn or damaged rear axleshaft spline.
10   Worn or damaged rear shock absorber mounting bushing.

11   Incorrect rear axle endplay.
12   See also causes of noises at the rear axle and driveshaft.

72 Excessive tire wear (not specific to one area)

1   Incorrect tire pressures.
2   Tires out of balance.
3   Wheels damaged. Inspect and replace as necessary.
4   Suspension or steering components worn (Chapter 1).
5   Front end alignment incorrect.
6   Lack of proper tire rotation routine. See Routine Maintenance Schedule, Chapter 1.

73 Excessive tire wear on outside edge

1   Incorrect tire pressure.
2   Excessive speed in turns.
3   Front end alignment incorrect.

74 Excessive tire wear on inside edge

1   Incorrect tire pressure.
2   Front end alignment incorrect.
3   Loose or damaged steering components (Chapter 1).

75 Tire tread worn in one place

1   Tires out of balance.
2   Damaged or buckled wheel. Inspect and replace if necessary.
3   Defective tire.

Chapter 1
Tune-up and routine maintenance

Contents

1

Specifications

Recommended lubricants and fluids

Engine oil
  Type .... API grade SG or SG/CC multigrade and fuel efficient oil
  Viscosity .... See accompanying chart

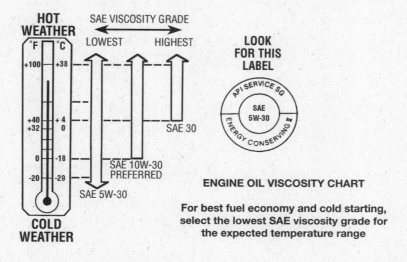

ENGINE OIL VISCOSITY CHART

For best fuel economy and cold starting, select the lowest SAE viscosity grade for the expected temperature range

Recommended lubricants and fluids (continued)

Brake fluid type	DOT 3 heavy duty brake fluid
Power steering fluid type	Type F automatic transmission fluid
Automatic transmission fluid type	MERCON automatic transmission fluid
Coolant type	50/50 mixture of ethylene glycol-based antifreeze and water
Chassis grease	SAE NLGI no. 2 chassis grease
Differential lubricant type	SAE 80W-90 GL-5 gear lubricant*

Trak-Lok axles add 4 oz. of friction modifier (Ford part no. C8AZ-19B546-A) when oil is changed.

Capacities*

Cooling system	14.1 qts
Engine oil (all)	5.0 qts
Automatic transmission	12.3 qts

All capacities approximate. Add as necessary to bring to appropriate level.

Radiator cap pressure

Standard	16 psi
Lower limit (must hold pressure)	13 psi
Upper limit (must relieve pressure)	18 psi

Brakes

Disc brake pad thickness (minimum)	1/8 inch
Drum brake shoe lining thickness (minimum)	1/8 inch

Idle speed (Idle speed solenoid connected and transmission in Drive) *

1973 and earlier	625 rpm
1974 through 1977	650 rpm
1978	580 rpm
1973 and earlier	625 rpm
1974 through 1977	650 rpm
1978 through 1980	625 rpm
1987 and 1988	550 to 600 rpm
1989 and later	550 to 600 rpm

Ignition system

Spark plug type and gap
1972 and earlier (all)

Type	Champion RF11YC or equivalent
Gap	0.035 inch

1973 (all)

Type	Champion RV17YC or equivalent
Gap	0.035-inch

1974
49 state

Type	Champion RV17YC or equivalent
Gap	0.054-inch

California

Type	Champion RV17YC or equivalent
Gap	0.044-inch

1975 and 1976 (all)

Type	Champion RV17YC or equivalent
Gap	0.044-inch

1977
49 state

Type	Champion RV17YC or equivalent
Gap	0.050-inch

California

Type	Champion RV17YC or equivalent
Gap	0.060-inch

1978 through 1984 (all)

Type	Champion RV17YC or equivalent
Gap	0.050-inch

1985
Mark VII 5.0L (302 cid) HO

Type	Champion RV17YC or equivalent
Gap	0.044-inch

Spark plug type and gap (continued)
  1985 (continued)
    All others
      Type .... Champion RV17YC or equivalent
      Gap 0.050-inch
  1986 through 1990 (all)
    Type .... Champion RS14LC or equivalent
    Gap 0.050-inch
  1991 and later
    5.0L (302 cid) OHV V8
      Type .... Champion RS14LC or equivalent
      Gap .... 0.050 inch
    4.6L OHC V8
      Type .... Champion RS12YC6 or equivalent
      Gap 0.054-inch
Distributor ignition points
  Point gap 0.017-inch
  Dwell .... 26 to 30-degrees
Firing order
  7.5L (460 cid) and 5.0L (302 cid) (non-H.O.) OHV engines 1-5-4-2-6-3-7-8
  All others 1-3-7-2-6-5-4-8
Ignition timing *
  1970 .... 6-degrees BTDC
  1971 .... 5-degrees BTDC
  1972 .... 10-degrees BTDC
  1973 through 1975 .... 14-degrees BTDC
  1976
    California models .... 14-degrees BTDC
    All others .... 8-degrees BTDC
  1977
    460 cid .... 16-degrees BTDC
    400 cid .... 8-degrees BTDC
  1978
    460 cid .... 16-degrees BTDC
    400 cid
      California models .... 16-degrees BTDC
      All others .... 0-degrees (TDC)
  1979
    460 cid .... 16-degrees BTDC
    400 cid
      California models .... 16-degrees BTDC
      All others .... 14-degrees BTDC
  1980
    5.0L (302 cid)
      Carbureted
        California models .... 8-degrees BTDC
        All others .... 6-degrees BTDC
      Fuel-injected .... Not adjustable
    5.8L (351W cid)
      California models .... Not adjustable
      All others .... 17-degrees BTDC (12-degrees BTDC on Calibration No. 012J-R10 models)
  1981
    5.0L (302 cid)
      Carbureted .... 8-degrees BTDC
      Fuel-injected .... Not adjustable
    5.8L (351W cid)
      California models .... Not adjustable
      All others .... 10-degrees BTDC
  1982
    5.8L (351W cid)
      California models .... Not adjustable
      All others .... 8-degrees BTDC (12-degrees BTDC on Calibration No. 2-24P-R10 models)
  1983
    5.0L (302 cid)
      Carbureted .... 10-degrees BTDC
      Fuel-injected .... Not adjustable
    5.8L (351W cid) .... 8-degrees BTDC

CYLINDER NUMBERING AND
DISTRIBUTOR LOCATION

FRONT

DISTRIBUTOR

FIRING ORDER AND ROTATION
COUNTERCLOCKWISE

CAP CLIP
POSITION

FIRING ORDER
5.0L-HO, 5.8L, 6.6L — 1-3-7-2-6-5-4-8

FIRING ORDER
5.0L, 7.5L — 1-5-4-2-6-3-7-8

Cylinder location and distributor rotation diagram

0806H

4.6L OHC V8 Cylinder and coil terminal location diagram

1

Ignition system (continued)

Ignition timing *
    1984
        5.0L (302 cid)
            Carbureted .... 10-degrees BTDC
            Fuel-injected .... Not adjustable
        5.8L (351W cid) .... 14-degrees BTDC
    1985 through 1991
        5.0L (302 cid) (all) .... 10-degrees BTDC **
        5.8L (351W cid) .... 14-degrees BTDC ***
    1992 on
        5.0L (302 cid) .... 10-degrees BTDC **
        4.6L .... Not adjustable

If the information on the Vehicle Emission Control Information label differs from the information printed here, follow the information on the label
**With SPOUT connector unplugged*
***Transmission in Drive*

Torque specifications

	Ft-lbs (unless otherwise noted)
Wheel lug nuts	85 to 105
Spark plugs	
Cast iron cylinder head	120 to 180 in-lbs
Aluminum cylinder head	72 in-lbs
Oil pan drain plug	15 to 25
Engine block drain plug	60 to 96 in-lbs
Automatic transmission	
Pan bolts	144 to 192 in-lbs
Filter bolt	80 to 120 in-lbs
Band adjustment locknut	35 to 45

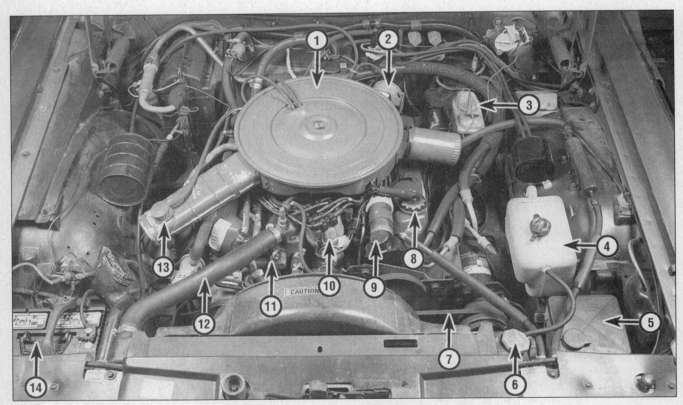

Typical engine compartment components (7.5L engine)

1	*Air cleaner housing*	*6*	*Radiator cap*	*11*	*Engine oil dipstick*
3	*Cruise control actuator*	*7*	*Power steering fluid reservoir*	*12*	*Upper radiator hose*
3	*Brake fluid reservoir*	*8*	*Oil filler cap*	*13*	*Thermostatic air cleaner motor*
4	*Coolant reservoir*	*9*	*Ignition coil*	*14*	*Battery*
5	*Windshield washer fluid reservoir*	*10*	*Distributor cap*		

Typical engine compartment components (5.0L engine)

1	Engine oil dipstick	6	Power steering fluid reservoir	11	Battery
2	Brake fluid reservoir	7	Distributor cap	12	Oil filler cap
3	Air cleaner housing	8	Spark plug wires	13	Automatic transmission fluid
4	Windshield washer fluid reservoir	9	Ignition coil		dipstick
5	Radiator cap	10	Upper radiator hose		

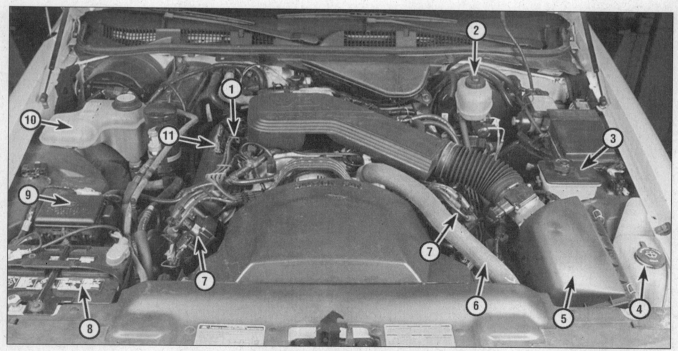

Typical engine compartment components (4.6L engine)

1	Spark plug wire	5	Air cleaner housing	9	Fuse block
2	Brake fluid reservoir	6	Upper radiator hose	10	Coolant expansion tank
3	Power steering fluid reservoir	7	Ignition coil	11	PCV valve
4	Windshield washer fluid reservoir	8	Battery		

Typical engine compartment underside components (1976 Continental with 7.5L engine)

1	Engine oil drain plug	3	Lower suspension balljoint	4	Tie-rod end grease fitting
2	Engine oil filter		grease fitting	5	Automatic transmission fluid pan

Typical engine compartment underside components (1988 Town Car with 5.0L engine)

1	Front engine oil drain plug	4	Lower suspension balljoint grease fitting
2	Rear engine oil drain plug	5	Pitman arm balljoint grease fitting
3	Tie-rod end grease fitting	6	Automatic transmission fluid pan

Typical rear underside components (1976 Continental)

1	Rear axle differential	3	Shock absorber
2	Gas tank Exhaust pipe	4	Parking brake cable

Typical rear underside components (1988 Town Car)

1	Gas tank	4	Rear axle differential
2	Exhaust pipe	5	Shock absorber
3	Fuel filter	6	Parking brake cable

1 Lincoln Maintenance schedule

The following maintenance intervals are based on the assumption that the vehicle owner will be doing the maintenance or service work, as opposed to having a dealer service department or other repair shop do the work. Although the time/mileage intervals are loosely based on factory recommendations, most have been shortened to ensure, for example, that such items as lubricants and fluids are checked/changed at intervals that promote maximum engine/driveline service life. Also, subject to the preference of the individual owner interested in keeping his or her vehicle in peak condition at all times, and with the vehicle's ultimate resale in mind, many of the maintenance procedures may be performed more often than recommended in the following schedule. We encourage such owner initiative.

When the vehicle is new it should be serviced initially by a factory authorized dealer service department to protect the factory warranty. In many cases the initial maintenance check is done at no cost to the owner (check with your dealer service department for more information).

Every 250 miles or weekly, whichever comes first

Check the engine oil level (Section 4)
Check the engine coolant level (Section 4)
Check the windshield washer fluid level (Section 4)
Check the brake fluid level (Section 4)
Check the tires and tire pressures (Section 5)

Every 3000 miles or 3 months, whichever comes first

All items listed above, plus:
Check the power steering fluid level (Section 6)
Check the automatic transmission fluid level (Section 7)
Change the engine oil and oil filter (Section 8)

Every 7500 miles or 6 months, whichever comes first

All items listed above, plus:
Inspect/replace the underhood hoses (Section 9)
Check the drivebelt(s) (Section 10)
Rotate the tires (Section 11)
Check the seat belt operation (Section 12)
Check/service the battery (Section 13)

Every 15,000 miles or 12 months, whichever comes first

All items listed above, plus:
Inspect/replace the windshield wiper blades (Section 14)
Replace the air filter (Section 15)*
Check the PCV valve (Section 16)
Check the fuel system (Section 17)
Inspect the cooling system (Section 18)
Check and adjust if necessary, the ignition timing (Section 19)
Check the Exhaust Gas Recirculation (EGR) valve (Section 20
Lubricate and check the exhaust control valve (Section 21)
Check the operation of the thermostatic air cleaner (Section 22)
Check and adjust if necessary, the ignition points (1974 and earlier models only) (Section 23)
Check and adjust if necessary, the engine idle speed (Section 24)
Inspect the exhaust system (Section 25)
Inspect the steering and suspension components (Section 26)
Inspect the brakes (Section 27)
Lubricate the automatic transmission control linkage (Section 28)
Check the rear axle (differential) lubricant level (Section 29)

Every 30,000 miles or 24 months, whichever comes first

Check the thermactor system (Section 30)
Replace the spark plugs (Section 31)
Check/replace the spark plug wires, distributor cap and rotor (Section 32)
Change the automatic transmission fluid and filter (Section 33)**
Adjust the automatic transmission bands (C6 transmission only) (Section 34)
Change the rear axle (differential) lubricant (Section 35)
Service the cooling system (drain, flush and refill) (Section 36)
Service the front wheel bearings (1991 and earlier models) (Section 37)
Lubricate the chassis components (Section 38)
Check the carburetor choke (Section 39)
Check the evaporative emissions system (Section 40)
Replace the fuel filter (Section 41)

* Replace more often if is the vehicle is driven in dusty areas
** If the vehicle is operated in continuous stop-and-go driving or in mountainous areas, change at 15,000 miles

2 Introduction

This Chapter is designed to help the home mechanic maintain the Lincoln Continental, Town Car and Mark Series with the goals of maximum performance, economy, safety and reliability in mind.

Included is a master maintenance schedule (page 1-6), followed by procedures dealing specifically with each item on the schedule. Visual checks, adjustments, component replacement and other helpful items are included. Refer to the accompanying illustrations of the engine compartment and the underside of the vehicle for the locations of various components.

Servicing the vehicle, in accordance with the mileage/time maintenance schedule and the step-by-step procedures will result in a planned maintenance program that should produce a long and reliable service life. Keep in mind that it is a comprehensive plan, so maintaining some items but not others at the specified intervals will not produce the same results.

As you service the vehicle, you will discover that many of the procedures can - and should - be grouped together because of the nature of the particular procedure you're performing or because of the close proximity of two otherwise unrelated components to one another.

For example, if the vehicle is raised for chassis lubrication, you should inspect the exhaust, suspension, steering and fuel systems while you're under the vehicle. When you're rotating the tires, it makes good sense to check the brakes since the wheels are already removed. Finally, let's suppose you have to borrow or rent a torque wrench. Even if you only need it to tighten the spark plugs, you might as well check the torque of as many critical fasteners as time allows.

The first step in this maintenance program is to prepare yourself before the actual work begins. Read through all the procedures you're planning to do, then gather up all the parts and tools needed. If it looks like you might run into problems during a particular job, seek advice from a mechanic or an experienced do-it-yourselfer.

3 Tune-up general information

The term tune-up is used in this manual to represent a combination of individual operations rather than one specific procedure.

If, from the time the vehicle is new, the routine maintenance schedule is followed closely and frequent checks are made of fluid levels and high wear items, as suggested throughout this manual, the engine will be kept in relatively good running condition and the need for additional work will be minimized.

More likely than not, however, there will be times when the engine is running poorly due to lack of regular maintenance. This is even more likely if a used vehicle, which has not received regular and frequent maintenance checks, is purchased. In such cases, an engine tune-up will be needed outside of the regular routine maintenance intervals.

The first step in any tune-up or diagnostic procedure to help correct a poor running engine is a cylinder compression check. A compression check (see Chapter 2) will help determine the condition of internal engine components and should be used as a guide for tune-up and repair procedures. If, for instance, a compression check indicates serious internal engine wear, a conventional tune-up will not improve the performance of the engine and would be a waste of time and money. Because of its importance, the compression check should be done by someone with the right equipment and the knowledge to use it properly.

The following procedures are those most often needed to bring a generally poor running engine back into a proper state of tune.

Minor tune-up

Check all engine related fluids (Section 4)
Check all underhood hoses (Section 9)
Check the drivebelts (Section 10)
Check the PCV valve (Section 16)
Clean, inspect and test the battery (Section 13)
Check the air/PCV filter (Section 15)

Check the cooling system (Section 18)
Replace the spark plugs (Section 31)
Replace the ignition points (1974 and earlier models only) (Section 23)
Check/adjust the idle speed (some models) (Section 24)
Inspect the spark plug and coil wires (Section 32)
Inspect the distributor cap and rotor (Section 32)
Check/adjust the ignition timing (some models) (Section 19)

Major tune-up

All items listed under Minor tune-up, plus . . .
Check the charging system (Chapter 5)
Replace the air/PCV filter (Section 15)
Check the fuel system (Section 17)
Replace the spark plug and coil wires (Section 32)
Replace the distributor cap and rotor (Section 32)

4 Fluid level checks (every 250 miles or weekly)

1 Fluids are an essential part of the lubrication, cooling, brake and windshield washer systems. Because the fluids gradually become depleted and/or contaminated during normal operation of the vehicle, they must be periodically replenished. See *Recommended lubricants and fluids* at the beginning of this Chapter before adding fluid to any of the following components. **Note:** *The vehicle must be on level ground when fluid levels are checked.*

Engine oil

Refer to illustrations 4.2a, 4.2b, 4.4, 4.6a and 4.6b
2 The oil level is checked with a dipstick, which is located at the front or side of the engine **(see illustrations)**. The dipstick extends

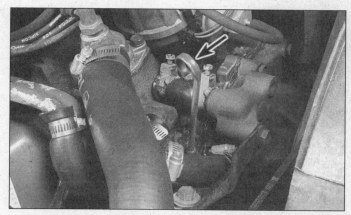

4.2a On the 7.5L (460 cu. in.), 400 and 351W cu. in. engines, the engine oil dipstick (arrow) is located up front, near the water pump

4.2b On the 4.6L OHC and 5.0L engines, the engine oil dipstick is located on the left (driver's) side

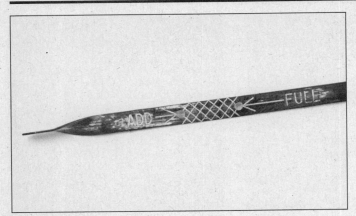

4.4 The oil level should be at or near the upper hatched area on the dipstick - if it isn't, add enough oil to bring the level to the upper mark (it takes one quart of oil to raise the level from the lower to upper mark)

4.6a On earlier models such as this 7.5L engine, the oil filler cap is located on the valve cover with a hose running to the PCV filter in the air cleaner housing

4.6b The oil filler cap on later models is clearly marked - always make sure the area around the opening is clean before unscrewing the cap to prevent dirt from contaminating the engine

4.9a Typical coolant reservoir - keep the level near the upper mark

4.9b The coolant expansion tank used on models with the 4.6L engine is located on the right (passenger) side of the engine compartment - keep the level near the arrow at the seam

through a metal tube down into the oil pan.

3   The oil level should be checked before the vehicle has been driven, or about 15 minutes after the engine has been shut off. If the oil is checked immediately after driving the vehicle, some of the oil will remain in the upper part of the engine, resulting in an inaccurate reading on the dipstick.

4   Pull the dipstick out of the tube and wipe all the oil from the end with a clean rag or paper towel. Insert the clean dipstick all the way back into the tube and pull it out again. Note the oil at the end of the dipstick. At its highest point, the level should be above the ADD mark, within the hatched marked section of the dipstick **(see illustration)**.

5   It takes one quart of oil to raise the level from the ADD mark to the FULL mark on the dipstick. Do not allow the level to drop below the ADD mark or oil starvation may cause engine damage. Conversely, overfilling the engine (adding oil above the FULL mark) may cause oil fouled spark plugs, oil leaks or oil seal failures.

6   To add oil, remove the filler cap located on valve cover **(see illustrations)**. After adding oil, wait a few minutes to allow the level to stabilize, then pull out the dipstick and check the level again. Add more oil if required. Install the filler cap and tighten it by hand only.

7   Checking the oil level is an important preventive maintenance step. A consistently low oil level indicates oil leakage through damaged seals, defective gaskets or past worn rings or valve guides. If the oil looks milky in color or has water droplets in it, the cylinder head gasket(s) may be blown or the head(s) or block may be cracked. The

engine should be checked immediately. The condition of the oil should also be checked. Whenever you check the oil level, slide your thumb and index finger up the dipstick before wiping off the oil. If you see small dirt or metal particles clinging to the dipstick, the oil should be changed (see Section 8).

Engine coolant

Refer to illustrations 4.9a and 4.9b

Warning: *Do not allow antifreeze to come in contact with your skin or painted surfaces of the vehicle. Flush contaminated areas immediately with plenty of water. Don't store new coolant or leave old coolant lying around where it's accessible to children or pets – they're attracted by its sweet smell. Ingestion of even a small amount of coolant can be fatal! Wipe up garage floor and drip pan spills immediately. Keep antifreeze containers covered and repair cooling system leaks as soon as they're noticed.*

8   All vehicles covered by this manual are equipped with a pressurized coolant recovery system. A white plastic coolant reservoir located at the front or an expansion tank located on the side of the engine compartment (1991 and later 4.6L engines) is connected by a hose to the radiator.

9   The coolant level in the tank should be checked regularly. **Warning:** Do not remove the radiator cap or expansion tank cap to check the coolant level when the engine is warm! The level in the tank

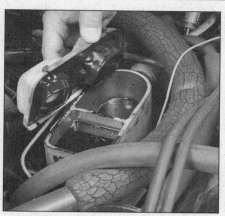

4.15a On earlier models, use a screwdriver to detach the spring retainer, then remove the cover to check the brake fluid level

4.15b The brake fluid level should within 1/4-inch of the top - this reservoir is quite low

4.15c The brake fluid level should be near the MAX line on the translucent plastic reservoir

varies with the temperature of the engine. When the engine is cold, the coolant level should be at or slightly above the FULL COLD mark on the reservoir or expansion tank. Once the engine has warmed up, the level should be at or near the FULL HOT mark. If it isn't, allow the engine to cool, then remove the cap from the tank and add a 50/50 mixture of ethylene glycol based antifreeze and water **(see illustrations)**.

10   Drive the vehicle and recheck the coolant level. If only a small amount of coolant is required to bring the system up to the proper level, water can be used. However, repeated additions of water will dilute the antifreeze and water solution. In order to maintain the proper ratio of antifreeze and water, always top up the coolant level with the correct mixture. Don't use rust inhibitors or additives. An empty plastic milk jug or bleach bottle makes an excellent container for mixing coolant.

11   If the coolant level drops consistently, there may be a leak in the system. Inspect the radiator, hoses, filler cap, drain plugs and water pump (see Section 18). If no leaks are noted, have the radiator cap or expansion tank cap pressure tested by a service station.

12   If you have to remove the radiator cap or expansion tank cap, wait until the engine has cooled completely, then wrap a thick cloth around the cap and turn it to the first stop (if you're removing an expansion tank cap, unscrew it slowly, stopping if you hear a hissing noise). If coolant or steam escapes, let the engine cool down longer, then remove the cap.

13   Check the condition of the coolant as well. It should be relatively clear. If it's brown or rust colored, the system should be drained, flushed and refilled. Even if the coolant appears to be normal, the corrosion inhibitors wear out, so it must be replaced at the specified intervals.

Brake fluid

Refer to illustrations 4.15a, 4.15b and 4.15c

14   The brake fluid level is checked by looking through the plastic reservoir mounted on the master cylinder. The master cylinder is mounted on the front of the power booster unit in the left (driver's side) rear corner of the engine compartment.

15   On earlier models, use a screwdriver to remove the cover and check the fluid level. **(see illustrations)**. On later models, the reservoir is translucent plastic and level can be checked visually. The level should be between the MAX and MIN lines on the side of the reservoir **(see illustration)**.

16   If the fluid level is low on later models, wipe the top of the reservoir and the cap with a clean rag to prevent contamination of the system as the cap is unscrewed.

17   Add only the specified brake fluid to the reservoir (refer to *Recommended lubricants and fluids* at the front of this Chapter or your

owner's manual). Mixing different types of brake fluid can damage the system. Fill the reservoir to the specified level (MAX line on later models). **Warning:** *Brake fluid can harm your eyes and damage painted surfaces, so use extreme caution when handling or pouring it. Do not use brake fluid that has been standing open or is more than one year old. Brake fluid absorbs moisture from the air, which can cause a dangerous loss of braking effectiveness.*

18   While the reservoir cap is off, check the master cylinder reservoir for contamination. If rust deposits, dirt particles or water droplets are present, the system should be drained and refilled by a dealer service department or repair shop.

19   After filling the reservoir to the proper level, make sure the cap is seated to prevent fluid leakage and/or contamination.

20   The fluid level in the master cylinder will drop slightly as the brake shoes or pads at each wheel wear down during normal operation. If the brake fluid level drops consistently, check the entire system for leaks immediately. Examine all brake lines, hoses and connections, along with the calipers, wheel cylinders and master cylinder (see Section 27).

21   When checking the fluid level, if you discover the reservoir is empty or nearly empty, the brake system should be bled (see Chapter 9).

Windshield washer fluid

Refer to illustration 4.22

22   Fluid for the windshield washer system is stored in a plastic reservoir located at the side of the engine compartment **(see illustration)**.

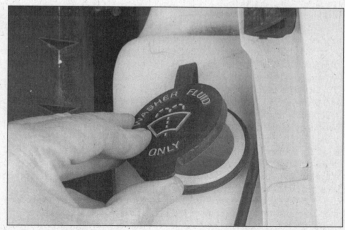

4.22 The windshield washer reservoir is located at the left front corner of the engine compartment on most models

23   In milder climates, plain water can be used in the reservoir, but it should be kept no more than 2/3 full to allow for expansion if the water freezes. In colder climates, use windshield washer system antifreeze, available at any auto parts store, to lower the freezing point of the fluid. Mix the antifreeze with water in accordance with the manufacturer's directions on the container. **Caution:** *Do not use cooling system antifreeze - it will damage the vehicle's paint.*

5   Tire and tire pressure checks (every 250 miles or weekly)

Refer to illustrations 5.2, 5.3, 5.4a, 5.4b and 5.8

1   Periodic inspection of the tires may spare you the inconvenience of being stranded with a flat tire. It can also provide you with vital information regarding possible problems in the steering and suspension systems before major damage occurs.
2   The original tires on this vehicle are equipped with 1/2-inch wide bands that will appear when tread depth reaches 1/16-inch (when the tires are worn out). Tread wear can be monitored with a simple, inexpensive device known as a tread depth indicator **(see illustration)**.
3   Note any abnormal tread wear **(see illustration)**. Tread pattern irregularities such as cupping, flat spots and more wear on one side than the other are indications of front end alignment and/or balance problems. If any of these conditions are noted, take the vehicle to a tire shop or service station to correct the problem.
4   Look closely for cuts, punctures and embedded nails or tacks. Sometimes a tire will hold air pressure for a short time or leak down very slowly after a nail has embedded itself in the tread. If a slow leak persists, check the valve stem core to make sure it is tight **(see illustration)**. Examine the tread for an object that may have embedded itself in the tire or for a "plug" that may have begun to leak (radial tire punctures are repaired with a plug that is installed in a puncture). If a puncture is suspected, it can be easily verified by spraying a solution of soapy water onto the puncture area **(see illustration)**. The soapy

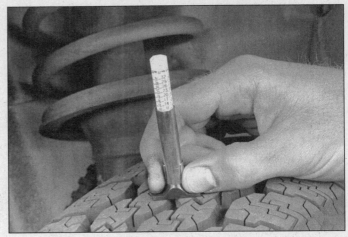

5.2 Use a tire tread depth indicator to monitor tire wear - they are available at auto parts stores and service stations and cost very little

solution will bubble if there is a leak. Unless the puncture is unusually large, a tire shop or service station can usually repair the tire.
5   Carefully inspect the inner sidewall of each tire for evidence of brake fluid leakage. If you see any, inspect the brakes immediately.
6   Correct air pressure adds miles to the lifespan of the tires, improves mileage and enhances overall ride quality. Tire pressure cannot be accurately estimated by looking at a tire, especially if it's a radial. A tire pressure gauge is essential. Keep an accurate gauge in the glove compartment. The pressure gauges attached to the nozzles of air hoses at gas stations are often inaccurate.
7   Always check tire pressure when the tires are cold. Cold, in this case, means the vehicle has not been driven over a mile in the three

Condition	Probable cause	Corrective action	Condition	Probable cause	Corrective action
Shoulder wear	• Underinflation (both sides wear) • Incorrect wheel camber (one side wear) • Hard cornering • Lack of rotation	• Measure and adjust pressure. • Repair or replace axle and suspension parts. • Reduce speed. • Rotate tires.	Feathered edge **Toe wear**	• Incorrect toe	• Adjust toe-in.
Center wear	• Overinflation • Lack of rotation	• Measure and adjust pressure. • Rotate tires.	**Uneven wear**	• Incorrect camber or caster • Malfunctioning suspension • Unbalanced wheel • Out-of-round brake drum • Lack of rotation	• Repair or replace axle and suspension parts. • Repair or replace suspension parts. • Balance or replace. • Turn or replace. • Rotate tires.

5.3 This chart will help you determine the condition of the tires, the probable cause(s) of abnormal wear and the corrective action necessary

5.4a If a tire loses air on a steady basis, check the valve stem core first to make sure it's snug (special inexpensive wrenches are commonly available at auto parts stores)

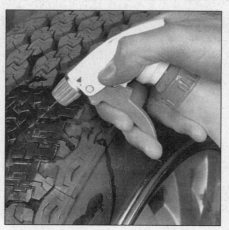

5.4b If the valve stem core is tight, raise the corner of the vehicle with the low tire and spray a soapy water solution onto the tread as the tire is turned slowly - leaks will cause small bubbles to appear

5.8 To extend the life of the tires, check the air pressure at least once a week with an accurate gauge (don't forget the spare!)

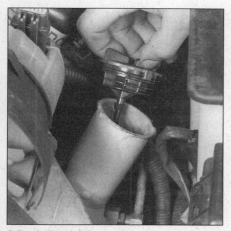

6.5a A dipstick is used to check the power steering fluid level on earlier models

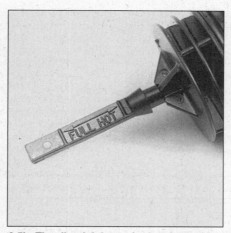

6.5b The dipstick is marked on both sides so the fluid can be checked hot . . .

6.5c . . . or cold

hours preceding a tire pressure check. A pressure rise of four to eight pounds is not uncommon once the tires are warm.

8   Unscrew the valve cap protruding from the wheel or hubcap and push the gauge firmly onto the valve stem **(see illustration)**. Note the reading on the gauge and compare the figure to the recommended tire pressure shown on the tire placard on the driver's side door. Be sure to reinstall the valve cap to keep dirt and moisture out of the valve stem mechanism. Check all four tires and, if necessary, add enough air to bring them up to the recommended pressure.

9   Don't forget to keep the spare tire inflated to the specified pressure (refer to your owner's manual or the decal usually found on the right door pillar). Note that the pressure recommended for the temporary (mini) spare is higher than for the tires on the vehicle.

6   Power steering fluid level check (every 3000 miles or 3 months)

Refer to illustrations 6.5a, 6.5b, 6.5c and 6.9

1   Check the power steering fluid level periodically to avoid steering system problems, such as damage to the pump. **Caution:** *DO NOT hold the steering wheel against either stop (extreme left or right turn) for more than five seconds. If you do, the power steering pump could be damaged.*

1991 and earlier models

2   The power steering pump, located at the front corner of the engine, is equipped with a twist-off cap with an integral fluid level dipstick.

3   Park the vehicle on level ground and apply the parking brake.

4   Run the engine until it has reached normal operating temperature. With the engine at idle, turn the steering wheel back-and-forth several times to get any air out of the steering system. Shut the engine off, remove the cap by turning it counterclockwise, wipe the dipstick clean and reinstall the cap. (Make sure it is seated.)

5   Remove the cap again and note the fluid level. It must be between the two lines designating the FULL HOT or FULL COLD range **(see illustration)**. Be sure to use the proper temperature range on the dipstick when checking the fluid level - the FULL COLD lines on the reverse side of the dipstick are only usable when the engine is cold **(see illustrations)**.

6   Add small amounts of fluid until the level is correct. **Caution:** *Do not overfill the pump. If too much fluid is added, remove the excess with a clean syringe or suction pump.*

7   If additional fluid is required, pour the specified type directly into the reservoir, using a funnel to prevent spills.

1992 and later models

8   The fluid reservoir for the power steering pump is located on the

6.9 The power steering fluid reservoir on later models is translucent so the fluid level can be checked without removing the cap - unscrew the cap to add fluid

7.4 The automatic transmission dipstick (arrow) is located at the rear of the engine

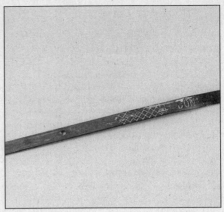

7.6 Check the fluid with the transmission at normal operating temperature - the level should be kept in the HOT range in the cross-hatched area (don't add fluid if the level is anywhere in the cross-hatched area)

inner fender panel near the front of the engine on the left (drivers) side of the engine compartment.

9   On these models the reservoir is translucent plastic and the fluid level can be checked visually **(see illustration)**.

10   The fluid level should be kept between the FULL and ADD marks on the reservoir.

11   Add small amounts of fluid until the level is correct. **Caution:** *Do not overfill the reservoir. If too much fluid is added, remove the excess with a clean syringe or suction pump.*

All models

12   If the reservoir requires frequent fluid additions, all power steering hoses, hose connections, the power steering pump and the steering gear assembly should be carefully checked for leaks.

7   Automatic transmission fluid level check (every 3000 miles or 3 months)

Refer to illustrations 7.4 and 7.6

1   The automatic transmission fluid level should be carefully maintained. Low fluid level can lead to slipping or loss of drive, while overfilling can cause foaming and loss of fluid. Either condition can cause transmission damage.

2   Since transmission fluid expands as it heats up, the fluid level should only be checked when the transmission is warm (at normal operating temperature). If the vehicle has just been driven over 20 miles (32 km), the transmission can be considered warm. **Caution:** *If the vehicle has just been driven for a long time at high speed or in city traffic in hot weather, or if it has been pulling a trailer, an accurate fluid level reading cannot be obtained.* Allow the transmission to cool down for about 30 minutes. You can also check the transmission fluid level when the transmission is cold. If the vehicle has not been driven for over five hours and the fluid is about room temperature (70 to 95-degrees F), the transmission is cold. However, the fluid level is normally checked with the transmission warm to ensure accurate results.

3   Immediately after driving the vehicle, park it on a level surface, set the parking brake and start the engine. While the engine is idling, depress the brake pedal and move the selector lever through all the gear ranges, beginning and ending in Park.

4   Locate the automatic transmission dipstick tube in the engine compartment **(see illustration)**.

5   With the engine still idling, pull the dipstick from the tube, wipe it off with a clean rag, push it all the way back into the tube and withdraw

it again, then note the fluid level.

6   If the transmission is cold, the level should be in the room temperature range on the dipstick (between the two holes); if it's warm, the fluid level should be in the operating temperature range (in the cross-hatched area) **(see illustration)**. If the level is low, add the specified automatic transmission fluid through the dipstick tube - use a funnel to prevent spills.

7   Add just enough of the recommended fluid to fill the transmission to the proper level. It takes about one pint to raise the level from the low mark to the high mark when the fluid is hot, so add the fluid a little at a time and keep checking the level until it's correct.

8   The condition of the fluid should also be checked along with the level. If the fluid is black or a dark reddish-brown color, or if it smells burned, it should be changed (see Section 33). If you are in doubt about its condition, purchase some new fluid and compare the two for color and smell.

8   Engine oil and filter change (every 3000 miles or 3 months)

Refer to illustrations 8.2, 8.7, 8.12 and 8.16

1   Frequent oil changes are the most important preventive maintenance procedures that can be done by the home mechanic. As engine oil ages, in becomes diluted and contaminated, which leads to premature engine wear.

2   Make sure that you have all the necessary tools before you begin this procedure **(see illustration)**. You should also have plenty of rags or newspapers handy for mopping up oil spills.

3   Access to the oil drain plug and filter will be improved if the vehicle can be lifted on a hoist, driven onto ramps or supported by jackstands. **Warning:** *Do not work under a vehicle supported only by a bumper, hydraulic or scissors-type jack - always use jackstands!*

4   If you haven't changed the oil on this vehicle before, get under it and locate the oil drain plug(s) and the oil filter. The exhaust components will be warm as you work, so note how they are routed to avoid touching them when you are under the vehicle.

5   Start the engine and allow it to reach normal operating temperature - oil and sludge will flow out more easily when warm. If new oil, a filter or tools are needed, use the vehicle to go get them and warm up the engine/oil at the same time. Park on a level surface and shut off the engine when it's warmed up. Remove the oil filler cap from the valve cover.

6   Raise the vehicle and support it on jackstands. Make sure it is safely supported!

7   Being careful not to touch the hot exhaust components, position a drain pan under the plug in the bottom of the engine, then remove the plug **(see illustration)**. Some models have two drain plugs and both must be removed to fully drain the pan. It's a good idea to wear a rubber glove while unscrewing the plug the final few turns to avoid being scalded by hot oil.

8   It may be necessary to move the drain pan slightly as oil flow slows to a trickle. Inspect the old oil for the presence of metal particles.

9   After all the oil has drained, wipe off the drain plug with a clean rag. Any small metal particles clinging to the plug would immediately contaminate the new oil.

10   Clean the area around the drain plug opening, reinstall the plug(s) and tighten it securely, but don't strip the threads.

11   Move the drain pan into position under the oil filter.

12   Loosen the oil filter by turning it counterclockwise with a filter wrench **(see illustration)**. Any standard filter wrench will work.

13   Sometimes the oil filter is screwed on so tightly that it can't be loosened. If it is, punch a metal bar or long screwdriver directly through it, as close to the engine as possible, and use it as a T-bar to turn the filter. Be prepared for oil to spurt out of the canister as it's punctured.

14   Once the filter is loose, use your hands to unscrew it from the block. Just as the filter is detached from the block, immediately tilt the open end up to prevent the oil inside the filter from spilling out.

15   Using a clean rag, wipe off the mounting surface on the block. Also, make sure that none of the old gasket remains stuck to the mounting surface. It can be removed with a scraper if necessary.

16   Compare the old filter with the new one to make sure they are the same type. Smear some engine oil on the rubber gasket of the new filter and screw it into place **(see illustration)**. Overtightening the filter will damage the gasket, so don't use a filter wrench. Most filter manufacturers recommend tightening the filter by hand only. Normally they should be tightened 3/4-turn after the gasket contacts the block, but be sure to follow the directions on the filter or container.

17   Remove all tools and materials from under the vehicle, being careful not to spill the oil in the drain pan, then lower the vehicle.

18   Add new oil to the engine through the oil filler cap in the valve cover. Use a funnel to prevent oil from spilling onto the top of the engine. Pour four quarts of fresh oil into the engine. Wait a few minutes to allow the oil to drain into the pan, then check the level on the dipstick (see Section 4 if necessary). If the oil level is in the SAFE range (hatched area), install the filler cap.

19   Start the engine and run it for about a minute. While the engine is running, look under the vehicle and check for leaks at the oil pan drain plug and around the oil filter. If either one is leaking, stop the engine and tighten the plug or filter slightly.

20   Wait a few minutes, then recheck the level on the dipstick. Add oil as necessary to bring the level into the SAFE range.

21   During the first few trips after an oil change, make it a point to check frequently for leaks and proper oil level.

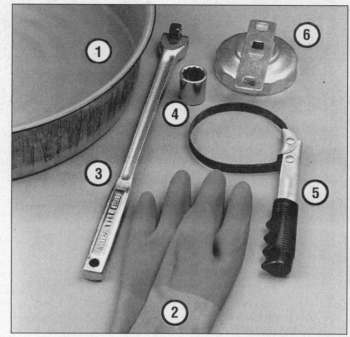

8.2 These tools are required when changing the engine oil and filter

1   **Drain pan** - It should be fairly shallow in depth, but wide to prevent spills

2   **Rubber gloves** - When removing the drain plug and filter, you will get oil on your hands (the gloves will prevent burns)

3   **Breaker bar** - Sometimes the oil drain plug is tight, and a long breaker bar is needed to loosen it

4   **Socket** – To be used with the breaker bar or a ratchet (must be the correct size to fit the drain plug - six-point preferred)

5   **Filter wrench** - This is a metal band-type wrench, which requires clearance around the filter to be effective

6   **Filter wrench** - This type fits on the bottom of the filter and can be turned with a ratchet or breaker bar (different-size wrenches are available for different types of filters)

22   The old oil drained from the engine cannot be reused in its present state and should be discarded. Oil reclamation centers, auto repair shops and gas stations will normally accept the oil, which can be recycled. After the oil has cooled, it can be drained into a container (plastic jugs, bottles, milk cartons, etc.) for transport to a disposal site.

8.7 Use a proper size box-end wrench or socket to remove the oil drain plug and avoid rounding it off

8.12 Since the oil filter (accessible from below) is usually on very tight, you'll need a special wrench for removal - DO NOT use the wrench to tighten the new filter

8.16 Lubricate the oil filter gasket with clean engine oil before installing the filter on the engine

9   Underhood hose check and replacement (every 7500 miles or 6 months)

Warning: *Replacement of air conditioning hoses must be left to a dealer service department or air conditioning shop that has the equipment to depressurize the system safely. Never remove air conditioning components or hoses until the system has been depressurized.*

General

1   High temperatures under the hood can cause deterioration of the rubber and plastic hoses used for engine, accessory and emission systems operation. Periodic inspection should be made for cracks, loose clamps, material hardening and leaks.
2   Information specific to the cooling system hoses can be found in Section 18.
3   Most (but not all) hoses are secured to the fittings with clamps. Where clamps are used, check to be sure they haven't lost their tension, allowing the hose to leak. If clamps aren't used, make sure the hose has not expanded and/or hardened where it slips over the fitting, allowing it to leak.

PCV system hose

4   To reduce hydrocarbon emissions, crankcase blow-by gas is vented through the PCV valve in the rocker arm cover to the intake manifold via a rubber hose on most models. The blow-by gases mix with incoming air in the intake manifold before being burned in the combustion chambers.
5   Check the PCV hose for cracks, leaks and other damage. Disconnect it from the valve cover and the intake manifold and check the inside for obstructions. If it's clogged, clean it out with solvent.

Vacuum hoses

6   It's quite common for vacuum hoses, especially those in the emissions system, to be color coded or identified by colored stripes molded into them. Various systems require hoses with different wall thicknesses, collapse resistance and temperature resistance. When replacing hoses, be sure the new ones are made of the same material.
7   Often the only effective way to check a hose is to remove it completely from the vehicle. If more than one hose is removed, be sure to label the hoses and fittings to ensure correct installation.
8   When checking vacuum hoses, be sure to include any plastic T-fittings in the check. Inspect the fittings for cracks and the hose where it fits over each fitting for distortion, which could cause leakage.
9   A small piece of vacuum hose (1/4-inch inside diameter) can be used as a stethoscope to detect vacuum leaks. Hold one end of the hose to your ear and probe around vacuum hoses and fittings, listening for the "hissing" sound characteristic of a vacuum leak. **Warning:** *When probing with the vacuum hose stethoscope, be careful not to come into contact with moving engine components such as drivebelts, the cooling fan, etc.*

Fuel hose

Warning: *Gasoline is extremely flammable, so take extra precautions when you work on any part of the fuel system. Don't smoke or allow open flames or bare light bulbs near the work area, and don't work in a garage where a natural gas-type appliance (such as a water heater or clothes dryer) with a pilot light is present. Since gasoline is carcinogenic, wear latex gloves when there's a possibility of being exposed to fuel, and, if you spill any fuel on your skin, rinse it off immediately with soap and water. Mop up any spills immediately and do not store fuel-soaked rags where they could ignite. On fuel injected engines the fuel system is under constant pressure, so, if any fuel lines are to be disconnected, the fuel pressure in the system must be relieved first (see Chapter 4 for more information). When you perform any kind of work on the fuel system, wear safety glasses and have a Class B type fire extinguisher on hand.*
10   The fuel lines are usually under pressure, so if any fuel lines are to be disconnected be prepared to catch spilled fuel. **Warning:** *If your vehicle is equipped with fuel injection you must relieve the fuel system pressure before servicing the fuel lines.* Refer to Chapter 4 for the fuel system pressure relief procedure.
11   Check all flexible fuel lines for deterioration and chafing. Check especially for cracks in areas where the hose bends and just before fittings, such as where a hose attaches to the fuel pump, fuel filter and carburetor or fuel injection unit.
12   On fuel-injected models, when replacing a hose, use only hose that is specifically designed for fuel injection systems.
13   Spring-type clamps are sometimes used on fuel return or vapor lines. These clamps often lose their tension over a period of time, and can be "sprung" during removal. Replace all spring-type clamps with screw clamps whenever a hose is replaced. Some fuel lines use spring-lock type couplings, which require a special tool to disconnect. See Chapter 4 for more information on these type of couplings.

Metal lines

14   Sections of metal line are often used for fuel line between the fuel pump and the carburetor or fuel injection unit. Check carefully to make sure the line isn't bent, crimped or cracked.
15   If a section of metal fuel line must be replaced, use seamless steel tubing only, since copper and aluminum tubing do not have the strength necessary to withstand vibration caused by the engine.
16   Check the metal brake lines where they enter the master cylinder and brake proportioning unit (if used) for cracks in the lines and loose fittings. Any sign of brake fluid leakage calls for an immediate thorough inspection of the brake system.

10   Drivebelt check and replacement (every 7500 miles or 6 months)

Refer to illustrations 10.3, 10.4, 10.5, 10.6a, 10.6b, 10.8, 10.13 and 10.15
1   The drivebelts are located at the front of the engine and play an important role in the overall operation of the vehicle and its components. Due to their function and material make-up, the drivebelts are prone to failure after a period of time and should be inspected and adjusted periodically to prevent major engine damage.
2   The number of belts used on a particular vehicle depends on the accessories installed. Drivebelts are used to turn the alternator, power steering pump, water pump, air pump and air-conditioning compressor. Depending on the pulley arrangement, more than one of these components may be driven by a single belt. On later models, a single self-adjusting serpentine drivebelt is used to drive all of the components.

Inspection

3   With the engine off, open the hood and locate the various belts at the front of the engine. Using your fingers (and a flashlight, if necessary), move along the belts checking for cracks and separation of the belt plies. Also check for fraying and glazing, which gives the belt a shiny appearance **(see illustration)**. Both sides of each belt should be

10.3 Here are some of the more common problems associated with drivebelts (check the belts very carefully to prevent an untimely breakdown)

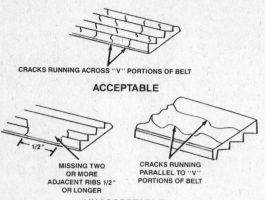

CRACKS RUNNING ACROSS "V" PORTIONS OF BELT

ACCEPTABLE

1/2"

MISSING TWO OR MORE ADJACENT RIBS 1/2" OR LONGER

CRACKS RUNNING PARALLEL TO "V" PORTIONS OF BELT

UNACCEPTABLE

10.4 Small cracks in the underside of a V-ribbed belt are acceptable - lengthwise cracks, or missing pieces that cause the belt to make noise, are cause for replacement

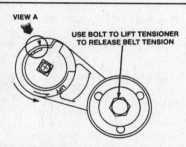

10.6a The serpentine drivebelt is automatically tensioned and requires no service as long as it is in good condition and the indicator is in the proper range (1994 and earlier)

VIEW A

USE BOLT TO LIFT TENSIONER TO RELEASE BELT TENSION

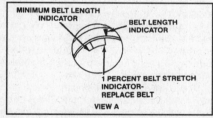

MINIMUM BELT LENGTH INDICATOR

BELT LENGTH INDICATOR

1 PERCENT BELT STRETCH INDICATOR- REPLACE BELT

VIEW A

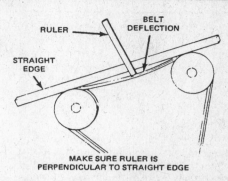

10.5 Measuring drivebelt deflection with a straightedge and ruler

RULER

BELT DEFLECTION

STRAIGHT EDGE

MAKE SURE RULER IS PERPENDICULAR TO STRAIGHT EDGE

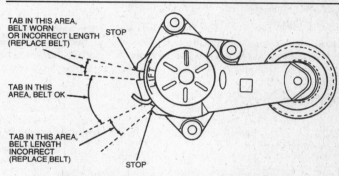

TAB IN THIS AREA, BELT WORN OR INCORRECT LENGTH (REPLACE BELT)

STOP

TAB IN THIS AREA, BELT OK

TAB IN THIS AREA, BELT LENGTH INCORRECT (REPLACE BELT)

STOP

10.6b The serpentine belt on 1995 and later models is also automatically tensioned - it operates the same way, except the position of the tab is used to indicate belt wear

10.8 Typical drivebelt details - 5.0L engine shown

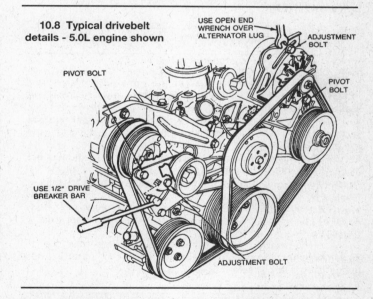

USE OPEN END WRENCH OVER ALTERNATOR LUG

ADJUSTMENT BOLT

PIVOT BOLT

PIVOT BOLT

USE 1/2" DRIVE BREAKER BAR

ADJUSTMENT BOLT

inspected, which means you will have to twist the belt to check the underside.

4   If your vehicle is equipped with serpentine belts, check the ribs on the underside of the belt. They should all be the same depth, with none of the surface uneven **(see illustration)**.

5   The tension of each belt on earlier models is checked by pushing on the belt at a distance halfway between the pulleys. Push firmly with your thumb and see how much the belt moves (deflects) **(see illustration)**. A rule of thumb is that if the distance from pulley center-to-pulley center is between 7 and 11 inches, the belt should deflect 1/4-inch. If the belt travels between pulleys spaced 12 to 16 inches apart, the belt should deflect 1/2-inch.

6   The tension of the belt on later models with serpentine belts is checked visually. Locate the belt tensioner at the front of the engine on the right (passenger) side, adjacent to the lower crankshaft pulley, then find the tensioner operating marks **(see illustrations)**. If the indicator mark is outside the operating range, the belt should be replaced.

7   If it is necessary to adjust the belt tension on earlier models, either to make the belt tighter or looser, it is done by moving the belt tensioner or the component, depending on which belt is being adjusted.

8   On some models, the adjustment is made by loosening adjustment and pivot bolts on the component, then moving the component in the required direction **(see illustration)**. Hold the component in position and tighten the adjustment bolt, followed by the pivot bolt.

9   On some later models the components adjustment is made with a tensioner. Loosen the adjustment and pivot bolts on the tensioner **(see**

illustration 10.8), Apply tension (on later models you can insert a 1/2-inch drive breaker bar into the square drive hole in the tensioner). Tighten the adjustment bolt when the desired tension is attained, followed by the pivot bolt.

Replacement

Non-serpentine belt models

10   Follow the above procedures for drivebelt adjustment but slip the belt off the pulleys and remove it. Since belts tend to wear out more or less at the same time, it's a good idea to replace all of them at the same time.

11   Take the old belts with you when purchasing new ones in order to make a direct comparison for length, width and design.

12   Adjust the belts as described earlier in this Section.

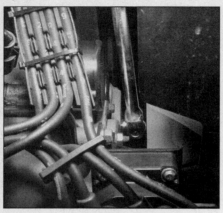

10.13 Place a socket over the tensioner bolt and lift up to release the belt tension

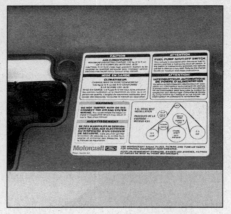

10.15 The routing schematic for the serpentine belt is usually found on the fan shroud (this one's for the 4.6L engine)

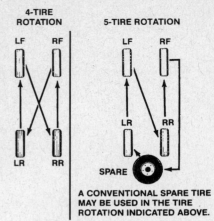

11.2 The recommended tire rotation pattern for these vehicles

Serpentine belt models

13   To replace the belt, lift the tensioner at the bolt **(see illustration)**. The tensioner will swing down once the tension of the belt is released.

14   Remove the belt from the auxiliary components and carefully release the tensioner.

15   Route the new belt over the various pulleys, again rotating the tensioner to allow the belt to be installed, then release the belt tensioner. Make sure the belt fits properly into the pulley grooves - it must be completely engaged. **Note:** *Most models have a drivebelt routing decal on the upper radiator panel to help during drivebelt installation* **(see illustration)**.

11   Tire rotation (every 7500 miles or 6 months)

Refer to illustration 11.2

1   The tires should be rotated at the specified intervals and whenever uneven wear is noticed. Since the vehicle will be raised and the tires removed anyway, check the brakes also (see Section 27).

2   Radial tires must be rotated in a specific pattern **(see illustration)**. If your vehicle has a compact spare tire, don't include it in the rotation pattern.

3   Refer to the information in *Jacking and towing* at the front of this manual for the proper procedure to follow when raising the vehicle and changing a tire. If the brakes must be checked, don't apply the parking brake as stated.

4   The vehicle must be raised on a hoist or supported on jackstands to get all four wheels off the ground. Make sure the vehicle is safely supported!

5   After the rotation procedure is finished, check and adjust the tire pressures as necessary and be sure to tighten the lug nuts to the torque listed in this Chapter's Specifications.

12   Seat belt check (every 7500 miles or 6 months)

1   Check seat belts, buckles, latch plates and guide loops for obvious damage and signs of wear.

2   See if the seat belt reminder light comes on when the key is turned to the Run or Start position. A chime should also sound. On passive restraint systems, the shoulder belt should move into position in the A-pillar.

3   The seat belts are designed to lock up during a sudden stop or impact, yet allow free movement during normal driving. Make sure the retractors return the belt against your chest while driving and rewind the belt fully when the buckle is unlatched.

4   If any of the above checks reveal problems with the seat belt system, replace parts as necessary.

13   Battery check, maintenance and charging (every 7500 miles or 6 months)

Refer to illustrations 13.1, 13.6a, 13.6b, 13.7a, 13.7b and 13.8

Warning: *Certain precautions must be followed when checking and servicing the battery. Hydrogen gas, which is highly flammable, is always present in the battery cells, so keep lighted tobacco and all other open flames and sparks away from the battery. The electrolyte inside the battery is actually dilute sulfuric acid, which will cause injury if splashed on your skin or in your eyes. It will also ruin clothes and painted surfaces. When removing the battery cables, always detach the negative cable first and hook it up last!*

1   A routine preventive maintenance program for the battery in your vehicle is the only way to ensure quick and reliable starts. But before performing any battery maintenance, make sure that you have the proper equipment necessary to work safely around the battery **(see illustration)**.

2   There are also several precautions that should be taken whenever battery maintenance is performed. Before servicing the battery, always turn the engine and all accessories off and disconnect the cable from the negative terminal of the battery.

3   The battery produces hydrogen gas, which is both flammable and explosive. Never create a spark, smoke or light a match around the battery. Always charge the battery in a ventilated area.

4   Electrolyte contains poisonous and corrosive sulfuric acid. Do not allow it to get in your eyes, on your skin on your clothes. Never ingest it. Wear protective safety glasses when working near the battery. Keep children away from the battery.

5   Note the external condition of the battery. If the positive terminal and cable clamp on your vehicle's battery is equipped with a rubber protector, make sure that it's not torn or damaged. It should completely cover the terminal. Look for any corroded or loose connections, cracks in the case or cover or loose hold-down clamps. Also check the entire length of each cable for cracks and frayed conductors.

6   If corrosion, which looks like white, fluffy deposits **(see illustration)** is evident, particularly around the terminals, the battery should be removed for cleaning. Loosen the cable clamp bolts with a wrench, being careful to remove the ground cable first, and slide them off the terminals **(see illustration)**. Then disconnect the hold-down clamp bolt and nut, remove the clamp and lift the battery from the engine compartment.

Cleaning

7   Clean the cable clamps thoroughly with a battery brush or a terminal cleaner and a solution of warm water and baking soda **(see illustration)**. Wash the terminals and the top of the battery case with

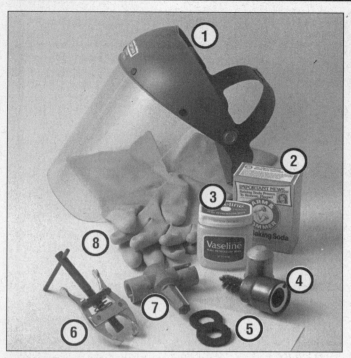

13.1 Tools and materials required for battery maintenance

1   *Face shield/safety goggles* - When removing corrosion with a brush, the acidic particles can easily fly up into your eyes

2   *Baking soda* - A solution of baking soda and water can be used to neutralize corrosion

3   *Petroleum jelly* - A layer of this on the battery posts will help prevent corrosion

4   *Battery post/cable cleaner* - This wire brush cleaning tool will remove all traces of corrosion from the battery posts and cable clamps

5   *Treated felt washers* - Placing one of these on each post, directly under the cable clamps, will help prevent corrosion

6   *Puller* - Sometimes the cable clamps are very difficult to pull off the posts, even after the nut/bolt has been completely loosened. This tool pulls the clamp straight up and off the post without damage

7   *Battery post/cable cleaner* - Here is another cleaning tool which is a slightly different version of Number 4 above, but it does the same thing

8   *Rubber gloves* - Another safety item to consider when servicing the battery; remember that's acid inside the battery!

13.6a Battery terminal corrosion usually appears as light, fluffy powder

13.6b Removing the cable from a battery post with a wrench - sometimes special battery pliers are required for this procedure if corrosion has caused deterioration of the nut hex (always remove the ground cable first and hook it up last!)

the same solution but make sure that the solution doesn't get into the battery When cleaning the cables, terminals and battery top, wear safety goggles and rubber gloves to prevent any solution from coming in contact with your eyes or hands. Wear old clothes too - even diluted, sulfuric acid splashed onto clothes will burn holes in them. If the terminals have been extensively corroded, clean them up with a terminal cleaner **(see illustration)**. Thoroughly wash all cleaned areas with plain water.

13.7a When cleaning the cable clamps, all corrosion must be removed (the inside of the clamp is tapered to match the taper on the post, so don't remove too much material)

13.7b Regardless of the type of tool used on the battery posts, a clean, shiny surface should be the result

13.8 Make sure the battery hold-down nuts or bolts are tight (arrows)

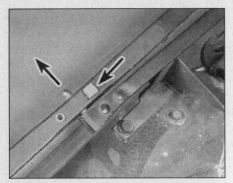

14.4a On earlier models, lift up on the lever and slide the blade assembly off

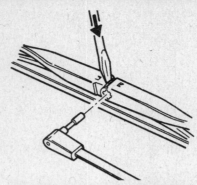

14.4b Press down on the spring with a screwdriver as shown to release the wiper assembly from the arm

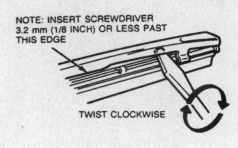

NOTE: INSERT SCREWDRIVER 3.2 mm (1/8 INCH) OR LESS PAST THIS EDGE

TWIST CLOCKWISE

14.6 Detach the element by twisting in a clockwise direction between the wiper frame and the element backing strip

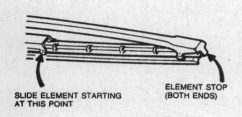

SLIDE ELEMENT STARTING AT THIS POINT

ELEMENT STOP (BOTH ENDS)

14.8a Slide the element into the wiper claws all the way up to the stops

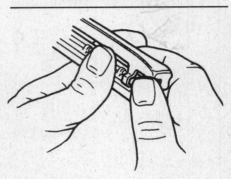

14.8b Lock the end of the element backing strip into place by twisting it into the end claw

15.2 Unscrew the wing-nut and lift the air cleaner cover off

8   Make sure that the battery tray is in good condition and the hold-down clamp bolts are tight **(see illustration)**. If the battery is removed from the tray, make sure no parts remain in the bottom of the tray when the battery is reinstalled. When reinstalling the hold-down clamp bolts, do not overtighten them.

9   Information on removing and installing the battery can be found in Chapter 5. Information on jump starting can be found at the front of this manual. For more detailed battery checking procedures, refer to the *Haynes Automotive Electrical Manual*.

10   Corrosion on the hold-down components, battery case and surrounding areas can be removed with a solution of water and baking soda. Thoroughly rinse all cleaned areas with plain water.

11   Any metal parts of the vehicle damaged by corrosion should be covered with a zinc-based primer, then painted.

Charging

Warning: *When batteries are being charged, hydrogen gas, which is very explosive and flammable, is produced. Do not smoke or allow open flames near a charging or a recently charged battery. Wear eye protection when near the battery during charging. Also, make sure the charger is unplugged before connecting or disconnecting the battery from the charger.*

12   Slow-rate charging is the best way to restore a battery that's discharged to the point where it will not start the engine. It's also a good way to maintain the battery charge in a vehicle that's only driven a few miles between starts. Maintaining the battery charge is particularly important in the winter when the battery must work harder to start the engine and electrical accessories that drain the battery are in greater use.

13   It's best to use a one or two-amp battery charger (sometimes called a "trickle" charger). They are the safest and put the least strain on the battery. They are also the least expensive. For a faster charge,

you can use a higher amperage charger, but don't use one rated more than 1/10th the amp/hour rating of the battery. Rapid boost charges that claim to restore the power of the battery in one to two hours are hardest on the battery and can damage batteries not in good condition. This type of charging should only be used in emergency situations.

14   The average time necessary to charge a battery should be listed in the instructions that come with the charger. As a general rule, a trickle charger will charge a battery in 12 to 16 hours.

14   Windshield wiper blade check and replacement (every 15,000 miles or 12 months)

Refer to illustrations 14.4a, 14.4b, 14.6, 14.8a and 14.8b

1   Road film can build up on the wiper blades and affect their efficiency, so they should be washed regularly with a mild detergent solution.

Check

2   The windshield wiper and blade assembly should be inspected periodically. Even if you don't use your wipers, the sun and elements will dry out the rubber portions, causing them to crack and break apart. If inspection reveals hardened or cracked rubber, replace the wiper blades. If inspection reveals nothing unusual, wet the windshield, turn the wipers on, allow them to cycle several times, then shut them off. An uneven wiper pattern across the glass or streaks over clean glass indicate that the blades should be replaced.

3   The operation of the wiper mechanism can loosen the fasteners, so they should be checked and tightened, as necessary, at the same time the wiper blades are checked (see Chapter 12 for further information regarding the wiper mechanism).

15.4 Lift the filter element out of
the housing

15.6 Pull the PCV filter out of the housing

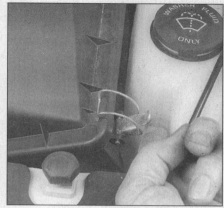

15.7a Lift up on the ends of the clips to
release them

Blade assembly replacement

4   Cycle the wiper assembly to a position on the windshield where removal of the blade assembly can be performed without difficulty. Turn the ignition key off at the desired position. With the blade assembly resting on the windshield, insert a small screwdriver into the release spring at the center of the blade and push down on the spring. Detach the assembly by lifting the release lever (early models) or pressing down with the screwdriver (later models) then pulling the wiper blade off the wiper arm pin (see illustrations).
5   To install the blade assembly, push it onto the pin until it snaps into place. Be sure that the blade assembly is securely attached to the wiper arm.

Blade element replacement

6   At one end of the rubber blade element, insert a small screwdriver between the blade and the metal backing strip (see illustration). Press down and in, then twist the screwdriver clockwise to release the element from the retaining claw.
7   Slide the blade element out of the retaining claws until the element is completely detached from the frame.
8   To install the element, slide the metal backing strip into the retaining claws starting with the second claw from either end (see illustration). Continue sliding the element up to the element stops, then secure the element by twisting the backing strip into the end claws (see illustration).
9   Make sure that all the claws are locked onto the metal backing strip before installing the blade on the wiper arm.

15 Air filter and PCV filter replacement (every 15,000 miles or 12 months)

1   At the specified intervals, the air filter, and on models so equipped, the PCV filter element should be replaced.

Carbureted models

Refer to illustrations 15.2, 15.4 and 15.6

2   The filter is located on top of the carburetor and is replaced by unscrewing the wing nut from the top of the filter housing and lifting off the cover (see illustration).
3   While the top plate is off, be careful not to drop anything down into the carburetor.
4   Lift the air filter element out of the housing (see illustration) and wipe out the inside of the air cleaner housing with a clean rag.
5   Place the new filter element in the air cleaner housing. Make sure it seats properly in the bottom of the housing.
6   On models equipped with a PCV filter element in the air cleaner housing, pull out the old filter and replace it with a new one (see illustration).

Fuel-injected models

Refer to illustrations 15.7a, 15.7b and 15.8

7   Detach the clips and lift the cover off the filter housing (see illustrations).
8   Remove the filter element (see illustration).

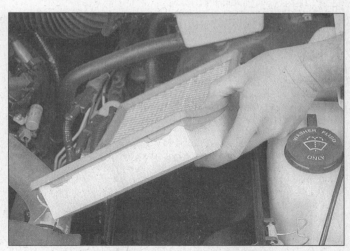

15.7b Raise the housing cover   15.8 Lift the filter out of the housing

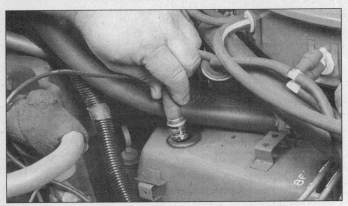

16.2 Pull the PCV valve out of the valve cover to check it

9   Wipe the inside of the air cleaner housing with a clean cloth.
10   Place the new air filter element in the housing. If the element is marked TOP be sure the marked side faces up.
11   Seat the tabs, rotate the cover into place and secure it with the clips.

16   Positive Crankcase Ventilation (PCV) valve check (every 15,000 miles or 12 months)

Refer to illustration 16.2
Note: *To maintain efficient operation of the PCV system, clean the hoses and check the PCV valve at the intervals recommended in the maintenance schedule. For additional information on the PCV system, refer to Chapter 6.*
1   The PCV valve is located in the valve cover.
2   Check the valve by first pulling it out of the valve cover **(see illustration)**. Shake it - if it rattles, reinstall it in the cover.
3   Start the engine and allow it to idle, then disconnect the PCV hose from the air cleaner housing and feel for vacuum at the hose. If vacuum is felt, the PCV valve/system is working properly (see Chapter 6 for additional PCV system information).
4   If no vacuum is felt, the oil filler cap, hoses or valve cover gasket may be leaking or the PCV valve may be bad. Check for vacuum leaks at the valve, filler cap and all hoses.
5   Pull straight up on the valve to remove it. Check the rubber grommet in the valve cover for cracks and distortion. If it's damaged, replace it.
6   If the valve is clogged, the hose is also probably plugged. Remove the hose between the valve and the intake manifold and clean it with solvent.
7   After cleaning the hose, inspect it for damage, wear and deterioration. Make sure it fits snugly on the fittings.
8   If necessary, install a new PCV valve.
9   Install the clean PCV system hose. Make sure that the PCV valve and hose are secure.

17   Fuel system check (every 15,000 miles or 12 months)

Warning: *Gasoline is extremely flammable, so take extra precautions when you work on any part of the fuel system. Don't smoke or allow open flames or bare light bulbs near the work area, and don't work in a garage where a natural gas-type appliance (such as a water heater or clothes dryer) with a pilot light is present. Since gasoline is carcinogenic, wear latex gloves when there's a possibility of being exposed to fuel, and, if you spill any fuel on your skin, rinse it off immediately with soap and water. Mop up any spills immediately and do not store fuel-soaked rags where they could ignite. When you perform any kind of work on the fuel system, wear safety glasses and have a Class B type fire extinguisher on hand. The fuel system on fuel-injected models is*

ALWAYS CHECK hose for chafed or burned areas that may cause an untimely and costly failure.

SOFT hose indicates inside deterioration. This deterioration can contaminate the cooling system and cause particles to clog the radiator.

HARDENED hose can fail at any time. Tightening hose clamps will not seal the connection or stop leaks.

SWOLLEN hose or oil soaked ends indicate danger and possible failure from oil or grease contamination. Squeeze the hose to locate cracks and breaks that cause leaks.

18.4a Hoses, like drivebelts, have a habit of failing at the worst possible time - to prevent the inconvenience of a blown radiator or heater hose, inspect them carefully as shown here

under constant pressure, so, before any lines are disconnected, the fuel system pressure must be relieved (see Chapter 4).
1   If you smell gasoline while driving or after the vehicle has been sitting in the sun, inspect the fuel system immediately.
2   Remove the gas filler cap and inspect if for damage and corrosion. The gasket should have an unbroken sealing imprint. If the gasket is damaged or corroded, install a new cap.
3   Inspect the fuel feed and return lines for cracks. Make sure that the connections between the fuel lines and the fuel injection system and between the fuel lines and the in-line fuel filter are tight. **Warning:** *If you vehicle is fuel injected, you must relieve the fuel system pressure before servicing fuel system components. The fuel system pressure relief procedure is outlined in Chapter 4.*
4   Since some components of the fuel system - the fuel tank and part of the fuel feed and return lines, for example - are underneath the vehicle, they can be inspected more easily with the vehicle raised on a hoist. If that's not possible, raise the vehicle and support it on jackstands.
5   With the vehicle raised and safely supported, inspect the gas tank and filler neck for punctures, cracks and other damage. The connection between the filler neck and the tank is particularly critical. Sometimes a rubber filler neck will leak because of loose clamps or deteriorated rubber. Inspect all fuel tank mounting brackets and straps to be sure that the tank is securely attached to the vehicle. **Warning:** *Do not, under any circumstances, try to repair a fuel tank (except rubber components). A welding torch or any open flame can easily cause fuel vapors inside the tank to explode.*
6   Carefully check all rubber hoses and metal lines leading away from the fuel tank. Check for loose connections, deteriorated hoses, crimped lines and other damage. Repair or replace damaged sections as necessary (see Chapter 4).

18   Cooling system check (every 15,000 miles or 12 months)

Refer to illustrations 18.4a and 18.4b
1   Many major engine failures can be attributed to a faulty cooling

18.4b A leak in the 4.6L V8 engine heater hose means the intake manifold will have to be removed for hose replacement - coolant coming out the back of the engine is the symptom

system. The cooling system also plays an important role in prolonging transmission life because it cools the fluid.

2 The engine should be cold for the cooling system check, so perform the following procedure before the vehicle is driven for the day or after it has been shut off for at least three hours.

3 If you're working on a 1990 or earlier model, remove the cap from the radiator. If you're working on a 1991 or later model, remove the cap from the expansion tank. Clean the cap thoroughly, inside and out, with clean water. Also clean the filler neck on the radiator or expansion tank. The presence of rust or corrosion in the filler neck means the coolant should be changed (see Section 36). The coolant inside the radiator should be relatively clean and transparent. If it's rust colored, drain the system and refill it with new coolant.

4 Carefully check the radiator hoses and the smaller diameter heater hoses **(see illustration)**. Inspect each coolant hose along its entire length, replacing any hose which is cracked, swollen or deteriorated. Cracks will show up better if the hose is squeezed. Pay close attention to hose clamps that secure the hoses to cooling system components. Hose clamps can pinch and puncture hoses, resulting in coolant leaks. Some hoses are hidden from view so sometimes you'll have to trace a coolant leak. For example, the heater hose on the 4.6L V8 engine connects to the water pump under the intake manifold. Should it leak, coolant will run out from the manifold and down the rear of the engine **(see illustration)**.

5 Make sure that all hose connections are tight. A leak in the cooling system will usually show up as white or rust colored deposits on the area adjoining the leak. If wire-type clamps are used on the hoses, it may be a good idea to replace them with screw-type clamps.

6 Clean the front of the radiator and air conditioning condenser with compressed air, if available, or a soft brush. Remove all bugs, leaves, etc. embedded in the radiator fins. Be extremely careful not to damage the cooling fins or cut your fingers on them.

7 If the coolant level has been dropping consistently and no leaks are detectable, have the radiator cap and cooling system pressure checked at a service station.

19 Ignition timing check and adjustment (every 15,000 miles or 12 months)

Refer to illustrations 19.2 and 19.5

1 All vehicles are equipped with an Emissions Control Information label inside the engine compartment. The label contains important ignition timing specifications and the proper timing procedure for your specific vehicle. If the information on the emissions label is different from the information included in this Section, follow the procedure on the label.

2 At the specified intervals, or when the distributor has been removed, the ignition timing must be checked and, if necessary,

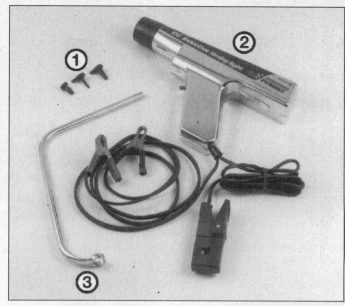

19.2 Tools needed to check and adjust the ignition timing

1 **Vacuum plugs -** *Vacuum hoses will, in most cases, have to be disconnected and plugged. Molded plugs in various shapes and sizes are available for this*

2 **Inductive pick-up timing light -** *Flashes a bright concentrated beam of light when the number one spark plug fires. Connect the leads according to the instructions supplied with the light*

3 **Distributor wrench -** *On some models, the hold-down bolt for the distributor is difficult to reach and turn with a conventional wrench or socket. A special wrench like this must be used*

19.5 The timing marks are the located on the crankshaft pulley and the pointer which is used as reference is attached to the front of the engine

adjusted. Tools required for this procedure include an inductive pick-up timing light, a tachometer, a distributor wrench and, in some cases, a means of plugging vacuum hoses **(see illustration)**.

3 Before you check the timing, make sure the idle speed is correct (see Section 24) and the engine is at normal operating temperature.

4 With the engine off, connect a timing light in accordance with the manufacturer's instructions. Usually, the light must be connected to the battery and the number one spark plug. The number one spark plug wire or terminal should be marked at the distributor; trace it back to the spark plug and attach the timing light lead near the plug.

5 Locate the timing marks on the crankshaft pulley **(see illustra-**

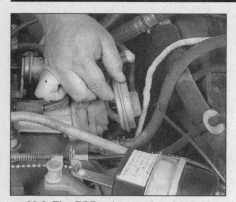

20.2 The EGR valve can be checked for free movement by pushing on the diaphragm

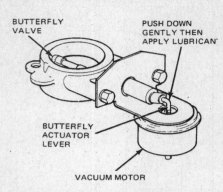

21.2 Exhaust heat control valve details

BUTTERFLY VALVE

PUSH DOWN GENTLY THEN APPLY LUBRICANT

BUTTERFLY ACTUATOR LEVER

VACUUM MOTOR

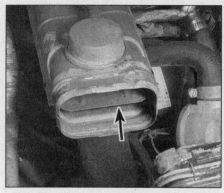

22.3 The damper door (arrow) is located in the air cleaner snorkel

tion). It may be necessary to have an assistant temporarily turn the ignition on and off in short bursts without starting the engine in order to bring the marks into a position where they can easily be cleaned and marked. **Warning:** *Stay clear of all moving engine components when the engine is turned over in this manner.*

6   Locate the pointer on the front the engine **(see illustration 19.5)**.
7   Use white soap-stone, chalk or paint to mark the pointer. Also, put a mark on the timing scale corresponding to the number of degrees specified on the Emission Control Information label in the engine compartment, or as listed in this Chapter's Specifications.
8   Aim the timing light at the marks, again being careful not to come into contact with moving parts. The marks made should appear stationary. If the marks are in alignment, the timing is correct. If the marks are not aligned, turn off the engine.
9   Loosen the hold-down bolt at the base of the distributor. Loosen the bolt only slightly, just enough to turn the distributor (see Chapter 5).
10   Now restart the engine and turn the distributor very slowly until the timing marks are aligned with the pointer.
11   Shut off the engine and tighten the distributor bolt, being careful not to move the distributor.
12   Start the engine and recheck the timing to make sure the marks are still in alignment.
13   Disconnect the timing light and tachometer and reconnect any components which were disconnected for this procedure.

20 Exhaust Gas Recirculation (EGR) valve check (every 15,000 miles or 12 months)

Refer to illustration 20.2
1   The EGR valve is usually located on the intake manifold, adjacent to the carburetor. Most of the time when a problem develops in the emissions system, it's due to a stuck or corroded EGR valve or a damaged or leaking hose or vacuum diaphragm.
2   With the engine cold to prevent burns, reach under the EGR valve and manually push on the diaphragm. Using moderate pressure, you should be able to press the diaphragm up and down inside the housing **(see illustration)**.
3   If the diaphragm doesn't move, or moves only with much effort, replace the EGR valve with a new one. If in doubt about the condition of the valve, compare the free movement of your EGR valve with a new valve.
4   Refer to Chapter 6 for more information on the EGR system.

21 Exhaust control valve lubrication and check (every 15,000 miles or 12 months)

Refer to illustration 21.2
1   Many earlier models are equipped with an exhaust heat control

valve, located near the junction of the exhaust manifold and the exhaust pipe. When the engine is cold, this valve redirects hot exhaust gases through a passage in the intake manifold to increase the fuel vaporization for better low speed driveability.
2   With the engine cold to prevent burns, press gently on the butterfly actuator lever to make sure it opens and closes freely **(see illustration)**. If the action isn't smooth, lubricate it by applying lithium base grease to the lever shaft while operating the shaft by hand to distribute it evenly.

22 Thermostatic air cleaner check (every 15,000 miles or 12 months)

Refer to illustration 22.3
1   Carbureted models are equipped with a thermostatically controlled air cleaner which draws air to the carburetor from different locations, depending upon engine temperature.
2   This is a visual check. If access is limited, a small mirror may have to be used.
3   Open the hood and locate the damper door inside the air cleaner assembly **(see illustration)**.
4   If there is a flexible air duct attached to the end of the air cleaner, disconnect it at the air cleaner. This will enable you to see the damper inside.
5   The check should be done when the engine is cold. Start the engine and look at the damper, which should move to a closed position. With the damper closed, air cannot enter through the air cleaner opening, but instead enters the air cleaner through a flexible duct attached to a heat stove on the exhaust manifold.
6   As the engine warms up to operating temperature, the damper should open to allow air through the air cleaner opening. Depending on outside temperature, this may take 10 to 15 minutes. To speed up this check you can reconnect the air duct, drive the vehicle, then check to see if the damper is completely open.
7   If the thermo-controlled air cleaner is not operating properly, see Chapter 6 for more information.

23 Ignition points check, replacement and adjustment (every 15,000 miles or 12 months)

Refer to illustrations 23.1 and 23.2

Check

1   The ignition points must be replaced at regular intervals on vehicles not equipped with electronic ignition. Occasionally, the rubbing block on the points will wear sufficiently to require readjustment. Several special tools are required to replace the points **(see illustration)**.

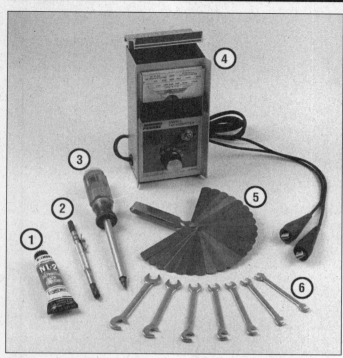

23.1 Tools and materials needed for ignition point replacement and dwell angle adjustment

1   Distributor cam lube - Sometimes this special lubricant comes with the new points; however, its a good idea to buy a tube and have it on hand

2   Screw starter - This tool has special claws which hold the screw securely as it is started, which helps prevent accidental dropping of the screw

3   Magnetic screwdriver - Serves the same purpose as 2 above. If you do not have one of these special screwdrivers, you risk dropping the point mounting screws down into the distributor body

4   Dwell meter - A dwell meter is the only accurate way to determine the point setting (gap). Connect the meter according to the instructions supplied with it

5   Blade-type feeler gauges - These required to set the initial point gap (space between the points when they are open)

6   Ignition wrenches - These special wrenches are made to work within the tight confines of the distributor. Specifically, they are needed to loosen the nut/bolt which secures the leads to the points

2   After removing the distributor cap and rotor, the point and condenser assembly are plainly visible **(see illustration)**. The points may be examined by gently prying them open to reveal the condition of the contact surfaces. If they are rough, pitted or dirty they should be replaced. **Caution:** *The following procedure requires the removal and installation of small screws which can easily fall into the distributor. To retrieve them, the distributor would have to be removed and disassembled. Use a magnetic or spring loaded screwdriver and exercise caution.*

Replacement

3   To replace the condenser, which should be replaced along with the points, remove the screw that secures the condenser to the point plate. Loosen the nut or screw retaining the condenser lead and the primary lead to the point assembly. Remove the condenser and mounting bracket.

4   Remove the point assembly mounting screw.

5   Attach the new point assembly to the distributor plate with the mounting screw.

23.2 The ignition points and related components are accessible after removing the distributor cap and rotor

1	*Condenser*	*5*	*Mounting screw*
2	*Primary lead*	*6*	*Adjusting slot*
3	*Point assembly*	*7*	*Point (distributor) cam*
4	*Primary/condenser lead connection*		

6   Install the new condenser and tighten the mounting screw.

7   Attach the primary ignition lead and the condenser lead to the point assembly. Make sure that the forked connectors for the primary ignition and condenser leads do not touch the distributor plate or any other grounded surface.

Adjustment

8   Two adjusting methods are available for setting the points. The first and most effective method involves an instrument called a dwell meter.

9   Connect one dwell meter lead to the primary ignition terminal of the point assembly or to the distributor terminal of the coil. Connect the other lead of the dwell meter to an engine ground. Some dwell meters may have different connecting instructions, so always follow the instrument manufacturer's directions.

10   Have an assistant crank the engine over or use a remote starter and crank the engine with the ignition switch turned to On.

11   Note the dwell reading on the meter and compare it to the Specifications found at the front of this chapter or on the engine tune-up decal. If the dwell reading is incorrect, adjust it by first loosening the point assembly mounting screw a small amount.

12   Move the point assembly plate with a screwdriver inserted into the slot provided next to the points. Closing the gap on the points will increase the dwell reading, while opening the gap will decrease the dwell.

13   Tighten the screw after the correct reading is obtained and recheck the setting.

14   If a dwell meter is unavailable, a feeler gauge can be used to set the points.

15   Have a helper crank the engine in short bursts until the rubbing block of the points rests on a high point of the cam assembly. The rubbing block must be exactly on the apex of one of the cam lobes for correct point adjustment. It may be necessary to rotate the front pulley of the engine with a socket and breaker bar to position the cam lobe exactly.

16   Measure the gap between the contact points with the correct size feeler gauge. If the gap is incorrect, loosen the mounting screw and move the point assembly until the correct gap is achieved.

17   Retighten the screw and recheck the gap one more time.

18   Apply a small amount of distributor cam lube to the point cam on the distributor shaft.

24.4 Adjusting the idle speed (1976 model shown, others similar)

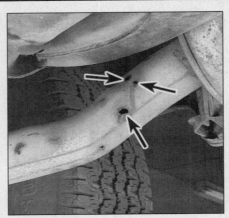

25.2 This exhaust pipe has rust holes (arrows), and should be replaced

26.6 This shock absorber has more than the normal amount of oil buildup, indicating that it should be replaced

24   Idle speed check and adjustment (carbureted models) (every 15,000 miles or 12 months)

Refer to illustration 24.4

1   Engine idle speed is the speed at which the engine operates when no accelerator pedal pressure is applied, as when stopped at a traffic light. This speed is critical to the performance of the engine itself, as well as many engine subsystems. Earlier models have fewer emissions and other controls on the carburetor so adjustment is a simpler procedure. Adjustment procedures for later model carbureted and fuel-injected engines may vary, so it is important to consult the emissions decal in the engine compartment before beginning work.

2   A hand-held tachometer must be used when adjusting idle speed to get an accurate reading. The exact hook-up for these meters varies with the manufacturer, so follow the particular directions included.

3   All vehicles covered in this manual should have a tune-up decal or Emissions Control Information label located on the inside of the hood. The printed instructions for setting idle speed can be found on this decal, and should be followed since they are for your particular engine. If your decal is missing, set the idle speed to the rpm listed in this Chapter's Specifications.

4   With the engine at normal operating temperature, the parking brake firmly set and the wheels blocked to prevent the vehicle from rolling, check the engine idle speed, following the instructions on the decal. Turn off all lights and accessories. Adjustment of the idle speed is made by turning the throttle screw on the carburetor until the specified idle speed is obtained **(see illustration).**

25   Exhaust system check (every 15,000 miles or 12 months)

Refer to illustration 25.2

1   With the engine cold (at least three hours after the vehicle has been driven), check the complete exhaust system from the engine to the end of the tailpipe. Ideally, the inspection should be done with the vehicle on a hoist to permit unrestricted access. If a hoist isn't available, raise the vehicle and support it securely on jackstands.

2   Check the exhaust pipes and connections for evidence of leaks, severe corrosion and damage **(see illustration).** Make sure that all brackets and hangers are in good condition and tight.

3   At the same time, inspect the underside of the body for holes, corrosion, open seams, etc. which may allow exhaust gases to enter the passenger compartment. Seal all body openings with silicone or body putty.

4   Rattles and other noises can often be traced to the exhaust system, especially the mounts and hangers. Try to move the pipes,

muffler and catalytic converter. If the components can come in contact with the body or suspension parts, secure the exhaust system with new mounts.

5   Check the running condition of the engine by inspecting inside the end of the tailpipe. The exhaust deposits here are an indication of engine state-of-tune. If the pipe is black and sooty or coated with white deposits, the engine may need a tune-up, including a thorough fuel system inspection and adjustment.

26   Steering and suspension check (every 15,000 miles or 12 months)

Refer to illustrations 26.6, 26.10 and 26.11

Note: *The steering linkage and suspension components should be checked periodically. Worn or damaged suspension and steering linkage components can result in excessive and abnormal tire wear, poor ride quality and vehicle handling and reduced fuel economy. For detailed illustrations of the steering and suspension components, refer to Chapter 10.*

Shock absorber check

1   Park the vehicle on level ground, turn the engine off and set the parking brake. Check the tire pressures.

2   Push down at one corner of the vehicle, then release it while noting the movement of the body. It should stop moving and come to rest in a level position within one or two bounces.

3   If the vehicle continues to move up-and-down or if it fails to return to its original position, a worn or weak shock absorber is probably the reason.

4   Repeat the above check at each of the three remaining corners of the vehicle.

5   Raise the vehicle and support it securely on jackstands.

6   Check the shock absorbers for evidence of fluid leakage **(see illustration).** A light film of fluid is no cause for concern. Make sure that any fluid noted is from the shocks and not from some other source. If leakage is noted, replace the shocks as a set.

7   Check the shock absorbers to be sure that they are securely mounted and undamaged. Check the upper mounts for damage and wear. If damage or wear is noted, replace the shock absorbers as a set (front or rear).

8   If the shock absorbers must be replaced, refer to Chapter 10 for the procedure.

Steering and suspension check

9   Visually inspect the steering system components for damage and distortion. Look for leaks and damaged seals, boots and fittings.

10   Clean the lower end of the steering knuckle. Have an assistant

26.10 Check the suspension balljoints by trying to move the lower edge of each tire in-and-out while watching/feeling for movement at the top of the tire and balljoints

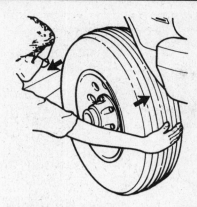

26.11 Grasp each front tire as shown and try to move it back-and-forth - if any play is noted, check the steering gear mounts and make sure that they're tight; if either tie-rod is worn or bent, replace it

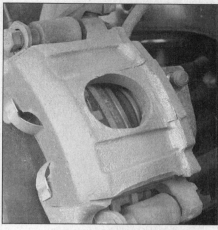

27.4 Determine the thickness of remaining pad material for both inner and outer pads

grasp the lower edge of the tire and move the wheel in-and-out **(see illustration)** while you look for movement at the steering knuckle-to-control arm balljoint. If there is any movement the suspension balljoint(s) must be replaced (see Chapter 10).

11   Grasp each front tire at the front and rear edges, push in at the front, pull out at the rear and feel for play in the steering system components **(see illustration)**. If any freeplay is noted, check the steering gear mounts and the tie-rod ends for looseness.

12   Check the steering gear mount bolt tightness. If the tie-rods are loose, the balljoints may be worn (check to make sure the nuts are tight). Additional steering and suspension system information and illustrations can be found in Chapter 10.

27 Brake system check (every 15,000 miles or 12 months)

Warning: *Brake system dust may contain asbestos, which is harmful to your health. Never blow it out with compressed air and don't inhale any of it. An approved filtering mask should be worn when working on the brakes. Do not, under any circumstances, use petroleum-based solvents to clean brake parts. Use brake system cleaner only!*

Note: For detailed photographs of the brake system, refer to Chapter 9.

1   In addition to the specified intervals, the brake system should be inspected each time the wheels are removed or a malfunction is suspected. Raise the vehicle and support it securely on jackstands. Remove the wheels (see Jacking and towing at the front of this book, or refer to your owner's manual, if necessary).

Disc brakes

Refer to illustration 27.4

2   Disc brakes are used at the front of these vehicles, and on some models at the rear as well. Extensive disc damage can occur if the pads are not replaced when needed.

3   The disc brake calipers, which contain the pads, are now visible. Each caliper has an outer and an inner pad - all pads should be checked.

4   Each caliper has an opening to inspect the pads **(see illustration)**. If the pad material has worn to about 1/8-inch thick or less, the pads should be replaced.

5   If you're unsure about the exact thickness of the remaining lining material, remove the pads for further inspection or replacement (refer to Chapter 9).

6   Before installing the wheels, check for leakage and/or damage at the brake hoses and connections. Replace the hose or fittings as necessary, referring to Chapter 9.

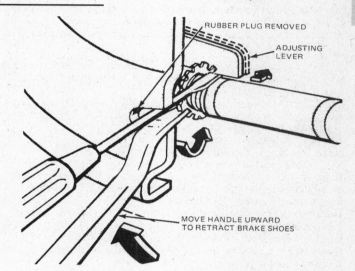

27.10 Turn the star wheel to adjust the brake shoe away from the drum

7   Check the condition of the brake disc. Look for score marks, deep scratches and overheated areas (they will appear blue or discolored). If damage or wear is noted, the disc can be removed and resurfaced by an automotive machine shop or replaced with a new one. Refer to Chapter 9 for more detailed inspection and repair procedures.

Drum brakes

Refer to illustrations 27.10, 27.11 and 27.13

8   Using a scribe or chalk, mark the drums and hub so the drum can be reinstalled in the same position on the hub.

9   Pull the brake drum off the hub and brake assembly. If this proves difficult, make sure the parking brake is released, then squirt some penetrating oil around the center hub area. Allow the oil to soak in and try to pull the drum off again.

10   If the drum still cannot be pulled off, the brake shoes will have to be retracted. This is done by first removing the rubber plug in the backing plate. Pull the self-adjusting lever off the star wheel and use a small screwdriver to turn the adjuster wheel, which will move the shoes away from the drum **(see illustration)**. With the drum removed, carefully wash off the accumulations of dirt and dust with brake system cleaner (see **Warning** above).

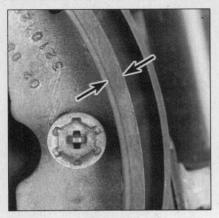

27.11 Measure the lining thickness from the outer surface to the metal shoe or rivet head

27.13 Check the wheel cylinders for signs of fluid leakage

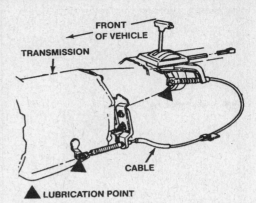

28.2 Lubricate the automatic transmission shift linkage at the points shown

11   Note the thickness of the lining material on the brake shoes. If the material is worn to within 1/16-inch of the recessed rivets or metal backing, the shoes should be replaced (see illustration). The shoes should also be replaced if they are cracked, glazed, (shiny surface) or contaminated with brake fluid.
12   Check to make sure all the brake assembly springs are connected and in good condition.
13   Check the brake components for signs of fluid leakage. Carefully pry back the rubber cups on the wheel cylinder, located on the top of the backing plate (see illustration). Any leakage is an indication that the wheel cylinders should be replaced or overhauled immediately (see Chapter 9). Also check the hoses and connections for signs of leakage.
14   Wipe the inside of the drum with a clean rag and brake cleaner or denatured alcohol.
15   Check the inside of the drum for cracks, score marks, deep scratches and hard spots, which will appear as small discolored areas. If imperfections cannot be removed with emery cloth or sandpaper, the drums must be taken to an automotive machine shop for resurfacing.
16   After the inspection process is complete, and if all the components are in good condition, reinstall the brake drums.

Parking brake

Lubrication
17   Apply the parking brake.
18   Apply multi-purpose grease to the parking brake linkage, adjuster assembly, connectors and the areas of the parking brake cable that come in contact with other parts of the vehicle.
19   Release the parking brake and repeat the lubrication procedure.
20   Install the wheels and lower the vehicle to the ground.

Check
21   The parking brake is operated by a foot pedal and locks the rear brake system. The easiest, and perhaps most obvious, method of periodically checking the parking brake is to park the vehicle on a steep hill with the parking brake set and the transmission in Neutral (remain in the car while performing this check). If the parking brake doesn't prevent the vehicle from rolling, it is in need of adjustment (see Chap-ter 9).

28   Automatic transmission control linkage lubrication (every 15,000 miles or 12 months)

Refer to illustration 28.2
1   Raise the front of the vehicle and support it securely on jackstands.
2   Clean the linkage pivot points and lubricate them with multi-purpose grease (see illustration).

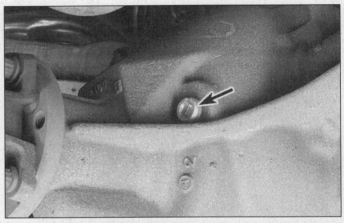

29.2 Use a 3/8-inch drive ratchet to remove the differential fill plug (arrow)

29   Rear axle (differential) lubricant level check (every 15,000 miles or 12 months)

Refer to illustration 29.2
1   The differential has a check/fill plug which must be removed to check the lubricant level. If the vehicle is raised to gain access to the plug, be sure to support it safely on jackstands - DO NOT crawl under the vehicle when it's supported only by the jack!
2   Remove the check/fill plug from the differential (see illustration).
3   Use your little finger as a dipstick to make sure the lubricant level is even with the bottom of the plug hole. If not, use a syringe to add the recommended lubricant until it just starts to run out of the opening. On some models a tag is located in the area of the plug which gives information regarding lubricant type, particularly on models equipped with a limited slip differential.
4   Install the plug and tighten it securely.

30   Thermactor system check (every 30,000 miles or 24 months)

Refer to illustration 30.2
1   The thermactor system reduces carbon monoxide and hydrocarbon emission by using a belt-driven pump to direct air to the exhaust manifold and in some instances the catalytic converter to aid in the combustion of unburned gasses.

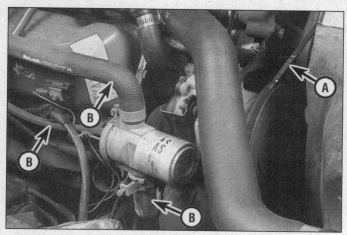

30.2 Inspect the thermactor drivebelt tension (A) and check for damage to the hoses (B)

2   Checking this system consists of making sure the thermactor pump drivebelt is properly tensioned (see Section 10) and inspecting hoses and connections for damage and leaks **(see illustration)**.
3   Refer to Chapter 6 for more information on the thermactor system.

31   Spark plug check and replacement (every 30,000 miles or 24 months)

Refer to illustrations 31.2, 31.5a, 31.5b, 31.6a, 31.6b, 31.8a, 31.8b, 31.10a and 31.10b

1   The spark plugs are located on the sides of the engine.
2   In most cases, the tools necessary for spark plug replacement include a spark plug socket which fits onto a ratchet (spark plug sockets are padded inside to prevent damage to the porcelain insulators on the new plugs), various extensions and a gap gauge to check and adjust the gaps on the new plugs **(see illustration)**. A special plug wire removal tool is available for separating the wire boots from the spark plugs, but it isn't absolutely necessary. A torque wrench should be used to tighten the new plugs.
3   The best approach when replacing the spark plugs is to purchase the new ones in advance, adjust them to the proper gap and replace the plugs one at a time. When buying the new spark plugs, be sure to

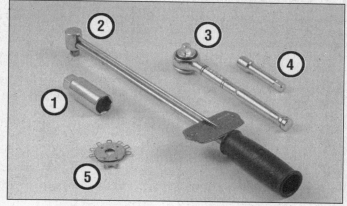

31.2 Tools required for changing spark plugs

1   **Spark plug socket** - *This will have special padding inside to protect the spark plug's porcelain insulator*
2   **Torque wrench** - *Although not mandatory, using this tool is the best way to ensure the plugs are tightened properly*
3   **Ratchet** - *Standard hand tool to fit the spark plug socket*
4   **Extension** - *Depending on model and accessories, you may need special extensions and universal joints to reach one or more of the plugs*
5   **Spark plug gap gauge** - *This gauge for checking the gap comes in a variety of styles. Make sure the gap for your engine is included*

obtain the correct plug type for your particular engine. This information can be found in the Specifications Section at the beginning of this Chapter, on the Emission Control Information label located under the hood or in the vehicle owner's manual. If differences exist between the plug specified on the emissions label, Specifications Section or in the owner's manual, assume that the emissions label is correct.
4   Allow the engine to cool completely before attempting to remove any of the plugs. 1991 and later models engines have aluminum cylinder heads, which can be damaged if the spark plugs are removed when the engine is hot. While you are waiting for the engine to cool, check the new plugs for defects and adjust the gaps.
5   The gap is checked by inserting the proper thickness gauge between the electrodes at the tip of the plug **(see illustration)**. The gap between the electrodes should be the same as the one specified on the Emissions Control Information label. The wire should just slide between the electrodes with a slight amount of drag. If the gap is

31.5a Spark plug manufacturers recommend using a wire-type gauge when checking the gap - if the wire does not slide between the electrodes with a slight drag, adjustment is required

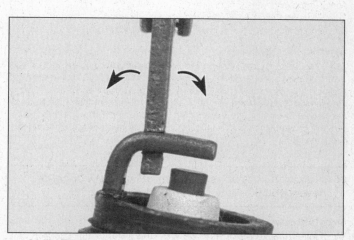

31.5b To change the gap, bend the side electrode only, as indicated by the arrows, and be very careful not to crack or chip the porcelain insulator surrounding the center electrode

Common spark plug conditions

NORMAL
Symptoms: Brown to grayish-tan color and slight electrode wear. Correct heat range for engine and operating conditions.
Recommendation: When new spark plugs are installed, replace with plugs of the same heat range.

WORN
Symptoms: Rounded electrodes with a small amount of deposits on the firing end. Normal color. Causes hard starting in damp or cold weather and poor fuel economy.
Recommendation: Plugs have been left in the engine too long. Replace with new plugs of the same heat range. Follow the recommended maintenance schedule.

CARBON DEPOSITS
Symptoms: Dry sooty deposits indicate a rich mixture or weak ignition. Causes misfiring, hard starting and hesitation.
Recommendation: Make sure the plug has the correct heat range. Check for a clogged air filter or problem in the fuel system or engine management system. Also check for ignition system problems.

ASH DEPOSITS
Symptoms: Light brown deposits encrusted on the side or center electrodes or both. Derived from oil and/or fuel additives. Excessive amounts may mask the spark, causing misfiring and hesitation during acceleration.
Recommendation: If excessive deposits accumulate over a short time or low mileage, install new valve guide seals to prevent seepage of oil into the combustion chambers. Also try changing gasoline brands.

OIL DEPOSITS
Symptoms: Oily coating caused by poor oil control. Oil is leaking past worn valve guides or piston rings into the combustion chamber. Causes hard starting, misfiring and hesitation.
Recommendation: Correct the mechanical condition with necessary repairs and install new plugs.

GAP BRIDGING
Symptoms: Combustion deposits lodge between the electrodes. Heavy deposits accumulate and bridge the electrode gap. The plug ceases to fire, resulting in a dead cylinder.
Recommendation: Locate the faulty plug and remove the deposits from between the electrodes.

TOO HOT
Symptoms: Blistered, white insulator, eroded electrode and absence of deposits. Results in shortened plug life.
Recommendation: Check for the correct plug heat range, over-advanced ignition timing, lean fuel mixture, intake manifold vacuum leaks, sticking valves and insufficient engine cooling.

PREIGNITION
Symptoms: Melted electrodes. Insulators are white, but may be dirty due to misfiring or flying debris in the combustion chamber. Can lead to engine damage.
Recommendation: Check for the correct plug heat range, over-advanced ignition timing, lean fuel mixture, insufficient engine cooling and lack of lubrication.

HIGH SPEED GLAZING
Symptoms: Insulator has yellowish, glazed appearance. Indicates that combustion chamber temperatures have risen suddenly during hard acceleration. Normal deposits melt to form a conductive coating. Causes misfiring at high speeds.
Recommendation: Install new plugs. Consider using a colder plug if driving habits warrant.

DETONATION
Symptoms: Insulators may be cracked or chipped. Improper gap setting techniques can also result in a fractured insulator tip. Can lead to piston damage.
Recommendation: Make sure the fuel anti-knock values meet engine requirements. Use care when setting the gaps on new plugs. Avoid lugging the engine.

MECHANICAL DAMAGE
Symptoms: May be caused by a foreign object in the combustion chamber or the piston striking an incorrect reach (too long) plug. Causes a dead cylinder and could result in piston damage.
Recommendation: Repair the mechanical damage. Remove the foreign object from the engine and/or install the correct reach plug.

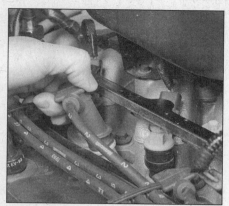

31.6a When removing the spark plug wires, pull only on the boot and twist it back-and-forth

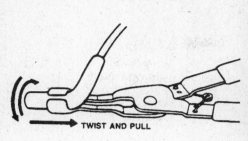

31.6b A spark plug wire removal tool makes the job easier

31.8a Use a spark plug socket wrench with a long extension to unscrew the spark plug

31.8b On 4.6L OHC engines the spark plug is mounted above the cylinder head, so it's more accessible

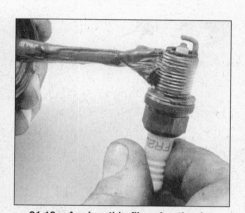

31.10a Apply a thin film of anti-seize compound to the spark plug threads to prevent damage to the cylinder head

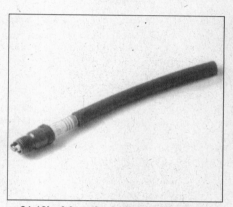

31.10b A length of 3/8-inch ID rubber hose will save time and prevent damaged threads when installing the spark plugs

incorrect, use the adjuster on the gauge body to bend the curved side electrode slightly until the specified gap is obtained **(see illustration)**. If the side electrode is not exactly over the center electrode, bend it with the adjuster until it is. Check for cracks in the porcelain insulator (if any are found, the plug should not be used).

6   With the engine cool, remove the spark plug wire from one spark plug. Pull only on the boot at the end of the wire - do not pull on the wire **(see illustration)**. A plug wire removal tool should be used if available **(see illustration)**.

7   If compressed air is available, use it to blow any dirt or foreign material away from the spark plug hole. A common bicycle pump will also work. The idea here is to eliminate the possibility of debris falling into the cylinder as the spark plug is removed.

8   Place the spark plug socket over the plug and remove it from the engine by turning it in a counterclockwise direction **(see illustrations)**. Withdraw the socket and remove the plug.

9   Compare the spark plug to those shown in the accompanying photos to get an indication of the general running condition of the engine.

10   Apply a small amount of anti-seize compound to the spark plug threads **(see illustration)**. If anti-seize compound isn't available, apply a drop of engine oil to the threads. Install one of the new plugs into the hole until you can no longer turn it with your fingers, then tighten it with a torque wrench (if available) or the ratchet. It is a good idea to slip a short length of rubber hose over the end of the plug to use as a tool to thread it into place **(see illustration)**. The hose will grip the plug well enough to turn it, but will start to slip if the plug begins to cross-thread in the hole - this will prevent damaged threads and the accompanying repair costs.

11   Before pushing the spark plug wire onto the end of the plug, inspect it following the procedures outlined in Section 32.

12   Attach the plug wire to the new spark plug, again using a twisting motion on the boot until it is seated on the spark plug.

13   Repeat the procedure for the remaining spark plugs, replacing them one at a time to prevent mixing up the spark plug wires.

32   Spark plug wire, distributor cap and rotor check and replacement (every 30,000 miles or 24 months)

Refer to illustrations 32.11a, 32.11b, 32.12a and 32.12b

Spark plug wires

Note: *Every time a spark plug wire is detached from a spark plug, the distributor cap or the coil, silicone dielectric compound (a white grease available at auto parts stores) must be applied to the inside of each boot before reconnection. Use a small standard screwdriver to coat the entire inside surface of each boot with a thin layer of the compound.*

1   The spark plug wires should be checked and, if necessary, replaced at the same time new spark plugs are installed.

2   The easiest way to identify bad wires is to make a visual check while the engine is running. In a dark, well-ventilated garage, start the engine and look at each plug wire. Be careful not to come into contact with any moving engine parts. If there is a break in the wire, you will see arcing or a small spark at the damaged area. If arcing is noticed, make a note to obtain new wires.

3   The spark plug wires should be inspected one at a time, begin-

32.11a Use a screwdriver to detach the distributor retaining clips

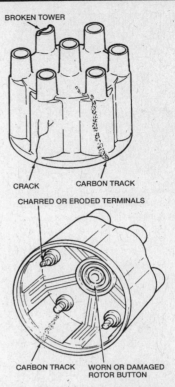

32.11b Shown here are some the common defects to look for when inspecting the distributor cap (if in doubt about its condition, install a new one)

ning with the spark plug for the number one cylinder, (the cylinder closest to the radiator on the right bank), to prevent confusion. Clearly label each original plug wire with a piece of tape marked with the correct number. The plug wires must be reinstalled in the correct order to ensure proper engine operation.

4   Disconnect the plug wire from the first spark plug. A removal tool can be used, or you can grab the wire boot, twist it slightly and pull the wire free. Do not pull on the wire itself, only on the rubber boot.

5   Push the wire and boot back onto the end of the spark plug. It should fit snugly. If it doesn't, detach the wire and boot once more and use a pair of pliers to carefully crimp the metal connector inside the wire boot until it does.

6   Using a clean rag, wipe the entire length of the wire to remove built-up dirt and grease.

7   Once the wire is clean, check for burns, cracks and other damage. Do not bend the wire sharply or you might break the conductor.

8   Disconnect the wire from the distributor (1990 and earlier models) or coil (1991 and later models). Pull only on the rubber boot. Check for corrosion and a tight fit. Reinstall the wire in the distributor or coils.

9   Inspect each of the remaining spark plug wires, making sure that each one is securely fastened at the distributor and spark plug when the check is complete.

10   If new spark plug wires are required, purchase a set for your specific engine model. Pre-cut wire sets with the boots already installed are available. Remove and replace the wires one at a time to avoid mix-ups in the firing order.

Distributor cap and rotor

Note: *It's common practice to install a new distributor cap and rotor each time new spark plug wires are installed. If you're planning to install new wires, install a new cap and rotor also. But if you're planning to reuse the existing wires, be sure to inspect the cap and rotor to make sure that they are in good condition. Models equipped with the EDIS ignition system do not have a distributor.*

11   Detach the clips and detach the cap from the distributor **(see illustration)**. Check it for cracks, carbon tracks and worn, burned or loose terminals **(see illustration)**.

12   Check the rotor for cracks and carbon tracks. Make sure the center terminal spring tension is adequate and look for corrosion and

32.12a Lift off the distributor cap for access to the rotor

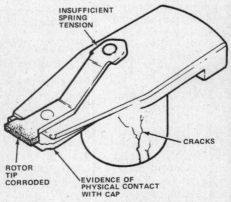

32.12b The rotor should be checked for wear and corrosion as indicated here (if in doubt about its condition, buy a new one)

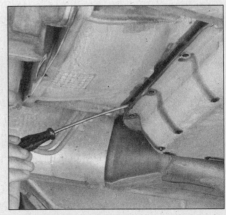

33.7 Pry the pan free of the gasket and allow the fluid to drain

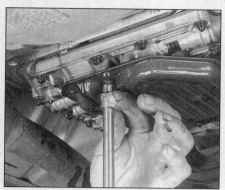

33.10 Use a socket and extension to remove the filter bolts

33.11a Install a new filter seal on the transmission . . .

33.11b . . . and a gasket on the filter itself (not all models)

wear on the rotor tip (see illustrations).

13 Replace the cap and rotor if damage or defects are found. Note that the rotor is indexed so it can only be installed one way. Before installing the cap, apply silicone dielectric compound to the rotor tip (see **Note** at beginning of this Section).

14 When installing a new cap, remove the wires from the old cap one at a time and attach them to the new cap in the exact same location - do not simultaneously remove all the wires from the old cap or firing order mix-ups may occur.

33 Automatic transmission fluid and filter change (every 30,000 miles or 24 months)

Refer to illustrations 33.7, 33.10, 33.11a, 33.11b and 33.12

1 At the specified intervals, the transmission fluid should be drained and replaced. Since the fluid will remain hot long after driving, perform this procedure only after the engine has cooled down completely.

2 Before beginning work, purchase the transmission fluid specified in Recommended lubricants and fluids at the front of this Chapter, a new filter and gaskets. Never reuse the old filter or gasket!

3 Other tools necessary for this job include jackstands to support the vehicle in a raised position, a drain pan capable of holding at least eight quarts, newspapers and clean rags.

4 Raise the vehicle and support it securely on jackstands.

5 With the drain pan in place, remove the front and side transmission pan mounting bolts.

6 Loosen the rear pan bolts approximately four turns.

7 Carefully pry the transmission pan loose with a screwdriver, allowing the fluid to drain (see illustration). Don't damage the pan or transmission gasket surfaces or leaks could develop.

8 Remove the remaining bolts, pan and gasket. Carefully clean the gasket surface of the transmission to remove all traces of the old

gasket and sealant.

9 Drain the fluid from the transmission pan, clean it with solvent and dry it with compressed air.

10 Remove the filter from the mount inside the transmission (see illustration).

11 Install a new seal, gasket and filter (see illustrations). Tighten the mounting bolts securely.

12 Make sure the gasket surface on the transmission pan is clean, then install a new gasket (see illustration). Put the pan in place against the transmission and install the bolts. Working around the pan, tighten each bolt a little at a time until the final torque figure is reached. Don't overtighten the bolts!

13 Lower the vehicle and add about four or five quarts of automatic transmission fluid through the filler tube (see Section 7).

14 With the transmission in Park and the parking brake set, run the engine at a fast idle, but don't race it.

15 Move the gear selector through each range and back to Park. Check the fluid level. Add fluid if needed to reach the correct level.

16 Check under the vehicle for leaks during the first few trips.

34 Automatic transmission band adjustment (C6 transmission only) (every 30,000 miles or 24 months)

Refer to illustration 34.4

1 The intermediate band on C6 transmissions must be adjusted at the specified intervals or a noticeable slip when shifting in or out of second gear will develop.

2 Raise the vehicle and support it securely on jackstands.

3 The intermediate band adjustment screw is located on the left (driver's) side of the transmission.

4 Loosen the locknut, use a torque wrench to tighten the adjusting screw to 120 inch-pounds, then back it off exactly 1-1/2 turns. Hold

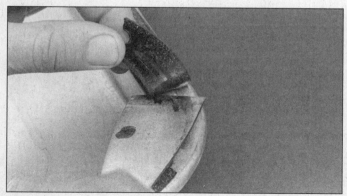

33.12 Be sure to clean all traces of the old gasket from the pan before installing a new one

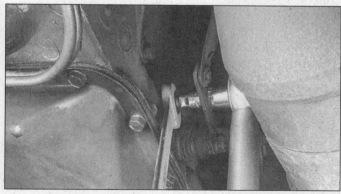

34.4 Hold the adjusting nut so that it can't move, then tighten the lock nut

35.4a Remove the bolts from the lower edge of the cover . . .

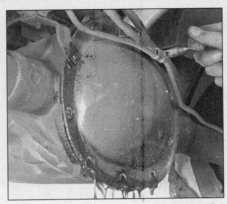

35.4b . . . then loosen the top bolts and let the lubricant drain

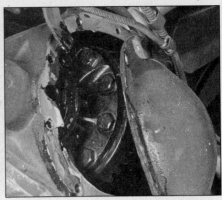

35.4c Once the lubricant has drained, remove the cover

the adjusting screw so it can't turn and tighten the locknut to the torque listed in the Specification Section at the beginning of this Chapter **(see illustration)**.

5   Lower the vehicle.

35   Rear axle (differential) lubricant change (every 30,000 miles or 24 months)

Refer to illustrations 35.4a, 35.4b, 35.4c and 35.6

1   Some models have a drain plug, while others don't. On models without a drain plug, a hand suction pump will be required to remove the differential lubricant through the filler hole. Some later models have a removable rear cover - if a suction pump isn't available, or the gasket is leaking, be sure to obtain a new gasket at the same time the gear lubricant is purchased because it will be necessary to remove the cover plate.

2   Raise the vehicle and support it securely on jackstands. Move a drain pan, rags, newspapers and wrenches under the vehicle.

3   Remove the fill plug from the differential (see Section 29). If a suction pump is being used, insert the flexible hose. Work the hose down to the bottom of the differential housing and pump the lubricant out.

4   If the differential is being drained by removing the cover plate, remove the bolts on the lower half of the plate **(see illustration)**. Loosen the bolts on the upper half and use them to keep the cover loosely attached **(see illustration)**. Allow the oil to drain into the pan, then completely remove the cover **(see illustration)**.

5   Using a lint-free rag, clean the inside of the cover and the accessible areas of the differential housing. As this is done, check for chipped gears and metal particles in the lubricant, indicating that the differential should be more thoroughly inspected and/or repaired.

6   Thoroughly clean the gasket mating surfaces of the differential housing and the cover plate. Use a gasket scraper or putty knife to remove all traces of the old gasket **(see illustration)**.

7   Apply a thin layer of RTV sealant to the cover flange, then press a new gasket into position on the cover. Make sure the bolt holes align properly.

8   Place the cover on the differential housing and install the bolts. Tighten the bolts securely.

9   Use a hand pump, syringe or funnel to fill the differential housing with the specified lubricant until it's level with the bottom of the plug hole.

10   Install the filler plug and make sure it is secure.

36   Cooling system servicing (draining, flushing and refilling) (every 30,000 miles or 24 months)

Refer to illustration 36.4

Warning: *Do not allow antifreeze to come in contact with your skin or painted surfaces of the vehicle. Rinse off spills immediately with plenty of water. Antifreeze is highly toxic if ingested. Never leave antifreeze lying around in an open container or in puddles on the floor; children and pets are attracted by it's sweet smell and may drink it. Check with local authorities about disposing of used antifreeze. Many communities have collection centers which will see that antifreeze is disposed of safely.*

1   Periodically, the cooling system should be drained, flushed and refilled to replenish the antifreeze mixture and prevent formation of rust and corrosion, which can impair the performance of the cooling system and cause engine damage. When the cooling system is serviced, all hoses and the radiator cap should be checked and replaced if necessary.

35.6 Carefully scrape off the old material to ensure a leak-free seal

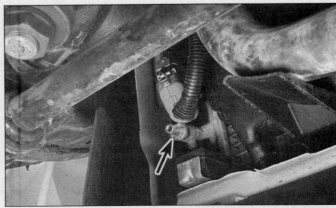

36.4 The radiator drain fitting is located at the lower corner of the radiator (arrow)

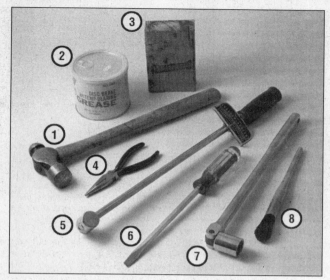

37.1 Tools and materials needed for front wheel bearing maintenance

1 **Hammer** - A common hammer will do just fine
2 **Grease** - High-temperature grease that is formulated for front wheel bearings should be used
3 **Wood block** - If you have a scrap piece of 2x4, it can be used to drive the new seal into the hub
4 **Needle-nose pliers** - Used to straighten and remove the cotter pin in the spindle
5 **Torque wrench** - This is very important in this procedure; if the bearing is too tight, the wheel won't turn freely - if it's too loose, the wheel will "wobble" on the spindle. Either way, it could mean extensive damage
6 **Screwdriver** - Used to remove the seal from the hub (a long screwdriver is preferred)
7 **Socket/breaker bar** - Needed to loosen the nut on the spindle if it's extremely tight
8 **Brush** - Together with some clean solvent, this will be used to remove old grease from the hub and spindle

Draining

2   Apply the parking brake and block the wheels. If the vehicle has just been driven, wait several hours to allow the engine to cool down before beginning this procedure.
3   Once the engine is completely cool, remove the cap from the radiator or expansion tank (some 1991 and later models).
4   Move a large container under the radiator drain to catch the coolant. Attach a 3/8-inch diameter hose to the drain fitting to direct the coolant into the container, then open the drain fitting (a pair of pliers may be required to turn it) **(see illustration)**.
5   While the coolant is draining, check the condition of the radiator hoses, heater hoses and clamps (refer to Section 18 if necessary).
6   Replace any damaged clamps or hoses (refer to Chapter 3 for detailed replacement procedures).
7   When the coolant reservoir is empty, remove the radiator cap, allow the radiator to drain, then, move the container under the engine block drain plug. Remove the plug and allow the coolant in the block to drain. **Note:** *Frequently, the coolant will not drain from the block after the plug is removed. This is due to a rust layer that has built up behind the plug. Insert a Phillips screw driver into the hole to break the rust barrier.*

Flushing

8   Once the system is completely drained, flush the radiator with fresh water from a garden hose until water runs clear at the drain. The flushing action of the water will remove sediments from the radiator but will not remove rust and scale from the engine and cooling tube surfaces.

9   These deposits can be removed by the chemical action of a cleaner available at auto parts stores. Follow the procedure outlined in the manufacturer's instructions. If the radiator is severely corroded, damaged or leaking, it should be removed (see Chapter 3) and taken to a radiator repair shop.
10   Remove the overflow hose from the coolant recovery reservoir. Drain the reservoir and flush it with clean water, then reconnect the hose.

Refilling

11   Close and tighten the radiator drain.
12   Place the heater temperature control in the maximum heat position.
13   Slowly add new coolant (a 50/50 mixture of water and antifreeze) to the radiator until it is full. Add coolant to the reservoir or expansion tank up to the Full Hot mark.
14   Leave the radiator or expansion tank cap off and run the engine in a well-ventilated area until the thermostat opens (coolant will begin flowing through the radiator and the upper radiator hose will become hot).
15   Turn the engine off and let it cool. Add more coolant mixture to bring the level back up to the lip on the radiator or expansion tank filler neck.
16   Squeeze the upper radiator hose to expel air, then add more coolant mixture if necessary. Replace the radiator or expansion tank cap.
17   Start the engine, allow it to reach normal operating temperature and check for leaks.

37   Front wheel bearing check, repack and adjustment (1991 and earlier models) (every 30,000 miles or 24 months)

Refer to illustrations 37.1, 37.6, 37.7, 37.11 and 37.15
1   In most cases the front wheel bearings will not need servicing until the brake pads are changed. However, the bearings should be checked whenever the front of the vehicle is raised for any reason. Several items, including a torque wrench and special grease, are required for this procedure **(see illustration)**.
2   With the vehicle securely supported on jackstands, spin each wheel and check for noise, rolling resistance and freeplay.
3   Grasp the top of each tire with one hand and the bottom with the other. Move the wheel in-and-out on the spindle. If there's any noticeable movement, the bearings should be checked and then repacked with grease or replaced if necessary.
4   Remove the wheel.
5   Remove the brake caliper (see Chapter 9) and hang it out of the way on a piece of wire. A wood block of the appropriate width can be slid between the brake pads to keep them separated, if necessary.
6   Pry the dust cap out of the hub using a screwdriver or hammer and chisel **(see illustration)**.

37.6 Dislodge the dust cap by working around the outer circumference with a hammer and chisel

37.7 Remove the cotter pin and discard it - use a new one when the hub is reinstalled

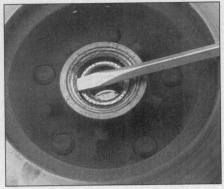

37.11 Use a large screwdriver to pry the grease seal out of the rear of the hub

37.15 Work the grease completely into the bearing rollers

7   Straighten the bent ends of the cotter pin, then pull the cotter pin out of the nut lock **(see illustration)**. Discard the cotter pin and use a new one during reassembly.

8   Remove the nut lock, nut and washer from the end of the spindle .

9   Pull the hub/disc assembly out slightly, then push it back into its original position. This should force the outer bearing off the spindle enough so it can be removed.

10   Pull the hub/disc assembly off the spindle.

11   Use a screwdriver to pry the seal out of the rear of the hub **(see illustration)**. As this is done, note how the seal is installed.

12   Remove the inner wheel bearing from the hub.

13   Use solvent to remove all traces of the old grease from the bearings, hub and spindle. A small brush may prove helpful; however make sure no bristles from the brush embed themselves inside the bearing rollers. Allow the parts to air dry.

14   Carefully inspect the bearings for cracks, heat discoloration, worn rollers, etc. Check the bearing races inside the hub for wear and damage. If the bearing races are defective, the hubs should be taken to a machine shop with the facilities to remove the old races and press new ones in. Note that the bearings and races come as matched sets and old bearings should never be installed on new races.

15   Use high-temperature front wheel bearing grease to pack the bearings. Work the grease completely into the bearings, forcing it between the rollers, cone and cage from the back side **(see illustration)**.

16   Apply a thin coat of grease to the spindle at the outer bearing seat, inner bearing seat, shoulder and seal seat.

17   Put a small quantity of grease inboard of each bearing race inside the hub. Using your finger, form a dam at these points to provide extra grease availability and to keep thinned grease from flowing out of the bearing.

18   Place the grease-packed inner bearing into the rear of the hub and put a little more grease outboard of the bearing.

19   Place a new seal over the inner bearing and tap the seal evenly into place with a hammer and blunt punch until it's flush with the hub.

20   Carefully place the hub assembly onto the spindle and push the grease-packed outer bearing into position.

21   Install the washer and spindle nut. Tighten the nut only slightly (no more than 12 ft-lbs of torque).

22   Spin the hub in a forward direction while tightening the spindle nut to approximately 20 ft-lbs to seat the bearings and remove any grease or burrs which could cause excessive bearing play later.

23   Loosen the spindle nut 1/4-turn, then using your hand (not a wrench of any kind), tighten the nut until it's snug. Install the nut lock and a new cotter pin through the hole in the spindle and the slots in the nut lock. If the nut lock slots don't line up, remove the nut lock and turn it slightly until they do.

24   Bend the ends of the cotter pin until they're flat against the nut. Cut off any extra length which could interfere with the dust cap.

25   Install the dust cap, tapping it into place with a hammer.

26   Place the brake caliper near the rotor and carefully remove the

wood spacer. Install the caliper (see Chapter 9).

27   Install the wheel on the hub and tighten the lug nuts.

28   Grasp the top and bottom of the tire and check the bearings in the manner described earlier in this Section.

29   Lower the vehicle.

---

38   Chassis lubrication (every 30,000 miles or 24 months)

Refer to illustrations 38.1 and 38.6

1   Refer to *Recommended lubricants and fluids* at the front of this Chapter to obtain the necessary grease, etc. You'll also need a grease gun **(see illustration)**. Occasionally plugs will be installed rather than grease fittings. If so, grease fittings will have to be purchased and installed.

2   Look under the vehicle and see if grease fittings or plugs are installed in the tie-rod ends. If there are plugs, remove them and buy

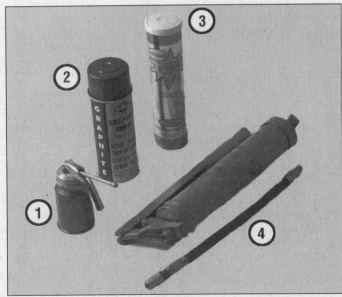

38.1 Materials required for chassis and body lubrication

1   *Engine oil - Light engine oil in a can like this can be used for door and hood hinges*

2   *Graphite spray - Used to lubricate lock cylinders*

3   *Grease - Grease, in a variety of types and weights, is available for use in a grease gun*

4   *Grease gun - A common grease gun, shown here with a detachable hose and nozzle, is needed for chassis lubrication. After use, clean it thoroughly!*

38.6 Pump the grease into the fitting until the rubber seal is firm to the touch

39.3 The choke plate (arrow) is located at the top of the carburetor air horn

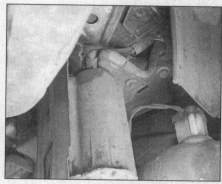

40.2 The evaporative emissions system canister is accessible from below on most models - check for damage to the canister and the hoses at the top

1

grease fittings, which will thread into the component. A dealer or auto parts store will be able to supply the correct fittings. Straight, as well as angled, fittings are available.

3   For easier access under the vehicle, raise it with a jack and place jackstands under the frame. Make sure it's safely supported by the stands. If the wheels are to be removed at this interval for tire rotation or brake inspection, loosen the lug nuts slightly while the vehicle is still on the ground.

4   Before beginning, force a little grease out of the nozzle to remove any dirt from the end of the gun. Wipe the nozzle clean with a rag.

5   With the grease gun and plenty of clean rags, crawl under the vehicle.

6   Wipe the tie-rod end grease fitting nipple clean and push the nozzle firmly over it. Squeeze the trigger on the grease gun to force grease into the component **(see illustration)**. They should be lubricated until the rubber seal is firm to the touch. Don't pump too much grease into the fitting as it could rupture the seal. If grease escapes around the grease gun nozzle, the nipple is clogged or the nozzle is not completely seated on the fitting. Resecure the gun nozzle to the fitting and try again. If necessary, replace the fitting with a new one.

7   Wipe the excess grease from the components and the grease fitting. Repeat the procedure for the remaining fitting.

8   While you're under the vehicle, clean and lubricate the parking brake cable, along with the cable guides and levers. This can be done by smearing some of the chassis grease onto the cable and its related parts with your fingers.

9   Open the hood and smear a little chassis grease on the hood latch mechanism. Have an assistant pull the hood release lever from inside the vehicle as you lubricate the cable at the latch.

10   Lubricate all the hinges (door, hood, etc.) with engine oil to keep them in proper working order.

11   The key lock cylinders can be lubricated with spray graphite or silicone lubricant, which is available at auto parts stores.

12   Lubricate the door weather-stripping with silicone spray. This will reduce chafing and retard wear.

39   Carburetor choke check (every 30,000 miles or 24 months)

Refer to illustration 39.3

1   The choke operates when the engine is cold, so this check can only be performed before the vehicle has been started for the day.

2   Open the hood and remove the top plate of the air cleaner assembly (see Section 15). If any vacuum hoses must be disconnected, make sure you tag the hoses for reinstallation in their original positions. Place the top plate and wing nut aside, out of the way of moving engine components.

3   Look at the center of the air cleaner housing. You will notice a flat plate at the carburetor opening **(see illustration)**.

4   Press the accelerator pedal to the floor. The plate should close completely. Start the engine while you watch the plate at the carburetor. **Warning:** *Do not position your face directly over the carburetor, as the engine could backfire, causing serious burns.* When the engine starts, the choke plate should open slightly.

5   Allow the engine to continue running at an idle speed. As the engine warms up to operating temperature, the plate should slowly open, allowing more air to enter through the top of the carburetor.

6   After a few minutes, the choke plate should be fully open to the vertical position. Lightly tap the accelerator to make sure the fast idle cam disengages.

7   You will notice that the engine speed corresponds with the plate opening. With the plate fully closed, the engine should run at a fast idle speed. As the plate opens and the throttle is moved to disengage the fast idle cam, the engine speed will decrease.

8   Refer to Chapter 4A for more information on adjusting and servicing the choke components.

40   Evaporative emissions system check (every 30,000 miles or 24 months)

Refer to illustration 40.2

1   The function of the evaporative emissions control system is to draw fuel vapors from the gas tank and fuel system, store them in a charcoal canister and route them to the intake manifold during normal engine operation.

2   The most common symptom of a fault in the evaporative emissions system is a strong fuel odor in the engine compartment. If a fuel odor is detected, inspect the charcoal canister, located in the engine compartment or under the vehicle **(see illustration)**. Check the canister and all hoses for damage and deterioration.

3   The evaporative emissions control system is explained in more detail in Chapter 6.

41   Fuel filter replacement (every 30,000 miles or 24 months)

Warning: *Gasoline is extremely flammable, so take extra precautions when you work on any part of the fuel system. Don't smoke or allow open flames or bare light bulbs near the work area, and don't work in a garage where a natural gas-type appliance (such as a water heater or clothes dryer) with a pilot light is present. Since gasoline is carcinogenic, wear latex gloves when there's a possibility of being exposed to fuel, and, if you spill any fuel on your skin, rinse it off immediately with soap and water. Mop up any spills immediately and do not store fuel-soaked rags where they could ignite. When you perform any kind of work on the fuel system, wear safety glasses and have a Class B type fire extinguisher on hand.*

41.5 On this type of fuel filter, loosen the screw clamp and disconnect the hose (A), then unscrew the filter nut (B)

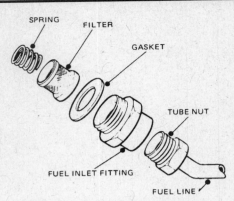

41.6 Carburetor mounted fuel filter details

41.9 Earlier models use a fuel filter that is mounted in a bracket (the arrow is pointing to the hairpin clip)

Carbureted models

Refer to illustrations 41.5 and 41.6

1   On these models the fuel filter is located at the carburetor.

2   The job should be done with the engine cold (after sitting for at least 3 hours). The necessary tools include open end wrenches (or better yet flare-nut wrenches that wrap around the fitting) to fit the fuel line fittings and on some models a screwdriver for the clamp screw.

3   Remove the air cleaner assembly.

4   Place some rags under the fuel inlet fittings to catch the fuel spilled when the fittings are disconnected.

5   On some models the filter is mounted on the outside of the carburetor. Loosen the screw clamp and disconnect the rubber hose, then unscrew the fitting and detach the filter from the carburetor **(see illustration)**. Installation is the reverse of removal.

6   On other models the filter is located inside the carburetor. With the proper size wrench, hold the large fuel inlet fitting immediately next to the carburetor and loosen the fitting at the end of the metal fuel line **(see illustration)**. Unscrew the fuel inlet tube nut and remove the gasket, filter and spring. Install the spring, new filter and gasket and secure it with the fuel inlet fitting, taking care not to cross thread it. Tighten the fitting securely, then install the fuel line and tighten the tube nut securely as well.

Fuel-injected models

Refer to illustrations 41.9, and 41.11

Warning: *The fuel system is under constant pressure, so, before removing the fuel filter, the fuel system pressure must be relieved* (see Chapter 4).

7   The fuel filter is located under the vehicle on the inside of either the left or right frame rail, near the fuel tank.

8   Inspect the hose fittings at both ends of the filter to see if they're clean. If more than a light coating of dust is present, clean the fittings before proceeding.

9   Relieve the fuel system pressure (see Chapter 4). Removal of the hairpin clip from each fitting is a two-stage procedure. First, spread the two clip legs apart about 1/8-inch to disengage them, then push in on them. Pull on the other end of the clip to detach it from the fitting **(see illustration)**. **Caution:** Don't use any tools or you may damage the plastic fuel line fittings. Use your fingers only.

10   On some models the filter is encased in a plastic housing (retainer) which will have to be unbolted from a bracket.

11   Remove the filter and retainer from the metal bracket **(see illustration)**. Remove the rubber insulator ring from the filter, then remove the filter from the retainer. Install the new filter (be sure to place an insulator on each end if the filter is mounted in a plastic housing), making sure the arrow on the side of the filter points towards the open end of the retainer. Install the bracket (if removed), tighten the bolts securely and connect the fuel lines.

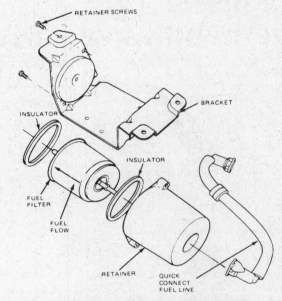

41.11 Bracket-mounted fuel filter details

12   On later models, once both hairpin clips are released, grasp the fuel hoses, one at a time, and pull them straight off the filter. Be prepared for fuel spillage.

13   After the hoses have been detached, check the clips for damage and distortion. If they were damaged in any way during removal, new ones must be used when the hoses are reattached to the new filter (if new clips are packaged with the filter, be sure to use them in place of the originals).

14   Remove the bolts and detach the filter and bracket assembly. Note which way the arrow on the filter is pointing - the new filter must be installed the same way. Use a screwdriver to loosen the clamp and remove the filter from the bracket.

15   Install the new filter with the arrow pointing the right direction and tighten the clamp. Install the filter/bracket assembly

16   Carefully push each hose onto the filter until it's seated against the collar on the fitting, then install the hairpin clips. **Warning:** Always use new clips. Make sure the clips are securely attached to the hose fittings - if they come off, the hoses could back off the filter and a fire could result!

All models

17   Start the engine and check for fuel leaks.

Chapter 2 Part A
Overhead valve (OHV) engines

Contents

Specifications

General

Cylinder numbers (front to rear)
    Right side 1-2-3-4
    Left (driver's side) 5-6-7-8
Firing order
    5.0L (302 cid)
        Standard 1-5-4-2-6-3-7-8
        HO 1-3-7-2-6-5-4-8
    7.5L (460 cid) engines 1-5-4-2-6-3-7-8
    5.8L (351 cid) and 6.6L (400 cid) engines 1-3-7-2-6-5-4-8

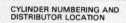

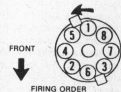

Camshaft

Lobe lift

  5.0L (302 cid) engine

    Standard

      Intake .... 0.2375 inch

      Exhaust .... 0.2474 inch

    HO

      Intake .... 0.2780 inch

      Exhaust .... 0.2780 inch

  5.8L (351 cid) engine

    Intake .... 0.2600 inch

    Exhaust .... 0.2600 inch

  6.6L (400 cid) engine

    Intake .... 0.2474 inch

    Exhaust .... 0.2500 inch

  7.5L (460 cid) engine

    Intake .... 0.2530 inch

    Exhaust .... 0.2780 inch

Maximum allowable lift loss .... 0.0050 inch

Endplay

  Standard .... 0.001 to 0.006 inch

  Service limit .... 0.009 inch

Journal diameter

  5.0L (302 cid) and 5.8L (351 cid) engines

    No. 1 .... 2.0805 to 2.0815 inches

    No. 2 .... 2.0655 to 2.0665 inches

    No. 3 .... 2.0505 to 2.0515 inches

    No. 4 .... 2.0355 to 2.0365 inches

    No. 5 .... 2.0205 to 2.0215 inches

  6.6L (400 cid) engine

    No. 1 .... 2.1238 to 2.1248 inches

    No. 2 .... 2.0655 to 2.0665 inches

    No. 3 .... 2.0505 to 2.0515 inches

    No. 4 .... 2.0355 to 2.0365 inches

    No. 5 .... 2.0205 to 2.0215 inches

  7.5L (460 cid) engine

    All journals .... 2.1238 to 2.1248 inches

Out-of-round limit .... 0.0005 inch (total indicator reading)

Runout limit (all) .... 0.005 inch (total indicator reading)

Journal-to-bearing (oil) clearance

  Standard .... 0.001 to 0.003 inch

  Service limit .... 0.006 inch maximum

Camshaft gear backlash .... 0.006 to 0.011 inch

Valve stem-to-rocker arm clearance (collapsed lifter)

  5.0L (302 cid) engines

    Standard .... 0.071 to 0.193 inch

    HO .... 0.098 to 0.198 inch

  5.8L (351 cid) engine .... 0.071 to 0.193 inch

  6.6L (400 cid) engine .... 0.100 to 0.200 inch

  7.5L (460 cid) engine .... 0.075 to 0.175 inch

Oil pump

Oil pressure (all)

  Hot at 2000 rpm .... 35 to 60 psi

  Normal operating pressure at curb idle .... 6 to 8 psi

Timing chain

Timing chain deflection (all) .... 0.500 inch maximum

Torque specifications

Ft-lb (unless otherwise indicated)

Camshaft sprocket bolt .... 40 to 45

Camshaft thrust plate screws .... 108 to 144 in-lbs

Timing cover bolts

  5.0L (302 cid) and 5.8L (351 cid) engines .... 15 to 21

  6.6L (400 cid) and 7.5L (460 cid) engines .... 12 to 15

Cylinder head bolts
    5.0L (302 cid) engine
        Step 1.. 55 to 65
        Step 2.. 65 to 72
    5.8L (351 cid) engine
        Step 1.. 85
        Step 2.. 95
        Step 3.. 105 to 112
    6.6L (400 cid) engine
        Step 1.. 75
        Step 2.. 95 to 105
    7.5L (460 cid) engine
        Step 1.. 70 to 80
        Step 2.. 100 to 110
        Step 3.. 130 to 140
Crankshaft pulley-to-vibration damper bolts.. 35 to 50
Engine mount to block.. 35 to 60
Engine mount through bolt nut .... 15 to 25
Exhaust manifold bolts
    5.0L (302 cid), 5.8L (351 cid) and 6.6L (400 cid) engines.................. 18 to 24
    7.5L (460 cid) engine .... 28 to 33
Flywheel/driveplate mounting bolts.. 75 to 85
Intake manifold-to-cylinder head bolts
    5.0L (302 cid) engine
        1988 and earlier .... 23 to 25*
        1989 and later 15*
    5.8L (351 cid) engine .... 23 to 25*
    6.6L (400 cid) engine
        3/8-inch bolts .... 22 to 32*
        5/16-inch bolts .... 19 to 25*
    7.5L (460 cid) engine .... 22 to 32*
Oil filter insert-to-engine block adapter bolt.. 20 to 30
Oil pan drain plug .... 15 to 25
Oil pan bolts
    1/4-inch bolts .... 72 to 108 in-lbs
    5/16-inch bolts .... 108 to 132 in-lbs
Oil pick-up tube-to-main bearing cap nut .... 22 to 32
Oil pick-up tube-to-oil pump bolts .... 12 to 18
Oil pump to block mounting bolts .... 22 to 32
Rocker arm fulcrum bolt/nut.. 18 to 25
Timing chain cover bolts.. 12 to 18
Valve cover bolts
    5.0L (302 cid) engine
        1987 and earlier .... 36 to 60 in-lbs
        1988 and later .... 72 to 108 in-lbs
    5.8L (351 cid) and 6.6L (400 cid) engines .... 36 to 60 in-lbs
    7.5L (460 cid) engine .... 60 to 72 in-lbs
Vibration damper-to-crankshaft bolt .... 70 to 90

* After assembly, re-tighten to the specified torque with the engine hot

2A

1   General information

Refer to illustrations 1.4a, 1.4b and 1.4c

    The following repair procedures are based on the assumption that the engine is installed in the vehicle. If the engine has been removed from the vehicle and mounted on a stand, many of the steps outlined in this Part of Chapter 2 will not apply.

    The Specifications included in this Part of Chapter 2 apply only to the procedures contained in this Part. Part C of Chapter 2 contains the Specifications necessary for cylinder head and engine block rebuilding.

    Several V8 engines of various displacements are covered by this manual. All engines covered in this Chapter are gasoline fueled with overhead valves (OHV) actuated by hydraulic lifters and have crankshafts supported by five main bearings.

    The engines covered in this manual are designated in either liters (L) or cubic inch displacement (cid), for example 5.0L (liter) and a 302 cid (cubic inch displacement) describe the same engine. Designations of liter or cubic inch varied through out the years covered by this manual.

    'Family' engine groupings **(see illustrations)** include the 5.0 liter (302 cubic inch), 5.8 liter (351"W" cubic inch) engines and the 6.6 liter (400 cubic inch) engines, these engines can be referred to as a "small block." **Note:** *Differences within engine groupings are indicated where applicable.* A 7.5 liter (460 cubic inch) engine was used through 1978 and can be referred to as a "big block." **Note:** *On 1992 and later models, the engine availability was limited to only a 4.6 liter (4.6L) Overhead Cam (OHC) engine (see Chapters 2B and 2C).* All information concerning engine removal, installation and/or engine block and cylinder head overhaul can be found in Part C of this Chapter.

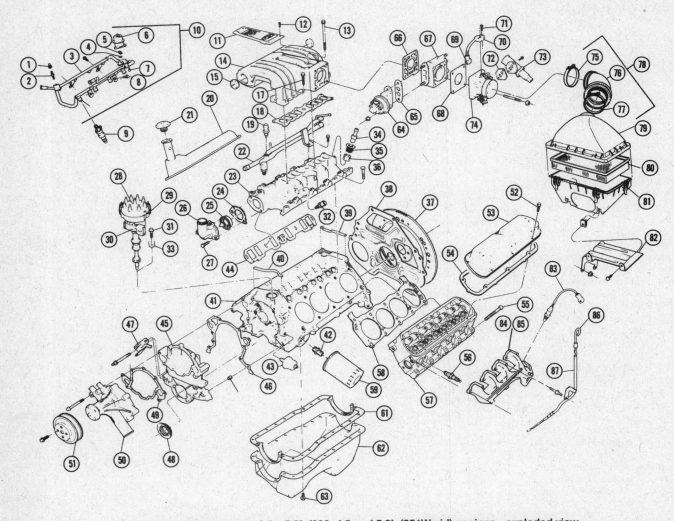

1.4a External components of the 5.0L (302 cid) and 5.8L (351W cid) engines - exploded view

1	Schrader valve cap	22	Heater water supply and	43	Oil pressure sending unit	67	EGR valve spacer
2	Schrader valve		return tube	44	Intake manifold gasket	68	Throttle body gasket
3	Fuel rail	23	Lower intake manifold	45	Front cover	69	Throttle Position Sensor
4	O-ring	24	Thermostat housing	46	Front cover gasket		connector
5	Fuel pressure regulator		gasket	47	Timing pointer	70	Throttle Position Sensor
	gasket	25	Thermostat	48	Crankshaft front oil seal	71	Screw
6	Fuel pressure regulator	26	Water outlet	49	Water pump gasket	72	Idle speed motor gasket
7	Screw	27	Bolt	50	Water pump	73	Idle bypass motor
8	Bolt	28	Distributor	51	Water pump pulley	74	Throttle body assembly
9	Fuel injector	29	Distributor adapter	52	Bolt	75	Clamp
10	Fuel rail assembly	30	Distributor module	53	Valve cover	76	Clean air tube
11	Upper manifold cover	31	Bolt	54	Valve cover gasket	77	Clamp
12	Screw	32	Air Charge Temperature	55	Bolt	78	Air inlet assembly
13	Bolt		sensor	56	Spark plug	79	Air cleaner tray top
14	Upper intake manifold	33	Distributor clamp	57	Cylinder head	80	Air cleaner element
	(plenum)	34	PCV valve	58	Cylinder head gasket	81	Air cleaner tray
15	Plug	35	PCV grommet	59	Oil filter	82	Air cleaner tray bracket
16	Bolt	36	Crankcase vent element	60	Not used	83	Oxygen sensor
17	Bolt	37	Flywheel	61	Oil pan gasket	84	Exhaust manifold (right)
18	Gasket	38	Rear cover	62	Oil pan	85	Exhaust manifold (left)
19	Sensor	39	Manifold end seal	63	Bolt	86	Dipstick
20	Valve cover	40	Manifold front seal	64	EGR valve	87	Dipstick tube
21	Oil filler cap	41	Cylinder block	65	EGR valve gasket		
		42	Oil filter mounting insert	66	EGR valve spacer gasket		

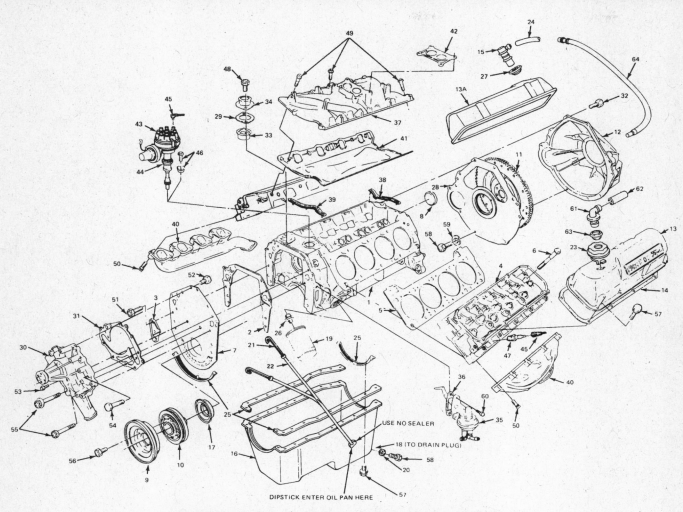

1.4b External components of the 6.6L (400 cid) engines - exploded view

1 Engine block
2 Front cover gasket
3 Timing pointer
4 Cylinder head
5 Cylinder head gaskets
6 Cylinder head bolt
7 Front cover plate
8 Camshaft rear bearing plug
9 Crankshaft pulley
10 Crankshaft damper
11 Flywheel
12 Flywheel housing
13 Left rocker cover assembly
13A Right rocker cover assembly
14 Rocker cover gasket
15 PCV assembly
16 Oil pan
17 Front cover oil seal
18 Oil pan drain plug

19 Oil filter
20 Drain plug gasket
21 Oil level dipstick
22 Dipstick tube
23 Oil filler cap
24 Crankcase ventilation hose
25 Oil pan gasket set
26 Oil filter mounting bolt insert
27 PCV grommet
28 Rear engine plate
29 Water outlet connection gasket
30 Water pump
31 Water pump housing gasket
32 Bolt (7/16-14 x 2-9/16)
33 Thermostat
34 Water outlet connection
35 Fuel pump
36 Fuel pump mounting gasket

37 Intake manifold
38 Intake manifold rear seal
39 Intake manifold front seal
40 Exhaust manifold
41 Intake manifold valley baffle
42 Carburetor mounting gasket
43 Distributor cap
44 Distributor
45 Spark plug wire set
46 Distributor holddown clamp
47 Spark plug
48 Screw and lockwasher
   (5/16-18 x 3/4)
49 Hex head bolt (5/16-18 x 2)
50 Washer head bolt
   (3/8-16 x 2)
51 Bolt (5/16-18 x 1-1/4)
52 Screw (5/16-18 x 1-1/4)
53 Screw (5/16-18 x 2-7/8)

54 Washer head bolt
   (5/16-18 x 1-7/8)
55 Washer head bolt
   (5/16-18 x 2-7/8)
56 Bolt (3/8-16 x 1)
57 Washer head bolt
   (1/4-20 x 5/8)
58 Bolt (5/16-18 x 3/4)
59 Lock washer
   (5/16 x 19/32 x 5/64)
60 Bolt (5/16-18 x 7/8)
61 Elbow (115° x 0.58 OD)
62 PCV system hose
63 Elbow grommet
64 PCV system tube

2 Repair operations possible with the engine in the vehicle

Many major repair operations can be accomplished without removing the engine from the vehicle.

Clean the engine compartment and the exterior of the engine with some type of pressure washer before any work is done. It will make the job easier and help keep dirt out of the internal areas of the engine.

It may help to remove the hood to improve access to the engine as repairs are performed (see Chapter 11 if necessary).

If vacuum, exhaust, oil or coolant leaks develop, indicating a need for gasket or seal replacement, the repairs can generally be made with the engine in the vehicle. The intake and exhaust manifold gaskets, timing cover gasket, oil pan gasket, crankshaft oil seals and cylinder head gaskets are all accessible with the engine in place.

Exterior engine components, such as the intake and exhaust

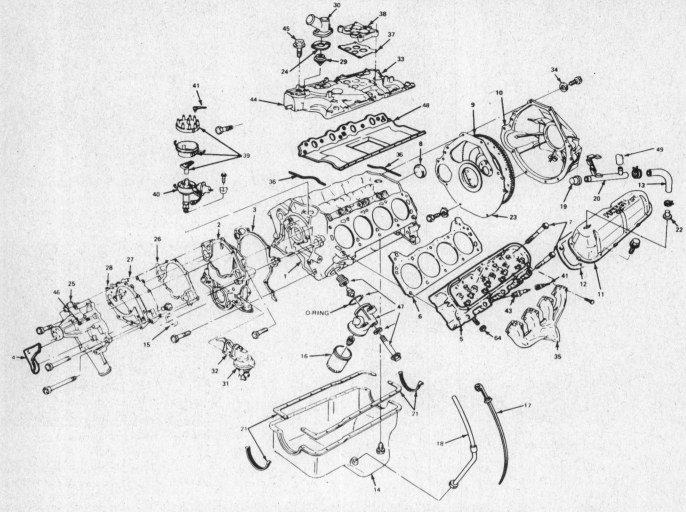

1.4c External components of the 7.5L (460 cid) engine - exploded view

1 Cylinder block	14 Oil pan	26 Water pump housing gasket	39 Distributor cap assembly
2 Front cover assembly	15 Front cover seal	27 Water pump cover	40 Distributor assembly
3 Front cover gasket	16 Oil filter	28 Water pump cover gasket	41 Spark plug wire set
4 Timing pointer	17 Oil level dipstick	29 Thermostat	42 Distributor holddown clamp
5 Cylinder head	18 Oil level dipstick tube	30 Water outlet connection	43 Spark plug
6 Cylinder head gasket	19 Oil filler cap	31 Fuel pump	44 Hot water connection tube
7 Cylinder head bolt	20 Oil filler pipe assembly	32 Fuel pump mounting gasket	45 Washer head bolt
8 Camshaft rear bearing plug	21 Oil pan gasket set	33 Intake manifold	46 Bolt (5/16-18 x 11/16)
9 Flywheel assembly	22 Oil filler adapter	34 Lockwasher (7/16)	47 Oil filter adapter assembly
10 Flywheel housing	23 Rear engine plate	35 Exhaust manifold	48 Intake manifold valley gasket
11 Rocker arm cover	24 Water outlet connection	36 Intake manifold gasket seals	49 Filler hose-to-carburetor hose
12 Rocker arm cover gasket	gasket	37 Carburetor gasket	
13 Oil filler pipe hose	25 Water pump	38 Carburetor-to-intake manifold spacer	

manifolds, the oil pan (and the oil pump), the water pump, the starter motor, the alternator, the distributor and the fuel system components can be removed for repair with the engine in place.

Since the cylinder heads can be removed without pulling the engine, valve component servicing can also be accomplished with the engine in the vehicle. **Note:** *Valve specifications are found in Chapter 2, Part C.* Replacement of the timing chain and sprockets is also possible with the engine in the vehicle.

In extreme cases caused by a lack of necessary equipment, repair or replacement of piston rings, pistons, connecting rods and rod bearings is possible with the engine in the vehicle. However, this practice is not recommended because of the cleaning and preparation work that must be done to the components involved.

3   Top Dead Center (TDC) for number one piston - locating

Refer to illustrations 3.4, 3.6 and 3.7

1   Top Dead Center (TDC) is the highest point in the cylinder that each piston reaches as it travels up-and-down when the crankshaft turns. Each piston reaches TDC on the compression stroke and again on the exhaust stroke, but TDC generally refers to piston position on the compression stroke. The timing marks on the vibration damper **(see illustration 3.6)** installed on the front of the crankshaft are referenced to the number one piston at TDC on the compression stroke.

2   Positioning the piston(s) at TDC is an essential part of many

3.4 Make marks (arrows) on the distributor cap and housing

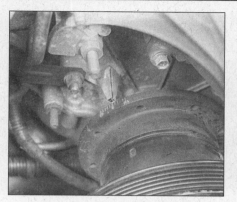

3.6 Turn the crankshaft clockwise until the zero on the vibration damper scale is lined up with the pointer

3.7 The rotor (upper arrow) should be directly above the mark (lower arrow) on the distributor housing

2A

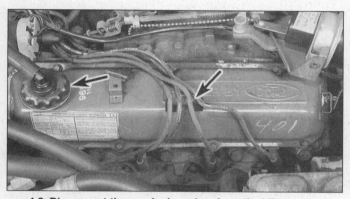

4.2 Disconnect the spark plug wires from the clips on the valve cover (arrow)

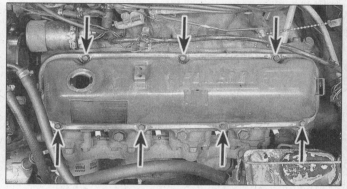

4.6 Location of the valve cover bolts (arrows)

procedures such as rocker arm removal, valve adjustment, timing chain and sprocket replacement and distributor removal.

3　In order to bring any piston to TDC, the crankshaft must be turned using one of the methods outlined below. When looking at the front of the engine, normal crankshaft rotation is clockwise. **Warning:** *Before beginning this procedure, be sure to place the transmission in Neutral and ground the coil wire attached to the center terminal of the distributor cap to disable the ignition system.*

　a)　*The preferred method is to turn the crankshaft with a large socket and breaker bar attached to the vibration damper bolt threaded into the front of the crankshaft.*
　b)　*A remote starter switch, which may save some time, can also be used. Attach the switch leads to the S (switch) and B (battery) terminals on the starter motor. Once the piston is close to TDC, use a socket and breaker bar as described in the previous paragraph.*
　c)　*If an assistant is available to turn the ignition switch to the Start position in short bursts, you can get the piston close to TDC without a remote starter switch. Use a socket and breaker bar as described in Paragraph a) to complete the procedure.*

4　Using a felt pen, make a mark on the distributor housing directly below the number one spark plug wire terminal on the distributor cap **(see illustration)**. **Note:** *The terminal numbers marked on the spark plug wires near the distributor are usually found on Original Equipment Manufactured (OEM) spark plug wires. So label the wires before removal, if numbering isn't found.*

5　Remove the distributor cap as described in Chapter 1.

6　Turn the crankshaft (see Paragraph 3 above) until the zero or groove on the vibration damper is aligned with the pointer or TDC mark **(see illustration)**. The pointer or TDC mark and vibration damper are located low on the front of the engine, near the pulley that turns the drivebelt.

7　The rotor should now be pointing directly at the mark on the distributor housing **(see illustration)**. If it isn't, the piston is at TDC on the exhaust stroke.

8　To get the piston to TDC on the compression stroke, turn the crankshaft one complete turn (360-degrees) clockwise. The rotor should now be pointing at the mark. When the rotor is pointing at the number one spark plug wire terminal in the distributor cap (which is indicated by the mark on the housing) and the ignition timing marks are aligned, the number one piston is at TDC on the compression stroke.

9　After the number one piston has been positioned at TDC on the compression stroke, TDC for any of the remaining cylinders can be located by turning the crankshaft and following the firing order (refer to the Specifications).

4　Valve covers - removal and installation

Removal

Refer to illustrations 4.2 and 4.6

1　Disconnect the battery cable from the negative terminal.

2　Note their locations, then detach the spark plug wire clips, if equipped, from the valve cover studs **(see illustration)**.

3　Refer to Chapter 1 and detach the spark plug wires from the plugs. Position the wires out of the way.

4　If so equipped, detach the diverter valve and hoses from the valve cover.

5　On vehicles with cruise control, disconnect the servo linkage at the carburetor or throttle body and remove the servo bracket.

6　Remove the valve cover bolts/nuts **(see illustration)**, then detach the cover from the head. **Note:** *If the cover is stuck to the head, bump one end with a wood block and a hammer to jar it loose. If that doesn't*

4.7 Being careful not to damage the mating surface of the cylinder head, carefully remove the valve cover gasket with a gasket scraper or putty knife

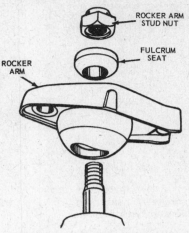

5.2a Early model rocker arm assembly

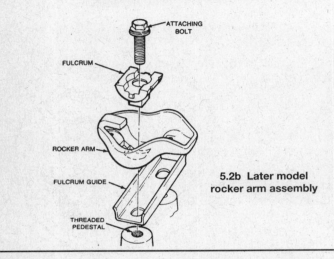

5.2b Later model rocker arm assembly

5.2c Loosen the nut or bolt (arrow) and pivot the rocker arm to the side to remove the pushrod

work, try to slip a flexible putty knife between the head and cover to break the gasket seal. Don't pry at the cover-to-head joint or damage to the sealing surfaces may occur (leading to oil leaks in the future). Some valve covers are made of plastic - be extra careful when tapping or pulling on them.

Installation

Refer to illustration 4.7

7   The mating surfaces of each cylinder head and valve cover must be perfectly clean when the covers are installed. Use a gasket scraper to remove all traces of sealant and old gasket material **(see illustration)**, then clean the mating surfaces with lacquer thinner or acetone. If there's sealant or oil on the mating surfaces when the cover is installed, oil leaks may develop.

8   Clean the mounting bolt threads with a die to remove any corrosion and restore damaged threads. Make sure the threaded holes in the head are clean - run a tap into them to remove corrosion and restore damaged threads. Apply a small amount of light oil to the bolt threads.

9   The gaskets should be mated to the covers before the covers are installed. Make sure the tabs on the gasket(s) engage in the slots in the cover(s).

10   Carefully position the cover on the head and install the bolts/nuts.

11   Tighten the bolts in two steps to the torque listed in this Chapter's Specifications. Wait two minutes between the first and the second round of tightening. **Caution:** *Be careful with plastic valve covers, if equipped. They can be easily distorted or damaged, so don't over tighten the bolts!*

12   The remaining installation steps are the reverse of removal.

13   Start the engine and check carefully for oil leaks as the engine warms up.

5   Rocker arms and pushrods - removal, inspection and installation

Removal

Refer to illustrations 5.2a, 5.2b, 5.2c and 5.4

1   Remove the valve cover(s) from the cylinder head(s) (see Section 4).

2   Beginning at the front of one cylinder head, remove the rocker arm fulcrum bolts, or stud nut **(see illustrations)**. **Note:** *If the pushrods are the only items being removed, loosen each bolt, or stud nut, just enough to allow the rocker arms to be rotated to the side so the pushrods can be lifted out* **(see illustration)**. Store them separately in marked containers to ensure that they will be reinstalled in their original locations.

3   Lift off the rocker arms, fulcrums and fulcrum guides (if equipped). Store them in the marked containers with the bolts (they must be reinstalled in their original locations).

4   Remove the pushrods and store them separately to make sure they don't get mixed up during installation **(see illustration)**.

Inspection

Refer to illustrations 5.5 and 5.8

5   Check each rocker arm for wear, cracks and other damage, especially where the pushrods and valve stems contact the rocker arm faces **(see illustration)**.

6   Make sure the hole at the pushrod end of each rocker arm is open.

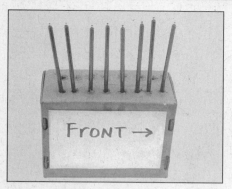

5.4 A perforated cardboard box provides ideal pushrod storage to ensure that they are reinstalled in their original locations

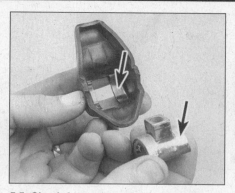

5.5 Check for wear on the rocker arm and fulcrum where contact is made (arrows)

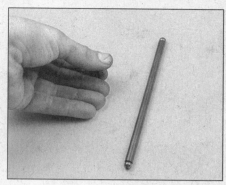

5.8 Roll each pushrod on flat, smooth surface, such as a plate of glass - if it wobbles, it's bent and must be replaced

5.12a A special tool is required to bleed down the lifters when checking the valve stem-to-rocker arm clearance

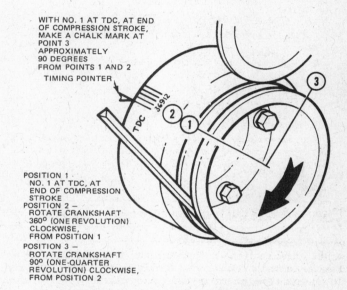

5.12b Crankshaft position for checking and adjusting valve clearances

7   Check each rocker arm pivot area and fulcrum for wear, cracks and galling. If the rocker arms are worn or damaged, replace them with new ones and use new fulcrums as well.

8   Inspect the pushrods for cracks and excessive wear at the ends. Roll each pushrod across a piece of plate glass to see if it's bent **(see illustration)**. If it wobbles when it rolls, check it with a feeler gauge - if you can get a gauge thicker than 0.008 inch between the pushrod and the surface, replace the pushrod.

Installation

Caution: *Make sure that both lifters for each cylinder are on the base circle of the cam lobe (both valves closed) before tightening the rocker arm bolts.*

9   Lubricate the lower end of each pushrod with clean engine oil or moly-base grease and install them in their original locations. Make sure each pushrod seats completely in the lifter.

10   Apply moly-base grease to the ends of the valve stems and the upper ends of the pushrods before positioning the rocker arms, fulcrums and guides.

11   Apply moly-base grease to the fulcrums to prevent damage to the mating surfaces before engine oil pressure builds up. Set the rocker arms and guides in place, then install the fulcrums and bolts.

Valve adjustment

Positive stop rocker arms

Refer to illustrations 5.12a and 5.12b

Note: *Adjustment is normally only needed after valve train components have been replaced or the valves and/or seats have been ground a considerable amount.*

12   Using Ford lifter bleed-down tool T70P-6513-A or equivalent **(see illustration)**, press on the rocker arm until the lifter leaks down. Check the clearance between the valve stem and rocker arm with a feeler gauge. Compare the results to the Specifications and write it down for future reference. Repeat the procedure for each valve in the order shown below. **Note:** *The arrangement of intake and exhaust valves is as follows:*

With the crankshaft in position 1, check the valves as follows **(see illustration):**

5.0L (except HO) and 460 cid engines:
    Intake - no. 1, 7 and 8
    Exhaust - no. 1, 4 and 5
All others:
    Intake - no. 1, 4 and 8
    Exhaust - no. 1, 3 and 7

13   Rotate the crankshaft to position 2 and check the following valves:

5.0L (except HO) and 460 cid engines:
    Intake - no. 4 and 5
    Exhaust - no. 2 and 6
All others:
    Intake - no. 3 and 7
    Exhaust - no. 2 and 6

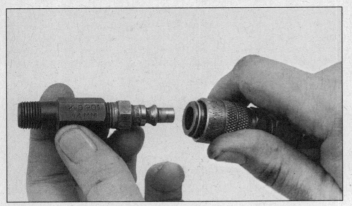

6.4 This is what the air hose adapter that threads into the spark plug hole looks like - they're commonly available from auto parts stores

6.9 Once the spring is depressed, the keepers can be removed with a small magnet

14   Rotate the crankshaft to position 3 and check the following valves:

    5.0L (except HO) and 460 cid engines:
        Intake - no. 2, 3 and 6
        Exhaust - no. 3, 7 and 8
    All others:
        Intake - no. 2, 5 and 6
        Exhaust - no. 4, 5 and 8

15   Clearance can be changed by using different length pushrods, available from your dealer parts department. If there isn't enough clearance, use a shorter pushrod; too much clearance, use a longer one.

6   Valve springs, retainers and seals - replacement

Refer to illustrations 6.4, 6.9, 6.10a, 6.10b, 6.15 and 6.17
Note: *Broken valve springs and defective valve stem seals can be replaced without removing the cylinder heads. Two special tools and a compressed air source are normally required to perform this operation, so read through this Section carefully and rent or buy the tools before beginning the job. If compressed air isn't available, a length of nylon rope can be used to keep the valves from falling into the cylinder during this procedure.*

1   Remove the valve cover from the cylinder head(s) (see Section 4). If all of the valve stem seals are being replaced, remove both valve covers.

2   Remove the spark plug from the cylinder with the defective component. If all of the valve stem seals are being replaced, all of the spark plugs should be removed.

3   Turn the crankshaft until the piston in the affected cylinder is at Top Dead Center on the compression stroke (see Section 3). If you're replacing all of the valve stem seals, begin with cylinder number one and work on the valves for one cylinder at a time. Move from cylinder-to-cylinder following the firing order sequence (see this Chapter's Specifications).

4   Thread an adapter into the spark plug hole **(see illustration)** and connect an air hose from a compressed air source to it. Most auto parts stores can supply the air hose adapter. **Note:** *Many cylinder compression gauges utilize a screw-in fitting that may work with your air hose quick-disconnect fitting.*

5   Remove the bolt, fulcrum and rocker arm for the valve with the defective component and pull out the pushrod. If all of the valve stem seals are being replaced, all of the rocker arms and pushrods should be removed (see Section 5).

6   Apply compressed air to the cylinder. **Warning:** *The piston may be forced down by compressed air, causing the crankshaft to turn suddenly. If the wrench used when positioning the number one piston*

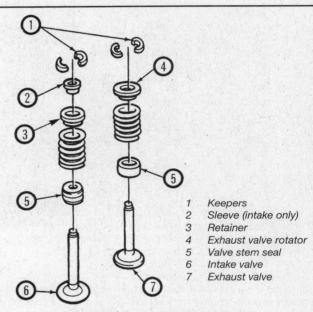

1	Keepers
2	Sleeve (intake only)
3	Retainer
4	Exhaust valve rotator
5	Valve stem seal
6	Intake valve
7	Exhaust valve

6.10a Valves and related components

at TDC is still attached to the bolt in the crankshaft nose, it could cause damage or injury when the crankshaft moves.

7   The valves should be held in place by the air pressure. If the valve faces or seats are in poor condition, leaks may prevent air pressure from retaining the valves - refer to the alternative procedure below.

8   If you don't have access to compressed air, an alternative method can be used. Position the piston at a point approximately 45-degrees before TDC on the compression stroke, then feed a long piece of nylon rope through the spark plug hole until it fills the combustion chamber. Be sure to leave the end of the rope hanging out of the engine so it can be removed easily. Use a large ratchet and socket to rotate the crankshaft in the normal direction of rotation until slight resistance is felt.

9   Stuff shop rags into the cylinder head holes above and below the valves to prevent parts and tools from falling into the engine, then use a valve spring compressor to compress the spring. Remove the keepers with small needle-nose pliers or a magnet **(see illustration).** **Note:** *A couple of different types of tools are available for compressing the valve springs with the head in place. One type, shown here, grips the lower spring coils and presses on the retainer as the knob is turned, while the other type utilizes the rocker arm bolt for leverage. Both types work very well, although the lever type is usually less expensive.*

10   Remove the spring retainer or rotator, sleeve (used on some

6.10b The seal can be pulled off the valve guide with a pair of pliers

6.15 A deep socket and hammer can be used to seat the new seals on the valve guides (not necessary with umbrella style seals, just push them on by hand)

6.17 Apply a small dab of grease to each keeper as shown here before installation - it'll hold them in place on the valve stem as the spring is released

2A

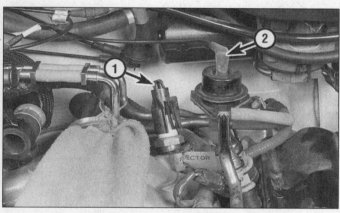

7.4 Label and disconnect the hoses and wiring

1 Sensor connector
2 Vacuum line to fuel pressure regulator

intake valves) and valve spring assembly, then remove the valve guide seal **(see illustrations)**. **Note:** *If air pressure fails to hold the valve in the closed position during this operation, the valve face or seat is probably damaged. If so, the cylinder head will have to be removed for additional repair.*

11 Wrap a rubber band or tape around the top of the valve stem so the valve won't fall into the combustion chamber, then release the air pressure. **Note:** *If a rope was used instead of air pressure, turn the crankshaft slightly in the direction opposite normal rotation.*

12 Inspect the valve stem for damage. Rotate the valve in the guide and check the end for eccentric movement, which would indicate that the valve is bent.

13 Move the valve up-and-down in the guide and make sure it doesn't bind. If the valve stem binds, either the valve is bent or the guide is damaged. In either case, the head will have to be removed for repair.

14 Reapply air pressure to the cylinder to retain the valve in the closed position, then remove the tape or rubber band from the valve stem. If a rope was used instead of air pressure, rotate the crankshaft in the normal direction of rotation until slight resistance is felt.

15 Lubricate the valve stem with engine oil and the valve stem tip with moly-base grease, then install a new guide seal **(see illustration)**. Lightly tap the seal into place with a socket and hammer as shown. **Note:** *Some seal manufacturers supply a plastic collar, that is slipped on the end of the valve tip, to avoid cutting or nicking the new seal during installation. There may even be an installation tool to be used in place of the socket shown.*

16 Install the spring in position over the valve.

17 Install the valve spring retainer or rotator. Some intake valves also have a sleeve that fits inside the retainer. Compress the valve spring and carefully position the keepers in the groove. Apply a small dab of grease to the inside of each keeper to hold it in place **(see illustration)**.

18 Remove the pressure from the spring tool and make sure the keepers are seated.

19 Disconnect the air hose and remove the adapter from the spark plug hole. If a rope was used in place of air pressure, pull it out of the cylinder.

20 Install the rocker arm(s) and pushrod(s) (see Section 5).

21 Install the spark plug(s) and hook up the wire(s) (see Chapter 1).

22 Install the valve cover(s) (see Section 4).

23 Start and run the engine, then check for oil leaks and unusual sounds coming from the valve cover area.

7 Intake manifold - removal and installation

Removal

Refer to illustrations 7.4, 7.7, 7.8a, 7.8b and 7.11

Warning: *The intake manifold is heavy. It is highly recommended to have help available when you lift the manifold off the engine to avoid injury.*

1 Drain the cooling system (see Chapter 1).

2 Remove the PCV and canister purge hoses.

3 Disconnect the accelerator cable, speed control linkage and automatic transmission cable. Remove the accelerator cable bracket (see Chapter 4).

4 Label and disconnect all electrical and vacuum connectors **(see illustration)** from the coolant temperature sending unit, air charge temperature sensor, throttle positioner, idle speed control solenoid, EGR sensors, fuel injectors and fuel charging assembly (see Chapter 4).

5 Remove the distributor (see Chapter 5).

6 Relieve the fuel system pressure (see Chapter 4) and disconnect the fuel supply and return lines. Remove the carburetor, if equipped (see Chapter 4).

7 Disconnect the radiator, heater and water pump bypass hoses from the water pump outlet **(see illustration)**. Disconnect the throttle body cooler hoses. **Note:** *The heater outlet and coolant bypass tubes are pressed in and cannot be removed.*

8 Unbolt the coolant pipes **(see illustrations)** which are attached to the manifold along the right side.

9 Remove the air intake plenum, if equipped (see Chapter 4).

10 Loosen the lower intake manifold bolts and nuts in 1/4-turn increments until they can be removed by hand.

11 The manifold will probably be stuck to the cylinder heads and force may be required to break the gasket seal. A prybar can be used to pry up the manifold **(see illustration)**, but make sure all bolts and

7.7 Disconnect all coolant hose connections (arrow) at the manifold

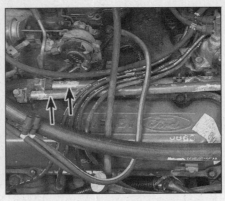

7.8a Once the hoses are disconnected from the manifold, move the steel coolant tubes (arrows) out of the way

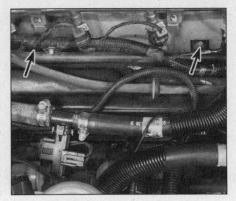

7.8b On fuel injected engines the coolant tubes are attached to the manifold (arrows) and must be removed

7.11 Pry against a casting protrusion to break the manifold loose

7.13 After covering the lifter valley, use a gasket scraper to remove all traces of sealant and old gasket material from the head and manifold mating surfaces

7.15 You can make your own guide studs for the intake manifold, using bolts with the heads cut off - make sure the studs are long enough to be easily screwed out, or cut a slot into the end with a hacksaw to allow use of a screwdriver, after the manifold is bolted into place

nuts have been removed first! **Caution:** *Don't pry between the block and manifold or the heads and manifold or damage to the gasket sealing surfaces may occur, leading to vacuum and oil leaks. Pry only at a manifold casting protrusion.*

Installation

Refer to illustrations 7.13, 7.15, 7.16, 7.17a, 7.17b, 7.18, 7.21a, 7.21b and 7.21c

Caution: *The mating surfaces of the cylinder heads, block and manifold must be perfectly clean when the manifold is installed. Gasket removal solvents in aerosol cans are available at most auto parts stores and may be helpful when removing old gasket material that's stuck to the heads and manifold (since some manifolds are made of aluminum, aggressive scraping can cause damage!). Be sure to follow directions printed on the container.*

Note: *Ford recommends the use of guide pins when installing the manifold. To make these, buy four extra manifold bolts. Cut the heads off the bolts, then grind a taper and cut a screwdriver slot in the cut ends.*

12   If the manifold was disassembled, reassemble it. Use electrically conductive sealant on the temperature sending unit threads. Use a new EGR valve gasket.

13   Use a gasket scraper to remove all traces of sealant and old gasket material, then clean the mating surfaces with lacquer thinner or acetone **(see illustration)**. If there's old sealant or oil on the mating surfaces when the manifold is installed, oil or vacuum leaks may

develop. When working on the heads and block, cover the lifter valley with shop rags to keep debris out of the engine. Use a vacuum cleaner to remove any gasket material that falls into the intake ports in the heads.

14   Use a tap of the correct size to chase the threads in the bolt holes, then use compressed air (if available) to remove the debris from the holes. **Warning:** *Wear safety glasses or a face shield to protect your eyes when using compressed air! Remove excessive carbon deposits and corrosion from the exhaust and coolant passages in the heads and manifold.*

15   Install the guide pins **(see illustration)**, as described in the note at the beginning of the installation Section.

16   Apply a 1/8-inch wide bead of RTV sealant to the four corners where the manifold, block and heads converge **(see illustration)**. **Note:** *This sealant sets up in 10 minutes. Do not take longer to install and tighten the manifold once the sealant is applied, or leaks may occur.*

17   Apply a small dab of gasket adhesive to the manifold gasket mating surface on each cylinder head. Position the gaskets on the cylinder heads **(see illustrations)**. The upper side of each gasket will have a TOP or THIS SIDE UP label stamped into it to ensure correct installation.

18   Position the end seals on the block **(see illustration)**, then apply a 1/8-inch wide bead of RTV sealant to the four points where the end seals meet the heads **(see illustration 7.16)**.

19   Make sure all intake port openings, coolant passage holes and bolt holes are aligned correctly.

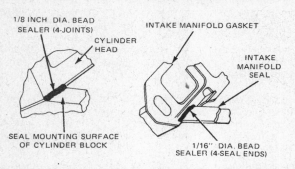

7.16 Apply a bead of RTV sealant to the corners where the block, heads and manifold meet before and after the gaskets are installed

7.17a Align the new intake manifold gaskets by seating them over the dowel pins or studs in the cylinder head (arrows)

7.17b If individual gaskets are used on each side of the intake manifold, make sure the intake manifold gaskets notch together with the cylinder head gaskets

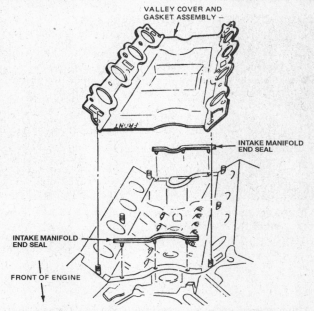

7.18 Once the intake-to-cylinder head gaskets are in place position the end seals carefully on the engine block - if necessary, use a small amount of sealant to hold them in place

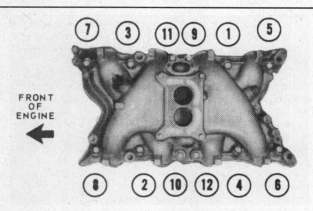

7.21a Intake manifold bolt tightening sequence - 6.6L (400 cid) engines

20   Carefully set the manifold in place while the sealant is still wet. **Caution:** *Don't disturb the gaskets and don't move the manifold fore-and-aft after it contacts the seals on the block. Make sure the end seals haven't been disturbed.*

21   Install the bolts and tighten them in the proper sequence to the torque listed in this Chapter's Specifications **(see illustrations).**

22   The remaining installation steps are the reverse of removal.

23   Change the engine oil and refill the cooling system (see Chapter 1).

24   Start the engine and check carefully for oil and coolant leaks at the intake manifold joints.

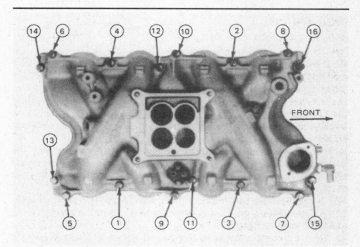

7.21b Intake manifold bolt tightening sequence - 7.5L (460 cid) engines

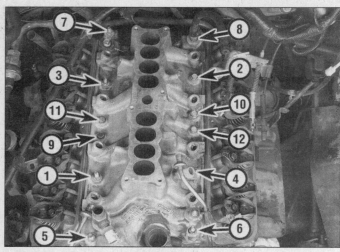

7.21c Intake manifold bolt tightening sequence - 5.0L (302 cid) and 5.8L (351 cid) engines

8   Exhaust manifolds - removal and installation

Removal

Refer to illustrations 8.3, 8.5a, 8.5b and 8.6

1   Disconnect the battery cable from the negative terminal of the battery.

2   Raise the vehicle and support it securely on jackstands (see Chapter 1).

3   Working under the vehicle, apply penetrating oil to the exhaust pipe-to-manifold studs and nuts **(see illustration)**.

4   Unplug the electrical connector for the oxygen sensor (see Chapter 4).

5   Lower the vehicle and remove the spark plug heat shields, if equipped **(see illustrations)**, and spark plugs (see Chapter 1).

6   Remove the manifold heat shields, if equipped **(see illustration)**.

7   Remove the air cleaner assembly and heat stove tube (if equipped).

Right side manifold

8   Remove the Thermactor hardware, if equipped.

9   Remove the automatic transmission fluid dipstick tube, if necessary.

Left side manifold

10   If it's in the way, remove the engine oil dipstick and tube.

Both manifolds

Refer to illustrations 8.11 and 8.12

11   Bend back the locking tabs **(see illustration)**, if equipped.

12   Remove the mounting bolts and separate the manifold from the head **(see illustration)**. Note the locations of the pilot bolts.

Installation

13   Check the manifold for cracks and make sure the bolt threads are clean and undamaged. The manifold and cylinder head mating

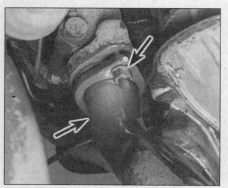

8.3 Remove the nuts (arrows) that hold the exhaust pipe flange to the exhaust manifold

8.5a First, remove the spark plug heat shield nuts (arrows)....

8.5b . . . and then remove the shield

8.6 On some models, it is necessary to remove the heat shield nuts (arrows) and the heat shield to gain access to the exhaust manifold bolts - use penetrating oil to make the fasteners easier to remove

8.11 Some models are equipped with manifold bolt locking tabs - bend these down before removing the bolts - use new locking assemblies on installation, bending the tabs up to lock the bolts in place

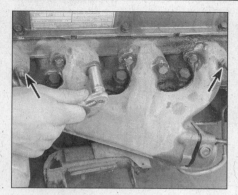

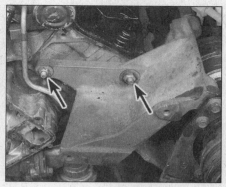

8.12 Use a deep socket to remove the special stud bolts used to retain the spark plug heat shield (arrows)

9.5 Unbolt and remove the Thermactor crossover tube (arrow) on each cylinder head, if applicable (power steering pump removed for clarity)

9.7 Remove the bracket mounting bolts (arrows) and set aside any mounting brackets and components that are attached to the cylinder heads

surfaces must be clean before the manifolds are reinstalled - use a gasket scraper to remove all carbon deposits and old gasket material.

14   Position the manifold and gasket (if used) on the head and install the mounting bolts.

15   When tightening the mounting bolts, work from the center to the ends and tighten the bolts in three equal steps to the torque listed in this Chapter's Specifications.

16   The remaining installation steps are the reverse of removal.

17   Start the engine and check for exhaust leaks.

9   Cylinder head(s) - removal and installation

Warning: *The cylinder heads are heavy. It is highly recommended to have an assistant help you lift them off the engine to avoid injury.*

Caution: *The engine must be completely cool when the heads are removed. Failure to allow the engine to cool off could result in head warpage.*

Removal

Both cylinder heads

Refer to illustration 9.5

1   Remove the valve cover(s) (see Section 4).

2   Remove the pushrods (see Section 5).

3   Remove the intake manifold (see Section 7).

4   Remove the drivebelts (see Chapter 1) and idler pulley bracket.

5   Remove the Thermactor diverter valve and pump and the crossover tube **(see illustration)** from the rear of the head (if applicable).

Left (driver's side) cylinder head

Refer to illustration 9.7

6   Unbolt the power steering pump and tie it aside in an upright position. Leave the hoses connected (see Chapter 10).

7   Remove the air conditioning compressor, and bracket(s) if necessary **(see illustration)**, and position it out of the way (see Chapter 3). DO NOT disconnect the hoses to the compressor!

8   Remove the exhaust manifold(s) (see Section 8).

9   Proceed to Step 12.

Right cylinder head

10   Detach the fuel line from the clip at the front of the head, if applicable.

Both cylinder heads

Refer to illustration 9.12

11   Remove the exhaust manifold(s) (see Section 8).

12   Using a new head gasket, outline the cylinders and bolt pattern on a piece of cardboard **(see illustration)**. Be sure to indicate the front

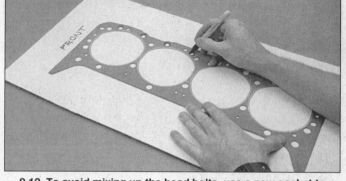

9.12 To avoid mixing up the head bolts, use a new gasket to transfer the bolt pattern to a piece of cardboard, then punch holes to accept the bolts

of the engine for reference. Punch holes at the bolt locations.

13   Loosen the head bolts in 1/4-turn increments until they can be removed by hand. Work from bolt-to-bolt in a pattern that's the reverse of the tightening sequence **(see illustration 9.22)**. Store the bolts in the cardboard holder as they're removed; this will ensure that the bolts are reinstalled in their original holes.

14   Lift the head(s) off the engine. If resistance is felt, DO NOT pry between the head and block as damage to the mating surfaces will result. To dislodge the head, place a wood block against the end of it and strike the wood block with a hammer. Store the heads on blocks of wood to prevent damage to the gasket sealing surfaces.

15   Cylinder head disassembly and inspection procedures are covered in detail in Chapter 2, Part C.

Installation

Refer to illustrations 9.16, 9.19 and 9.22

16   The mating surfaces of the cylinder heads and block must be perfectly clean when the heads are installed. Use a gasket scraper to remove all traces of carbon and old gasket material **(see illustration)**, then clean the mating surfaces with lacquer thinner or acetone. If there's oil on the mating surfaces when the heads are installed, the gaskets may not seal correctly and leaks may develop. When working on the block, cover the lifter valley with shop rags to keep debris out of the engine. Use a vacuum cleaner to remove any debris that falls into the cylinders.

17   Check the block and head mating surfaces for nicks, deep scratches and other damage. If damage is slight, it can be removed with a file - if it's excessive, machining may be the only alternative.

18   Use a tap of the correct size to chase the threads in the head bolt holes. Mount each bolt in a vise and run a die down the threads to

2A

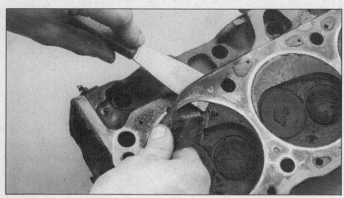

9.16 Use a scraper to remove all traces of old gasket material

9.19 Be certain that the cylinder head gaskets are positioned with the correct side up (note the *Front* mark on the type used here)

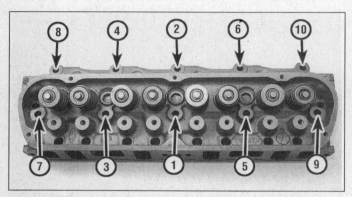

9.22 Cylinder head bolt tightening sequence (all engines)

10.5a Mark the pulley and vibration damper before removing the four pulley bolts - the large vibration damper bolt (arrow) is usually very tight, so use a six-point socket and a breaker bar to loosen it

remove corrosion and restore the threads. Dirt, corrosion, sealant and damaged threads will affect torque readings.

19   Position the new gasket(s) over the locating dowels in the block. Make sure it's facing the correct direction and that all bolt and coolant passage holes are aligned. **Note:** *Most gaskets will either be marked FRONT or TOP to be sure the gasket is positioned correctly* **(see illustration).**

20   Carefully position the head(s) on the block without disturbing the gasket(s).

21   Before installing the head bolts, lightly oil the threads on all of the bolts.

22   Install the bolts in their original locations and tighten them finger tight. Follow the recommended sequence and tighten the bolts, in two or three steps, to the torque listed in this Chapter's Specifications **(see illustration).**

23   The remaining installation steps are the reverse of removal.

24   Change the engine oil and filter (see Chapter 1), then start the engine and check carefully for oil and coolant leaks.

10 Crankshaft pulley/vibration damper - removal and installation

Removal

Refer to illustrations 10.5a and 10.5b

1   Remove the bolts attaching the fan shroud to the radiator and position the shroud back over the fan.

2   Remove the fan/clutch assembly and the shroud (see Chapter 3).

3   Remove the drivebelts (see Chapter 1).

4   Mark the crankshaft pulley and vibration damper so they can be reassembled in the same relative position to each other. This is important, since the damper and pulley are initially balanced as a unit.

Unbolt and remove the pulley.

5   Remove the bolt from the front of the crankshaft **(see illustration).** You'll most likely have to prevent the crankshaft from turning. Remove the torque converter access cover and wedge a large screwdriver between the teeth of the starter ring gear, allowing the screwdriver to rest against the transmission housing. Use a puller to detach the vibration damper **(see illustration). Caution:** *Don't use a puller with jaws that grip the outer edge of the damper. The puller must be the type shown in the illustration that utilizes bolts to apply force to the damper hub only. Clean the crankshaft nose and the seal contact surface on the vibration damper with lacquer thinner or acetone. Leave the Woodruff key in place in the crankshaft keyway.*

Installation

Refer to illustrations 10.6a and 10.6b

6   Lubricate the oil seal contact surface of the vibration damper hub with multi-purpose grease or clean engine oil **(see illustration),** then install the damper on the end of the crankshaft. The keyway in the damper must be aligned with the Woodruff key in the crankshaft nose. If the damper cannot be seated by hand, slip the large washer over the bolt, install the bolt and tighten it to pull the damper into place. An alternative method that can be used is to use a soft face/dead blow hammer or a wood block and a steel hammer to drive the damper into place **(see illustration). Caution:** *Never use a steel hammer directly on the damper.* Tighten the bolt to the torque listed in this Chapter's Specifications.

7   The remaining installation steps are the reverse of removal.

8   Add coolant and check the oil level. Run the engine and check for oil and coolant leaks.

10.5b Use the recommended puller to remove the vibration damper - if a puller that applies force to the outer edge is used, the damper will be damaged

10.6a Apply white grease to the inside of the vibration damper to ease installation and prevent the formation of rust

10.6b A soft-face hammer can be used to tap the vibration damper onto the crankshaft - DON'T use a steel hammer

2A

11 Timing chain cover - removal and installation

Removal

Refer to illustrations 11.5a, 11.5b, 11.7, 11.9

1   Perform all water pump removal steps except actual removal of the pump. The pump may be removed or left attached to the timing chain cover during removal (see Chapter 3).
2   Drain the engine oil and remove the oil filter (see Chapter 1).
3   Disconnect and plug fuel inlet hose at the fuel pump (see Chapter 4).
4   Remove the crankshaft vibration damper (see Section 10).
5   On the 7.5L (460 cid) engine, slide the sleeve off the end of the crankshaft **(see illustration). Caution:** *Check the sleeve for wear. The oil seal rides on the sleeve* **(see illustration)** *and should be replaced if a groove can be felt. If in doubt, replace the part to avoid a possible oil leak after reassembly.*
6   Unbolt and remove all accessory brackets attached to the timing chain cover.
7   From underneath the vehicle, remove the oil pan-to-timing chain cover bolts **(see illustration)**.
8   Use a razor knife (thin blade) or razor blade to cut the oil pan gasket flush with the engine block face before separating the cover from the engine block.
9   Remove the remaining bolts and separate the timing chain cover from the block. If it's stuck, tap it gently with a soft-face hammer **(see illustration). Caution:** *DO NOT use excessive force or you may crack the cover. If the cover is difficult to remove, double check to make sure all of the bolts are out.*

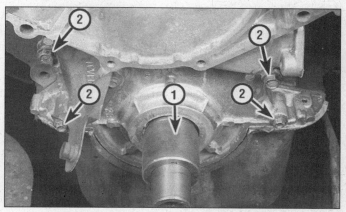

11.5a On the 7.5L (460 cid) engine, slide the sleeve off of the crankshaft and remove the remaining timing chain cover-to-block bolts

1   Crankshaft spacer/sleeve
2   Timing chain cover to block bolts

Installation

Refer to illustration 11.17

10   Remove the circular rubber seal from the front of the oil pan and stuff a shop rag into the oil pan opening to keep debris out of the engine. Use a gasket scraper to remove all traces of old gasket

11.5b Inspect the sleeve, if applicable, for excessive wear in the area the front oil seal rides on (arrow), replace if necessary

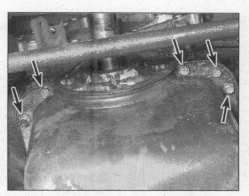

11.7 When removing the timing chain cover, remove only those bolts from the oil pan that attach directly to the cover (arrows)

11.9 Gently tap the timing chain cover loose with a soft face hammer

11.17 Before positioning the new pan gasket pieces, apply a bead of RTV-type sealant at the junction of the oil pan and block as shown

12.5 Install a dial indicator to measure timing chain deflection (this setup can also be used to check camshaft lobe lift)

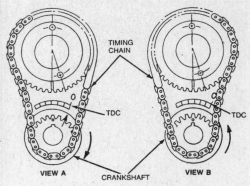

12.6 Timing chain deflection check - dial indicator measurement procedure

material and sealant from the cover, oil pan and engine block, then clean them with lacquer thinner or acetone.

11   Cut two sections out of a new oil pan gasket to install between the oil pan and timing chain cover. **Note:** *Some gasket sets come with the correct size gasket pieces for these two areas already precut.*

12   Attach the gasket sections to the oil pan with gasket contact adhesive.

13   Apply a 1/8-inch bead of RTV sealant to the oil pan-to-block joints.

14   Install a new circular rubber seal in the oil pan cutout (use contact adhesive to hold it in place).

15   Lubricate the timing chain and crankshaft front oil seal lips with engine oil.

16   Apply a thin coat of RTV sealant to the block side of the new cover gasket, then position it on the engine. The dowel pins will hold it in place as the cover is installed.

17   Before positioning the pan gasket pieces, apply a bead of RTV sealant at the junction of the oil pan, block and timing chain cover **(see illustration)**

18   Apply a thin coat of RTV sealant to the gasket surface of the cover and attach it to the engine. Don't dislodge the circular rubber seal or the gaskets.

19   It may be necessary to compress the rubber seal by forcing the cover down before installing the bolts. Temporarily slip the vibration damper onto the crankshaft to align the cover. **Caution:** *Install the sleeve, on engines so equipped* **(see illustration 11.5).**

20   Apply pipe sealant with Teflon to the threads, then install the bolts. Tighten the oil pan-to-cover bolts to the torque listed in this Chapter's Specifications while aligning the cover with the damper, or sleeve. Make sure the gaskets and seal stay in place.

21   Tighten the cover-to-block bolts to the torque listed in this Chapter's Specifications, then remove the vibration damper.

22   Install the remaining parts in the reverse order of removal.

23   Add engine oil and coolant (see Chapter 1).

24   Run the engine and check for leaks.

12   Timing chain and sprockets - inspection, removal and installation

Timing chain inspection (cover on engine)

Refer to illustrations 12.5 and 12.6

1   Disconnect the battery cable from the negative battery terminal.

2   Place the number one cylinder at Top Dead Center (TDC) on the compression stroke (see Section 3).

3   Rotate the crankshaft 360-degrees. Place the timing indicator several degrees before TDC (BTDC).

4   Remove the right side valve cover (see Section 4).

5   Attach a dial indicator to the cylinder head with the plunger in-line with and resting on the number one cylinder rocker arm at the end contacting the pushrod **(see illustration).**

6   Turn the crankshaft clockwise until the number one piston is at TDC. This will take up the slack on the right side of the timing chain **(see illustration).**

7   Zero the dial indicator.

8   Slowly turn the crankshaft counterclockwise until the slightest movement is seen on the dial indicator. Stop and note how far the crankshaft has moved away from the TDC mark by looking at the timing marks.

9   If the mark has moved more than 10-degrees, install a new timing chain and sprockets.

Timing chain and gear inspection (cover removed from engine)

Refer to illustration 12.16

10   Disconnect the battery cable from the negative battery terminal.

11   Detach any accessories such as the power steering pump, alternator and air conditioning compressor that block access to the timing chain cover. Leave the hoses/wires connected and tie the units aside. Refer to Chapters 3, 5 and 10 for additional information. Unbolt the accessory brackets from the front of the engine.

12   Position the number one piston at TDC on the compression stroke (see Chapter 2C). **Caution:** *Once this has been done, do not turn the crankshaft until the timing chain and sprockets have been reinstalled (if they are removed for replacement).*

13   Remove the vibration damper (see Section 10).

14   Remove the mounting bolts and separate the timing chain cover from the block and oil pan (see Section 11). **Caution:** *The cover is easily damaged, so DO NOT attempt to pry it off.*

15   Rotate the crankshaft in a counterclockwise direction to take up the slack in the left side (drivers side) of the chain.

16   Establish a reference point on the block and measure from that point to the chain **(see illustration).**

17   Reinstall the vibration damper bolt. Using this bolt, turn the crankshaft clockwise with a wrench until the slack is taken up on the right side of the chain.

18   Force the left side of the chain out with your fingers and measure the distance between the reference point and the chain. The difference between the two measurements is the deflection.

19   If the deflection exceeds 1/2-inch, install a new timing chain and sprockets. **Note:** *Whenever a new timing chain is required, the entire set (chain, camshaft and crankshaft sprockets) must be replaced as an assembly.*

Inspection

20   Inspect the camshaft gear for damage or wear, the teeth can be grooved or worn enough to cause a poor meshing of the gear and the

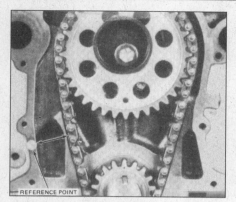

12.16 Timing chain deflection check - timing chain cover removed

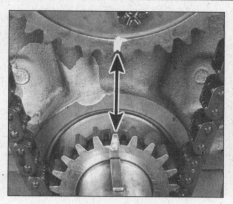

12.24 Align the timing marks on the crankshaft and camshaft sprockets (arrows) as shown here before removing the sprockets from the shafts

12.25 Slide the oil slinger (1) off of the crankshaft, remove the camshaft sprocket bolt and the fuel pump drive eccentric (2)

12.26 Remove both timing gears and the chain as a unit (be sure to align the timing gear marks first)

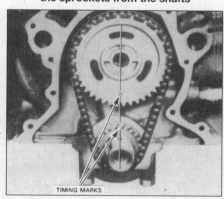

12.33 Correctly aligned timing marks

12.34 When reassembling the fuel pump drive (regardless of type used), make sure the tang on the drive is installed in the hole in the camshaft gear (arrows)

2A

chain and cause timing chain failure. **Caution:** *The camshaft gear on early models* **may** *have been an aluminum gear with a nylon coating on the teeth. This nylon coating may be cracked or flaking off in small pieces. These pieces tend to end up in the oil pan and may eventually plug the oil pump pick-up screen. If the pieces have come off the camshaft gear, the oil pump should be removed to properly clean or replace the oil pump pick-up screen. It is preferred to replace the gear set with steel camshaft gear.*

21   Inspect the crankshaft gear for damage or wear. The crankshaft gear is a steel gear, but the teeth can be grooved or worn enough to also cause a poor meshing of the gear and the chain which can lead to chain failure.

Timing chain and sprocket removal

Refer to illustrations 12.24, 12.25 and 12.26

22   Make sure the number one piston is at TDC (see Section 3).

23   Remove the timing chain cover (see Section 11). Try to avoid turning the crankshaft during vibration damper removal.

24   Make sure the crankshaft and camshaft sprocket timing marks are aligned **(see illustration)**. If they aren't, install the vibration damper bolt and use it to turn the crankshaft clockwise until the two marks are aligned.

25   Remove the camshaft sprocket mounting bolt(s) and remove the fuel pump drive eccentric **(see illustration)**.

26.   Pull the sprocket/chain off the camshaft and detach the chain from the crankshaft sprocket **(see illustration)**. Don't lose the pin in the end of the camshaft.

27   The crankshaft sprocket can be levered off, if necessary, with two large screwdrivers or a prybar.

Timing chain and sprocket installation

Refer to illustrations 12.33 and 12.34

28   Use a gasket scraper to remove all traces of old gasket material and sealant from the cover and engine block. Stuff a shop rag into the opening at the front of the oil pan to keep debris out of the engine. Wipe the cover and block sealing surfaces with a cloth saturated with lacquer thinner or acetone.

29   Check the cover flange for distortion, particularly around the bolt holes. **Note:** *If the timing chain cover oil seal has been leaking, refer to Section 18 and install a new one.*

30   Align the keyway in the crankshaft sprocket with the Woodruff key in the end of the crankshaft. Press the sprocket onto the crankshaft with the vibration damper bolt, a large socket and some washers or tap it gently into place until it's completely seated. **Caution:** *If resistance is encountered, DO NOT hammer the sprocket onto the shaft. It may eventually move into place, but it may be cracked in the process and fail later, causing extensive engine damage.*

31   Turn the crankshaft until the key is facing up (12 o'clock position).

32   Drape the chain over the camshaft sprocket and turn the sprocket until the timing mark faces down (6 o'clock position). Mesh the chain with the crankshaft sprocket and position the camshaft sprocket on the end of the camshaft. If necessary, turn the camshaft so the dowel pin fits into the sprocket hole.

33   When correctly installed, a straight line should pass through the center of the camshaft, the camshaft timing mark (in the 6 o'clock position), the crankshaft timing mark (in the 12 o'clock position) and the center of the crankshaft **(see illustration)**. DO NOT proceed until the valve timing is correct!

34   Install the fuel pump drive to the camshaft gear and install the

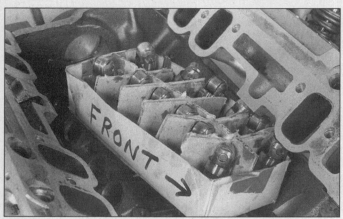

**13.3 Be sure to store the lifters in an organized manner to make
sure they're reinstalled in their original locations**

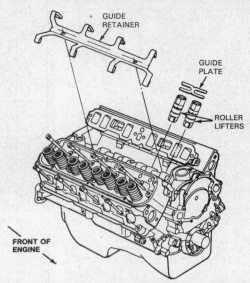

13.4a Roller lifter guide plate and retainer locations

13.4b Remove the bolts (arrows) and guide plate retainer

hardened washer and bolt. Caution; There is a tang that must fit into
the camshaft gear **(see illustration)** when assembled.

35   Apply Loc-tite to the threads and install the camshaft sprocket
bolt(s). Tighten the bolt(s) to the torque listed in this Chapter's Specifications.

36   Reinstall the timing chain cover (see Section 11).

37   Lubricate the oil seal contact surface of the vibration damper hub
with moly-base grease or clean engine oil, then install the damper on
the end of the crankshaft. The keyway in the damper must be aligned
with the Woodruff key in the crankshaft nose. If the damper cannot be
seated by hand, slip the large washer over the bolt, install the bolt and
tighten it to pull the damper into place. Tighten the bolt to the torque
listed in this Chapter's Specifications.

38   Reinstall the remaining parts in the reverse order of removal.

39   Add coolant and check the oil level. Run the engine and check for
oil and coolant leaks.

---

13   Valve lifters - removal, inspection and installation

Removal

Refer to illustrations 13.3, 13.4a, 13.4b, 13.4c, 13.5a and 13.5b

1   Remove the intake manifold (Section 7).

2   Remove the rocker arms and pushrods (Section 5).

3   Before removing the lifters, arrange to store them in a clearly
labeled box to ensure that they're reinstalled in their original locations
(see illustration).

4   On engines equipped with roller lifters, the guide retainer and

guide plates must be removed before the lifters are withdrawn **(see
illustrations)**. Remove the lifters and store them where they won't get
dirty.

5   There are several ways to extract the lifters from the bores.
Special tools designed to grip and remove lifters are manufactured by
many tool companies and are widely available, but may not be needed
in every case **(see illustration)**. On newer engines without a lot of
varnish buildup, the lifters can often be removed with a small magnet
or even with your fingers **(see illustration)**. A machinist's scribe with a
bent end can be used to pull the lifters out by positioning the point
under the retainer ring in the top of each lifter. **Caution:** *Don't use
pliers to remove the lifters unless you intend to replace them with new
ones (along with the camshaft). The pliers may damage the precision
machined and hardened lifters, rendering them useless. On engines
with a lot of sludge and varnish, work the lifters up and down, using
carburetor cleaner spray to loosen the deposits.*

Inspection

Conventional lifters

Refer to illustrations 13.7a, 13.7b ,13.7c and 13.7d

6   Clean the lifters with solvent and dry them thoroughly without
mixing them up.

7   Each lifter foot (the surface that rides on the cam lobe) must be
slightly convex, although this can be difficult to determine by eye. If the
base of the lifter is concave **(see illustrations)**, the lifters and camshaft
must be replaced. If the lifter walls are damaged or worn (which is not
very likely), inspect the lifter bores in the engine block as well. If the
pushrod seats are worn **(see illustration)**, check the pushrod ends.

8   If new lifters are being installed, a new camshaft must also be
installed. If a new camshaft is installed, then use new lifters as well.
Never install used lifters unless the original camshaft is used and the
lifters can be installed in their original locations.

Roller lifters

Refer to illustration 13.9

9   Check the rollers carefully for wear and damage, as described in
the steps 6 through 8 and make sure they turn freely without excessive
play **(see illustration)**.

10   Check each lifter wall and pushrod seat for scuffing, score marks
and uneven wear.

11   Unlike conventional lifters, used roller lifters can be reinstalled
with a new camshaft and the original camshaft can be used if new
lifters are installed, provided the used parts are in good condition.

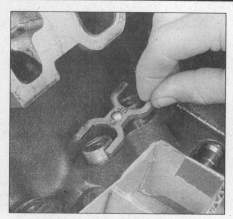

13.4c With the guide plate retainer removed the guide plates can lifted off the lifters, notice the UP stamped on the guide plates for proper reassembly

13.5a The lifters in an engine that has accumulated many miles may have to be removed with a special tool

13.5b You may be able to remove the lifters with a magnet

2A

13.7a If the lifters are pitted or rough, they shouldn't be re-used

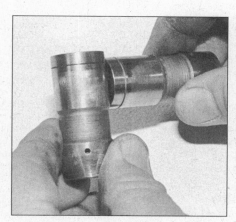

13.7b The foot of each lifter should be slightly convex - the side of another lifter can be used as a straightedge to check it

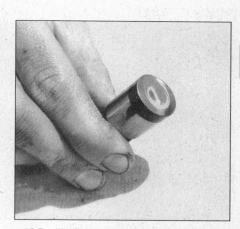

13.7c If the bottom of any lifter is worn concave, scratched or galled, replace the camshaft and all the lifters

Installation

12   Before installing the lifter(s) the air should be bled out of them as much a possible. Stand the lifter(s) upright in a container with enough oil to cover them. Use one of the pushrods to work the plunger to "prime" (fill with oil) the lifter and remove all the air.

13   The original lifters, if they're being reinstalled, must be returned to their original locations. Coat them with moly-base grease or engine assembly lube.

14   Install the lifters in the bores.

15   Install the guide plates and retainer.

16   Install the pushrods and rocker arms.

17   Install the intake manifold and valve covers.

18   Reinstall the remaining parts in the reverse order of removal.

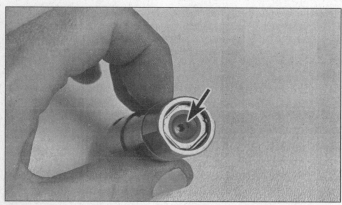

13.7d Inspect the pushrod seat (arrow) in the top of each lifter for wear

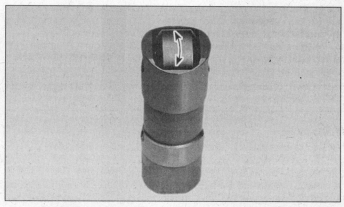

13.9 The roller on roller lifters must turn freely - check for wear and excessive play as well

14.11 Remove the camshaft thrust plate bolts (arrows) and remove the thrust plate

14.12a Thread a long bolt into the camshaft sprocket bolt hole to use as a handle

14.12b Remove the camshaft carefully to avoid damaging the bearings (note that in this case the lifters aren't stored in a box because they will be discarded along with the camshaft)

14   Camshaft - removal, inspection and installation

Camshaft lobe lift check

1   In order to determine the extent of cam lobe wear, the lobe lift should be checked prior to camshaft removal. Remove the valve covers (see Section 4).

2   Position the number one piston at TDC on the compression stroke (see Section 3).

3   Beginning with the number one cylinder, mount a dial indicator on the engine and position the plunger in-line with and resting on the first rocker arm **(see illustration 12.5)**.

4   Zero the dial indicator, then very slowly turn the crankshaft in the normal direction of rotation until the indicator needle stops and begins to move in the opposite direction. The point at which it stops indicates maximum cam lobe lift.

5   Record this figure for future reference, then reposition the piston at TDC on the compression stroke.

6   Move the dial indicator to the remaining number one cylinder pushrod and repeat the check. Be sure to record the results for each valve.

7   Repeat the check for the remaining valves. Since each piston must be at TDC on the compression stroke for this procedure, work from cylinder-to-cylinder following the firing order sequence.

8   After the check is complete, compare the results to this Chapter's Specifications. If camshaft lobe lift is less than specified, cam lobe wear has occurred and a new camshaft should be installed.

Removal

Refer to illustrations 14.11, 14.12a and 14.12b

9   Refer to the appropriate Sections and remove the pushrods, the valve lifters and the timing chain and camshaft sprocket. The radiator should be removed as well (see Chapter 3). You also may have to remove the air conditioning condenser and the grille, but wait and see if the camshaft can be pulled out of the engine.

10   Check the camshaft endplay with a dial indicator. If it's greater than specified, replace the thrust plate with a new one when the camshaft is reinstalled.

11   Remove the camshaft thrust plate bolts and thrust plate **(see illustration)**.

12   Thread a long bolt into the camshaft that can be used to pull the cam from the block and also provide leverage to support the cam so the lobes don't get nicked or gouged on the bearings as it's withdrawn **(see illustrations)**.

Inspection

Refer to illustration 14.14

13   After the camshaft has been removed from the engine, cleaned with solvent and dried, inspect the bearing journals for uneven wear, pitting and evidence of seizure. If the journals are damaged, the bearing inserts in the block are probably damaged as well. Both the camshaft and bearings will have to be replaced (see bearing replacement in Step 16).

14   Measure the bearing journals with a micrometer **(see illustration)**, to determine if they are excessively worn or out-of-round.

15   Check the camshaft lobes for heat discoloration, score marks, chipped areas, pitting and uneven wear. If the lobes are in good condition and if the lobe lift measurements are as specified in this Chapter, the camshaft can be reused.

Bearing replacement

16   Camshaft bearing replacement requires special tools and expertise that make it a difficult job to do at home.

    However, the special tool required for bearing removal/installation is available at many stores that carry automotive tools, possibly even found at a tool rental company. follow the specific instructions that accompany the special tool for the removal and installation of the camshaft bearings.

    It is advisable though, if the bearings are bad, that the engine be removed and the block taken to an automotive machine shop to ensure that the job is done correctly.

Installation

Refer to illustration 14.17

17   Lubricate the camshaft bearing journals and cam lobes with engine assembly grease or camshaft installation lube **(see illustration)**.

18   Slide the camshaft into the engine. Support the cam near the block and be careful not to scrape or nick the bearings.

19   Apply moly-base grease or engine assembly lube to both sides of the thrust plate, then position it on the block. Install the bolts and tighten them to the torque listed in this Chapter's Specifications.

20   Refer to the appropriate Sections and install the lifters, pushrods, rocker arms, timing chain/sprocket, timing chain cover and valve covers.

21   The remaining installation steps are the reverse of removal.

22   Before starting and running the engine, change the oil and install a new oil filter (see Chapter 1).

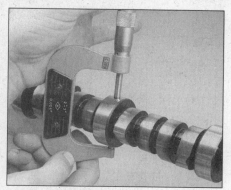

14.14 Check the diameter of each camshaft bearing journal to pinpoint excessive wear and out-of-round conditions

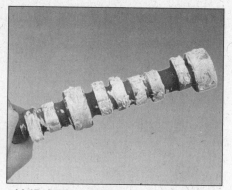

14.17 Apply an engine assembly grease or camshaft installation lube to the camshaft lobes and journals prior to installation

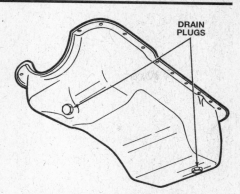

15.8 If your vehicle has a dual-sump pan, as shown, drain the oil from both plugs before removing the pan

15 Oil pan - removal and installation

Removal

Refer to illustrations 15.8, 15.17 and 15.21

1   Disconnect the battery cable from the negative battery terminal.
2   Remove the air cleaner assembly (see Chapter 4).
3   Remove the fan shroud mounting bolts and position the shroud back over the fan (see Chapter 3).
4   Remove the oil level dipstick and disconnect the oil level sensor switch on the side of the oil pan (if equipped).
5   If so equipped, remove the screws attaching the vacuum solenoids to the firewall behind the engine. Position the solenoids out of the way without disconnecting them.
6   Disconnect and lower the exhaust crossover pipe from the manifolds (see Section 8).
7   Carefully unbolt the exhaust pipe-to-catalytic converter connection (remember - it's already unbolted from the engine) and remove the exhaust pipe(s) section.
8   Drain the engine oil and remove the oil filter (see Chapter 1). **Note:** *If the vehicle has a dual-sump pan be sure to drain oil from both plugs before removing the pan* **(see illustration).**
9   Disconnect the shift linkage where it goes from the body to the transmission (see Chapter 7).
10   Disconnect the transmission cooler lines at the radiator (see Chapter 3).
11   Remove the four torque converter cover retaining bolts and detach the cover.
12   Remove the starter motor (see Chapter 5).
13   Disconnect the fuel lines. **Warning:** *On fuel injected models, the*

pressure must be relieved at the Schrader valve on the fuel charging assembly before disconnecting fuel supply and return lines (see Chapter 4).
14   Disconnect the steering flex coupling and remove the two bolts attaching the steering gear to the subframe (see Chapter 10). Let the steering gear rest on the subframe away from the oil pan.
15   Loosen the nuts holding the transmission mount to the crossmember, but don't remove them completely.
16   Remove the through bolts from the front engine mounts. Place a wood block under the oil pan and lift the engine slightly with a jack. **Caution:** *When raising the engine, watch the clearance between the transmission dipstick tube and the Thermactor air tube going to the catalytic converter. If the tubes contact before adequate mount-to-sub frame clearance is achieved, lower the engine and remove the dipstick tube and air tube. A clamp cutter and crimping tool (Ford tool no. T78P-9481-A or equivalent) are recommended to disconnect the tube from the converter.*
17   Place wooden blocks between the mounts and sub frame **(see illustration).**
18   Remove the oil pan mounting bolts. Most models are equipped with a reinforcement strip on each side of the pan which may come loose as the bolts are removed.
19   Carefully separate the pan from the block. Don't pry between the block and pan or damage to the sealing surfaces may result and oil leaks could develop. Instead, dislodge the pan with a large rubber mallet or a wood block and a hammer.
20   Reach in and remove the oil pump and pick-up tube fasteners (see Section 16) and allow them to drop into the oil pan (the pan can't be removed with them bolted to the block - there's not enough room).
21   Rotate the crankshaft as required for clearance and remove the oil pan from the vehicle **(see illustration).**

15.17 Place a wood block between the mount and subframe

15.21 Slip the oil pan out, turning it slightly to clear the driveplate

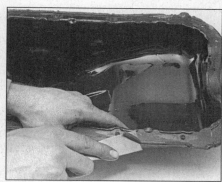

15.22 Scrape away all traces of gasket material and sealant, then clean the gasket surfaces with lacquer thinner or acetone

2A

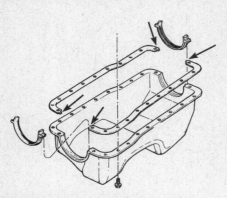

15.25a Typical engine oil pan gaskets and rubber seals - (later models use a one-piece gasket)

15.25b Use a small screwdriver to tuck the rubber seal into the block

15.25c Apply a thin bead of RTV sealant into the corners where the cork gasket and the rubber gasket notch together

Installation

Refer to illustrations 15.22, 15.25a, 15.25b and 15.25c

Note: *Several different oil pan gasket configurations are found on engines covered by this manual. Early model engines are equipped with rubber seals at the rear main bearing cap and timing chain cover, while conventional gaskets are used to seal the sides of the pan. Later model engines use a one-piece oil pan gasket. RTV is needed at the junctions of engine components regardless of the style of gasket being used. Be sure to follow the installation instructions included with an OEM or aftermarket gasket set - they supersede the information included here.*

22   Remove the gasket(s) using a gasket scraper or putty knife, if necessary, to remove all traces of old gasket material and sealant from the pan and block **(see illustration)**.

23   Clean the mating surfaces with lacquer thinner or acetone. Make sure the bolt holes in the block are clean.

24   Check the oil pan flange for distortion, particularly around the bolt holes. If necessary, place the pan on a wood block and use a hammer to flatten and restore the gasket surface.

25   On the four-piece style gasket, remove the old rubber seals from the rear main bearing cap and timing chain cover, then clean the grooves and install new seals. Use RTV sealant or gasket contact adhesive to hold the new seals in place, then apply a bead of RTV sealant to the block-to-seal junctions **(see illustrations)**.

26   Install the oil pump along with the pan. Attach the oil pump to the block.

27   Carefully position the pan against the block and install the bolts finger tight (don't forget the reinforcement strips, if used). Make sure the seal(s)/gasket(s) haven't shifted, then tighten the bolts in three steps to the torque listed in this Chapter's Specifications. Start at the center of the pan and work out toward the ends in a spiral pattern.

28   The remaining steps are the reverse of removal. **Caution:** *Don't forget to refill the engine with oil and replace the filter before starting it* (see Chapter 1).

29   Start the engine and check carefully for oil leaks at the oil pan.

16 Oil pump - removal and installation

Removal

Refer to illustrations 16.2, 16.3 and 16.4

1   Unbolt and lower the oil pan.(see Section 15).

2   Remove the oil pick-up tube-to-main bearing cap nut **(see illustration)**.

3   Remove the oil pump pick-up tube mounting bolts **(see illustration)**.

4   Remove the oil pump mounting bolts **(see illustration)** and lower the oil pump assembly into the oil pan and lift them both out together. If the pump is faulty, or you suspect that it's faulty, install a new one - do not attempt to repair the original. **Note:** *As complete oil pumps, new or remanufactured, have become more inexpensive, reliable and readily available, service parts for oil pump overhaul/repair have become increasingly difficult and unnecessary to find.*

Installation

5   Prime the oil pump prior to installation. Pour clean oil into the pick-up and turn the pump shaft by hand.

16.2 Remove the nut (arrow) . . .

16.3 . . . and the two bolts (arrows) to detach the oil pick-up tube

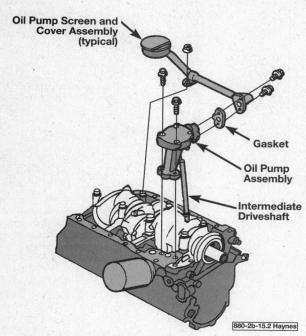

16.4 Typical oil pump installation details

6   If you separated the pump from the pick-up tube, use a new gasket and tighten the bolts securely when reattaching them.

7   As the pump is reinstalled, fit the oil pump driveshaft into the pump. It must seat all the way. DO NOT try to force it. If it doesn't align, turn the pump slightly and try again.

8   Install the mounting bolts/nut and tighten them to the torque listed in this Chapter's Specifications.

17   Driveplate - removal and installation

1   Disconnect the battery cable from the negative battery terminal.

2   Raise the vehicle and support it securely on jackstands (see Chapter 1), then refer to Chapter 7 and remove the transmission. If it's leaking, now would be a very good time to have the automatic transmission front pump seal/O-ring replaced.

3   Look for factory paint marks that indicate driveplate-to-crankshaft alignment. If they aren't there, use paint or a center-punch to make alignment marks on the driveplate and crankshaft to ensure correct alignment during reinstallation (see illustration 16.2 in Chapter 2, Part B).

4   Remove the bolts that secure the driveplate to the crankshaft. If the crankshaft turns, wedge a screwdriver through the starter opening to jam the driveplate. **Note:** *The driveplate can also be held in place, with the help of an assistant, by using a socket and breaker bar on the damper bolt at the front end of the crankshaft.*

5   Remove the driveplate from the crankshaft. Since the driveplate is fairly heavy, be sure to support it while removing the last bolt.

6   Clean the driveplate to remove grease and oil. Inspect the surface for cracks, rivet grooves, burned areas and score marks. Light scoring can be removed with emery cloth. Check for cracked and broken ring gear teeth. Lay the flywheel on a flat surface and use a straightedge to check for warpage.

7   Clean and inspect the mating surfaces of the driveplate and the crankshaft. If the crankshaft rear seal is leaking, replace it before reinstalling the driveplate.

8   Position the driveplate against the crankshaft. Be sure to align the marks made during removal. Note that some engines have an alignment dowel or staggered bolt holes to ensure correct installation.

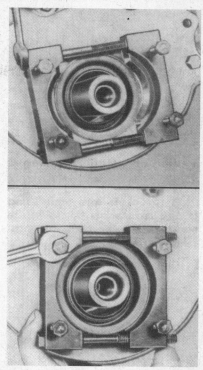

18.5a On all except the 7.5L (460 cid) engine, removing the crankshaft front oil seal is most easily accomplished with the use of a special Ford tool or an equivalent found at a local auto parts store but . . .

Before installing the bolts, apply Teflon pipe sealant to the threads.

9   Wedge a screwdriver through the starter motor opening to keep the driveplate from turning as you tighten the bolts to the torque listed in this Chapter's Specifications.

10   The remainder of installation is the reverse of the removal procedure.

18   Crankshaft oil seals - replacement

Front seal

Timing chain cover in place

Note: *Replacement of the front crankshaft oil seal, with the timing chain cover in place, applies to all engines except the 7.5L (460 cid) engine. The 7.5L (460 cid) engine requires removal of the timing chain cover to replace the seal.*

Refer to illustrations 18.5a, 18.5b, 18.7a and 18.7b

1   Remove the bolts attaching the fan shroud to the radiator and position the shroud back over the fan.

2   Remove the fan/clutch assembly and the shroud (Chapter 3).

3   Remove the drivebelts (see Chapter 1).

4   Remove the bolt from the front of the crankshaft, then use a puller to detach the vibration damper (see Section 10). **Caution:** *Don't use a puller with jaws that grip the outer edge of the damper. The puller must be the type shown in the illustration that utilizes bolts to apply force to the damper hub only. Clean the crankshaft nose and the seal contact surface on the vibration damper with lacquer thinner or acetone. Leave the Woodruff key in place in the crankshaft keyway.*

5   The crankshaft front oil seal can be removed with the use of a special tool such as the one the manufacturer recommends or it can be removed from the cover with the careful use of a small chisel and hammer **(see illustrations)**. Be careful not to damage the cover or

18.5b . . . a small chisel and hammer can be used to work the seal out of the timing chain cover - be very careful not to damage the cover or nick the crankshaft!

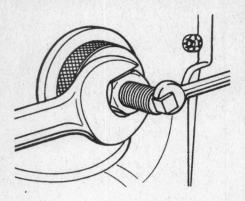

18.7a On all except the 7.5L (460 cid) engine, the front oil seal may be installed as shown with the special Ford tool . .

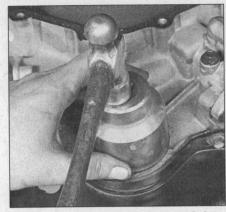

18.7b . . . or you can drive it squarely into the opening with a large socket and a hammer - don't damage the seal in the process and make sure it's completely seated

18.13 On the 7.5l (460 cid) engine, the timing chain cover must be removed and the seal driven out towards the inside of the cover (be sure to support the cover solidly on wooden blocks as shown)

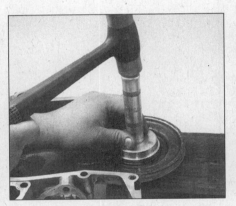

18.15 Drive the seal into the cover with a hammer and driver (driver sets of various sizes can be found at most auto parts stores), a large socket or piece of pipe would also work if it is the correct size to fit the seal

18.17 If you're very careful not to damage the crankshaft or the seal bore, the rear seal can be pried out with a screwdriver

scratch the wall of the seal bore. If the engine has accumulated a lot of miles, apply penetrating oil to the seal-to-cover joint and allow it to soak in before attempting to remove the seal.

6   Check the seal bore and crankshaft, as well as the seal contact surface on the vibration damper for nicks and burrs. Position the new seal in the bore with the open end of the seal facing IN. A small amount of oil applied to the outer edge of the new seal will make installation easier.

7   The seal can be reinstalled in either of two ways. Either use a special tool such as the one recommended by the manufacturer or the seal can be driven into the bore with a large socket and hammer until it's completely seated **(see illustrations)**. Select a socket that's the same outside diameter as the seal (a section of pipe can be used if a socket isn't available).

8   **Note:** *If a new vibration damper is being installed, balance pins must be located in the new damper in the same relative positions as the original. Also, the pulley must be attached to the damper with the same orientation to the pins as on the original. Apply clean engine oil to the seal contact surface of the vibration damper and coat the keyway (groove) with a thin layer of RTV sealant.*

9   Install the damper on the end of the crankshaft. The keyway in the damper bore must be aligned with the Woodruff key in the crankshaft nose. If the damper can't be seated by hand, tap it into place with a soft-face hammer or slip a large washer over the bolt, install the bolt and tighten it to push the damper into place. Remove the large washer,

then install the bolt and tighten it to the torque listed in this Chapter's Specifications.

10   Install the remaining parts removed for access to the seal.

11   Start the engine and check for leaks at the seal-to-cover joint.

Timing chain cover removed
Refer to illustrations 18.13 and 18.15

12   Remove the timing chain cover (see Section 11).

13   Use a punch or screwdriver and hammer to drive the seal out. On all engines except the 7.5L (460 cid), the seal is driven out from the back side. On the 7.5L (460 cid) engine, the seal must be driven out from the front side of the timing chain cover **(see illustration)**. Support the cover as close to the seal bore as possible. Be careful not to distort the cover or scratch the wall of the seal bore. If the engine has accumulated a lot of miles, apply penetrating oil to the seal-to-cover joint on each side and allow it to soak in before attempting to drive the seal out.

14   Clean the bore to remove any old seal material and corrosion. Support the cover on blocks of wood and position the new seal in the bore with the open end of the seal facing IN. A small amount of oil applied to the outer edge of the new seal will make installation easier.

15   Drive the seal into the bore with a large socket and hammer until it's completely seated **(see illustration)**. Select a socket that's the same outside diameter as the seal (a section of pipe can be used if a socket isn't available).

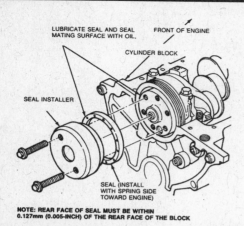

18.19 Rear main oil seal installation should be done with a special Ford tool (or equivalent) to ensure that the seal isn't damaged

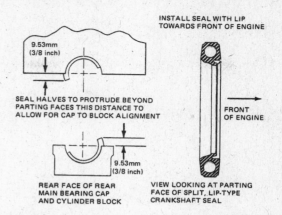

18.26 Correct installation of the crankshaft rear oil seal for the two-piece seal

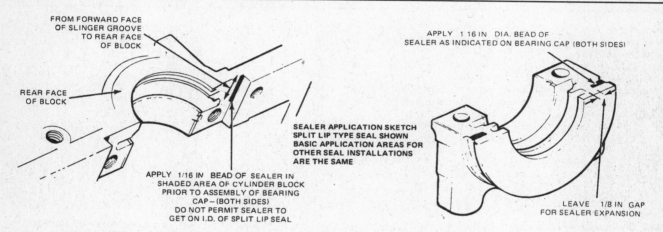

18.29 Apply RTV sealant as shown to the main bearing cap and block during rear seal installation (two-piece seal)

2A

Rear main oil seal

One-piece seal

Refer to illustrations 18.17 and 18.19

16   Refer to Chapter 7 and remove the transmission, then detach the driveplate and the rear cover plate from the engine (see Section 17).

17   The old seal can be removed by prying it out with a screwdriver **(see illustration)**. Be sure to note how far it is recessed into the bore before removing it; the new seal will have to be recessed an equal amount. **Caution:** *Be very careful not to scratch or otherwise damage the crankshaft or the bore in the housing or oil leaks could develop!*

18   Clean the crankshaft and seal bore with lacquer thinner or acetone. Check the seal contact surface very carefully for scratches and nicks that could damage the new seal lip and cause oil leaks. **Caution:** *If the crankshaft is damaged, the only alternative is a new or different crankshaft.*

19   Make sure the bore is clean, then apply a thin coat of engine oil to the outer edge of the new seal. Apply moly-base grease to the seal lips. The seal must be pressed squarely into the bore, so hammering it into place is not recommended. If you don't have access to Ford tool no. T82L-6701-A **(see illustration)**, you may be able to tap the seal in with a large section of pipe and a hammer. If you must use this method, be very careful not to damage the seal or crankshaft! And work the seal lip carefully over the end of the crankshaft with a blunt tool such as the rounded end of a socket extension.

20   Reinstall the engine rear cover plate, the driveplate and the transmission.

Two-piece seal

Refer to illustrations 18.26 and 18.29

21   Remove the oil pan to gain access to the seal (see Section 15).

22   Loosen the main bearing cap bolts slightly to allow the crankshaft to drop no more than 1/32 inch.

23   Remove the rear main bearing cap and detach the oil seal from the cap. To remove the portion of the rear main seal housed in the block, install a small sheet metal screw in one end of the seal and pull on the screw to rotate the seal out of the block groove. **Caution:** *Exercise extreme care during this procedure to prevent scratching or damaging the crankshaft seal surfaces.*

24   Carefully clean the seal grooves in the cap and block with a brush dipped in solvent.

25   Dip both new seal halves in clean engine oil.

26   Carefully install the upper seal into the groove with the lip of the seal toward the front of the engine. It will be necessary to rotate it into the seal seat. Make sure that 3/8-inch of the seal protrudes on one side below the parting surface of the bearing cap **(see illustration)**.

27   Tighten all but the rear main bearing cap bolts to the torque listed in the Chapter 2, Part C Specifications.

28   Install the lower seal into the rear bearing cap with the undercut side of the seal towards the front of the engine, allow the seal to protrude 3/8-inch above the parting surface on the opposite side of the upper protruding seal to properly mate with the upper seal **(see illustration 18.26)**.

29   Apply a thin coat of RTV sealant to the rear main bearing cap at

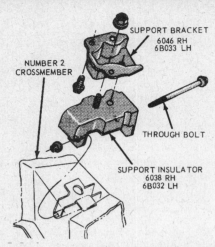

19.8a Typical early model engine mount details

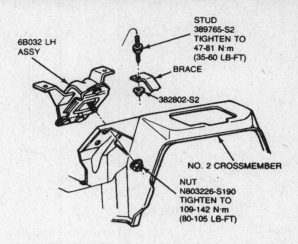

19.8b Typical mid-to-later model engine mount details

the top of the mating surface and to the block surface **(see illustration)**. Make sure that no sealant is permitted to get on the inside of the split lip seal.

30   Install the rear main bearing cap and make sure that the parting surfaces of the seals meet each other as shown.

31   Tighten the crankshaft main bearing cap bolts to the torque listed in the Chapter 2, Part C Specifications, making sure that no sealant has worked its way forward of the seal side groove.

32   Install the oil pan and oil pump (see Sections 15 and 16).

33   The remainder of the installation procedure is the reverse of removal.

34   Fill the engine with oil and coolant (see Chapter 1).

35   Start and operate the engine at a fast idle and check for leaks of any type.

19   Engine mounts - check and replacement

1   Engine mounts seldom require attention, but broken or deteriorated mounts should be replaced immediately or the added strain placed on the driveline components may cause damage or wear.

Check

2   During the check, the engine must be raised slightly to remove the weight from the mounts.

3   Raise the vehicle and support it securely on jackstands, then position a jack under the engine oil pan. Place a large wood block between the jack head and the oil pan, then carefully raise the engine just enough to take the weight off the mounts. **Warning:** *DO NOT place any part of your body under the engine when it's supported only by a jack!*

4   Check the mounts to see if the rubber is cracked, hardened or separated from the metal plates. Sometimes the rubber will split right down the center.

5   Check for relative movement between the mount plates and the engine or frame (use a large screwdriver or prybar to attempt to move

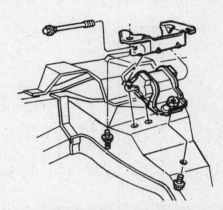

19.8c Typical later model engine mount details

the mounts). If movement is noted, lower the engine and tighten the mount fasteners.

6   Rubber preservative should be applied to the mounts to slow deterioration.

Replacement

Refer to illustration 19.8a, 19.8b and 19.8c

7   Disconnect the negative battery cable from the battery, then raise the vehicle and support it securely on jackstands (if not already done).

8   Remove the nut or through bolt to disconnect the mount from the frame **(see illustrations)**. Disconnect the automatic transmission shift linkage (see Chapter 7).

9   Raise the engine slightly with a jack or hoist (make sure the fan doesn't hit the radiator or shroud). Remove the mount-to-block bolts and detach the mount.

10   Installation is the reverse of removal. Use thread locking compound on the mount bolts and be sure to tighten them securely.

Chapter 2 Part B
Overhead cam (OHC) engine

Contents

Specifications

General

Displacement	4.6 liters (281 CID)
Bore and stroke	3.5539 X 3.5460 inches
Cylinder numbers (front to rear)	
Right side	1-2-3-4
Left (driver's) side	5-6-7-8
Firing order	1-3-7-2-6-5-4-8

Cylinder location and coil terminal location

Camshaft
Lobe lift
   Intake .... 0.02596 inch
   Exhaust... 0.02596 inch

Endplay
   Standard.. 0.0010 to 0.0065 inch
   Service limit .... 0.0075 inch maximum
Journal diameter (all) .... 1.0623 to 1.0613 inches
Bearing inside diameter (all) .... 1.0643 to 1.0633 inches
Journal-to-bearing (oil) clearance
   Standard.. 0.0010 to 0.003 inch
   Service limit .... 0.0048 inch maximum

Torque specifications
Ft-lbs (unless otherwise indicated)

Camshaft(s) sprocket bolt	81 to 95
Timing chain cover bolts	15 to 22
Cylinder head bolts (new bolts)	
Step 1	15 to 22
Step 2	Rotate an additional 85 to 95 degrees
Step 3	Rotate an additional 85 to 95 degrees
Vibration damper-to-crankshaft bolt	114 to 121
Valve cover bolts	70 to 106 in-lbs
Oil pan-to-block bolts	15 to 22
Exhaust manifold-to-cylinder head bolts	15 to 22
Intake manifold-to-cylinder head bolts	15 to 22
Oil filter insert-to-engine block adapter bolt	15 to 22
Oil pump-to-block mounting bolts	70 to 106 in-lbs
Oil pick-up tube-to-main bearing cap nut	15 to 22
Oil pick-up tube-to-oil pump bolts	70 to 106 in-lbs
Driveplate mounting bolts	75 to 85
Timing chain tensioners/guides	15 to 22
Engine mount-to-block bolts	15 to 22
Engine mount through bolts	15 to 22

After assembly, retorque with the engine hot

1   General information

This Part of Chapter 2 is devoted to in-vehicle repair procedures for the 4.6L Single Overhead Cam (OHC) V8 engine. All information concerning engine removal and installation and engine block and cylinder head overhaul can be found in Part C of this Chapter.

The following repair procedures are based on the assumption that the engine is installed in the vehicle. If the engine has been removed from the vehicle and mounted on a stand, many of the steps outlined in this Part of Chapter 2 will not apply.

The Specifications included in this Part of Chapter 2 apply only to the procedures contained in this Part. Part C of Chapter 2 contains the Specifications necessary for cylinder head and engine block rebuilding.

2   Repair operations possible with the engine in the vehicle

Refer to illustration 2.5

Many major repair operations can be accomplished without removing the engine from the vehicle.

If possible, clean the engine compartment and the exterior of the engine with some type of pressure washer before any work is started. It will make the job easier and help keep dirt out of the internal areas of the engine.

It may help to remove the hood to improve access to the engine as repairs are performed (refer to Chapter 11 if necessary).

If vacuum, exhaust, oil or coolant leaks develop, indicating a need for gasket or seal replacement, the repairs can generally be made with the engine in the vehicle. The intake and exhaust manifold gaskets, timing cover gasket, oil pan gasket, crankshaft oil seals and cylinder head gaskets are all accessible with the engine in place.

Exterior engine components, such as the intake and exhaust manifolds, the oil pan, the water pump, the starter motor, the alternator and the fuel system components can be removed for repair with the engine in place **(see illustration)**.

Since the cylinder heads can be removed without pulling the engine, valve component servicing can also be accomplished with the engine in the vehicle. Replacement of the timing chain and sprockets and oil pump is also possible with the engine in the vehicle.

In extreme cases caused by a lack of necessary equipment, repair or replacement of piston rings, pistons, connecting rods and rod bearings is also possible with the engine in the vehicle. However, this practice is not recommended because of the cleaning and preparation work that must be done to the components involved.

3   Top Dead Center (TDC) for number one piston - locating

Refer to illustration 3.1

Refer to Chapter 2, Part A for the TDC locating procedure, but use the illustration provided with this Section for the appropriate reference marks and the following exceptions.

a) *Disable the ignition system by disconnecting the primary electrical connectors at the ignition coil pack/modules (see Chapter 5).*

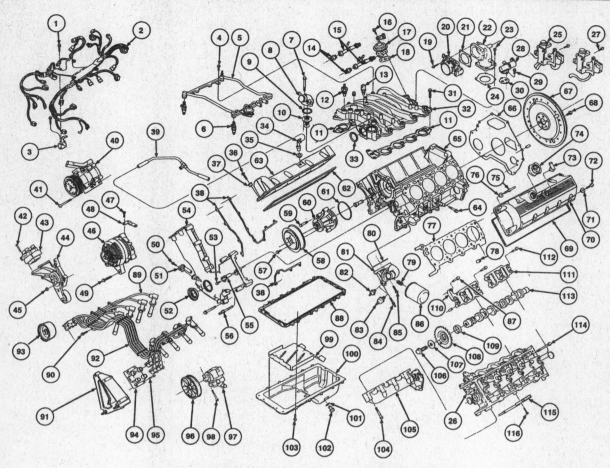

2.5 4.6L Overhead Cam (OHC) engine - exploded view

1	Bolt	27	Bolt	58	Pulley, water pump	89	Spark plug wire set
2	Fuel injection wiring	28	Idle air control valve	59	Bolt	90	Bolt
3	Accelerator shaft bracket	29	Bolt	60	Water pump	91	Coil bracket
4	Bolt	30	Air bypass valve gasket	61	O ring	92	Spark plug wire separator
5	Fuel injection supply manifold	31	Bolt	62	Valve cover gasket	93	Idler pulley
6	Fuel injector	32	Intake manifold	63	Valve cover (right hand)	94	Coil pack
7	Nut	33	Core plug	64	Side bolt and washer	95	Bolt
8	Thermostat housing	34	Crankcase ventilation valve	65	Cylinder block	96	Power steering pump pulley
9	O-ring	35	Grommet	66	Plate	97	Power steering pump
10	Thermostat	36	Bolt	67	Flywheel	98	Bolt
11	Intake manifold gasket	37	Seal	68	Bolt	99	Baffle
12	Coolant temperature switch	38	Engine front cover seal	69	Valve cover gasket	100	Oil pan
13	Coolant temperature sensor	39	PCV hose	70	Valve cover (left hand)	101	Seal
14	EGR valve tube to manifold connector	40	Air conditioning compressor	71	Seal	102	Drain plug
15	EGR valve to exhaust manifold tube	41	Bolt	72	Bolt	103	Bolt
		42	Bolt	73	Fitting	104	Bolt
16	Bolt	43	Ignition coil pack	74	Oil filler cap	105	Exhaust manifold
17	EGR valve	44	Tensioner assembly	75	Stud	106	Bolt
18	EGR valve gasket	45	Nut	76	Seal	107	Washer
19	Screw and washer	46	Generator	77	Cylinder head gasket	108	Camshaft sprocket
20	Throttle-body	47	Screw and washer	78	Dowel	109	Camshaft bearing
21	Throttle body to intake manifold gasket	48	Bracket, generator	79	Adapter	110	Camshaft bearing cap
22	Throttle body to intake manifold spacer	49	Bolt	80	Oil filter adapter gasket	111	Camshaft bearing cap
		50	Bolt	81	Oil filter adapter	112	Bolt
23	Bolt	51	Crankshaft sensor	82	Oil pressure sender	113	Camshaft
24	Intake manifold upper gasket	52	Crankshaft front oil seal	83	Oil pressure sensor	114	Cylinder head bolt
25	EGR vacuum regulator bracket	53	Bolt	84	Stud	115	Oil level indicator
		54	Engine front cover assembly	85	Bolt	116	Bolt
26	Cylinder head	55	Camshaft position sensor	86	Oil filter		
		56	Stud	87	Bolt		
		57	Screw and washer	88	Oil pan gasket		

3.1 When placing the engine at Top Dead Center (TDC), be sure to align the notch in the crankshaft damper (arrow) with the correct indicator on the timing chain cover

b) *Turn the crankshaft clockwise with a socket and breaker bar as described in Chapter 2, Part A while you hold your finger over the number one spark plug hole.*

c) *When the piston approaches TDC, air pressure will be felt escaping at the spark plug hole. Continue turning the crankshaft until the notch in the crankshaft damper is aligned with the TDC mark on the front cover* (**see illustration**). *At this point number one cylinder is at TDC on the compression stroke.*

4   Valve covers - removal and installation

Removal

Refer to illustrations 4.2, 4.5, 4.7a, 4.7b and 4.10

1   Disconnect the cable from the negative battery terminal.
2   Note their locations, then detach the spark plug wire clips from the rocker arm cover studs (**see illustration**).
3   Detach the spark plug boots and wires from the plugs (see Chapter 1). Position the wires out of the way.
4   Disconnect the hose from the breather fitting on the left valve cover (**see illustration 4.2**).
5   Remove the PCV valve from the right valve cover (**see illustration**).
6   Remove the left (drivers side) DIS module by removing the two nuts and one bolt that hold it to the timing chain cover. This will provide enough clearance for the valve cover to be moved forward, as it is lifted, for removal.

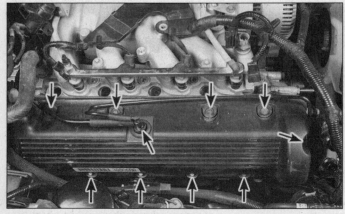

4.5 The valve cover can be removed after removing the PCV valve (arrow) and the bolts around the perimeter (arrows)

4.2 Remove the spark plug wires and clips from the valve cover studs (arrows) and remove the breather hose from the fitting (arrow)

7   Remove the three bolts attaching the wiper module support bracket and remove the bracket (**see illustrations**).
8   Remove the valve cover bolts (**see illustration 4.5**).
9   Remove the right valve cover from the cylinder head. **Note:** *If the cover is stuck to the head, bump one end with a wood block and a hammer to jar it loose. If that doesn't work, try to slip a flexible putty knife between the head and cover to break the gasket seal. Don't pry at the cover-to-head joint or damage to the sealing surfaces may occur (leading to oil leaks in the future). Some valve covers are made of plastic - be extra careful when tapping or pulling on them.*
10   To remove the left valve cover, LIGHTLY pry up the wiper module (**see illustration**). Lift the valve cover over the camshaft and off the cylinder head. **Note:** *The fuel lines running over the left valve cover DO NOT have to be disconnected for the valve to be removed.*

Installation

11   The mating surfaces of each cylinder head and valve cover must be perfectly clean when the covers are installed. Remove all traces of sealant, and clean the mating surfaces with lacquer thinner or acetone. If there's sealant or oil on the mating surfaces when the cover is installed, oil leaks may develop.
12   Clean the mounting stud threads with a die to remove any corrosion and restore damaged threads. Apply a small amount of light oil to the stud threads.
13   The gaskets should be mated to the covers before the covers are installed. Make sure the gasket is pushed all the way into the groove in the valve cover.
14   Carefully position the cover on the head and install the nuts.
15   Tighten the nuts in two steps to the torque listed in this Chapter's

4.7a Remove three attaching bolts (arrows) . . .

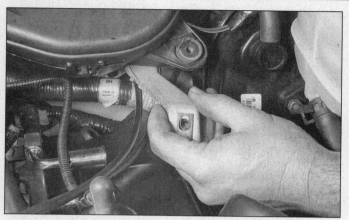

4.7b . . .and remove the wiper module support bracket (arrow)

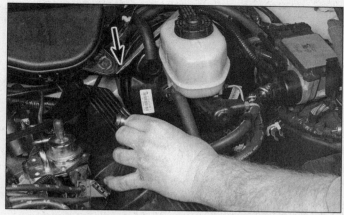

4.10 By prying up very slightly on the wiper module, the valve cover on the drivers side can be removed from the cylinder head

Specifications. Wait two minutes between the first and the second round of tightening. **Caution:** *Be careful with plastic valve covers, don't over tighten the bolts!*

16   The remaining installation steps are the reverse of removal.

17   Start the engine and check for oil leaks as the engine warms up.

5   Crankshaft pulley/vibration damper - removal and installation

Removal

Refer to illustration 5.4

1   Remove the bolts attaching the fan shroud to the radiator and position the shroud back over the fan (see Chapter 3).

2   Remove the fan/clutch assembly and the shroud (see Chapter 3).

3   Remove the accessory drivebelt (see Chapter 1).

4   Remove the bolt from the front of the crankshaft, and using a suitable puller, detach the vibration damper **(see illustration)**. Leave the Woodruff key in place in the crankshaft keyway. **Caution:** *Don't use a puller with jaws that grip the outer edge of the damper. The puller must be the type shown in the illustration that utilizes bolts to apply force to the damper hub only.*

Installation

Refer to illustration 5.5

5   Lubricate the oil seal contact surface of the vibration damper hub **(see illustration)** with moly-base grease or clean engine oil. Apply a

silicone based sealer (Ford number D6AZ-19562-AA or equivalent) to the crankshaft keyway before installing the damper.

6   Install the damper on the end of the crankshaft. The keyway in the damper must be aligned with the Woodruff key in the crankshaft nose. If the damper cannot be seated by hand, slip the large washer over the bolt, install the bolt and tighten it to pull the damper into place. Tighten the bolt to the torque listed in this Chapter's Specifications.

7   The remaining installation steps are the reverse of removal.

8   Check the oil level. Run the engine and check for oil leaks.

6   Timing chain(s) cover - removal and installation

Removal

Refer to illustrations 6.5, 6.6 and 6.7

1   Disconnect the cable from the negative battery terminal.

2   Drain the engine oil and remove the oil filter (see Chapter 1).

3   Remove the drivebelt and the water pump pulley. Remove the crankshaft pulley/vibration damper (see Section 5).

4   Disconnect the electrical connector to the camshaft sensor. Disconnect the electrical connector to the crankshaft sensor. Disconnect, unbolt and remove both DIS modules, one is attached to each side of the timing chain cover.

5   Remove the bolts securing the power steering pump to the engine. **Note:** *The front lower bolt on the power steering pump will not come all the way out.* Position the pump aside and secure it out of the way. Remove the accessory drivebelt idler from the timing chain cover

5.4 After the bolt has been removed, use a puller that bolts to the damper to remove the damper from the end of the crankshaft

5.5 Inspect the damper for signs of damage or excessive wear

1   Oil seal surface
2   Woodruff keyway

6.5 Remove the bolt (arrow) and accessory drivebelt idler pulley from the timing chain cover

2B

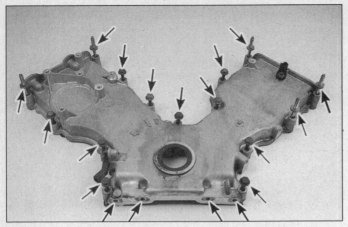

6.6 There are eighteen bolts (arrows) to be removed (note the locations of special studded bolts) before the timing chain cover can be removed

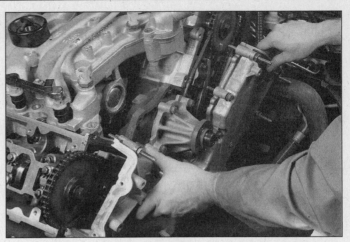

6.7 Separate the timing chain cover from the engine, using a soft-faced hammer if necessary to break the gasket seal

(see illustration) to gain access to one of the cover bolts.

6   Remove both valve covers (see Section 4). Remove the timing chain cover-to-block bolts **(see illustration)**. Note: *Be sure to remove the four oil pan-to-timing chain cover bolts from underneath.*

7   Separate the timing chain cover from the block **(see illustration)**. If it's stuck, tap it gently with a soft-face hammer just enough to break the gasket's bond. **Caution:** *DO NOT use excessive force or you may crack the cover. If the cover is difficult to remove, double check to make sure all of the bolts have been removed.*

Installation

8   Apply a 1/8-inch bead of RTV sealant to the junctions of the oil pan, timing chain cover and engine block.

9   Lubricate the timing chains and the lip of the front crankshaft oil seal with clean engine oil.

10   Install the front cover on the engine. Tighten the cover-to-block bolts to the torque listed in this Chapter's Specifications.

11   Install the remaining parts in the reverse order of removal.

12   Add the proper type and quantity of engine oil (see Chapter 1). Run the engine and check for leaks.

---

7   Timing chains, tensioners and sprockets - inspection, removal and installation

---

Caution: *At no time, once the timing chain(s) have been removed, can the crankshaft or the camshafts be rotated. If moved, damage to the valves and/or pistons can occur. Special tools, available from your local Ford dealer, are necessary to prevent the camshafts from moving when the timing chain is removed.*

Note: *Because this engine is not a "freewheeling" engine, if it has "jumped time," there will be damage to the valves and/or pistons and will require removal of the cylinder heads.*

Removal

Refer to illustrations 7.5, 7.6a, 7.6b, 7.6c, 7.7 and 7.9

1   Disconnect the cable from the negative battery terminal.

2   Position the number one cylinder on TDC (see Section 3).

3   Remove all necessary components to access the timing chain cover (see Section 6).

4   Remove the timing chain cover (see Section 6).

5   Remove the crankshaft position sensor toothed-wheel **(see illustration)** by sliding it off the end of the crankshaft nose. Note the stamped word "rear" on the wheel to be sure it's reinstalled in the correct direction.

6   Install the appropriate camshaft holding tools **(see illustrations)**. The tool locks the camshaft from moving in either direction when the

timing chain(s) are removed. **Caution:** *The camshaft(s) MUST be kept at TDC. Any movement will cause the valve timing to be off when the timing chain(s) are reinstalled. This misalignment will cause severe problems when the engine is started.* In 1991 the camshaft holding tool (Ford number T91P-6256-A) is installed on the "flats" of the camshaft (located at the center of the cam, between the two camshaft cluster caps). On 1992 and later models, the holding tool (Ford number T92P-6256-A), or equivalent is installed into the rear of the camshaft

7.5 The crankshaft sensor tooth wheel has a specific direction to be installed, look for the word "rear" stamped into the gear (arrow)

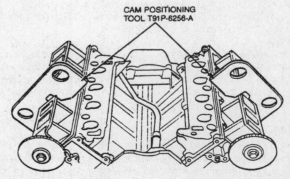

7.6a There is a special service tool for locking the camshaft in place while removing the timing chain, this one is for the 1991 model vehicle which engages the two flat sides on the camshaft

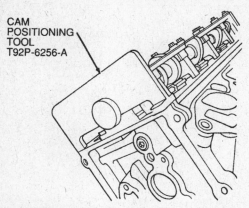

7.6b For 1992 and later models, the tool is positioned at the rear of the camshaft . . .

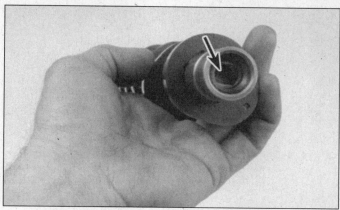

7.6c . . . and inserts into a flat-sided hole (arrow)

7.7 To remove the timing chain tensioner from the block, remove the two bolts from the tensioner (arrows) and detach the guide assembly from the dowel at the opposite end

7.9 The stationary chain guide is removed by removing the two bolts at the mount plate (arrows) and detaching the guide from the dowel at the opposite end

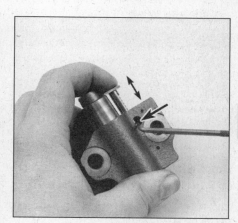

7.14a To fully retract the tensioner, release the plunger lock (arrow) and push the plunger into the tensioner body

2B

and holds the cam in place by locking into the specially shaped hole in the rear of the camshaft (see illustration). This will prevent any movement of the camshafts in either direction, due to valve spring pressure, when the timing chains are removed. **Note:** *When the engine is placed at TDC, the flat sides of the camshaft hole are parallel with the machined valve cover gasket surface.*

7 Remove the right side timing chain tensioner (see illustration).
8 Remove the right timing chain from the crankshaft and camshaft sprockets.
9 Remove the right side stationary guide (see illustration).
10 Remove the left side timing chain tensioner. Remove the chain from the crankshaft and camshaft sprockets.
11 Remove the left side stationary guide.
12 If necessary, remove the crankshaft sprockets, camshaft sprockets and camshaft sprocket spacers, noting the position of each sprocket so it may be reinstalled in its original location. The camshaft sprockets should only be removed from the camshafts if replacement of one of the components is necessary.

Inspection

Refer to illustrations 7.14a and 7.14b

13 Inspect the individual sprocket teeth and keyways for wear and damage. Check the chain for cracked plates, pitted or worn rollers. Check the plastic surface of the chain guides for wear and damage. Replace any excessively worn or defective parts with new ones. **Caution:** *If excessive plastic material is missing from the chain guides, the oil pan should be removed and cleaned of all debris. Check the oil*

pick-up tube and screen. Replace the assembly if it is clogged.
14 Check the tensioner for proper operation:
a) *Release the plunger lock (see illustration) and make sure the piston moves freely.*
b) *Submerge the tensioner in a can of oil or solvent, remove from the fluid and depress the plunger to make sure the oil feed oil is not plugged (see illustration).* **Note:** *Also inspect the oil feed hole in the block to be certain it's not plugged.*

7.14b Check the tensioner oil feed hole (arrow) to be sure it's not plugged by debris

7.17 When installing the timing chain, align one of the bright links in the timing chain with the dimple on the camshaft (arrows)

Installation

Refer to illustrations 7.17, 7.19 and 7.22

15   Install the stationary chain guides, for both sides, and tighten the bolts to the torque listed in this Chapter's Specifications.

16   If removed, install the crankshaft sprockets. Place the left chain crankshaft sprocket on the crankshaft with the beveled hub of the sprocket facing forward. Place the right chain sprocket on the crankshaft with the beveled hub facing towards the engine. When the two sprockets are placed correctly the hubs will be facing each other and there will be the maximum space possible between the two sprockets. The timing marks on each sprocket will also align.

17   Install the left timing chain on the camshaft sprocket, aligning the bright link with the dimple **(see illustration)**. Loop the timing chain under the crankshaft sprocket and align the bright link with the alignment mark on the crankshaft sprocket. The timing marks on the crankshaft sprockets should be in the 6-o'clock position **(see illustration 7.22)**.

18   Install the cam sprocket and chain on the camshaft. Install the camshaft sprocket bolt and, holding the camshaft stationary, tighten the bolt to the torque listed in this Chapter's Specifications. Install the right chain and sprocket in the same manner. Verify that all timing marks are in alignment **(see illustration 7.22)**.

7.22 Once everything is assembled, recheck all the timing chain alignment points (arrows) to be certain they are properly aligned

7.19 Lock the timing chain tensioner in the fully retracted position by placing a paper clip into the hole in the tensioner body (arrow)

19   The steps for installing the timing chain tensioner/guide are the same for both sides, either side can be done first. Before assembling the tensioner with the chain guide, compress the tensioner and lock it in this position with a paper clip, Allen wrench or drill bit **(see illustration)**.

20   Install the tensioner and guide assembly to the block in the retracted position. Tighten the bolts to the torque listed in this Chapter's Specifications.

21   Remove the paper clip and apply pressure against the tensioner chain guide so the tensioner fully extends against the chain guide and all slack is removed from the chain.

22   Recheck all the timing marks to make sure they are still in alignment **(see illustration)**.

23   Slowly rotate the crankshaft in the normal direction of rotation (clockwise) at least two revolutions and again bring the engine to TDC. If you feel any resistance, stop and find out why. Check all alignment marks to verify that everything is properly assembled.

24   The remainder of installation is the reverse of removal.

8   Camshaft(s) - removal, inspection and installation

Removal

Refer to illustration 8.4

1   Remove the valve cover(s) (see Section 4).

2   Remove the timing chain(s), camshaft sprocket(s) and spacers (see Section 6). **Caution:** *Don't mix up the gears, they are marked, as RB (right bank) and LB (left bank), and must go back on the same camshaft.*

3   Measure the thrust clearance (endplay) of the camshaft(s) with a dial indicator. If the clearance is greater than the value listed in this Chapter's Specifications, replace the camshaft and/or the cylinder head.

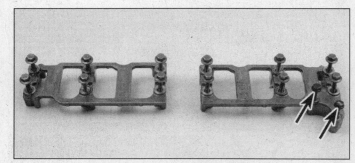

8.4 Each camshaft has two "camshaft cap clusters", rather than individual bearing caps, that hold the camshaft in place on the cylinder head. Note the position of the bolts (arrows)

8.9a Areas to look for excessive wear or damage on the camshafts are; the bearing surfaces and the camshaft lobes (arrows)

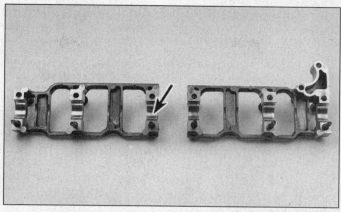

8.9b Inspect the bearing surfaces of the "camshaft cap clusters" (arrow) for signs of excessive wear, damage or overheating

4 There are two "camshaft cap clusters", for each camshaft. The configuration of the two cap clusters are different and must be placed in their original locations. Mark the camshaft cap clusters with a front and rear indication, for both the left and right cylinder heads. **Note:** *Two bolts used on one of the camshaft cap clusters are different than the others* **(see illustration)**, *be sure they go back in the same locations on reassembly.*

5 Before removing the camshaft caps and camshafts, rotate the crankshaft 45-degrees counterclockwise (as you are facing the engine) from TDC. This will place the crankshaft keyway in the 9'o-clock position. Once at this position it ensures that all pistons are below the level of the block deck, and low enough in the cylinders to avoid any valve contact.

6 It's IMPORTANT to loosen the bearing cap cluster bolts only 1/4-turn at a time, following the reverse sequence of the tightening procedure **(see illustration 8.16)**, until they can be removed by hand.

7 Remove the two cap clusters and lift the camshaft off the cylinder head. Don't mix up the camshafts or any of the components. They must all go back on the same positions, and on the same cylinder head they were removed from.

8 Repeat this procedure for removal of the other camshaft.

Inspection

Refer to illustrations 8.9a, 8.9b, 8.10a, 8.10b, 8.10c, 8.11a, 8.11b and 8.13

9 Visually examine the cam lobes and bearing journals for score marks, pitting, galling and evidence of overheating (blue, discolored areas). Look for flaking of the hardened surface of each lobe **(see illustrations)**.

10 Using a micrometer, measure the diameter of each camshaft journal and the lift of each camshaft lobe **(see illustrations)**. Compare your measurements with the Specifications listed at the front of this Chapter, and if the diameter of any one of these is less than specified, replace the camshaft.

2B

8.10a Measure the camshaft bearing journal diameter

8.10b Measure the camshaft lobe at its greatest dimension . . .

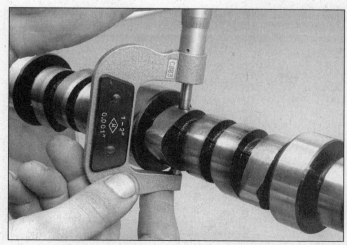

8.10c . . . and subtract the camshaft lobe diameter at its smallest dimension to obtain the lobe lift specification

8.11a Lay a strip of Plastigage on each of the camshaft journals

8.11b Compare the width of the crushed Plastigage to the scale on the envelope to determine the oil clearance

8.13 Oil is delivered to the timing chain tensioner by a feed tube and reservoir in the cylinder head

1   *Tensioner oil feed tube*
2   *Reservoir*

11 Check the oil clearance for each camshaft journal as follows:
   a) *Clean the bearing surfaces and the camshaft journals with lacquer thinner or acetone.*
   b) *Carefully lay the camshaft(s) in place in the head. Don't install the lifters and don't use any lubrication.*
   c) *Lay a strip of Plastigage on each journal* (see illustration).
   d) *Install the camshaft cap clusters.*
   e) *Tighten the cluster cap bolts, a little at a time, to the torque listed in this Chapter's Specifications.* **Note:** *Don't turn the camshaft while the Plastigage is in place.*
   f) *Remove the bolts and detach the caps.*
   g) *Compare the width of the crushed Plastigage (at its widest point) to the scale on the Plastigage envelope* (see illustration).
   h) *If the clearance is greater than specified, and the diameter of any journal is less than specified, replace the camshaft. If the journal diameters are within specifications but the oil clearance is too great, the cylinder head is worn and must be replaced.*
12 Scrape off the Plastigage with your fingernail or the edge of a credit card - don't scratch or nick the journals or bearing surfaces.
13 Finally, be sure to check the timing chain tensioner oil feed tube and reservoir (see illustration) before installing the cam cap cluster. it must be absolutely clean and free of all obstructions or it will affect the operation of the timing chain tensioner.

Installation

Refer to illustration 8.16
14 If the lash adjusters and/or camshaft followers have been removed, install them in their original locations (see Section 9).
15 Apply moly-base grease or camshaft installation lube to the camshaft lobes and bearing journals, then install the camshaft(s).
16 Install the camshaft cap clusters in the correct locations, and following the correct bolt tightening sequence (see illustration), tighten the bolts in 1/4 turn increments to the torque listed in this Chapter's Specifications.
17 Rotate the crankshaft 45-degrees clockwise, to bring it **back** to top dead center (TDC) before reinstalling the timing chain(s).
18 Install the camshaft sprockets, timing chain(s), tensioners and timing chain cover (see Section 7).
19 The remainder of installation is the reverse of the removal procedure.

---

9   Valve lash adjusters and roller cam followers - removal, inspection and installation

---

There are two methods described in this Section. The method

recommended by the manufacturer accomplishes the removal of the camshaft roller followers without the removal of the camshaft(s). Although it does require the use of two special tools specified by the manufacturer; a valve spring spacer (T91P-6565-AH) and a valve spring compressor (T91P-6565-A) which are made specifically for the overhead cam engine. The valve spring compressor uses the camshaft as a pivot point and, with a ratchet attached, pushes down on the spring to release tension on the cam follower. The spring spacer keeps the spring from collapsing too far and hitting the valve stem seal. The alternative method requires the removal of the camshaft (see Section 8) in order to remove the cam followers. Either method will achieve the same results, but it is much easier using the manufacturers recommended procedure, if the correct tools can be located.

Removal

1   Remove the valve cover(s) (see Section 4).
2   Position the cylinder being serviced so that the cam followers are on the base of each camshaft lobe. Install valve spring compressor (Ford tool no. T91P-6565-A) and valve spring spacer (Ford tool no. T91P-6565-AH). If the spacer isn't in place between one of the valve coils, the spring can be compressed to far and damage the valve seal will result.
3   Compress the spring and remove the camshaft roller follower. Camshaft roller followers and hydraulic lash adjusters, MUST be reinstalled with the same camshaft lobe that they were removed from. Label and store all components to avoid confusion during reassembly.
4   Remove the hydraulic lash adjuster(s). If there are many miles on the vehicle, the adjusters may have become varnished and difficult to remove. Apply a little penetrating oil around the lash adjuster to help loosen the varnish.

Alternative procedure

5   Remove the camshaft (see Section 8).
6   Lift the camshaft roller followers from the head. Camshaft roller followers and hydraulic lash adjusters, MUST be reinstalled with the same camshaft lobe that they were removed from. Label and store all components to avoid confusion during reassembly.
7   Remove the hydraulic lash adjusters

Inspection

Refer to illustrations 9.8 and 9.10
8   Inspect each adjuster carefully for signs of wear or damage. The areas of possible wear are the ball tip that contacts the cam follower and the sides of the adjuster that contacts the bore in the cylinder head (see illustration). Since the lash adjusters frequently become clogged as mileage increases, we recommend replacing them if you're

8.16 The camshaft cap cluster bolt tightening sequence, notice that each cap is tightened separately and has its own sequence

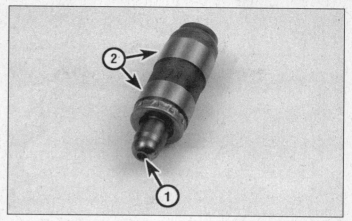

9.8 Inspect the lash adjuster for signs of excessive wear or damage, such as pitting, scoring or signs of overheating (bluing or discoloration), where the tip contacts the camshaft follower (1) and the side surfaces that contact the lifter bore in the cylinder head (2)

2B

concerned about their condition or if the engine is exhibiting valve "tapping" noises.

9   A thin wire or paper clip can be placed in the oil hole to move the plunger and make sure it's not stuck. **Note:** *The lash adjuster must have no more than 1.5 mm of total plunger travel. It's recommended that if replacement of any of the adjusters is necessary, that the entire set be replaced. This will avoid the need to repeat the repair procedure as the others require replacement in the future.*

10   Inspect the roller cam follower for signs of wear or damage. The areas of wear are the ball socket that contacts the lash adjuster and the roller where the follower contacts the camshaft **(see illustration)**.

Installation

11   Before installing the lash adjuster(s) as much air as possible should be bled out of them. Stand the adjuster(s) upright in a container of oil. Use a thin wire or paper clip to work the plunger up and down. This "primes" the adjuster and removes most of the air. Leave the adjusters in the oil until ready to install.

12   Lubricate the valve stem tip, roller follower and the lash adjuster bore with clean engine oil.

13   Install the lash adjuster(s) and roller cam follower(s).

14   The remainder of installation is the reverse of the removal procedures.

15   When re-starting the engine after replacing the adjusters, the adjusters will normally make some "tapping" noises, until all the air is bled from the lash adjusters. After the engine is warmed-up, raise the speed from idle to 3,000 rpm for one minute. Stop the engine and let it cool down. All of the noise should be gone the next time the engine is started.

10 Valve springs, retainers and seals - replacement

Broken valve springs and/or defective valve stem seals can be replaced without removing the cylinder heads. There are two methods described in this Section. The method recommended by the manufacturer accomplishes the removal of the valve springs and seals without the removal of the camshafts. Although it does require the use of two special tools specified by the manufacturer; a valve spring spacer (T91P-6565-AH) and a valve spring compressor (T91P-6565-A) which are made specifically for the overhead cam engine. The valve spring compressor uses the camshaft as a pivot point and, with a ratchet attached, pushes down on the spring to release tension on the cam follower. The spring spacer keeps the spring from collapsing too far and hitting the valve stem seal. The alternative method uses a more

commonly available tool, but will require the removal of the camshaft (see Section 8) in order to remove the valve spring. Either method will achieve the same results, but it is much easier using the manufacturers recommended procedure, if the correct tools can be located.

In either repair procedure, a compressed air source is normally required to perform this operation, so read through this Section carefully and rent or buy the tools before beginning the job. If compressed air isn't available, a length of nylon rope can be used to keep the valves from falling into the cylinder during this procedure.

Removal

Refer to illustrations 10.4 and 10.9

1   Remove the valve cover (see Section 4).

2   Remove the spark plug from the cylinder with the defective component. If all of the valve stem seals are being replaced, remove all the spark plugs.

3   Turn the crankshaft until the piston in the affected cylinder is at Top Dead Center (TDC) on the compression stroke (see Section 3). If you're replacing all of the valve stem seals, begin with cylinder number one and work on the valves for one cylinder at a time. Move from cylinder-to-cylinder following the firing order sequence (see this Chapter's Specifications).

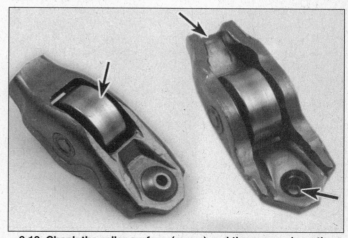

9.10 Check the roller surface (arrow) and the areas where the valve stem and lash adjuster contact the camshaft follower (arrows) for signs of excessive wear or damage, such as pitting, scoring or signs of overheating (bluing or discoloration)

10.4 This is the air hose adapter that threads into the spark plug hole - they're commonly available from auto parts stores

4   Thread an air hose adapter into the spark plug hole **(see illustration)** and connect an air hose from a compressed air source to it. Most auto parts stores can supply the air hose adapter. **Note:** *Many cylinder compression gauges utilize a screw-in fitting that may work with your air hose quick-disconnect fitting.*

5   Apply compressed air to the cylinder. **Warning:** *The piston may be forced down by compressed air, causing the crankshaft to turn suddenly. If the wrench used when positioning the number one piston at TDC is still attached to the bolt in the crankshaft nose, it could cause damage or injury when the crankshaft moves.*

6   The valves should be held in place by the air pressure.

7   If you don't have access to compressed air, an alternative method can be used. Position the piston at a point a few degrees before TDC on the compression stroke, then feed a long piece of nylon rope through the spark plug hole until it fills the combustion chamber. Be sure to leave the end of the rope hanging out of the engine so it can be removed easily. Use a large ratchet and socket to rotate the crankshaft in the normal direction of rotation until slight resistance is felt.

8   Stuff shop rags into the cylinder head holes above and below the valves to prevent parts and tools from falling into the engine.

9   Install valve spring compressor (Ford tool no. T91P-6565-A) and valve spring spacer (Ford tool no. T91P-6565-AH). **Caution:** *If the spacer isn't in place between one of the valve coils, the spring can be compressed to far and damage the valve seal* **(see illustration).**

10   Compress the spring and remove the camshaft roller follower. Camshaft roller followers and hydraulic lash adjusters, MUST be reinstalled with the same camshaft lobe that they were removed from. Label and store all components to avoid confusion during reassembly.

11   Keeping the spring compressed remove the keepers with small needle-nose pliers or a magnet **(see illustration 10.14)**. Remove the spring retainer and valve spring. Remove the valve stem seal **(see illustration 10.16)**. If air pressure fails to hold the valve in the closed position during this operation, the valve face and/or seat is probably damaged. If so, the cylinder head will have to be removed for additional repair operations.

Alternative procedure

Refer to illustrations 10.13, 10.14 and 10.16

12   Remove the camshaft and roller followers (see Section 8).

13   Install the valve spring compressor **(see illustration)**.

14   Compress the spring and remove the keepers with small needle-nose pliers or a magnet **(see illustration)**.

15   Remove the spring retainer and valve spring.

16   Remove the stem seal **(see illustration)**. If air pressure is being used, and it fails to hold the valve in the closed position during this operation, the valve face and/or seat is probably damaged. If so, the cylinder head will have to be removed for additional repair operations.

Installation

Refer to illustrations, 10.21a, 10.21b and 10.23

17   Wrap a rubber band or tape around the top of the valve stem so

the valve won't fall into the combustion chamber, then release the air pressure. If rope was used instead of air pressure, turn the crankshaft slightly in the direction opposite normal rotation.

18   Inspect the valve stem for damage. Rotate the valve in the guide and check the end for eccentric movement, which would indicate that the valve is bent.

19   Move the valve up-and-down in the guide and make sure it doesn't bind. If the valve stem binds, either the valve is bent or the guide is damaged. In either case, the head will have to be removed for repair.

20   Reapply air pressure to the cylinder to retain the valve in the closed position, then remove the tape or rubber band from the valve stem. If a rope was used instead of air pressure, rotate the crankshaft in the normal direction of rotation until slight resistance is felt.

21   Lubricate the valve stem with engine oil and install a new seal **(see illustration)**. There is a special tool for the installation of the valve seal (Ford tool no. T91P-6571-A). If the tool isn't available, a socket that will fit over the seal and make contact with the seat **(see illustration)**, can be used to carefully tap the new seal into place. **Caution:** *The valve seal used on the OHC engine is a combination seal and spring seat. Never place a valve spring directly against the aluminum head, the hardened spring would damage the cylinder head.*

22   Install the spring in position over the valve.

23   Install the valve spring retainer. Compress the valve spring and carefully position the keepers in the groove. Apply a small dab of

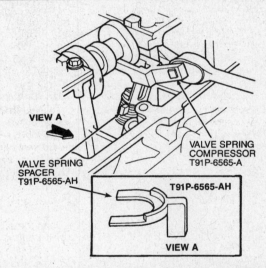

10.9 Installation setup for the factory recommended special valve spring compressor and spacer tools

10.13 Installation of a valve spring compressor more commonly available at local automotive parts stores (note the camshaft must be removed for the use of this type of valve spring compressor)

10.14 Once the spring is compressed remove the keepers with a needle nose pliers or a magnet, as shown here

10.16 Use pliers, of any type, to firmly grasp the old seal and pull it off the valve guide

2B

10.21a The valve stem seals used on the OHC engines combines a seal with the valve spring seat

10.21b There is special valve seal installation tool (Ford tool no. T91P-6571-A) available, but a deep socket that fits over the seal can be used to gently tap the seal into place

10.23 Apply a small dab of grease to each keeper as shown here before installation - it'll hold them in place on the valve stem as the spring is released

grease to the inside of each keeper to hold it in place if necessary **(see illustration)**.

24 Remove the pressure from the spring tool and make sure the keepers are seated.

25 Disconnect the air hose and remove the adapter from the spark plug hole. If a rope was used in place of air pressure, pull it out of the cylinder.

26 If the camshaft(s) were removed, reinstall them at this time (see Section 8).

27 Install the spark plug(s) and connect the wire(s).

28 The remaining installation steps are the reverse of removal.

29 Start and run the engine, then check for oil leaks and unusual sounds coming from the valve cover area.

11 Intake manifold - removal and installation

Note: *Removal and installation of the intake manifold on the 1996 models is the same as on previous years. The only difference is that it is manufactured of plastic instead of aluminum and the throttle body is now attached to a throttle body spacer that is attached to the center of the intake manifold.*

Removal

Refer to illustration 11.10, 11.16 and 11.23

1 Relieve the fuel system pressure (see Chapter 4B). Disconnect the cable from the negative battery terminal.

2 Drain the cooling system and remove the drivebelt (see Chapter 1.)

3 Disconnect the radiator, heater and water pump bypass hoses from the water outlet (see Chapter 3).

4 Remove the thermostat housing (see Chapter 3). The thermostat housing bolts also retain the intake manifold.

5 Remove the air inlet tube.

6 Label and disconnect the intake manifold vacuum lines.

7 Remove the PCV and canister purge hoses from the valve covers (see Section 4).

8 Disconnect the accelerator cable, automatic transmission cable and speed control linkage (if so equipped).

9 Disconnect the ignition wire brackets, boots and wires and set them out of the way.

10 Remove the two bolts holding the alternator to the intake manifold **(see illustration)**.

11.10 Remove the two bolts attaching the alternator bracket to the intake manifold (arrows)

11.16 Separate the wire loom bracket from the intake manifold extension

11   Disconnect the alternator electrical connectors and remove the alternator (see Chapter 5).

12   Disconnect both ignition coils and the CID sensor (see Chapter 5).

13   Disconnect the electrical connectors from the ignition coils and CID sensor, coolant temperature sending unit, air charge temperature sensor, throttle positioner, idle speed control solenoid, EGR sensors, fuel injectors and fuel charging assembly (see Chapter 5).

14   Remove the 42-pin engine harness electrical connector from the retainer bracket on the vacuum brake booster and disconnect it from the main electrical harness.

15   Remove the upper intake manifold (see Chapter 4).

16   Separate the wire loom bracket from the intake manifold extension, at the rear of the manifold **(see illustration).**

17   Raise the vehicle with a jack and place it securely on jackstands.

18   Disconnect the EGR tube from the right exhaust manifold (see Chapter 4).

19   Disconnect the electrical connector at the oil pressure sending unit (see Chapter 2, Part C).

20   Lower the vehicle and position the harness out of the way.

21   Disconnect the fuel supply and return lines (see Chapter 4).

22   Loosen the lower intake manifold bolts and nuts in 1/4-turn increments, following the reverse order of the tightening sequence **(see illustration 11.30)**, until they can be removed by hand. The injectors and fuel rails can be left on the intake manifold during removal.

23   Lift the manifold from the cylinder heads **(see illustration).** The manifold may be stuck to the cylinder heads and force may be required to break the gasket seal. A prybar can be used to pry up the manifold, but make sure all bolts and nuts have been removed first!

Caution: *On 1995 and earlier models, the cylinder heads and the intake manifold are aluminum. The intake manifold on 1996 models is plastic. Don't pry between the block and manifold or the cylinder heads or damage to the gasket sealing surface may occur, leading to vacuum and oil leaks. Pry only at the manifold casting protrusion.*

24   Remove the intake manifold gaskets and clean all traces of gasket or sealant material from the sealing surfaces of the cylinder heads and intake manifold.

Installation

Refer to illustration 11.30

Caution: *The mating surfaces of the cylinder heads, block and manifold must be perfectly clean when the manifold is installed. Gasket removal solvents in aerosol cans are available at most auto parts stores and may be helpful when removing old gasket material that's stuck to the heads and manifold. Since the cylinder heads are aluminum and the intake manifold is aluminum or plastic, aggressive scraping can cause damage! Be sure to follow the directions printed on the container.*

25   If the manifold was disassembled, reassemble it or if being replaced, transfer all components to the new intake manifold. Use electrically conductive sealant on the temperature sending unit threads. Use a new EGR valve gasket.

26   Use a gasket scraper to remove all traces of sealant and old gasket material, then clean the mating surfaces with lacquer thinner or acetone. If there's old sealant or oil on the mating surfaces when the manifold is installed, oil or vacuum leaks may develop. When working on the heads and block, cover the open engine areas with shop rags to keep debris out of the engine. Use a vacuum cleaner to remove any gasket material that falls into the intake ports in the heads.

27   Use a tap of the correct size to chase the threads in the bolt holes, then use compressed air (if available) to remove the debris from the holes. **Warning:** *Wear safety glasses or a face shield to protect your eyes when using compressed air!* Remove excessive carbon deposits and corrosion from the exhaust and coolant passages in the heads and manifold.

28   Install the gaskets on the cylinder heads. Make sure all alignment tabs, intake port openings, coolant passage holes and bolt holes are aligned correctly.

29   Carefully set the manifold in place. Don't disturb the gaskets and don't move the manifold fore-and-aft after it contacts the gaskets on the block.

30   Install the nine intake manifold bolts and, following the correct tightening sequence **(see illustration)**, tighten them to the torque listed in this Chapter's Specifications. Replace the O-ring seal on the

11.23 Make sure there is nothing else attached to the manifold (fuel injector rails and injectors can stay on the intake) and remove the manifold from the engine

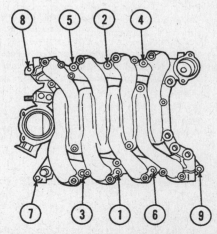

11.30 Intake manifold bolt tightening sequence

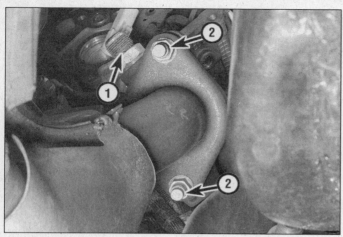

12.4a On the right side exhaust manifold disconnect the EGR pipe (1) and remove the two manifold-to-exhaust pipe nuts (2)

thermostat housing. Install the thermostat housing and tighten the bolts to the torque listed in Chapter 3 Specifications.
31   The remaining installation steps are the reverse of removal. Start the engine and check carefully for oil and coolant leaks at the intake manifold joints.

12 Exhaust manifolds - removal and installation

Removal

Refer to illustrations 12.4a, 12.4b and 12.8
1   Disconnect the cable from the negative battery terminal.
2   Raise the vehicle and support it securely on jackstands.
3   Working under the vehicle, apply penetrating oil to the exhaust pipe-to-manifold studs and nuts (they're usually corroded or rusty).
4   Remove the nuts holding the exhaust pipe(s) to the manifold(s) **(see illustrations)**. In extreme cases you may have to heat them with a propane or acetylene torch in order to loosen them. **Note:** *There is very little room to get at the lower row of exhaust manifold bolts from the top, although it's possible. It's easier to remove the bolts from underneath at the same time that the exhaust pipes are being separated from the manifolds.*
5   Disconnect the EGR tube connector from the right side manifold **(see illustration 12.4a)**.
6   Remove the through bolts for the engine mounts (see Section 18).
7   Slowly raise the engine with a floor jack, using a piece of wood between the jack and the oil pan, until the fan just touches the fan shroud. **Caution:** *Since none of the coolant, air conditioning and power steering hoses or other connections are being separated from the engine, be careful that nothing is being pulled or stretched to tightly. Areas to watch for are; the wiper module at the left rear valve cover, the cooling fan and shroud and the fuel lines at the manifold connections.*
8   Remove the left side engine mount from the block **(see illustration)**, if necessary, to get to all the manifold bolts. It isn't necessary to remove the right side engine mount.
9   Remove the exhaust manifold(s)-to-cylinder head bolts **(see illustration 12.8)** and separate the manifold(s) from the cylinder head(s).

Installation

10   Check the manifold for cracks and make sure the bolt threads are clean and undamaged. The manifold and cylinder head mating surfaces must be clean before the manifolds are reinstalled - use a gasket scraper to remove all carbon deposits.
11   Position the manifold on the head and install the mounting bolts.
12   When tightening the mounting bolts, work from the center to the

ends and be sure to use a torque wrench. Tighten the bolts in three equal steps to the torque listed in this Chapter's Specifications.
13   The remaining installation steps are the reverse of removal.
14   Start the engine and check for exhaust leaks.

13 Cylinder heads - removal and installation

Caution: *The engine must be completely cool when the heads are removed. Failure to allow the engine to cool off could result in head warpage.*

Removal

Refer to illustrations 13.6, 13.7, 13.8, 13.11 and 13.12
1   Disconnect the cable from the negative battery terminal. Remove the valve cover(s) (Section 4).
2   Remove the intake manifold (Section 11).
3   Remove the timing chain cover (see Section 7).
4   Remove the timing chains (see Section 7). **Caution:** *Use the required camshaft holding fixture to lock the camshafts in place. Leave the holding fixtures in place until after the reassembly is complete.*

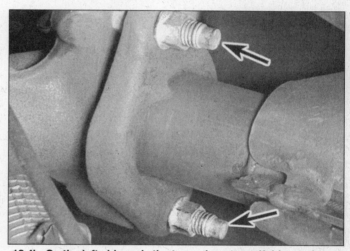

12.4b On the left side, only the two exhaust manifold-to-exhaust pipe nuts need to be removed (arrows)

12.8 The engine mount on the left side may have to be removed to be able to get to all the lower exhaust manifold bolts
  1   Exhaust manifold-to-cylinder head bolts
  2   Engine mount-to-block bolts

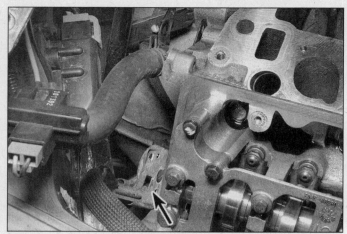

13.6 Loosen the bolt on the back of the right cylinder head and slip the battery cable bracket (arrow) up and off the cylinder head

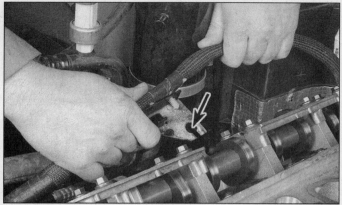

13.7 Loosen the bolt on the side of the right cylinder head and slip the battery cable bracket (arrow) up and off the cylinder head and set the cable out of the way for cylinder head removal

13.8 At the back of the right cylinder head, remove nut and disconnect the ground strap

13.11 Use a breaker bar and deep socket to loosen the cylinder head bolts, 1/4 turn at a time until they can be removed by hand (head bolts CANNOT be reused)

13.12 Lift the cylinder head from the block, it may be necessary to break the gasket bond by placing a wood block on the head and striking it with a hammer (DO NOT pry between the head and the cylinder block)

5   Separate the exhaust manifold-to-exhaust pipe(s) (Section 12).

6   Detach the positive battery cable bracket at the rear of the cylinder head **(see illustration)**.

7   Loosen the nut and slide the positive battery cable bracket up and off the stud on the right side of the cylinder head **(see illustration)**

8   At the rear of the right cylinder head remove the ground strap **(see illustration)**.

9   Disconnect the heater hose at the pipe fastened at the rear of the right side cylinder head. The pipe can remain attached to the head during removal.

10   Remove the exhaust manifold(s), if desired (see Section 12). **Note:** *Even though the exhaust manifold adds extra weight to the removal of the cylinder head, the difficulty of getting at the bolts to remove the manifold makes leaving the manifold attached to the head during removal easier than separating the manifold from the head while in the vehicle.*

11   Remove the head bolts by loosening them 1/4 turn at a time **(see illustration)**, following the reverse of the tightening sequence **(see illustration 13.21a)** until they can be removed by hand. The lower rear head bolt on the right cylinder head, once loosened, cannot be removed because of the location of the heater/air conditioning case. Use a rubber band to hold the bolt out of the block during cylinder head removal. Discard the head bolts - New bolts MUST be used when reinstalling the head(s).

12   Lift the head(s) off the engine **(see illustration)**. If resistance is felt, DO NOT pry between the head and block as damage to the mating surfaces will result. To dislodge the head, place a wood block against the end and strike the wood block with a hammer. Store the heads on wood blocks to prevent damage to the gasket sealing surfaces.

13   Remove the old head gasket(s). Before removing, note which gasket goes on which side, they are different and cannot be interchanged.

14   Cylinder head disassembly and inspection procedures are covered in detail in Chapter 2, Part C.

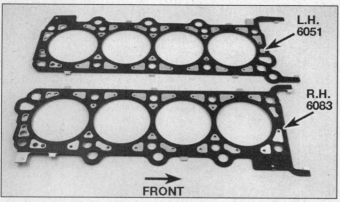

13.18 Identify the left and right cylinder head gaskets, the shapes are different and cannot be interchanged

13.19 Position the gaskets on the correct cylinder banks, push them down over the alignment dowels (arrows)

13.21a Cylinder head bolt tightening sequence

13.21b By marking each head bolt with a stripe (arrow) . .

13.21c . . .it will be easier to keep track of the head bolts that have had the additional turn (arrows)

Installation

Refer to illustrations 13.18, 13.19, 13.21a, 13.21b and 13.21c

15 The mating surfaces of the cylinder heads and block must be perfectly clean when the heads are installed. Use a gasket scraper to remove all traces of carbon and old gasket material, then clean the mating surfaces with lacquer thinner or acetone. If there's oil on the mating surfaces when the heads are installed, the gaskets may not seal correctly and leaks may develop. When working on the block, cover the open areas of the engine with shop rags to keep debris out during repair and reassembly. Use a vacuum cleaner to remove any debris that falls into the cylinders.

16 Check the block and head mating surfaces for nicks, deep scratches and other damage. If damage is slight, it can be removed with a file - if it's excessive, machining may be the only alternative.

17 Use a tap of the correct size to chase the threads in the head bolt holes. Dirt, corrosion, sealant and damaged threads will affect torque readings.

18 Make sure the new gaskets are on the correct cylinder banks **(see illustration)**. They are not interchangeable.

19 Position the new gasket(s) over the alignment dowels **(see illustration)** in the block.

20 Before placing the cylinder heads back on the block, rotate the crankshaft counterclockwise , as you are facing the engine, so the keyway is in the 9 o'clock position. **Caution:** *If the crankshaft isn't placed in the position described, damage will occur to either pistons and/or valve train parts.*

21 Carefully position the head(s) on the block without disturbing the gasket(s). Install the NEW head bolts and follow the recommended sequence **(see illustration)** and tighten the bolts, in three steps, as listed in this Chapter's Specifications. Mark a stripe on each of the head bolts **(see illustrations)**. This will help keep track of the bolts that have been turned the additional 90 degrees. **Note:** *The method used for the head bolt tightening procedure is referred to as "torque-angle" or "torque-to-yield" method. The first tightening sequence will be to a specified torque. The second and third tightening steps use an "torque-angle", which uses a predetermined angle, such as an additional 85 to 95-degrees, to get the correct bolt "stretch". This has been shown to give a more uniform clamping load for better head gasket sealing.*

22 The remaining installation steps are the reverse of removal.

23 Change the engine oil and filter (Chapter 1), then start the engine and check carefully for oil and coolant leaks.

2B

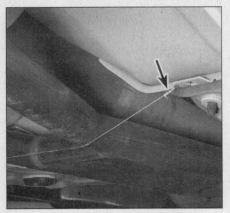
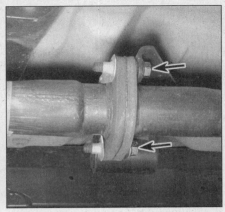
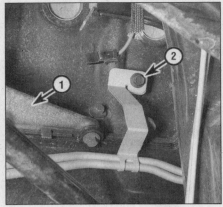

14.4 Support the exhaust pipes, just ahead of the catalytic converters at the H-pipe, with a length of mechanics wire (arrow)

14.5 Remove the two bolts (arrows) that connect the two exhaust pipe sections, and remove the front exhaust section from the under the vehicle

14.8 Remove the reinforcement brackets from each side of the block (1), and remove the transmission line bracket bolt (2)

14 Oil pan - removal and installation

Removal

Refer to illustrations 14.4, 14.5, 14.8, 14.9, 14.15, 14.17a and 14.17b

1   Disconnect the cable from the negative battery terminal.
2   Drain the engine oil and remove the oil filter (Chapter 1).
3   Disconnect the exhaust pipe from the manifolds (see Section 12).
4   Support the exhaust pipe, with a length of mechanics wire, just ahead of the catalytic converters, at the H-pipe section of the exhaust pipes **(see illustration)**.
5   Disconnect and remove the section of exhaust pipe between the manifolds and converters **(see illustration)**. **Warning:** *When the bolts are removed, the exhaust pipe section will fall out if not supported. Be prepared to handle and remove the pipe before the bolts are taken out.*
6   Remove the fan shroud mounting bolts and position the shroud back over the fan.
7   Remove the starter motor (see Chapter 5).
8   Remove the reinforcement bracket on both right and left sides of the engine block and remove the transmission line bracket bolt **(see illustration)**.
9   Loosen the nuts holding the transmission mount to the crossmember, but don't remove them completely **(see illustration)**. This will allow the engine/transmission assembly to be moved up, providing clearance for oil pan removal.
10   Remove the through bolts from the front engine mounts (see Section 18).
11   Place a jack under the oil pan, using a wood block between the jack head and the oil pan. Raise the engine until the valve cover just

makes contact with the wiper module, which is located at the firewall behind the left valve cover (see Section 4). Place a wood block between the exhaust manifold and the frame **(see illustration 18.9)**.
12   Move the jack to the right side of the engine and raise the right side of the engine, it will twist and allow the right to raise slightly higher than the left side. Raise it as far as possible.
13   Place wood block between the exhaust manifold and the frame on the right side.
14   Lower the engine onto the wood block and remove the jack.
15   Remove the oil pan mounting bolts **(see illustration)**.

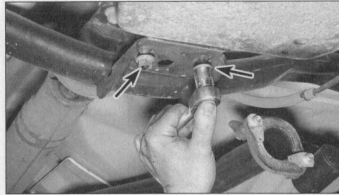

14.9 Loosen the transmission rear mount bolts (arrows), but do not remove, this allows the rear of the transmission to be raised enough to clear the oil pan

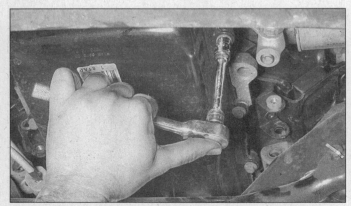

14.15 Remove the sixteen oil pan bolts from around the perimeter of the pan and lower the pan to the frame crossmember

14.17a The oil pick-up tube and screen must be unbolted at the number two main cap (arrow)

14.17b Remove the two bolts at the oil pump body (arrows), lower the pick-up into the pan and removed the tube and screen with the oil pan (oil pan removed for clarity)

16   Carefully separate the pan from the engine block and let it hang down as far as possible. **Caution:** *Don't pry between the block and pan or damage to the sealing surfaces may result and oil leaks could develop. Instead, dislodge the pan with a large rubber mallet or a wood block and a hammer.*

17   Reach in between the oil pan and the cylinder block, and remove the oil pump pick-up tube/screen bolts **(see illustrations)** and allow the pick-up to drop into the oil pan. The pan can't be removed with the pick-up tube bolted to the block - there's not enough room.

18   Maneuver the pan out the front, between the subframe and engine.

Installation

Refer to illustrations 14.22 and 14.23

19   Remove all traces of old gasket material and sealant from the pan and block.

20   Clean the mating surfaces with lacquer thinner or acetone. Make sure the bolt holes in the block are clean.

21   The oil pan has a reinforcement rail welded to the oil pan, check the flange for distortion, particularly around the bolt holes. If necessary, place the pan on a wood block and use a hammer to flatten and restore the gasket surface.

22   Check the O-ring **(see illustration)** on the pick-up tube. Replace if necessary.

23   Place the oil pan gasket on the oil pan. The gasket has alignment tabs that will keep it in place on the oil pan **(see illustration)**.

24   Place the pick-up tube in the oil pan and reinstall the oil pan and pick-up tube to the engine. Tighten the bolts to the torque listed in this Chapter's Specifications. When tightening the oil pan bolts, start at the center of the oil pan and work out toward the ends in a spiral pattern.

25   The remaining steps are the reverse of removal.

26   Fill the engine with the correct type and quantity of oil (see Chapter 1). Start the engine and check for oil leaks at the oil pan.

15   Oil pump - removal and installation

Refer to illustration 15.4

Note: *The oil pump is available as a complete replacement unit only. No service parts or repair specifications are available from the manufacturer.*

1   Unbolt and lower the oil pan as described in Section 14. It's not necessary to completely remove the oil pan.

2   Remove the two bolts that attach the oil pump pick-up tube to the oil pump **(see illustration 14.17b)**.

3   Remove the timing cover, timing chains, chain guides and crankshaft sprockets (see Section 7).

4   Remove the four oil pump mounting bolts **(see illustration)** and separate the pump from the block.

14.22 Before the pick-up tube is reinstalled into the oil pump, inspect the O-ring (arrow) and replace it if necessary

5   Prime the oil pump prior to installation. Pour clean oil into the pick-up port and turn the pump by hand.

6   Inspect the O-ring gasket on the pick-up tube, if damaged replace it.

7   Install the oil pump to the engine and tighten the bolts to the torque listed in this Chapter's Specifications.

8   The remainder of installation is the reverse of removal procedure.

9   Fill the engine with the correct type and quantity of oil. Start the engine and check for leaks.

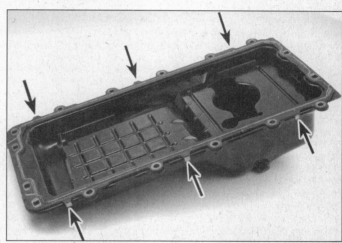

14.23 Place the gasket on the oil pan, the locating tabs (arrows) on each side of the gasket will keep the gasket aligned during installation

15.4 Remove the four oil pump mounting bolts (arrows) and oil pump from the engine block

2B

16 Driveplate - removal and installation

Removal

Refer to illustration 16.2

1   Disconnect the cable from the negative battery terminal. Raise the vehicle and support it securely on jackstands, refer to Chapter 7 and remove the transmission. Inspect the transmission, if it's leaking, now would be a very good time to have the transmission front pump seal/O-ring replaced. **Note:** *The driveplate-to-torque converter bolts can be accessed for removal through the large rubber plug on the right rear of the engine block*

2   Look for factory paint marks that indicate driveplate-to-crankshaft alignment. If they aren't there, scribe or paint marks on the driveplate and crankshaft to ensure correct alignment during reassembly **(see illustration)**.

3   Remove the bolts that secure the driveplate to the crankshaft. If the crankshaft turns, wedge a screwdriver through the starter opening to jam the driveplate.

4   Remove the driveplate from the crankshaft. Be sure to support it while removing the last bolt. **Note:** *After the driveplate is removed, there is an reinforcement/mounting plate that is located between the engine block and the driveplate. It doesn't need to be removed, unless being replaced.*

Installation

Refer to illustration 16.5

5   If removed, be sure the reinforcement plate is installed as shown **(see illustration)**, so it is correctly positioned for the starter installation.

6   Clean and inspect the mating surfaces of the driveplate and the crankshaft. If the crankshaft rear seal is leaking, replace it before reinstalling the driveplate.

7   Check for cracked, broken or missing ring gear teeth. If any of these conditions are found, replace the driveplate.

8   Install the driveplate to the engine aligning the marks made during removal. Note that some engines have an alignment dowel or staggered bolt holes to ensure correct installation. Before installing the bolts, apply Ford sealant with Teflon (D8AZ-19554-A), or equivalent, to the threads.

9   Wedge a screwdriver through the starter motor opening to keep the driveplate from turning as you tighten the bolts to the torque listed in this Chapter's Specifications.

10   The remainder of installation is the reverse of the removal procedure.

16.2 Make an alignment mark (arrow), if not already on the driveplate, to reassure proper reassembly

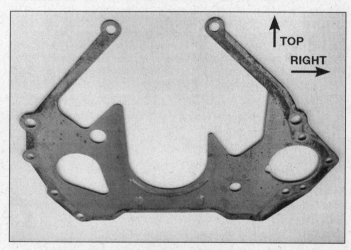

16.5 If the reinforcement plate is removed, for any reason, it should be reinstalled in the direction shown here

17.4 Using a special seal removal tool (a screwdriver will also work) remove the front crankshaft oil seal, being very careful not to scratch the crankshaft during seal removal

17.6 There is special tool for installing the front oil seal into the timing chain cover, but if the tool is unavailable a large socket, the same diameter as the seal can be used to drive the seal into place

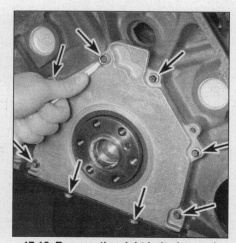

17.16 Remove the eight bolts (arrows) and separate the seal retainer from the block

17.17 Support the seal retainer on two wood blocks and drive out the old seal with a punch and hammer

17.18 Support the seal retainer and drive the new seal into the housing with a wood block or a section of pipe, be sure not to cock the seal in the bore while installing

17   Crankshaft oil seals - replacement

Front seal

Refer to illustrations 17.4 and 17.6

1   Remove the fan/clutch assembly and the fan shroud (Chapter 3).
2   Remove the drivebelt (Chapter 1).
3   Remove the crankshaft pulley/vibration damper (see Section 5).
4   Carefully remove the seal from the cover with a seal removal tool **(see illustration)**, a screwdriver will also work. If the timing cover is removed, use a chisel or small punch and hammer to drive the seal out of the cover from the back side. Support the cover as close to the seal bore as possible with two wood blocks. Be careful not to damage the cover or scratch the wall of the seal bore.
5   Check the seal bore and crankshaft, as well as the seal contact surface on the vibration damper for nicks and burrs. Position the new seal in the bore with the open end of the seal facing IN. A small amount of oil or grease applied to the outer edge of the new seal will make installation easier - but don't overdo it!
6   Drive the seal into the bore with a large socket and hammer until it's completely seated **(see illustration)**. If the cover is removed, support the cover on wood blocks. Select a socket that's the same outside diameter as the seal (a section of pipe can be used if a socket isn't available).
7   Lubricate the lip of the seal with clean engine oil and install the damper on the end of the crankshaft. The keyway in the damper bore must be aligned with the Woodruff key in the crankshaft nose.
8   If the damper can't be seated by hand, tap it into place with a soft-face hammer, or install the bolt and washer and tighten it to push the damper into place.
9   Tighten the damper bolt to the torque listed in this Chapter's Specifications.
10   Install the drivebelt.
11   Install the fan/clutch assembly and fan shroud.
12   Install the remaining parts removed for access to the seal.
13   Start the engine and check for leaks.

Rear seal

Refer to illustrations 17.16, 17.17, 17.18 and 17.19

14   Disconnect the cable from the negative battery terminal. Refer to Chapter 7 and remove the transmission.
15   Remove the driveplate and the rear cover plate from the engine (Section 16).
16   Remove the bolts, detach the seal retainer **(see illustration)** and clean off all the old gasket and/or sealant material from both the engine block and the seal retainer.

17   Support the seal and retainer assembly on wood blocks and drive the old seal out from the back side with a chisel or a punch and hammer **(see illustration)**.
18   Drive the new seal into the retainer with a wood block **(see illustration)**.
19   Clean the crankshaft and seal bore with lacquer thinner or acetone. Check the seal contact surface on the crankshaft very carefully for scratches or nicks that could damage the new seal lip and cause oil leaks **(see illustration)**. If the crankshaft is damaged, the only alternative is a new or different crankshaft.
20   Lubricate the crankshaft seal journal and the lip of the new seal with engine oil.
21   Place a small bead (1.5 mm wide) of RTV sealant on either the engine block **or** the seal retainer.
22   Install the oil seal retainer by slowly and carefully pushing the seal onto the crankshaft. The seal lip is stiff, so work it onto the crankshaft with a smooth object such as the end of a socket extension as you push the retainer against the block.
23   Install and tighten the retainer bolts to the torque listed in this Chapter's Specifications.
24   Reinstall the engine rear cover plate, driveplate and the transmission.
25   The remaining steps are the reverse of removal.
26   Check the oil level and add if necessary, run the engine and check for oil leaks.

17.19 Inspect the seal contact surface on the crankshaft (arrow) for signs of excessive wear or grooves

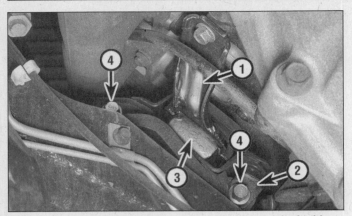

18.4 Inspect the engine mount components for cracked rubber insulators, missing through bolts or cracked metal engine mounts

1 *Engine mount (block half)*	3 *Rubber insulator*
2 *Engine mount (frame half)*	4 *Through bolts*

18 Engine mounts - check and replacement

Check

Refer to illustration 18.4

1   Engine mounts seldom require attention, but broken or deteriorated mounts should be replaced immediately or the added strain placed on the driveline components may cause damage or wear.

2   During the check, the engine must be raised slightly to remove the weight from the mounts.

3   Raise the vehicle and support it securely on jackstands, then position a jack under the engine oil pan. Place a large wood block between the jack head and the oil pan, then carefully raise the engine just enough to take the weight off the mounts.

4   Check the mounts to see if the rubber is cracked, hardened or separated from the metal plates **(see illustration)**. Sometimes the rubber will split right down the center.

5   Check for relative movement between the mount plates and the engine or frame (use a large screwdriver or pry bar to attempt to move the mounts). If movement is noted, lower the engine and tighten the mount fasteners.

6   Rubber preservative should be applied to the mounts to slow deterioration.

18.8 Using a flex-socket and a long extension, remove the through bolts (there are two on the left engine mount and only one on the right side mount)

Replacement

Refer to illustrations 18.8, 18.9, 18.10 and 18.11

7   Disconnect the cable from the negative battery terminal. Raise the vehicle and support it securely on jackstands (if not already done). Place a large wood block between the jack head and the oil pan, then carefully raise the engine just enough to take the weight off the mounts and through bolts.

8   Remove the through bolts that connect the upper and lower motor mount halves **(see illustration)**. **Note:** *There are two through bolts for the left hand engine mount and one through bolts used on the right hand mount.*

9   Once the bolts have been removed from the mounts on both sides of the engine, raise the engine up until the fan blades just meet the fan shroud. Place a wood block between the frame and the exhaust manifold, on both sides of the engine **(see illustration)**.

10   Remove the mount-to-block bolts and detach the mount **(see illustration)**.

11   If the mounts are being replaced, the bolts attaching them to the frame can be reached with a socket and long extension through the access holes in the frame **(see illustration)**.

12   Installation is the reverse of removal. Use thread locking compound on the mount bolts and tighten them to the torque listed in this Chapter's Specifications.

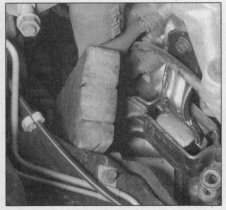

18.9 With the engine raised, place a wood block between the frame and the exhaust manifold, on both sides, to support the engine and provide enough clearance for engine mount removal

18.10 Remove the three bolts (arrows) and mount from the engine block

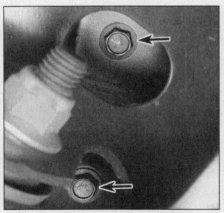

18.11 If the lower half of the engine mount needs to be removed or replaced, unbolt the mount from the frame through access holes in the frame (arrows)

Chapter 2 Part C
General engine overhaul procedures

Contents

Specifications

General

Oil pressure	
OHV (engine hot at 2000 rpm)	35 to 60 psi
OHC (engine hot at 1500 rpm)	20 to 45 psi
Cylinder head warpage limit	0.003 (in any 6 inches)/0.006 inch overall

Cylinder bore
OHV engine
Bore
  5.0L (302 cid)... 4.000 to 4.0048 inches
  5.8L (351 cid)... 4.000 to 4.0048 inches
  6.6L (400 cid)... 4.000 to 4.0048 inches
  7.5L (460 cid)... 4.360 to 4.3632 inches
Stroke
  5.0L (302 cid)... 3.00 inches
  5.8L (351 cid)... 3.50 inches
  6.6L (400 cid)... 4.00 inches
  7.5L (460 cid)... 3.850 inches
Out-of-round
  Standard.. 0.0015 inch
  Service limit... 0.005 inch
Taper .... 0.010 inch maximum

OHC engine
Bore
  Standard.. 3.5539 inches
    Coded red 1.. 3.5539 to 3.5544 inches
    Coded blue 2... 3.5544 to 3.5549 inches
    Coded yellow 3.. 3.5549 to 3.5554 inches
Stroke .... 3.546 inches
Out-of-round
  Standard.. 0.0006 inch
  Service limit... 0.0008 inch
Taper .... 0.0002 inch maximum

Valves and related components
Valve arrangement (front-to-rear) - all engines
Left (driver's side) cylinder head.. E-I-E-I-E-I-E-I
Right cylinder head... I-E-I-E-I-E-I-E

OHV engines
Intake valve
Seat angle.. 45-degrees
Seat width... 0.060 to 0.080 inch
Seat runout limit
  5.0L (302 cid), 5.8L (351 cid)
    and 6.6L (400 cid) .... 0.002 inch maximum (total indicator reading)
  7.5L (460 cid)... 0.0015 inch maximum (total indicator reading)
Stem diameter
  Standard.. 0.3416 to 0.3423 inch
  0.015 oversize.. 0.3566 to 0.3573 inch
  0.030 oversize.. 0.3716 to 0.3723 inch
Valve stem-to-guide clearance
  Standard.. 0.0010 to 0.0027 inch
  Service limit... 0.0055 inch maximum
Valve face angle.. 44-degrees
Valve face runout limit .... 0.002 inch maximum

Exhaust valve
Seat angle.. 45-degrees
Seat width... 0.060 to 0.080 inch
Seat runout limit
  5.0L (302 cid), 5.8L (351 cid)
    and 6.6L (400 cid) .... 0.002 inch maximum (total indicator reading)
  7.5L (460 cid)... 0.0015 inch maximum (total indicator reading)
Stem diameter
  5.0L (302 cid), 5.8L (351 cid)
    and 6.6L (400 cid)
      Standard .... 0.3411 to 0.3418 inch
      0.015 oversize... 0.3561 to 0.3568 inch
      0.030 oversize... 0.3711 to 0.3718 inch
  7.4L (460 cid)
      Standard .... 0.3416 to 0.3423 inch
      0.015 oversize... 0.3566 to 0.3573 inch
      0.030 oversize... 0.3716 to 0.3723 inch

Valve stem-to-guide clearance
   Standard.. 0.0015 to 0.0032 inch
   Service limit .... 0.0055 inch maximum
Valve face angle.. 44-degrees
Valve face runout limit .... 0.002 inch maximum

OHC engine
Intake
Seat angle.. 45 degrees
Seat width.. 0.0749 to 0.0827 inch
Seat runout limit.. 0.0010 inch maximum (total indicator reading)
Stem diameter
   Standard.. 0.2756 to 0.2748 inch
   0.015 oversize .... 0.2906 to 0.2898 inch
   0.030 oversize .... 0.2985 to 0.3048 inch
Valve stem-to-guide clearance...................................... 0.00749 to 0.0027 inch
Valve face angle.. 45.5 degrees
Valve face runout limit .... 0.0020 inch maximum

Exhaust
Seat angle.. 45 degrees
Seat width.. 0.0749 to 0.0827 inch
Seat runout limit.. 0.0010 inch maximum (total indicator reading)
Stem diameter
   Standard.. 0.02746 to 0.2738 inch
   0.015 oversize .... 0.2896 to 0.2898 inch
   0.030 oversize .... 0.3046 to 0.3038 inch
Valve stem-to-guide clearance...................................... 0.0018 to 0.0037 inch
Valve face angle.. 45.5 degrees
Valve face runout limit .... 0.0020 inch maximum

Valve spring
OHV engine
Free length
   5.0L (302 cid) and 5.8L (351 cid)
      Intake .... 2.04 inches
      Exhaust .... 1.88 inches
   6.6L (400 cid)
      Intake .... 2.06 inches
      Exhaust .... 1.93 inches
   7.5L (460 cid).. 2.07 inches
Installed height
   5.0L (302 cid) and 5.8L (351 cid)
      Intake .... 1-3/4 to 1-13/16 inches
      Exhaust .... 1-37/64 to 1-41/64 inches
   6.6L (400 cid).. 1-13/16 to 1-27/32 inches
   7.5L (460 cid).. 1-51/64 to 1-53/64 inches
Out-of-square limit (all) .... 5/64 inch

OHC engine
Free length
   Intake .... 1.9523 inches
   Exhaust.. 1.9523 inches
Out-of-square limit .... 2 degrees maximum
Installed height
   Intake .... 1.1576 inches
   Exhaust.. 1.1576 inches

Hydraulic lash adjuster (lifter)
OHV engine
Diameter .... 0.8740 to 0.8745 inch
Lifter-to-bore clearance
   Standard.. 0.0007 to 0.0027 inch
   Service limit... 0.005 inch maximum

OHC engine
Diameter
   Standard.. 0.6304 to 0.6299 inch
Lifter-to-bore clearance
   Standard.. 0.0007 to 0.0027 inch
   Service limit... 0.0006 inch maximum

2C

Crankshaft and connecting rods

Crankshaft
OHV engine
Endplay
    Standard.. 0.004 to 0.008 inch
    Service limit.. 0.012 inch maximum
Runout to rear face of block .... 0.005 inch maximum (total indicator reading)

OHC engine
Endplay .... 0.0051 to 0.0099 inch
Runout to rear face of block
    Standard.. 0.002 inch
    Service limit.. 0.005 inch maximum

Main bearing journal
OHV engine
Diameter
    5.0L (302 cid) and 5.8L (351 cid) .... 2.2490 to 2.2482 inches
    6.6L (400 cid) and 7.5L (460 cid) .... 2.9994 to 3.0002 inches
Out-of-round limit .... 0.0006 inch
Taper limit .... 0.0006 inch
Bearing oil clearance .... 0.0008 to 0.0015 inch

OHC engine
Diameter .... 2.6595 inches
Bearing oil clearance .... 0.0011 to 0.0027 inch

Connecting rods
OHV engine
Connecting rod journal
Diameter
    5.0L (302 cid)... 2.1228 to 2.1236 inches
    6.6L (400 cid) and 5.8L (351 cid) .... 2.3103 to 2.3111 inches
    7.5l (460 cid) .... 2.4992 to 2.5000 inches
Out-of-round/taper limit.. 0.0006 inch
Bearing oil clearance .... 0.0008 to 0.0015 inch
Connecting rod side clearance (endplay)
    Standard.. 0.010 to 0.020 inch
    Service limit.. 0.023 inch maximum

OHC engine
Connecting rod journal
    Diameter.. 2.0882 inches
Bearing oil clearance .... 0.0011 to 0.0027 inch
Connecting rod side clearance (endplay)
    Standard.. 0.0006 to 0.0177 inch
    Service limit.. 0.0197 inch

Pistons and rings

Piston diameter
OHV engine
    5.0L (302 cid) and 5.8L (351 cid)
        Coded red .... 3.9978 to 3.9984 inches
        Coded blue .... 3.9990 to 3.9996 inches
        Coded yellow .... 4.0014 to 4.0020 inches
    6.6L (400 cid)
        Coded red .... 3.9982 to 3.9988 inches
        Coded blue .... 3.9994 to 4.0000 inches
        0.003 oversized.. 4.0006 to 4.0012 inches
    7.5L (460 cid)
        Coded red .... 4.3585 to 4.3591 inches
        Coded blue .... 4.3597 to 4.3603 inches
        0.003 oversized.. 4.3609 to 4.3615 inches

OHC engine
Coded red 1... 3.5526 to 3.5531 inches
Coded blue 2.. 3.5531 to 3.5536 inches
Coded yellow 3... 3.5536 to 3.5541 inches

Piston-to-bore clearance limit

OHV engine..	0.0014 to 0.0022 inch
OHC engine	0.0008 to 0.0018 inch

Piston ring end gap

OHV engine

Compression rings...	0.010 to 0.020 inch
Oil ring (steel rail)	0.015 to 0.055 inch

OHC engine

Compression rings...	0.0394 inch
Oil ring (steel rail)	0.0493 inch

Piston ring side clearance

OHV engine

Compression rings...	0.002 to 0.004 inch
Service limit	0.006 inch
Oil ring	Snug fit

OHC engine

Compression ring (top)	0.0016 to 0.0035 inch
Compression ring (bottom).......................................	0.0012 to 0.0032 inch
Service limit	0.0006 inch maximum
Oil ring	Snug fit

Torque specifications

Ft-lbs (unless otherwise indicated)

OHV engine

Main bearing cap bolts	
5.0L (302 cid)...	60 to 70
All except 5.0L (302 cid)......................................	95 to 105
Connecting rod cap nuts	
5.0L (302 cid)...	19 to 24
All except 5.0L (302 cid)......................................	40 to 45

OHC engine

Main bearing cap bolts (tighten first)	
First step	22 to 25
Second step	rotate and additional 85 to 95 degrees
Main bearing cap - jack screws (tighten second)	
First step	44 in-lbs
Second step	80 to 97 in-lbs
Main bearing cap - side bolts (tighten third)	
First step	84 in-lbs
Second step	14 to 17
Connecting rod cap nuts	
First step	18 to 25
Second step	rotate an additional 85 to 95 degrees

* **Note:** *Refer to Part A and B for additional torque specifications.*

2C

1   General information

Refer to illustrations 1.2 a, 1.2b, 1.2c and 1.2d

Included in this portion of Chapter 2 are the general overhaul procedures for the cylinder head(s) and internal engine components.

The information ranges from advice concerning preparation for an overhaul and the purchase of replacement parts to detailed, step-by-step procedures covering removal and installation of internal engine components and the inspection of parts **(see illustrations)**. Note: *For engine "Family" identification see Chapter 2, Part A, Section 1.*

The following Sections have been written based on the assumption that the engine has been removed from the vehicle. For information concerning in-vehicle engine repair, as well as removal and installation of the external components necessary for the overhaul, see Parts A and B of this Chapter and Section 7 of this Part.

The Specifications included in this Part are only those necessary for the inspection and overhaul procedures which follow. Refer to Parts A and B for additional Specifications.

2   Engine overhaul - general information

Refer to illustrations 2.4a, 2.4b and 2.4c

It is not always easy to determine when, or if, an engine should be completely overhauled, as a number of factors must be considered.

High mileage is not necessarily an indication that an overhaul is needed, while low mileage does not preclude the need for an overhaul. Frequency of servicing is probably the most important consideration. An engine that has had regular and frequent oil and filter changes, as

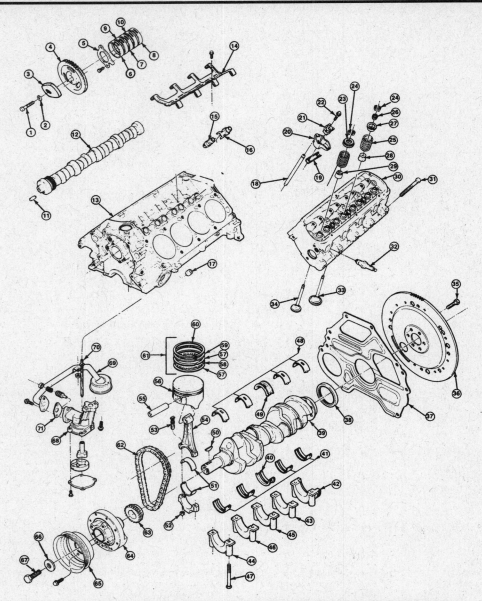

1.2a Internal components - 5.0L (302 cid) and 5.8L (351W) Overhead valve (OHV) engines

1	Bolt	19	Rocker arm fulcrum guide	39	Crankshaft	53	Connecting rod bolt
2	Washer	20	Rocker arm	40	Crankshaft thrust bearing (lower)	54	Connecting rod
3	Eccentric	21	Fulcrum			55	Piston wrist pin
4	Camshaft sprocket	22	Screw and washer	41	Crankshaft main bearings (lower)	56	Piston
5	Camshaft thrust plate	23	Exhaust valve rotator			57	Oil ring side rail
6	Camshaft bearing (front)	24	Valve spring retainer keys	42	Rear main bearing cap	58	Oil ring expander
7	Camshaft bearing (center)	25	Valve spring	43	Main bearing cap (rear intermediate)	59	Compression ring (lower)
8	Camshaft bearing (rear)	26	Valve spring sleeve			60	Compression ring (upper)
9	Camshaft bearing (front intermediate)	27	Valve spring retainer	44	Main bearing cap (front)	61	Ring set
		28	Valve guide seal	45	Main bearing cap (center)	62	Timing chain
10	Camshaft bearing (rear intermediate)	29	Valve stem seal	46	Main bearing cap (front intermediate)	63	Crankshaft sprocket
		30	Cylinder head			64	Crankshaft damper
11	Dowel pin	31	Bolt	47	Bolt	65	Crankshaft pulley
12	Camshaft	32	Spark plug	48	Crankshaft main bearings (upper)	66	Washer
13	Cylinder block	33	Intake valve			67	Bolt
14	Lifter guide retaining plate	34	Exhaust valve	49	Crankshaft thrust bearing (upper)	68	Oil pump
15	Roller lifter	35	Bolt			69	Oil pump pick-up
16	Valve lifter guide plate	36	Driveplate	50	Key	70	Oil pump driveshaft
17	Dowel pin	37	Rear engine plate	51	Connecting rod bearing	71	Oil pump gasket
18	Pushrod	38	Rear main oil seal	52	Connecting rod nut		

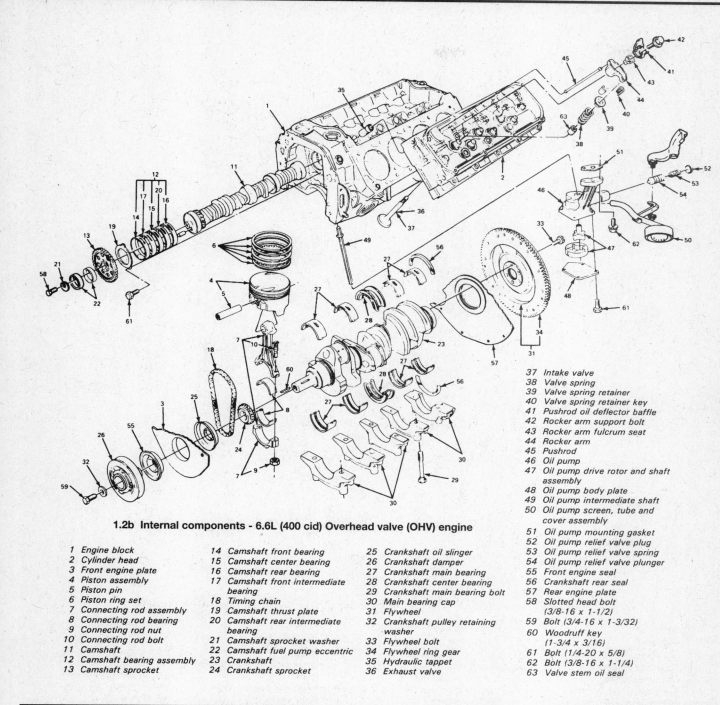

1.2b Internal components - 6.6L (400 cid) Overhead valve (OHV) engine

1   Engine block
2   Cylinder head
3   Front engine plate
4   Piston assembly
5   Piston pin
6   Piston ring set
7   Connecting rod assembly
8   Connecting rod bearing
9   Connecting rod nut
10 Connecting rod bolt
11 Camshaft
12 Camshaft bearing assembly
13 Camshaft sprocket

14 Camshaft front bearing
15 Camshaft center bearing
16 Camshaft rear bearing
17 Camshaft front intermediate bearing
18 Timing chain
19 Camshaft thrust plate
20 Camshaft rear intermediate bearing
21 Camshaft sprocket washer
22 Camshaft fuel pump eccentric
23 Crankshaft
24 Crankshaft sprocket

25 Crankshaft oil slinger
26 Crankshaft damper
27 Crankshaft main bearing
28 Crankshaft center bearing
29 Crankshaft main bearing bolt
30 Main bearing cap
31 Flywheel
32 Crankshaft pulley retaining washer
33 Flywheel bolt
34 Flywheel ring gear
35 Hydraulic tappet
36 Exhaust valve

37 Intake valve
38 Valve spring
39 Valve spring retainer
40 Valve spring retainer key
41 Pushrod oil deflector baffle
42 Rocker arm support bolt
43 Rocker arm fulcrum seat
44 Rocker arm
45 Pushrod
46 Oil pump
47 Oil pump drive rotor and shaft assembly
48 Oil pump body plate
49 Oil pump intermediate shaft
50 Oil pump screen, tube and cover assembly
51 Oil pump mounting gasket
52 Oil pump relief valve plug
53 Oil pump relief valve spring
54 Oil pump relief valve plunger
55 Front engine seal
56 Crankshaft rear seal
57 Rear engine plate
58 Slotted head bolt (3/8-16 x 1-1/2)
59 Bolt (3/4-16 x 1-3/32)
60 Woodruff key (1-3/4 x 3/16)
61 Bolt (1/4-20 x 5/8)
62 Bolt (3/8-16 x 1-1/4)
63 Valve stem oil seal

well as other required maintenance, will most likely give many thousands of miles of reliable service. Conversely, a neglected engine may require an overhaul very early in its life.

Excessive oil consumption is an indication that piston rings and/or valve guides are in need of attention. Make sure that oil leaks are not responsible before deciding that the rings and/or guides are bad. Test the cylinder compression (see Section 3) or have a leak down test performed by an experienced tune-up mechanic to determine the extent of the work required.

If the engine is making obvious knocking or rumbling noises, the connecting rod and/or main bearings are probably at fault. To accurately test oil pressure, temporarily connect an oil pressure gauge

in place of the oil pressure sending unit (see illustrations). Compare the reading to the pressure listed in this Chapter's Specifications. If the pressure is extremely low, the bearings and/or oil pump are probably worn out.

Loss of power, rough running, excessive valve train noise and high fuel consumption rates may also point to the need for an overhaul, especially if they are all present at the same time. If a complete tune-up does not remedy the situation, major mechanical work is the only solution.

An engine overhaul involves restoring the internal parts to the specifications of a new engine. During an overhaul, the piston rings are replaced and the cylinder walls are reconditioned (rebored and/or

2C

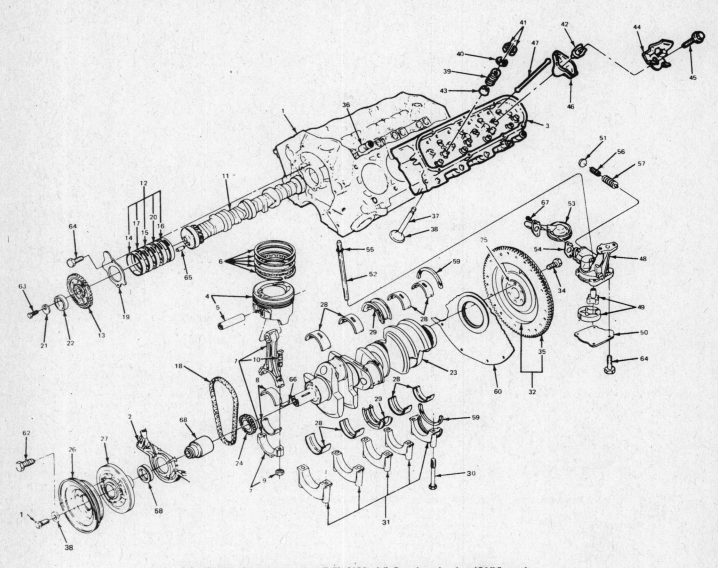

1.2c Internal components - 7.5L (460 cid) Overhead valve (OHV) engine

1 Engine block	20 Camshaft rear intermediate
2 Front cover assembly	bearing
3 Cylinder head	21 Camshaft sprocket washer
4 Piston assembly	22 Camshaft fuel pump eccentric
5 Piston pin	23 Crankshaft
6 Piston ring set	24 Crankshaft sprocket
7 Connecting rod assembly	25 Crankshaft-to-flywheel
8 Connecting rod bearing	mounting flange
9 Connecting rod nut	26 Crankshaft outer pulley
10 Connecting rod bolt	27 Crankshaft damper
11 Camshaft	28 Crankshaft main bearing
12 Camshaft bearing assembly	29 Crankshaft center main
13 Camshaft sprocket	bearing
14 Camshaft front bearing	30 Crankshaft main bearing cap
15 Camshaft center bearing	bolt
16 Camshaft rear bearing	31 Main bearing cap
17 Camshaft front intermediate	32 Flywheel
bearing	33 Crankshaft pulley retaining
18 Timing chain	washer
19 Camshaft thrust plate	34 Flywheel bolt

35 Flywheel ring gear	53 Oil pump screen, tube and
36 Hydraulic tappet	cover assembly
37 Exhaust valve	54 Oil pump inlet tube gasket
38 Intake valve	55 Oil pump intermediate shaft
39 Valve spring	ring
40 Valve spring retainer	56 Oil pump relief valve spring
41 Valve spring retainer key	57 Oil pump relief valve plunger
42 Rocker arm fulcrum	58 Front cover oil seal
43 Valve stem seal	59 Crankshaft rear packing
44 Oil deflector	60 Engine rear plate
45 Rocker arm attaching bolt	61 Bolt (5/8-18 x 2)
46 Rocker arm	62 Bolt (3/8-16 x 1)
47 Pushrod	63 Bolt (3/8-16 x 1-1/2)
48 Oil pump	64 Bolt (1/4-20 x 5/8)
49 Oil pump rotor and shaft	65 Dowel pin (5/16 x 1-3/8)
assembly	66 Woodruff key
50 Oil pump body plate	(1-3/4 x 3/16)
51 Oil pump relief valve plug	67 Bolt (5/16-18 x 7/8)
52 Oil pump intermediate shaft	68 Crankshaft pulley spacer

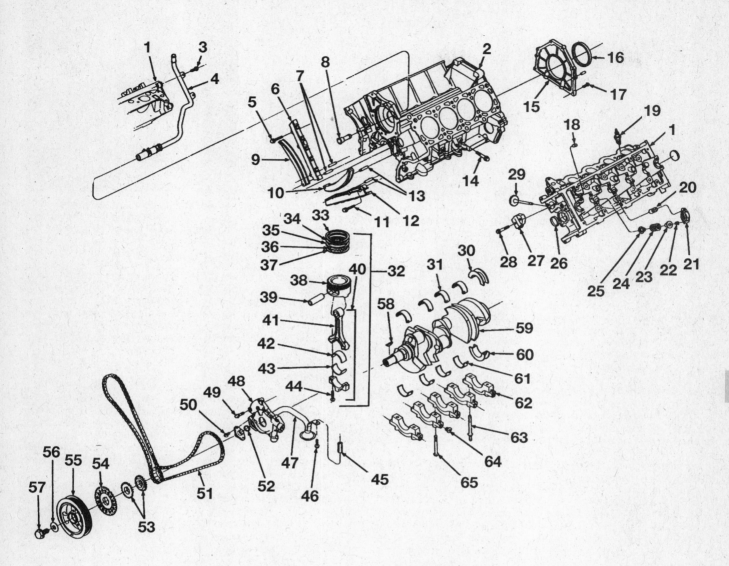

1.2d Internal components - 4.6L Overhead cam (OHC) engine

1	Cylinder head	17	Bolt	34	Piston compression ring	52	O-ring
2	Cylinder block	18	Dowel	35	Oil ring rail	53	Timing chain sprocket
3	Screw and washer	19	Spark plug	36	Oil ring expander	54	Crankshaft sensor toothed wheel
4	Heater hose	20	Lash adjuster	37	Oil ring rail		
5	Bolt	21	Roller follower	38	Piston	55	Crankshaft pulley
6	Timing chain guide	22	Valve spring keeper	39	Piston pin	56	Washer
7	Dowel	23	Valve spring retainer	40	Connecting rod assembly	57	Bolt
8	Heater bypass tube	24	Valve spring	41	Connecting rod	58	Woodruff key
9	Timing chain tensioner arm	25	Valve spring seal	42	Connecting rod bearing	59	Crankshaft
10	Timing chain tensioner arm	26	Core plug	43	Connecting rod bearing	60	Crankshaft main/thrust bearing
		27	Timing chain tensioner	44	Bearing cap screw		
11	Bolt	28	Bolt	45	Stud spacer	61	Crankshaft main bearing
12	Timing chain guide	29	Valve	46	Bolt	62	Main bearing cap
13	Dowel	30	Crankshaft main/thrust bearing	47	Oil screen	63	Main bearing cap bolt (with stud)
14	Bolt			48	Oil pump		
15	Engine rear cover	31	Crankshaft main bearing	49	Bolt	64	Jack screw
16	Crankshaft rear oil seal	32	Piston and rod assembly	50	Bolt	65	Main bearing cap bolt
		33	Piston compression ring	51	Timing chain		

2.4a The oil pressure sending unit is located either at the left side of the front engine cover (arrow), or on top of the engine block at the rear of the intake manifold, on OHV engines

2.4b The oil pressure sending unit is located at the lower left (driver's side) corner of the engine, near the oil filter, on OHC engines

2.4c Thread an oil pressure gauge in place of the sending unit, as shown, and check actual engine oil pressure

honed). If a re-bore is done, new pistons are required. The main bearings, connecting rod bearings and camshaft bearings are generally replaced with new ones and, if necessary, the crankshaft may be reground to restore the journals. Generally, the valves are serviced as well, since they are usually in less-than-perfect condition at this point. While the engine is being overhauled, other components, such as the distributor, starter and alternator, can be rebuilt as well. The end result should be a like-new engine that will give many trouble free miles. **Note:** *Critical cooling system components such as the hoses, the drivebelts, the thermostat and the water pump MUST be replaced with new parts when an engine is overhauled. The radiator should be checked carefully to ensure that it isn't clogged or leaking. If in doubt, replace it with a new one. Also, we do not recommend overhauling the oil pump - always install a new one when an engine is rebuilt.*

Before beginning the engine overhaul, read through the entire procedure to familiarize yourself with the scope and requirements of the job. Overhauling an engine is not difficult, but it is time consuming. Plan on the vehicle being tied up for a minimum of two weeks, especially if parts must be taken to an automotive machine shop for repair or reconditioning. Check on availability of parts and make sure that any necessary special tools and equipment are obtained in advance. Most work can be done with typical hand tools, although a number of precision measuring tools are required for inspecting parts to determine if they must be replaced. Often an automotive machine shop will handle the inspection of parts and offer advice concerning reconditioning and replacement. **Note:** *Always wait until the engine has been completely disassembled and all components, especially the engine block, have been inspected before deciding what service and repair operations must be performed by an automotive machine shop.* Since the block's condition will be the major factor to consider when determining whether to overhaul the original engine or buy a rebuilt one, never purchase parts or have machine work done on other components until the block has been thoroughly inspected. As a general rule, time is the primary cost of an overhaul, so it does not pay to install worn or substandard parts.

As a final note, to ensure maximum life and minimum trouble from a rebuilt engine, everything must be assembled with care in a spotlessly clean environment.

---

3   Cylinder compression check

Refer to illustration 3.6

1   A compression check will tell you what mechanical condition the upper end (pistons, rings, valves, head gaskets) of your engine is in. Specifically, it can tell you if the compression is down due to leakage

caused by worn piston rings, defective valves and seats or a blown head gasket. **Note:** *The engine must be at normal operating temperature for this check and the battery must be fully charged.*

2   Begin by cleaning the area around the spark plugs before you remove them (compressed air works best for this). This will prevent dirt from getting into the cylinders as the compression check is being done.

3   Remove all of the spark plugs from the engine (see Chapter 1).

4   Block the throttle wide open.

5   Disconnect the primary (low voltage) wires from the coil(s).

6   With the compression gauge in the number one spark plug hole, crank the engine over at least four compression strokes and watch the gauge **(see illustration)**. The compression should build up quickly in a healthy engine. Low compression on the first stroke, followed by gradually increasing pressure on successive strokes, indicates worn piston rings. A low compression reading on the first stroke, which does not build up during successive strokes, indicates leaking valves or a blown head gasket (a cracked head could also be the cause). Record the highest gauge reading obtained.

7   Repeat the procedure for the remaining cylinders and compare the results to the Specifications.

8   Add some engine oil (about three squirts from a plunger-type oil can) to each cylinder, through the spark plug hole, and repeat the test.

9   If the compression increases after the oil is added, the piston rings are definitely worn. If the compression does not increase signifi-

3.6 A compression gauge with a threaded fitting for the spark plug hole is preferred over the type that requires hand pressure to maintain the seal - be sure to open the throttle valve as far as possible during the compression check

cantly, the leakage is occurring at the valves or head gasket. Leakage past the valves may be caused by burned valve seats and/or faces or warped, cracked or bent valves.

10   If two adjacent cylinders have equally low compression, there is a strong possibility that the head gasket between them is blown. The appearance of coolant in the combustion chambers or the crankcase would verify this condition.

11   If the compression is unusually high, the combustion chambers are probably coated with carbon deposits. If that is the case, the cylinder heads should be removed and decarbonized.

12   If compression is way down or varies greatly between cylinders, it would be a good idea to have a leak-down test performed by an automotive repair shop. This test will pinpoint exactly where the leakage is occurring and how severe it is.

4   Vacuum gauge diagnostic checks

A vacuum gauge provides valuable information about what is going on in the engine at a low-cost. You can check for worn rings or cylinder walls, leaking head or intake manifold gaskets, incorrect carburetor adjustments, restricted exhaust, stuck or burned valves, weak valve springs, improper ignition or valve timing and ignition problems.

Unfortunately, vacuum gauge readings are easy to misinterpret, so they should be used in conjunction with other tests to confirm the diagnosis.

Both the absolute readings and the rate of needle movement are important for accurate interpretation. Most gauges measure vacuum in inches of mercury (in-Hg). The following references to vacuum assume the diagnosis is being performed at sea level. As elevation increases (or atmospheric pressure decreases), the reading will decrease. For every 1,000 foot increase in elevation above approximately 2000 feet, the gauge readings will decrease about one inch of mercury.

Connect the vacuum gauge directly to intake manifold vacuum, not to ported (throttle body) vacuum. Be sure no hoses are left disconnected during the test or false readings will result.

Before you begin the test, allow the engine to warm up completely. Block the wheels and set the parking brake. With the transmission in Park, start the engine and allow it to run at normal idle speed. **Warning:** *Carefully inspect the fan blades for cracks or damage before starting the engine. Keep your hands and the vacuum gauge clear of the fan and do not stand in front of the vehicle or in line with the fan when the engine is running.*

Read the vacuum gauge; an average, healthy engine should normally produce about 17 to 22 inches of vacuum with a fairly steady needle. Refer to the following vacuum gauge readings and what they indicate about the engine's condition:

a) *A low steady reading usually indicates a leaking gasket between the intake manifold and carburetor or throttle body, a leaky vacuum hose, late ignition timing or incorrect camshaft timing. Check ignition timing with a timing light and eliminate all other possible causes, utilizing the tests provided in this Chapter before you remove the timing chain cover to check the timing marks.*

b) *If the reading is three to eight inches below normal and it fluctuates at that low reading, suspect an intake manifold gasket leak at an intake port or a faulty fuel injector.*

c) *If the needle has regular drops of about two-to-four inches at a steady rate, the valves are probably leaking. Perform a compression check or leak-down test to confirm this.*

d) *An irregular drop or down-flick of the needle can be caused by a sticking valve or an ignition misfire. Perform a compression check or leak-down test and read the spark plugs.*

e) *A rapid vibration of about four in.-Hg vibration at idle combined with exhaust smoke indicates worn valve guides. Perform a leak-down test to confirm this. If the rapid vibration occurs with an increase in engine speed, check for a leaking intake manifold gasket or head gasket, weak valve springs, burned valves or ignition misfire.*

f) *A slight fluctuation, say one inch up and down, may mean ignition problems. Check all the usual tune-up items and, if necessary, run the engine on an ignition analyzer.*

g) *If there is a large fluctuation, perform a compression or leak-down test to look for a weak or dead cylinder or a blown head gasket.*

h) *If the needle moves slowly through a wide range, check for a clogged PCV system, incorrect idle fuel mixture, carburetor/throttle body or intake manifold gasket leaks.*

i) *Check for a slow return after revving the engine by quickly snapping the throttle open until the engine reaches about 2,500 rpm and let it shut. Normally the reading should drop to near zero, rise above normal idle reading (about 5 in.-Hg over) and then return to the previous idle reading. If the vacuum returns slowly and doesn't peak when the throttle is snapped shut, the rings may be worn. If there is a long delay, look for a restricted exhaust system (often the muffler or catalytic converter). An easy way to check this is to temporarily disconnect the exhaust ahead of the suspected part and redo the test.*

5   Engine removal - methods and precautions

If you have decided that an engine must be removed for overhaul or major repair work, several preliminary steps should be taken.

Locating a suitable work area is extremely important. A shop is, of course, the most desirable place to work. Adequate work space, along with storage space for the vehicle, will be needed. If a shop or garage is not available, at the very least a flat, level, clean work surface made of concrete or asphalt is required.

Cleaning the engine compartment and engine before beginning the removal procedure will help keep tools clean and organized.

An engine hoist or A-frame will be needed. Make sure that the equipment is rated in excess of the combined weight of the engine and its accessories. Safety is of primary importance, considering the potential hazards involved in lifting the engine out of the vehicle.

If the engine is being removed by a novice, a helper should be available. Advice and aid from someone more experienced would also be helpful. There are many instances when one person cannot simultaneously perform all of the operations required when lifting the engine out of the vehicle.

Plan the operation ahead of time. Arrange for or obtain all of the tools and equipment you will need prior to beginning the job. Some of the equipment necessary to perform engine removal and installation safely and with relative ease are (in addition to an engine hoist) a heavy duty floor jack, complete sets of wrenches and sockets as described in the front of this manual, wooden blocks and plenty of rags and cleaning solvent for mopping up spilled oil, coolant and gasoline. If the hoist is to be rented, make sure that you arrange for it in advance and perform beforehand all of the operations possible without it. This will save you money and time.

Plan for the vehicle to be out of use for a considerable amount of time. A machine shop will be required to perform some of the work which the do-it-yourselfer cannot accomplish due to a lack of special equipment. These shops often have a busy schedule, so it would be wise to consult them before removing the engine in order to accurately estimate the amount of time required to rebuild or repair components that may need work.

Always use extreme caution when removing and installing the engine. Serious injury can result from careless actions. Plan ahead, take your time and a job of this nature, although major, can be accomplished successfully.

6   Engine - removal and installation

Refer to illustrations 6.6, 6.19a, 6.19b, 6.21, 6.26, 6.27, 6.28 and 6.29
Warning 1: *The air conditioning system is under high pressure! Have a dealer service department or service station discharge the system before disconnecting any air conditioning system hoses or fittings.*

2C

6.6 Use masking tape to mark each end of the various electrical connectors, hoses and vacuum lines before disconnecting them

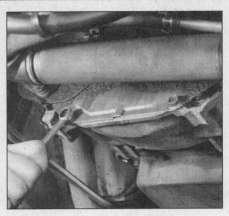

6.19a Remove the bolts (arrows) and remove the torque converter access cover

6.19b Mark the relationship of the torque converter to the driveplate

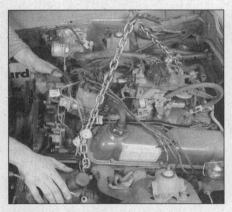

6.21 Center the chain, or sling, on the engine hoist to balance the engine, keeping as much remaining coolant from spilling out onto the floor as possible

6.26 Use a prybar or a large screwdriver and pry the engine from the transmission bellhousing

6.27 Mark the relationship of the driveplate to the crankshaft so they can be correctly aligned on reassembly

Warning 2: *Gasoline is extremely flammable, so take extra precautions when you work on any part of the fuel system. Don't smoke or allow open flames or bare light bulbs near the work area, and don't work in a garage where a natural gas-type appliance (such as a water heater or a clothes dryer) with a pilot light is present. Since gasoline is carcinogenic, wear latex gloves when there's a possibility of being exposed to fuel, and, if you spill any fuel on your skin, rinse it off immediately with soap and water. Mop up any spills immediately and do not store fuel-soaked rags where they could ignite. The fuel system on fuel-injected models is under constant pressure, so, if any fuel lines are to be disconnected, the fuel pressure in the system must be relieved first (see Chapter 4 for more information). When you perform any kind of work on the fuel system, wear safety glasses and have a Class B type fire extinguisher on hand.*

Removal

1   Relieve the fuel system pressure on fuel-injected models (see Chapter 4B).

2   Disconnect the negative cable from the battery.

3   Cover the fenders and cowl and remove the hood (see Chapter 11). Special pads are available to protect the fenders, but an old bedspread or blanket will also work.

4   Remove the air cleaner assembly.

5   Drain the cooling system (see Chapter 1).

6   Label the vacuum lines, emissions system hoses, electrical connectors, ground straps and fuel lines that would interfere with engine removal, to ensure correct reinstallation, then detach them.

Pieces of masking tape with numbers or letters written on them work well **(see illustration)**. If there's any possibility of confusion, make a sketch of the engine compartment and clearly label the lines, hoses and wires.

7   Label and detach all coolant hoses from the engine.

8   Remove the cooling fan, shroud and radiator (see Chapter 3).

9   Remove the drivebelt(s) (see Chapter 1).

10   Disconnect the accelerator cable and Throttle Valve (TV) linkage/speed control cable from the engine (see Chapter 4).

11   Unbolt the power steering pump (see Chapter 10). Leave the lines/hoses attached and make sure the pump is kept in an upright position in the engine compartment (use wire or rope to restrain it out of the way).

12   On air conditioned models, unbolt the compressor (see Chapter 3) and set it aside. Do not disconnect the hoses.

13   Remove the air inlet tube.

14   On OHC engine models, remove the 42-pin connector from the retaining bracket on the vacuum booster and separate the 42-pin connector from the transmission harness and position it out of the way (see Chapter 2B).

15   Drain the engine oil (see Chapter 1) and remove the filter.

16   Remove the starter motor (see Chapter 5).

17   Remove the alternator (see Chapter 5).

18   Unbolt the exhaust system from the engine.

19   Remove the torque converter access cover **(see illustration)**. Mark the torque converter and driveplate **(see illustration)**, so they can be reassembled in the same position to one another, and remove

6.28 Use long high-strength bolts (arrows) to hold the engine block on the engine stand - make sure they are tight before lowering the hoist and placing the entire weight of the engine on the stand

6.29 Use a piece of pipe or chain to support the transmission once the engine has been removed, then remove the floor jack supporting the transmission during engine removal

the torque converter-to-driveplate fasteners.

20   Support the transmission with a jack. Position a wood block between them to prevent damage to the transmission. Special transmission jacks with safety chains are available - use one if possible.

21   Attach an engine sling or a length of chain to the engine and then to the engine hoist **(see illustration)**.

22   Roll the hoist into position and connect the sling to it. Take up the slack in the sling or chain, but don't lift the engine. **Warning:** *DO NOT place any part of your body under the engine when it's supported only by a hoist or other lifting device.*

23   Remove the transmission-to-engine block bolts (see Chapter 7).

24   Remove the engine mount through bolts from both sides (see Chapter 2, Part A or B, depending which engine is being worked on).

25   Recheck to be sure nothing is still connecting the engine to the transmission or vehicle. Disconnect anything still remaining.

26   Raise the engine slightly. Carefully work it forward to separate it from the transmission **(see illustration)**. If you're working on a vehicle with an automatic transmission, be sure the torque converter stays in the transmission (clamp a pair of vise-grips to the transmission housing to keep the converter from sliding out). If you're working on a vehicle with a manual transmission, the input shaft must be completely disengaged from the clutch. Slowly raise the engine out of the engine compartment. Check carefully to make sure nothing is hanging up.

27   Remove the driveplate **(see illustration)**.

28   Mount the engine on an engine stand **(see illustration)**.

29   Once the engine is removed, support the transmission with a chain or pipe that crosses from side to side to hold the transmission as the floor jack is removed **(see illustration)**.

Installation

30   Check the engine and transmission mounts. If they're worn or damaged, replace them.

31   Carefully lower the engine into the engine compartment - make sure the engine mounts line up.

32   Guide the torque converter into the crankshaft following the procedure outlined in Chapter 7.

33   Install the transmission-to-engine bolts and tighten them securely. **Caution:** *DO NOT use the bolts to force the transmission and engine together!*

34   Reinstall the remaining components in the reverse order of removal.

35   Add coolant and oil as needed. Run the engine and check for leaks and proper operation of all accessories, then install the hood and test drive the vehicle.

7   Engine rebuilding alternatives

The do-it-yourselfer is faced with a number of options when performing an engine overhaul. The decision to replace the engine block, piston/connecting rod assemblies and crankshaft depends on a number of factors, with the number one consideration being the condition of the block. Other considerations are cost, access to machine shop facilities, parts availability, time required to complete the project and the extent of prior mechanical experience on the part of the do-it-yourselfer.

Some of the rebuilding alternatives include:

Individual parts - If the inspection procedures reveal that the engine block and most engine components are in reusable condition, purchasing individual parts may be the most economical alternative. The block, crankshaft and piston/connecting rod assemblies should all be inspected carefully. Even if the block shows little wear, the cylinder bores should be surface honed.

Crankshaft kit - This rebuild package consists of a reground crankshaft and a matched set of pistons and connecting rods. The pistons will already be installed on the connecting rods. Piston rings and the necessary bearings will be included in the kit. These kits are commonly available for standard cylinder bores, as well as for engine blocks which have been bored to a regular oversize.

Short block - A short block consists of an engine block with a crankshaft and piston/connecting rod assemblies already installed. All new bearings are incorporated and all clearances will be correct. The existing cylinder head(s), camshaft, valve train components and external parts can be bolted to the short block with little or no machine shop work necessary.

Long block - A long block consists of a short block plus an oil pump, oil pan, cylinder head(s), valve cover(s), camshaft and valve train components, timing sprockets, belt or chain and timing cover. All components are installed with new bearings, seals and gaskets incorporated throughout. The installation of manifolds and external parts is all that is necessary.

Give careful thought to which alternative is best for you and discuss the situation with local automotive machine shops, auto parts dealers or parts store countermen before ordering or purchasing replacement parts.

8   Engine overhaul - disassembly sequence

1   It's much easier to disassemble and work on the engine if it's

2C

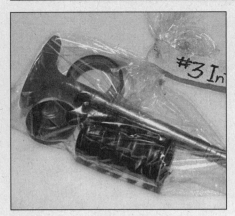

9.1 A small plastic bag, with an appropriate label, can be used to store the valve train components so they can be kept together and reinstalled in their original position

9.2a Use a valve spring compressor to compress the spring, then remove the keepers from the valve stem with needle nose pliers . . .

9.2b . . . or use a magnet, as shown here on the OHC engine

mounted on a portable engine stand. A stand can often be rented quite cheaply from an equipment rental yard. Before the engine is mounted on a stand, the flywheel/driveplate should be removed from the engine.

2   If a stand isn't available, it's possible to disassemble the engine with it blocked up on the floor. Be extra careful not to tip or drop the engine when working without a stand.

3   If you're going to obtain a rebuilt engine, all external components must come off first, to be transferred to the replacement engine, just as they will if you're doing a complete engine overhaul yourself. These include:

Alternator and brackets
Emissions control components
Distributor (if equipped)
Spark plug wires and spark plugs
Thermostat and housing cover
Water pump
EFI components or carburetor
Intake/exhaust manifolds
Oil filter (replace)
Engine mounts
Driveplate
Engine rear plate

Note: *When removing the external components from the engine, pay close attention to details that may be helpful or important during installation. Note the installed position of gaskets, seals, spacers, pins, brackets, washers, bolts and other small items.*

4   If you're obtaining a short block, which consists of the engine block, crankshaft, pistons and connecting rods all assembled, then the cylinder head(s), oil pan and oil pump will have to be removed as well. See *Engine rebuilding alternatives* for additional information regarding the different possibilities to be considered.

5   If you're planning a complete overhaul, the engine must be disassembled and the internal components removed in the following order:

Driveplate
Valve covers
Intake manifold
Exhaust manifolds
Rocker arms and pushrods (OHV engines)
Valve lifters (OHV engines)
Vibration damper
Timing chain cover
Timing chain and sprockets (OHV engines)
Camshafts (OHV engines)
Timing chains, sprockets, guides and tensioners (OHC engine)
Camshaft and followers (OHC engine)
Valve lifters (OHC engine)

Cylinder heads
Oil pan
Oil pump (replace)
Piston/connecting rod assemblies
Crankshaft and main bearings ((replace)

6   Before beginning the disassembly and overhaul procedures, make sure the following items are available. Also, refer to *Engine overhaul - reassembly sequence* for a list of tools and materials needed for engine reassembly.

Common hand tools
Small cardboard boxes or plastic bags for storing parts
Gasket scraper
Ridge reamer
Vibration damper puller
Micrometers
Telescoping gauges
Dial indicator set
Valve spring compressor
Cylinder surfacing hone
Piston ring groove cleaning tool
Electric drill motor
Tap and die set
Wire brushes
Oil gallery brushes
Cleaning solvent

9   Cylinder head - disassembly

Refer to illustrations 9.1, 9.2a, 9.2b, 9.2c and 9.4

Note: *New and rebuilt cylinder heads are commonly available for most engines at dealerships and auto parts stores. Due to the fact that some specialized tools are necessary for the disassembly and inspection procedures, and replacement parts may not be readily available, it may be more practical and economical for the home mechanic to purchase replacement head(s) rather than taking the time to disassemble, inspect and recondition the original(s).*

1   Cylinder head disassembly involves removal of the intake and exhaust valves and related components. If they're still in place, remove the rocker arm nuts, pivot balls and rocker arms from the cylinder head studs. Label the parts or store them separately **(see illustration)** so they can be reinstalled in their original locations and in the same valve guides they are removed from.

2   Compress the springs on the first valve with a spring compressor and remove the keepers **(see illustrations)**. **Note:** *If the keepers are stuck to the retainer, try releasing them by placing a socket against the retainer and hitting it sharply with a hammer* **(see illustration)**.

9.2c If the valve keepers won't break loose from the retainer when compressed, it may be necessary to use a socket (as shown) and strike it sharply to loosen the keepers (they may pop out of the retainer when struck)

9.4 If the valve won't pull through the guide, deburr the edge of the stem end and the area around the top of the keeper groove with a file or whetstone

3   Carefully release the valve spring compressor and remove the retainer, sleeve (if used), the spring and the spring seat (if used).
4   Pull the valve out of the head, then remove the oil seal from the guide. If the valve binds in the guide (won't pull through), push it back into the head and deburr the area around the keeper groove with a fine file or whetstone **(see illustration)**.
5   Repeat the procedure for the remaining valves. Remember to keep all the parts for each valve together so they can be reinstalled in the same locations.
6   Once the valves and related components have been removed and stored in an organized manner, the head should be thoroughly cleaned and inspected. If a complete engine overhaul is being done, finish the engine disassembly procedures before beginning the cylinder head cleaning and inspection process.

---

10   Cylinder head - cleaning and inspection

---

1   Thorough cleaning of the cylinder head(s) and related valve train components, followed by a detailed inspection, will enable you to decide how much valve service work must be done during the engine overhaul. **Note:** *If the engine was severely overheated, the cylinder head is probably warped (see Step 12).*

Cleaning

2   Scrape all traces of old gasket material and sealing compound off the head gasket, intake manifold and exhaust manifold sealing surfaces. Be very careful not to gouge the cylinder head. **Caution:** *Be extremely careful when cleaning 4.6L aluminum cylinder heads. If gouged, or the gasket surfaces damaged, may require replacement.* Special gasket removal solvents that soften gaskets and make removal much easier are available at auto parts stores.
3   Remove all built up scale from the coolant passages.
4   Run a stiff wire brush through the various holes to remove deposits that may have formed in them.
5   Run an appropriate size tap into each of the threaded holes to remove corrosion and thread sealant that may be present. If compressed air is available, use it to clear the holes of debris produced by this operation. **Warning:** *Wear eye protection when using compressed air!*
6   Clean the exhaust manifold stud threads, if equipped. Clean the rocker arm pivot stud threads (if applicable) with a wire brush.
7   Clean the cylinder head with solvent and dry it thoroughly. Compressed air will speed the drying process and ensure that all holes and recessed areas are clean. **Note:** *Decarbonizing chemicals are available and may prove very useful when cleaning cylinder heads and valve train components. They are very caustic and should be used with*

caution. Be sure to follow the instructions on the container.
8   Clean the rocker arms, fulcrums and bolts and pushrods with solvent and dry them thoroughly (don't mix them up during the cleaning process). **Note:** *Compressed air will speed the drying process and can be used to clean out the oil passages.*
9   Clean all the valve springs, spring seats, keepers and retainers (or rotators) with solvent and dry them thoroughly. Do the components from one valve at a time to avoid mixing up the parts.
10   Scrape off any heavy deposits that may have formed on the valves, then use a motorized wire brush to remove deposits from the valve heads and stems. Again, make sure the valves don't get mixed up.

Inspection

Note: *Be sure to perform all of the following inspection procedures before concluding that machine shop work is required. Make a list of the items that need attention.*

Cylinder head

Refer to illustrations 10.12 and 10.14
11   Inspect the head very carefully for cracks, evidence of coolant leakage and other damage. If cracks are found, check with an automotive machine shop concerning repair. If repair isn't possible, a new cylinder head should be obtained.
12   Using a straightedge and feeler gauge, check the head gasket

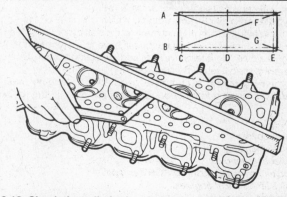

10.12 Check the cylinder head gasket surface for warpage by trying to slip a feeler gauge under the straightedge (see this Chapter's Specifications for the maximum warpage allowed and use a feeler gauge of that thickness); check for both "twist" and "bulge" warpage by positioning the straightedge diagonally as well as straight across the gasket surface

2C

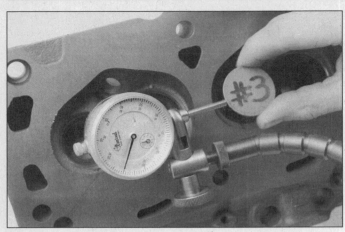

10.14 Lay the head on its edge, pull each valve out about 1/8 inch, set up a dial indicator with the probe touching the valve stem, wiggle the valve and measure its movement

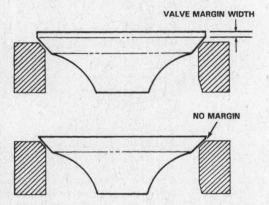

10.16 The margin width on each valve must be at least 1/32-inch (if no margin exists, the valve cannot be reused)

mating surface for warpage **(see illustration)**. If the warpage exceeds the limit listed in this Chapter's Specifications, it can be resurfaced at an automotive machine shop. **Note:** *If the OHV cylinder heads are resurfaced, the intake manifold flanges will also require machining.*

13   Examine the valve seats in each of the combustion chambers. If

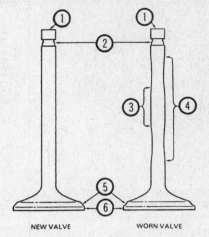

10.15 Check for valve wear at the points shown here

1	*Valve tip*	4	*Stem (most worn area)*
2	*Keeper groove*	5	*Valve face*
3	*Stem (least worn area)*	6	*Margin*

they're pitted, cracked or burned, the head will require valve service.

14   Check the valve stem-to-guide clearance by measuring the lateral movement of the valve stem with a dial indicator attached securely to the head **(see illustration)**. The valve must be in the guide and approximately 1/16-inch off the seat. The total valve stem movement indicated by the gauge needle must be divided by two to obtain the actual clearance. After this is done, if there's still some doubt regarding the condition of the valve guides they should be checked by an automotive machine shop (the cost should be minimal).

Valves

Refer to illustrations 10.15 and 10.16

15   Carefully inspect each valve face for uneven wear, deformation, cracks, pits and burned areas **(see illustration)**. Check the valve stem for scuffing and galling and the neck for cracks. Rotate the valve and check for any obvious indication that it's bent. Look for pits and excessive wear on the end of the stem. The presence of any of these conditions indicates the need for valve service by an automotive machine shop.

16   Measure the margin width on each valve **(see illustration)**. Any valve with a margin narrower than 1/32-inch will have to be replaced with a new one.

10.17 Measure the free length of each valve spring with a dial or vernier caliper

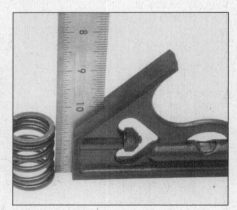

10.18 Check each valve spring for squareness, if it is bent it should be replaced

10.19 The exhaust valve rotators, if equipped, can be checked by turning the inner and outer sections in opposite directions to feel for smooth movement and excessive play

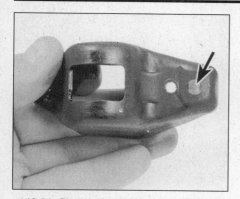

10.21 Check the rocker arm surfaces (OHV engines) that contact the valve stem and pushrod . . .

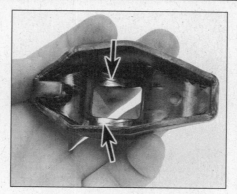

10.22a . . . the fulcrum seats in the rocker arm . . .

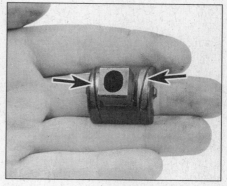

10.22b . . . and the fulcrums themselves for wear and galling (arrows)

Valve components

Refer to illustrations 10.17, 10.18 and 10.19

17   Check each valve spring for wear (on the ends) and pits. Measure the free length and compare it to the Specifications **(see illustration)**. Any springs that are shorter than specified have sagged and should not be reused. The tension of all springs should be checked with a special fixture before deciding that they're suitable for use in a rebuilt engine (take the springs to an automotive machine shop for this check).

18   Stand each spring on a flat surface and check it for squareness **(see illustration)**. If any of the springs are distorted or sagged, replace all of them with new parts.

19   Check the spring retainers (or rotators) and keepers for obvious wear and cracks. Any questionable parts should be replaced with new ones, as extensive damage will occur if they fail during engine operation. Make sure the rotators operate smoothly with no binding or excessive play **(see illustration)**.

Rocker arm components (OHV engines)

Refer to illustrations 10.21, 10.22a and 10.22b

20   Clean all the parts thoroughly. Make sure all oil passages are open.

21   Check the rocker arm faces (the areas that contact the pushrod ends and valve stems) for pits, wear, galling, score marks and rough spots **(see illustration)**.

22   Check the rocker arm pivot contact areas and fulcrums **(see illustrations)**. Look for cracks in each rocker arm and bolt (or nut on some very early OHV engines).

23   Inspect the pushrod ends for scuffing and excessive wear. Roll each pushrod on a flat surface, like a piece of plate glass, to determine if it's bent.

24   Check the rocker arm studs in the cylinder heads (if applicable) for damaged threads and secure installation.

25   Any damaged or excessively worn parts must be replaced with new ones.

26   If the inspection process indicates that the valve components are in generally poor condition and worn beyond the limits specified, which is usually the case in an engine that's being overhauled, reassemble the valves in the cylinder head and refer to Section 11 for valve servicing recommendations.

Cam followers (OHC engine)

Refer to illustration 10.28

27   Clean all the parts thoroughly. Make sure all oil passages are open.

28   Check the cam follower pads (the areas that contact the lifter and valve stems end) for pits, wear, galling, score marks and rough spots **(see illustration)**.

29   Check the cam follower roller (the area that contacts the camshaft) for pits, wear, galling, score marks and rough spots.

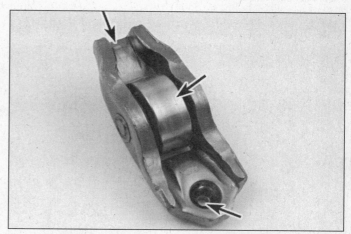

10.28 On OHC engines, check the camshaft followers for signs of wear or damage to the areas that contact the cam, lifter or valve stem tip (arrows)

30   Any damaged or excessively worn parts must be replaced with new ones.

31   If the inspection process indicates that the valve components are in generally poor condition and worn beyond the limits specified, which is usually the case in an engine that's being overhauled, reassemble the valves in the cylinder head and refer to Section 11 for valve servicing recommendations.

11   Valves - servicing

1   Because of the complex nature of the job and the prohibitive cost of the special tools and equipment needed, servicing of the valves, the valve seats and the valve guides, commonly known as a valve job, is usually more easily, and inexpensively, done by an automotive machine shop.

2   The home mechanic can remove and disassemble the head, do the initial cleaning and inspection, then reassemble and deliver it to a dealer service department or an automotive machine shop for the actual service work. Doing the inspection will enable you to see what condition the head and valve train components are in and will ensure that you know what work and new parts are required when dealing with an automotive machine shop.

3   The dealer service department or automotive machine shop will remove the valves and springs, recondition or replace the valves and valve seats, recondition the valve guides, check and replace the valve springs, spring retainers or rotators and keepers (as necessary), replace the valve seals with new ones, reassemble the valve

2C

12.3a On models with the type of seal shown, use a hammer and a seal installer (or a deep socket, as shown here) to drive the seal onto the valve guide/head casting boss (umbrella-type seals don't need to be driven into place)

12.3b Installing a valve stem seal on an OHC engine - the socket must contact the flange (spring seat) of the seal

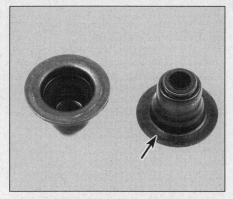

12.6 OHC engines use valve stem seals that are a valve spring seat and seal combined (arrow) - make sure replacement parts are the same as the ones removed earlier

12.7a Apply a small dab of grease to each keeper as shown here before installation - it'll hold them in place on the valve stem as the spring is released

12.7b Compress the springs with a valve spring compressor and position the keepers in the upper groove on the valve stem (arrow), then slowly release the compressor and make sure the keepers seat properly

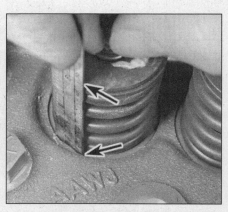

12.9 Valve spring installed height is the distance from the spring seat on the head to the bottom of the spring retainer (arrows)

components and make sure the installed spring height, and pressure, is correct. The cylinder head gasket surface will also be resurfaced if it's warped, if not beyond service limits. **Note:** *It may be advisable to have the cylinder head pressure checked for internal coolant leaks, especially if the engine has been overheated.*

4   After the valve job has been performed, the head will be in like-new condition. When the head is returned, be sure to clean it again before installation on the engine to remove any metal particles and abrasive grit that may still be present from the valve service or head resurfacing operations. Use compressed air, if available, to blow out all the oil holes and passages.

12   Cylinder head - reassembly

Refer to illustrations 12.3a, 12.3b, 12.6, 12.7a, 12.7b and 12.9

1   Regardless of whether or not the head was sent to an automotive repair shop for valve servicing, make sure it's clean before beginning reassembly.

2   If the head was sent out for valve servicing, the valves and related components will already be in place. Begin the reassembly procedure with Step 9.

3   On all engines, lubricate and install the valves, then install new

seals on each of the valve guides. Using a hammer and deep socket, gently tap each seal into place until it's seated on the guide **(see illustrations)**. Don't twist or cock the seals during installation or they will not seat properly on the valve stems.

4   On OHC engines, reinstall the valve lifters.

5   Beginning at one end of the head, lubricate and install the first valve. Apply moly-base grease or clean engine oil to the valve stem.

6   Drop the spring seat or shim(s) over the valve guide and set the valve spring, retainer (or rotator) and sleeve (if used) in place. **Note:** *On OHC engines, the valve seal has the spring seat/shim incorporated into one piece* **(see illustration)**. *A valve spring should never sit directly against an aluminum cylinder head.*

7   Apply a small dab of grease to each keeper to hold it in place **(see illustration)**. Compress the springs with a valve spring compressor and carefully install the keepers in the upper groove **(see illustration)**, then slowly release the compressor and make sure the keepers seat properly.

8   Repeat the procedure for the remaining valves. Be sure to return the components to their original locations - don't mix them up!

9   Check the installed valve spring height with a ruler graduated in 1/32-inch increments or a dial caliper. If the head was sent out for service work, the installed height should be correct (but don't automatically assume that it is). The measurement is taken from the top of each spring seat or shim(s) to the bottom of the retainer **(see illustration)**. If

13.1 A ridge reamer is required to remove the ridge from the top of each cylinder - do this before removing the pistons!

13.3a Check the connecting rod side clearance (endplay) with a dial indicator . . .

13.3b . . . or with a feeler gauge

13.4 Mark the rod bearing caps in order, from the front of the engine to the rear

13.6a Remove the rod and bearing insert together

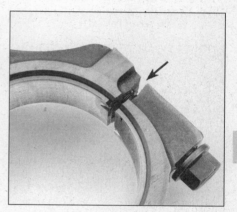

13.6b On OHC engine connecting rods the method used to manufacture and machine the rod cap is unique; they "fracture" (break) the cap from the rod to give a perfect match upon reassembly

2C

the height is greater than the figure listed in this Chapter's Specifications, shims can be added under the springs to correct it. **Caution:** *Don't, under any circumstances, shim the springs to the point where the installed height is less than specified.*
10   Apply moly-base grease to the rocker arm faces and the fulcrums, then install the rocker arms and fulcrums on the cylinder head studs.

13 Pistons/connecting rods - removal

Refer to illustrations 13.1, 13.3a, 13.3b, 13.4, 13.6a, 13.6b, 13.7 and 13.8
Note: *Prior to removing the piston/connecting rod assemblies, remove the cylinder head(s), the oil pan and the oil pump (on OHV engines) by referring to the appropriate Sections in Chapter 2, Part A or Part B, depending which engine is being overhauled.*
1   Use your fingernail to feel if a ridge has formed at the upper limit of ring travel (about 1/4-inch down from the top of each cylinder). If carbon deposits or cylinder wear have produced ridges, they must be completely removed with a special tool **(see illustration)**. Follow the manufacturer's instructions provided with the tool. Failure to remove the ridges before attempting to remove the piston/connecting rod assemblies may result in piston breakage. **Note:** *Do not let the tool cut into the ring travel area more than 1/32-inch.*
2   After the cylinder ridges have been removed, turn the engine

upside-down so the crankshaft is facing up.
3   Before the connecting rods are removed, check the connecting rod side clearance (sometimes also called endplay) with a dial indicator **(see illustration)** or with feeler gauges **(see illustration)**. Slide them between the first connecting rod and the crankshaft throw until the play is removed. The clearance is equal to the thickness of the feeler gauge(s). If the clearance exceeds the service limit, new connecting rods will be required. **Note:** *It is possible that the excessive connecting rod side clearance may be caused by the lack of a crankshaft journal radius. If this is the case the crankshaft will either have to be repaired, if possible, or replaced. If new rods (or a new crankshaft) are installed, the clearance may fall under the specified minimum (if it does, the rods will have to be machined to restore it - consult an automotive machine shop for advice if necessary).* Repeat the procedure for the remaining connecting rods.
4   Check the connecting rods and caps for identification marks. If they aren't plainly marked, use a small center-punch, number stamping die **(see illustration)**, or scribe, to make the appropriate number of indentations, or marks, on each rod and cap (1, 2, 3, etc., depending on the engine type and cylinder they're associated with).
5   Loosen each of the connecting rod cap nuts or bolts 1/2-turn at a time until they can be removed by hand.
6   Remove the connecting rod cap and bearing insert **(see illustrations)**. Don't drop the bearing insert out of the cap.
7   If the connecting rod has studs with attaching nuts (rather than cap bolts as shown in illustration 13.6a) slip a short length of plastic or rubber hose over each connecting rod cap bolt to protect the

13.7 To prevent damage to the crankshaft journals and cylinder walls, slip sections of hose over the rod bolts (on OHV engines) before removing the piston/rod assemblies

13.8 Use a hammer handle to drive the piston and connecting assembly down and out of the cylinder block, being very careful not to nick the crankshaft on the way out

14.1 Checking crankshaft endplay with a dial indicator

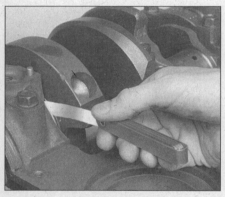

14.3 Checking crankshaft endplay with a feeler gauge

14.4a The main bearing caps are usually marked to indicate their locations (arrows). They should be numbered consecutively from the front of the engine to the rear

14.4b Mark the main bearing caps with number stamping dies or a center punch if they aren't numbered

crankshaft journal and cylinder wall as the piston is removed **(see illustration)**.

8   Remove the bearing insert and push the connecting rod/piston assembly out through the top of the engine. Use a wooden or plastic hammer handle to push on the upper bearing surface in the connecting rod **(see illustration)**. If resistance is felt, double-check to make sure that all of the ridge was removed from the cylinder.

9   Repeat the procedure for the remaining cylinders.

10   After removal, reassemble the connecting rod caps and bearing inserts in their respective connecting rods and install the cap nuts finger tight. Leaving the old bearing inserts in place until reassembly will help prevent the connecting rod bearing surfaces from being accidentally nicked or gouged.

11   Don't separate the pistons from the connecting rods (see Section 18 for additional information).

14 Crankshaft - removal

Refer to illustrations 14.1, 14.3, 14.4a and 14.4b
Note: *The crankshaft can be removed only after the engine has been removed from the vehicle. It's assumed that the flywheel or driveplate, vibration damper, timing chain(s) or gears, oil pan, oil pump and piston/connecting rod assemblies have already been removed.*

1   Before the crankshaft removal procedure is started, check the endplay. Mount a dial indicator with the stem in line with the crankshaft

and just touching the end of the crankshaft **(see illustration)**.

2   Push the crankshaft all the way to the rear and zero the dial indicator. Next, pry the crankshaft to the front as far as possible and check the reading on the dial indicator. The distance that it moves is the endplay. If it's greater than limit listed in this Chapter's Specifications, check the crankshaft thrust surfaces for wear. If no wear is evident, new main bearings should correct the endplay.

3   If a dial indicator isn't available, feeler gauges can be used. Gently pry or push the crankshaft all the way to the front of the engine. Slip feeler gauges between the crankshaft and the front face of the thrust main bearing to determine the clearance **(see Illustration)**.

4   Check the main bearing caps to see if they're marked to indicate their locations **(see illustration)**. They should be numbered consecutively from the front of the engine to the rear. If they aren't, mark them with number stamping dies or a center-punch **(see illustration)**. Main bearing caps generally have a cast-in arrow, which points to the front of the engine.

OHV engines

Note: *The thrust bearing on the OHV engines is the number three main bearing cap location. It has an upper and lower thrust bearing shell.*

5   Loosen the main bearing cap bolts 1/4-turn at a time each, until they can be removed by hand. Loosen the bolts starting from the center main cap and work towards the outer caps. Note if any stud bolts are used and make sure they're returned to their original locations when the crankshaft is reinstalled.

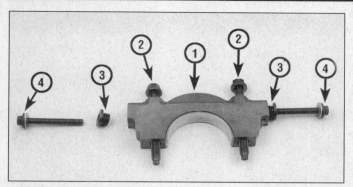

14.6 On OHC engines, the main bearing caps are fastened to the block with a set of cap bolts, side bolts and jack screws

1 Main bearing cap
2 Main bearing bolts
3 Jack screws (left handed thread)
4 Side bolts

14.7 Remove the side bolts

OHC engines

Refer to illustrations 14.6, 14.7 and 14.9

6 The OHC engines have a more complex crankshaft removal and assembly procedure than OHV engines because of the number of bolts used to fasten the main cap to the cylinder block **(see illustration)**. There are two main cap bolts, two jack screws and two side bolts on each of the number one through number four main caps. **Note:** *The number five main bearing cap is the thrust bearing location and has upper and lower thrust bearing halves. It is bolted to the block with two main cap bolts; no jack screws or side bolts are used, although it is drilled for jack screws. It is extremely important to follow the removal and the installation procedure to ensure correct assembly and operation.*

7 Remove all side bolts **(see illustration)**.
8 Bottom all jack screws (which are 8 mm, Allen head screws, with left hand threads) against the main bearing caps **(see illustration 14.6)**.
9 Remove the main bearing cap bolts **(see illustration)**. **Caution:** *The main bearing cap bolts are "angle-torque" bolts and are NOT reusable. A pre-determined stretch of the bolt, calculated by the manufacturer, gives the added rigidity required with this cylinder block. Once removed they must be discarded and replaced. The side bolts and jack screws are reusable.*

All engines

10 Gently tap the caps with a soft-face hammer, then separate them from the engine block. If necessary, use the bolts as levers to remove

the caps. Try not to drop the bearing inserts if they come out with the caps.
11 Carefully lift the crankshaft out of the engine. It may be a good idea to have an assistant available, since the crankshaft is quite heavy. With the bearing inserts in place in the engine block and main bearing caps, return the caps to their respective locations on the engine block and tighten the bolts finger tight.

15 Engine block - cleaning

Refer to illustrations 15.1a, 15.1b, 15.8 and 15.10
Caution: *The core plugs (also known as freeze plugs or soft plugs) may be difficult or impossible to retrieve if they're driven into the block coolant passages.*

1 Using the wide end of a punch **(see illustration)** tap in on the outer edge of the core plug to turn the plug sideways in the bore. Then, using a pair of pliers, pull the core plug from the engine block **(see illustration)**. Don't worry about the condition of the old core plugs as they are being removed because they will be replaced on reassembly with new plugs.
2 Using a gasket scraper, remove all traces of gasket material from the engine block. Be very careful not to nick or gouge the gasket sealing surfaces.
3 Remove the main bearing caps and separate the bearing inserts from the caps and the engine block (see Section 14). Tag the bearings, indicating which cylinder they were removed from and whether they were in the cap or the block, then set them aside.

2C

14.9 Following the reverse order of the tightening sequence (see illustration 23.35), remove the main bearing cap bolts, loosening them 1/4-turn at a time until they can be removed by hand

15.1a A hammer and a large punch can be used to knock the core plugs sideways in their bores

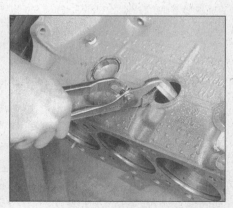

15.1b Pull the core plugs from the block with pliers

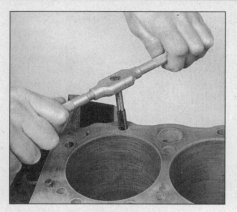

15.8 All bolt holes in the block - particularly the main bearing cap and head bolt holes - should be cleaned and restored with a tap (be sure to remove debris from the holes after this is done)

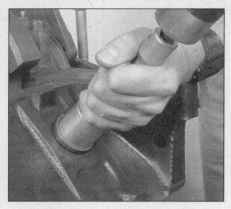

15.10 A large socket on an extension can be used to drive the new core plugs into the bores

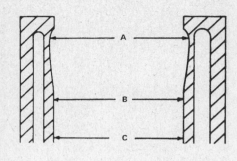

16.4a Measure the diameter of each cylinder just under the wear ridge (A), at the center (B) and at the bottom (C)

4   Remove all of the threaded oil gallery plugs from the block. The plugs are usually very tight - they may have to be drilled out and the holes re tapped. Use new plugs when the engine is reassembled.

5   If the engine is extremely dirty it should be taken to an automotive machine shop to be cleaned.

6   After the block is returned, clean all oil holes and oil galleries one more time. Brushes specifically designed for this purpose are available at most auto parts stores. Flush the passages with warm water until the water runs clear, dry the block thoroughly and wipe all machined surfaces with a light, rust preventive oil. If you have access to compressed air, use it to speed the drying process and to blow out all the oil holes and galleries. **Warning:** *Wear eye protection when using compressed air!*

7   If the block isn't extremely dirty or sludged up, you can do an adequate cleaning job with hot soapy water and a stiff brush. Take plenty of time and do a thorough job. Regardless of the cleaning method used, be sure to clean all oil holes and galleries very thoroughly, dry the block completely and coat all machined surfaces with light oil.

8   The threaded holes in the block must be clean to ensure accurate torque readings during reassembly. Run the proper size tap into each of the holes to remove rust, corrosion, thread sealant or sludge and restore damaged threads **(see illustration)**. If possible, use compressed air to clear the holes of debris produced by this operation. Now is a good time to clean the threads on the head bolts and the main bearing cap bolts as well.

9   Reinstall the main bearing caps and tighten all bolts finger tight.

10   After coating the sealing surfaces of the new core plugs with Permatex no. 2 sealant, install them in the engine block **(see illustration)**. Make sure they're driven in straight and seated properly or leakage could result. Special tools are available for this purpose, but a large socket, with an outside diameter that will just slip into the core plug, a 1/2-inch drive extension and a hammer will work just as well.

11   Apply non-hardening sealant (such as Permatex no. 2 or Teflon pipe sealant) to the new oil gallery plugs and thread them into the holes in the block. Make sure they're tightened securely.

12   If the engine isn't going to be reassembled right away, cover it with a large plastic trash bag to keep it clean.

16 Engine block - inspection

Refer to illustrations 16.4a, 16.4b and 16.4c

1   Before the block is inspected, it should be cleaned as described in Section 15.

2   Visually check the block for cracks, rust and corrosion. Look for stripped threads in the threaded holes. It's also a good idea to have the block checked for hidden cracks by an automotive machine shop that has the special equipment to do this type of work. If defects are found, have the block repaired, if possible, or replaced.

3   Check the cylinder bores for scuffing and scoring.

4   Measure the diameter of each cylinder at the top (just under the ridge area), center and bottom of the cylinder bore, parallel to the crankshaft axis **(see illustrations)**.

16.4b The ability to "feel" when the telescoping gauge is at the correct point will be developed over time, so work slowly and repeat the check until you're satisfied the bore measurement is accurate

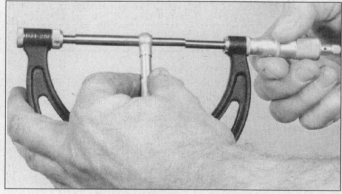

16.4c The gauge is then measured with a micrometer to determine the bore size

17.3a A "bottle brush" hone will produce better results if you've never honed cylinders before

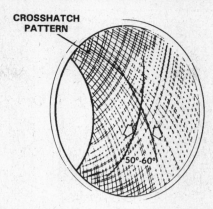

CROSSHATCH
PATTERN

50°-60°

17.3b The cylinder hone should leave a smooth, crosshatch pattern with the lines intersecting at approximately a 60-degree angle

5   Next, measure each cylinder's diameter at the same three locations across the crankshaft axis. Compare the results to this Chapter's Specifications.

6   If the required precision measuring tools aren't available, the piston-to-cylinder clearances can be obtained, though not quite as accurately, using feeler gauge stock. Feeler gauge stock comes in 12-inch lengths and various thickness' and is generally available at auto parts stores.

7   To check the clearance, select a feeler gauge and slip it into the cylinder along with the matching piston. The piston must be positioned exactly as it normally would be. The feeler gauge must be between the piston and cylinder on one of the thrust faces (90-degrees to the piston pin bore).

8   The piston should slip through the cylinder (with the feeler gauge in place) with moderate pressure.

9   If it falls through or slides through easily, the clearance is excessive and a new piston will be required. If the piston binds at the lower end of the cylinder and is loose toward the top, the cylinder is tapered. If tight spots are encountered as the piston/feeler gauge is rotated in the cylinder, the cylinder is out-of-round.

10   Repeat the procedure for the remaining pistons and cylinders.

11   If the cylinder walls are badly scuffed or scored, or if they're out-of-round or tapered beyond the limits given in this Chapter's Specifications, have the engine block rebored and honed at an automotive machine shop. If a rebore is done, oversize pistons and rings will be required.

12   If the cylinders are in reasonably good condition and not worn to the outside of the limits, and if the piston-to-cylinder clearances can be maintained properly, then they don't have to be rebored. Honing is all that's necessary (see Section 17).

17 Cylinder honing

Refer to illustrations 17.3a and 17.3b

1   Prior to engine reassembly, the cylinder bores must be honed so the new piston rings will seat correctly and provide the best possible combustion chamber seal. **Note:** *If you don't have the tools or don't want to tackle the honing operation, most automotive machine shops will do it for a reasonable fee.*

2   Before honing the cylinders, install the main bearing caps and tighten the bolts to the torque listed in this Chapter's Specifications.

3   Two types of cylinder hones are commonly available - the flex hone or "bottle brush" type and the more traditional surfacing hone with spring-loaded stones. Both will do the job, but for the less experienced mechanic the "bottle brush" hone will probably be easier to use. You'll also need some kerosene or honing oil, rags and an electric drill motor. Proceed as follows:

a)   Mount the hone in the drill motor, compress the stones and slip it into the first cylinder **(see illustration)**. Be sure to wear safety goggles or a face shield!

b)   Lubricate the cylinder with plenty of honing oil, turn on the drill and move the hone up-and-down in the cylinder at a pace that will produce a fine crosshatch pattern on the cylinder walls. Ideally, the crosshatch lines should intersect at approximately a 60-degree angle **(see illustration)**. Be sure to use plenty of lubricant and don't take off any more material than is absolutely necessary to produce the desired finish. **Note:** *Piston ring manufacturers may specify a smaller crosshatch angle than the traditional 60-degrees - read and follow any instructions included with the new rings.*

c)   Don't withdraw the hone from the cylinder while it's running. Instead, shut off the drill and continue moving the hone up-and-down in the cylinder until it comes to a complete stop, then compress the stones and withdraw the hone. If you're using a "bottle brush" type hone, stop the drill motor, then turn the chuck in the normal direction of rotation while withdrawing the hone from the cylinder.

d)   Wipe the oil out of the cylinder and repeat the procedure for the remaining cylinders.

4   After the honing job is complete, chamfer the top edges of the cylinder bores with a small file so the rings won't catch when the pistons are installed. Be very careful not to nick the cylinder walls with the end of the file.

5   The entire engine block must be washed again very thoroughly with warm, soapy water to remove all traces of the abrasive grit produced during the honing operation. **Note:** *The bores can be considered clean when a lint-free white cloth - dampened with clean engine oil - used to wipe them out doesn't pick-up any more honing residue, which will show up as gray areas on the cloth. Be sure to run a brush through all oil holes and galleries and flush them with running water.*

6   After rinsing, dry the block and apply a coat of light rust preventive oil to all machined surfaces. Wrap the block in a plastic trash bag to keep it clean and set it aside until reassembly.

18 Pistons/connecting rods - inspection

Refer to illustrations 18.4a, 18.4b, 18.10 and 18.11

1   Before the inspection process can be carried out, the piston/connecting rod assemblies must be cleaned and the original piston rings removed from the pistons. **Note:** *Always use new piston rings when the engine is reassembled.*

2   Using a piston ring installation tool, carefully remove the rings from the pistons **(see illustration 22.11)**. Be careful not to nick or

2C

18.4a The piston ring grooves can be cleaned with a special tool, as shown here . . .

18.4b . . . or a section of a broken ring

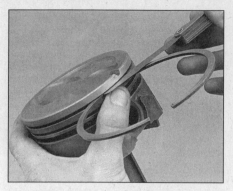

18.10 Check the ring side clearance with a feeler gauge at several points around the groove

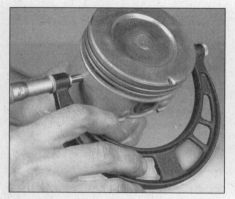

18.11 Measure the piston diameter at a 90-degree angle to the piston pin and in line with it

19.1 The oil holes should be chamfered so sharp edges don't gouge or scratch the new bearings

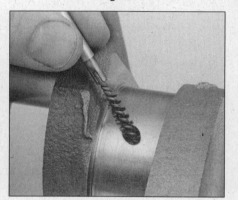

19.2 Use a wire or stiff plastic bristle brush to clean the oil passages in the crankshaft

gouge the pistons in the process.

3   Scrape all traces of carbon from the top of the piston. A hand-held wire brush or a piece of fine emery cloth can be used once the majority of the deposits have been scraped away. Do not, under any circumstances, use a wire brush mounted in a drill motor to remove deposits from the pistons. The piston material is soft and may be eroded away by the wire brush.

4   Use a piston ring groove cleaning tool to remove carbon deposits from the ring grooves. If a tool isn't available, a piece broken off the old ring will do the job **(see illustrations)**. Be very careful to remove only the carbon deposits - don't remove any metal and do not nick or scratch the sides of the ring grooves.

5   Once the deposits have been removed, clean the piston/rod assemblies with solvent and dry them with compressed air (if available). Make sure the oil return holes in the back sides of the ring grooves are clear.

6   If the pistons and cylinder walls aren't damaged or worn excessively, and if the engine block is not rebored, new pistons won't be necessary. Normal piston wear appears as even vertical wear on the piston thrust surfaces and slight looseness of the top ring in its groove. New piston rings, however, should always be used when an engine is rebuilt.

7   Carefully inspect each piston for cracks around the skirt, at the pin bosses and at the ring lands.

8   Look for scoring and scuffing on the thrust faces of the skirt, holes in the piston crown and burned areas at the edge of the crown. If the skirt is scored or scuffed, the engine may have been suffering from overheating and/or abnormal combustion, which caused excessively high operating temperatures. The cooling and lubrication systems should be checked thoroughly. A hole in the piston crown is an indication that abnormal combustion (pre-ignition) was occurring. Burned areas at the edge of the piston crown are usually evidence of

spark knock (detonation). If any of the above problems exist, the causes must be corrected or the damage will occur again. The causes may include intake air leaks, incorrect fuel/air mixture, incorrect ignition timing and EGR system malfunctions.

9   Corrosion of the piston, in the form of small pits, indicates that coolant is leaking into the combustion chamber and/or the crankcase. Again, the cause must be corrected or the problem may persist in the rebuilt engine.

10   Measure the piston ring side clearance by laying a new piston ring in each ring groove and slipping a feeler gauge in beside it **(see illustration)**. **Note:** *Piston ring side clearance is only measured on the compression rings.* Check the clearance at three or four locations around each groove. Be sure to use the correct ring for each groove - they are different. If the side clearance is greater than the figure listed in this Chapter's Specifications, new pistons will have to be used.

11   Check the piston-to-bore clearance by measuring the bore (see Section 16) and the piston diameter. Make sure the pistons and bores are correctly matched. Measure the piston across the skirt, at a 90-degree angle to and in line with the piston pin **(see illustration)**. Subtract the piston diameter from the bore diameter to obtain the clearance. If it's greater than specified, the block will have to be rebored and new pistons and rings installed.

12   Check the piston-to-rod clearance by twisting the piston and rod in opposite directions. Any noticeable play indicates excessive wear, which must be corrected. The piston/connecting rod assemblies should be taken to an automotive machine shop to have the pistons and rods resized and new pins installed.

13   If the pistons must be removed from the connecting rods for any reason, they should be taken to an automotive machine shop. While they are there have the connecting rods checked for bend and twist, since automotive machine shops have special equipment for this purpose. **Note:** *Unless new pistons and/or connecting rods must be*

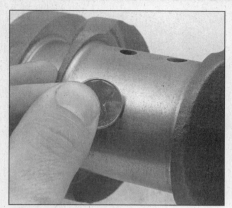

19.3 Rubbing a penny lengthwise on each journal will reveal its condition - if copper rubs off and is embedded in the crankshaft, the journals should be reground

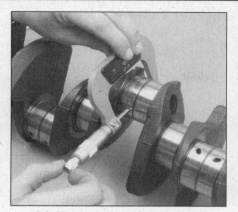

19.6 Measure the diameter of each crankshaft journal at several points to detect taper and out-of-round conditions

19.8 If the seals have worn grooves in the crankshaft journals, or if the seal contact surfaces are nicked or scratched, the new seals will leak

installed, do not disassemble the pistons and connecting rods.

14   Check the connecting rods for cracks and other damage. Temporarily remove the rod caps, lift out the old bearing inserts, wipe the rod and cap bearing surfaces clean and inspect them for nicks, gouges and scratches. After checking the rods, replace the old bearings, slip the caps into place and tighten the nuts finger tight. **Note:** *If the engine is being rebuilt because of a connecting rod knock, be sure to install new rods.*

19 Crankshaft - inspection

Refer to illustrations 19.1, 19.2, 19.3, 19.6 and 19.8

1   Remove all burrs from the crankshaft oil holes with a stone, file or scraper **(see illustration)**.
2   Clean the crankshaft with solvent and dry it with compressed air (if available). Be sure to clean the oil holes with a stiff brush **(see illustration)** and flush them with solvent.
3   Rub a penny across each journal several times **(see illustration)**. If a journal picks up copper from the penny, it's too rough and must be reground.
4   Check the main and connecting rod bearing journals for uneven wear, scoring, pits and cracks.
5   Check the rest of the crankshaft for cracks and other damage. It should be magnafluxed to reveal hidden cracks - an automotive machine shop will handle the procedure.
6   Using a micrometer, measure the diameter of the main and connecting rod journals and compare the results to this Chapter's Specifications **(see illustration)**. By measuring the diameter at a number of points around each journal's circumference, you'll be able to determine whether or not the journal is out-of-round. Take the measurement at each end of the journal, near the crank throws, to determine if the journal is tapered.
7   If the crankshaft journals are damaged, tapered, out-of-round or worn beyond the limits given in the Specifications, have the crankshaft reground by an automotive machine shop. Be sure to use the correct size bearing inserts if the crankshaft is reconditioned. **Note:** *If the crankshaft is being reground, have the machine shop provide bearings that are matched to that crankshaft.*
8   Check the oil seal journals at each end of the crankshaft for wear and damage. If the seal has worn a groove in the journal, or if it's nicked or scratched **(see illustration)**, the new seal may leak when the engine is reassembled. In some cases, an automotive machine shop may be able to repair the journal by pressing on a thin sleeve. If repair isn't feasible, a new or different crankshaft should be installed.
9   Refer to Section 19 and examine the main and rod bearing inserts.

20 Main and connecting rod bearings - inspection

Refer to illustration 20.1

1   Even though the main and connecting rod bearings should be replaced with new ones during the engine overhaul, the old bearings should be retained for close examination, as they may reveal valuable information about the condition of the engine **(see illustration)**.
2   Bearing failure occurs because of lack of lubrication, the presence of dirt or other foreign particles, overloading the engine and corrosion. Regardless of the cause of bearing failure, it must be corrected before the engine is reassembled to prevent it from happening again.
3   When examining the bearings, remove them from the engine block, the main bearing caps, the connecting rods and the rod caps and lay them out on a clean surface in the same general position as their location in the engine. This will enable you to match any bearing problems with the corresponding crankshaft journal.
4   Dirt and other foreign particles get into the engine in a variety of

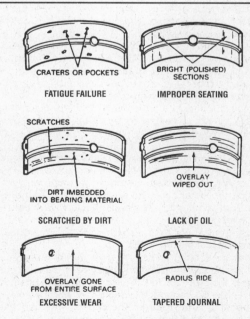

20.1 Typical bearing failures

ways. It may be left in the engine during assembly, or it may pass through filters or the PCV system. It may get into the oil, and from there into the bearings. Metal chips from machining operations and normal engine wear are often present. Abrasives are sometimes left in engine components after reconditioning, especially when parts are not thoroughly cleaned using the proper cleaning methods. Whatever the source, these foreign objects often end up embedded in the soft bearing material and are easily recognized. Large particles will not embed in the bearing and will score or gouge the bearing and journal. The best prevention for this cause of bearing failure is to clean all parts thoroughly and keep everything spotlessly clean during engine assembly. Frequent and regular engine oil and filter changes are also recommended.

5   Lack of lubrication (or lubrication breakdown) has a number of interrelated causes. Excessive heat (which thins the oil), overloading (which squeezes the oil from the bearing face) and oil leakage or throw off (from excessive bearing clearances, worn oil pump or high engine speeds) all contribute to lubrication breakdown. Blocked oil passages, which usually are the result of misaligned oil holes in a bearing shell, will also oil starve a bearing and destroy it. When lack of lubrication is the cause of bearing failure, the bearing material is wiped or extruded from the steel backing of the bearing. Temperatures may increase to the point where the steel backing turns blue from overheating.

6   Driving habits can have a definite effect on bearing life. Full throttle, low speed operation (lugging the engine) puts very high loads on bearings, which tends to squeeze out the oil film. These loads cause the bearings to flex, which produces fine cracks in the bearing face (fatigue failure). Eventually the bearing material will loosen in pieces and tear away from the steel backing. Short trip driving leads to corrosion of bearings because insufficient engine heat is produced to drive off the condensed water and corrosive gases. These products collect in the engine oil, forming acid and sludge. As the oil is carried to the engine bearings, the acid attacks and corrodes the bearing material.

7   Incorrect bearing installation during engine assembly will lead to bearing failure as well. Tight fitting bearings leave insufficient bearing oil clearance and will result in oil starvation. Dirt or foreign particles trapped behind a bearing insert result in high spots on the bearing which lead to failure.

21 Engine overhaul - reassembly sequence

1   Before beginning engine reassembly, make sure you have all the necessary new parts, gaskets and seals as well as the following items on hand:

> *Common hand tools*
> *A 1/2-inch drive torque wrench*
> *A 3/8-inch drive torque wrench (inch-lb measurement)*
> *Piston ring installation tool*
> *Piston ring compressor*
> *Vibration damper installation tool*
> *Short lengths of rubber or plastic hose to fit over connecting*
> *   rod bolts*
> *Plastigage*
> *Feeler gauges*
> *A fine-tooth file*
> *New engine oil*
> *Engine assembly lube or moly-base grease*
> *Gasket sealant*
> *Thread locking compound*

2   In order to save time and avoid problems, engine reassembly must be done in the following general order:

OHV engines

> *New camshaft bearings (recommended to be done by an*
> *   automotive machine shop)*
> *Crankshaft and main bearings*
> *Piston rings*

> *Piston/connecting rod assemblies*
> *Oil pump*
> *Oil pan*
> *Camshaft(s)*
> *Valve lifters*
> *Timing chain(s) and sprockets*
> *Timing chain cover*
> *Cylinder heads*
> *Rocker arms and pushrods*
> *Intake and exhaust manifolds*
> *Valve covers*
> *Driveplate*

OHC engines

> *Crankshaft and main bearings*
> *Piston rings*
> *Piston/connecting rod assemblies*
> *Oil pump*
> *Oil pan*
> *Cylinder heads*
> *Valve lifters*
> *Camshaft followers*
> *Camshaft(s)*
> *Camshaft cap cluster assemblies*
> *Timing chain(s) and sprockets*
> *Timing chain guides and tensioners*
> *Timing chain cover*
> *Intake and exhaust manifolds*
> *Valve covers*
> *Driveplate*

22 Piston rings - installation

Refer to illustrations 22.3, 22.4, 22.8a, 22.8b and 22.11

1   Before installing the new piston rings, the ring end gaps must be checked. It's assumed that the piston ring side clearance has been checked and verified correct (see Section 18).

2   Lay out the piston/connecting rod assemblies and the new ring sets so the ring sets will be matched with the same piston and cylinder during the end gap measurement and engine assembly.

3   Insert the top (number one) ring into the first cylinder and square it up with the cylinder walls by pushing it in with the top of the piston **(see illustration)**. The ring should be near the bottom of the cylinder, at the lower limit of ring travel.

4   To measure the end gap, slip feeler gauges between the ends of the ring until a gauge equal to the gap width is found **(see illustration)**. The feeler gauge should slide between the ring ends with a slight amount of drag. Compare the measurement to this Chapter's Specifications. If the gap is larger or smaller than specified, double-check to make sure you have the correct rings before proceeding. If there is any doubt contact the parts department where the rings were purchased, to verify that the correct ring set is being used.

5   Excess end gap isn't critical unless it's greater than 0.040-inch. Again, double-check to make sure you have the correct rings for your engine.

6   Repeat the procedure for each ring that will be installed in the first cylinder and for each ring in the remaining cylinders. Remember to keep rings, pistons and cylinders matched up.

7   Once the ring end gaps have been checked/corrected, the rings can be installed on the pistons.

8   The oil control ring (lowest one on the piston) is usually installed first. It's composed of three separate components. Slip the spacer/expander into the groove **(see illustration)**. Next, install the lower side rail. Don't use a piston ring installation tool on the oil ring side rails, as they may be damaged. Instead, place one end of the side rail into the groove between the spacer/expander and the ring land, hold it firmly in place and slide a finger around the piston while pushing the rail into the groove **(see illustration)**. Next, install the upper side rail in the same manner.

22.3 When checking piston ring end gap, the ring must be square in the cylinder bore (this is done by pushing the ring down with the top of a piston as shown)

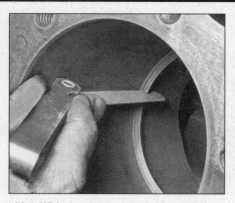

22.4 With the ring square in the cylinder, measure the end gap with a feeler gauge

22.8a Installing the spacer/expander in the oil control ring groove . . .

9   After the three oil ring components have been installed, check to make sure that both the upper and lower side rails can be turned smoothly in the ring groove.

10   The number two (middle) ring is installed next. It's usually stamped with a mark which must face up, toward the top of the piston. **Note:** *Always follow the instructions printed on the ring package or box - different manufacturers may require different approaches. Do not mix up the top and middle rings, as they have different cross sections.*

11   Use a piston ring installation tool and make sure the identification mark is facing the top of the piston, then slip the ring into the middle groove on the piston **(see illustration)**. Don't expand the ring any more than necessary to slide it over the piston.

12   Install the number one (top) ring in the same manner. Make sure the mark is facing up. Be careful not to confuse the number one and number two rings.

13   Repeat the procedure for the remaining pistons and rings.

---

23   Crankshaft - installation and main bearing oil clearance check

---

1   Crankshaft installation is the first step in engine reassembly. It's assumed at this point that the engine block and crankshaft have been cleaned, inspected and repaired or reconditioned.

2   Position the engine with the bottom facing up.

3   Remove the main bearing cap bolts and lift out the caps. Lay them out in the proper order to ensure correct installation.

4   If they're still in place, remove the original bearing inserts from the block and the main bearing caps. Wipe the bearing surfaces of the block and caps with a clean, lint-free cloth. They must be kept spotlessly clean.

Main bearing oil clearance check

Refer to illustrations 23.11 and 23.15

5   Clean the back sides of the new main bearing inserts and lay one in each main bearing saddle in the block. If one of the bearing inserts from each set has a large groove in it, make sure the grooved insert is installed in the block. Lay the other bearing from each set in the corresponding main bearing cap. Make sure the tab on the bearing insert fits into the recess in the block or cap. **Caution:** *The oil holes in the block must line up with the oil holes in the bearing insert. Do not hammer the bearing into place and don't nick or gouge the bearing faces. No lubrication should be used at this time.*

6   The flanged thrust bearing must be installed in the third cap and saddle on OHV engines, or the fifth cap and saddle on OHC engines.

7   Clean the faces of the bearings in the block and the crankshaft main bearing journals with a clean, lint-free cloth.

8   Check or clean the oil holes in the crankshaft, as any dirt here can go only one way - straight through the new bearings.

9   Once you're certain the crankshaft is clean, carefully lay it in position in the main bearings.

10   Before the crankshaft can be permanently installed, the main bearing oil clearance must be checked.

11   Cut several pieces of the appropriate size Plastigage (they must be slightly shorter than the width of the main bearings) and place one piece on each crankshaft main bearing journal, parallel with the journal axis **(see illustration).**

12   Clean the faces of the bearings in the caps and install the caps in their respective positions (don't mix them up) with the arrows pointing toward the front of the engine. Don't disturb the Plastigage.

13   Starting with the center main and working out toward the ends, tighten the main bearing cap bolts, in three steps, to the torque listed

22.8b . . . followed by the side rails - DO NOT use a piston ring installation tool when installing the oil ring side rails

22.11 Installing the compressor rings with a ring expander - the mark (arrow) must face up

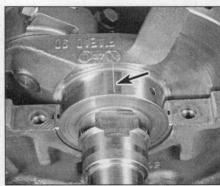

23.11 Lay the Plastigage strips (arrow) on the main bearing journals, parallel to the crankshaft centerline

2C

23.15 Compare the width of the crushed Plastigage to the scale on the envelope to determine the main bearing oil clearance (always take the measurement at the widest point of the Plastigage); be sure to use the correct scale - standard and metric ones are included

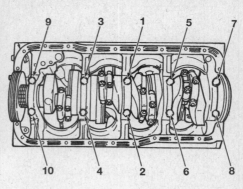

23.27 Tighten all the main bearing cap bolts in the sequence shown (OHV engine)

23.35 Tighten all the main bearing cap bolts in the sequence shown (OHC engine)

in this Chapter's Specifications. **Note:** *On the OHC engine it is not necessary to install the jack screws or the side bolts for Plastigage measurement purposes. Don't rotate the crankshaft at any time during this operation.*

14   Remove the bolts and carefully lift off the main bearing caps. Keep them in order. Don't disturb the Plastigage or rotate the crankshaft. If any of the main bearing caps are difficult to remove, tap them gently from side-to-side with a soft-face hammer to loosen them.

15   Compare the width of the crushed Plastigage on each journal to the scale printed on the Plastigage envelope to obtain the main bearing oil clearance **(see illustration)**. Check the Specifications to make sure it's correct.

16   If the clearance is not as specified, the bearing inserts may be the wrong size (which means different ones will be required). Before deciding that different inserts are needed, make sure that no dirt or oil was between the bearing inserts and the caps or block when the clearance was measured. If the Plastigage was wider at one end than the other, the journal may be tapered (refer to Section 19).

17   Carefully scrape all traces of the Plastigage material off the main bearing journals and/or the bearing faces. Use your fingernail or the edge of a credit card - don't nick or scratch the bearing faces.

Final crankshaft installation

18   Carefully lift the crankshaft out of the engine.

19   Clean the bearing faces in the block, then apply a thin, uniform layer of moly-base grease or engine assembly lube to each of the bearing surfaces. Be sure to coat the thrust faces as well as the journal face of the thrust bearing.

20   Make sure the crankshaft journals are clean, then lay the crankshaft back in place in the block.

21   Clean the faces of the bearings in the caps, then apply lubricant to them.

22   Install the caps in their respective positions with the arrows pointing toward the front of the engine.

OHV engines

Refer to illustration 23.27

23   Install the main cap bolts.

24   Tighten all, except the thrust bearing cap bolts (number 3) to the specified torque (work from the center out and approach the final torque in three steps).

25   Tighten the thrust bearing cap bolts finger tight.

26   Pry the crankshaft forward and while holding pressure on the crankshaft, pry the thrust bearing cap backward. Forcing these two in opposite directions, against each other, will align the thrust bearing surfaces.

27   While keeping forward pressure on the crankshaft, re-tighten ALL main bearing cap bolts to the specified torque, following the proper tightening sequence **(see illustration)**.

28   Rotate the crankshaft a number of times by hand to check for any

obvious binding.

29   As a final step, check the crankshaft endplay with a feeler gauge or a dial indicator (see Section 14) The endplay should be correct if the crankshaft thrust faces aren't worn or damaged and new bearings have been installed.

30   Install the rear main oil seal (see Chapter 2, Part A).

OHC engines

Refer to illustrations 23.35, 23.36a, 23.36b, 23.37a and 23.37b

31   Install the jack screws into the main caps and bottom them lightly against the caps, this must be done before the caps are placed into the block.

32   Place the main caps on their correct journals and tap the caps into place with a brass or soft-face hammer. **Caution:** *All main bearing caps MUST be tapped into position prior to tightening. Failure to do so may result in improper torque.*

33   Install the main cap bolts and tighten them to 10-to-12 ft-lbs.

34   Push the crankshaft forward using a screwdriver or prybar to seat the thrust bearing. **Caution:** *Once the crankshaft is pushed fully forward, to seat the thrust bearing, leave the screwdriver in position so that pressure stays placed on the crankshaft until after all main bearing cap bolts have been tightened.*

35   Tighten the main bearing cap bolts in two steps in the sequence shown **(see illustration)** and to the torque listed in this Chapter's Specifications.

36   Tighten all jack screws in two steps and in the sequence shown **(see illustrations)** to the torque listed in this Chapter's Specifications.

37   Tighten all side bolts in two steps and in the sequence shown **(see illustrations)** to the torque listed in this Chapter's Specifications.

38   Check crankshaft endplay again and verify that it is correct.

39   Rotate the crankshaft a number of times by hand to check for any obvious binding.

40   Install the rear main oil seal (see Chapter 2, Part B).

24   Pistons/connecting rods - installation and rod bearing oil clearance check

1   Before installing the piston/connecting rod assemblies, the cylinder walls must be perfectly clean, the top edge of each cylinder must be chamfered, and the crankshaft must be in place.

2   Remove the cap from the end of the number one connecting rod (refer to the marks made during removal). Remove the original bearing inserts and wipe the bearing surfaces of the connecting rod and cap with a clean, lint-free cloth. They must be kept spotlessly clean.

Connecting rod bearing oil clearance check

Refer to illustrations 24.3, 24.5, 24.9, 24.11, 24.13 and 24.17

3   Clean the back side of the new upper bearing insert, then lay it in place in the connecting rod **(see illustration)**. Make sure the tab on the

23.36a On an OHC engine, place the Allen wrench through the side bolt hole and tighten the jack screw (arrow) against the cylinder block . . .

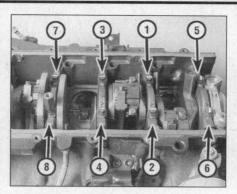

23.36b . . . in two steps, following the sequence shown, to the torque listed in this Chapter's Specifications

23.37a Tighten the side bolts . . .

bearing fits into the recess in the rod. Don't hammer the bearing insert into place and be very careful not to nick or gouge the bearing face. Don't lubricate the bearing at this time.

4   Clean the back side of the other bearing insert and install it in the rod cap (see illustration 24.3). Again, make sure the tab on the bearing fits into the recess in the cap, and don't apply any lubricant. It's critically important that the mating surfaces of the bearing and connecting rod are perfectly clean and oil free when they're assembled.

5   Position the piston ring gaps at intervals around the piston (see illustration).

6   On OHV engines, slip a section of plastic or rubber hose over each connecting rod bolt (see illustration 13.7). Note: OHC engines use cap bolts that are screwed into the rod after the rod and cap are assembled on the crankshaft.

7   Lubricate the piston and rings with clean engine oil and attach a piston ring compressor to the piston. Leave the skirt protruding about 1/4-inch to guide the piston into the cylinder. The rings must be compressed until they're flush with the piston.

8   Rotate the crankshaft until the number one connecting rod journal is at BDC (bottom dead center) and apply a coat of engine oil to the cylinder walls.

9   With the arrow or notches on top of the piston (see illustration) facing the front of the engine, gently insert the piston/connecting rod assembly into the number one cylinder bore and rest the bottom edge of the ring compressor on the engine block. Caution: Re-check and re-tighten the ring compressor. Any edge of a piston ring, no matter how little, that is outside the piston ring groove will cause the ring to be broken when tapping the piston into the cylinder.

10   Tap the top edge of the ring compressor to make sure it's contacting the block around its entire circumference.

23.37b . . . in two steps, following the sequence shown, to the torque listed in this Chapter's Specifications

11   Gently tap on the top of the piston with the end of a wooden hammer handle (see illustration) while guiding the end of the connecting rod into place on the crankshaft journal. The piston rings may try to pop out of the ring compressor just before entering the cylinder bore, so keep some down pressure on the ring compressor. Work slowly, and if any resistance is felt as the piston enters the cylinder, stop immediately. Find out what's hanging up and fix it before proceeding. Do not, for any reason, force the piston into the cylinder - you might break a ring and/or the piston.

12   Once the piston/connecting rod assembly is installed, the connecting rod bearing oil clearance must be checked before the rod cap is permanently bolted in place.

24.3 Insert the connecting rod bearing halves, making sure the bearing tab (arrows) are in the notches in the rod and cap

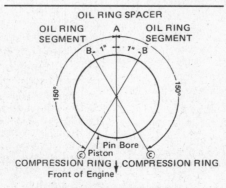

24.5 Ring end gap positions

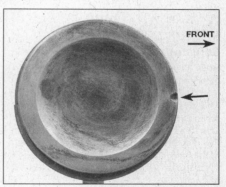

24.9 Turn the piston when installing it to make sure the notch in the piston (arrow) faces the front of the engine as they are installed

2C

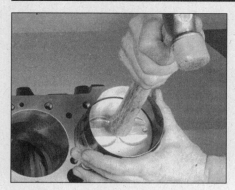

24.11 The piston can be driven gently into the cylinder bore with the end of a wooden or plastic hammer handle

24.13 Lay the Plastigage strips on each rod bearing journal, parallel to the crankshaft centerline

24.17 Measuring the width of the crushed Plastigage to determine the rod bearing oil clearance (be sure to use the correct scale - standard and metric ones are included)

13   Cut a piece of the appropriate size Plastigage slightly shorter than the width of the connecting rod bearing and lay it in place on the number one connecting rod journal, parallel with the journal axis **(see illustration)**.

14   Clean the connecting rod cap bearing face, remove the protective hoses from the connecting rod bolts and install the rod cap. Make sure the mating mark on the cap is on the same side as the mark on the connecting rod.

15   Install the nuts and tighten them to the torque listed in this Chapter's Specifications, working up to it in three steps. **Note:** *Use a thin-wall socket to avoid erroneous torque readings that can result if the socket is wedged between the rod cap and nut/bolt. If the socket tends to wedge itself between the nut/bolt and the cap, lift up on it slightly until it no longer contacts the cap. Do not rotate the crankshaft at any time during this operation.*

16   Remove the nuts/bolts and detach the rod cap, being very careful not to disturb the Plastigage.

17   Compare the width of the crushed Plastigage to the scale printed on the Plastigage envelope to obtain the oil clearance **(see illustration)**. Compare it to the Specifications to make sure the clearance is correct.

18   If the clearance is not as specified, the bearing inserts may be the wrong size (which means different ones will be required). Before deciding that different inserts are needed, make sure that no dirt or oil was between the bearing inserts and the connecting rod or cap when the clearance was measured. Also, recheck the journal diameter. If the Plastigage was wider at one end than the other, the journal may be tapered (refer to Section 18).

Final connecting rod installation

19   Carefully scrape all traces of the Plastigage material off the rod journal and/or bearing face. Be very careful not to scratch the bearing - use your fingernail or the edge of a credit card.

20   Make sure the bearing faces are perfectly clean, then apply a uniform layer of clean moly-base grease or engine assembly lube to both of them. You'll have to push the piston into the cylinder to expose the face of the bearing insert in the connecting rod - be sure to slip the protective hoses over the rod bolts first.

21   Slide the connecting rod back into place on the journal, remove the protective hoses from the rod cap bolts, install the rod cap and tighten the nuts to the specified torque. Again, work up to the torque in three steps.

22   Repeat the entire procedure for the remaining pistons/connecting rods.

23   The important points to remember are:

a) *Keep the back sides of the bearing inserts and the insides of the connecting rods and caps perfectly clean when assembling them.*

b) *Make sure you have the correct piston/rod assembly for each cylinder.*

c) *The notches or mark on the piston must face the FRONT of the engine.*

d) *Lubricate the cylinder walls with clean oil.*

e) *Lubricate the bearing faces when installing the rod caps after the oil clearance has been checked.*

24   After all the piston/connecting rod assemblies have been properly installed, rotate the crankshaft a number of times by hand to check for any obvious binding.

25   As a final step, the connecting rod endplay must be checked. Refer to Section 13 for this procedure.

26   Compare the measured endplay to the Specifications to make sure it's correct. If it was correct before disassembly and the original crankshaft and rods were reinstalled, it should still be right. If new rods or a new crankshaft were installed, the endplay may be inadequate. If so, the rods will have to be removed and taken to an automotive machine shop for resizing.

25   Initial start-up and break-in after overhaul

Warning: *Have a fire extinguisher handy when starting the engine for the first time.*

1   Once the engine has been installed in the vehicle, double-check the engine oil and coolant levels.

2   With the spark plugs out of the engine and the ignition system disabled (see Chapter 1), crank the engine until oil pressure registers on the gauge or the light goes out.

3   Install the spark plugs, hook up the plug wires and restore the ignition system functions.

4   Start the engine. It may take a few moments for the fuel system to build up pressure, but the engine should start without a great deal of effort. **Note:** *If backfiring occurs through the carburetor or throttle body, recheck the valve timing and ignition timing.*

5   After the engine starts, it should be allowed to warm up to normal operating temperature. While the engine is warming up, make a thorough check for fuel, oil and coolant leaks.

6   Shut the engine off and recheck the engine oil and coolant levels.

7   Drive the vehicle to an area with minimum traffic, accelerate from 30 to 50 mph, then allow the vehicle to slow to 30 mph with the throttle closed. Repeat the procedure 10 or 12 times. This will load the piston rings and cause them to seat properly against the cylinder walls. Check again for oil and coolant leaks.

8   Drive the vehicle gently for the first 500 miles (no sustained high speeds) and keep a constant check on the oil level. It is not unusual for an engine to use oil during the break-in period.

9   At approximately 500 to 600 miles, change the oil and filter.

10   For the next few hundred miles, drive the vehicle normally. Do not pamper it or abuse it.

11   After 2000 miles, change the oil and filter again and consider the engine broken in.

Chapter 3
Cooling, heating and air conditioning systems

Contents

3

Specifications

Capacity	17 to 19 quarts*
Coolant type	50/50 mixture of non-phosphate ethylene glycol antifreeze
Thermostat	
Opening temperature	185 to 195 degrees
Fully open temperature	212 to 221 degrees
Radiator pressure cap	
Specified cap pressure	16 psi
Minimum (must maintain)	13 psi
Maximum (must relieve)	19 psi

*The cooling system capacity varies slightly by model and year. Always bring coolant up to the proper level.

Torque specifications

	Ft-lbs (unless otherwise indicated)
Fan-to-fan clutch bolts	
OHV engines	12 to 18
OHC engine	15 to 20
Fan clutch-to-water pump bolts (OHV engines)	12 to 18
Fan clutch-to-water pump hub (OHC engine only)	37 to 46
Water pump-to-engine bolts	
OHV engines	12 to 18
OHC engine	15 to 22
Transmission oil line fitting-to-radiator	12 to 18
Fan shroud-to-radiator	24 to 48 inch-lbs
Thermostat housing bolts	
OHV engines	12 to 18
OHC engine	15 to 22

1   General information

The cooling system consists of a radiator and coolant reserve system, a radiator pressure cap, a thermostat (of varying temperatures depending on year and model), a four, five or seven blade fan, and a crankshaft pulley-driven water pump.

The radiator cooling fan is mounted on the front of the water pump. There are two types of fans used, one incorporates a fluid drive fan clutch (viscous fan clutch) saves horsepower and reduces noise, the second is a basic fan with a solid hub attaching to the water pump. On both styles a fan shroud is mounted on the rear of the radiator to direct air flow over the engine.

The system is pressurized by a spring-loaded radiator cap, which, by maintaining pressure, increases the boiling point of the coolant. If the coolant temperature goes above this increased boiling point, the extra pressure in the system forces the radiator cap valve off its seat and exposes the overflow pipe or hose . The overflow pipe/hose leads to a coolant recovery system. This consists of a plastic reservoir into which the coolant that normally escapes due to expansion is retained. When the engine cools, the excess coolant is drawn back into the radiator by the vacuum created as the system cools, maintaining the system at full capacity. This is a continuous process and provided the level in the reservoir is correctly maintained, it is not necessary to add coolant to the radiator.

Coolant in the right side of the radiator circulates up the lower radiator hose to the water pump, where it is forced through the water passages in the cylinder block. The coolant then travels up into the cylinder head, circulates around the combustion chambers and valve seats, travels out of the cylinder head past the open thermostat into the upper radiator hose and back into the radiator.

When the engine is cold, the thermostat restricts the circulation of coolant to the engine. When the minimum operating temperature is reached, the thermostat begins to open, allowing coolant to return to the radiator.

Automatic transmission-equipped models have a cooler element incorporated into the radiator to cool the transmission fluid.

The heating system works by directing air through the heater core mounted in the dash and then to the interior of the vehicle by a system of ducts. Temperature is controlled by mixing heated air with fresh air, using a system of flapper doors in the ducts, and a heater motor.

Air conditioning is an optional accessory, consisting of an evaporator core located under the dash, a condenser in front of the radiator, a receiver-drier in the engine compartment and a belt-driven compressor mounted at the front of the engine.

2   Antifreeze - general information

Warning: *Do not allow antifreeze to come in contact with your skin or painted surfaces of the vehicle. Rinse off spills immediately with plenty of water. Antifreeze is highly toxic if ingested. Never leave antifreeze lying around in an open container or in puddles on the floor; children and pets are attracted by it's sweet smell and may drink it. Check with local authorities about disposing of used antifreeze. Many communities have collection centers which will see that antifreeze is disposed of safely.*
Note: *Non-Toxic antifreeze is now manufactured and available at local auto parts stores.*

The cooling system should be filled with a water/ethylene glycol based antifreeze solution which will prevent freezing down to at least -20-degrees F (even lower in cold climates). It also provides protection against corrosion and increases the coolant boiling point.

The cooling system should be drained, flushed and refilled at least every other year (see Chapter 1). The use of antifreeze solutions for periods of longer than two years is likely to cause damage and encourage the formation of rust and scale in the system.

Before adding antifreeze to the system, check all hose connections. Antifreeze can leak through very minute openings.

The exact mixture of antifreeze to water which you should use depends on the relative weather conditions. The mixture should contain at least 50-percent antifreeze, but should never contain more than 70-percent antifreeze.

3   Thermostat - check and replacement

Warning: *The engine must be completely cool when this procedure is performed.*
Note: *Don't drive the vehicle without a thermostat! The engine may not reach the required temperature for the computer to go into closed loop operation and emissions and fuel economy will suffer.*

Check

Refer to illustration 3.5

1   Before condemning the thermostat, check the coolant level, drivebelt tension and temperature gauge (or light) operation.
2   If the engine takes a long time to warm up, the thermostat is probably stuck open. Replace the thermostat.
3   If the engine runs hot, check the temperature of the upper radiator hose. If the hose isn't hot, the thermostat is probably stuck shut. Replace the thermostat.
4   If the upper radiator hose is hot, it means the coolant is circulating and the thermostat is open. Refer to the Troubleshooting section for the cause of overheating.
5   If an engine has been overheated, you may find damage such as leaking head gaskets, scuffed pistons and warped or cracked cylinder heads. **Note:** *The same tool* **(see illustration)** *that many shops use to*

3.5 Special tools are available, referred to as block tester or block checker, to check for traces of hydrocarbons from combustion gases which would be found in the coolant if the head gasket has an internal leak

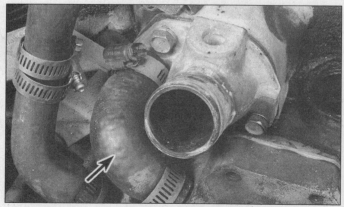

3.8 Disconnect the coolant bypass hose (arrow) if attached to the thermostat housing

3.9 Remove the vacuum line connection from the switching valve (arrow) - pull straight out or the plastic fittings on the sensor will break

3.10a Remove the bolts from the thermostat housing

check for combustion hydrocarbons in coolant, which indicates a head gasket leak, is available at local auto parts stores.

Replacement

Refer to illustrations 3.8, 3.9, 3.10a, 3.10b, 3.11 and 3.13

6   Drain coolant (about 1 gallon) from the radiator, until the coolant level is below the thermostat housing (See Chapter 1).

7   On some models of the OHV engines, it may be necessary to remove the distributor cap in order to remove the thermostat housing (see Chapter 5).

8   Disconnect the upper radiator hose from the thermostat housing. Disconnect the by-pass hose from the thermostat housing on OHV engines **(see illustration)**.

9   Some models may have a vacuum switching valve attached to the thermostat housing **(see illustration)**, disconnect the vacuum lines before removal. **Caution:** *The vacuum lines and the switching valve tend to become brittle with age and can easily be broken if trying to remove stuck lines. Either cut the rubber vacuum line or be extremely careful when removing the lines from the connections.*

10   Remove the bolts and lift the cover off **(see illustrations)**. It may be necessary to tap the cover with a soft-face hammer to break the gasket seal on a OHV engines. Remove the O-ring seal on a OHC engine.

11   Note how it's installed, then remove the thermostat **(see illustration)**. Be sure to use a replacement thermostat with the correct opening temperature (see this Chapter's Specifications).

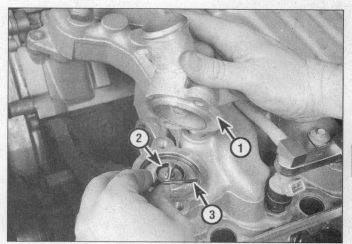

3.10b Once the bolts are removed, separate the housing from the intake manifold in order to remove the gasket and thermostat (OHC engine shown)

1	Thermostat housing cover	2	Thermostat
		3	O-ring seal

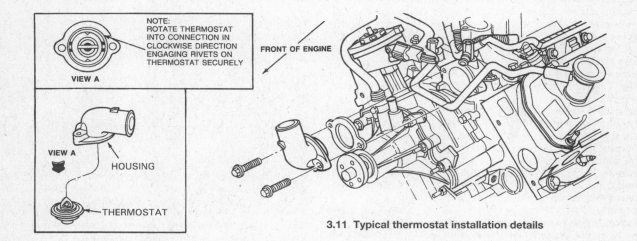

3.11 Typical thermostat installation details

3.13 When installing the thermostat pay special attention to the direction in which it's placed in the engine, the spring will go into the intake manifold

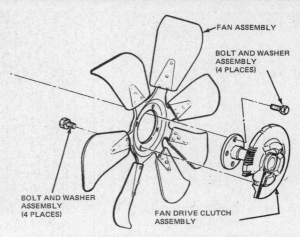

4.2 A typical clutch-equipped cooling fan assembly, the fan blades can be metal, as shown, or plastic

4.10a Remove the fan shroud bolts (arrows) and set the fan shroud back over the water pump

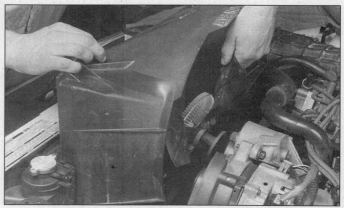

4.10b Lift the fan shroud out of the engine compartment

12   Use a scraper or putty knife to remove all traces of old gasket material and sealant from the mating surfaces. **Note:** *On OHC engines the gasket has been replaced by an O-ring* **(see illustration 3.10b)**. Make sure no gasket material falls into the coolant passages; it is a good idea to stuff a rag in the passage. Wipe the mating surfaces with a rag saturated with lacquer thinner or acetone.

13   Install the thermostat and make sure the correct end faces out **(see illustration)** - the spring is directed toward the engine.

14   On models that use a conventional paper gasket, apply a thin coat of RTV sealant to both sides of the new gasket and position it on

the engine side, over the thermostat, and make sure the gasket holes line up with the bolt holes in the housing. **Caution:** *No RTV sealant should be used on the later model O-ring seal.*

15   On models that use an O-ring seal, install the new O-ring into the intake manifold.

16   Carefully position the cover and install the bolts. Tighten them to the torque listed in this Chapter's Specifications - do not over tighten them or the cover may be cracked or distorted.

17   Reattach the radiator hose to the cover and tighten the clamp - now may be a good time to check and replace the hoses and clamps (see Chapter 1).

18   Refer to Chapter 1 and refill the system, then run the engine and check carefully for leaks.

19   Repeat steps 1 through 5 to be sure the repairs corrected the previous problem(s).

4   Engine cooling fan and clutch - check, removal and installation

Check

Refer to illustration 4.2

1   Disconnect the cable from the negative battery terminal.

2   The clutch-type fan uses rigid fan blades, metal or plastic, bolted to a fan clutch/hub assembly **(see illustration)**.

3   Check carefully for cracks, especially at the base of each blade. Blades cannot be replaced individually. Replace the fan blades immediately if any damage is found upon inspection.

4.11a The fan assembly is attached to the water pump with four bolts (arrow) on an OHV engine

4.11b Loosen the large hex-nut (arrow) on the fan clutch shaft (right hand thread) to remove the cooling fan from the water pump on a OHC engine

4.14a To separate the fan clutch from the fan blades on an OHC engine, remove the four attaching bolts (arrows)

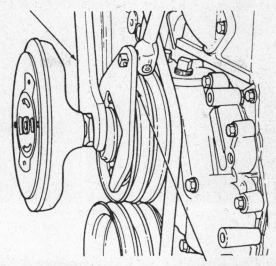

4.11c Loosening the large hex nut may require the use of special wrenches ((available at most auto parts stores) to keep the pulley from turning while loosening the nut with a open-end wrench

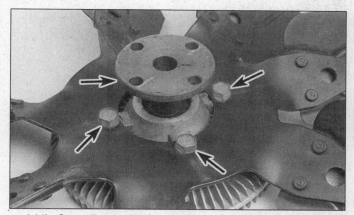

4.14b On earlier models, the fan blades are bolted to the fan clutch as shown (arrows)

4.14c When storing the fan clutch after removal, always place it with this side down, to prevent silicone fluid from leaking out or into the bearing

4   Symptoms of failure of the fan clutch include; continuous noisy operation, looseness or vibration and silicone fluid leaks.
5   Rock the fan back and forth by hand to check for excessive bearing play. If the blades wobble, replace the fan clutch.
6   With the engine cold, turn the blades by hand. The fan should turn freely.
7   Visually inspect for substantial fluid leakage from the clutch assembly, a deformed bi-metal spring or grease leakage from the cooling fan bearing. If any of these conditions exist, replace the fan clutch.
8   Turn the fan by hand. Some resistance should be felt. If the fan turns easily, replace the fan clutch.

Removal and installation

Refer to illustrations 4.10a, 4.10b, 4.11a, 4.11b, 4.11c, 4.14a, 4.14b and 4.14c

9   On later models, separate the lower radiator hose from the fastener along the bottom of the radiator, if routed this way.
10   Remove the fan shroud bolts and set the fan shroud back over the water pump **(see illustration)**. This should give enough room to remove the fan and clutch assembly. If more room is needed, once the fan has been unbolted from water pump, it may be necessary to remove the fan clutch assembly together with the shroud **(see illustration)**.
11   Loosen the fan clutch-to-water pump bolts (OHV engines) or the large hex-nut on the fan clutch shaft (OHC engines) **(see illustrations)**.
12   Loosen or remove the drivebelts from the water pump pulley on OHV engines (see Chapter 1).
13   Unbolt the fan assembly and detach it from the water pump.
14   The fan clutch can be unbolted from the fan blade assembly for replacement **(see illustrations)**. **Caution:** *To prevent silicone fluid from draining from the clutch assembly into the fan drive bearing and ruining the lubricant, DON'T place the drive unit in a position with the rear of the shaft pointing down* **(see illustration)**.
15   Installation is the reverse of removal.

5.2   Pump the cooling system tester until pressure equals the rating on the radiator cap (usually about 16 psi), then look for leaks and watch the gauge on the tester for a pressure drop

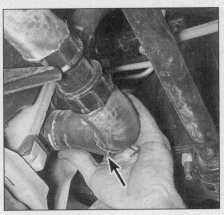

5.3   When removing the hoses, use pliers to squeeze the tangs together and slide the clamp away from the end of the hose (arrow), then pull the hose from the radiator connection (OHC engine shown)

5.4   Use a flare-nut wrench on the fluid line (arrows) and a back up wrench at the radiator fitting, as shown, to prevent damage to the transmission cooler lines when removing them from the radiator

5   Radiator and coolant reservoir tank - removal and installation

Warning: *The engine must be completely cool when this procedure is performed.*

Removal

Refer to illustrations 5.2, 5.3, 5.4, 5.5 and 5.8

1   Disconnect the cable from the negative battery terminal.

2   If a radiator or cooling system leak is suspected, pressure test the system to determine the exact location of the leak. A cooling system pressure tester **(see illustration)** is available at most local auto parts stores. **Note:** *Don't forget to check the radiator cap. It is one of the most commonly replaced (and overlooked) parts of the cooling system. See the specifications at the beginning of this Chapter.*

3   Drain the cooling system as described in Chapter 1, then disconnect the overflow hose, upper radiator hose and lower radiator hose from the radiator **(see illustration)**.

4   If equipped with an automatic transmission or engine oil cooler, remove the cooler lines from the radiator **(see illustration)** - be careful not to damage the lines or fittings. Plug the ends of the disconnected

lines to prevent leakage and stop dirt from entering the system. Have a drip pan ready to catch any spills.

5   Remove the radiator mounting bolts **(see illustration)**.

6   Unbolt the fan shroud and slip it back over the fan.

7   Lift the radiator from the engine compartment. Take care not to contact the fan blades.

8   Prior to installation of the radiator, replace any damaged rubber mounts **(see illustration)**, hose clamps and radiator hoses.

Installation

9   Radiator installation is the reverse of removal. When installing the radiator, make sure it seats properly in the lower saddles and that the rubber mounts are intact **(see illustration 5.8)**.

10   After installation, fill the system with the proper mixture of antifreeze, and also check the automatic transmission fluid level.

Coolant reservoir tank

Removal and installation

Refer to illustration 5.11

11   Remove the coolant overflow hoses from the reservoir **(see illustration)**.

12   Remove the bolts and detach the reservoir.

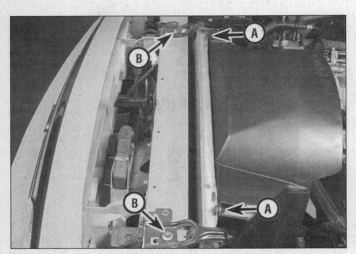

5.5   The cooling fan shroud is held in place by two bolts (A) as is the radiator support bracket (B). Both the shroud and the bracket must be removed before the radiator can be removed

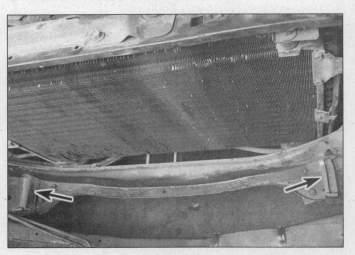

5.8   Check to make sure that the rubber mounts (arrows) are in place and in good shape, if they're beginning to deteriorate, now is the time to replace them

5.11 Locate the two hoses attached to the coolant reservoir bottle (arrows) and disconnect them

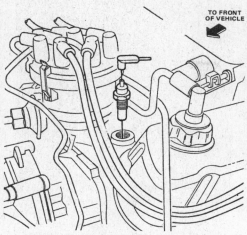

6.1a The coolant temperature sending unit, on OHV engines, is located at the front of the intake manifold near the distributor

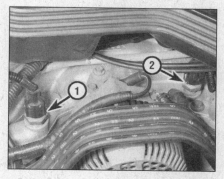

6.1b On the OHC engine, the coolant temperature sending unit is one of two at the front of the intake manifold, be sure to select the correct one for the repair procedure

1 *Coolant temperature sending unit (gauge)*
2 *Coolant temperature sensor (computer)*

13 Prior to installation make sure the reservoir is clean and free of debris which could be drawn into the radiator (wash it with soap and water if necessary).
14 Installation is the reverse of removal.

6 Coolant temperature sending unit - check and replacement

Refer to illustrations 6.1a and 6.1b
Warning: *Wait until the engine is completely cool before beginning this procedure.*

Check

1 The coolant temperature indicator system is composed of a light or temperature gauge mounted in the dash and a coolant temperature sending unit mounted on the engine **(see illustration)**. Some vehicles have more than one sending unit **(see illustration)**, but only one is used for the indicator system and the other is used to send engine temperature information to the computer.
2 If an overheating indication occurs, check the coolant level in the system. Make sure the wiring between the light or gauge and the sending unit is secure and all fuses are intact.
3 When the ignition switch is turned on and the starter motor is turning, the indicator light (if equipped) should glow (bulb check).
4 If the light is not on, the bulb may be burned out, the ignition switch may be faulty or the circuit may be open. Test the circuit by grounding the wire to the sending unit while the ignition is on (engine NOT running for safety). If the gauge deflects full scale or the light comes on, replace the sending unit.
5 As soon as the engine starts, the light should go out and remain out unless the engine overheats. Failure of the light to go out may be due to a grounded wire between the light and the sending unit, a defective sending unit or a faulty ignition switch. Also, check the coolant to make sure it's of the proper type and mixture.

Replacement

6 If the sending unit must be replaced, disconnect the electrical connector and simply unscrew the sensor from the engine and install the replacement. **Caution:** *The sending unit is made up of metal and plastic and is fragile. Use care when removing not to crack the unit.* Use sealant on the threads. Make sure the engine is cool before removing the defective sending unit. There will be some coolant loss as the unit is removed, so be prepared to catch it. Check the coolant level after the replacement unit has been installed.

7 Water pump - check

Refer to illustrations 7.3 and 7.5
1 Water pump failure can cause overheating and serious damage to the engine. There are three ways to check the operation of the water pump while it's installed on the engine. If any one of the three following quick checks indicates water pump problems, it should be replaced immediately.
2 Start the engine and warm it up to normal operating temperature. Squeeze the upper radiator hose. If the water pump is working properly, you should feel a pressure surge as the hose is released.
3 A seal protects the water pump impeller shaft bearing from contamination by engine coolant. If this seal fails, a weep hole in the water pump snout will leak coolant **(see illustration)** (an inspection mirror can be used to look at the underside of the pump if the hole isn't on top). If the weep hole is leaking, shaft bearing failure will follow. Replace the water pump immediately.
4 Besides contamination by coolant after a seal failure, the water pump impeller shaft bearing can also prematurely wear out. If a noise is coming from the water pump during engine operation, the shaft bearing has failed - replace the water pump immediately. **Note:** *Do not confuse drivebelt noise with bearing noise. Loose or glazed drivebelts may emit a high-pitched squealing noise.*
5 To identify excessive bearing wear before the bearing actually fails, grasp the water pump pulley and try to force it up-and-down or

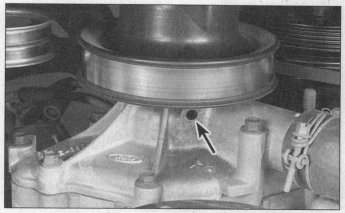

7.3 If there's coolant leaking from the weep hole (arrow) the water pump should be replaced

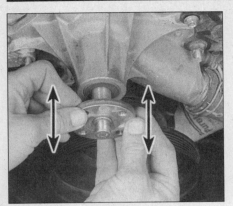

7.5 Rock the shaft back and forth to check for play and the need for replacement

8.8 Loosen the clamps, then twist the hoses (arrows) to detach them from the pump fittings

8.9a On OHV engines, after the belt-driven accessory brackets have been removed, remove the hoses and the water pump retaining bolts (note the bolts that have an additional mounting stud for accessory brackets)

from side-to-side **(see illustration)**. If the pulley can be moved either horizontally or vertically, the bearing is nearing the end of its service life. Replace the water pump.

8   Water pump - removal and installation

Removal

Refer to illustrations 8.8, 8.9a, 8.9b and 8.9c
1   Disconnect the cable from the negative battery terminal.
2   With the engine cold, drain the cooling system (see Chapter 1).
3   Remove the fan shroud and the fan assembly (see Section 4).
4   Remove the drivebelt(s) (see Chapter 1) and remove the water pump pulley.
5   On OHV engines, if the power steering pump bracket is retained at the water pump, the power steering pump should be completely removed and laid to one side to facilitate removal of the bracket.
6   On OHV engines equipped with air conditioning, remove the idler pulley and bracket assembly.
7   Remove any accessory brackets that attach to the water pump.
8   On OHV engines, remove the lower radiator hose, the heater hose and the by-pass hose from the water pump **(see illustration)**. **Note:** *The heater and bypass hoses of models and years covered by this manual don't always attach directly to the water pump. Disconnect the hose(s) only if necessary to remove the pump.*
9   On all engines, remove the water pump retaining bolts and

remove the water pump. On OHV engines, take note of the installed positions of the various length bolts and bolts that have mounting studs **(see illustrations)** for accessory mounting.

Installation

Refer to illustrations 8.10, 8.11a, 8.11b and 8.14
10   Before installation, remove and clean all gasket or sealant material from the water pump, cylinder front cover, or cylinder block **(see illustration)**.
11   On OHC engines, inspect the O-ring and sealing surface of the water pump housing in the block for dirt and/or debris **(see illustrations)**. Clean thoroughly before reassembly. **Note:** *On the OHC engine, it is recommended that the O-ring be replaced any time the water pump is removed.*
12   On OHV engines, position new gaskets on the water pump and coat them on both sides with RTV sealant. On OHC engines, lubricate a new O-ring seal with a clean antifreeze and install it to the water pump.
13   On OHV engine water pumps, it may be necessary to transfer some hose ports and/or fittings from the old pump if you are replacing it with a new one.
14   On OHV engine water pumps, there is a plate between the water pump and front cover **(see illustration)**. Some early styles are not bolted to the water pump, while others have been bolted to the pump. In either case be sure to replace the gaskets (or reseal) on both sides of the plate during installation. **Caution:** *If the old water pump is being reused, remove the plate and replace the gasket or it will leak coolant*

8.9b On OHC engines, remove the four bolts (arrows) . . .

8.9c . . . and remove the water pump from out of the engine block

8.10 Remove all traces of old gasket material, being careful not to gouge the aluminum housing

8.11a On OHC engines, install a new O-ring seal on the water pump

8.11b Inspect the sealing surface (arrow) in the pump cavity for dirt or signs of pitting

8.14 On engines so equipped, don't forget to replace the gaskets and install this plate before placing the water pump on the timing chain cover

into the timing chain cover and oil pan.

15   Install the water pump and tighten the bolts to the torque listed in this Chapter's Specifications.

16   On OHV engines, install the lower radiator hose, heater hose and by-pass hose to the water pump **(see illustration 8.8)**. Replace the hose clamps with new, if necessary.

17   Install the remaining components to the water pump and engine in the reverse order of removal.

18   Fill the cooling system with the proper coolant mixture.

19   Start the engine and make sure there are no leaks. Check the level frequently during the first few weeks of operation to ensure there are no leaks and that the level in the system is stable.

---

9   Heater and air conditioning blower motor and circuit - check and switch replacement

---

Check

1   Check the fuse and all connections in the circuit for looseness and corrosion. Make sure the battery is fully charged.

2   With the transmission in Park, the parking brake securely set, turn the ignition switch to the run position. It isn't necessary to start the vehicle.

3   Connect a voltmeter to the blower motor connector **(see illustration 10.1a or 10.1b)**.

4   Move the blower switch through each of its positions and note the voltage readings. Changes in voltage indicates that the motor speeds will also vary as the switch is moved to the different positions.

Thermal limiter resistor assembly

Refer to illustrations 9.5 and 9.6

5   The thermal limiter relay assembly is located on the evaporator case in the engine compartment **(see illustration)**. There are three resistance elements mounted on the resistor board to provide four blower speeds. **Note:** *The high blower setting bypasses the resistors to give the fourth blower speed.*

6   Remove the thermal resistor relay from the heater case mounting location and visually check for damage. Check the resistor block for continuity between all terminals. A thermal limiter resistor is integrated into the circuits to prevent heat damage to the evaporator case assembly **(see illustration)**. If the thermal limiter circuit has been opened as a result of excessive heat, it should be replaced only with the identical replacement part. A standard limiter cannot be used.

Blower motor operates at only one speed

Refer to illustration 9.9

7   If there is voltage, but the blower motor does not operate connect a jumper wire between the motor ground terminal (or case) and a good chassis ground. Connect a fused jumper wire between the battery positive terminal and the positive terminal on the motor. If the motor now works, remove the jumper wire, and if the motor stops working when the ground wire is removed, check for bad ground and re-test. If the motor still doesn't work, the blower motor is probably faulty.

8   If there's no voltage at the motor, remove the resistor block connector and check it for voltage. If there's voltage at any of the connector terminals, check the resistor block and the wiring between the resistor block and the motor for an open or short.

9   If there's no voltage at any of the terminals in the resistor block

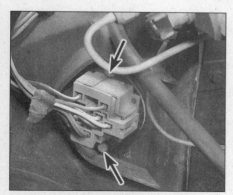

9.5 Remove the two mounting screws (arrows) and remove the blower motor resistor from the heater/air-conditioning case

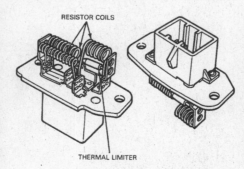

9.6 Typical blower motor resistor assembly

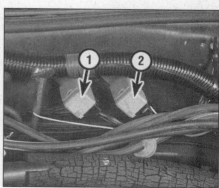

9.9 Check for power at the high blower relay (1) or the range relay (2) (if equipped), if no power is found at the blower resistor

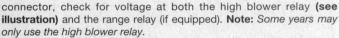

10.1a Unplug the electrical connector at the blower motor (arrow), shown here on an early model . . .

10.1b . . .or as shown here on a later model, and using a voltmeter, test for power at the motor

connector, check for voltage at both the high blower relay **(see illustration)** and the range relay (if equipped). **Note:** *Some years may only use the high blower relay.*

10   If there's no voltage to the high blower relay (or range relay if equipped) remove the heater control panel (if necessary) and, with the ignition ON, check for voltage at the connector for the blower motor switch.

11   If there's no voltage, check the wiring between the fuse panel and the switch for an open or a short.

12   If there's voltage, connect one end of a jumper wire to the terminal of the switch connector with voltage. Connect the other end of the jumper to each of the terminals that carry voltage to the resistor block. If the motor now operates normally, replace the switch.

Blower motor doesn't operate at any speed

13   Again, check the fuse, if not already done.

14   With the ignition and blower motor switch on, check for voltage at the motor positive connector. If there's no voltage, check the wiring between the fuse panel and the motor for an open or short. If there's voltage, test the motor, as described in step 5.

15   If the motor works when tested, remove the heater control panel and use a jumper wire to ground each terminal of the blower motor switch connector. Make sure the ignition switch is on. If the motor now

works, check for a bad ground at the switch. If the switch ground is good, replace the switch.

Switch replacement

16   Remove the control assembly from the instrument panel(see Section 11).

17   Remove the screw, from the beneath the assembly, that holds the switch to the main assembly and remove the switch.

---

10   Heater blower motor - removal and installation

Removal (all except 1982 through 1987 Continental and 1984 through 1992 Mark VII)

Refer to illustrations 10.1a, 10.1b and 10.3

1   Disconnect the blower motor electrical connector from the motor **(see illustrations)**.

2   Remove the cooling tube from the underside of the blower motor.

3   Remove the retaining screws from the blower motor mounting plate **(see illustration)**.

4   Turn the blower motor slightly to the right so that the bottom edge

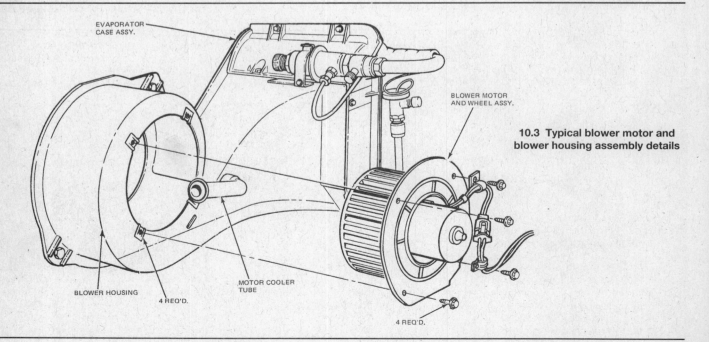

EVAPORATOR CASE ASSY.

BLOWER MOTOR AND WHEEL ASSY.

10.3 Typical blower motor and blower housing assembly details

BLOWER HOUSING
4 REQ'D.

MOTOR COOLER TUBE

4 REQ'D.

10.5 Remove the retaining clip (arrow)

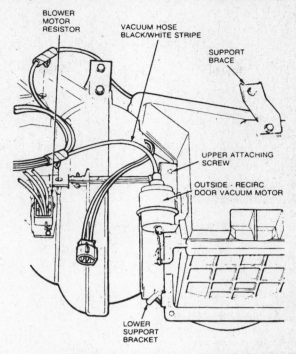

10.9 Blower housing components

of the mounting plate aligns with the contour of the wheel well splash panel. While still in the blower housing, lift the motor assembly up and maneuver it out of the heater housing assembly.

Installation

Refer to illustration 10.5

5   Position the motor and fan assembly so that the bottom edge (the straight portion) follows the contour of the wheel well splash panel. **Note:** *If the blower motor is being replaced, the fan wheel should be transferred to the new motor at this time* **(see illustration)**. *It is attached to the blower motor shaft with a push nut. Grasp the nut with a pliers and pull it off or get a small screw driver under it and pry it off, being careful not to crack the push nut. To reinstall the nut, simply push it on to the shaft.* Maneuver the assembly past the wheel well splash panel and into the top portion of the housing opening, then down into position.

6   The remainder of the installation is the reverse of removal.

Removal - 1982 through 1987 Continental and 1984 through 1992 Mark VII

Refer to illustrations 10.9, 10.15a and 10.15b

7   Disconnect the negative battery cable.

8   Remove the glove compartment liner by squeezing the sides

together and disengaging the tabs (see Chapter 11).

9   Working through the glove compartment opening, disconnect the hose from the recirculation door vacuum motor **(see illustration)**.

10   Disconnect the blower motor electrical connector by depressing the locking tabs and pulling the connector off.

11   Remove the support brace at the top of the air inlet duct.

12   Unbolt and remove the lower right side cowl trim panel from the instrument panel.

13   Remove the nut which connects the evaporator case to the lower support brace.

14   Remove the screw which attaches the inlet duct to the heater assembly.

15   Separate the air duct and blower case from the heater housing

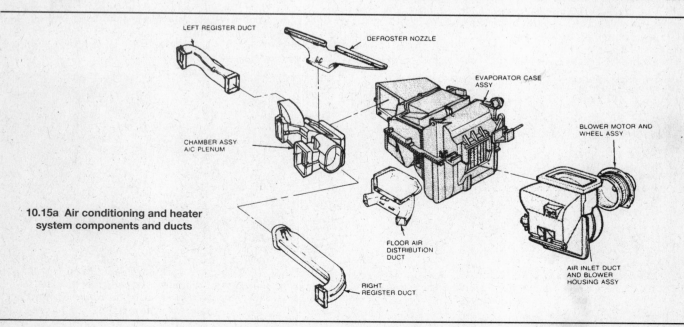

10.15a Air conditioning and heater system components and ducts

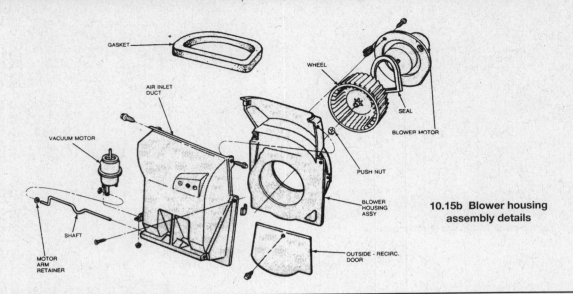

**10.15b Blower housing
assembly details**

and remove it **(see illustrations)**.

16   Remove the blower motor from the housing. Pull the motor and mounting plate out as a unit.

17   If the motor is being replaced, transfer the fan to the new motor by removing the hub clamp and pulling the fan off the shaft.

Installation

Note: *If the blower motor is being replaced, the fan wheel should be transferred to the new motor at this time. It is attached to the blower motor shaft with a push nut. Grasp the nut with a pliers and pull it off or get a small screw driver under it and pry it off, being careful not to crack the push nut. To reinstall the nut, simply push it on to the shaft.*

18   Tape the blower motor power lead to the air intake duct to keep the wire away from the blower outlet during installation.

19   Position the blower motor and fan assembly into the blower housing with the flat side of the flange near the blower outlet. Install the retaining screws. Ensure the blower wire is routed to the passenger side of the evaporator case.

20   Install the air intake duct and the blower housing to the evaporator case.

21   Hold the outside-recirculation door open and rotate the blower wheel to ensure it operates freely. If an interference exists, remove the blower motor and correct the condition.

22   Reconnect the blower motor electrical connector.

23   Install the air inlet duct-to-cowl support brace attaching screw.

24   Connect the vacuum hose to the vacuum motor.

25   Install the glove compartment liner and door.

26   Install the lower right side instrument panel bolt.

27   Reinstall the lower right cowl trim and connect the battery cable.

11   Heater and air conditioning control assembly - removal and installation

Refer to illustrations 11.3, 11.4, 11.5a and 11.5b

1   Disconnect the cable from the negative battery terminal. **Warning:** *Some models have airbags. Always disconnect the negative battery cable, then the positive battery cable and wait 2 minutes before working in the vicinity of the impact sensors, steering column or instrument panel to avoid the possibility of accidental deployment of the airbag, which could cause personal injury (see Chapter 12).*

2   Remove the instrument panel trim pieces necessary to gain access to the heater and air conditioning control assembly (see Chapter 11).

3   Remove the screws retaining the heater and air conditioning control assembly to the dash **(see illustration)**.

4   Pull the control out of the instrument panel far enough to remove the control cables (if equipped) and the vacuum and electrical connectors **(see illustration)**.

**11.3 After the trim is removed, remove the four control assembly
retaining screws (arrows)**

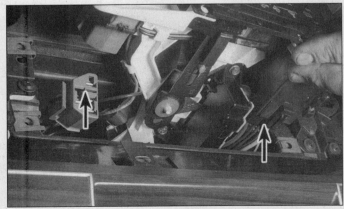

**11.4 Carefully pull the control assembly out of the dash far
enough to disconnect the cables and the electrical and vacuum
connections (arrows)**

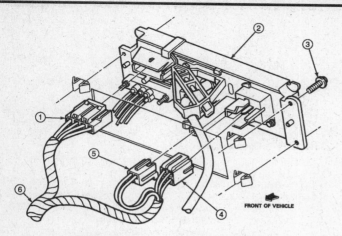

11.5a Typical heater control assembly details

1   To heater mode switch   5   To air conditioner
2   Control assembly   illumination
3   Screw   6   Wiring assembly
4   To air conditioner blower
    switch

5   Disconnect the electrical connectors to the control assembly and blower switch. Remove the retainers securing the vacuum harness to the control assembly and remove the harness as an assembly from the vacuum selector valve (see illustrations).
6   Installation is the reverse of the removal procedure.

12 Heater core - removal and installation

Warning : The air conditioning system is under high pressure. DO NOT loosen any fittings or remove any components until after the system has been discharged. Air conditioning refrigerant should be properly discharged into an EPA-approved container at a dealer service department or an automotive air conditioning repair facility. Always wear eye protection when disconnecting air conditioning system fittings.

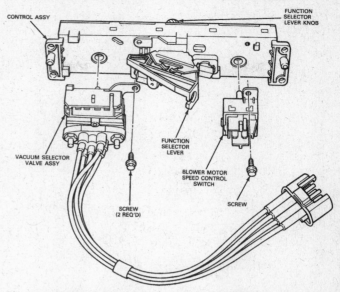

11.5b Typical heater control assembly vacuum harness connection details

Note: The following procedures require the removal of several interior trim parts. Refer to Chapter 11 for specific removal and installation procedures.

Removal - 1981 and later Town Car
Refer to illustrations 12.2a, 12.2b and 12.21
1   Disconnect the cable from the negative battery terminal.
Warning: Some models have airbags. Always disconnect the negative battery cable, then the positive battery cable and wait 2 minutes before working in the vicinity of the impact sensors, steering column or instrument panel to avoid the possibility of accidental deployment of the airbag, which could cause personal injury (see Chapter 12).
2   Drain the cooling system and disconnect the heater hoses from

3

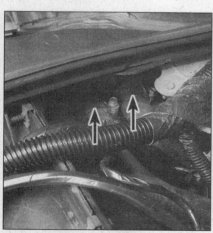

12.2a Loosen the clamps and remove the heater hoses from the heater core inlet and outlet pipes (arrows)

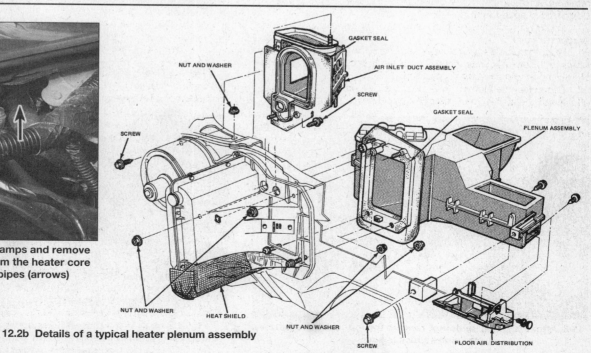

12.2b Details of a typical heater plenum assembly

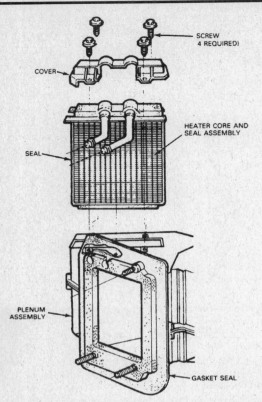

SCREW
4 REQUIRED)

COVER

HEATER CORE AND
SEAL ASSEMBLY

SEAL

PLENUM
ASSEMBLY

GASKET SEAL

12.21 Remove the four screws and retaining cover, then lift the heater core from the plenum assembly

the heater core inlet and outlet tubes **(see illustrations)**.

3   The heater core is located in the plenum assembly, which is in the passenger compartment under the instrument panel. Plug the heater core tubes to avoid spilling any coolant during the plenum removal.

4   Remove three nuts located below the windshield wiper motor that hold the left end of the plenum to the firewall.

5   Remove the nut holding the upper left side corner of the evaporator case to the firewall.

6   Disconnect the two vacuum supply hoses from the vacuum source. Push the grommet and the vacuum supply hose into the passenger compartment.

7   Remove the instrument panel trim moldings and remove the left side and right side lower instrument trim panel insulators. On 1987 and earlier models, remove the screws from around the perimeter of the dash pad, including the two screws in each defroster outlet and the screws on each end, and remove the pad.

8   On 1988 and later models, remove the upper and lower steering column covers, disconnect the PRNDL cable from the column and remove the reinforcement brace from under the steering column.

9   On 1988 and later models, position the wheels in the straight ahead position and remove the nuts retaining the steering column to the instrument panel. Lower the steering column as far as possible and support it securely.

10   Open the glove compartment door, depress the tabs and lower the door. Reaching through the left side of the glove compartment opening, remove the bolts retaining the instrument panel to the dash brace. Close the glove compartment door.

11   Loosen both the left and right side door sill plates and remove both left and right side cowl trim panels. Remove the bolts on each end of the instrument panel retaining the instrument panel to the A-pillars.

12   Remove the defroster grille, support the instrument panel and remove the instrument panel to cowl retaining screws.

13   Pull the instrument panel back as far as possible without disconnecting any wiring harnesses electrical connectors.

14   Remove the cross body brace and disconnect the wiring harness from the temperature blend door actuator and disconnect the temperature control sensor tube from the evaporator case connector.

15   Disconnect the vacuum jumper harness at the multiple vacuum connector near the floor air distribution duct.

16   Disconnect the vacuum hose from the outside-recirculation door vacuum motor **(see illustration 10.9)**.

17   Remove the plastic push fastener retaining the floor air distribution duct to the left end of the plenum.

18   Remove the left side screw and loosen the right side screw on the rear of the plenum and remove the floor air distribution duct.

19   Remove two nuts from the two studs along the lower edge of the plenum.

20   Carefully move the plenum rearward to allow the heater core tubes and the stud at the top of the plenum to clear the holes in the dash panel. Remove the plenum from the vehicle by rotating the top of the plenum forward, down and out from under the instrument panel. Carefully pull the lower edge of instrument panel as necessary while rolling the plenum from behind the instrument panel.

21   Remove the four retaining screws from the heater core cover and remove the cover to expose the heater core **(see illustration)**. Then pull the heater core and seal from the plenum assembly.

Installation

22   Route the vacuum supply hose through the dash panel and seat the grommet in the opening.

23   Install the new heater core in the plenum. Position the plenum under the instrument panel with the register duct opening up and the heater core tubes down. Rotate the plenum up behind the instrument panel and position the plenum to the dash panel. Insert the heater core tubes and mounting studs through their respective holes in the dash panel and the evaporator case.

24   The remainder of the installation is the reverse of removal.

Removal - 1982 through 1987 Continental and 1984 through 1992 Mark VII

Refer to illustration 12.33

25   If your vehicle has air conditioning, take it to a dealer service department or automotive air conditioning repair facility and have the refrigerant gas discharged.

26   Disconnect the cable from the negative battery terminal. Drain the cooling system (see Chapter 1).

27   Remove the instrument panel (see Chapter 11).

28   On air conditioning equipped vehicles, disconnect the refrigerant lines which go through the firewall. Use a backup wrench to prevent twisting the tubing. Cap all open ends.

29   Disconnect the heater hoses going through the firewall. Cap all open ends.

30   Remove the screw attaching the air inlet duct and blower housing assembly support brace to the cowl top panel.

31   Disconnect the black vacuum supply hose from the inline vacuum check valve in the engine compartment.

32   Disconnect the blower motor wiring.

33   Working under the hood, remove the two nuts retaining the evaporator case to the dash panel **(see illustration)**.

34   In the passenger compartment, remove the screw attaching the evaporator case support bracket to the cowl top panel.

35   Remove the nut retaining the bracket below the evaporator case to the dash panel.

36   Carefully pull the evaporator case away from the dash panel and remove the evaporator case assembly from the vehicle.

37   Remove the five heater core access cover screws and detach the access cover **(see illustration 12.33)**.

38   Lift the heater core and seals from the evaporator case.

39   Remove the seal from the evaporator case.

Installation

40   Install the heater core tube seal on the heater core tubes, the thin seal first.

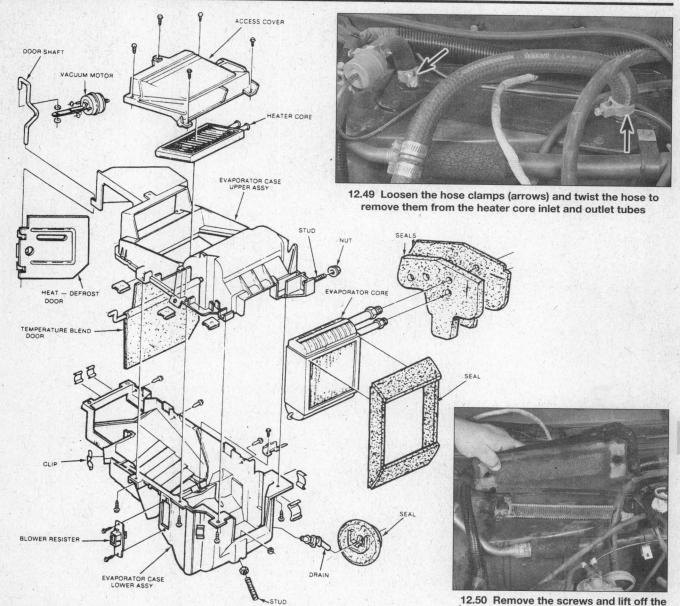

12.49 Loosen the hose clamps (arrows) and twist the hose to remove them from the heater core inlet and outlet tubes

12.33 Exploded view of heater/air conditioning evaporator case (1982 through 1987 Continental and 1984 through 1992 Mark series vehicles)

12.50 Remove the screws and lift off the cover and gasket from the evaporator case assembly

41   Install the heater core in the evaporator case with the seals on the outside of the case.
42   Position the heater core access cover on the evaporator case. Install the four attaching screws.
43   Install the evaporator case assembly in the vehicle in the reverse order of removal.
44   Refill the cooling system and check for leaks.
45   Return the vehicle to the shop which discharged the air conditioning for evacuating, recharging and leak testing the system. Ford recommends that the air conditioner accumulator be replaced before recharging the system—consult your dealer.

Removal - 1973 through 1979 Continental and Mark series

Refer to illustrations 12.49 and 12.50
46   The heater core can be removed without discharging the air conditioning system.

47   Disconnect the cable from the negative battery terminal.
48   Drain the cooling system (see Chapter 1).
49   Disconnect the heater hoses from the heater core tubes **(see illustration)**.
50   Remove the screws from the heater core cover and remove the cover and gasket **(see illustration)**.
51   Lift out the heater core and the lower mounting gasket.

Installation

52   Installation is the reverse of the removal procedure. **Note:** *Replace the lower gasket if it has deteriorated and no longer insulates the heater core from the housing.*

Removal - 1970 through 1972 Continental and Mark series

Refer to illustration 12.60
53   Disconnect the cable from the negative battery terminal.

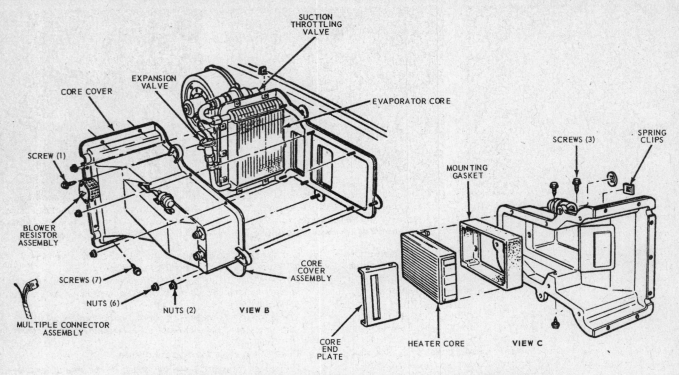

12.60 Exploded view of the early model evaporator/heater case and heater core

54   Drain the cooling system (see Chapter 1).
55   Remove the multiple connector from the blower resistor (see Section 9).
56   Disconnect the vacuum junction valve from the dash panel and move the valve and vacuum hoses away from the case.
57   Disconnect the speed control servo and bracket assembly from the dash panel (if equipped) and move it away from the case.
58   Disconnect the heater hoses from the heater core, and the hose support bracket from the case. Move the hoses and water valve away from the heater case.
59   Disconnect the vacuum hose from the restrictor air door vacuum motor.
60   Remove the case cover-to-case flange attaching screws **(see illustration)**.
61   Remove the case cover-to-back plate stud nuts.
62   Remove the upper case-to-dash panel mounting screw from the case.
63   Remove the case-to-dash panel mounting stud nuts; one on the inboard mounting flange and the one below the case on the lower flange.
64   Carefully move the heater core cover assembly forward to clear the mounting studs and lift it up and out of the vehicle.
65   Remove the two springs clips from the heater core tubes.
66   Remove the end plate and remove the heater core and gasket from the cover. Remove the gasket from the core.

Installation

67   Assemble the heater core and gasket and position them in the heater core cover. Install the end plate.
68   Install the two spring clips over the heater core tubes.
69   Carefully position the heater core cover assembly on the mounting studs. The rest of the installation is the reverse of the removal procedure.
70   Fill the cooling system with coolant, start the engine and check for heater system leaks.

13   Heater control valve and thermal blower lockout switch - replacement

Note: *Not all model years are equipped with a heater control valve.*

Check

Refer to illustrations 13.1 and 13.6

1   The heater control valve (hot water valve) is located in the inlet heater hose to the heater core. The valve controls the flow of engine coolant through the heater core by opening or closing to varying degrees. The amount of valve opening is controlled by vacuum applied to the control unit. Locate the heater control valve **(see illustration)**.
2   Manually move the lever to be certain that it isn't stuck and has a full range of movement from fully open to fully closed.
3   If the valve operates manually, next check the vacuum source to the valve **(see illustration 13.1)**.
4   Set the parking brake and start the engine.
5   Disconnect the vacuum line at the valve **(see illustration 13.1)** and while operating the heater control, check for vacuum at the hose. If vacuum is present, next check the vacuum valve. If no vacuum is present repair the vacuum source where necessary.
6   With a hand vacuum pump, apply vacuum to the valve and watch for movement **(see illustration)**. If no movement is seen replace the valve.

Thermal blower lockout switch
Check

Refer to illustration 13.7

7   On computer controlled vehicles, the thermal blower lockout switch is located in the inlet heater hose **(see illustration)**, just as is the heater control valve. **Note:** *The thermal blower lockout switch doesn't control coolant flow, it works as a coolant temperature sensor/switch for the computer controlled automatic heater/air conditioning system. The switch only allows blower operation and*

13.1 The heater control valve assembly (arrow) is located in the heater inlet hose

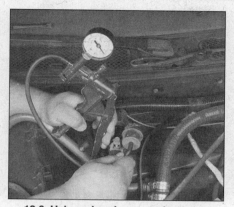
13.6 Using a hand operated vacuum pump at the valve, check for lever movement when vacuum is applied

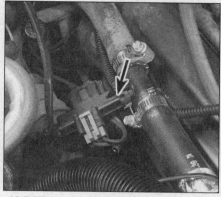
13.7 The thermal blower lockout (arrow) is also located in the heater inlet hose on later model vehicles

opening of the outside-recirculation door to outside air, based upon coolant temperature. When coolant temperature reaches 120-degrees F, the electrical portion of the switch closes (allowing blower operation) and the vacuum valve opens (allowing outside-recirculation door to open to outside air).

8   To check for a faulty thermal blower lockout switch, remove the connector from the switch and check for continuity through switch with the engine warm.

9   Check the condition of the vacuum lines and electrical connections before and after the switch. Repair and/or replace as necessary.

Replacement - all

10   When removing the control valve or the thermal blower lockout switch, a small amount of coolant may be lost. To minimize the amount of coolant lost, clamp off the heater hoses on either side of the control valve.

11   Loosen the hose clamps and slide them up the hoses, away from the valve.

12   Separate the hoses from both sides of the valve and replace the valve.

13   Place the hose clamps back into position and tighten the hose clamps on the heater hoses.

14   Check the operation of the heater system.

14 Air conditioning and heating system - check and maintenance

Warning : *The air conditioning system is under high pressure. DO NOT loosen any fittings or remove any components until after the system has been discharged. Air conditioning refrigerant should be properly discharged into an EPA-approved container at a dealer service department or an automotive air conditioning repair facility. Always wear eye protection when disconnecting air conditioning system fittings.*

Note: *The 1993 and earlier air conditioning systems use R-12 refrigerant. 1994 and later models, the refrigerant system was changed to use the new, "environmentally friendly", R-134a refrigerant. Each system uses similar components and locations but components are NOT interchangeable. All discharging of refrigerant, for part replacement or maintenance, should be done by an approved air conditioning facility with the proper refrigerant recovery equipment.*

1   The following maintenance steps should be performed on a regular basis to ensure that the air conditioning system continues to operate at peak efficiency.

a) *Check the tension of the drivebelt and adjust if necessary (see Chapter 1).*

b) *Check the condition of the hoses. Look for cracks, hardening and deterioration.* **Warning:** *Do not replace air conditioning hoses*

until the system has been discharged by a dealer service department or air conditioning repair facility.

c) *Check the fins of the condenser for leaves, bugs and other foreign material. A soft brush and compressed air can be used to remove them.*

d) *Check the wire harness for correct routing, broken wires, damaged insulation, etc. Make sure the harness connections are clean and tight.*

e) *Maintain the correct refrigerant charge.*

2   The system should be run for about 10 minutes at least once a month. This is particularly important during the winter months because long-term non-use can cause hardening of the internal seals.

3   Because of the complexity of the air conditioning system and the special equipment required to effectively work on it, accurate troubleshooting of the system should be left to a professional technician. One probable cause for poor cooling that can be determined by the home mechanic is low refrigerant charge. Should the system lose its cooling ability, the following procedure will help you pinpoint the cause.

Check

4   Warm the engine up to normal operating temperature.

5   Place the air conditioning temperature selector at the coldest setting and put the blower at the highest setting. Open the doors (to make sure the air conditioning system doesn't cycle off as soon as it cools the passenger compartment).

6   With the compressor engaged - the clutch will make an audible click and the center of the clutch will rotate - inspect the sight glass, if equipped. If the refrigerant looks foamy, it's low. Charge the system as described later in this Section. If the refrigerant appears clear, the system is properly charged.

Adding refrigerant

Note: *Because of recent Federal regulations proposed by the Environmental Protection Agency, 14-ounce cans of R-12 refrigerant, or R-134a refrigerant on 1993 and later vehicles, may not be available in your area. If this is the case, it will be necessary to take the vehicle to a licensed air conditioning technician for charging. If you decide to add refrigerant from one of the large 30 lb. cans available, you will need a set of manifold gauges, all the necessary fittings, adapters and hoses to hook everything up and a copy of Haynes Automotive Heating and Air Conditioning manual before tackling this job.*

15 Air conditioning compressor - removal and installation

Warning: *The air conditioning system is under high pressure. DO NOT loosen any fittings or remove any components until after the system has been discharged. Air conditioning refrigerant should be properly*

3

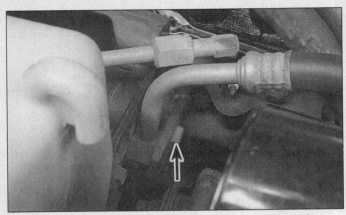

15.3a Remove the bolt (arrow) and fitting block from the compressor or . . .

15.3b . . .remove the lines from the manifold if the refrigerant lines are threaded fittings

discharged into an EPA-approved container at a dealer service department or an automotive air conditioning repair facility. Always wear eye protection when disconnecting air conditioning system fittings.

Removal

Refer to illustrations 15.3a, 15.3b, 15.3c, 15.4, 15.5a, 15.5b, and 15.5c

Caution: *Whenever a compressor is replaced, it will be necessary to replace the accumulator/drier or the receiver /drier with fixed orifice, whichever system the vehicle is equipped with (see Section 18).*

1   Remove the accessory drivebelt(s) (see Chapter 1).

2   Have the system discharged by a dealer service department or an automotive air conditioning repair facility.

3   Remove the refrigerant lines from the compressor **(see illustrations)**. **Note:** *Some compressor models may have separate refrigerant lines threaded to connections, or the fitting block may be bolted to the side or top of the compressor.*

4   Disconnect the electrical connection at the compressor clutch **(see illustration)**.

5   Remove the compressor mounting bolts **(see illustrations)**.

6   Remove the compressor from the mounting location.

7   Drain and measure the refrigerant oil from the compressor.

Installation

8   If the compressor is being replaced, add the appropriate amount of refrigerant oil to maintain the correct level. Add refrigerant oil to the component being replaced based on the following guidelines:

   a) *If the amount removed was **between** three and five ounces, add the same amount of clean refrigerant oil to the new compressor.*

   b) *If the amount of oil removed was **greater than** five ounces, add only five ounces to the component before installation.*

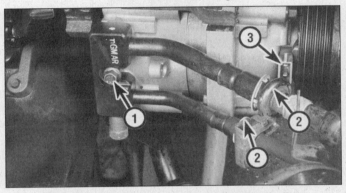

15.3c Details of the air conditioning refrigerant lines (OHC engine)

1   *Refrigerant line fitting block*
2   *Spring lock couplers*
3   *Compressor clutch electrical connection*

   c) *If the amount of oil removed was **less than** three ounces, add three ounces to the component before reinstallation.*

This will maintain the correct oil level in the system after the repairs are completed.

9   Installation procedures are the reverse of those for removal. **Note:** *If connections were disassembled that use O-ring seals, use new O-rings and lubricate them with clean refrigerant oil upon reassembly.*

10   After the compressor is installed have the system evacuated, recharged and leak tested by a dealer service department or an air conditioning repair facility.

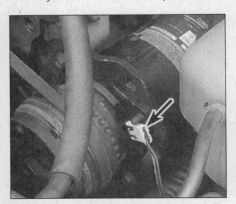

15.4 Disconnect the compressor clutch electrical connection (arrow)

15.5a Remove the mounting bolts (arrows) to remove the air conditioning compressor on a 5.0L (302 cid) engine

15.5b Remove the mounting bolts (arrows) to remove the air conditioning compressor on a 7.4L (460 cid) engine

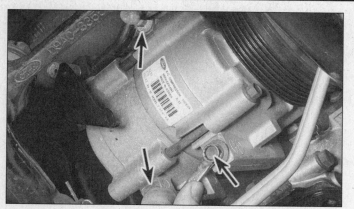

15.5c Remove the mounting bolts (arrows) to remove the air conditioning compressor (OHC engine)

16 Air conditioning condenser - removal and installation

Warning: *The air conditioning system is under high pressure. DO NOT loosen any fittings or remove any components until after the system has been discharged. Air conditioning refrigerant should be properly discharged into an EPA-approved container at a dealer service department or an automotive air conditioning repair facility. Always wear eye protection when disconnecting air conditioning system fittings.*

Note: *Special spring lock coupling tools are required on 1982 and later air conditioning systems, to release the connectors used on the refrigerant lines through out the air conditioning system. There are different Ford special tools for each line size, they are as follows:*

> 3/8 and 1/2 inch - Ford tool no. T81P-19623-G
> 3/8 inch - Ford tool no. T81P-19623-G1
> 1/2 inch - Ford tool no. T81P-19623-G2
> 5/8 inch - Ford tool no. T83P-19623-C
> 3/4 inch - Ford tool no. T85L-19623-A

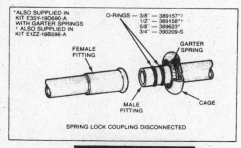

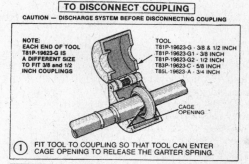

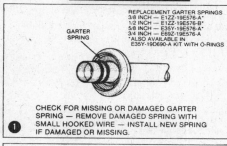

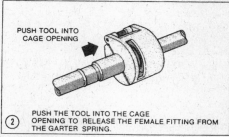

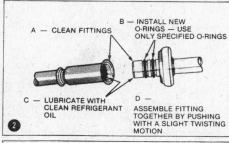

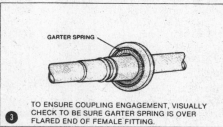

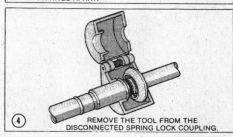

16.2a To release the spring lock couplers on the refrigerant lines fitted with quick-disconnect fittings, follow the instructions as shown

16.2b On early models disconnect the threaded refrigerant line fittings on both the right and left side of the condenser

16.5 Remove the condenser bracket bolts on at the top of the condenser (arrows)

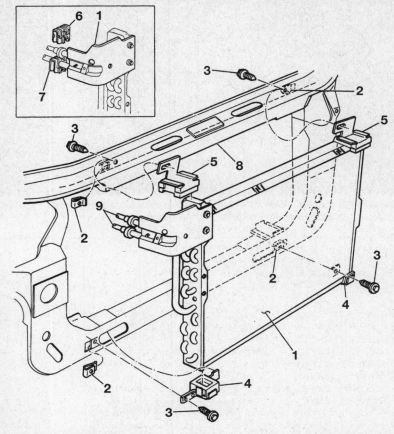

16.6 Typical later model air conditioning condenser installation details

1	Condenser assembly	6	Spring lock coupling
2	U-nuts	7	Spring lock coupling
3	Bolts	8	Radiator support
4	Lower mounting bracket assemblies	9	Refrigerant line connections
5	Upper mounting bracket assemblies		

Aftermarket equivalents of these tools can usually be found at local auto parts stores. Many times the necessary coupling tool may be included in the kit used for parts replacement.

Removal

Refer to illustrations 16.2a, 16.2b, 16.5 and 16.6

1   Disconnect the cable at the negative battery terminal.
2   Have the system discharged by a dealer service department or an automotive air conditioning repair facility. Disconnect the coupled hose and liquid line fittings. The connections will be either a threaded fitting or the spring lock coupler style **(see illustrations)**.
3   Remove the screws retaining the top radiator shroud (see Section 4).
4   Carefully tilt the radiator to the rear (see Section 5).
5   Remove the bolts holding the condenser to the top radiator support **(see illustration)** and lift the condenser out of the bottom cradle supports.

Installation

6   If the condenser is being replaced with a new one, transfer the brackets and mounts from the old unit to the new one **(see illustration)**.
7   When replacing the condenser add one ounce of refrigerant oil to the condenser before reassembly. This will maintain the correct oil level in the system after the repairs are completed.
8   Before installation, check the bracket assemblies and mounts for

excessive wear or damage. Replace them if necessary.
9   The installation procedures are the reverse of those for removal. **Note:** *If connections were disassembled that use O-ring seals, use new O-rings and lubricate them with clean refrigerant oil upon reassembly.*
10   After the condenser is installed have the system evacuated, recharged and leak tested by a dealer service department or an air conditioning repair facility.

---

17 Air conditioning receiver/accumulator-drier - removal and installation

Note: *Two different systems were used from 1970 through 1995. 1970 through 1979 used a receiver/drier with an expansion valve, while 1980 and later vehicles use an accumulator/drier with a fixed orifice tube.*

Removal

Refer to illustrations 17.2a, 17.2b, 17.2c

Warning: *The air conditioning system is under high pressure. DO NOT loosen any fittings or remove any components until after the system has been discharged. Air conditioning refrigerant should be properly discharged into an EPA-approved container at a dealer service department or an automotive air conditioning repair facility. Always wear eye protection when disconnecting air conditioning system fittings.*

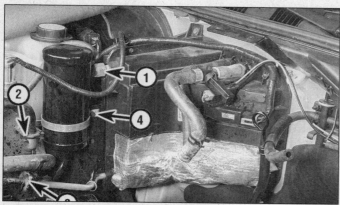

17.2a On later models, disconnect the two refrigerant lines at the accumulator/drier, one is a conventional nut and the other is a spring lock coupling

1   *Accumulator/drier suction line (threaded fitting)*
2   *Accumulator/drier liquid line (spring lock coupler)*
3   *Evaporator core liquid refrigerant line (spring lock coupler)*
4   *Mounting bracket and screw*

Note: *Special spring lock coupling tools may be required, on 1982 and later models, to release the connectors used on the refrigerant lines through out the air conditioning system (see Section 16).*
1   Have the system discharged by a dealer service department or an automotive air conditioning repair facility. Disconnect the cable at the negative battery terminal.
2   Disconnect the refrigerant inlet and outlet lines **(see illustrations)**. Cap or plug the open lines immediately.
3   Remove the mounting bolt(s) **(see illustrations in Step 2)** and slide the receiver-drier assembly up and out of the mounting bracket.

Installation

4   If you are replacing either a receiver or accumulator, drain the refrigerant oil from the old part. Add the same amount plus two ounces of clean refrigerant oil to the new part. This will maintain the correct oil level in the system after the repairs are completed.
5   Place the new receiver or accumulator into position, tighten the mounting bracket screw securely.
6   Install the inlet and outlet lines. Lubricate the O-rings using clean refrigerant and tighten the through-bolt and refrigerant line connections securely.
7   Connect the cable to the negative terminal of the battery.
8   Have the system evacuated, recharged and leak tested by a dealer service department or an air conditioning repair facility.

18 Expansion valve - removal and installation

Warning: *The air conditioning system is under high pressure. DO NOT loosen any fittings or remove any components until after the system has been discharged. Air conditioning refrigerant should be properly discharged into an EPA-approved container at a dealer service department or an automotive air conditioning repair facility. Always wear eye protection when disconnecting air conditioning system fittings.*
Note: *This information applies only to air conditioning systems on 1970 through 1979 models, which use a receiver/drier and expansion valve. Later models use an accumulator/drier with a fixed orifice tube. Refer to illustration 18.4*

Removal

1   Have the system discharged by a dealer service department or an automotive air conditioning repair facility.
2   Disconnect the cable at the negative battery terminal.

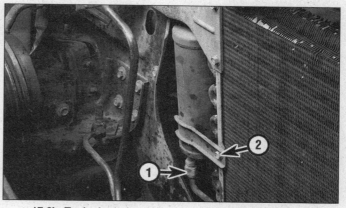

17.2b Typical receiver/drier mounted at the condenser

1   *Refrigerant line connections*
2   *Mounting bracket (additional bracket on front side of condenser)*

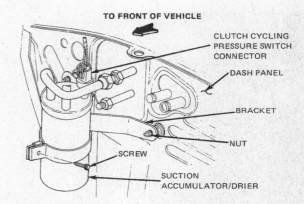

17.2c The accumulator/drier is mounted to the firewall, at the evaporator core connections, on 1982 through 1987 Continental and 1984 through 1992 Mark VII

3   Remove the insulation from the expansion valve, if equipped.
4   Disconnect the fitting and remove the high pressure hose from the expansion valve **(see illustration)**.
5   Loosen the clamp and remove the sensing bulb from the clamp.
6   Loosen the refrigerant line fitting and remove the expansion valve from the evaporator core inlet tube.

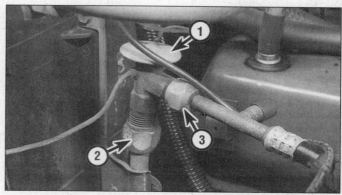

18.4 Typical expansion valve details

1   *Expansion valve*   3   *Liquid refrigerant line*
2   *Evaporator inlet tube*

3

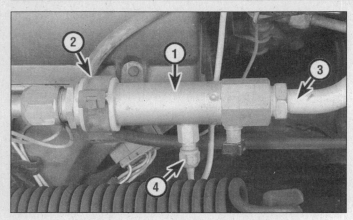

19.1 Typical suction throttling valve details

1	Suction throttling valve	3	Evaporator outlet line
2	Clam	4	Liquid bleed line

Installation

7   Installation is the reverse of the removal procedure.
8   Install all removed components using new O-ring seals. Always lubricate the o-ring with clean refrigerant oil before assembly.
9   Have the system evacuated, recharged and leak tested by a dealer service department or an air conditioning repair facility.

19   Suction Throttling Valve - removal and installation

Warning: *The air conditioning system is under high pressure. DO NOT loosen any fittings or remove any components until after the system has been discharged. Air conditioning refrigerant should be properly discharged into an EPA-approved container at a dealer service department or an automotive air conditioning repair facility. Always wear eye protection when disconnecting air conditioning system fittings.*

Removal

Refer to illustration 19.1
1   Have the system discharged by a dealer service department or an automotive air conditioning repair facility. Disconnect the suction line from the suction throttling valve **(see illustration)**. Immediately cap or plug open refrigerant lines.
2   Disconnect the cable at the negative battery terminal.
3   Disconnect the liquid bleed line from the suction throttling valve and cap or plug the bleed line.
4   Remove the clamp from the suction throttling valve and disconnect the suction throttling valve from the evaporator core outlet tube. Cap the evaporator outlet tube if the valve isn't being replaced immediately.

Installation

5   Assemble the suction throttling valve to the evaporator core using a new O-ring lubricated with clean refrigerant oil.
6   Reinstall the clamp on the valve.
7   Connect the liquid bleed line and suction lines to the suction throttling valve using a new O-ring in each location. Be sure to use clean refrigerant oil on the O-rings before assembly.
8   Have the system evacuated, recharged and leak tested by a dealer service department or an air conditioning repair facility.

20   Fixed orifice tube - removal and installation

Warning: *The air conditioning system is under high pressure. DO NOT loosen any fittings or remove any components until after the system*

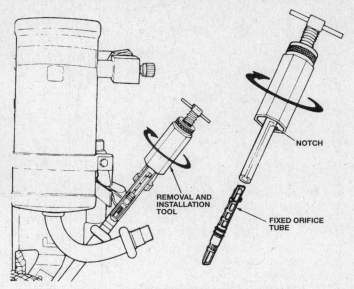

20.4 Fixed orifice tube removal details

has been discharged. Air conditioning refrigerant should be properly discharged into an EPA-approved container at a dealer service department or an automotive air conditioning repair facility. Always wear eye protection when disconnecting air conditioning system fittings.
Note: *This information applies only to air conditioning on 1980 through 1995 models, which use an accumulator/drier with a fixed orifice tube.*

Removal

Refer to illustration 20.4
Note: *Special spring lock coupling tools are required to release the connectors used on the refrigerant lines through out the air conditioning system (see Section 16).*
1   Have the system discharged by a dealer service department or an automotive air conditioning repair facility. Disconnect the cable at the negative battery terminal.
2   Disconnect the liquid line from the evaporator core at the accumulator/drier **(see illustration 17.2a)**.
3   Pour a small amount of refrigerant oil into the evaporator core tube to lubricate the O-rings seals on the orifice tube during removal.
4   Using the special tool (D80I-19990-A or Motorcraft YT-1008 or equivalent), engage the tool on the fixed orifice tube **(see illustration)** and remove it from the liquid refrigerant line. **Caution:** *DON'T try to remove or install the fixed orifice tube with anything except the special tool recommended by Ford, tool number T83L-19990-A or equivalent. To try to remove any other way will break the fixed orifice tube inside the evaporator core tube, and may require the replacement of the evaporator core.*
5   Cap or plug the open refrigerant lines immediately to prevent any dirt or excessive moisture from entering the system.

Installation

6   Lubricate the O-rings on the new fixed orifice tube with clean refrigerant oil.
7   Place the new fixed orifice tube into the special tool (the same tool is used for removal and installation) and insert it into the evaporator core tube until the orifice tube is seated at the stop.
8   Remove the tool.
9   Replace the O-ring at the refrigerant line spring lock coupling.
10   Reconnect the refrigerant lines.
11   Have the system evacuated, recharged and leak tested by a dealer service department or an air conditioning repair facility.

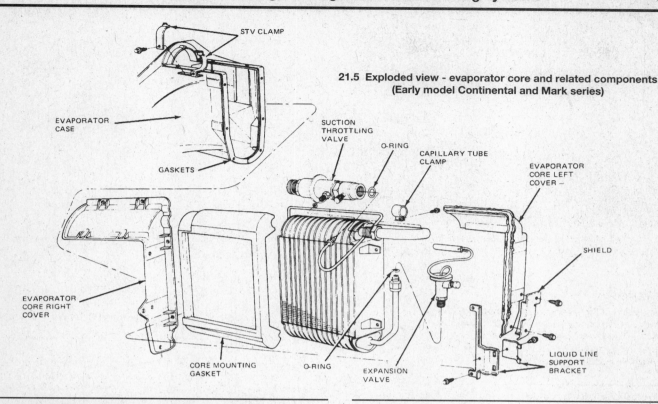

21.5 Exploded view - evaporator core and related components (Early model Continental and Mark series)

21 Air conditioning evaporator core - removal and installation

Warning: *The air conditioning system is under high pressure. DO NOT loosen any fittings or remove any components until after the system has been discharged. Air conditioning refrigerant should be properly discharged into an EPA-approved container at a dealer service department or an automotive air conditioning repair facility. Always wear eye protection when disconnecting air conditioning system fittings.*

Removal - 1970 through 1981 Continental and 1970 through 1983 Mark series

Refer to illustration 21.5
1   Have the system discharged by a dealer service department or an automotive air conditioning repair facility.
2   Disconnect the cable at the negative battery terminal.
3   Remove the expansion valve (see Section 18).
4   Remove the suction throttling valve (see Section 19).
5   Remove the liquid line support bracket **(see illustration)**.
6   Remove the cover flange screws that attach the cover halves to each other. **Note:** *There is a rope seal between the two cover halves that must be replaced during installation of the covers.*
7   Remove the case-to-cover screws and remove the left cover half, exposing the evaporator core. **Note:** *Each cover half will have screws attaching it to the case as well as each other.*
8   Remove right cover with the evaporator core from the case.
9   Separate the evaporator core from the right cover half and remove the mounting gasket.
10   Repair or replace the evaporator, as necessary.

Installation
11   Installation is the reverse of the removal procedure.
12   Install all removed components using new O-ring seals. Always lubricate the O-ring with clean refrigerant oil before assembly.
13   Have the system evacuated, recharged and leak tested by a dealer service department or an air conditioning repair facility.

Removal - 1982 through 1987 Continental and 1984 through 1992 Mark series

14   Have the system discharged by a dealer service department or an automotive air conditioning repair facility. Disconnect the cable from the negative battery terminal.
15   Drain the cooling system (see Chapter 1).
16   Remove the instrument panel (see Chapter 11).
17   On air conditioning equipped vehicles, disconnect the refrigerant lines which go through the firewall **(see illustration 12.33)**. Use a backup wrench to prevent twisting the tubing. Cap all open ends.
18   Disconnect the heater hoses which goes through the firewall. Cap all open ends.
19   Remove the screw attaching the air inlet duct and blower housing assembly support brace to the cowl top panel.
20   Disconnect the black vacuum supply hose from the inline vacuum check valve in the engine compartment.
21   Disconnect the blower motor wiring.
22   Working under the hood, remove the two nuts retaining the evaporator case to the dash panel.
23   In the passenger compartment, remove the screw attaching the evaporator case support bracket to the cowl top panel.
24   Remove the nut retaining the bracket below the evaporator case to the dash panel.
25   Carefully pull the evaporator case away from the dash panel and remove the evaporator case assembly from the vehicle.
26   Separate the upper case assembly **(see illustration 12.33)**.
27   Lift out the evaporator core and seal.
28   Separate the seal from the evaporator core and repair or replace the core, as necessary.

Installation
29   Installation is the reverse of the removal procedure.
30   Install all removed components using new O-ring seals. Always lubricate the O-ring with clean refrigerant oil before assembly.
31   Have the system evacuated, recharged and leak tested by a dealer service department or an air conditioning repair facility.

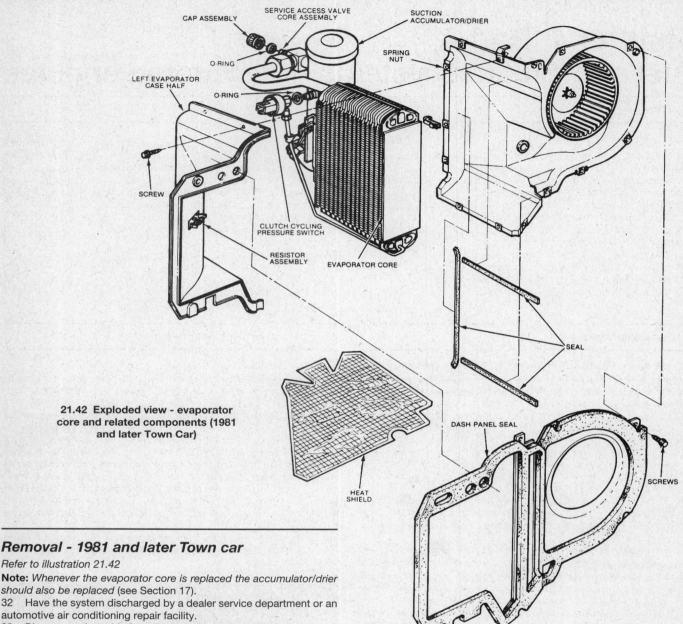

21.42 Exploded view - evaporator core and related components (1981 and later Town Car)

Removal - 1981 and later Town car

Refer to illustration 21.42

Note: *Whenever the evaporator core is replaced the accumulator/drier should also be replaced* (see Section 17).

32   Have the system discharged by a dealer service department or an automotive air conditioning repair facility.

33   Disconnect the cable from the negative battery terminal.

34   Disconnect the accumulator/drier suction line and the evaporator core liquid line **(see illustration 17.2a)**. Cap the open lines to prevent dirt and moisture from entering and position them out of the way.

35   Drain the cooling system and remove the heater hoses from the heater core inlet and outlet tubes.

36   Disconnect the electrical connectors to the blower motor and pressure switch. Position the wiring harness and any hoses that may interfere with removal out of the way.

37   Remove the hood seal from the right side of the engine compartment, if necessary.

38   From inside the passenger compartment, fold down the carpet on the right side of the floor and remove the bottom left screw of the two screws that support the recirculation air duct.

39   From under the hood, remove the nuts and screws from around the perimeter of the evaporator case.

40   Pull the evaporator case away from the firewall, disengaging it from the studs. Maneuver the case over the wheel well splash panel and out from under the hood. On some models, it may be necessary to loosen

the wheel well splash panel and push it down slightly for extra clearance.

41   Remove the evaporator case to dash panel seal and the insulator from the bottom of the housing.

42   Remove the screws retaining the two case halves and separate the housing **(see illustration)**.

43   Remove the evaporator core and accumulator/drier from the housing and disconnect the accumulator drier from the evaporator core.

Installation

44   Installation is the reverse of the removal procedure.

45   Install all removed components using new O-ring seals. Always lubricate the O-ring with clean refrigerant oil before assembly.

46   Have the system evacuated, recharged and leak tested by a dealer service department or an air conditioning repair facility.

Chapter 4 Part A
Fuel and exhaust systems - carbureted engines

Contents

1 General information

Warning: *Gasoline is extremely flammable, so take extra precautions when you work on any part of the fuel system. Don't smoke or allow open flames or bare light bulbs near the work area, and don't work in a garage where a natural gas-type appliance (such as a water heater or a clothes dryer) with a pilot light is present. Since gasoline is carcinogenic, wear latex gloves when there's a possibility of being exposed to fuel, and, if you spill any fuel on your skin, rinse it off immediately with soap and water. Mop up any spills immediately and do not store fuel-soaked rags where they could ignite. When you perform any kind of work on the fuel system, wear safety glasses and have a Class B type fire extinguisher on hand.*

The fuel system on all models consists of a fuel tank mounted in various locations on the chassis, a mechanically operated fuel pump and a carburetor. A combination of metal and rubber fuel hoses is used to connect these components.

The electric-assist choke system consists of a thermostatic spring and cover (choke assembly), temperature sensing switch and a ceramic heater. At temperatures below 60-degrees, the switch is open and no current is supplied to the ceramic heater located within the thermostatic spring. At temperatures above 60-degrees F, the temperature sensing switch closes and current is supplied to the ceramic heater. As the heater warms, it causes the spring to pull the choke plate open within 1 to 1-1/2 minutes.

The carburetor is either a two or four-barrel type, depending on engine displacement and year of production. Later models are equipped with electronic feedback carburetors. These carburetors are linked with a variety of sensors and output actuators to help control the amount of emissions.

Here is a list of the various carburetors used on these models:

Two-barrel carburetors
2150 2V Motorcraft carburetor
2700 VV variable venturi carburetor for Canada
7200 VV feedback carburetor

Four-barrel carburetors
4300 4V Autolite carburetor
4350 4V Motorcraft carburetor

The fuel system is interrelated with the emissions control systems on all models produced for sale in the United States. Components of the emissions control systems are described in Chapter 6.

2 Fuel pump/fuel pressure check

Refer to illustration 2.1
Warning: *Gasoline is extremely flammable, so take extra precautions when you work on any part of the fuel system.* **See Warning in Section 1.**
Note: *It is a good idea to check the fuel pump and lines for any obvious damage or fuel leakage. Also check all hoses from the tank to the pump, particularly the suction hoses at the fuel tank and pump which, if they have are cracked, may not allow fuel to the fuel pump. It is also possible for the fuel pump diaphragm to rupture internally and leak fuel into the crankcase. If you have excess fuel consumption or fuel smell, and you can't find any external leaks, check the condition of the engine oil for any signs of fuel mixing with the engine oil; the oil level will usually be abnormally high and the oil will be thinned out and have a fuel smell.*

1 Disconnect the fuel line from the carburetor and install a T-fitting. Connect a fuel pressure gauge to the T-fitting with a section of fuel hose **(see illustration)**.

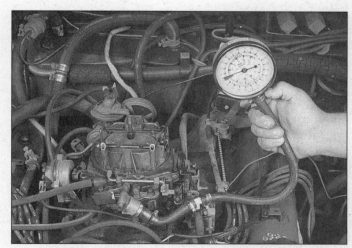

2.1 Connect a fuel pressure gauge to a T-fitting and install the assembly between the fuel inlet and the carburetor bowl inlet valve at the carburetor

4A

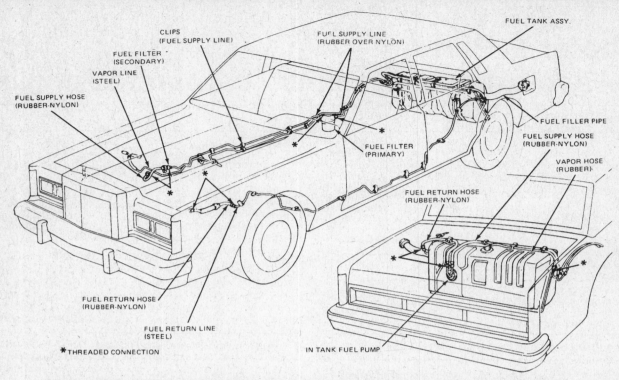

3.2a Typical fuel line arrangement in a carbureted model (1981 Lincoln Continental Mark VI shown)

2   Start the engine and allow it to idle. The pressure on the gauge should be 2-1/2 to 8 psi. It should remain constant and return to zero slowly when the engine is shut off. **Note:** *If the engine will not start, crank the engine until you get a reading on the gauge.*

3   An instant pressure drop indicates a faulty outlet valve and the fuel pump must be replaced.

4   If the pressure is too high, check the air vent to see if it is plugged before replacing the pump.

5   If the pressure is too low, be sure the fuel hoses and lines are in good shape and not plugged, then replace the pump.

3   Fuel lines and fittings - repair and replacement

Warning: *Gasoline is extremely flammable, so take extra precautions when you work on any part of the fuel system.* **See Warning in Section 1.**

Inspection

Refer to illustrations 3.2a and 3.2b

1   Once in a while, you will have to raise the vehicle to service or replace some component (an exhaust pipe hanger, for example). Whenever you work under the vehicle, always inspect the fuel lines and fittings for possible damage or deterioration.

2   Check all hoses and pipes for cracks, kinks, deformation or obstructions **(see illustrations)**.

3   Make sure all hose and pipe clips attach their associated hoses or pipes securely to the underside of the vehicle.

4   Verify all hose clamps attaching rubber hoses to metal fuel lines or pipes are snug enough to assure a tight fit between the hoses and pipes.

Replacement

5   If you must replace any damaged sections, use hoses approved for use in fuel systems or pipes made from steel only (it's best to use an original-type pipe from a dealer that's already flared and pre-bent).

3.2b Carefully inspect the fuel lines that extend from the fuel pump and fuel tank to the metal lines attached to the chassis of the vehicle (also check the entire length of the metal lines)

Do not install substitutes constructed from inferior or inappropriate material, as this could result in a fuel leak and a fire.

6   Always, before detaching or disassembling any part of the fuel line system, note the routing of all hoses and pipes and the orientation of all clamps and clips to assure that replacement sections are installed in exactly the same manner.

7   Before detaching any part of the fuel system, be sure to relieve the fuel tank pressure by removing the fuel filler cap.

8   Always use new hose clamps after loosening or removing them.

9   While you're under the vehicle, it's a good idea to check the following related components:

a)   *Check the condition of the fuel filter - make sure that it's not clogged or damaged* (see Chapter 1).

b)   *Inspect the evaporative emission control (EVAP) system. Verify that all hoses are attached and in good condition (see Chapter 6).*

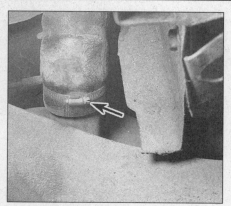

4.7 Loosen the clamp (arrow) and remove the fuel filler hose from the fuel tank

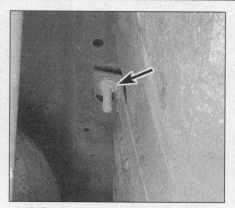

4.10 Remove the nuts from the fuel tank retaining straps

4.12 The auxiliary tank (if equipped) can be removed from the trunk by removing the bolts (arrows)

4   Fuel tank - removal and installation

Refer to illustrations 4.7, 4.10 and 4.12

Warning: *Gasoline is extremely flammable, so take extra precautions when you work on any part of the fuel system.* **See Warning in Section 1.**

Note: *The following procedure is much easier to perform if the fuel tank is empty. Some tanks have a drain plug for this purpose. If the tank does not have a drain plug, drain the fuel into an approved fuel container using a commercially available siphoning kit (NEVER start the siphoning action by mouth) or wait until the fuel tank is nearly empty, if possible.*

1   Remove the fuel tank filler cap to relieve fuel tank pressure.

2   Detach the cable from the negative terminal of the battery.

3   If the tank still has fuel in it, you can drain it at the fuel filler hose after raising the vehicle. If the tank has a drain plug, remove it and allow the fuel to collect in an approved gasoline container.

4   Raise the vehicle and place it securely on jackstands.

5   Remove the screws from the top of the fuel filler neck and disconnect the fuel filler neck from the body of the vehicle.

6   Disconnect the fuel lines and the vapor return line. **Note:** *The fuel feed and return lines and the vapor return line are three different diameters, so reattachment is simplified. If you have any doubts, however, clearly label the three lines and the fittings. Be sure to plug the hoses to prevent leakage and contamination of the fuel system.*

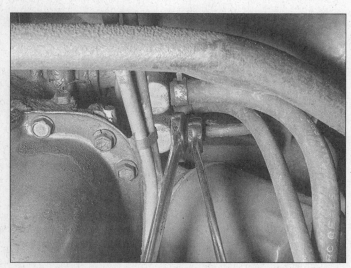

6.3 Use a back-up wrench and a flare-nut wrench when removing the fuel feed line

7   Loosen the hose clamp(s) and detach the fuel filler neck from the tank **(see illustration)**. If there is still fuel in the tank, siphon it out from the fuel feed port. Remember - NEVER start the siphoning action by mouth! Use a siphoning kit, which can be purchased at most auto parts stores.

8   If the fuel tank is equipped with a protective shield, remove the nuts and detach it from the underside of the chassis.

9   Support the fuel tank with a floor jack. Position a piece of wood between the jack head and the fuel tank to protect the tank.

10   Disconnect both fuel tank retaining straps and pivot them down until they are hanging out of the way **(see illustration)**.

11   Lower the tank enough to disconnect the wires and ground strap from the fuel pump/fuel gauge sending unit, if you have not already done so. Remove the tank from the vehicle.

12   Some models are equipped with an auxiliary fuel tank. Removal of these tanks is similar to the main fuel tank, but instead of being retained by straps, they are retained by bolts around the flange of the tank **(see illustration)**.

13   Installation is the reverse of removal.

5   Fuel tank cleaning and repair - general information

1   All repairs to the fuel tank or filler neck should be carried out by a professional who has experience in this critical and potentially dangerous work. Even after cleaning and flushing of the fuel system, explosive fumes can remain and ignite during repair of the tank.

2   If the fuel tank is removed from the vehicle, it should not be placed in an area where sparks or open flames could ignite the fumes coming out of the tank. Be especially careful inside garages where a natural gas-type appliance is located, because the pilot light could cause an explosion.

6   Fuel pump - removal and installation

Refer to illustrations 6.3 and 6.4

Warning: *Gasoline is extremely flammable, so take extra precautions when you work on any part of the fuel system.* **See Warning in Section 1.**

1   The fuel pump is located on the left (driver's) side of the engine, on the timing chain cover.

2   Place rags under the fuel pump to catch any gasoline which may be spilled during removal.

3   Carefully unscrew the fuel line fittings and detach the lines from the pump. A flare-nut wrench along with a back-up wrench should be used on the pressure-side fitting to prevent damage to the line and fittings **(see illustration)**.

4A

6.4 Remove the two bolts (arrows) from the fuel pump

4   Unbolt and remove the fuel pump **(see illustration)**.

5   Before installation, coat both sides of the gasket surface with RTV sealant, position the gasket and fuel pump against the block and install the bolts, tightening them securely.

6   Attach the lines to the pump and tighten the pressure fitting securely (use a flare-nut wrench, if one is available, to prevent damage to the fittings). Use a new hose clamp on the fuel hose.

7   Run the engine and check for leaks.

---

7   Fuel level sending unit - check and replacement

Refer to illustration 7.7

Warning: *Gasoline is extremely flammable, so take extra precautions when you work on any part of the fuel system.* **See Warning in Section 1.**

Check

1   Raise the vehicle and support it securely on jackstands.

2   If the fuel level gauge on the instrument panel hasn't been working properly, first check the operation of the gauge. If the gauge works in accordance with the following tests, the gauge and its circuit are OK - the problem must lie in the fuel level sending unit.

Models with an analog gauge

3   Disconnect the electrical connector for the fuel level sending unit. Turn on the ignition key. The needle on the gauge should deflect past the Full mark on the gauge.

4   Next, using a test light, probe the terminals on the electrical connector to find the one with battery voltage present. Using a jumper wire, ground the terminal **without** battery voltage - the needle on the gauge should now swing past the Empty mark. If the gauge works as described, it is functioning properly

Models with a digital instrument cluster

5   Disconnect the electrical connector for the fuel level sending unit. Turn on the ignition key. Using a voltmeter or test light, probe the terminals on the electrical connector to find the one with battery voltage present. Using a jumper wire and a 15-ohm resistor, ground the sending unit terminal **without** battery voltage. The gauge should indicate Empty (or nearly empty).

6   Next, remove the 15-ohm resistor, install a 150-ohm resistor in its place and ground it. The gauge should now indicate Full (or nearly Full). If the gauge works as described, it is functioning properly. **Note:** *If the resistance in the sending unit circuit is greater than 168-ohms or less than 11-ohms, only the top and bottom bars of the fuel gauge will illuminate.*

All models

7   A more accurate check of the sending unit can be made by removing it from the fuel tank and checking its resistance while

7.7 A more accurate check of the fuel level sending unit can be performed with the assembly on the bench, the ohmmeter probes on the connector and the float positioned on "empty" (bottom) and "full" (top). Check for a smooth change in resistance between these positions

manually operating the float arm **(see illustration)**.

Replacement

8   Remove the fuel tank from the vehicle if access to the sending unit is restricted (see Section 4). If there is plenty of room around the sending unit, siphon the fuel from the tank into an approved fuel container.

9   If necessary, carefully peel back the insulation material from the top of the fuel tank without damaging it.

10   Using a brass punch and hammer, tap the sending unit lock ring until the tabs align with the cutouts on the fuel tank retaining ring.

11   Lift the sending unit from the tank. Carefully angle the sending unit out of the opening without damaging the fuel level float located at the bottom of the assembly.

12   Disconnect the electrical connector from the sending unit.

13   Installation is the reverse of removal. Be sure to use a new O-ring between the tank and the sending unit cover.

---

8   Air cleaner housing - removal and installation

1   Remove the air filter from the air cleaner housing (see Chapter 1).

2   Disconnect any vacuum hoses or electrical connectors that would interfere with air cleaner removal and mark them with pieces of numbered tape for reassembly purposes.

3   Lift the air cleaner housing from the engine compartment.

4   Installation is the reverse of removal.

---

9   Accelerator cable - removal, installation and adjustment

Refer to illustrations 9.1, 9.2 and 9.5

Removal

1   Remove the accelerator cable from the throttle linkage by prying the cable end **(see illustration)** off the shaft using a small screwdriver.

2   Loosen the accelerator cable locknut and remove the cable from the bracket assembly **(see illustration)**.

3   Detach the screws and the clips retaining the lower instrument

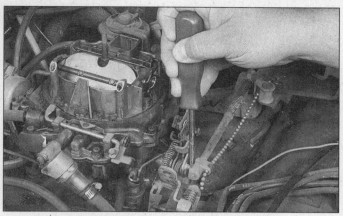

9.1 Pry the cable end off the throttle lever

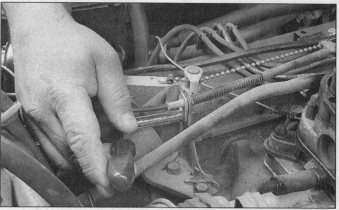

9.2 Remove the bolt and separate the accelerator cable from the bracket

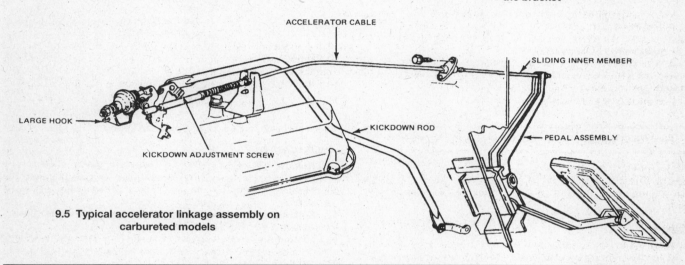

9.5 Typical accelerator linkage assembly on carbureted models

trim panel on the driver's side and remove the trim piece.

4   Pull the cable end out and then up from the accelerator pedal recess.

5   To disconnect the cable at the firewall, remove the cable retainer bracket bolts **(see illustration)** and push the cable assembly through the firewall from inside the passenger compartment.

Installation

6   Installation is the reverse of removal. **Note:** *To prevent possible interference, flexible components (hoses, wires, etc.) must not be routed within two inches of moving parts, unless routing is controlled.*

7   Operate the accelerator pedal and check for any binding condition by completely opening and closing the throttle.

8   If necessary, at the engine compartment side of the firewall, apply sealant around the accelerator cable to prevent water from entering the passenger compartment.

Adjustment

9   There is no specific adjustment on these type of accelerator cables but it will be necessary to adjust the kickdown cable for the automatic transmission (see Chapter 7).

10 Carburetor - diagnosis and overhaul

Warning: *Gasoline is extremely flammable, so take extra precautions when you work on any part of the fuel system.* **See Warning in Section 1.**

Diagnosis

1   A thorough road test and check of carburetor adjustments should be done before any major carburetor service. Specifications for some adjustments are listed on the *Vehicle Emissions Control Information* (VECI) label found in the engine compartment.

2   Carburetor problems usually show up as flooding, hard starting, stalling, severe backfiring and poor acceleration. A carburetor that's leaking fuel and/or covered with wet looking deposits definitely needs attention.

3   Some performance complaints directed at the carburetor are actually a result of loose, out-of-adjustment or malfunctioning engine or electrical components. Others develop when vacuum hoses leak, are disconnected or are incorrectly routed. The proper approach to analyzing carburetor problems should include the following items:

a) *Inspect all vacuum hoses and actuators for leaks and correct installation (see Chapters 1 and 6).*

b) *Tighten the intake manifold and carburetor mounting nuts/bolts evenly and securely.*

c) *Perform a compression test and vacuum test (see Chapter 2C).*

d) *Clean or replace the spark plugs as necessary (see Chapter 1).*

e) *Check the spark plug wires (see Chapter 1).*

f) *Inspect the ignition primary wires.*

g) *Check the ignition timing (follow the instructions printed on the Emissions Control Information label).*

h) *Check the fuel pump pressure/volume (see Section 2).*

i) *Check the heat control valve in the air cleaner for proper operation (see Chapter 1).*

j) *Check/replace the air filter element (see Chapter 1).*

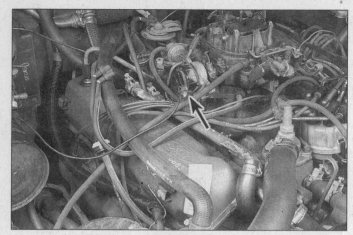

11.1a Apply battery voltage to the choke coil terminal and confirm that the choke slowly opens

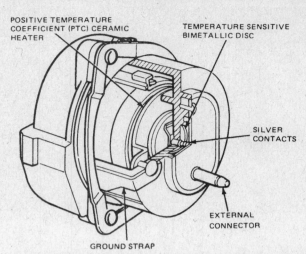

11.1b Typical electrically assisted carburetor choke system (2150 2V carburetor shown)

k) *Check the PCV system (see Chapter 6).*
l) *Check/replace the fuel filter (see Chapter 1). Also, the strainer in the tank could be restricted.*
m) *Check for a plugged exhaust system.*
n) *Check EGR valve operation (see Chapter 6).*
o) *Check the choke - it should be completely open at normal engine operating temperature (see Chapter 1).*
p) *Check for fuel leaks and kinked or dented fuel lines (see Chapters 1 and 4)*
q) *Check accelerator pump operation with the engine off (remove the air cleaner cover and operate the throttle as you look into the carburetor throat - you should see a stream of gasoline enter the carburetor).*
r) *Check for incorrect fuel or bad gasoline.*
s) *Check the valve clearances (if applicable) and camshaft lobe lift (see Chapters 1 and 2).*
t) *Have a dealer service department or other repair shop check the electronic engine and carburetor controls.*

4   Diagnosing carburetor problems may require that the engine be started and run with the air cleaner off. While running the engine without the air cleaner, backfires are possible. This situation is likely to occur if the carburetor is malfunctioning, but just the removal of the air cleaner can lean the fuel/air mixture enough to produce an engine backfire. **Warning:** *Do not position any part of your body, especially your face, directly over the carburetor during inspection and servicing procedures. Wear eye protection!*

Overhaul

Note: *Holley provides a replacement carburetor as a substitute for the Motorcraft feedback carburetors installed at the factory. Consult your automotive or performance parts store for availability and prices. Also, be aware that some of these substitute carburetors are not emissions legal and it will necessary to verify their legality with the EPA offices in your state.*

5   Once it's determined that the carburetor needs an overhaul, several options are available. If you're going to attempt to overhaul the carburetor yourself, first obtain a good-quality carburetor rebuild kit (which will include all necessary gaskets, internal parts, instructions and a parts list). You'll also need some special solvent and a means of blowing out the internal passages of the carburetor with air.

6   An alternative is to obtain a new or rebuilt carburetor. They are readily available from dealers and auto parts stores. Make absolutely sure the exchange carburetor is identical to the original. A tag is usually attached to the top of the carburetor or a number is stamped on the float bowl. It will help determine the exact type of carburetor you have. When obtaining a rebuilt carburetor or a rebuild kit, make sure the kit or carburetor matches your application exactly. Seemingly insignificant

differences can make a large difference in engine performance.

7   If you choose to overhaul your own carburetor, allow enough time to disassemble it carefully, soak the necessary parts in the cleaning solvent (usually for at least one-half day or according to the instructions listed on the carburetor cleaner) and reassemble it, which will usually take much longer than disassembly. When disassembling the carburetor, match each part with the illustration in the carburetor kit and lay the parts out in order on a clean work surface. Overhauls by inexperienced mechanics can result in an engine which runs poorly or not at all. To avoid this, use care and patience when disassembling the carburetor so you can reassemble it correctly.

8   Because carburetor designs are constantly modified by the manufacturer in order to meet increasingly more stringent emissions regulations, it isn't feasible to include a step-by-step overhaul of each type. You'll receive a detailed, well illustrated set of instructions with the carburetor overhaul kit.

11   Electric choke heater - testing

Refer to illustrations 11.1a and 11.1b
Caution: *If there is any loss of electrical current to the choke heater, operation of any type, including idling, should be avoided. Loss of power to the choke will cause the choke to remain partly closed during engine operation. A very rich air/fuel mixture will be created and result in abnormally high exhaust system temperatures, which may cause damage to the catalytic converter or other underbody parts of the vehicle.*

1   With the engine cold, connect a jumper wire from the choke heater terminal to the positive battery terminal. The choke heater housing should start becoming hot and the choke plate in the carburetor should slowly open after some time. Be sure it opens completely in about five minutes or replacement is necessary **(see illustration). Note:** *As the heater is heating the choke coil, occasionally tap the accelerator to allow the choke to open.* **Note:** *The electric assist choke system consists of a thermostatic spring and cover (choke assembly), temperature sensing switch and a ceramic (positive temperature coefficient) heater* **(see illustration).** *At temperatures below 60-degrees, the switch is open and no current is supplied to the ceramic heater located within the thermostatic spring. At temperatures above 60-degrees F, the temperature sensing switch closes and current is supplied to the ceramic heater. As the heater warms, it causes the spring to pull the choke plate open within 1 to 1-1/2 minutes.*

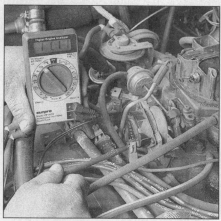

11.2 With the ignition key ON, check for battery voltage to the choke coil

12.4a Remove the three screws (arrows) that retain the thermostatic spring housing

12.4b Lift the spring housing from the carburetor

2   If the choke heater tests okay, but the choke valve does not open in normal operation, check for voltage to the choke heater when the engine is cold and the ignition switch is in the ON position **(see illustration)**.

3   If no voltage is present in Step 2, repair the open in the power circuit to the choke heater (be sure to check the fuse first!).

12 Carburetor adjustments

Note: *These carburetor adjustments are strictly in-vehicle adjustments. During overhaul, refer to the instructions included in the overhaul kit for complete procedures and any additional adjustments that are required.*

Choke plate opening and choke plate pulldown

Refer to illustrations 12.4a, 12.4b, 12.6a, 12.6b, 12.9 and 12.11

Note: *For more information on the choke system, refer to Chapter 1 and Section 11 on the electric choke heater system.*

1   The choke plate opening is a critical carburetor adjustment directly involved with cold-running conditions and choke enrichment during cranking. The choke unloader is a mechanical device that partially opens the choke valve at wide open throttle to eliminate choke enrichment during hard acceleration.

2   Engines which have been stalled or flooded by excessive choke enrichment can be cleared by the use of the choke unloader. With the throttle valve at wide open throttle, the choke plate should be slightly open to allow a sufficient amount of intake air into the carburetor venturi.

4300 4V and 4350 4V carburetors

3   The 4300 4V and 4350 4V carburetors installed on models covered by this manual are equipped with an integral choke system. When the engine is first started the choke plate is pulled to an initial pulldown position by engine vacuum. First adjust the choke plate pulldown and then check the choke plate opening.

4   Remove the air cleaner housing, then mark the position of the outer choke housing and remove the retaining screws from the housing **(see illustrations)**. Remove the choke thermostatic spring housing assembly.

5   Open the throttle about halfway and make sure the fast idle screw is not touching the fast idle cam.

6   Bend a piece of wire (0.036 inch) to a 90-degree angle approximately 1/8-inch from the end **(see illustrations)**. Insert the bent end of the wire between the choke piston and the slot near the upper edge of the piston housing and slowly lift the piston. This will lock the piston in a stationary position.

7   Rotate the choke thermostat lever counterclockwise until the gauge (bent wire) is snug in the piston slot. Hold the gauge in position with light force on the choke thermostat lever and move the top of the choke rod away from the carburetor while moving the bottom of the rod toward the carburetor to remove the endplay from the linkage.

8   Use a drill bit (1/8-inch) and place it against the inner wall of the choke airhorn approximately in the middle of the carburetor. The choke plate should rest against the drill. If not, adjust the choke plate.

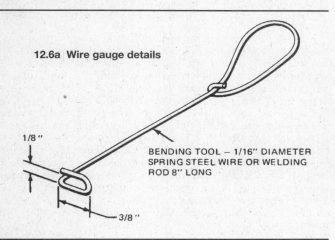

12.6a Wire gauge details

1/8"

BENDING TOOL – 1/16" DIAMETER SPRING STEEL WIRE OR WELDING ROD 8" LONG

3/8"

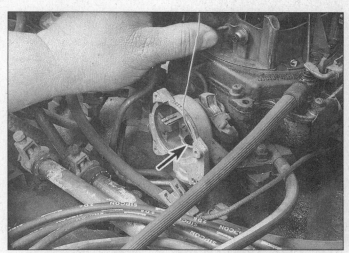

12.6b Insert the gauge into the slot in the upper edge of the cylinder and slowly lift the piston to lock it into place

4A

12.9 Adjust the choke plate until it touches the drill bit and tighten the pivot bolt (counterclockwise)

12.11 If the choke plate is not closing enough, turn the choke cover counterclockwise (the marks on the housing and cover are used for reference)

9   Turn the lock nut on the choke plate shaft (see illustration) to loosen (clockwise because the threads are left handed) and move the choke plate until it contacts the drill. Tighten the screw (counterclockwise). Note: Be sure the wire gauge is in place and the bottom of the rod is toward the carburetor and the linkage does not have freeplay.
10   Reinstall the choke thermostatic spring housing onto the carburetor but leave them loose.
11   Since choke coils lose their tension over time, you may find, on older coils, that lining up the marks does not provide enough choke. Readjust the coil by rotating the cover counterclockwise until the choke plate closes completely, then rotate it clockwise until the plate just moves away from the fully closed position (about 1/16-inch, measured at the rear of the air horn) (see illustration).
12   Re-tighten the three cover screws. Note: The metal clips beneath the screws must be positioned so they exert their maximum spring force against the cover. If they're installed backwards, the choke cover will have a tendency to rotate, changing the choke setting.

2150 2V carburetor
Refer to illustrations 12.15, 12.16, 12.17 and 12.18
13   Run the engine until it is up to operating temperature (about 5 minutes) and then shut it off.
14   Remove the air cleaner housing (see Section 8).
15   Rotate the choke housing to the rich setting which will lightly close the choke plate (see illustration). Rotate the housing an additional 90-degrees.
16   Push the choke pulldown diaphragm to the CLOSED position (see illustration).
17   Use a 1/2 inch drill bit shank to measure the clearance between the air horn wall and lower edge of the choke plate (see illustration).
18   To decrease the choke pulldown, turn the adjusting screw clockwise and to increase it, turn the screw counterclockwise (see illustration).
19   The fast idle cam must be adjusted after choke vacuum pulldown has been adjusted.

2700 VV and 7200 VV carburetors
Refer to illustrations 12.25, 12.29 and 12.34
Note: The choke pulldown adjustment on 2700 VV and 7200 VV carburetors will require the cold enrichment rod, the control vacuum regulator (CVR) and the choke control diaphragm to be adjusted.
20   Remove the choke cap. The choke cap on 2700/7200VV carburetors is held in place by three screws or in the case of California vehicles, three rivets.
21   To remove the choke cap, remove the three screws and lift the cap and gasket away from the carburetor. On California vehicles, the two top rivets are removed by drilling them out. The bottom rivet is located in a blind hole and must be tapped out, using a suitable punch and hammer. The choke cap, gasket and retainer can then be removed from the carburetor.
22   Installation is the reverse of removal on choke caps retained with screws. California models require the use of a suitable rivet gun and three rivets. It may be necessary to remove the carburetor when installing the rivets.
23   Remove the choke pulldown diaphragm and spring.
24   Install a choke weight on the choke bi-metal lever (Ford part T77L-9848-A or equivalent). Place the fast idle pick-up lever on the first highest step of the fast idle cam.
25   Install a dial indicator (Ford tool 4201-C or equivalent) on the carburetor so that the indicator tip contacts the top surface of the cold enrichment rod (see illustration) and adjust the dial to zero. Slightly raise the choke weight and then release it, making sure that the zero reading repeats.
26   Remove the choke weight.
27   After installing the stator cap at the index position, the dial indicator should read to specification. If it doesn't, adjust the rod height by turning the adjusting nut clockwise to increase height and counterclockwise to decrease it.
28   To check the setting, repeat steps 3 through 6.
29   To adjust the control vacuum regulator (CVR), remove the stator cap and leave the dial indicator installed (see illustration) but not reset to zero.

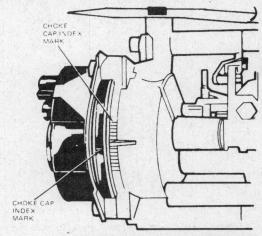

12.15 2150 2V carburetor choke housing

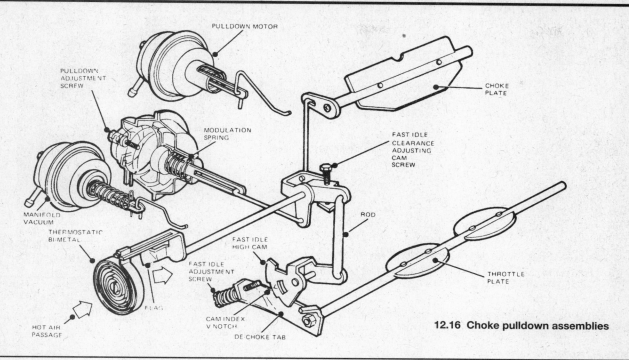

12.16 Choke pulldown assemblies

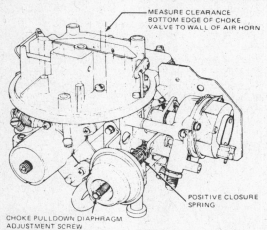

12.17 Measuring the 2150 carburetor choke plate clearance

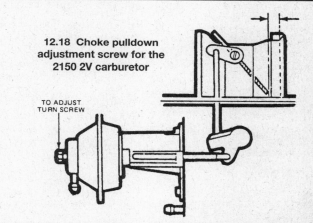

12.18 Choke pulldown adjustment screw for the 2150 2V carburetor

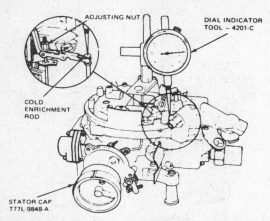

12.25 Raise the choke weight then release it, making sure the dial indicator returns back to zero

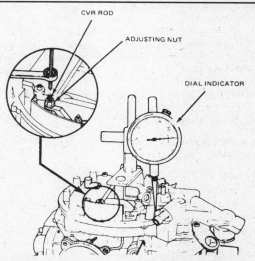

12.29 Control vacuum regulator (CVR) adjustment for the 2700 VV and the 7200 VV carburetors

4A

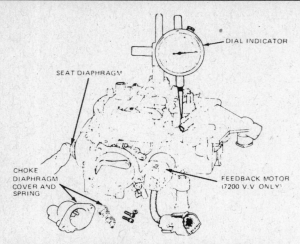

12.34 Choke diaphragm adjustment for the 2700 VV and 7200 VV carburetors

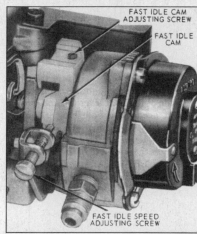

12.38 Place the fast idle adjustment screw on the middle step of the fast idle cam (4300 4V carburetor)

30   Set the fast idle on the highest step.

31   Press the CVR rod down until it bottoms in its seat and read the travel on the dial indicator.

32   If adjustment is necessary, place a 1/2-inch box-end wrench on the CVR adjusting nut to prevent it from turning.

33   Using a 3/32-inch Allen wrench, turn the CVR rod counter-clockwise to increase its travel or clockwise to decrease it.

34   With the stator cap removed and dial indicator still installed but not reset to zero, seat the choke diaphragm assembly in the direction of the fast idle cam **(see illustration)**.

35   If the dial indicator reading is not within specification, turn the choke diaphragm clockwise to decrease or counterclockwise to increase the height as shown.

36   The cold idle enrichment rod height must be checked after each adjustment of the CVR and choke control diaphragm.

Fast idle cam - adjustment

4300 4V and 4350 4V carburetors

Refer to illustration 12.38

37   Adjust the position of the choke spring housing to align with the main index mark **(see illustration 12.11)**, then rotate the housing an additional 90-degrees counterclockwise. Tighten the screws in this position.

38   Position the fast idle speed screw on the middle step on the fast idle cam **(see illustration)**. Close the choke plate as far down as it will go. Check the clearance between the lower edge of the choke plate and the air horn wall. Turn the fast idle cam adjusting screw in to increase the clearance or out to decrease the clearance. **Note:** *Make sure the fast idle speed adjusting screw remains positioned on the middle step.*

39   Loosen the adjusting screws on the thermostatic choke housing and adjust it to the specified index mark.

40   Adjust the engine idle speed and the fuel mixture (see Chapter 1).

2150 2V carburetor

Refer to illustrations 12.43 and 12.45

41   With the choke housing rotated to the rich position, push the throttle open to set the fast idle cam.

42   Close the choke.

43   Open the throttle while watching the fast idle cam and idle speed screw. The cam should drop to the kickdown step and idle speed screw should be opposite the V notch on the cam **(see illustration)**.

44   To align the fast idle speed screw with the V notch, turn the hex-headed screw in the plastic fast idle cam lever as shown.

45   De-choke after adjusting the choke plate lower edge and the air horn wall **(see illustration 12.18)**. To adjust the clearance, bend the metal tang on the fast idle speed lever **(see illustration)**.

46   After all adjustments are made reset the choke thermostat housing to the specifications on the emissions decal.

2700 VV and 7200 VV carburetors

Refer to illustration 12.49

47   Remove the choke cap.

48   Counting the highest step as the first, install the fast idle lever in the corner of the step specified on the emissions label.

49   Install the stator cap and rotate it clockwise until the lever contacts the adjusting screw **(see illustration)**.

50   Line up the index mark on the stator cap with the specified mark on the choke casing by turning the fast idle cam adjusting screw. This screw may be hard to turn as it was coated with a thread locking compound at the factory.

51   Remove the stator cap and re-install the choke cap to the setting specified on the emissions label.

Fast-idle speed

Note: *In order to adjust the fast idle speed on engines equipped with feedback carburetor systems (Models 2700 VV and 7200 VV), it may be necessary to prevent certain systems (EVAP, EGR, Oxygen sensor feedback, idle stop solenoid, etc.) from operating. Refer to the VECI label for your particular model for a list of the steps necessary to make this adjustment.*

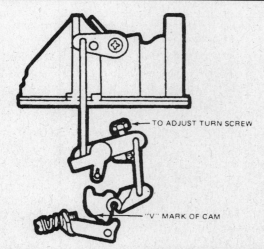

12.43 Fast idle cam adjustment screw on the 2150 2V carburetor

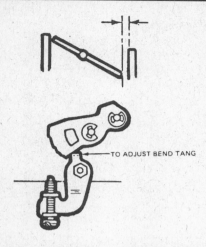

12.45 Adjusting the fast idle speed tang on the 2150 2V carburetor

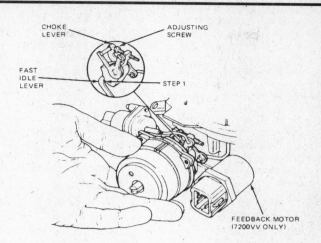

12.49 Fast idle cam setting on the 2700 VV and 7200 VV carburetors

4300 4V and 4350 4V carburetors

Refer to illustration 12.55

52   Place the fast idle speed adjusting screw on the second highest step on the fast idle cam.

53   Connect a tachometer in accordance with the tool manufacturer's instructions.

54   Start and run the engine to normal operating temperature.

55   With the choke fully open, turn the fast idle adjusting screw until the correct fast idle speed is obtained **(see illustration)**. Doublecheck to make sure the fast idle adjusting screw remains on the second highest step of the cam. Refer to the VECI label in the engine compartment. If the label is not available, set the fast idle speed at approximately 1,700 rpm.

56   To verify the fast idle speed is correct, return the engine to idle, then reposition the adjusting screw on the second highest step of the fast idle cam. Readjust the fast idle speed if necessary.

2150 2V carburetor

Refer to illustration 12.66

57   Start the engine and run it up to operating temperature. Shut the engine off and remove the air cleaner. The air cleaner assembly must be in position when engine speeds are measured.

58   Apply the parking brake and block the rear wheels.

59   Check, and adjust if necessary, the choke and throttle linkage for freedom of movement.

60   When applicable, turn the air conditioner OFF.

61   Disconnect the evaporative purge line from the carburetor and plug it with a suitable tool.

62   Connect a tachometer in accordance with the tool manufacturer's instructions.

63   Disconnect the EGR vacuum hose and plug it. If the vehicle is equipped with a ported vacuum switch (PVS), do not disconnect the EGR line.

64   Disconnect the distributor vacuum hose from the advance side of the distributor and plug it.

65   Follow the vacuum hose from the thermactor dump valve to the carburetor and disconnect the dump valve vacuum hose nearest the carburetor. Plug the original vacuum source and connect the dump valve directly to the manifold vacuum.

66   With the transmission in Park (automatic) or Neutral (manual) and the choke plate fully open, run the engine at 2500 rpm for 15 seconds. Place the fast idle lever on the step of the fast idle cam specified on the emissions decal **(see illustration)**. Allow the engine speed to stabilize (10 to 15 seconds) and measure the fast idle rpm.

4A

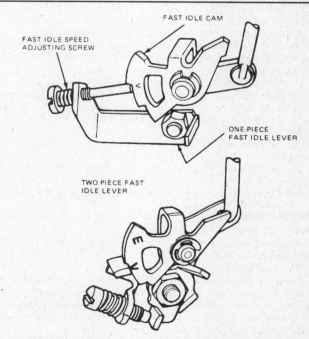

12.66 Fast idle adjustment screws and linkage components on the 2150 2V carburetor

12.55 Fast idle speed adjustment on the 4350 4V carburetor

67   Repeat this procedure three times and adjust the fast idle rpm if not as specified on the VECI label.

68   Before adjusting the curb idle, it is necessary to determine which of the various throttle positioners and engine speed control devices the carburetor is equipped with. Refer to Chapter 6 for a description of these devices.

69   Make all adjustments after determining the curb idle speed (see Chapter 1).

70   If the carburetor is equipped with a dashpot to control the throttle closing, the dashpot plunger must be collapsed with the engine off. Check the clearance between the plunger and the throttle lever pad and adjust, if necessary, to the specifications on the emissions label. Each time the curb idle is adjusted, the dashpot clearance must also be adjusted .

2700 VV and 7200 VV

Refer to illustration 12.76

71   Connect a tachometer in accordance with the tool manufacturer's instructions.

72   Disconnect the EGR hose from the valve and plug the hose.

73   With the choke off and the engine running at normal operating temperature, raise the speed of the engine to 2,500 rpm for 15 seconds. Place the fast idle lever on the specified step of the fast idle cam (refer to the emission decal in the engine compartment).

74   Allow the engine speed to stabilize and measure the engine speed (rpm). Depending upon the engine and the state of tune, it may require anywhere from 15 seconds to 2 minutes for the engine speed to stabilize.

75   Repeat the above step three times to ensure accuracy.

76   Adjust the fast idle screw as necessary **(see illustrations)**.

77   Repeat the rpm check if an adjustment has been made.

78   Turn the engine off and reconnect the EGR hose.

79   Set the parking brake and block the wheels. Remove the air cleaner and place the fast-idle speed adjusting screw on the second highest step on the fast-idle cam.

80   Connect a tachometer according to the tool manufacturer's instructions.

81   Start and run the engine to normal operating temperature.

82   With the choke fully open, turn the fast-idle adjusting screw until the correct fast-idle speed is obtained. Double-check to make sure the fast idle adjusting screw remains on the second highest step of the cam. Refer to the VECI label in the engine compartment. If the label is not available, set the fast-idle speed to approximately 1,700 rpm.

83   To verify the fast-idle speed is correct, return the engine to idle, then reposition the adjusting screw on the second highest step of the fast-idle cam. Readjust the fast-idle speed, if necessary.

Idle mixture

Refer to illustrations 12.85a, 12.85b, 12.85c and 12.85d

Note 1: *Be sure to check the ignition timing, the dwell on the ignition points (1970 through 1973 models), the condition of the spark plugs and spark plug wires and, if necessary, perform a complete tune-up before attempting to make the following carburetor adjustment. Often, problems with the mixture are due to a vacuum leak (see* Troubleshooting *at the front of this manual and the vacuum gauge checks in Chapter 2C).*

Note2: *On models with limiter caps on the mixture screws, do not adjust the mixture any richer than the caps will allow (do not break off the caps). If the engine runs too rich at the factory settings, there's something wrong with the choke or the carburetor is faulty. If the engine is running too lean at the factory settings, there's a vacuum leak or the carburetor is faulty. If necessary, have the system diagnosed by a qualified shop.*

Note 3: *On 7200 VV feedback carburetors, the base idle mixture is adjusted using a special tool. Consult your local auto parts store or a specialty tool company that deals with carburetor tools.*

84   After the engine has reached normal operating temperature, set the parking brake and block the wheels, then remove the air cleaner and turn the idle speed adjusting screw out as far as possible without

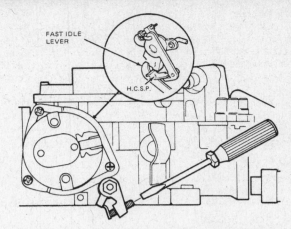

12.76 Fast idle speed adjustment on the 2700 VV and the 7200 VV carburetors

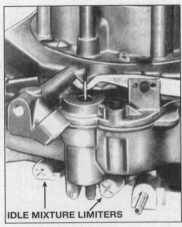

12.85a Idle mixture adjusting limiters on the 4300 4V carburetor

12.85b On 7200 VV carburetors, install a pick or sharp tool into the carburetor to remove the concealment plugs. Note: *While performing the adjustment procedure, you'll have to insert a vacuum plug into the opposite hole.*

the engine running rough, since the throttle plate(s) must be as nearly closed as possible when adjusting the idle mixture.

85   Working with one idle mixture screw at a time, turn the screw clockwise until the idle speed drops a noticeable amount **(see illustrations)**. Now slowly turn the screw out until the maximum idle

speed is reached, but no further.

86   Repeat the procedure for the other idle mixture screw. Keep track of the number of turns each screw is off the seat to be sure they are each out approximately the same number of turns. This will verify that the idle circuit is operating properly and balance is maintained. **Note:** *If it was necessary to turn the idle speed screw in (to keep the engine running) before setting the idle mixture, adjust the idle speed, then perform the mixture adjustment procedure again. This will ensure that the idle mixture is set with the throttle plates fully closed, so the engine is drawing the fuel mixture only from the idle circuit. If you're working on a 2700/7200 VV carburetor, install new concealment plugs.*

Idle speed

See Chapter 1 for the idle speed adjustment procedure.

Venturi valve limiter (2700/7200VV carburetors only) - adjustment

Refer to illustration 12.90

87   Remove the carburetor.
88   Remove the venturi valve cover, gasket and roller bearings.
89   Using a suitable punch, remove the expansion plug at the rear of the main body on the throttle side.
90   Remove the venturi valve limiter screw assembly using a 5/32-inch Allen wrench **(see illustration)** and block the throttle plates open.
91   Lightly close the venturi valve and check the gap between the valve and the air horn wall. Adjust if necessary.
92   Move the venturi valve to the wide open position and insert an Allen wrench into the stop screw hole. To adjust the flap, turn the limiter adjusting screw counterclockwise to decrease the clearance and clockwise to increase it.
93   Remove the allen wrench, lightly close the valve and re-check the gap.
94   Re-install the venturi valve limiter stop screw and turn it clockwise

12.85c Special carburetor mixture jet adjusting tool for 7200 VV carburetors

12.85d Install the special tool into the carburetor and slowly turn the mixture screw clockwise until a noticeable change in rpm occurs. Be sure to follow the directions on the VECI label and block airflow to the thermactor system

until it contacts the valve.
95   Open the venturi valve all the way and check the gap between the valve and the air horn. Adjust the stop screw to specification if necessary.
96   After installing a new expansion plug, re-install the venturi valve cover, gasket and bearing and re-install the carburetor.

13   Carburetor - removal and installation

Warning: *Gasoline is extremely flammable, so take extra precautions when you work on any part of the fuel system.* **See Warning in Section 1.**

Removal

1   Remove the fuel filler cap to relieve fuel tank pressure.
2   Remove the air cleaner housing (see Section 8).
3   Disconnect the accelerator cable from the throttle lever (see Section 9).
4   If the vehicle is equipped with an automatic transmission, disconnect the kickdown cable or linkage from the throttle lever.
5   Clearly label all vacuum hoses and fittings, then disconnect the hoses.
6   Disconnect the fuel line from the carburetor.
7   Label the wires and terminals, then unplug all the electrical connectors.
8   Remove the mounting fasteners and detach the carburetor from the intake manifold. Remove the carburetor mounting gasket. Stuff a rag into the intake manifold openings to prevent debris from entering.

Installation

9   Use a gasket scraper to remove all traces of gasket material and sealant from the intake manifold (and the carburetor, if it's being reinstalled), then remove the shop rag from the manifold openings. Clean the mating surfaces with lacquer thinner or acetone.
10   Place a new gasket on the intake manifold.
11   Position the carburetor on the gasket and install the mounting fasteners.
12   To prevent carburetor distortion or damage, tighten the fasteners to approximately 16 ft-lbs in a criss-cross pattern, 1/4-turn at a time.
13   The remaining installation steps are the reverse of removal.
14   Check and, if necessary, adjust the idle speed (see Section 12).
15   If the vehicle is equipped with an automatic transmission, refer to Chapter 7B for the kickdown cable or linkage adjustment procedure.
16   Start the engine and check carefully for fuel leaks.

4A

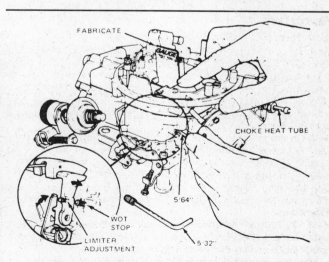

12.90 Venturi valve limiter adjustment on the 2700 VV and 7200 VV carburetors

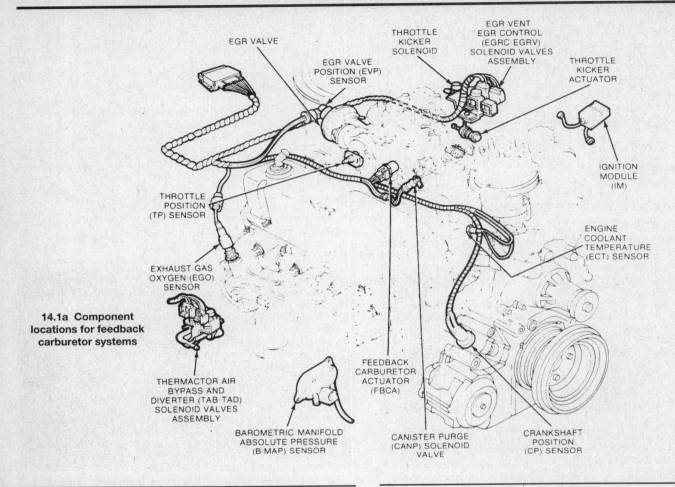

14.1a Component locations for feedback carburetor systems

EGR VALVE

EGR VALVE POSITION (EVP) SENSOR

THROTTLE KICKER SOLENOID

EGR VENT EGR CONTROL (EGRC/EGRV) SOLENOID VALVES ASSEMBLY

THROTTLE KICKER ACTUATOR

IGNITION MODULE (IM)

THROTTLE POSITION (TP) SENSOR

ENGINE COOLANT TEMPERATURE (ECT) SENSOR

EXHAUST GAS OXYGEN (EGO) SENSOR

THERMACTOR AIR BYPASS AND DIVERTER (TAB/TAD) SOLENOID VALVES ASSEMBLY

BAROMETRIC MANIFOLD ABSOLUTE PRESSURE (B/MAP) SENSOR

FEEDBACK CARBURETOR ACTUATOR (FBCA)

CANISTER PURGE (CANP) SOLENOID VALVE

CRANKSHAFT POSITION (CP) SENSOR

14   Electronic feedback carburetor systems - general information

Refer to illustrations 14.1a, 14.1b and 14.1c

1   The electronic feedback carburetor (EEC-III) emission system relies on an electronic signal, which is generated by an exhaust gas oxygen (EGO) sensor, to control a variety of devices and keep emissions within limits **(see illustrations)**. The system works in conjunction with a three-way catalyst to control the levels of carbon monoxide, hydrocarbons and oxides of nitrogen. The EEC-III system also works in conjunction with the computer. The two systems share certain sensors and output actuators; therefore, diagnosing the EEC-III system will require a thorough check of all the feedback carburetor components.

2   The system operates in two modes: open loop and closed loop. When the engine is cold, the air/fuel mixture is controlled by the computer in accordance with a program designed in at the time of production. The air/fuel mixture during this time will be richer to allow for proper engine warm-up. When the engine is at operating temperature, the system operates in closed loop and the air/fuel mixture is varied depending on the information supplied by the exhaust gas oxygen sensor.

3   Here is a list of the various sensors and output actuators involved with these feedback carburetor systems:

Coolant temperature sensor (ECT)
Exhaust Gas Oxygen (EGO) sensor
Electronic ignition (DuraSpark III)
EGR vent/control solenoid valves (EGRC/EGRV)
Feedback carburetor actuator (FBCA)
EEC-III computer

Throttle Position Sensor (TPS)
Barometric Manifold Absolute Pressure (B/MAP) sensor
EGR valve position (EVP) sensor
Thermactor air bypass and diverter (TAB/TAD) solenoid valves
Canister purge (CANP) solenoid valve
Crankshaft Position (CP) sensor

4   Refer to Section 15 for the diagnostic checks for the feedback carburetor system components

15   Electronic feedback carburetor information sensors and output actuators - check and replacement

Engine Coolant Temperature (ECT) sensor

Refer to illustration 15.2

General description

1   The coolant sensor is a thermistor (a resistor which varies the value of its resistance in accordance with temperature changes). The change in the resistance values will directly affect the voltage signal from the computer. As the sensor temperature DECREASES, the resistance values will DECREASE. As the sensor temperature INCREASES, the resistance values will INCREASE.

Check

2   To check the sensor, connect the probes of an ohmmeter to the terminals of the coolant temperature sensor **(see illustration)** while it is completely cold (50 to 80-degrees F = 1,500 to 3,000 ohms). Next, start the engine and warm it up until the engine reaches normal operating temperature **(see illustration)**. The resistance should be

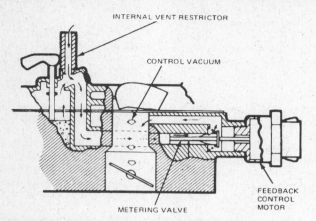

14.1b Backsuction feedback system on the 7200 VV carburetor

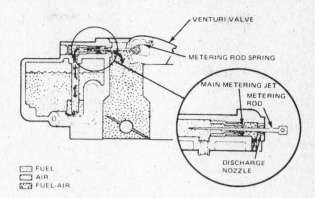

14.1c Variable venturi main metering system on the 7200 VV carburetor

15.2 Working on the sensor side, check the resistance of the coolant temperature sensor

15.8 The oxygen sensor creates a very small voltage signal. A quick oxygen sensor check is to backprobe the signal wire using a pin and monitor the millivolt readings as the engine warms up

4A

higher (180 to 200-degrees F = 8,000 to 10,000 ohms). **Note:** *Access to the coolant temperature sensor makes it difficult to position test probes on the terminals. If necessary, remove the sensor and perform the tests in a pan of heated water to simulate the conditions.*

Replacement
Warning: *Wait until the engine is completely cool before performing this procedure.*
3   Before installing the new sensor, wrap the threads with Teflon sealing tape to prevent leakage and thread corrosion.
4   To remove the sensor, release the locking tab, unplug the electrical connector, then carefully unscrew the sensor.
5   Install the new sensor as quickly as possible to minimize coolant loss. Check the coolant level and add some, if necessary (see Chapter 1).

Exhaust gas oxygen (EGO) sensor
Refer to illustration 15.8
Note 1: *The oxygen sensor is used only on 1980 and later models that are equipped with a feedback carburetor.*
Note 2: *A faulty oxygen sensor is one of the most common causes of high fuel consumption and poor driveability on a vehicle equipped with a feedback carburetor.*

General description and check
6   The oxygen sensor, which is located in the exhaust manifold, monitors the oxygen content of the exhaust gas stream. The oxygen content in the exhaust reacts with the oxygen sensor to produce a voltage output which varies from 0.1-volt (high oxygen, lean mixture) to 0.9-volts (low oxygen, rich mixture). The electronic control unit

constantly monitors this variable voltage output to determine the ratio of oxygen to fuel in the mixture. The electronic control unit alters the air/fuel mixture ratio by controlling the pulse width (open time) of the mixture control solenoid. A mixture ratio of 14.7 parts air to 1 part fuel is the ideal mixture ratio for minimizing exhaust emissions, thus allowing the catalytic converter to operate at maximum efficiency. It is this ratio of 14.7 to 1 which the electronic control unit and the oxygen sensor attempt to maintain at all times.
7   The oxygen sensor produces no voltage when it is below its normal operating temperature of about 600-degrees F. During this initial period before warm-up, the system operates in open loop mode.
8   If the engine reaches normal operating temperature and/or has been running for two or more minutes, and if the oxygen sensor is producing a steady signal voltage between 0.1 and 0.9-volts **(see illustration)**, the oxygen sensor is working properly.
9   The proper operation of the oxygen sensor depends on four conditions:

a) **Electrical** - *The low voltages generated by the sensor depend upon good, clean connections which should be checked whenever a malfunction of the sensor is suspected or indicated.*
b) **Outside air supply** - *The sensor is designed to allow air circulation to the internal portion of the sensor. Whenever the sensor is removed and installed or replaced, make sure the air passages are not restricted.*
c) **Proper operating temperature** - *The electronic control unit will not react to the sensor signal until the sensor reaches approximately 600-degrees F. This factor must be taken into consideration when evaluating the performance of the sensor.*

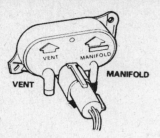

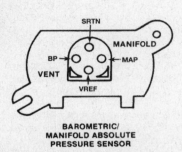

15.20 Connect the negative probe of the voltmeter to the SRTN terminal and the positive probe to the MAP terminal and check for voltage with and without vacuum

BAROMETRIC/
MANIFOLD ABSOLUTE
PRESSURE SENSOR

d) *Unleaded fuel - The use of unleaded fuel is essential for proper operation of the sensor. Make sure the fuel you are using is of this type.*

10   In addition to observing the above conditions, special care must be taken whenever the sensor is serviced.

a) *The oxygen sensor has a permanently attached pigtail and electrical connector which should not be removed from the sensor. Damage or removal of the pigtail or electrical connector can adversely affect operation of the sensor.*
b) *Grease, dirt and other contaminants should be kept away from the electrical connector and the louvered end of the sensor.*
c) *Do not use cleaning solvents of any kind on the oxygen sensor.*
d) *Do not drop or roughly handle the sensor.*
e) *The silicone boot must be installed in the correct position to prevent the boot from being melted and to allow the sensor to operate properly.*

Replacement

Note: *Because it is installed in the exhaust manifold or pipe, which contracts when cool, the oxygen sensor may be very difficult to loosen when the engine is cold. Rather than risk damage to the sensor (assuming you are planning to reuse it in another manifold or pipe), start and run the engine for a minute or two, then shut it off. Be careful not to burn yourself during the following procedure.*

11   Disconnect the cable from the negative terminal of the battery.
12   Raise the vehicle and place it securely on jackstands.
13   Carefully disconnect the electrical connector from the sensor.
14   Carefully unscrew the sensor from the exhaust manifold. **Caution:** *Excessive force may damage the threads.*
15   Anti-seize compound must be used on the threads of the sensor to facilitate future removal. The threads of new sensors will already be coated with this compound, but if an old sensor is removed and reinstalled, recoat the threads.
16   Install the sensor and tighten it securely.
17   Reconnect the electrical connector of the pigtail lead to the main engine wiring harness.
18   Lower the vehicle and reconnect the cable to the negative terminal of the battery.

Barometric/Manifold Absolute Pressure (B/MAP) sensor

General description

19   The Manifold Absolute Pressure (MAP) sensor monitors the intake manifold pressure changes resulting from changes in engine load and speed and converts the information into a voltage output. The EEC-III computer uses the MAP sensor to control fuel delivery. The EEC-III computer will receive information as a voltage signal that will vary from 1.0 to 1.5 volts at closed throttle (high vacuum) to 4.0 to 4.5 volts at wide open throttle (low vacuum).

Check

Refer to illustration 15.20

20   With the ignition key ON (engine not running), backprobe terminals MAP and SRTN **(see illustration)** of the B/MAP electrical connector.
21   Without vacuum applied to the B/MAP sensor (idle condition) the voltmeter should register high (3.5 to 4.5 volts).
22   Using a hand-held vacuum pump, apply approximately 20 inches Hg of vacuum to the B/MAP sensor and observe the voltage. **Note:** *Apply vacuum to the MANIFOLD side of the B/MAP sensor using a hand-held vacuum pump.* It should decrease to 1.0 to 2.0 volts.
23   If the measurements are incorrect, replace the B/MAP sensor with a new part.

Replacement

24   Disconnect the harness electrical connector from the MAP sensor.
25   Remove the mounting bolts and lift the MAP sensor from the engine compartment. Installation is the reverse of removal.

Feedback carburetor actuator (FBCA) motor

Check

Refer to illustrations 15.27 and 15.28

26   The function of the feedback carburetor actuator is to provide limited regulation of the fuel-air ratio of a feedback carburetor in response to the electronic signals sent by the computer. This is accomplished by metering the main fuel jets in the carburetor with the use of a fuel metering pintle that extends into the fuel passage and shuts the fuel off (lean) and on (rich), allowing the fuel/air mixture ratio to change. By controlling the duration of this voltage signal, the ratio of power ON-time versus the power OFF-time is called the duty cycle.
27   Maintain an engine speed of 1500 rpm. Disconnect the feedback carburetor actuator motor connector from the solenoid **(see illustration)**. Average engine speed should increase a minimum of 50 rpm.
28   Reconnect the feedback carburetor actuator motor connector. The engine speed should slowly return to 1500 rpm. If rpm does not change as specified, there's a problem in the feedback carburetor system, possibly the feedback motor, although the oxygen sensor is usually the cause. First check for battery voltage to the FBCA electrical connector **(see illustration)**, then check the oxygen sensor. If the oxygen sensor is OK and all connections are OK, the fuel metering pintle is probably bad.

15.27 Disconnect the FBC actuator from the motor and confirm a change in engine rpm

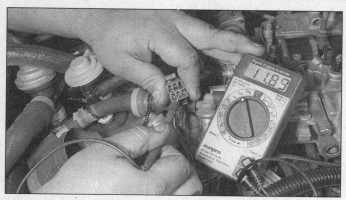

15.28 Check for battery voltage to the FBC Actuator motor with the ignition key ON (engine not running)

Component replacement
29 Disconnect the cable from the negative battery terminal.
30 Disconnect the electrical connector from the FBCA motor.
31 Use an open end wrench and remove the FBCA motor.
32 Installation is the reverse of removal.

Throttle Position Sensor (TPS)
General description
33 The Throttle Position Sensor (TPS) is located on the end of the throttle shaft on the throttle body. By monitoring the output voltage from the TPS, the EEC can determine fuel delivery based on throttle valve angle (driver demand). A broken or loose TPS can cause an unstable idle because the computer thinks the throttle is moving.

Check
Refer to illustration 15.34
34 To check the TPS, turn the ignition switch to ON (engine not running) and connect the probes of the voltmeter to the ground wire (GRND) and signal wire (SIG) terminals on the backside of the electrical connector **(see illustration)**. This test checks for the proper signal voltage from the TPS. **Note:** *Be careful when backprobing the electrical connector. Do not damage the wiring harness or pull on any connectors to make clean contact. Be sure the probes are placed in the correct position.*
35 The sensor should read 0.5 to 1.0-volt at idle. Have an assistant depress the accelerator pedal to simulate full throttle and the sensor should increase voltage to 5.0 to 8.0-volts. If the TPS voltage readings are incorrect, replace it with a new unit.
36 Also, check the TPS reference voltage. With the ignition key ON (engine not running), connect the positive (+) probe of the voltmeter to the voltage reference wire (REF). There should be approximately 5.0 volts sent from the EEC to the TPS.
37 Also, check the resistance of the potentiometer within the TPS. Disconnect the TPS electrical connector and working on the sensor

side, connect the probes of the ohmmeter to the ground wire and the TPS signal wire. With the throttle valve fully closed, the TPS should read between 3.0 and 4.0 K-ohms.
38 Now open the throttle with one hand and check the resistance again. Slowly advance the throttle until fully open. The resistance should be approximately 350 ohms. The potentiometer should exhibit a smooth change in resistance as it travels from fully closed to wide open throttle. Any deviations indicate a possible worn or damaged TPS.

Removal
39 Detach the cable from the negative terminal of the battery.
40 Unplug the wire harness electrical connector from the TPS connector.
41 Remove the TPS connector bracket retaining screw and detach the bracket and connector from the throttle body.
42 Remove the TPS retaining screws.
43 Slide the TPS off the throttle shaft.

Adjustment
44 Turn the ignition key to ON (engine not running).
45 With the TPS bolts in place and slightly loose, rotate the sensor counter-clockwise.
46 Remove the vacuum hose from the throttle kicker actuator and make sure the throttle is off the fast idle cam.
47 The voltage should read between 0.5 and 2.0 volts (idle).
48 If the voltage reading is incorrect, continue to rotate the TPS until the correct voltage is present.
49 Tighten the adjustment bolts.

Crankshaft Position (CP) sensor
General information
Refer to illustration 15.50
50 The CP sensor and the Pulse Ring work in conjunction to provide the EEC system with a signal indicating the crankshaft position **(see illustration)**. The pulse ring is pressed onto the vibration damper (see Chapter 2A) at 10-degrees BTDC. The sensor is mounted on the timing chain cover and picks up a magnetic pulse as the ring turns.

Check
51 Disconnect the CP sensor electrical connector and using an ohmmeter, probe the terminals. Check the resistance.
52 The sensor should read between 100 and 640 ohms.
53 If the resistance is too high or low, replace the sensor with a new part.

Replacement
54 Detach the cable from the negative terminal of the battery.
55 Unplug the wire harness electrical connector from the CP sensor connector.
56 Remove the CP sensor bracket retaining screws and detach the bracket and sensor from the timing chain cover.
57 Installation is the reverse of removal.

4A

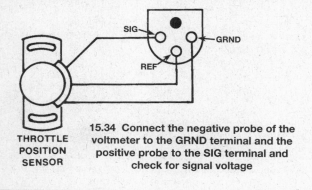

15.34 Connect the negative probe of the voltmeter to the GRND terminal and the positive probe to the SIG terminal and check for signal voltage

THROTTLE POSITION SENSOR

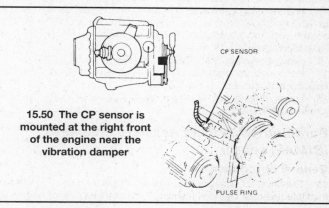

15.50 The CP sensor is mounted at the right front of the engine near the vibration damper

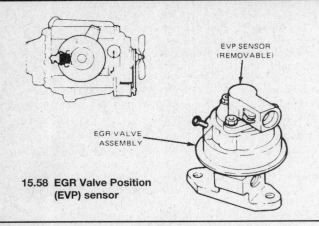

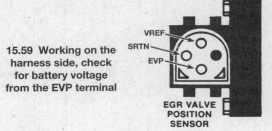

15.58 EGR Valve Position (EVP) sensor

15.59 Working on the harness side, check for battery voltage from the EVP terminal

EGR Valve Position (EVP) sensor

General Description

Refer to illustration 15.58

58   Many of the EEC III feedback carburetor systems are equipped with the EGR valve position sensor mounted near the EGR valve **(see illustration)**. This sensor detects the position of the EGR valve. The information is sent to the ECA (computer) and in turn the air/fuel ratio is regulated by the FBCA motor.

Check

Refer to illustration 15.59

59   Disconnect the electrical connector for the EGR valve position sensor and working on the harness side **(see illustration),** measure the voltage available to the sensor on terminal EVP with the ignition key ON (engine not running). There should be battery voltage.

60   If battery voltage is not available, check the wiring harness and computer for possible shorts or damage. If battery voltage is available, have the EGR valve position sensor checked by a dealer service department or other qualified repair shop.

Replacement

61   Disconnect the harness connector for the EGR valve position sensor and remove the bolts that retain the assembly to the EGR valve.

62   Installation is the reverse of removal.

Electronic Control Assembly (ECA) computer

General Information

Refer to illustration 15.63

63   The ECA assembly is the "brain" of the electronic control system. This computer processes and calibrates information it receives from the sensor and output actuators **(see illustration)**. This computer receives information from the coolant temperature sensor, EGR valve position sensor, EGO sensor, atmospheric pressure sensor. B/MAP sensor, TPS and CP sensor. The information is used by the processor to activate various engine control systems such as air/fuel ratio, EGR flow, spark advance, canister purge and thermactor to give optimum fuel and emissions control.

Ignition module

See Chapter 5 for information on the ignition module.

16   Exhaust system - servicing and general information

Warning: *Inspection and repair of exhaust system components should be done only after enough time has elapsed after driving the vehicle to allow the system components to cool completely. Also, when working under the vehicle, make sure it is securely supported on jackstands.*

1   The exhaust system consists of the exhaust manifold(s), the catalytic converter(s), the muffler, the tailpipe and all connecting pipes,

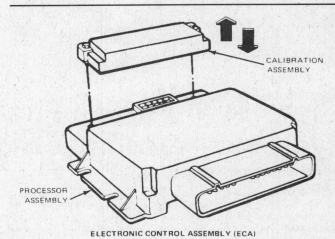

15.63 Electronic Control Assembly (ECA)

brackets, hangers and clamps. The exhaust system is attached to the body with mounting brackets and rubber hangers. If any of the parts are improperly installed, excessive noise and vibration will be transmitted to the body.

2   Conduct regular inspections of the exhaust system to keep it safe and quiet. Look for any damaged or bent parts, open seams, holes, loose connections, excessive corrosion or other defects which could allow exhaust fumes to enter the vehicle. Deteriorated exhaust system components should not be repaired; they should be replaced with new parts.

3   If the exhaust system components are extremely corroded or rusted together, welding equipment will probably be required to remove them. The convenient way to accomplish this is to have a muffler repair shop remove the corroded sections with a cutting torch. If, however, you want to save money by doing it yourself (and you don't have a welding outfit with a cutting torch), simply cut off the old components with a hacksaw. If you have compressed air, special pneumatic cutting chisels can also be used. If you do decide to tackle the job at home, be sure to wear safety goggles to protect your eyes from metal chips and work gloves to protect your hands.

4   Here are some simple guidelines to follow when repairing the exhaust system:

a) *Work from the back to the front when removing exhaust system components.*

b) *Apply penetrating oil to the exhaust system component fasteners to make them easier to remove.*

c) *Use new gaskets, hangers and clamps when installing exhaust system components.*

d) *Apply anti-seize compound to the threads of all exhaust system fasteners during reassembly.*

e) *Be sure to allow sufficient clearance between newly installed parts and all points on the underbody to avoid overheating the floor pan and possibly damaging the interior carpet and insulation. Pay particularly close attention to the catalytic converter and heat shield.*

Chapter 4 Part B Fuel and exhaust systems - fuel-injected engines

Contents

Specifications

Fuel pressure

CFI

Fuel system pressure (at idle)	35 to 45 psi

SEFI

Fuel system pressure with key on, engine off	35 to 45 psi
Fuel system pressure (at idle)	
Vacuum hose attached	30 to 45 psi
Vacuum hose detached	40 to 50 psi
Fuel system hold pressure (after 5 minutes)	30 to 40 psi
Fuel pump pressure (maximum)	65 psi
Fuel pump hold pressure	50 psi

Injector resistance

Injector resistance	13.5 to 19 ohms

Torque specifications

	Ft-lbs (unless otherwise indicated)
Air intake plenum mounting bolts (5.0L engine)	12 to 18
Throttle body mounting bolts (4.6L engine)	
1995 and earlier	12 to 18
1996	71 to 106 in-lbs
Throttle body mounting nuts (5.0L engine)	12 to 18
EGR valve-to-throttle body (5.0L engine)	12 to 18
Fuel rail mounting bolts	70 to 105 in-lbs
Exhaust pipe-to-exhaust manifold bolts	25 to 35

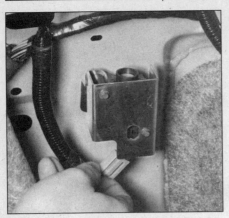

2.1 The inertia switch is located in the trunk. Disconnect the electrical connector to disable the fuel pump

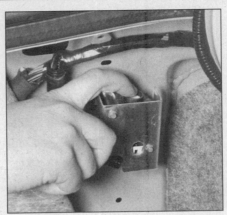

2.4 If necessary, push the reset button after connecting the inertia switch to energize the fuel pump

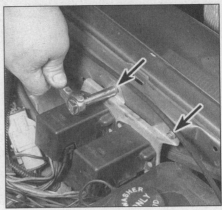

3.2a Remove the bolts (arrows) from the relay cluster bracket assembly (1988 5.0L shown)

1   General information

Warning: *Gasoline is extremely flammable, so take extra precautions when you work on any part of the fuel system. Don't smoke or allow open flames or bare light bulbs near the work area, and don't work in a garage where a natural gas-type appliance (such as a water heater or a clothes dryer) with a pilot light is present. Since gasoline is carcinogenic, wear latex gloves when there's a possibility of being exposed to fuel, and, if you spill any fuel on your skin, rinse it off immediately with soap and water. Mop up any spills immediately and do not store fuel-soaked rags where they could ignite. The fuel system is under constant pressure, so, if any fuel lines are to be disconnected, the fuel pressure in the system must be relieved first. When you perform any kind of work on the fuel system, wear safety glasses and have a Class B type fire extinguisher on hand.*

The fuel system on fuel-injected engines consists of a fuel tank, an electric fuel pump (located in the fuel tank), a fuel pump relay, fuel injectors, an air cleaner assembly and a throttle body unit. Fuel-injected engines, which start in 1981, are equipped with either a Central Fuel Injection (CFI) system or a Sequential Electronic Fuel Injection (SEFI) system. Most engines are equipped with SEFI after 1987. The two systems are easily distinguished. The CFI system uses a large throttle body unit mounted upright directly in the middle of the engine while the SEFI system uses separate injectors mounted in the intake manifold and positioned over the intake valves.

Central Fuel Injection (CFI)

The Central Fuel Injection system incorporates two injectors mounted in a throttle body similar to that of a conventional carburetor. This system produces greatly improved fuel metering in all running conditions and since most of the control mechanism is electronic, CFI reduces maintenance and minor repair problems.

The Electronic Engine Control (EEC) Module automatically adjusts the air/fuel mixture according to engine load and performance. A fuel pressure regulator mounted in the fuel charging assembly regulates the electric pump generated fuel pressure at a constant 39 psi. The injectors consist of a solenoid activated pintle valve and a small inline fuel filter. They are energized by time modulated electronic pulses from the EEC (computer).

Sequential Electronic Fuel Injection (SEFI) system

Sequential Electronic Fuel Injection uses timed impulses to inject the fuel directly into the intake port of each cylinder according to its firing order. The injectors are controlled by the Powertrain Control Module (PCM). The PCM monitors various engine parameters and delivers the exact amount of fuel required into the intake ports. The throttle body serves only to control the amount of air passing into the system. Because each cylinder is equipped with its own injector, much better control of the air/fuel mixture is possible.

Fuel pump and lines

Fuel is circulated from the fuel tank to the fuel injection system, and back to the fuel tank, through a pair of metal lines running along the underside of the vehicle. An electric fuel pump is located inside the fuel tank. A vapor return system routes all vapors back to the fuel tank through a separate return line.

The fuel pump will operate as long as the engine is cranking or running and the PCM is receiving ignition reference pulses from the electronic ignition system. If there are no reference pulses, the fuel pump will shut off after two or three seconds.

Exhaust system

The exhaust system includes an exhaust manifold fitted with an exhaust oxygen sensor, a catalytic converter, an exhaust pipe, and a muffler.

The catalytic converter is an emission control device added to the exhaust system to reduce pollutants. A single-bed converter is used in conjunction with a three-way (reduction) catalyst. Refer to Chapter 6 for more information regarding the catalytic converter.

2   Fuel pressure relief procedure

Refer to illustrations 2.1 and 2.4
Warning: *Gasoline is extremely flammable, so take extra precautions when you work on any part of the fuel system.* **See Warning in Section 1.**

1   The fuel pump inertia switch, which shuts off fuel to the engine in the event of a collision, affords a simple and convenient means by which fuel pressure can be relieved before servicing fuel injection components. The switch is located in the luggage compartment **(see illustration)** and is usually covered by the carpet which comes up the sides of the trunk.

2   Unplug the inertia switch electrical connector.

3   Start the engine and allow it to run until it stops. This should take only a few seconds.

4   The fuel system pressure is now relieved. Disconnect the cable from the negative terminal of the battery before performing any work on the fuel system. When you're finished working on the fuel system, simply plug the electrical connector back into the switch. If the inertia switch was "popped" (activated) during this procedure, push the reset button on the top of the switch **(see illustration)**.

5   After the fuel pressure has been relieved. it's a good idea to lay a shop towel over any fuel connection to be disconnected, to absorb the residual fuel that may leak out when servicing the fuel system.

3.2b Use a jumper wire and connect the power wire (battery voltage) to the fuel pump (1988 5.0L shown)

3.2c On models with the 4.6L engine, first lift the relay control assembly from the fuse center and press the tab on the cover . . .

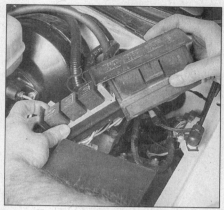

3.2d . . . then slide the cover off the relay control panel (4.6L engine)

3.2e Relay control panel

1	PCM power relay	3	Air conditioning
2	Fuel pump relay		cutout relay

3   Fuel pump/fuel pressure - check

Warning: *Gasoline is extremely flammable, so take extra precautions when you work on any part of the fuel system.* **See Warning in Section 1.**

Note 1: *To perform the fuel pressure test, you will need to obtain a fuel pressure gauge and adapter set (fuel line fittings).*

Note 2: *After the fuel pressure has been relieved. it's a good idea to lay a shop towel over any fuel connection to be disassembled, to absorb the residual fuel that may leak out when servicing the fuel system.*

Preliminary inspection

Refer to illustrations 3.2a through 3.2h and 3.3a through 3.3e

1   Should the fuel system fail to deliver the proper amount of fuel, or any fuel at all, inspect it as follows. Remove the fuel filler cap. Have an assistant turn the ignition key to the On position (engine not running) while you listen at the fuel filler opening. You should hear a whirring sound that lasts for a couple of seconds.

2   If you don't hear anything, check the fuel pump fuse (see Chapter 12). If the fuse is blown, replace it and see if it blows again. If it does, trace the fuel pump circuit for a short. If it isn't blown, remove the fuel pump relay and install a jumper wire into the fuel pump relay terminals that power the fuel pump **(see illustrations)**. Listen at the fuel filler opening again - if you now hear the whirring sound, the fuel pump relay or its control circuit is faulty. If there is still no whirring sound, there is a problem in the fuel pump circuit from the relay panel to the fuel pump, defective power relay or a defective fuel pump.

3   Check for battery voltage to the fuel pump relay connector and

3.2f Use a jumper wire and jump the connector to power the fuel pump (yellow wire and green/yellow wire) (4.6L engine shown)

4B

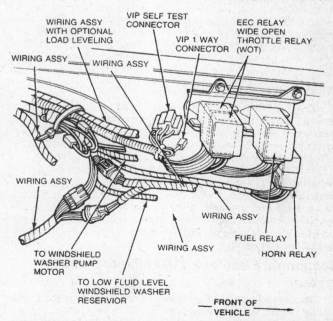

3.2g Location of the fuel pump relay on models with the 5.0L engine with SEFI

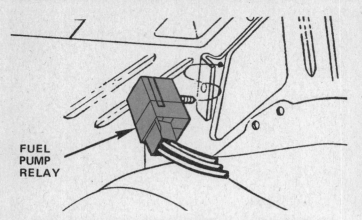

3.2h Location of the fuel pump relay on model with the 5.0L engine with CFI

3.3a Checking for battery voltage on the fuel pump relay power supply terminal (5.0L engine with SEFI shown)

3.3b Checking for battery voltage on the power relay supply terminal (5.0L engine with SEFI shown)

3.3c Checking for battery voltage on the fuel pump relay power supply terminal (4.6L engine shown)

3.3d Checking for battery voltage on the power relay supply terminal (4.6L engine shown)

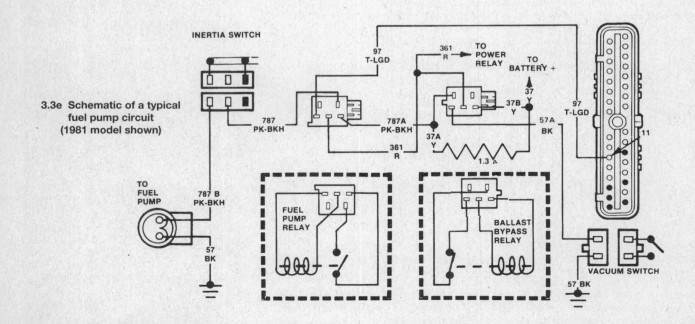

3.3e Schematic of a typical fuel pump circuit (1981 model shown)

the power relay connector (see illustrations). If there is battery voltage present, have the relay(s) tested at a dealer service department or other qualified automotive repair shop.

4   If there is no voltage present, check the fuse(s) and the wiring circuit for the fuel pump relay and/or power relay (see Chapter 12).

Operating pressure check

Refer to illustrations 3.7a, 3.7b, 3.7c and 3.8

5   Relieve the fuel system pressure (see Section 2).

6   Detach the cable from the negative battery terminal.

7   Remove the cap from the fuel pressure test port and attach a fuel pressure gauge (see illustrations). If you don't have the correct adapter for the test port, remove the Schrader valve and connect the gauge hose to the fitting. Tighten the hose clamp securely.

8   Attach the cable to the negative battery terminal. Turn the ignition key ON (engine not running). Locate the Diagnostic Test connector and install a jumper wire from terminal Fp (see illustrations) to ground. This will activate the fuel pump without running the engine.

9   Note the fuel pressure and compare it with the pressure listed in this Chapter's Specifications.

10   Next, remove the jumper wire from the Diagnostic Test connector and start the engine. With the engine idling, measure the fuel pressure. It should be as listed in this Chapter's Specifications. Detach the vacuum hose from the fuel pressure regulator - the fuel pressure reading should immediately increase. Compare the pressure with the value listed in this Chapter's Specifications. If the pressure doesn't rise when the hose is disconnected, check for vacuum at the disconnected hose. If vacuum is present, the fuel pressure regulator is faulty. Reconnect the vacuum hose.

11   If the fuel pressure is too high, check for a pinched or clogged fuel return hose or pipe. If the fuel return line is not obstructed, replace the fuel pressure regulator (see Section 12).

12   If the pressure is lower than specified, inspect the fuel filter - make sure it's not clogged. Look for a pinched or clogged fuel hose between the fuel tank and the fuel injection assembly. If the fuel feed line is OK, pinch the fuel return hose with a pair of pliers. If the pressure rises, replace the fuel pressure regulator (see Section 12). If the pressure is still low, check the fuel pump (see below).

13   Turn the ignition switch to Off, wait five minutes and recheck the pressure on the gauge. Compare the reading with the hold pressure listed in this Chapter's Specifications. If the hold pressure is less than specified:

a) The fuel lines may be leaking.
b) The fuel pressure regulator may be allowing the fuel pressure to bleed through to the return line.
c) A fuel injector (or injectors) may be leaking.
d) The fuel pump may be defective.

3.7a If you don't have the correct adapter, it is possible to remove the Schrader valve from the fitting and install a standard fuel pressure gauge, using a hose clamp (5.0L engine with SEFI shown)

Fuel pump output pressure check (dead-head pressure)

Warning: *For this test it is necessary to use a fuel pressure gauge with a bleeder valve in order to relieve the fuel pressure after the test is completed (the normal procedure for pressure relief will not work because the gauge is connected directly to the fuel pump).*

14   Relieve the system fuel pressure (see Section 2).

15   Detach the cable from the negative battery terminal.

16   Attach a fuel pressure gauge directly to the fuel feed line at the fuel tank.

17   Attach the cable to the negative battery terminal.

18   Using a jumper wire, bridge the terminals on the Diagnostic Test connector located under the engine compartment (see illustration 3.8).

19   Note the pressure reading on the gauge and compare the reading to the value listed in this Chapter's Specifications.

20   If the indicated pressure is less than specified, inspect the fuel line for leaks between the pump and gauge. If no leaks are found, replace the fuel pump.

21   Turn the ignition key to Off and wait five minutes. Note the reading on the gauge and compare it to the hold pressure listed in this Chapter's Specifications. If the hold pressure is less than specified, check the fuel line between the pump and gauge for leaks. If no leaks are found, replace the fuel pump.

22   Remove the jumper wire from the diagnostic test connector.

4B

3.7b Checking the fuel pressure on a 4.6L engine

3.7c Location of the Schrader valve (arrow) on a CFI system

3.8 With the ignition key ON (engine not running) ground terminal Fp to activate the fuel pump

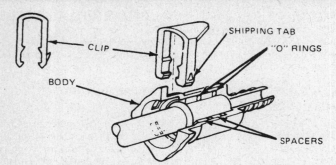

4.5 Details of the hairpin clip type push-connect fitting

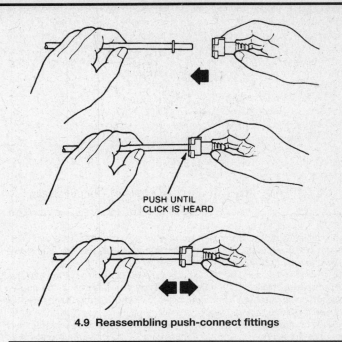

4.9 Reassembling push-connect fittings

23   Open the bleeder valve on the gauge and allow the pressurized fuel drain into an approved fuel container. Remove the gauge and reconnect the fuel line.

---

4   Fuel line fittings - service procedures

Refer to illustrations 4.5, 4.9, 4.10, 4.13, 4.14, 4.26a, 4.26b and 4.26c
Warning: *Gasoline is extremely flammable, so take extra precautions when you work on any part of the fuel system.* **See Warning in Section 1.**

Push-connect fittings - disassembly and reassembly

1   Ford uses two different push-connect fitting designs. Fittings used with 3/8 and 5/16-inch diameter lines have a "hairpin" type clip; fittings used with 1/4-inch diameter lines have a "duck bill" type clip. The procedure used for releasing each type of fitting is different. The clips should be replaced whenever a connector is disassembled.
2   Disconnect all push-connect fittings from fuel system components such as the fuel filter, the fuel charging assembly, the fuel tank, etc. before removing the assembly.

3/8 and 5/16-inch fittings (hairpin clip)

3   Inspect the internal portion of the fitting for accumulations of dirt. If more than a light coating of dust is present, clean the fitting before disassembly.
4   Some adhesion between the seals in the fitting and the line will occur over a period of time. Twist the fitting on the line, then push and pull the fitting until it moves freely.
5   Remove the hairpin clip from the fitting by bending the shipping tab down until it clears the body **(see illustration)**. Then, using nothing but your hands, spread each leg about 1/8-inch to disengage the body and push the legs through the fitting. Finally, pull lightly on the triangular end of the clip and work it clear of the line and fitting. Remember, don't use any tools to perform this part of the procedure.
6   Grasp the fitting and hose and pull it straight off the line.
7   Do not reuse the original clip in the fitting. A new clip must be used.

8   Before reinstalling the fitting on the line, wipe the line end with a clean cloth. Inspect the inside of the fitting to ensure that it's free of dirt and/or obstructions.
9   To reinstall the fitting on the line, align them and push the fitting into place. When the fitting is engaged, a definite click will be heard. Pull on the fitting to ensure that it's completely engaged **(see illustration)**. To install the new clip, insert it into any two adjacent openings in the fitting with the triangular portion of the clip pointing away from the fitting opening. Using your index finger, push the clip in until the legs are locked on the outside of the fitting.

1/4-inch fittings (duck bill clip)

10   The duck bill clip type fitting consists of a body, spacers, O-rings and the retaining clip **(see illustration)**. The clip holds the fitting securely in place on the line. One of the two following methods must be used to disconnect this type of fitting.
11   Before attempting to disconnect the fitting, check the visible internal portion of the fitting for accumulations of dirt. If more than a light coating of dust is evident, clean the fitting before disassembly.
12   Some adhesion between the seals in the fitting and line will occur over a period of time. Twist the fitting on the line, then push and pull the fitting until it moves freely.
13   The preferred method used to disconnect the fitting requires a special tool. To disengage the line from the fitting, align the slot in the push-connect disassembly tool (Ford Part No. T82L-9500-AH or equivalent tool) with either tab on the clip (90-degrees from the slots on the side of the fitting) and insert the tool **(see illustration)**. This disengages the duck bill from the line. **Note:** *Some fuel lines have a*

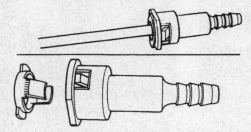

4.10 A push-connect fitting with a duck bill clip

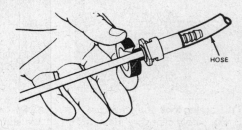

4.13 Duck bill clip fitting disassembly using the special Ford tool

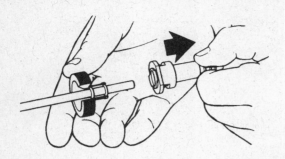

4.14 Pulling off the duck bill clip type push-connect fitting

secondary bead which aligns with the outer surface of the clip. The bead can make tool insertion difficult. If necessary, use the alternative disassembly method described in Step 16.

14   Holding the tool and the line with one hand, pull the fitting off **(see illustration)**. **Note:** *Only moderate effort is necessary if the clip is properly disengaged. The use of anything other than your hands should not be required.*

15   After disassembly, inspect and clean the line sealing surface. Also inspect the inside of the fitting and the line for any internal parts that may have been dislodged from the fitting. Any loose internal parts should be immediately reinstalled (use the line to insert the parts).

16   The alternative disassembly procedure requires a pair of small adjustable pliers. The pliers must have a jaw width of 3/16-inch or less.

17   Align the jaws of the pliers with the openings in the side of the fitting and compress the portion of the retaining clip that engages the body. This disengages the retaining clip from the body (often one side of the clip will disengage before the other - both sides must be disengaged).

18   Pull the fitting off the line. **Note:** *Only moderate effort is required if the retaining clip has been properly disengaged.*

19   Once the fitting is removed from the line end, check the fitting and line for any internal parts that may have been dislodged from the fitting. Any loose internal parts should be immediately reinstalled (use the line to insert the parts).

20   The retaining clip will remain on the line. Disengage the clip from the line bead to remove it. Do not reuse the retaining clip - install a new one!

21   Before reinstalling the fitting, wipe the line end with a clean cloth. Check the inside of the fitting to make sure that it's free of dirt and/or obstructions.

22   To reinstall the fitting, align it with the line and push it into place.

When the fitting is engaged, a definite click will be heard. Pull on the fitting to ensure that it's fully engaged.

23   Install the new replacement clip by inserting one of the serrated edges on the duck bill portion into one of the openings. Push on the other side until the clip snaps into place.

Spring lock couplings - disassembly and reassembly

24   The fuel supply and return lines used on SEFI engines utilize spring lock couplings at the engine fuel rail end instead of plastic push-connect fittings. The male end of the spring lock coupling, which is girded by two O-rings, is inserted into a female flared end engine fitting. The coupling is secured by a garter spring which prevents disengagement by gripping the flared end of the female fitting. On later models, a cup-tether assembly provides additional security.

25   To disconnect the 1/2-inch (12.7 mm) spring lock coupling supply fitting, you will need to obtain a spring lock coupling tool D87L-9280-B or its equivalent; for the 3/8-inch (9.52 mm) return fitting, get tool D87L-9280-A or its equivalent.

26   Study the accompanying illustrations carefully before detaching either spring lock coupling fitting **(see illustrations)**.

5   Fuel pump - removal and installation

Warning: *Gasoline is extremely flammable, so take extra precautions when you work on any part of the fuel system.* **See Warning in Section 1.**

Note: *Forward mounted fuel pumps are accessible without having to remove the fuel tank. This will be easily recognizable by the fuel lines that are mounted directly with the fuel pump assembly. Rear mounted fuel pumps will have only the fuel level sending unit mounted forward in the fuel tank with the fuel pump mounted on the rear. If the vehicle is equipped with a rear mounted fuel pump, it will be necessary to remove the fuel tank for access to the fuel pump.*

1   Unless the vehicle has been driven far enough to completely empty the tank, it's a good idea to siphon the residual fuel out before removing the fuel pump from the vehicle. **Warning:** *DO NOT start the siphoning action by mouth! Use a siphoning kit (available at most auto parts stores).*

2   Relieve the fuel pressure (refer to Section 2).

3   Detach the cable from the negative terminal of the battery.

4   Raise the rear of the vehicle and support it securely on jackstands.

5   Disconnect the fuel lines from the fuel pump/fuel level sender assembly (see Section 3).

6   Disconnect the fuel pump/fuel level sender electrical connector.

4B

4.26a If the spring lock couplings are equipped with safety clips, pry them off with a small screwdriver

4.26b Open the spring-loaded halves of the spring lock coupling tool and place it in position around the coupling, then close it

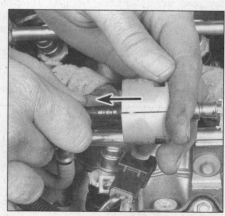

4.26c To disconnect the coupling, push the tool into the cage opening to expand the garter spring and release the female fitting, then pull the male and female fittings apart

5.7 Use a brass punch to turn the locking ring on the fuel pump/sending unit assembly counterclockwise (forward mounted fuel pump shown)

5.8 Carefully angle the fuel pump/sending unit out of the fuel tank without damaging the fuel strainer or sending unit

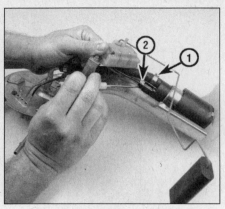

5.11 Remove the clamp (1) and disconnect the electrical connector (2) from the fuel pump, then separate the pump from the sending unit assembly

5.15 Disconnect the electrical connector from the fuel pump assembly

5.17 Carefully angle the fuel pump out of the fuel tank

5.20a Remove the clamp from the fuel line

Forward-mounted fuel pumps

Refer to illustrations 5.7, 5.8 and 5.11

7   Using a brass punch or wood dowel only, tap the lock ring counterclockwise until it's loose (see illustration).

8   Carefully pull the fuel pump/sending unit assembly from the tank (see illustration).

9   Remove the old lock ring gasket and discard it.

10   If you're planning to reinstall the original fuel pump/sending unit, remove the strainer by prying it off with a screwdriver, wash it in clean solvent, then push it back onto the metal pipe on the end of the pump. If you're installing a new pump/sending unit, the assembly will include a new strainer.

11   To separate the fuel pump from the assembly, remove the clamp (see illustration) and disconnect the electrical connector from the fuel pump.

12   Clean the fuel pump mounting flange and the tank mounting surface and seal ring groove.

13   Installation is the reverse of removal. Apply a thin coat of heavy grease to the new seal ring to hold it in place during assembly.

Rear-mounted fuel pumps

Refer to illustrations 5.15, 5.17, 5.20a and 5.20b

14   Unbolt the fuel tank straps (see Chapter 4A, Section 4) and lower the fuel tank part way down.

15   Disconnect the fuel lines from the fuel pump and disconnect the electrical connector from the unit (see illustration).

16   Using a brass punch or wood dowel only, tap the lock ring counterclockwise until it's loose.

17   Carefully pull the fuel pump assembly from the tank (see illustration).

18   Remove the old lock ring gasket and discard it.

19   If you're planning to reinstall the original fuel pump, remove the strainer by prying it off with a screwdriver, wash it with carburetor cleaner, then push it back onto the end of the pump. If you're installing a new pump, the assembly will include a new strainer.

20   To separate the fuel pump from the assembly, remove the clamp (see illustrations) and disconnect the electrical connector from the fuel pump.

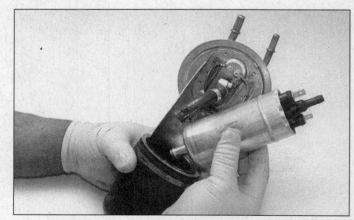

5.20b Slide the fuel pump out of the rubber holder

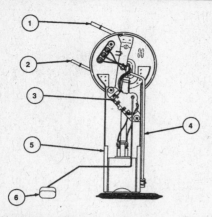

6.4 Details of the fuel pump/sending unit assembly

1	Fuel supply line	4	Fuel return tube
2	Fuel return line	5	Electric fuel pump
3	Fuel gauge sender	6	Float

21   Clean the fuel pump mounting flange and the tank mounting surface and seal ring groove.
22   Installation is the reverse of removal. Apply a thin coat of heavy grease to the new seal ring to hold it in place during assembly.

6   Fuel level sending unit – check and replacement

Refer to illustration 6.4

Check

Refer to Chapter 4A, Section 7, for the fuel level sending unit checking procedure.

Replacement

1   Remove the fuel pump/sending unit assembly from the vehicle (see Section 7).

7.2a Remove the mounting bolt and clamp (arrow) from the air intake assembly (4.6L engine shown)

2   Carefully angle the sending unit out of the opening without damaging the fuel level float located at the bottom of the assembly.
3   Remove the sending unit electrical connector from the fuel pump assembly.
4   On fuel level sending unit/fuel pump assembly types, remove the screws that secure the sending unit to the fuel pump assembly **(see illustration)**.
5   Installation is the reverse of removal.
6   If the float arm and float wire loop were damaged or bent during removal and installation, adjust the angle and travel distance.
7   Be sure to install a new rubber gasket.

7   Air cleaner assembly - removal and installation

Refer to illustrations 7.2a, 7.2b, 7.2c, 7.2d, 7.5a and 7.5b
1   Detach the cable from the negative terminal of the battery.
2   Loosen the bolt(s) from the air intake assembly on the intake manifold and the clamps on the air cleaner housing and remove the air intake assembly from the engine compartment **(see illustrations)**.

4B

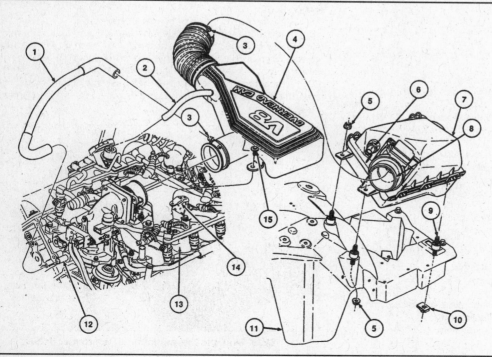

7.2b Exploded view of the air intake system on the 4.6L engine

1   Idle air control valve inlet tube
2   Crankcase ventilation tube
3   Clamp
4   Air intake assembly
5   Nut
6   IAT sensor
7   Air cleaner assembly
8   MAF sensor
9   Air cleaner studs
10   Nut
11   Left side fender apron
12   BPA-ISC valve inlet
13   Intake manifold
14   Accelerator cable bracket
15   Bolt

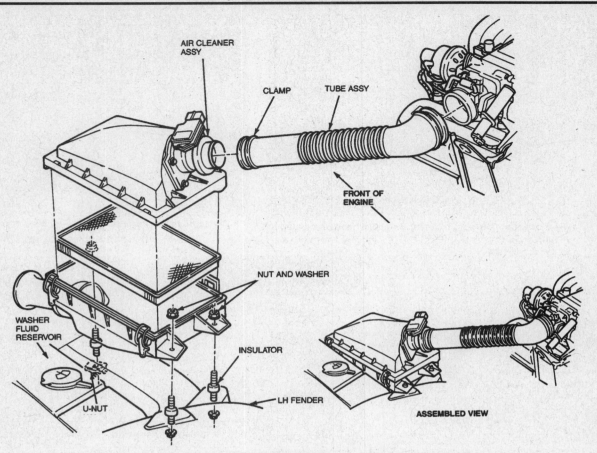

7.2c Air cleaner housing mounting details (5.0L engine with SEFI, California models)

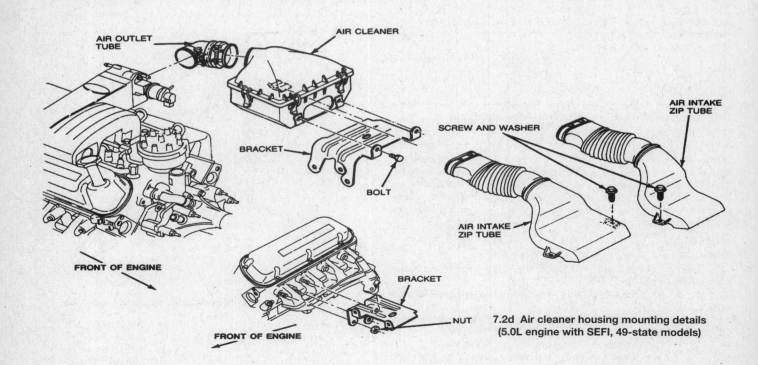

7.2d Air cleaner housing mounting details
(5.0L engine with SEFI, 49-state models)

7.5a Remove the mounting bolts (arrows) from the air cleaner housing (5.0L engine with SEFI shown - 49-state model)

7.5b Remove the mounting nuts (arrows) from the air cleaner housing (4.6L engine shown)

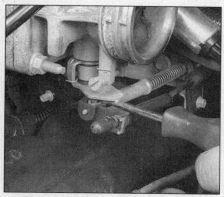

8.2a On 5.0L engines with SEFI, pry the end of the accelerator cable off using a screwdriver

8.2b Carefully remove the accelerator cable from the throttle lever by twisting (if necessary, pry it off with a screwdriver) (4.6L engine shown)

8.3 Remove the bolt (arrow) and separate the cruise control cable from the bracket (4.6L engine shown)

3   Unclip the upper half of the air cleaner housing assembly and remove it (see Chapter 1).
4   Remove the air filter element.
5   Remove the air cleaner housing mounting nuts **(see illustration)** and detach the assembly.
6   Installation is the reverse of removal.

8 Accelerator cable - removal, installation and adjustment

Note: *Removal and installation of the accelerator cable on 1996 models is the same as on previous years. The only difference is the throttle body is now attached to a throttle body spacer that is attached to the center of the plastic intake manifold. The throttle body is now positioned transversely to the engine instead of in-line to the engine as on previous models.*

Removal

Refer to illustrations 8.2a, 8.2b, 8.3, 8.5 and 8.6

1   Remove the air intake duct from the throttle body and intake manifold area (see Section 9).
2   Detach the accelerator cable from the throttle lever **(see illustrations)**.
3   Remove the cruise control cable from the cable bracket **(see illustration)**.
4   Separate the accelerator cable from the cable bracket.
5   Pull the cable end out from the accelerator pedal recess in the driver's compartment **(see illustration)**.
6   Disconnect the accelerator cable clips mounted on the intake

4B

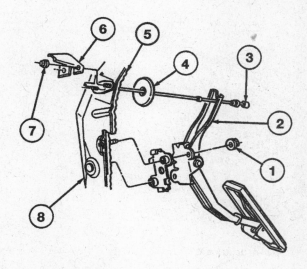

8.5 Exploded view of the accelerator pedal and cable

1	Nut	5	Insulator
2	Accelerator pedal	6	Brace
3	Cable end	7	Nut
4	Cable retainer	8	Firewall

manifold and valve cover **(see illustration)**.

7   Remove the cable through the firewall from the engine compartment.

Installation

8   Installation is the reverse of removal. Be sure the cable is routed correctly.

9   If necessary, at the engine compartment side of the firewall, apply sealant around the accelerator cable to prevent water from entering the passenger compartment.

Adjustment

10   Measure the freeplay at the accelerator pedal **(see illustration 8.5)**. Freeplay should be 3/64 to 1/8-inch.

11   To adjust, loosen the locknut on the cable bracket and adjust the deflection until it is within the specified range.

---

9   Electronic fuel injection system - general information

Central Fuel Injection

Refer to illustration 9.1

The Central Fuel Injection (CFI) system **(see illustration)** is a single point, pulse time modulated injection system. Fuel is metered into the air intake stream in accordance with engine demands by two solenoid injection valves mounted in a throttle body on the intake manifold.

Fuel is supplied from the fuel tank by a low pressure, electric fuel pump mounted in the fuel tank. The fuel is filtered and sent to the

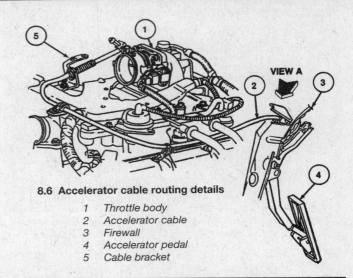

8.6 Accelerator cable routing details

1   *Throttle body*
2   *Accelerator cable*
3   *Firewall*
4   *Accelerator pedal*
5   *Cable bracket*

throttle body, where a regulator maintains the fuel delivery pressure at a constant value of 39 psi. A pair of injector nozzles are mounted vertically above the throttle plates and connected in series with the fuel pressure regulator. Excess fuel supplied by the pump but not needed by the engine is returned to the fuel tank by a steel fuel return line.

The fuel charging assembly consists of five individual components which perform the fuel and air metering function. The throttle

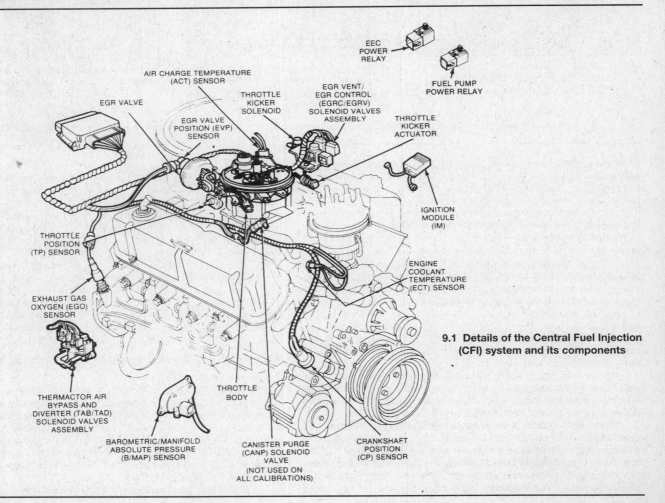

9.1 Details of the Central Fuel Injection (CFI) system and its components

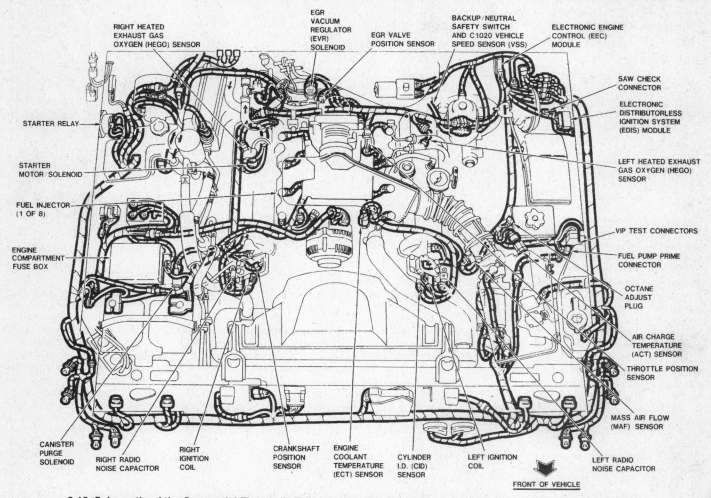

9.12 Schematic of the Sequential Electronic Fuel Injection (SEFI) system and its components (typical 4.6L engine)

4B

body assembly is attached to the conventional carburetor mounting pad on the intake manifold and houses the air control system, fuel injector nozzle, fuel pressure regulator, fuel pressure diagnostic valve, cold engine speed control and throttle position sensor.

Airflow to the engine is controlled by a single butterfly valve mounted in a two piece, die-cast aluminum housing called a throttle body. The butterfly valve is identical in configuration to the throttle plates of a conventional carburetor.

The fuel injector nozzle is mounted vertically above the throttle plate and is an electro-mechanical device which meters and atomizes the fuel delivered to the engine. The injector valve body consists of a solenoid actuated ball and seat valve assembly.

An electric control signal from the EEC electronic processor activates the solenoid, causing the ball to move off the seat and allowing fuel to flow. The injector flow orifice is fixed and the fuel supply is constant. Therefore, fuel flow to the engine is controlled by how long the solenoid is energized.

The pressure regulator is integral to the fuel charging main body near the rear of the air horn surface. The regulator is located so as to nullify the effects of the supply line pressure drops. Its design is such that it is not sensitive to back pressure in the return line to the tank.

A second function of the pressure regulator is to maintain fuel supply pressure upon fuel pump shutdown. The regulator functions as a downstream check valve and traps the fuel between itself and the fuel pump. The constant fuel pressure level after engine shutdown precludes fuel line vapor formation and allows for rapid restarts and stable idle operation immediately thereafter.

The throttle actuator controls idle speed by modulating the throttle lever for the required air flow to maintain the desired engine rpm for any operating condition, from an idling cold engine to a warm engine at normal operating temperature. An idle tracking switch (ITS) determines when the throttle lever has contacted the actuator, signaling the need to control engine rpm. The DC motor extends or retracts a shaft through a gear reduction system. The motor direction is determined by the polarity of the applied voltage.

A throttle position sensor (non-adjustable) is mounted to the throttle shaft on the choke side of the fuel charging assembly and is used to supply a voltage output proportional to the change in the throttle position. The TP sensor is used by the computer (EEC) to determine the operation mode (closed throttle, part throttle and wide open throttle) for selection of the proper fuel mixture, spark and EGR at all engine speeds and loads.

Sequential Electronic Fuel Injection (SEFI)

Refer to illustration 9.12

The Sequential Electronic Fuel Injection (SEFI) system **(see illustration)** known as a multi-point, pulse timed, speed density control fuel injection system. On the SEFI system, fuel is metered into each intake port in sequence with the engine firing order in accordance with engine demand through eight injectors mounted on a tuned intake manifold. The two-piece air intake manifold on the 5.0L engines includes an air intake plenum. The 4.6L engine incorporates a single intake manifold (see Section 12).

This system incorporates an on-board Electronic Engine Control

10.9 Use a stethoscope to determine if the injectors are working properly - they should make a steady clicking sound that rises and falls with engine speed changes

10.10 Install the "noid" light into the fuel injector electrical connector and confirm that it blinks when the engine is running

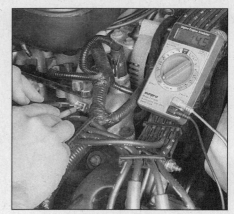

10.11 Measure the resistance of each injector. It should be within Specifications

(EEC-IV) computer that accepts inputs from various engine sensors to compute the required fuel flow rate necessary to maintain a prescribed air/fuel ratio throughout the entire engine operational range. The computer then outputs a command to the fuel injectors to meter the approximate quantity of fuel. The system automatically senses and compensates for changes in altitude, load and speed.

The fuel delivery systems include an electric in-tank fuel pump which forces pressurized fuel through a series of metal and plastic lines and an inline fuel filter/reservoir to the fuel charging manifold assembly. The SEFI system uses a single high-pressure pump mounted inside the tank.

The fuel charging manifold assembly incorporates electrically actuated fuel injectors directly above each intake port. When energized, the injectors spray a metered quantity of fuel into the intake air stream.

A constant fuel pressure drop is maintained across the injector nozzles by a pressure regulator. The regulator is positioned downstream from the fuel injectors. Excess fuel passes through the regulator and returns to the fuel tank through a fuel return line.

On the SEFI system, each injector is energized once every other crankshaft revolution in sequence with engine firing order. The period of time that the injectors are energized (known as "on time" or "pulse width") is controlled by the EEC-IV computer. Air entering the engine is sensed by speed, pressure and temperature sensors. The outputs of these sensors are processed by the EEC-IV computer. The computer determines the needed injector pulse width and outputs a command to the injector to meter the exact quantity of fuel.

10 Electronic fuel injection system – check

Warning: *Gasoline is extremely flammable, so take extra precautions when you work on any part of the fuel system.* **See Warning in Section 1.**
Note: *The following procedure is based on the assumption that the fuel pump is working and the fuel pressure is adequate (see Section 3).*

Preliminary checks

1   Check all electrical connectors that are related to the system. Loose electrical connectors and poor grounds can cause many problems that resemble more serious malfunctions.
2   Check to see that the battery is fully charged, as the control unit and sensors depend on an accurate supply voltage in order to properly meter the fuel.
3   Check the air filter element - a dirty or partially blocked filter will severely impede performance and economy (see Chapter 1).
4   If a blown fuse is found, replace it and see if it blows again. If it does, search for a grounded wire in the harness to the fuel pump (see Chapter 12).

System checks

5   Check the condition of the vacuum hoses connected to the intake manifold.

Central Electronic Fuel Injection (CFI) systems

6   First, start the engine and observe that each injector in the throttle body unit is spraying fuel evenly into the venturi. To observe the spray pattern of the injectors, remove the air cleaner housing and point a flashlight into the CFI unit.
7   Another test of the spray pattern is to install a timing light according with the tool manufacturer's instructions and point the light into the CFI unit. Watch the spray pattern from each injector. Make sure they are even and constant. Vary the idle rpm's and watch also. There should not be any intermittent breaks or weak spray patterns.
Caution: *Make sure all timing light electrical chords and any engine wire(s) are carefully tucked away into the engine wiring harness to avoid any accidental contact with the fan blades during testing.*

Sequential Electronic Fuel Injection (SEFI) systems

Refer to illustrations 10.9, 10.10 and 10.11
8   Remove the air intake duct from the throttle body and check for dirt, carbon or other residue build-up in the throttle body, particularly around the throttle plate. If it's dirty, clean it with carburetor cleaner and a toothbrush.
9   With the engine running, place an automotive stethoscope against each injector, one at a time, and listen for a clicking sound, indicating operation **(see illustration)**. If you don't have a stethoscope, you can place the tip of a long screwdriver against the injector and listen through the handle.
10   If an injector isn't functioning (not clicking), purchase a special injector test light (sometimes called a "noid" light) and install it into the injector electrical connector **(see illustration)**. Start the engine and check to see if the noid light flashes. If it does, the injector is receiving proper voltage. If it doesn't flash, further diagnosis should be performed by a dealer service department or other repair shop.
11   With the engine OFF and the fuel injector electrical connectors disconnected, measure the resistance of each injector **(see illustration)**. Compare the resistance readings with the values listed in this Chapter's Specifications.
12   The remainder of the system checks can be found in Section 12.

11 Central Fuel Injection (CFI) system - component check and replacement

Warning: *Gasoline is extremely flammable, so take extra precautions when you work on any part of the fuel system.* **See Warning in Section 1.**

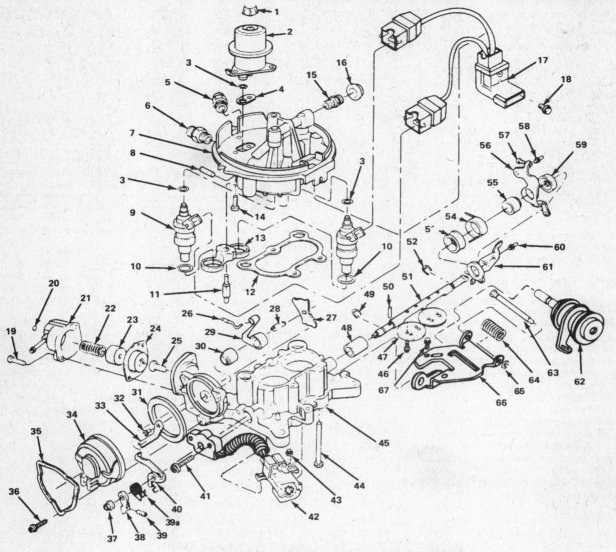

11.1 Central Fuel Injection assembly - exploded view

1	Fuel pressure regulator adjusting screw plug
2	Fuel pressure regulator
3	O-ring
4	Fuel pressure regulator gasket
5	Connector
6	Connector
7	Fuel charging main body
8	Plug
9	Injector assembly
10	O-ring
11	Fuel injector retaining screw
12	Fuel charging body gasket
13	Fuel injector retainer
14	Screw
15	Diagnostic valve
16	Fuel pressure relief valve cap
17	Fuel charging wiring assembly
18	Screw
19	Screw and washer
20	Ball
21	Control diaphragm
22	Control modulator spring
23	Pulldown diaphragm retainer
24	Pulldown control diaphragm
25	Pulldown control adjuster
26	Fast idle control rod
27	Fast idle cam
28	Choke housing shaft
29	Fast idle control rod positioner
30	Choke housing bushing
31	Thermostat housing gasket
32	Screw and washer
33	Choke thermostat lever
34	Thermostat housing
35	Retainer
36	Screw
37	Nut and washer
38	Fast idle cam adjuster lever
39	Screw
40	Fast idle lever
41	Screw and washer
42	Throttle position sensor
43	Screw
44	Screw
45	Fuel charging throttle body
46	Screw
47	Throttle plate
48	Throttle control linkage bearing
49	E-clip
50	Pin
51	Throttle shaft
52	C-ring
53	Throttle control linkage bearing
54	Throttle return spring
55	Bushing
56	Transmission linkage lever
57	Screw
58	Transmission linkage lever pin
59	Throttle shaft spacer
60	Throttle lever ball
61	Throttle lever
62	Throttle positioner
63	Adjusting screw
64	Throttle positioner retaining spring
65	E-clip
66	Throttle positioner bracket
67	Screw

4B

CFI assembly

Refer to illustration 11.1

1   When buying replacement parts for the CFI assembly **(see illustrations)**, always check the number on the identification tag on the side of the CFI assembly to make sure that you are getting the right parts.

2   Relieve the fuel system pressure (see Section 2). Detach the cable from the negative terminal of the battery.

3   Remove the air cleaner housing (see Section 7).

4   Detach the accelerator cable and, if equipped, cruise control cable from the throttle lever (see Section 8).

5   If your vehicle is equipped with an automatic transmission, detach the kickdown rod.

6   Unplug the electrical connectors to the fuel injectors, the Idle Speed Control (ISC) and the Throttle Position (TP) sensor.

7   Remove the fuel line bracket bolt.

8   Using a backup wrench, detach the fuel feed and return lines.
Note: *If either line proves difficult to pull out, carefully wiggle it up and down - do not strike the lines with a tool or attempt to pry them loose or you may dent them.*

9   Detach the PCV hose.

10   Remove the four mounting nuts.

11   Installation is the reverse of removal.

Idle Speed Control (ISC) motor

Check

12   With the engine idling, disconnect the electrical connector from the ISC motor and observe a change in engine rpm. If the idle is not affected, have the ISC system diagnosed at a dealer service department or other qualified repair shop.

Replacement

13   Detach the cable from the negative terminal of the battery and unplug the electrical connector from the ISC motor.

14   Remove the downshift lever return spring.

15   Remove the two mounting bolts and detach the ISC motor.

16   Installation is the reverse of removal.

Throttle Position Sensor (TPS)

General description

Refer to illustration 11.18

17   The Throttle Position Sensor (TPS) is located on the end of the throttle shaft on the throttle body. By monitoring the output voltage from the TPS, the EEC can determine fuel delivery based on throttle valve angle (driver demand). A broken or loose TPS can cause intermittent bursts of fuel from the injector and an unstable idle because the EEC thinks the throttle is moving.

Check

18   To check the TPS, turn the ignition switch to ON (engine not running) and connect the probes of a voltmeter into the ground wire and signal wire on the backside of the electrical connector **(see illustration)**. This test checks for the proper signal voltage from the TPS.
Note: *Be careful when backprobing the electrical connector. Do not damage the wiring harness or pull on any connectors to make clean contact. Be sure the probes are placed in the correct position.*

19   The sensor should read 0.5 to 1.0-volt with the throttle closed. Have an assistant depress the accelerator pedal to simulate full throttle and the sensor should increase voltage to 5.0 to 8.0-volts. If the TPS voltage readings are incorrect, replace it with a new unit.

20   Also, check the TPS reference voltage. With the ignition key ON (engine not running), connect the positive (+) probe of the voltmeter to the voltage reference wire. There should be approximately 5.0 volts sent from the EEC to the TPS.

21   Also, check the resistance of the potentiometer within the TPS. Disconnect the TPS electrical connector and working on the sensor side, connect the probes of the ohmmeter to the ground wire and the TPS signal wire. With the throttle valve fully closed, the TPS should read between 3.0 and 4.0 K-ohms.

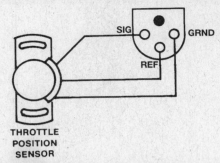

11.18 Connect the negative probe to the GRND terminal and the positive probe to the SIG terminal on the TPS electrical connector and check for signal voltage. It should be approximately 0.5 to 1.0 volts at idle and 5.0 to 8.0 volts with the throttle wide open

22   Now open the throttle with one hand and check the resistance again. Slowly advance the throttle until fully open. The resistance should be approximately 350 ohms. The potentiometer should exhibit a smooth change in resistance as it travels from fully closed to wide open throttle. Any deviations indicate a possible worn or damaged TPS.

Replacement

Note: *It is not necessary to remove the CFI assembly to replace the TPS.*

23   Detach the cable from the negative terminal of the battery.

24   Unplug the electrical connector from the TPS.

25   Remove the bracket retaining screw from the TPS electrical connector and detach the bracket and connector from the throttle body.

26   Remove the TPS retaining screws.

27   Slide the TPS off the throttle shaft. Installation is the reverse of removal.

Adjustment

28   Turn the ignition key to ON (engine not running).

29   With the TPS screws in place and slightly loose, rotate the TPS counterclockwise.

30   Remove the vacuum hose from the throttle kicker actuator and make sure the throttle is off the fast idle cam.

31   The voltage should read between 0.5 and 2.0 volts (idle).

32   If the voltage reading is incorrect, continue to rotate the TPS until the correct voltage is present.

33   Tighten the adjustment bolts.

Fuel injector

Check

34   First, start the engine and confirm that each injector in the throttle body unit is spraying fuel evenly into the venturi. To observe the spray pattern of the injectors, remove the air cleaner housing and point a flashlight into the CFI unit.

35   Another test of the spray pattern is to install a timing light according to the tool manufacturer's instructions and point the light into the CFI unit. Watch the spray pattern from each injector. Make sure they are even and constant. Vary the idle speed and watch also. There should not be any intermittent breaks or weak spray patterns.
Warning: *Make sure all timing light electrical cords and any engine wire(s) are carefully tucked away into the engine wiring harness to avoid any accidental contact with the fan blades during testing.*

Replacement

Refer to illustration 11.38

36   Remove the CFI assembly from the intake manifold.

37   Remove the air cleaner stud.

38   Remove the four throttle body-to-main body screws and separate the throttle body and main body assemblies. **Caution:** *Do not remove the three screws which attach the pressure regulator to the main body assembly* **(see illustration)**.

11.38 Do not remove these three screws (arrows) - they attach the pressure regulator to the fuel charging assembly

39 Clearly mark the positions of the injectors. **Caution:** *The injectors must not be mixed up during reassembly.*
40 Unplug the injector electrical connectors. Pull on the connector plugs, not on the wires.
41 Remove the fuel injector retainer screw and retainer.
42 Carefully pull up on the injector while using a twisting motion.

43 Discard the old O-rings and replace them with new ones. Use a light grade oil to lubricate the new O-rings before installing them.
44 Installation is the reverse of removal.

12 Sequential Electronic Fuel Injection (SEFI) system - component check and replacement

Air intake plenum (upper intake manifold) (5.0L engine) with throttle body

Refer to illustrations 12.2, 12.8a, 12.8b and 12.8c
Warning: *Wait until the engine is completely cool before beginning this procedure.*

Removal

1 Detach the cable from the negative terminal of the battery.
2 Unplug the electrical connectors at the air bypass valve, throttle position sensor and EGR position sensor **(see illustration)**.
3 Detach the accelerator cable (see Section 8) and transmission linkage (see Chapter 7) from the throttle body assembly.
4 Remove the accelerator cable/throttle valve (TV) cable bracket from the plenum (see Section 8) and position the bracket and cables out of the way.
5 Clearly label, then detach, the vacuum lines from the upper intake manifold vacuum tree, the EGR valve and the fuel pressure regulator.
6 Detach the PCV system by disconnecting the hose from the fitting on the rear of the upper manifold.
7 If equipped, detach the canister purge line or lines from the

12.2 Exploded view of the air intake plenum and surrounding components on the 5.0L engine

1 Schrader valve
2 Cap
3 Fuel rail assembly
4 O-ring seal
5 Gasket
6 Fuel pressure regulator
7 Plenum cover
8 Screw
9 Bolt
10 EGR spacer gasket
11 EGR spacer
12 TPS electrical connector
13 Screw
14 TPS
15 Throttle air bypass valve
16 Throttle air bypass valve gasket
17 Throttle body assembly
18 Throttle body gasket
19 Gasket EGR valve
20 EGR valve assembly
21 PCV valve assembly
22 PCV grommet
23 PCV filter element
24 Lower intake manifold
25 Thermostat housing gasket
26 Thermostat
27 Bolt
28 Thermostat housing
29 Coolant supply and return tube
30 Coolant temperature sensor

31 Air intake plenum gasket
32 Bolt
33 Cover
34 Plug

35 Air intake plenum
36 Screw
37 Fuel rail bolt
38 Fuel injector

4B

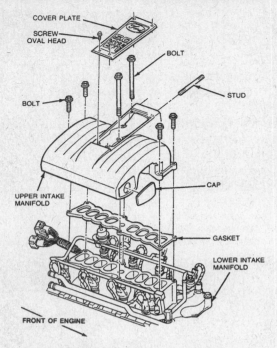

12.8a Air intake plenum mounting details

12.8b Remove the four screws that retain the plate on the top of the plenum . . .

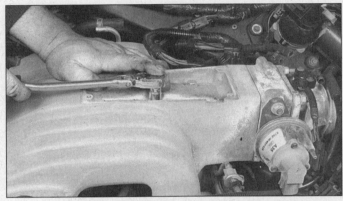

12.8c . . . then remove the bolts underneath the plate

throttle body and detach the EGR spacer coolant lines from the EGR spacer. Plug the lines to prevent excessive coolant leakage.

8   Remove the six plenum retaining bolts **(see illustrations)**.
9   Remove the plenum and throttle body as an assembly from the lower intake manifold.

Installation

10   Be sure to clean and inspect the mounting faces of the lower intake manifold (see Chapter 2A) and the air intake plenum before positioning the new gasket(s) onto the lower intake mounting face. Install the air intake plenum and throttle body assembly onto the lower intake manifold. The use of alignment studs may be helpful. Ensure the gasket remains in place (if alignment studs are not used). Install the six upper intake manifold retaining bolts and tighten them to the torque listed in this Chapter's Specifications. Be sure to install the long bolts in the middle and the short bolts in the ends. Installation is otherwise

the reverse of removal. Check the coolant level and add some, if necessary (see Chapter 1).

Throttle body (5.0L and 4.6L engines)

Removal

Refer to illustrations 12.15a and 12.15b
11   Detach the cable from the negative terminal of the battery.
12   Detach the throttle position sensor and throttle air bypass valve electrical connectors.
13   Disconnect the accelerator cable (see Section 8) and the Throttle

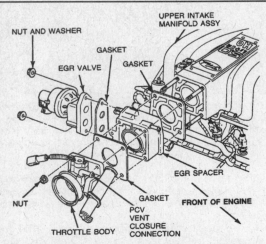

12.15a Exploded view of the throttle body assembly on the 5.0L engine

12.15b Remove the four nuts or bolts (arrows) from the throttle body (5.0L engine shown)

12.23a Push down to release the safety clamp from the fuel line connectors

12.23b Install the correct diameter spring lock coupling tool and push away from the fuel rail to release the internal locking mechanism

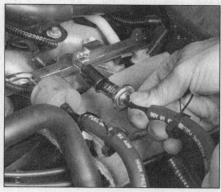

12.23c Detach the fuel line from the fuel rail

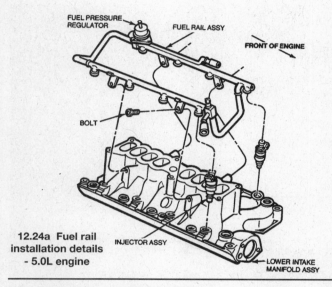

12.24a Fuel rail installation details - 5.0L engine

12.24b Remove the four bolts (arrows) from the fuel rail assembly - 4.6L engine

12.24c It will be necessary to disconnect the wiring harness from all the engine components (air conditioning compressor, power steering pressure switch, oil pressure switch etc.) in order to be able to lift the fuel rail assembly as a complete unit from the 4.6L engine

Valve (TV) cable from the throttle body.

14   If equipped, remove the PCV vent closure hose at the throttle body.

15   Remove the four throttle body mounting nuts (see illustrations).

16   On 5.0L engines, carefully separate the throttle body from the EGR spacer (see illustration 12.15a).

17   Remove and discard the gasket between the throttle body and the EGR spacer (5.0L engines only).

Installation

18   Clean the gasket mating surfaces. If scraping is necessary, be careful not to damage the gasket surfaces or allow material to drop into the manifold. Installation is the reverse of removal. Be sure to tighten the throttle body mounting nuts to the torque listed in this Chapter's Specifications.

Throttle Position (TP) sensor

19   Refer to Chapter 6, Section 7 for the check and replacement procedures for the TP sensor on SEFI engines.

Fuel rail assembly

Refer to illustrations 12.23a, 12.23b, 12.23c, 12.24a, 12.24b and 12.24c

Note: *Removal and installation of the fuel rail on models since 1996 is the same as on previous years. The illustrations shown in this procedure are shown on a pre-1996 4.6L engine which is equipped with a different type of intake manifold.*

Removal

20   Relieve the fuel pressure (see Section 2).

21   Detach the cable from the negative terminal of the battery.

22   On 5.0L engines, remove the air intake plenum assembly (see Steps 1 through 9). On 4.6L engines, remove the air intake assembly (see Section 9).

23   Using the special spring lock coupler tool D87L-9280-A or equivalent, disconnect the fuel feed and return lines from the fuel rail assembly (see illustrations). **Note:** *Refer to Section 4 for additional information on disconnecting fuel lines.*

24   Remove the four fuel rail assembly retaining bolts (two on each

4B

12.35a Remove the two fuel rail bolts (arrows) . . .

12.35b . . . and carefully lift one side to install a Torx drive tool into the fuel pressure regulator bolts (4.6L engine shown)

12.42a Remove the fuel rail bolts and . . .

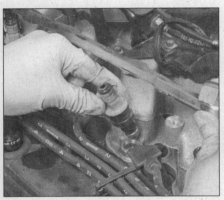

12.42b . . . wiggle the injector out of the manifold (4.6L engine shown)

12.45a Remove the O-ring from the top of the fuel injector . . .

12.45b . . . then remove the lower O-ring from the injector

side) (see illustrations).

25 Carefully disengage the fuel rail from the fuel injectors and remove the fuel rail. **Note:** *It may be easier to remove the injectors with the fuel rail as an assembly.*

26 Use a rocking, side-to-side motion while lifting to remove the injectors from the fuel rail.

Installation

Note: *It's a good idea to replace the injector O-rings whenever the fuel rail is removed.*

27 Ensure that the injector caps are clean and free of contamination.

28 Place the fuel injector fuel rail assembly over each of the injectors and seat the injectors into the fuel rail. Ensure that the injectors are well seated in the fuel rail assembly. **Note:** *It may be easier to seat the injectors in the fuel rail and then seat the entire assembly in the lower intake manifold.*

29 Secure the fuel rail assembly with the four retaining bolts and tighten them to the torque listed in this Chapter's Specifications.

30 The remainder of installation is the reverse of removal.

Fuel pressure regulator

Check

Refer to illustrations 12.35a, 12.35b, 12.40a and 12.40b

Note: *This procedure assumes the fuel filter is in good condition.*

31 Refer to Section 3 for the fuel pressure regulator check procedure (it's part of the fuel pressure check).

Replacement

Refer to illustrations 12.35a and 12.35b

Note: *Removal and installation of the fuel pressure regulator on models since 1996 is the same as on previous years. The illustrations shown in this procedure are shown on a pre-1996 4.6L engine which is equipped with a different type of intake manifold.*

32 Relieve the fuel pressure from the system (see Section 2). Disconnect the cable from the negative terminal of the battery.

33 Clean any dirt from around the fuel pressure regulator.

34 Detach the vacuum hose from the fuel pressure regulator.

35 On 4.6L engines, remove the bolts from one side of the fuel rail **(see illustration)** and carefully lift one side of the fuel rail assembly to gain access to the fuel pressure regulator mounting bolts **(see illustration)**.

36 Remove the bolts that retain the fuel pressure regulator and detach the regulator from the fuel rail.

37 Install new O-rings on the pressure regulator and lubricate them with a light coat of oil.

38 Installation is the reverse of removal. Tighten the pressure regulator mounting bolts securely.

Fuel injector

Refer to illustrations 12.42a, 12.42b, 12.45a and 12.45b

Removal

39 Relieve the system fuel pressure (see Section 2).

40 If you're working on a 5.0L engine, remove the air intake plenum assembly (see Steps 1 through 9). On 4.6L engines, remove the air intake assembly (see Section 9).

41 Remove the fuel rail assembly (see above).

42 If you're working on a 4.6L engine, remove the fuel rail bolts from the fuel rail and carefully lift the assembly to gain access to the

12.51 Check for battery voltage to the BPA-ISC valve with the ignition key ON (engine not running)

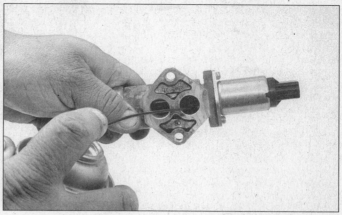

12.52 Spray carburetor cleaner into the valve to remove any carbon or sludge build-up inside the valve

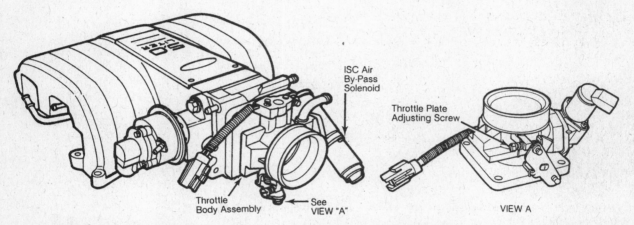

12.54 On 1988 models, turn the throttle plate adjusting screw until 550 to 600 rpm are attained, then back out the adjusting screw an additional 1/2 turn

4B

injectors **(see illustrations)**. **Note:** *If all of the injectors are going to be replaced, remove the entire fuel rail.*

43   Carefully detach the electrical connectors from the individual injectors as required.

44   Grasping the injector body, pull up while gently rocking the injector from side-to-side.

45   Inspect the injector O-rings (two per injector) for signs of deterioration **(see illustrations)**. Replace as required. **Note:** *As long as you have the fuel rail off (or the injector(s) removed), it's a good idea to replace the O-rings.*

46   Inspect the injector plastic "hat" (covering the injector pintle) and washer for signs of deterioration. Replace as required. If the hat is missing, look for it in the intake manifold.

Installation

47   Lubricate the new O-rings with light grade oil and install two on each injector. **Caution:** *Do not use silicone grease. It will clog the injectors.*

48   Using a light twisting motion, install the injector(s).

49   The remainder of installation is the reverse of removal.

Bypass air valve and idle speed

Refer to illustrations 12.51, 12.52, 12.54 and 12.60

Note: *The minimum idle speed is pre-set at the factory and should not require adjustment under normal circumstances; however, if the throttle body has been replaced or you suspect the minimum idle speed has been tampered with (for example, if the idle stop screw was removed) follow this procedure.*

Check

50   The bypass air valve (BPA-ISC) controls the amount of air that bypasses the throttle body assembly throttle valve and consequently controls the engine idle speed. This output actuator is mounted on the throttle body and is controlled by voltage pulses sent from the computer. The BPA-ISC valve body moves in or out allowing more or less intake air into the system according to the engine conditions. To increase idle speed, the computer extends the BPA-ISC valve body from the seat and allows more air to bypass the throttle bore. To decrease idle speed, the computer retracts the BPA-ISC valve body towards the seat, reducing the air flow.

51   To check the system, first check for battery voltage to the BPA-ISC. Turn the ignition key On (engine not running) and with a voltmeter, probe the wires of the terminals of the BPA-ISC valve electrical connector. It should be approximately 10.5 volts **(see illustration)**.

52   Next, remove the valve (proceed to Step 59) and check the pintle for excessive carbon deposits. If necessary, clean it with carburetor cleaner spray **(see illustration)**. Also clean the valve housing to remove any deposits.

Adjustment (5.0L engines)

53   Place the transmission in Park and set the emergency brake for safety. Start the engine and allow it to run until it reaches normal operating temperatures. **Note:** *On 1989 through 1992 models, go to Step 6 for the adjustment procedure.*

54   On 1988 models, raise the engine speed to 1,800 rpm and hold the pedal there for 30 seconds. Allow the engine to return to idle, position the transmission selector in Drive and check idle speed. Install

a tachometer according to the tool manufacturer's instructions and set the idle speed between 550 and 600 rpm by turning the throttle plate adjusting screw clockwise **(see illustration)**, then back the screw OUT an additional 1/2-turn.

55   On 1989 through 1992 models, place the transmission in Park and set the emergency brake. With the engine off, back out the throttle plate stop screw so it does not touch the throttle lever pad. Insert a 0.10-inch feeler gauge between the throttle plate stop screw and the throttle lever pad.

56   Tighten the screw until it touches the feeler gauge. Remove the feeler gauge and turn the screw IN an additional 1-1/2 turns.

57   Start the engine and allow it to stabilize for two minutes, then depress the accelerator quickly and allow the engine rpm to settle back down to idle. The computer and BPA-ISC valve should adjust the idle from this point. If idle quality suffers (high or low) run a complete diagnosis of the fuel injection and emission control system (see Chapter 6). Also, check the throttle valve (TV) cable adjustment (see Chapter 7).

Adjustment (4.6L engines)

58   The idle speed on the 4.6L is not adjustable. This procedure requires a special SCAN tool to extract working parameters (voltage signals) from the EEC-IV system while it is running. Have the vehicle repaired at a dealer service department or other qualified repair shop.

Removal

59   Unplug the electrical connector from the BPA-ISC valve.

60   Remove the two valve attaching screws and withdraw the assembly **(see illustration)**.

61   Check the condition of the O-ring. If it's hardened or deteriorated, replace it.

62   Clean the sealing surface and the bore of the throttle body

12.60 Remove the two bolts (arrows) and lift the BPA-ISC valve from the intake manifold (4.6L engine shown)

assembly to ensure a good seal. **Caution:** *The BPA-ISC valve itself is an electrical component and must not be soaked in any liquid cleaner, as damage may result.*

Installation

63   Position the new O-ring on the BPA-ISC valve. Lubricate the O-ring with a light film of engine oil.

64   Install the BPA-ISC valve and tighten the screws securely.

65   Plug in the electrical connector at the BPA-ISC valve assembly.

Chapter 5
Engine electrical systems

Contents

Specifications

Battery voltage

Engine off	12-volts
Engine running	14-to-15 volts

Firing order

See Chapter 2

Ignition coil-to-distributor cap wire resistance

SSI and DuraSpark systems	5,000 ohms per inch (maximum)
TFI-IV system	5,000 ohms per foot (maximum)

Ignition coil resistance

Solid State Ignition systems - 1974 through 1976

Primary resistance	1.0 to 2.0 ohms
Secondary resistance	7.0 to 13.0 K-ohms

DuraSpark I systems - 1977 and 1978

Primary resistance	0.7 to 0.8 ohms
Secondary resistance	7.0 to 9.3 K-ohms

DuraSpark I systems - 1979

Primary resistance	0.7 to 0.8 ohms
Secondary resistance	7.0 to 8.3 K-ohms

DuraSpark II systems - 1977 and 1978

Primary resistance	1.0 to 2.0 ohms
Secondary resistance	7.0 to 13.0 K-ohms

DuraSpark II systems - 1979

Primary resistance	1.10 to 1.25 ohms
Secondary resistance	7.0 to 13.0 K-ohms

DuraSpark II systems - 1980

Primary resistance	1.10 to 1.25 ohms
Secondary resistance	7.7 to 9.6 K-ohms

5

DuraSpark II systems -1981
    Primary resistance... 1.0 to 2.0 ohms
    Secondary resistance.. 7.7 to 9.6 K-ohms
DuraSpark III systems -1979 through 1981
    Primary resistance... 1.10 to 1.25 ohms
    Secondary resistance.. 7.7 to 9.6 K-ohms
DuraSpark II and III systems - 1982 through 1987
    Primary resistance... 0.8 to 1.6 ohms
    Secondary resistance.. 7.7 to 10.5 K-ohms
TFI-IV system
    Primary resistance... 0.3 to 1.0 ohms
    Secondary resistance.. 6.5 to 11.5 K-ohms
EDIS system
    Primary resistance... 8.0 to 9.0 ohms
    Secondary resistance.. 13.0 to 14.0 K-ohms

Ballast resistor wire

Solid State Ignition - 1974 through 1976...................................... 1.4 ohms
DuraSpark I - 1977 through 1979 .... None
DuraSpark II and III - 1977 through 1981 .... 1.05 to 1.15 ohms
DuraSpark II and III - 1982 through 1987 .... 0.8 to 1.6 ohms

Ignition coil primary winding-to-case resistance .... 10-M ohms

Ignition stator (pick-up coil) resistance

Solid State Ignition - 1974 through 1977...................................... 400 to 800 ohms
DuraSpark I - 1977 and 1978 .... 400 to 800 ohms
DuraSpark I - 1979 .... 400 to 1,000 ohms
DuraSpark II - 1977 and 1978 .... 400 to 800 ohms
DuraSpark II - 1979 through 1987 .... 400 to 1,000 ohms
Air Gap... Not adjustable

Alternator brush length

New... 1/2 inch
Minimum .... 1/4 inch

1   General information

The engine electrical systems include all ignition, charging and starting components. Because of their engine-related functions, these components are considered separately from chassis electrical devices like the lights, instruments, etc.

Be very careful when working on the engine electrical components. They are easily damaged if checked, connected or handled improperly. The alternator is driven by an engine drivebelt which could cause serious injury if your hands, hair or clothes become entangled in it with the engine running. Both the starter and alternator are connected directly to the battery and could arc or even cause a fire if mishandled, overloaded or shorted out.

Never leave the ignition switch on for long periods of time with the engine off. Don't disconnect the battery cables while the engine is running. Correct polarity must be maintained when connecting battery cables from another source, such as another vehicle, during jump starting. Always disconnect the negative cable first and hook it up last or the battery may be shorted by the tool being used to loosen the cable clamps.

Additional safety related information on the engine electrical systems can be found in *Safety first* near the front of this manual. It should be referred to before beginning any operation included in this Chapter.

2   Battery - removal and installation

Refer to illustration 2.2

1   Disconnect both cables from the battery terminals. **Caution:** *Always disconnect the negative cable first and hook it up last or the battery may be shorted by the tool being used to loosen the cable clamps.*

2   Locate the battery hold-down clamp straddling the top of the battery. Remove the bolt and nut and the hold-down clamp **(see illustration)**.

3   Lift out the battery. Use the special straps that attach to the battery posts - lifting and moving the battery is much easier if you use one.

4   Installation is the reverse of removal.

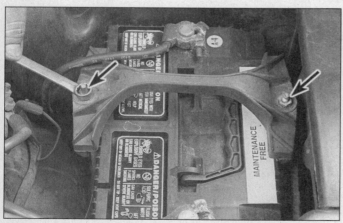

2.2 Detach the battery cables (negative first, then positive) then remove the nut and bolt from the battery hold-down clamp (arrows)

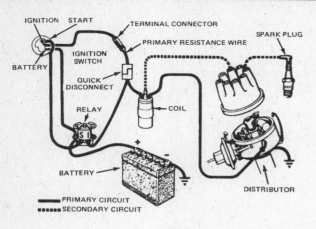

5.3 Diagram of a typical breaker (points) type ignition system

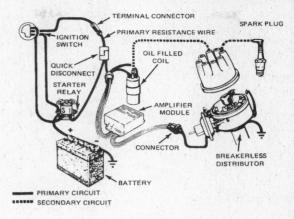

5.4a Diagram of a typical Solid State Ignition (SSI) system

3   Battery - emergency jump starting

Refer to the *Booster battery (jump) starting* procedure at the front of this manual.

4   Battery cables - check and replacement

1   Periodically inspect the entire length of each battery cable for damage, cracked or burned insulation and corrosion. Poor battery cable connections can cause starting problems and decreased engine performance.

2   Check the cable-to-terminal connections at the ends of the cables for cracks, loose wire strands and corrosion. The presence of white, fluffy deposits under the insulation at the cable terminal connection is a sign that the cable is corroded and should be replaced. Check the terminals for distortion, missing mounting bolts and corrosion.

3   When replacing the cables, always disconnect the negative cable first and hook it up last or the battery may be shorted by the tool used to loosen the cable clamps. Even if only the positive cable is being replaced, be sure to disconnect the negative cable from the battery first.

4   Disconnect and remove the cable. Make sure the replacement cable is the same length and diameter.

5   Clean the threads of the relay or ground connection with a wire brush to remove rust and corrosion. Apply a light coat of petroleum jelly to the threads to prevent future corrosion.

6   Attach the cable to the relay or ground connection and tighten the mounting nut/bolt securely.

7   Before connecting the new cable to the battery, make sure that it reaches the battery post without having to be stretched. Clean the battery posts thoroughly and apply a light coat of petroleum jelly to prevent corrosion.

8   Connect the positive cable first, followed by the negative cable.

5   Ignition system - general information

Refer to illustrations 5.3, 5.4a, 5.4b, 5.5, 5.12 and 5.14

1   The ignition system is designed to ignite the fuel/air charge entering each cylinder at just the right moment. It does this by producing a high voltage spark between the electrodes of each spark plug.

2   The types of ignition systems installed on these vehicles evolved through the years to accommodate more strict emissions standards adopted by the major automotive manufacturers. Some of the changes in the ignition systems overlapped in certain years and others changed with certain models while some did not. Here is a general listing of the various systems.

Breaker-points type ignition system

3   This ignition system controls the ignition spark using the conventional points and condenser arrangement **(see illustration)** and timing is controlled by mechanical advance components. This system is installed on 1970 through 1973 models only.

Breakerless type ignition system (SSI, DuraSpark I-II-III and TFI-IV)

4   Early electronic (breakerless) ignition systems include the Solid State Ignition (SSI) and the DuraSpark I, II and III versions. 1974 through 1976 models are equipped with a simplified system referred to as Solid State Ignition (3 and 4 wire electrical connector on module) **(see illustration)**. DuraSpark I **(see illustration)** and II systems were first installed on 1977 models. DuraSpark I and II (2 and 4 wire electrical connector on module) are similar in operation and almost identical in appearance. Each system is used for a specific emission systems application. The DuraSpark I uses a special control module which senses current flow through the ignition coil and adjusts the dwell (on-time) for maximum spark intensity. If the DuraSpark module senses that the ignition is ON and the distributor shaft is not turning, the current to the ignition coil is turned OFF by the module. DuraSpark II systems do not have this capability. Here the ignition coil is energized the full amount of time that the ignition switch is ON. **Caution:** *The ignition system on DuraSpark II could inadvertently fire (spark) during a simple ignition procedures such as distributor cap removal, ignition wire removal etc. with the ignition key ON.*

The DuraSpark II system is easily identified with its two-piece distributor cap. DuraSpark II was installed on models up to 1987.

5   In 1980 the DuraSpark III system **(see illustration)** was introduced on models equipped with the EEC II and III systems (feedback carburetors). Basically the same as the previous systems, DuraSpark III differs from the earlier systems in that the input signal is controlled by the computer rather than by the ignition timing and distributor armature position. The DuraSpark III distributor does not contain a pick-up coil and armature, rather it has been moved and positioned down near the crankshaft and now it is called the crankshaft sensor (CP). If the computer malfunctions in the DuraSpark III system, the unit will switch into a limited operation mode while fixing the spark timing at 10 degrees BTDC. The emission controls will shut down and the vehicle will run (poorly) back home or to a shop for repairs. Although the modules look similar between the DuraSpark II

5

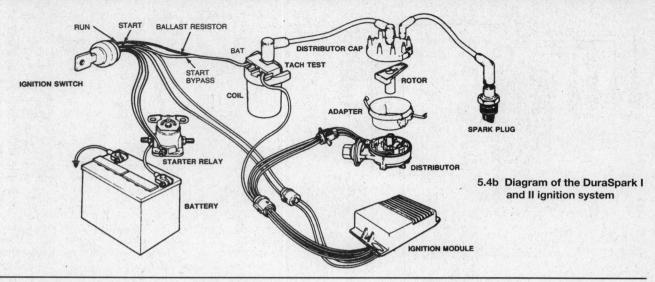

5.4b Diagram of the DuraSpark I and II ignition system

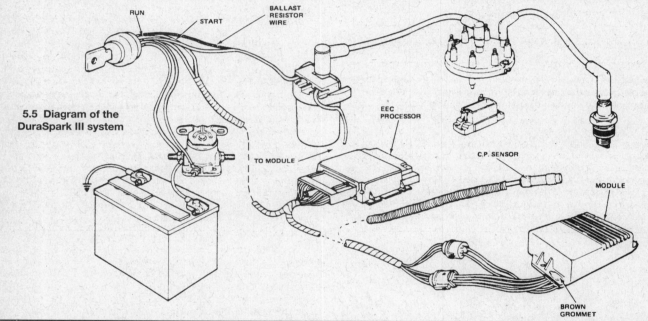

5.5 Diagram of the DuraSpark III system

and III systems, do not interchange these parts or the system will become damaged.

6   These ignition systems are a solid state electronic design consisting of an ignition module, coil, distributor, the spark plug wires and the spark plugs. Mechanically, the system is similar to a breaker point system, except that the distributor cam and ignition points are replaced by an armature and magnetic pick-up unit. The coil primary circuit is controlled by an amplifier module.

7   When the ignition is switched on, the ignition primary circuit is energized. When the distributor armature "teeth" or "spokes" approach the magnetic coil assembly, a voltage is induced which signals the amplifier to turn off the coil primary current. A timing circuit in the amplifier module turns the coil current back on after the coil field has collapsed.

8   When it's on, current flows from the battery through the ignition switch, the coil primary winding, the amplifier module and then to ground. When the current is interrupted, the magnetic field in the ignition coil collapses, inducing a high voltage in the coil secondary windings. The voltage is conducted to the distributor where the rotor directs it to the appropriate spark plug. This process is repeated continuously.

DuraSpark I, II and III

9   These systems are equipped with a gear driven distributor with a die cast base housing a "Hall Effect" vane switch stator assembly and a device for fixed octane adjustment.

10   DuraSpark distributors have a two piece cap. When removing the cap, the upper half is removed, then the rotor is removed, then the lower half of the cap is removed. TFI-IV distributors have a conventional one-piece cap.

11   However, there are a few differences between earlier Canadian and US distributors. The distributors on earlier Canadian vehicles are equipped with centrifugal and vacuum advance mechanisms which control the actual point of ignition based on engine speed and load. As engine speed increases, two weights move out and alter the position of the armature in relation to the distributor shaft, advancing the ignition timing. As engine load increases (when climbing hills or accelerating, for example), a drop in intake manifold vacuum causes the base plate to move slightly in the opposite direction (clockwise) under the action of the spring in the vacuum unit, retarding the timing and counteracting the centrifugal advance. Under light loads (moderate steady speeds, for example), the comparatively high intake

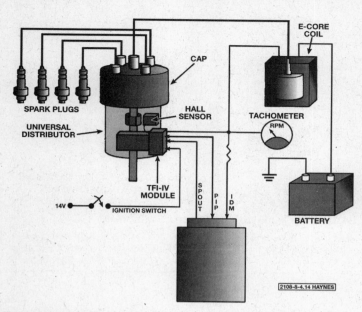

5.12 Diagram of the Thick Film Integrated (TFI-IV) ignition system

13   The TFI-IV/EEC-IV type distributor is similar to the DuraSpark II model but has neither a centrifugal nor a vacuum advance mechanism (advance is handled by the computer instead). The computer uses information from the Profile Ignition Pick-up (PIP) and Cylinder Identification (CID) to determine the proper point to fire the coil. The ignition control module sends the Spark Output (SPOUT) signal to the TFI module to turn the coil ON and OFF. The TFI module also generates an Ignition Diagnostic Monitor (IDM) signal so that the EEC module can check the TFI operation. These signals are important in diagnosing problems with the ignition system.

Electronic Distributorless Ignition (EDIS) type

14   The Electronic Distributorless Ignition System (EDIS) **(see illustration)** is a completely electronically controlled ignition system that does not incorporate a distributor or rotor and cap. The EDIS system consists of a crankshaft timing sensor (Variable Reluctance Sensor [VRS]), EDIS module, two ignition coil packs, the Spark Angle Word (SAW) signal from the EEC IV module, the spark plug wires and the spark plugs. This engine is equipped with an ignition coil for each pair of spark plugs. The EDIS system features a waste-spark method of spark distribution. Each cylinder is paired with its companion cylinder in the firing order (1-6, 5-3, 4-7, 2-8) so one cylinder under compression fires simultaneously with its opposing cylinder, where the piston is on the exhaust stroke. Since the cylinder on the exhaust stroke requires very little of the available voltage to fire its plug, most of the voltage is used to fire the plug under compression.

15   This ignition system does not have any moving parts (no distributor) and all engine timing and spark distribution is handled electronically. This system has fewer parts that require replacement and provides more accurate spark timing. During engine operation, the EDIS ignition module calculates spark angle and determines the turn-on and firing time of the ignition coil.

16   The crankshaft timing sensor is a variable reluctance-type sensor consisting of a 35-tooth trigger wheel with one missing tooth that is incorporated into the crankshaft front damper. The signal generated by this sensor is called a Variable Reluctance Sensor signal (VRS) and it provides the base timing and engine RPM information to the EDIS ignition modules. The main function of the EDIS module is to synchronize the ignition coils so they are turned ON an OFF in the proper sequence for accurate spark control.

manifold vacuum acting on the vacuum advance diaphragm causes the base plate assembly to move in a counterclockwise direction to provide a greater amount of timing advance.

TFI-IV

12   Later models use the Thick Film Integrated IV (TFI-IV) **(see illustration)** ignition module, which is housed in a molded thermoplastic box mounted on the base of the distributor. "Thick Film" refers to the type of manufactured solid state trigger and power units in the module. The important difference between the DS-II and TFI-IV modules is that the TFI-IV module is controlled by the Electronic Engine Control IV (EEC-IV), while the DuraSpark II modules are not.

5

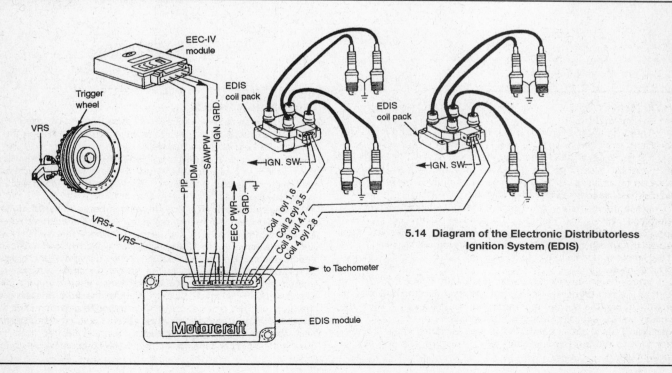

5.14 Diagram of the Electronic Distributorless Ignition System (EDIS)

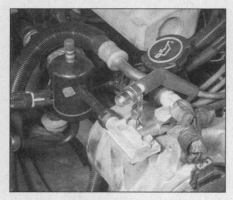

6.1 To use a calibrated ignition tester, simply disconnect a spark plug wire, connect it to the tester, clip the tester to a convenient ground and operate the starter - if there is enough power to fire the plug, sparks will be visible between the electrode tip and the tester body

6.6 Check for battery voltage to the coil with the ignition key on

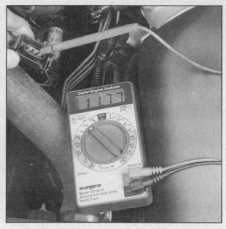

6.16 It is better to use a voltmeter but a test light is adequate to check for battery voltage on the center terminal of the ignition coil electrical connector

6.8 Check the resistance of the ignition ballast resistor wire by placing the probes of the ohmmeter on the coil BATT terminal and the red wire on the module connector

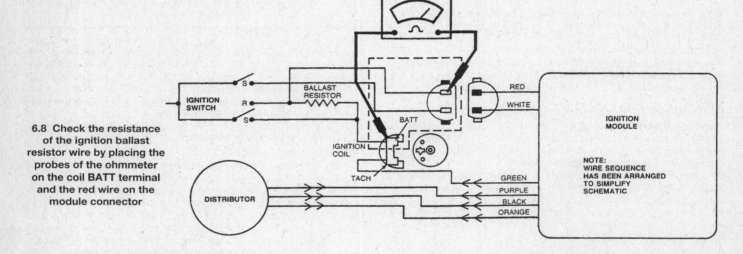

6   Ignition system - check

Warning: *Because of the high voltage generated by the ignition system, extreme care should be taken whenever an operation is performed involving ignition components. This not only includes the igniter (electronic ignition), coil, distributor and spark plug wires, but related components such as spark plug connectors, tachometer and other test equipment.*

All distributor-type ignition systems

Refer to illustrations 6.1, 6.6 and 6.8

1   If the engine will not start even though it turns over, check for spark at the spark plug by installing a calibrated ignition system tester to one of the spark plug wires **(see illustration)**. Note: *The tool is available at most auto parts stores. Be sure to get the correct tool for your particular ignition system (breaker type [points] or breakerless type [electronic]).*

2   Connect the clip on the tester to a ground such as a metal bracket or valve cover bolt, crank the engine and watch the end of the tester for bright blue, well defined sparks.

3   If sparks occur, sufficient voltage is reaching the plugs to fire the engine. However the plugs themselves may be fouled, so remove and check them as described in Chapter 1 or replace them with new ones.

4   If no sparks occur, detach the coil secondary wire from the distributor cap, connect the tester to the coil wire and repeat the test.

5   If sparks occur, the distributor cap, rotor, spark plug wires or spark plugs may be defective. Remove the distributor cap and check the cap, rotor and spark plug wires as described in Chapter 1. Replace defective parts as necessary. If moisture is present in the distributor cap, use WD-40 or something similar to dry out the cap and rotor, then reinstall the cap and repeat the spark test at the spark plug wire.

6   If no sparks occur at the coil wire, check the primary wire connections at the coil to make sure they are clean and tight. Check for voltage to the ignition coil **(see illustration)**.

7   The coil-to-cap wire may be bad, check the resistance with an ohmmeter and compare it to the Specifications. Make any necessary repairs and repeat the test.

8   If no sparks occur, check the ballast resistor wire. On breakerless ignition types, measure the resistance of the ballast resistor between the BATT terminal of the ignition coil connector and the module harness connector red wire **(see illustration)**. It will be necessary to disconnect the electrical connector and measure the resistance from the ballast resistor side. Refer to the Specifications listed in this Chapter for the correct value. If the test results are incorrect, replace it with a new resistor wire (see Section 7).

9   If there's still no spark, the ignition coil, module or other internal components may be defective.

Breaker-points type ignition systems

10   If there is still no spark (see Step 1), check the ignition points (refer to Chapter 1). If the points appear to be in good condition (no pits or burned spots on the point surface) and the primary wires are hooked up correctly, adjust the points as described in Chapter 1.

11   Measure the voltage at the points with a voltmeter. With the ignition ON (engine not running), the points should produce a voltmeter reading of at least 10.5 volts. If not, the battery must be recharged or replaced. If the reading is 10.5 volts or more, record the reading for future reference.

12   If there is still no spark at the plugs, check for a ground or open circuit in the distributor/points circuit. There may be a damaged points terminal causing the ignition voltage to become shorted or diminished.

Electronic Distributorless Ignition (EDIS) system

Refer to illustration 6.16

13   If the engine turns over but won't start, disconnect the spark plug lead from any spark plug and attach it to a calibrated ignition tester (available at most auto parts stores). Make sure the tester is designed for Ford ignition systems if a universal tester isn't available.

14   Connect the clip on the tester to a bolt or metal bracket on the engine **(see illustration 6.1)**, crank the engine and watch the end of the tester to see if bright blue, well-defined sparks occur.

15   If sparks occur, sufficient voltage is reaching the spark plug to fire it (repeat the check at the remaining plug wires to verify that all the ignition coils and wires are functioning). However, the plugs themselves may be fouled, so remove and check them as described in Chapter 1 or install new ones.

16   If no spark or intermittent spark occurs, check for battery voltage to the ignition coil **(see illustration)**. Check for a bad spark plug wire by swapping wires. Check the coils and EDIS ignition module.

Alternative method (all ignition systems)

Note: *If you're unable to obtain a calibrated ignition tester, the following method will allow you to determine if the ignition system has spark, but it won't tell you if there's enough voltage produced to actually initiate combustion in the cylinders.*

17   Remove the wire from one of the spark plugs. Using an insulated tool, hold the wire about 1/4-inch from a good ground and have an assistant crank the engine.

18   If bright blue, well-defined sparks occur, sufficient voltage is reaching the plug to fire it. However, the plug(s) may be fouled, so remove and check them as described in Chapter 1 or install new ones.

19   If there's no spark, check the remaining wires in the same manner. A few sparks followed by no spark is the same condition as no spark at all.

20   If no sparks occur, remove the distributor cap and check the cap and rotor as described in Chapter 1. If moisture is present, dry out the cap and rotor, then reinstall the cap and repeat the spark test.

21   If there's still no spark, disconnect the secondary coil wire from the distributor cap, hold it about 1/4-inch from a good engine ground and crank the engine again.

22   If no sparks occur, check the primary (small) wire connections at the coil to make sure they're clean and tight.

23   If sparks now occur, the distributor cap and rotor (DuraSpark II and TFI-IV systems only), plug wire(s) or spark plug(s) (or all of them) may be defective.

24   If there's still no spark, the coil-to-cap wire may be bad (check the resistance with an ohmmeter and compare it to the Specifications). If a known good wire doesn't make any difference in the test results, the ignition coil, module or other internal components may be defective. Refer further testing to a Ford dealer or qualified electrical specialist.

7   Ballast resistor wire - replacement

Note: *A special ignition resistance wire is installed into the wiring loom between the ignition key and the ignition coil. This wire, often called the*

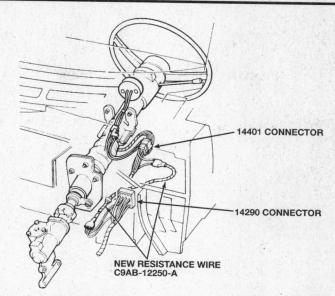

7.2 Locate the steering column and the 14290 connector and drill a hole between them being very careful not to damage any wiring or vacuum circuits

ballast resistor, reduces the voltage to the ignition coil when the engine is running. Because it is rated at a specified resistance, do not replace it with a piece of wire that is not rated for the correct resistance, or damage to the coil will result. Replace it only with the manufacturer's specified resistor wire. When a new resistor wire is installed, the old one must be isolated from the system.

1970 through 1976 models

Refer to illustrations 7.2 and 7.3

1   Disconnect the negative battery cable.

2   Working in the engine compartment, locate the dash panel directly next to the steering column **(see illustration)** and drill a 5/8 inch hole between the column bracket and the 14290 wire harness connector. This hole will be close to the 14401 harness connector and it will allow the special grommet (part number 354972) to be inserted when the resistor wire is in place. The grommet will act as an insulator as well as a guide for the wire. **Note:** *Before drilling the firewall, make sure the drill will not contact any vacuum hoses or wires.*

3   Cut the old resistor wire approximately two inches from the 14401 connector **(see illustration on following page)**.

4   Install a bullet connector on each end of the wire that was just cut and plug the two ends into the fixed connector on the special resistor wire (part number C9AB - 12250-A). One end will be a dead circuit. Be sure continuity exists when the resistor wire is completely installed.

5   Thread the new resistor wire through the hole in the dash and install the special grommet (part number 354972-S) into the vacant hole.

6   Cut the number 16 wire (red/light blue stripe wire) of the number 14401 connector and install a bullet connector onto each end of this wire. This wire is equivalent to the number 16 wire to the ignition coil.

7   Check and make sure there is continuity on the new circuit.

1977 through 1987 models

Refer to illustrations 7.9 and 7.13

Note: *On 1977 through 1987 models, the procedure that follows should be used when making a replacement of a damaged ignition resistor wire. The resistor wire is located in the steering column wiring harness about three inches from the ignition switch connector and is routed to the fuse panel and connects with the engine compartment wiring harness on the left side of the dash panel.*

8   Disconnect the negative battery cable.

5

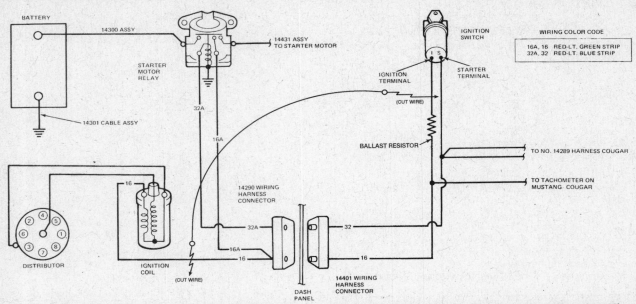

7.3 Install the new resistor wire from the old ballast resistor (wire 16) through the firewall to the ignition coil wire (number 16) on the engine compartment side

9   Working in the engine compartment, disconnect the wiring connector from the wiring harness and fuse panel **(see illustration)**.
10   To gain access to the unit, remove the lower trim panel and disconnect the steering column from the instrument panel.
11   Detach the wiring connector from the back of the fuse panel.
12   Pull the connector from the fuse panel.
13   Locate the number 16A (red/light green stripe) wire in the connector and retract the terminal retaining tab with a small screwdriver or large paper clip and separate the female terminal from the connector **(see illustration)**.
14   Cut the damaged resistor wire as close to the wiring harness as possible and seal the cut end with electrical tape.
15   Locate the ignition switch connector and unwrap the tape covering and expose the circuits that are welded into the harness.

16   Cut the 16A wire about 1-1/2 inches directly at the weld and trim each end of the wire. Install a bullet connector onto each end using a crimping tool. Plug both ends into a double connector **(see illustration 7.13)**.
17   Install one end of the new resistor wire into the remaining opening of the double connector. **Note:** *This wire must be of the specified resistance and length. Consult your dealer parts department for the correct part.*
18   Route the new resistor wire to the connector behind the fuse panel and tape it to the harness using plastic tape.
19   Cut a four inch piece of number 16 gauge wire (part number B6A-14296-C) from stock and strip 3/8 inch of insulation from the ends. Install a female terminal on one end and a bullet terminal onto the other end.

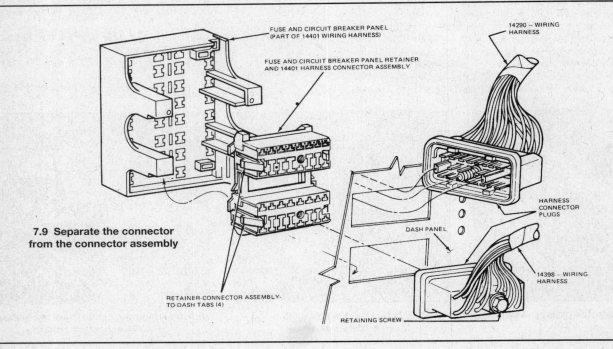

7.9 Separate the connector from the connector assembly

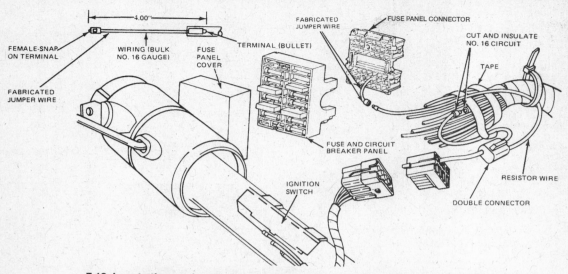

7.13 Locate the number 16 wire (red/light green stripe) and remove it from the terminal

20   Install the female terminal into the vacated cavity of the fuse panel connector where the damaged 16A wire was removed. Push the terminal firmly into place until the locking tabs snap.
21   Connect the free end of the new resistor wire to the free end of the jumper wire using a single connector.
22   Install the connector to the back of the fuse panel and connect it with the wiring harness of the dash panel.
23   Reconnect the battery terminal and start the engine. Check to make sure the lock cylinder releases and returns to the RUN position. The new resistor allows for a slightly higher current to the coil.

8   Ignition coil - check and replacement

Breaker-points type ignition systems

Refer to illustrations 8.4 and 8.5
1   Mark the wires and terminals with pieces of numbered tape, then remove the primary wires and the high-tension wire from the coil.
2   Remove the coil assembly from its mount, clean the outer case and check it for cracks and other damage.
3   Inspect the coil primary terminals and the coil tower terminal for corrosion. Clean them with a wire brush if any corrosion is found.
4   Check the coil primary resistance by attaching the leads of an ohmmeter to the primary terminals **(see illustration)**. Compare the

measured resistance to the Specifications listed in this Chapter.
5   Check the coil secondary resistance by hooking one of the ohmmeter leads to one of the primary terminals and the other ohmmeter lead to the coil high-tension terminal **(see illustration)**. Compare the measured resistance to the Specifications listed in this Chapter.
6   If the measured resistances are not as specified, the coil is defective and should be replaced with a new one.
7   It is essential for proper ignition system operation that all coil terminals and wire leads to be kept clean, tight and dry.
8   Install the coil in its mount and hook up the wires. Installation is the reverse of removal.

Breakerless type ignition systems
Check

Primary and secondary coil resistance
Refer to illustrations 8.9 and 8.10
Caution: *If the coil terminals touch a ground source, the coil and/or stator (pick-up coil) could be damaged.*
9   With the ignition off, disconnect the wires from the coil. Connect an ohmmeter across the coil primary (small wire) terminals **(see illustration)**. The resistance should be as listed in this Chapter's Specifications. If not, replace the coil.
10   Connect an ohmmeter between the negative primary terminal and

8.4 Checking the coil primary resistance

8.5 Checking the coil secondary resistance

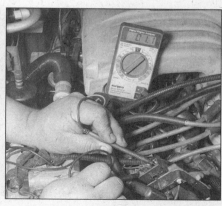

8.9 Checking the coil primary resistance on a TFI-IV ignition system

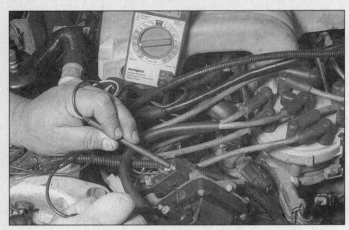

**8.10 Checking the coil secondary resistance on a
TFI-IV ignition system**

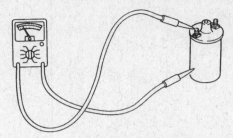

**8.11 Checking the primary winding-to-case resistance on
the ignition coil**

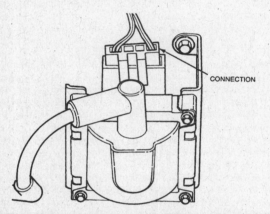

CONNECTION

**8.15 To replace the ignition coil, detach the cable from the
negative terminal of the battery, unplug the coil primary
connection, detach the coil secondary lead and remove both coil
bracket bolts (TFI-IV coil shown)**

**8.19 To check the primary resistance of the EDIS coil, connect
the probes to the center terminal and outer terminal of the coil.
Be sure to check the other coil pack (opposite terminal) and then
the other coil pack assembly mounted on the right engine bank.
The resistance should be the same for all four tests**

**8.20 Check the coil secondary resistance by probing the paired
companion cylinders (7/4, 8/2, 1/6 and 3/5)**

the secondary terminal **(see illustration)** (the one that the distributor cap wire connects to). The resistance should be as listed in this Chapter's Specifications. If not, replace the coil.

Ignition coil primary winding-to-case resistance

Refer to illustration 8.11

11   Measure the resistance from the positive primary terminal to the case of the ignition coil **(see illustration)**.

12   If the indicated resistance is less than the resistance listed in this Chapter's Specifications, replace the ignition coil.

13   Reconnect the ignition coil wires.

Replacement

Refer to illustration 8.15

14   Detach the cable from the negative terminal of the battery.

15   Detach the wires from the primary terminals on the coil (some coils have a single electrical connector for the primary wires) **(see illustration)**.

16   Unplug the coil secondary lead.

17   Remove both bracket bolts and detach the coil.

18   Installation is the reverse of removal.

Electronic Distributorless Ignition (EDIS) system

Check

Refer to illustrations 8.19 and 8.20

19   With the ignition off, disconnect the electrical connector(s) from

the coil. Connect an ohmmeter across the coil primary (center terminal) terminal and the outer terminal **(see illustration)**. The resistance should be as listed in this Chapter's Specifications. If not, replace the coil.

20   Connect an ohmmeter between the secondary terminals **(see illustration)** (the one that the spark plug wires connect to) of each coil pack. The resistance should be as listed in this Chapter's Specifications. **Note:** *Each coil pack is paired 7/4, 8/2, 1/6 and 3/5. Be sure to check resistance with these designated terminals only.* If not, replace the coil.

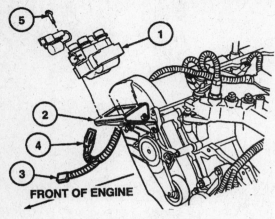

8.24 EDIS coil mounting details

1	Coil pack	4	Ignition coil harness
2	Bracket		connector
3	Radio/ignition capacitor	5	Bolt

Replacement

Refer to illustration 8.24

21   Disconnect the negative cable from the battery.

22   Disconnect the ignition coil electrical connector(s) from each individual coil pack.

23   Disconnect the ignition wires by squeezing the locking tabs and twisting while pulling. DO NOT just pull on the wires to disconnect them.

24   Remove the bolts securing the ignition coil to the mounting bracket on the engine **(see illustration)**.

25   Installation is the reverse of the removal procedure with the following additions:

   a) *Prior to installing the spark plug lead into the ignition coil, coat the entire interior of the rubber boot with Silicone Dielectric Compound (Ford part No. D7AZ-19A331-A) or equivalent.*

   b) *Insert each spark plug wire into the proper terminal of the ignition coil. Push the wire into the terminal and make sure the boots are fully seated and both locking tabs are engaged properly.*

Note: *Refer to the EDIS firing order schematic in Chapter 2 Specifications to correctly identify each cylinder and its corresponding coil pack terminal.*

9   Distributor - removal and installation

Removal

Refer to illustrations 9.3, 9.5a and 9.5b

1   Unplug the primary lead from the coil.

2   Unplug the electrical connector for the module. Follow the wires as they exit the distributor to find the connector.

3   Note the raised "1" on the distributor cap **(see illustration)**. This marks the location for the number one cylinder spark plug wire terminal.

4   Remove the distributor cap (see Chapter 1) and turn the engine over until the rotor is pointing toward the number one spark plug terminal (see the TDC locating procedure in Chapter 2).

5   Make a mark on the edge of the distributor base directly below the rotor tip and in line with it **(see illustration)**. Also, mark the distributor base and the engine block to ensure that the distributor is installed correctly **(see illustration)**.

6   Remove the distributor hold-down bolt and clamp, then pull the distributor straight up to remove it. Be careful not to disturb the intermediate driveshaft. **Caution:** *DO NOT turn the engine while the distributor is removed, or the alignment marks will be useless.*

Installation

7   Insert the distributor into the engine in exactly the same relationship to the block that it was in when removed.

8   To mesh the helical gears on the camshaft and the distributor, it may be necessary to turn the rotor slightly. If the distributor doesn't seat completely, the hex shaped recess in the lower end of the distributor shaft is not mating properly with the oil pump shaft. Recheck the alignment marks between the distributor base and the block to verify that the distributor is in the same position it was in before removal. Also check the rotor to see if it's aligned with the mark you made on the edge of the distributor base. **Note:** *If the crankshaft has been moved while the distributor is out, locate Top Dead Center (TDC) for the number one piston (see Chapter 2) and position the distributor and rotor accordingly.*

9   Place the hold-down clamp in position and loosely install the bolt.

10   Install the distributor cap and tighten the cap screws securely.

11   Plug in the module electrical connector.

12   Reattach the spark plug wires to the plugs (if removed).

13   Connect the cable to the negative terminal of the battery.

14   Check and, if necessary, adjust the ignition timing (refer to Chapter 1) and tighten the distributor hold-down bolt securely.

5

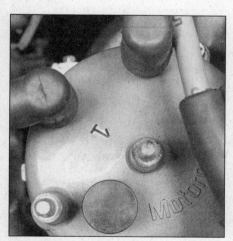

9.3 The number "1" on the distributor cap marks the location of the spark plug wire terminal for the number 1 cylinder spark plug

9.5a Make a mark on the perimeter of the distributor body that marks the position of the rotor (arrow)

9.5b Make a mark on the base of the distributor body and the engine block to clearly define the position of the distributor (arrow)

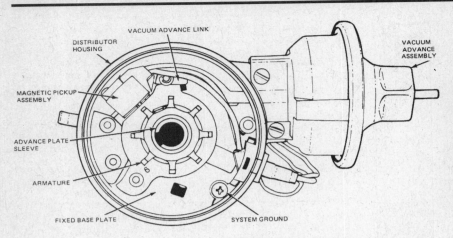

10.1 Diagram of a breakerless type distributor

10.5 Observe the timing mark with the timing light while applying vacuum with the vacuum pump. There should be a noticeable increase in timing advance.

10   Distributor centrifugal and vacuum advance system - check

General information

Refer to illustration 10.1

1   To provide the proper spark timing during different speeds and throttle openings, most distributors (carbureted models only) are equipped with a vacuum advance **(see illustration)** and a centrifugal advance mechanism in the distributor. These parts may stick, wear out or become defective after years of service. **Note:** *On the models covered in this manual, the vacuum advance unit governs ignition timing according to engine load, while the centrifugal advance unit governs ignition timing according to engine speed.* **Note:** *Some models are equipped with dual diaphragm vacuum advance units that provide additional timing retard during engine cranking to aid in starting and also reduce emissions during idle and during coast down.*

2   Both the vacuum advance and the centrifugal advance systems can be tested using the timing light method. After the initial test to determine its working capabilities, the different systems must be checked separately.

Timing light test

Refer to illustration 10.5

3   Disconnect the vacuum line to the vacuum advance and run the engine at approximately 1,200 rpm.

4   Install a timing light and observe the paint mark on the pulley while slowly raising the engine rpm to 4,000. The timing mark should move smoothly and without any hesitations or sudden movements. If the timing mark jumps around, it will be necessary to remove the distributor cap and check the centrifugal weights for binding, missing parts or defective parts (see Step 7).

5   Next, check the operation of the vacuum advance unit. Run the engine at a steady 1,200 rpm and point the timing light at the timing mark **(see illustration).**

6   Note the exact position of the timing mark and raise the rpm while observing the mark. When the vacuum line is connected the timing mark should advance quickly and completely. Most systems will advance the timing approximately 35 degrees when opened to wide open throttle. If it doesn't, see Step 9.

Centrifugal advance check

7   With the ignition OFF, and the distributor cap removed from the distributor, advance the timing plate manually using the rotor and release the mechanism. It should snap back to its original position very quickly and without hesitation. Try oiling the weights and springs with a spray penetrant and repeat the test several times to loosen the springs and weights if they show signs of sticking or binding.

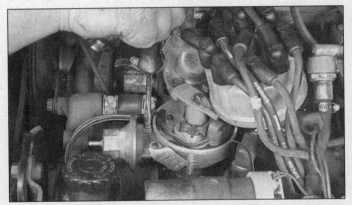

10.14 Remove the screws that retain the vacuum advance to the distributor body

8   Repeat the test several more times until the timing can be advanced without trouble.

Vacuum advance check

9   The diaphragm assembly is attached to the distributor breaker plate. A vacuum line attaches the diaphragm housing to a ported vacuum source. As vacuum changes from idle to acceleration through deceleration and back to idle, the timing changes accordingly.

10   With the engine OFF check the condition of the vacuum hose from the distributor to the vacuum source. Make sure the hose is connected and the ends sealed.

11   Disconnect and plug the vacuum hose to the distributor. Connect a vacuum pump to the vacuum diaphragm and apply between 15 to 20 in-Hg. to the advance unit.

12   Make sure the vacuum advance diaphragm holds vacuum. If the vacuum bleeds down, replace the unit with a new vacuum advance.

Vacuum advance removal

Refer to illustration 10.14

13   Remove the distributor cap and the vacuum line to the advance unit.

14   Remove the two screws that retain the vacuum advance unit to the distributor body **(see illustration).**

15   Remove the clip that retains the vacuum advance plate to the vacuum advance link. Be very careful not to drop it into the distributor or somewhere in the engine compartment.

16   Remove the old vacuum advance unit and replace it with a new part.

17   Installation is the reverse of removal.

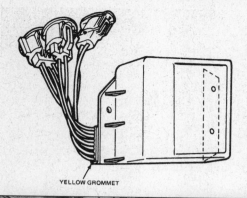
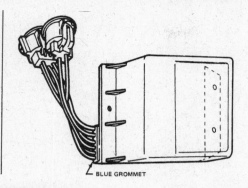

YELLOW GROMMET

BLUE GROMMET

11.1 DuraSpark ignition systems will have one or the other of the above ignition modules - the one on the left, known as a Universal Ignition Module (UIM), has three electrical connectors; the one on the right is the standard DuraSpark I and II module with two electrical connectors

11.2a Check battery voltage on the red wire to the ignition module

11.2b Electrical schematic of the SSI ignition system on 1974 models

11 Ignition module and stator assembly - check and replacement

Caution: *The ignition module is a delicate and relatively expensive electronic component. Failure to follow the step-by-step procedures could result in damage to the module and/or other electronic devices, including the EEC-IV microprocessor itself. Additionally, all devices under computer control are protected by a Federally mandated extended warranty. Check with your dealer concerning this warranty before attempting to diagnose and replace the module yourself.*

Note: *On some models, a special DuraSpark II ignition module is used with altitude compensation features that aid in spark timing and engine performance at high altitudes. This special module along with the altitude sensor, ignition timing vacuum switch or ignition pressure switch, allows the base engine timing to be modified to suit either altitude or engine load conditions.*

SSI and DuraSpark ignition modules
Check

Refer to illustrations 11.1, 11.2a through 11.2f, 11.3 and 11.4a through 11.4c

Note: *Be aware of an intermittent no-start condition the ignition module exhibits on certain years and models of SSI and DuraSpark ignition systems. The engine will start momentarily and then shut down instantly or the engine will start and run the duration of the trip until the engine is shut off and from there it will not re-start. This intermittent condition will not remedy itself but it is possible to strike the module with a rubber mallet or to apply heat to the module using a heat lamp (bulb) to try and bring the module "back to life". This will only confirm the ignition module as defective.*

1   DuraSpark ignition systems are equipped with a two or three-connector module **(see illustration)**. Do not be confused with these

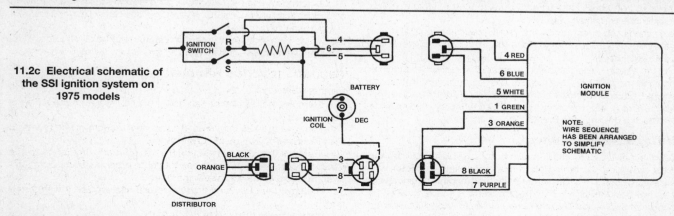

11.2c Electrical schematic of the SSI ignition system on 1975 models

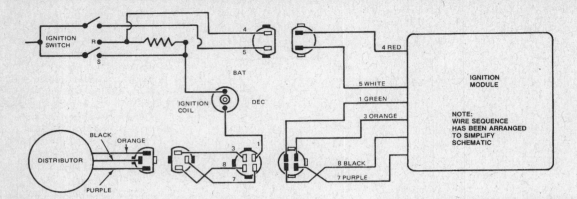

11.2d Electrical schematic of the SSI, DuraSpark I and II systems on 1976 through 1981 models

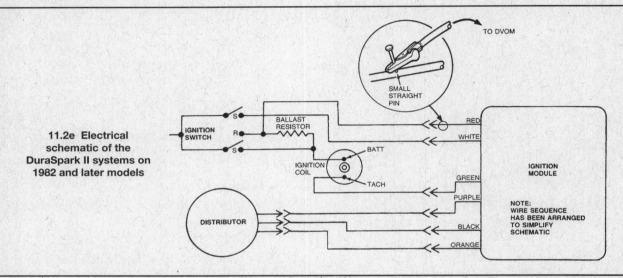

11.2e Electrical schematic of the DuraSpark II systems on 1982 and later models

ignition modules but instead follow the same color code for all diagnostic voltage and resistance checks as designated on the schematics.

2   Check for power to the ignition module. Using a voltmeter, probe the red wire from the module **(see illustrations)**. With the ignition ON (engine not running), there should be battery voltage.

3   Check the resistance of the distributor stator **(see accompanying illustration and illustrations 11.2b through 11.2f)**. Using an ohmmeter, probe the orange and purple wires at the distributor electrical connector and check the resistance. It should be between 400 and

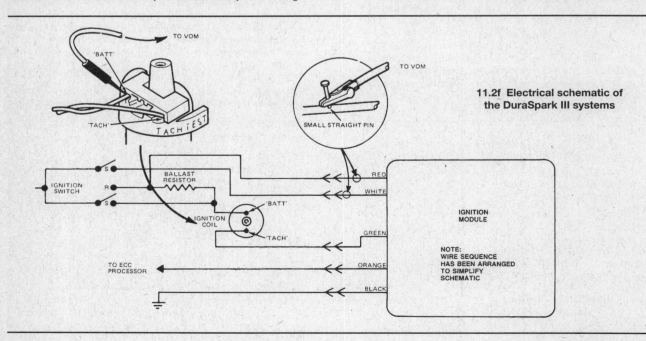

11.2f Electrical schematic of the DuraSpark III systems

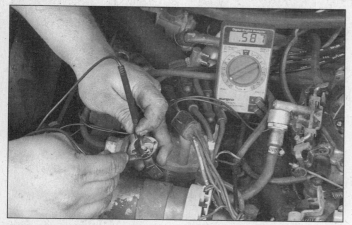

11.3a Check the stator resistance on the orange and purple wires

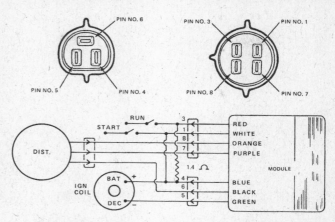

11.3b Use pin number 7 and number 8 to check the stator resistance on 1974 SSI ignition systems

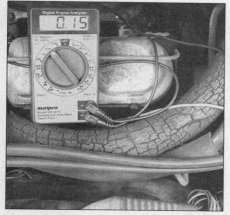

11.4a Checking the ground circuit voltage

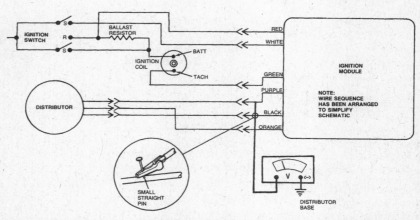

11.4b Check the ground circuit continuity on DuraSpark II ignition systems. The ignition key should be ON (engine not running) and the voltmeter should read approximately 0.5 volt

1,000 ohms. Refer to the Specifications listed in this Chapter for the correct value. If not, replace the stator assembly within the distributor. **Note:** *On DuraSpark III systems, check the resistance of the crankshaft position sensor (see Chapter 4A). This system does not use a stator in the distributor but instead the CP sensor acts as an impulse generator for the ignition system.*

4   Check the ground circuit continuity. Using a voltmeter, probe the black wire from the ignition module **(see illustrations)**. With the ignition ON (engine not running), there should be approximately 0.5 volts or greater.

5

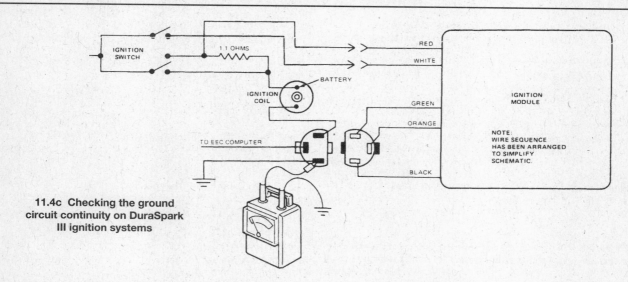

11.4c Checking the ground circuit continuity on DuraSpark III ignition systems

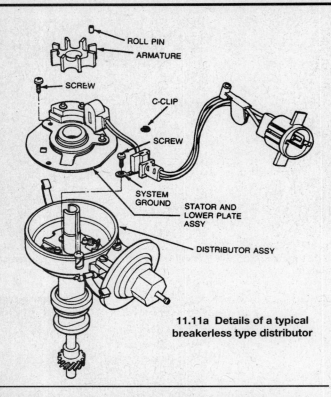

ROLL PIN
ARMATURE
SCREW
C-CLIP
SCREW
SYSTEM GROUND
STATOR AND LOWER PLATE ASSY
DISTRIBUTOR ASSY

11.11a Details of a typical breakerless type distributor

11.11b Using two screwdrivers, carefully pry the armature off the distributor shaft

11.12 Remove the retaining screw from the baseplate

5   If battery voltage is not reaching the ignition module, trace the circuit to the ignition switch and battery (see Chapter 12) and check for open circuits or a damaged wire harness. If any of the other test results are incorrect, replace the ignition module with a new part.

Replacement
Ignition module

6   Detach the cable from the negative terminal of the battery.
7   Unplug the electrical connectors.
8   Remove the mounting screws and detach the module.
9   Installation is the reverse of removal.

Stator

Refer to illustrations 11.11a, 11.11b, 11.12, 11.13, 11.14, 11.15, 11.16, and 11.17
Note: *On some models it will be possible to perform this procedure in the vehicle. It is recommended that the distributor be placed on a clean bench to avoid any problems with losing parts.*

10   Detach the cable from the negative terminal of the battery.
11   Using two screwdrivers, carefully pry the armature up and off the distributor shaft **(see illustrations)**.
12   Remove the set screw for the harness connector **(see illustration)**.
13   Remove the circlip that retains the vacuum advance to the pick-up assembly **(see illustration)**.
14   Remove the vacuum advance **(see illustration)**.
15   Remove the center clip **(see illustration)** from the distributor shaft.
16   Lift the stator assembly from the distributor **(see illustration)**.
17   Installation is the reverse of removal. Be sure to lubricate the new stator assembly to allow free movement for proper advancing charac-

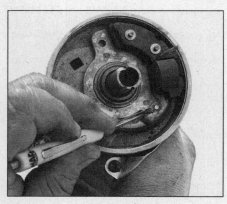

11.13 Pry the circlip off the advance plate

11.14 Remove the vacuum advance from the distributor

11.15 Pry the center clip off the shaft

11.16 Lift the stator assembly from the distributor

11.17 Be sure to install the pin into the grooved section of the distributor shaft and the armature

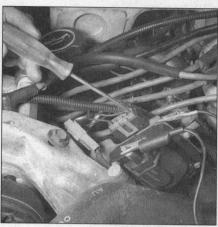

11.19 Checking the ignition coil primary circuit using a test light on the ignition coil TACH terminal

11.23 Checking for battery voltage on terminal number 3 (TFI PWR) with the ignition key ON (engine not running). If the probes of the voltmeter do not penetrate the electrical connector, install a pin into the terminal and place the probe onto the pin

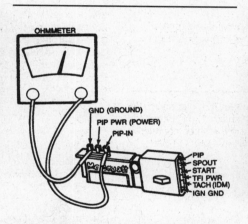

11.26 Ignition module terminal identification on the TFI-IV system

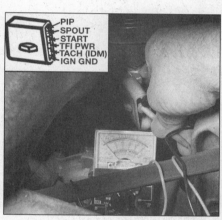

11.31 Check the resistance of the PIP to SPOUT circuit with an ohmmeter. It should be less than 7,000 ohms

5

teristics. Also, drive in the lock pin (see illustration) to secure the armature.

TFI-IV ignition module

Check

Ignition coil primary circuit

Refer to illustration 11.19

18 Unplug the ignition wiring harness connectors and inspect them for dirt, corrosion and damage, then reconnect them.

19 Attach a 12 volt test light between the coil TACH terminal and a good engine ground (see illustration).

20 Remove the coil wire from the ignition coil and use a suitable jumper wire to ground the secondary terminal.

21 Crank the engine.

22 The test light should flash with each output signal from the coil primary circuit as the engine turns over.

Ignition module checks

Refer to illustrations 11.23, 11.26 and 11.31

23 Check for power to the ignition module. Using a voltmeter, probe terminal number 3 (ICM PWR) from the module (see illustration). With the ignition ON (engine not running), there should be battery voltage.

24 Remove the distributor from the engine (see Section 9).

25 Remove the module from the distributor.

26 Using an ohmmeter, ensure that the resistance between terminals GND and PIP IN is greater than 500 ohms (see illustration).

27 Ensure resistance between terminals PIP PWR and PIP IN is less than 2,000 ohms.

28 Ensure resistance between terminals PIP PWR and TFI PWR is less than 200 ohms.

29 Ensure resistance between terminals GND and IGN GND is less than 2 ohms.

30 Ensure resistance between terminals PIP IN and PIP is less than 200 ohms.

31 Ensure resistance between terminals PIP and SPOUT is less than 7,000 ohms (see illustration).

32 If any of these test results are incorrect, replace the ignition module with a new part.

33 If all these tests are correct, replace the stator (see Steps 34 through 38).

Replacement

Ignition module

Refer to illustrations 11.35, 11.36 and 11.37

34 Remove the distributor from the engine (see Section 9) if access to the module is blocked.

11.35 To remove the TFI-IV ignition module from the distributor base, remove the two screws (arrows) . . .

11.36 . . . then pull the module straight down to detach the spade terminals from the stator connector

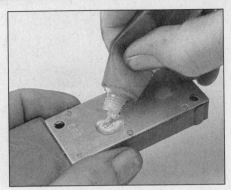

11.37 Be sure to wipe the back side of the module clean and apply a film of dielectric grease (essential for cool operation of the module) - DO NOT use any other type of grease

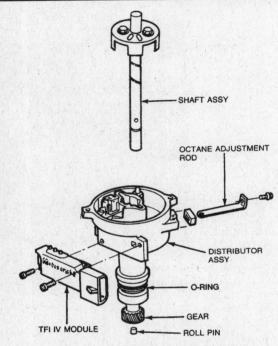

11.41 Typical TFI-IV distributor details

- SHAFT ASSY
- OCTANE ADJUSTMENT ROD
- DISTRIBUTOR ASSY
- O-RING
- GEAR
- ROLL PIN
- TFI IV MODULE

35   Remove the two module mounting screws with a 1/4-inch drive 7/32-inch deep socket **(see illustration)**.

36   Pull straight down on the module to disconnect the spade connectors from the stator connector **(see illustration)**.

37   Whether you are installing the old module or a new one, wipe the back side of the module clean with a soft, clean rag and apply a film of silicone dielectric grease to the back side of the module **(see illustration)**.

38   Installation is the reverse of removal. When plugging in the module, make sure that the three terminals are inserted all the way into the stator connector.

Stator

Refer to illustrations 11.41, 11.42, 11.43, 11.44 and 11.46

39   Detach the cable from the negative terminal of the battery. Remove the distributor (see Section 9).

40   Remove the rotor and the ignition module from the distributor.

41   Using the appropriate size pin-punch, remove the roll pin from the gear and shaft assembly **(see illustration)**.

42   Using a small gear puller, remove the gear from the shaft **(see illustration)**. Be very careful not to chip or break the gear teeth when removing the gear.

43   Remove the shaft assembly from the housing. Note the position of the spacer washer for reassembly and remove the washer **(see illustration)**.

44   Remove the octane rod and the stator from the distributor **(see illustration)**.

45   Reassemble the distributor in the reverse order of disassembly.

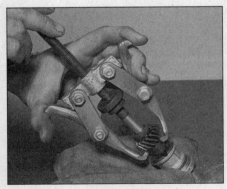

11.42 After removing the roll pin, use a small gear puller to remove the gear from the shaft

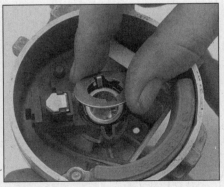

11.43 After removing the shaft, note the position of the spacer washer and remove the washer

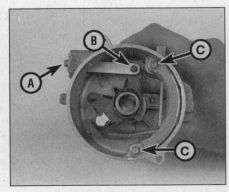

11.44 Remove the octane rod retaining screw (A) and lift the end of the rod off the post (B) - remove the stator retaining screws (C) and remove the stator from the housing

11.46 Align the holes and carefully drive the gear on the shaft - if the holes do not align perfectly, remove the gear and reposition it before installing the roll-pin

11.49 Connect a test light between the coil outer terminals on the ignition coil connectors and watch for a blinking light when the engine is cranked

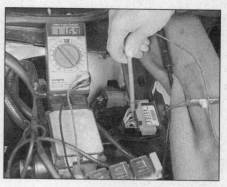

11.51a Probe terminal number 6 terminal (black/orange stripe wire) and check for battery voltage from the power relay

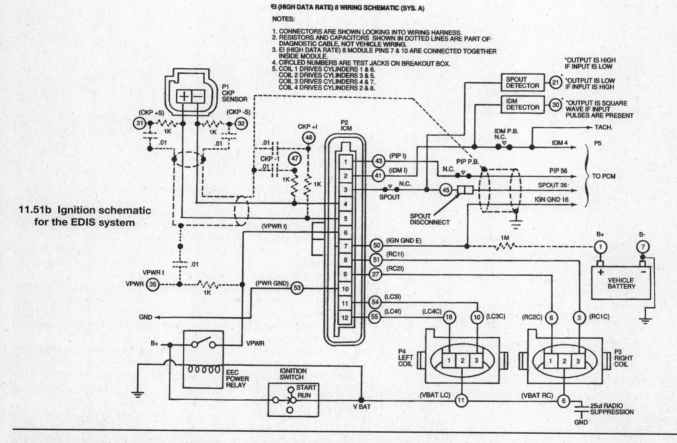

11.51b Ignition schematic for the EDIS system

Apply a light coat of engine oil to the distributor shaft before installing it in the housing.

46   Using a deep socket and a hammer, lightly tap the gear onto the shaft. Make sure the hole in the gear and the hole in the shaft are perfectly aligned or the roll pin cannot be installed **(see illustration)**.

47   Replace the O-ring at the base of the distributor, install the ignition module and rotor and install the distributor in the engine (see Section 9).

EDIS ignition module
Refer to illustrations 11.49, 11.51a, 11.51b, 11.52 and 11.53

Ignition coil primary circuit

48   Unplug the ignition coil wiring harness connectors and inspect them for dirt, corrosion and damage.

49   Attach a 12 volt test light to the battery positive (+) terminal and the coil electrical connector **(see illustration)** and crank the engine.

50   The test light should flash with each output signal from the EDIS ignition module through the coil primary circuit. **Note:** *It will be necessary to check each circuit that governs each coil pack. Install the test light into the opposite terminal on the harness connector (outside terminals) and repeat the test. Follow the same procedure for the other coil assembly also.*

Ignition module checks

51   Check for power to the ignition module. Using a voltmeter, probe terminal number 6 (black/orange stripe) and check for battery voltage through the power relay **(see illustrations)**. With the ignition ON

11.52 Make sure the SPOUT circuit maintains continuity from the ignition module (terminal number 3) and the SPOUT connector

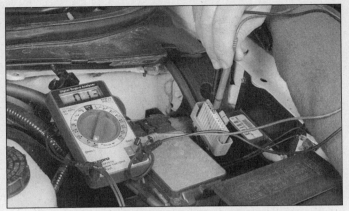

11.53 Check the crankshaft sensor resistance on terminal numbers 4 and 5. It should be between 1.0 and 1.5 ohms

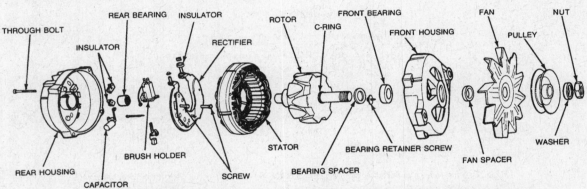

12.2a Typical side terminal type alternator (EVR) (externally regulated charging system)

(engine not running), there should be battery voltage.

52   Check the circuit from the ignition module to the SPOUT connector (terminal number 3) for a complete circuit **(see illustration)**. Continuity should exist.

53   Also check the resistance of the crankshaft sensor **(see illustration)**. It should be between 1.0 and 1.5 ohms.

54   If battery voltage is not reaching the ignition module, trace the electrical circuit to the ignition and battery (see Chapter 12) and check for open circuits or a damaged wire harness. If any of the other test results are incorrect, replace the ignition module with a new one.

Replacement

55   Disconnect the negative cable from the battery.

56   Disconnect the electrical connector from the EDIS ignition module.

57   Remove the screws securing the EDIS module to the fenderwell.

58   Installation is the reverse of the removal procedure.

12   Charging system - general information and precautions

Refer to illustrations 12.2a and 12.2b

The charging system includes the alternator, either an internal or an external voltage regulator **(see illustrations)**, a charge indicator or warning light, the battery, a fusible link and the wiring between all the components. The charging system supplies electrical power for the ignition system, the lights, the radio, etc. The alternator is driven by a drivebelt at the front of the engine.

The purpose of the voltage regulator is to limit the alternator's voltage to a preset value. This prevents power surges, circuit

overloads, etc., during peak voltage output. On EVR (external voltage regulator) systems, the regulator is mounted on the right fender apron of the vehicle. On IAR (Integral Alternator/Regulator) systems, a solid state regulator is housed inside a plastic module mounted on the alternator itself.

The fusible link is a short length of insulated wire integral with the engine compartment wiring harness. The link is several wire gauges smaller in diameter than the circuit it protects. Production fusible links and their identification flags are identified by the flag color. Refer to Chapter 12 for additional information on fusible links.

The charging system doesn't ordinarily require periodic maintenance. However, the drivebelt, battery and wires and connections should be inspected at the intervals outlined in Chapter 1.

Be very careful when making electrical circuit connections to a vehicle equipped with an alternator and note the following:

a) *When reconnecting wires to the alternator from the battery, be sure to note the polarity.*

b) *Before using arc welding equipment to repair any part of the vehicle, disconnect the wires from the alternator and the battery terminals.*

c) *Never start the engine with a battery charger connected.*

d) *Always disconnect both battery cables before using a battery charger (negative cable first, positive cable last).*

13   Charging system - check

Refer to illustration 13.2

1   If a malfunction occurs in the charging circuit, do not immediately assume that the alternator is causing the problem. First check the

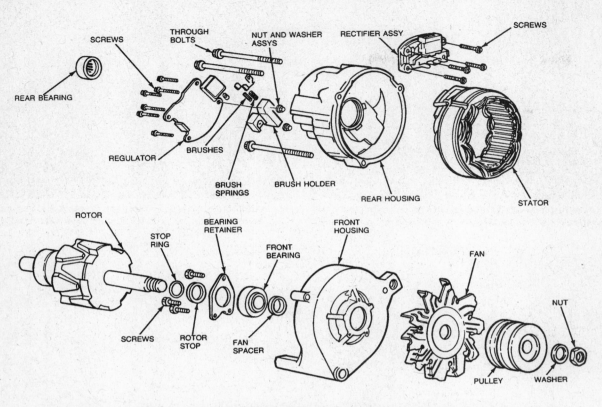

12.2b Typical Integral Alternator/Regulator (IAR) (internally regulated charging system)

following items:

a) *The battery cables where they connect to the battery. Make sure the connections are clean and tight.*
b) *The battery electrolyte specific gravity. If it is low, charge the battery.*
c) *Check the external alternator wiring and connections.*
d) *Check the drivebelt condition and tension (see Chapter 1).*
e) *Check the alternator mounting bolts for tightness.*
f) *Run the engine and check the alternator for abnormal noise.*

2   Using a voltmeter, check the battery voltage with the engine off. It should be approximately 12-volts **(see illustration)**.
3   Start the engine and check the battery voltage again. It should now be approximately 14 to 15-volts.
4   If the indicated voltage reading is less or more than the specified charging voltage, replace the voltage regulator. If replacing the regulator fails to restore the voltage to the specified range, the problem may be within the alternator.
5   Due to the special equipment necessary to test or service the alternator, it is recommended that if a fault is suspected the vehicle be taken to a dealer or a shop with the proper equipment. Because of this, the home mechanic should limit maintenance to checking connections and the inspection and replacement of the brushes.
6   Some models are equipped with an ammeter on the instrument panel that indicates charge or discharge - current passing in or out of the battery. With all electrical equipment switched ON, and the engine idling, the gauge needle may show a discharge condition. At fast idle or normal driving speeds the needle should stay on the charge side of the gauge, with the charged state of the battery determining just how far over (the lower the battery state of charge, the farther the needle should swing toward the charge side).
7   Some models are equipped with a voltmeter on the instrument panel that indicates battery voltage with the key on and engine off, and

13.2 To measure battery voltage, attach the voltmeter leads to the battery terminals - to measure charging voltage, start the engine

alternator output when the engine is running.
8   The charge light on the instrument panel illuminates with the key on and engine not running, and should go out when the engine runs.
9   If the gauge does not show a charge when it should or the alternator light (if equipped) remains on, there is a fault in the system. Before inspecting the brushes or replacing the alternator, the battery condition, alternator belt tension and electrical cable connections should be checked.

14.2 Be sure to mark each electrical connector (arrows) before unplugging them from the alternator

14.3a Remove the bolt(s) (arrow) that retain the alternator to the brackets

14.3b Remove the bolts (arrows) from the alternator bracket and separate the bracket from the intake manifold (4.6L OHC engine)

14.3c The lower mounting bolts (arrows) can be reached without removing the fan shroud (4.6L OHC engine)

15.2 Scribe a line across the alternator housing for alignment reference

15.3 Remove the bolts (arrows) that retain the alternator body sections together

14   Alternator - removal and installation

Refer to illustrations 14.2, 14.3a, 14.3b and 14.3c
1   Detach the cable from the negative terminal of the battery.
2   Unplug the electrical connectors from the alternator **(see illustration)**.
3   Loosen the alternator bolts **(see illustrations)** and detach the drivebelt.
4   On 4.6L engines, remove the ignition wire assembly from the intake manifold area.
5   Remove the adjustment and pivot bolts and separate the alternator from the engine.
6   Installation is the reverse of removal.
7   After the alternator is installed, adjust the drivebelt tension (see Chapter 1).

15   Alternator brushes (EVR type alternator) - replacement

Note: *Internal replacement parts for alternators may not be readily available. Check the availability of replacement parts before proceeding.*

Rear terminal alternator

Refer to illustrations 15.2, 15.3, 15.4, 15.5 and 15.7
1   Remove the alternator as described in Section 14.

2   Scribe a line across the length of the alternator housing to ensure correct reassembly **(see illustration)**.
3   Remove the housing through-bolts from the rear housing **(see illustration)**. Make a careful note of all insulator locations.
4   Withdraw the rear housing section from the stator, rotor and front housing assembly **(see illustration)**.
5   Remove the brush holder, brushes and springs from the rear housing **(see illustration)**.
6   Check the length of the brushes against the wear dimensions given in the Specifications and replace the brushes with new ones if necessary.
7   Install the springs and brushes in the holder assembly and hold them in place by inserting a piece of stiff wire through the rear housing and brush terminal insulator **(see illustration)**. Make sure enough wire protrudes through the rear housing so it can be withdrawn after assembly.
8   Attach the rear housing, rotor and front housing assembly to the stator, making sure the scribed marks are aligned.
9   Install the housing through-bolts and rear end insulators and nuts but do not tighten the nuts at this time.
10   Carefully extract the piece of wire from the rear housing and make sure that the brushes are seated on the slip ring. Install the through-bolts and tighten securely.
11   Install the alternator as described in Section 14.

Side terminal alternator

Refer to illustration 15.18
12   Remove the alternator as described in Section 14 and scribe a mark on both end housings and the stator for ease of reassembly.

15.4 Separate the two sections

15.5 Remove the screws (arrows) and detach the brush holder and the brushes

15.7 Insert a paper clip through the hole in the back to retain the brushes

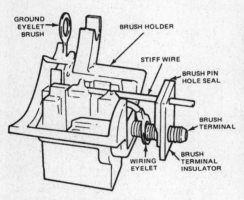

15.18 A piece of stiff wire is used to hold the brushes in place on a side terminal alternator

16.2 The external voltage regulator is located in the corner of the engine compartment and is retained by two bolts (arrows)

17.3 To detach the voltage regulator/brush holder assembly, remove the four screws

13   Remove the through-bolts and separate the front housing and rotor from the rear housing and stator. Be careful that you do not separate the rear housing and stator.

14   Use a soldering iron to unsolder and disengage the brush holder from the rear housing. Remove the brushes and springs from the brush holders.

15   Remove the two brush holder attaching screws and lift the brush holder from the rear housing.

16   Remove any sealing compound from the brush holder and rear housing.

17   Inspect the brushes for damage and check their dimensions against the Specifications. If they are worn, replace them with new ones.

18   To reassemble, install the springs and brushes in the brush holders, inserting a piece of stiff wire to hold them in place **(see illustration)**.

19   Place the brush holder in position in the rear housing, using the wire to retract the brushes through the hole in the rear housing.

20   Install the brush holder attaching screws and push the holder toward the shaft opening as you tighten the screws. **Caution:** *The rectifier can be overheated and damaged if the soldering is not done quickly. Press the brush holder lead onto the rectifier lead and solder them in place.*

21   Place the rotor and front housing in position in the stator and rear housing. After aligning the scribe marks, install the through-bolts.

22   Turn the fan and pulley to check for binding in the alternator.

23   Withdraw the wire which is retracting the brushes and seal the

hole with waterproof cement. **Caution:** *Do not use RTV-type sealant on the hole.*

16   External Voltage Regulator (EVR) - replacement

Refer to illustration 16.2

1   Detach the cable from the negative terminal of the battery.

2   Locate the voltage regulator on the right side of the engine compartment **(see illustration)**.

3   If necessary, remove the battery or air cleaner duct to gain access to the voltage regulator.

4   Unplug the electrical connector from the voltage regulator.

5   Remove the regulator mounting bolts.

6   Remove the regulator.

7   Installation is the reverse of removal.

17   Voltage regulator/alternator brushes (IAR-type alternator) - replacement

Refer to illustrations 17.3, 17.4, 17.5 and 17.9

1   Remove the alternator (see Section 14).

2   Set the alternator on a clean workbench.

3   Remove the four voltage regulator mounting screws **(see illustration)**.

5

17.4 Lift the assembly from the alternator

17.5 To remove the brushes from the voltage regulator/brush holder assembly, detach the rubber plugs from the two brush lead screws and remove both screws (arrows)

17.9 Before installing the voltage regulator/brush holder assembly, insert a paper clip as shown to hold the brushes in place during installation - after installation, simply pull the paper clip out

4   Detach the voltage regulator/brush holder assembly **(see illustration)**.

5   Detach the rubber plugs and remove the brush lead retaining screws and nuts to separate the brush leads from the holder **(see illustration)**. Note that the screws have Torx heads and require a special screwdriver.

6   After noting the relationship of the brushes to the brush holder assembly, remove both brushes. Don't lose the springs.

7   If you're installing a new voltage regulator, insert the old brushes into the brush holder of the new regulator. If you're installing new brushes, insert them into the brush holder of the old regulator. Make sure the springs are properly compressed and the brushes are properly inserted into the recesses in the brush holder.

8   Install the brush lead retaining screws and nuts.

9   Insert a short section of wire, like a paper clip, through the hole in the voltage regulator **(see illustration)** to hold the brushes in the retracted position during regulator installation.

10   Carefully install the regulator. Make sure the brushes don't hang up on the rotor.

11   Install the voltage regulator screws and tighten them securely.

12   Remove the wire or paper clip.

13   Install the alternator (see Section 14).

18   Starting system - general information and precautions

Refer to illustrations 18.3a and 18.3b

1   The function of the starting system is to crank the engine to start it. The system is composed of the starter motor, starter relay, battery, switch and connecting wires.

2   Turning the ignition key to the Start position actuates the starter relay through the starter control circuit. The starter relay then connects

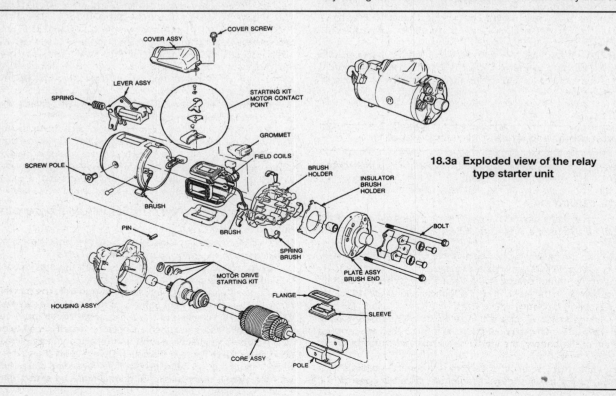

18.3a Exploded view of the relay type starter unit

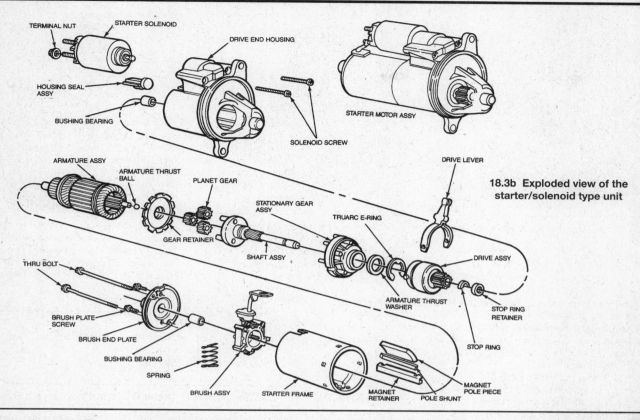

18.3b Exploded view of the starter/solenoid type unit

the battery to the starter. The battery supplies the electrical energy to the starter motor, which does the actual work of cranking the engine.

3   Early models are equipped with an external relay mounted on the fenderwell along with a starter unit to engage the starter motor with the flywheel **(see illustration)** while later models are equipped with a starter/solenoid assembly **(see illustration)** that is mounted to the transmission bellhousing.

4   All vehicles are equipped with a Neutral start switch in the starter control circuit, which prevents operation of the starter unless the shift lever is in Neutral or Park.

5   Never operate the starter motor for more than 15 seconds at a time without pausing to allow it to cool for at least two minutes. Excessive cranking can cause overheating, which can seriously damage the starter.

19   Starter motor and circuit - in-vehicle check

Note: *Before diagnosing starter problems, make sure the battery is fully charged.*

General check

1   If the starter motor doesn't turn at all when the switch is operated, make sure the shift lever is in Neutral or Park.

2   Make sure the battery is charged and that all cables at the battery and starter relay/solenoid terminals are secure.

3   If the starter motor spins but the engine doesn't turn over, then the drive assembly in the starter motor is slipping and the starter motor must be replaced (see Section 20 or 21).

4   If, when the switch is actuated, the starter motor doesn't operate at all but the starter relay/solenoid operates (clicks), then the problem lies with either the battery, the starter relay/solenoid contacts or the starter motor connections.

5   If the starter relay/solenoid doesn't click when the ignition switch is actuated, either the starter relay/solenoid circuit is open or the

relay/solenoid itself is defective. Check the starter relay/solenoid circuit (see the wiring diagrams at the end of this book) or replace the relay or solenoid (see Section 20).

6   To check the starter relay/solenoid circuit, remove the push-on connector from the relay/solenoid wire. Make sure that the connection is clean and secure and the relay bracket is grounded. If the connections are good, check the operation of the relay/solenoid with a jumper wire. To do this, place the transmission in Park. Remove the push-on connector from the relay/solenoid. Connect a jumper wire between the battery positive terminal and the exposed terminal on the relay/solenoid. If the starter motor now operates, the starter relay/solenoid is okay. The problem is in the ignition switch, Neutral start switch or in the starting circuit wiring (look for open or loose connections).

7   If the starter motor still doesn't operate, replace the starter relay/solenoid (see Section 20 and 21).

8   If the starter motor cranks the engine at an abnormally slow speed, first make sure the battery is fully charged and all terminal connections are clean and tight. Also check the connections at the starter relay/solenoid and battery ground. Eyelet terminals should not be easily rotated by hand. Also check for a short to ground. If the engine is partially seized, or has the wrong viscosity oil in it, it will crank slowly.

Starter cranking circuit test (relay type starter)

Refer to illustration 19.13

Note: *To determine the location of excessive resistance in the starter circuit, perform the following simple series of tests.*

9   Disconnect the ignition coil wire from the distributor cap and ground it on the engine.

10   Connect a remote control starter switch from the battery terminal of the starter relay/solenoid to the S terminal of the relay/solenoid.

11   Connect a voltmeter positive lead to the starter motor terminal of the starter relay/solenoid, then connect the negative lead to ground.

12   Actuate the ignition switch and take the voltmeter readings as soon as a steady figure is indicated. Do not allow the starter motor to turn for more than 15 seconds at a time. A reading of 9-volts or more, with the starter motor turning at normal cranking speed, is normal. If

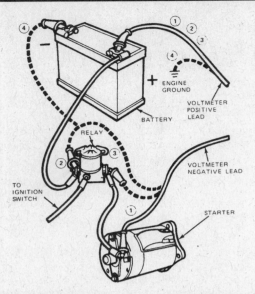

19.13 The four test lead connections for the starter cranking circuit test on a relay type starting system. This test applies to the starter/solenoid starting system also

the reading is 9-volts or more but the cranking speed is slow, the motor is faulty. If the reading is less than 9-volts and the cranking speed is slow, the relay/solenoid contacts are probably burned.

13   Make the test connections as shown **(see illustration)**. Refer to this illustration as you perform the following four tests.

14   Operate the ignition switch and take the voltmeter readings as soon as a steady figure is indicated. Don't allow the starter motor to turn for more than 15 seconds at a time.

15   The voltage drop in the circuit will be indicated by the voltmeter (put the voltmeter on the 0-to-2 volt range). The maximum allowable voltage drop should be:

a) *0.5-volt with the voltmeter negative lead connected to the starter terminal and the positive lead connected to the battery positive terminal (Connection 1 in* **illustration 19.13***).*

b) *0.1-volt with the voltmeter negative lead connected to the starter relay/solenoid (battery side) and the positive lead connected to the positive terminal of the battery (Connection 2).*

c) *0.3-volt with the voltmeter negative lead connected to the starter relay (starter side) and the positive lead connected to the positive terminal of the battery (Connection 3).* **Note:** *This particular test will not apply for starter/solenoid assemblies equipped on later models.*

d) *0.3-volt with the voltmeter negative lead connected to the negative terminal of the battery and the positive lead connected to the engine ground (Connection 4).*

20   Starter motor - removal and installation

Relay type starter

1   Detach the cable from the negative terminal of the battery.
2   Raise the vehicle and support it securely on jackstands.
3   Disconnect the large cable from the terminal on the starter motor.
4   Remove the starter motor mounting bolts and detach the starter from the engine.
5   If necessary, turn the wheels to one side to provide removal access.
6   Installation is the reverse of removal.

Solenoid/starter assembly type

Refer to illustrations 20.10a and 20.10b

7   Detach the cable from the negative terminal of the battery.
8   Raise the vehicle and support it securely on jackstands.
9   Disconnect the large cable from the terminal on the starter motor and the solenoid terminal connections.
10   Remove the starter motor mounting bolts **(see illustrations)** and detach the starter from the engine.
11   If necessary, turn the wheels to one side to provide removal access.
12   Installation is the reverse of removal.

21   Starter relay - removal and installation

Refer to illustration 21.2

1   Detach the cable from the negative terminal of the battery.
2   Label the wires and the terminals then disconnect the Neutral safety switch wire, the battery cable, the fusible link and the starter cable from the relay terminals **(see illustration)**.
3   Remove the mounting bolts and detach the relay.
4   Installation is the reverse of removal.

22   Starter solenoid - replacement

Early Continentals (1970 through 1976) are equipped with starter solenoid motor assembly units that have a removable solenoid, however, it is recommended that the starter assembly be replaced as a complete unit.

The solenoid on the 4.6L engine can only be replaced as a complete unit along with the starter assembly.

20.10a Remove the starter/solenoid assembly bolts (arrow) and separate the assembly from the transmission bellhousing. The top bolts are hidden from view (4.6L OHC engine shown)

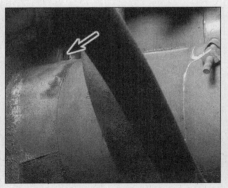

20.10b Detach the solenoid electrical connector (arrow) and bellhousing bolts (arrows) to separate the starter unit from the engine

21.2 To remove the starter relay, detach the neutral safety switch wire, the fusible link, the battery positive lead and the starter motor leads (arrows), then remove the relay mounting bracket bolts (arrows)

Chapter 6
Emissions and engine control systems

Contents

1   General information

Refer to illustrations 1.1a, 1.1b, 1.1c and 1.7

To prevent pollution of the atmosphere from incompletely burned and evaporating gases, and to maintain good driveability and fuel economy, a number of emission control systems are incorporated **(see illustrations)**. They include the:

EGR with vacuum amplifier
Automatic choke system
Thermactor (air injection) system
Coolant Temperature Actuated Vacuum System (CTAV)
Inlet air temperature control system
Feedback carburetors
Evaporative Emission Control (EVAP) system
Electronic Engine Control system (EEC-III)
Electronic Engine Control system (EEC-IV)
Electronic Engine Control system (EEC-V) (1995 models only)
Positive Crankcase Ventilation (PCV) system

Exhaust Gas Recirculation (EGR) system (electronic)
Catalytic converter

All of these systems are linked, directly or indirectly, to the emission control system.

The Sections in this Chapter include general descriptions, checking procedures within the scope of the home mechanic and component replacement procedures (when possible) for each of the systems listed above.

Before assuming that an emissions control system is malfunctioning, check the fuel and ignition systems carefully. The diagnosis of some emission control devices requires specialized tools, equipment and training. If checking and servicing become too difficult or if a procedure is beyond your ability, consult a dealer service department. Remember, the most frequent cause of emissions problems is simply a loose or broken vacuum hose or wire, so always check the hose and wiring connections first.

This doesn't mean, however, that emission control systems are particularly difficult to maintain and repair. You can quickly and easily perform many checks and do most of the regular maintenance at home

1.1a Emission and engine control system component locations (1976 Continental with a 460 cid engine)

1	*EGR valve (hidden from view)*	*4*	*Thermal vacuum switching valve*
2	*Cruise control actuator*	*5*	*Air pump*
3	*Temperature Vacuum Switch (TVS)*	*6*	*Air bypass valve*
	(Hot Air Intake system)	*7*	*Vacuum motor (Hot Air Intake system)*

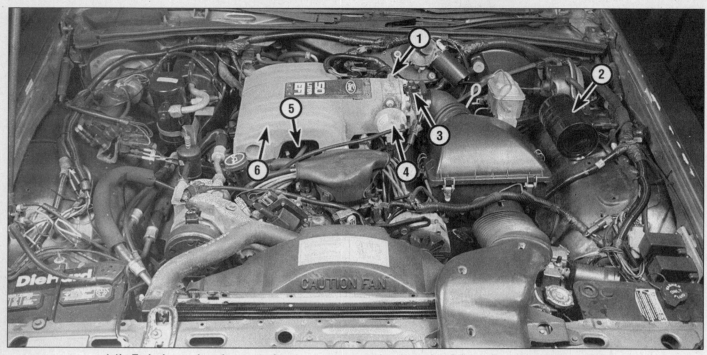

1.1b Emission and engine control system component locations (1988 Town Car with a 5.0L engine)

1	BPA-ISC valve	3	TPS	5	Coolant temperature sensor
2	Vacuum canister	4	EGR valve	6	Air intake plenum

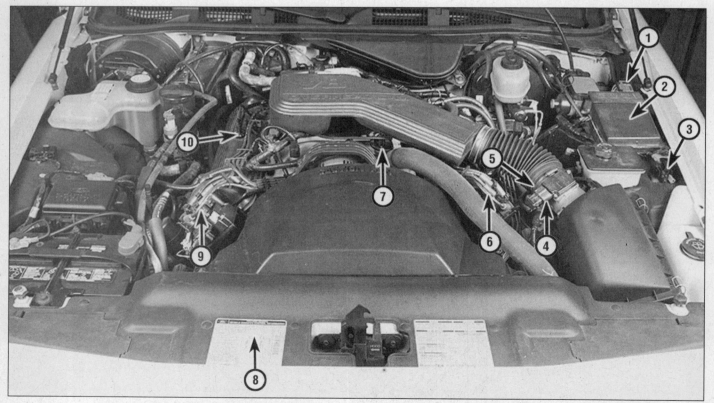

1.1c Emission and engine control system component locations (1993 4.6L engine)

1	EDIS module	5	IAT sensor	9	Coil pack
2	Relays	6	Coil pack	10	Positive Crankcase Ventilation
3	Diagnostic connector	7	Coolant temperature sensor		(PCV) valve
4	MAF sensor	8	VECI label		

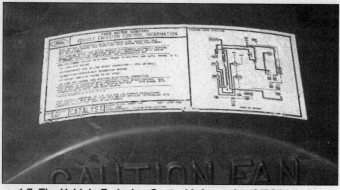

1.7 The Vehicle Emission Control Information (VECI) label is located in the engine compartment on the radiator support and contains information on the emission devices on your vehicle, vacuum line routing, etc.

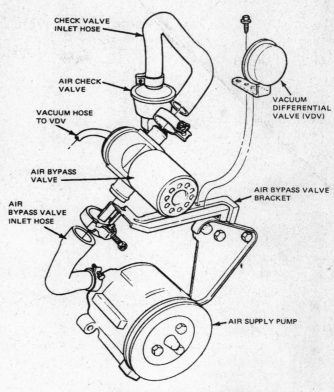

2.1a Typical thermactor system

with common tune-up and hand tools. **Note:** *Because of a federally mandated extended warranty which covers the emission control system components, check with your dealer about warranty coverage before working on any emissions-related systems. Once the warranty has expired, you may wish to perform some of the component checks and/or replacement procedures in this Chapter to save money.*

Pay close attention to any special precautions outlined in this Chapter. It should be noted that the illustrations of the various systems may not exactly match the system installed on the vehicle you're working on because of changes made by the manufacturer during production or from year-to-year.

A Vehicle Emissions Control Information (VECI) label is located in the engine compartment **(see illustration)**. This label contains important emissions specifications and adjustment information, as well as a vacuum hose schematic with emissions components identified. When servicing the engine or emissions systems, the VECI label in your particular vehicle should always be checked for up-to-date information.

2   Thermactor system

General description

Refer to illustrations 2.1a and 2.1b

1   The thermactor (air injection) exhaust emission control system

(see illustrations) reduces carbon monoxide and hydrocarbon content in the exhaust gases by injecting fresh air into the hot exhaust gases leaving the exhaust ports. When fresh air is mixed with hot exhaust gases, oxidation is increased, reducing the concentration of hydrocarbons and carbon monoxide and converting them into harmless carbon dioxide and water.

2   Many of the early models utilize either a conventional thermactor system or a "managed air" thermactor system. The two systems are basically the same. The managed air thermactor system diverts thermactor air either upstream to the exhaust manifold check valve or downstream to the rear section check valve and dual bed catalyst. An

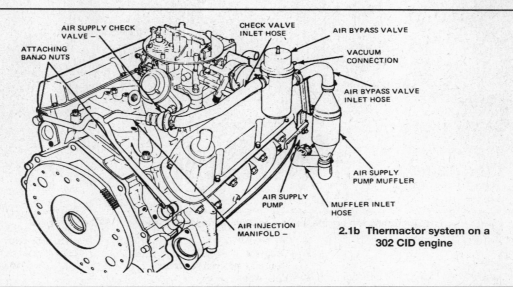

2.1b Thermactor system on a 302 CID engine

6

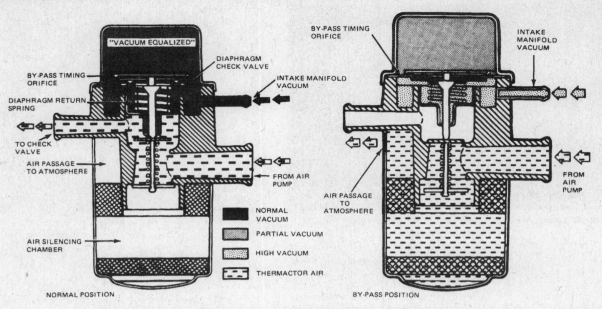

2.13 Cross-sectional view of a typical bypass valve (open and closed)

extended idle air bypass system in carbureted models also vents thermactor air to the atmosphere during extended idling.

3   On managed air systems, an air control valve directs the air upstream or downstream. An air bypass valve is used to dump air to the atmosphere. In some applications, the two valves are combined into a single air bypass/control valve.

Check

Air supply pump

4   Check and adjust the drivebelt tension (see Chapter 1).
5   Disconnect the air supply hose at the air bypass valve inlet.
6   The pump is operating satisfactorily if airflow is felt at the pump outlet with the engine running at idle, increasing as the engine speed is increased.
7   If the air pump doesn't pass the above tests, replace it with a new or rebuilt unit.

Air bypass valve

Refer to illustration 2.13
8   With the engine running at idle, disconnect the hose from the valve outlet.
9   Remove the vacuum hose from the port and remove or bypass any restrictors or delay valves in the vacuum hose.
10   Verify that vacuum is present in the vacuum hose by putting your finger over the end.
11   Reconnect the vacuum hose to the port.
12   With the engine running at 1500 rpm, the air pump supply air should be felt or heard at the air bypass valve outlet.
13   With the engine running at 1500 rpm, disconnect the vacuum hose. Air at the valve outlet **(see illustration)** should be decreased or shut off and air pump supply air should be felt or heard at the silencer ports.
14   Reconnect all hoses.
15   If the normally closed air bypass valve doesn't successfully pass the above tests, check the air pump (refer to Steps 4 through 7).
16   If the air pump is operating satisfactorily, replace the air bypass valve with a new one.

Check valve

17   Disconnect the hoses from both ends of the check valve, carefully noting the installed position of the valve and the hoses.

18   Blow through both ends of the check valve, verifying that air flows in one direction only.
19   If air flows in both directions or not at all, replace the check valve with a new one.
20   When reconnecting the valve, make sure it is installed in the proper direction.

Thermactor system noise test

21   The thermactor system is not completely noiseless. Under normal conditions, noise rises in pitch as the engine speed increases. To determine if noise is the fault of the air injection system, detach the drivebelt (after verifying that the belt tension is correct) and operate the engine. If the noise disappears, proceed with the following diagnosis.
Caution: *The pump must accumulate 500 miles (vehicle miles) before the following check is valid.*
22   If the belt noise is excessive:
a) *Check for a loose belt and tighten as necessary (refer to Chapter 1).*
b) *Check for a seized pump and replace it if necessary.*
c) *Check for a loose pulley. Tighten the mounting bolts as required.*
d) *Check for loose, broken or missing mounting brackets or bolts. Tighten or replace as necessary.*
23   If there is excessive mechanical noise:
a) *Check for an overtightened mounting bolt.*
b) *Check for an overtightened drivebelt (see Chapter 1).*
c) *Check for excessive flash on the air pump adjusting arm boss and remove as necessary.*
d) *Check for a distorted adjusting arm and, if necessary, replace the arm.*
24   If there is excessive thermactor system noise (whirring or hissing sounds):
a) *Check for a leak in the hoses (use a soap and water solution to find the leaks) and replace the hose(s) as necessary.*
b) *Check for a loose, pinched or kinked hose and reassemble, straighten or replace the hose and/or clamps as required.*
c) *Check for a hose touching other engine parts and adjust or reroute the hose to prevent further contact.*
d) *Check for an inoperative bypass valve (refer to Step 8) and replace if necessary.*
e) *Check for an inoperative check valve (refer to Step 17) and replace if necessary.*

2.26 To replace the air bypass valve, label, then detach the following

1   Air bypass valve-to-right exhaust manifold hose
2   Vacuum line to control solenoid
3   Air bypass valve-to-left exhaust manifold hose

f)   Check for loose pump or pulley mounting fasteners and tighten as necessary.
g)   Check for a restricted or bent pump outlet fitting. Inspect the fitting and remove any casting flash blocking the air passageway. Replace bent fittings.
h)   Check for air dumping through the bypass valve (only at idle). On many vehicles, the thermactor system has been designed to dump air at idle to prevent overheating the catalytic converter. This condition is normal. Determine that the noise persists at higher speeds before proceeding.
i)   Check for air dumping through the bypass valve (the decel and idle dump). On many vehicles, the thermactor air is dumped into the air cleaner or the remote silencer. Make sure that the hoses are connected properly and not cracked.

25   If there is excessive pump noise, make sure the pump has had sufficient break-in time (at least 500 miles). Check for a worn or damaged pump and replace as necessary.

Component replacement

Refer to illustrations 2.26 and 2.27

26   To replace the air bypass valve, air supply control valve, check valve, combination air bypass/air control valve **(see illustration)** or the silencer, clearly label, then disconnect, the hoses leading to them,

2.27 To remove the air pump, loosen the hose clamp (arrow) and detach the hose to the bypass valve, then remove the mounting bracket bolts

replace the faulty component and reattach the hoses to the proper ports. Make sure the hoses are in good condition. If not, replace them with new ones.
27   To replace the air supply pump, first loosen the engine drivebelt (see Chapter 1), then remove the pump mounting bolts **(see illustration)** from the mounting bracket. Label all wires and hoses as
28   If you're replacing either of the check valves on a Pulse Air System (Thermactor II), be sure to use a back-up wrench.
29   After the new pump is installed, adjust the drivebelts (see Chapter 1).

3   Cold Temperature Activated Vacuum (CTAV) system

General Information

Refer to illustration 3.2

1   The CTAV system is used to coordinate spark advance characteristics with engine requirements under cold operating conditions. The system can select from two vacuum sources for spark advance, depending upon the air temperature within the air cleaner assembly. If the ambient air temperature is below 49-degrees F, the system will select spark PORT vacuum for distributor modulation. If the temperature is above 65-degrees F, the system will select EGR vacuum. In between these temperatures, the system will select either

6

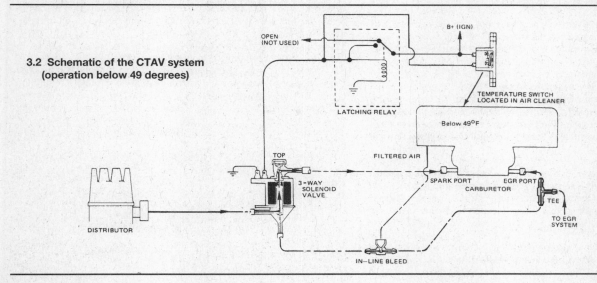

3.2 Schematic of the CTAV system (operation below 49 degrees)

4.4 A typical temperature vacuum switch (TVS) installation in the air cleaner housing assembly

4.5 A typical Cold Weather Modulator (CWM) installation in the air cleaner housing assembly

4.20 To remove the TVS, label and detach the hoses, then pry off the retaining clip with a small screwdriver

port, depending upon which cycle it is in.

2   The CTAV system consists of a ambient temperature switch, a three way vacuum switch, and an in-line vacuum bleed and a latching relay **(see illustration on previous page)**. Vacuum from the spark port and the EGR port is supplied to the three-way solenoid valve. The ambient temperature switch provides the signal that determines which of the sources will be selected. The latching relay provides only one cycle when the ignition key is turned ON.

Component checks

3   With the engine temperature below 49-degrees F, start the engine and check for vacuum to the vacuum advance unit on the distributor (see Chapter 5).

4   If no vacuum is present, check the 3-way solenoid valve for power. Using a voltmeter, test for battery voltage.

5   If no voltage is present at the solenoid valve, check for voltage at the latching relay, There should be battery voltage present.

6   If the relay does not transfer any voltage to the solenoid valve, check the temperature switch.

7   If any of the components are not operating properly, replace them with new parts.

4   Inlet air temperature control system

General description

Refer to illustrations 4.4 and 4.5

1   The inlet air temperature control system (carburetor and CFI equipped vehicles) provides heated intake air during warm-up, then maintains the inlet air temperature within a 70-degrees F to 105-degrees F operating range by mixing warm and cool air. This allows leaner fuel/air mixture settings for the carburetor or CFI system, which reduces emissions and improves driveability.

2   Two fresh air inlets - one warm and one cold - are used. The balance between the two is controlled by intake manifold vacuum, a temperature vacuum switch and a time delay valve. A vacuum motor, which operates a heat duct valve in the air cleaner, is controlled by the vacuum switch.

3   When the underhood temperature is cold, warm air radiating off the exhaust manifold is routed by a shroud which fits over the manifold up through a hot air inlet tube and into the air cleaner **(see illustration)**. This provides warm air for the carburetor or CFI, resulting in better driveability and faster warm-up. As the underhood temperature rises, a heat duct valve is gradually closed by a vacuum motor and the air cleaner draws air through a cold air duct instead. The result is a consistent intake air temperature.

4   A temperature vacuum switch **(see illustration)** mounted on the

air cleaner housing monitors the temperature of the inlet air heated by the exhaust manifold. A bimetal disc in the temperature vacuum switch orients itself in one of two positions, depending on the temperature. One position allows vacuum through a hose to the motor; the other position blocks vacuum.

5   The vacuum motor itself is regulated by a Cold Weather Modulator (CWM), mounted in the side of the air cleaner housing assembly, between the temperature vacuum switch and the motor **(see illustration)**, which provides the motor with a range of graduated positions between fully open and fully closed.

Check

Note: *Make sure the engine is cold before beginning this test.*

6   Always check the vacuum source and the integrity of all vacuum hoses between the source and the vacuum motor before beginning the following test. Do not proceed until they're okay.

7   Apply the parking brake and block the wheels.

8   Detach, but do not remove, the air cleaner housing and element (see Chapter 4).

9   Turn the air cleaner housing upside down so the vacuum motor door is visible. The door should be open. If it isn't, it may be binding or sticking. Make sure that it's not rusted in an open or closed position by attempting to move it by hand. If it's rusted, it can usually be freed by cleaning and oiling the hinge. If it fails to work properly after servicing, replace it.

10   If the vacuum motor door is okay but the motor still fails to operate correctly, check carefully for a leak in the hose leading to it. Check the vacuum source to and from the bimetal sensor and the time delay valve as well. If no leak is found, replace the vacuum motor (see Step 26).

11   Start the engine. If the duct door has moved or moves to the "heat on" (closed to fresh air) position, go to Step 15.

12   If the door stays in the "heat off" (closed to warm air) position, place a finger over the bimetal sensor bleed. The duct door must move rapidly to the "heat on" position. If the door doesn't move to the "heat on" position, stop the engine and replace the vacuum motor (see Step 26). Repeat this Step with the new vacuum motor.

13   With the engine off, allow the bimetal sensor and the cold weather modulator to cool completely.

14   Restart the engine. The duct door should move to the "heat on" position. If the door doesn't move or moves only partially, replace the TVS (see Step 18).

15   Start and run the engine briefly (less than 15 seconds). The duct door should move to the "heat on" position.

16   Shut off the engine and watch the duct door. It should stay in the "heat on" position for at least two minutes.

17   If it doesn't stay in the "heat on" position for at least two minutes, replace the CWM (see Step 23).

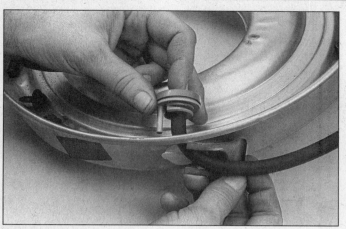

4.24 To remove the CWM, label and detach the hoses, then slide off the retaining clip and pull the CWM out of the mounting hole

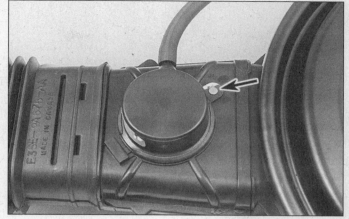

4.28 To remove the vacuum motor, label and detach the hoses, then drill out the rivet (arrow) and slide out the retaining strap

Component replacement

Refer to illustrations 4.20, 4.24 and 4.28

Temperature vacuum switch (TVS)

18   Clearly label, then detach both vacuum hoses from the TVS (one is coming from the vacuum source at the manifold and the other is going to the vacuum motor underneath the air cleaner housing).

19   Remove the air cleaner housing cover assembly (see Chapter 4A).

20   Pry the TVS retaining clip off with a screwdriver **(see illustration)**.

21   Remove the TVS.

22   Installation is the reverse of removal.

Cold Weather Modulator (CWM)

23   Locate the CWM, then detach both vacuum hoses and remove the CWM.

24   Slide the CWM retaining clip off **(see illustration)** and remove the CWM.

25   Installation is the reverse of removal.

Vacuum motor

26   Remove the air cleaner housing (see Chapter 4A) and place it on a workbench.

27   Detach the vacuum hose from the motor.

28   Drill out the vacuum motor retaining strap rivet **(see illustration)**.

29   Remove the motor.

30 · Installation is the reverse of removal. Use a sheet metal screw of the appropriate size to replace the rivet.

---

5   Electronic Engine Control (EEC-IV) system and trouble codes

---

Note 1: *This procedure does not include the diagnostic codes or the procedure on engines equipped with the Central Fuel Injection system (CFI) or the EEC III system. These codes require a special Rotunda Breakout Box for proper diagnosis.*

Note 2: *This procedure also does not include the diagnostic codes or the procedure on engines (1995 models) equipped with the EEC V system or OBD II system. These codes require a special Scan tool in order to read out the various levels of coded information.*

General description

1   Later models (1987 through 1994 with SEFI) use the Electronic Engine Control (EEC-IV) system. The EEC-IV system consists of an onboard computer, known as the Powertrain Control Module (PCM), and information sensors, which monitor various functions of the engine and send data to the PCM. Based on the data and the information programmed into the computer's memory, the PCM generates output signals to control various engine functions via control relays, solenoids and other output actuators.

2   The PCM, located under the instrument panel, is the "brain" of the EEC-IV system. It receives data from a number of sensors and other electronic components (switches, relays, etc.). Based on the information it receives, the PCM generates output signals to control various relays, solenoids and other actuators. The PCM is specifically calibrated to optimize the emissions, fuel economy and driveability of the vehicle.

3   Because of a federally mandated extended warranty which covers the EEC-IV system components and because any owner-induced damage to the PCM, the sensors and/or the control devices may void the warranty, it isn't a good idea to attempt diagnosis or replacement of the PCM at home while the vehicle is under warranty. Take the vehicle to a dealer service department if the PCM or a system component malfunctions.

Information sensors

4   When battery voltage is applied to the air conditioning compressor clutch, a signal is sent to the PCM, which interprets the signal as an added load created by the compressor and increases engine idle speed accordingly to compensate.

5   The Intake Air Temperature sensor (IAT), threaded into a runner of the intake manifold (see Section 7), provides the PCM with fuel/air mixture temperature information. The PCM uses this information to control fuel flow, ignition timing and EGR system operation.

6   The Engine Coolant Temperature (ECT) sensor, which is threaded into a coolant passage in the intake manifold, monitors engine coolant temperature. The ECT sends the PCM a constantly varying voltage signal which influences PCM control of the fuel mixture, ignition timing and EGR operation.

7   The Heated Exhaust Gas Oxygen (HEGO) sensors, which are threaded into the exhaust manifolds, constantly monitor the oxygen content of the exhaust gases. A voltage signal which varies in accordance with the difference between the oxygen content of the exhaust gases and the surrounding atmosphere is sent to the PCM. The PCM converts this exhaust gas oxygen content signal to the fuel/air ratio, compares it to the ideal ratio for current engine operating conditions and alters the signal to the injectors accordingly.

8   The Throttle Position Sensor (TPS), which is mounted on the side of the throttle body (see Section 4) and connected directly to the throttle shaft, senses throttle movement and position, then transmits an electrical signal to the PCM. This signal enables the PCM to determine when the throttle is closed, in its normal cruise condition or wide open.

9   The Mass Air Flow (MAF) sensor, which is mounted in the air cleaner intake passage, measures the mass of the air entering the engine (see Section 4). Because air mass varies with air temperature

6

(cold air is denser than warm air), measuring air mass provides the PCM with a very accurate way of determining the correct amount of fuel to obtain the ideal fuel/air mixture.

Output devices

10   The EEC power relay, which is activated by the ignition switch, supplies battery voltage to the EEC-IV system components when the switch is in the Start or Run position.

11   The canister purge solenoid (CANP) switches manifold vacuum to operate the canister purge valve when a signal is received from the PCM. Vacuum opens the purge valve when the solenoid is energized, allowing fuel vapor to flow from the canister to the intake manifold.

12   The solenoid-operated fuel injectors are located above the intake ports (see Chapter 4). The PCM controls the length of time the injector is open. The "open" time of the injector determines the amount of fuel delivered. For information regarding injector replacement, refer to Chapter 4.

13   The fuel pump relay is activated by the PCM with the ignition switch in the On position. When the ignition switch is turned to the On position, the relay is activated to supply line pressure to the system. For information regarding fuel pump check and replacement, refer to Chapter 4.

14   The EDIS ignition module (see Chapter 5) installed on all 4.6L engines, mounted on a bracket between the upper intake manifold and the valve cover, triggers the ignition coils and determines dwell. The PCM uses a signal from the Profile Ignition Pick-Up (PIP) to determine crankshaft position. Ignition timing is determined by the PCM, which then signals the module to fire the coil. For further information regarding the ignition module, refer to the appropriate Section in Chapter 5.

Obtaining codes

15   The diagnostic codes for the EEC-IV systems are arranged in such a way that a series of tests must be completed in order to extract ALL the codes from the system. If one portion of the test is performed without the others, there may be a chance the trouble code that will pinpoint a problem in your particular vehicle will remain stored in the PCM without detection. The tests start first with a Key On, Engine Off (KOEO) test followed by a computed timing test then finally a Engine Running (ER) test. Here is a brief overview of the code extracting procedures of the EEC-IV system followed by the actual test:

Quick Test - Key On Engine Off (KOEO)

16   The following tests are all included with the key on, engine off:

Self test codes - These codes are accessed on the test connector by using a jumper wire and an analog voltmeter or the factory diagnostic tool called the Star tester. These codes are also called *Hard Codes.*

Separator pulse codes - After the initial Hard Codes, the system will flash a code 11 (separator pulse) (1990 and earlier) or code 111 (1991 through 1994) and then will flash a series of Soft (or Continuous Memory) Codes.

Continuous Memory Codes - These codes indicate a fault that may or may not be present at the time of testing. These codes usually indicate an intermittent failure. Continuous Memory codes are stored in the system and they will flash after the normal Hard Codes. These codes are either two digit (1990 and earlier) or three digit codes (1991 through 1994). These codes can indicate chronic or intermittent problems. Also called *Soft Codes.*

Fast codes - These codes are transmitted 100 times faster than normal codes and can only be read by a Star Tester from Ford or an equivalent SCAN tool.

Engine running codes (KOER) or (ER)

17   **Running tests** - These tests make it possible for the PCM to pick-up a diagnostic trouble code that cannot be set while the engine is in KOEO. These problems usually occur during driving conditions. Some codes are detected by cold or warm running conditions, some are detected at low rpm or high rpm and some are detected at closed throttle or WOT.

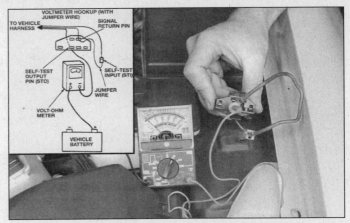

5.19 To read any stored trouble codes, connect a voltmeter to the Diagnostic Test connector as shown, then connect a jumper wire between the self test input and pin number 2 on the larger connector - turn the ignition key ON and watch the voltmeter needle (or CHECK ENGINE light on later models) (4.6L engine shown)

I.D. Pulse codes - These codes indicate the type of engine (4, 6 or 8 cylinder) or the correct module and Self Test mode access.

Computed engine timing test - This engine running test determines base timing for the engine and starts the process of allowing the engine to store running codes.

Wiggle test - This engine running test checks the wiring system to the sensors and output actuators as the engine performs

Cylinder balance test - This engine running test determines injector balance as well as cylinder compression balance. **Note:** *This test should be performed by a dealer service department.*

Beginning the test

Refer to illustration 5.19

18   Position the parking brake ON, Shift lever in PARK, block the drive wheels and turn off all electrical loads (air conditioning, radio, heater fan blower etc.). Make sure the engine is warmed to normal operating temperature (if possible).

19   Perform the KOEO tests:

a)   *Turn the ignition key off for at least 10 seconds*

b)   *Locate the Diagnostic Test connector inside the engine compartment. Install the voltmeter leads onto the battery and pin number 4 (STO) of the test connector* (see illustration). *Install a jumper wire from the test terminal to pin number 2 of the Diagnostic Test terminal (STI).*

c)   *Turn the ignition key ON (engine not running) and observe the needle sweeps on the voltmeter. For example code 23, the voltmeter will sweep once, pause 1/2 second and sweep again. There will be a two second pause between digits and then there will be three distinct sweeps of the needle to indicate the second digit of the code number. On three digit codes, the sequence is the same except there will be an additional sequence of numbers (sweeps) to indicate the third digit in the code. Additional codes will be separated by a four second pause and then the indicated sweeps on the voltmeter. Be aware that the code sequence may continue into the continuous memory codes (read further).* **Note:** *Later models will flash the CHECK ENGINE light on the dash in place of the voltmeter.*

20   Interpreting the continuous memory codes:

a)   *After the KOEO codes are reported, there will be a short pause and any stored Continuous Memory codes will appear in order. Remember that the "Separator" code is 11, or 111 on 1991 through 1994 models. The computer will not enter the Continuous Memory mode without flashing the separator pulse code. The Continuous Memory codes are read the same as the initial codes* or "Hard Codes". Record these codes onto a piece of paper and continue the test.

21   Perform the Engine Running (ER) tests.

a) Remove the jumper wires from the Diagnostic Test connector to start the test.

b) Run engine until it reaches normal operating temperature.

c) Turn the engine OFF for at least 10 seconds.

d) Connect the jumper wire to the Diagnostic Test connector **(see illustration 5.19)** and start the engine.

e) Observe that the voltmeter or CHECK ENGINE light will flash the engine identification code. This code indicates 1/2 the number of cylinders of the engine. For example, 4 flashes represent an 8 cylinder engine, or 3 flashes represent a six cylinder engine.

f) Within 1 to 2 seconds of the I.D. code, turn the steering wheel at least 1/2 turn and release. This will store any power steering pressure switch trouble codes.

g) Depress the brake pedal and release. **Note:** Perform the steering wheel and brake pedal procedure in succession immediately (1 to 2 seconds) after the I.D. codes are flashed.

h) Observe all the codes and record them on a piece of paper. Be sure to count the sweeps or flashes very carefully as you jot them down.

22   On some models the PCM will request a Dynamic Response check. This test quickly checks the operation of the TPS, MAF or MAP sensors in action. This will be indicated by a code 1 or a single sweep of the voltmeter needle (one flash on CHECK ENGINE light). This test will require the operator to simply full throttle ("goose") the accelerator pedal for one second. DO NOT throttle the accelerator pedal unless it is requested.

23   The next part of this test makes sure the system can advance the timing. This is called the Computed Timing test. After the last ER code has been displayed, the PCM will advance the ignition timing a fixed amount and hold it there for approximately 2 minutes. Use a timing light to check the amount of advance. The computed timing should equal the base timing plus 20-degrees BTDC. The total advance should equal 27 to 33-degrees advance. If the timing is out of specification, have the system checked at a dealer service department. **Note:** Remember to remove the SPOUT from the connector as described in the ignition timing procedure in Chapter 1. This will remove the computer from the loop and give base timing.

24   Finally perform the Wiggle Test. This test can be used to recreate a possible intermittent fault in the harness wiring system.

a) Use a jumper wire to ground the STI lead on the Diagnostic Test connector **(see illustration 5.19)**.

b) Turn the ignition key ON (engine not running).

c) Now deactivate the self test mode (remove the jumper wire) and then immediately reactivate the self-test mode. Now the system has entered Continuous Monitor Test Mode.

d) Carefully wiggle, tap or remove any suspect wiring to a sensor or output actuator. If a problem exists, a trouble code will be stored that indicates a problem with the circuit that governs the particular component. Record the codes that are indicated.

e) Next, enter Engine Running Continuous Monitor Test Mode to check for wiring problems only when the engine is running. Start first by deactivating the Diagnostic Test connector and turning the ignition key OFF. Now start the engine and allow it to idle.

f) Use a jumper wire to ground the STI lead on the Diagnostic Test connector **(see illustration 5.19)**. Wait ten seconds and then deactivate the test mode and reactivate it again (install jumper wire). This will enter Engine Running Continuous Monitor Test Mode.

g) Carefully wiggle, tap or remove any suspect wiring to a sensor or output actuator. If a problem exists, a trouble code will be stored that indicates a problem with the circuit that governs the particular component. Record the codes that are indicated.

25   If necessary, perform the Cylinder Balance Test. This test must be performed by a dealer service department.

Clearing codes

To clear the codes from the PCM memory, start the KOEO self test diagnostic procedure **(see illustration 5.19)** and install the jumper wire into the Diagnostic Test connector. When the codes start to display themselves on the voltmeter or CHECK ENGINE light, remove the jumper wire from the Diagnostic Test connector. This will erase any stored codes within the system. **Caution:** Do not disconnect the battery from the vehicle to clear the codes. This will erase stored operating parameters from the KAM (Keep Alive Memory) and cause the engine to run rough for a period of time while the computer relearns the information.

2 Digit Trouble Codes

Code	Test Condition*	Probable Cause
11	O,C,R	Pass (separator code)
12	R	RPM not within Self-test upper limit
13	R	RPM not within Self-test lower limit
14	C	Profile Ignition Pick-up circuit fault
15	O	Read Only Memory test failed
15	C	Keep Alive Memory test failed
16	R	RPM too low to perform Oxygen Sensor/fuel test
18	C	Loss of TACH input to PCM; SPOUT circuit grounded
18	R	SPOUT circuit open
19	O	Failure in EEC reference voltage
21	O,R	Coolant Temperature Sensor out of range
22	O,C	Manifold Absolute/Baro Pressure Sensor out of range
23	O,R	Throttle Position Sensor out of range
24	O,R	Intake Air Temperature sensor out of range
26	O,R	Mass Air Flow Sensor out of range
29	C	No input from Vehicle Speed Sensor
31	O,C,R	EGR Valve Position Sensor out of range (low)
32	O,C,R	EGR valve not seated; closed voltage low
33	C,R	EGR valve not opening; Insufficient flow detected

* O = Key On, Engine Off; C = Continuous Memory; R = Engine Running

2 Digit Trouble Codes (continued)

Code	Test Condition*	Probable Cause
34	O,C,R	EGR Valve Pressure Transducer/Position Sensor sonic voltage above closed limit
35	O,C,R	EGR Valve Pressure Transducer/Position Sensor voltage out of range (high)
41	R	Heated Oxygen Sensor circuit indicates system lean, right side
41	C	No Heated Oxygen Sensor switch detected, right side
42	R	Heated Oxygen Sensor circuit indicates system rich, right side
44	R	Thermactor Air system inoperative, right side
45	R	Thermactor Air upstream during Self-test (5.0L only)
46	R	Thermactor Air not by-passed during Self-test (5.0L only)
51	O,C	Coolant Temperature sensor circuit open
53	O,C	Throttle Position sensor out of range (high)
54	O,C	Intake Air Temperature sensor circuit open
56	O,C	Mass Air Flow sensor out of range (high)
61	O,C	Coolant Temperature sensor circuit grounded
63	O,C	Throttle Position sensor circuit out of range (low)
64	O,C	Intake Air Temperature sensor circuit grounded
66	C	Mass Air Flow sensor circuit out-of-range (low)
67	O	Neutral Drive Switch circuit open
72	R	Insufficient Mass Air Flow change during Dynamic Response Test
73	R	Insufficient Throttle Position output during Dynamic Response Test
74	R	Brake On/Off switch failure
75	R	Brake On/Off circuit failure
77	R	Wide Open Throttle not sensed during Self-test
79	O	Air conditioning on during self-test
81	O	Air Management 2 circuit failure (5.0L only)
82	O	Air Management 1 circuit failure (5.0L only)
84	O	EGR Vacuum Regulator circuit failure
85	O	Canister Purge circuit failure
87	O,C	Primary Fuel Pump circuit failure
91	R	Heated oxygen sensor indicates system lean, left side
91	C	No heated oxygen sensor switching indicated, left side
92	R	Heated oxygen sensor indicates system rich, left side
94	R	Thermactor Air system inoperative, left side (5.0L only)
95	O,C	Fuel Pump circuit open, PCM to motor
96	O,C	Fuel Pump circuit open, Battery to PCM
98	R	Hard Fault present

3 Digit Trouble Codes

Code	Test Condition*	Probable Cause
111	O,C,R	Pass
112	O,R	Intake Air Temperature sensor circuit indicates circuit grounded/above 245 degrees F
113	O,R	Intake Air Temperature sensor circuit indicates open circuit/below -40 degrees F
114	O,R	Intake Air Temperature sensor out of self-test range
116	O,R	Coolant Temperature sensor out of self-test range
117	O,C	Coolant Temperature circuit below minimum voltage/indicates above 245 degrees F
118	O,C	Coolant Temperature sensor circuit above maximum voltage/ indicates below -40 degrees F
121	O,C,R	Throttle Position sensor out of self-test range
122	O,C	Throttle Position sensor below minimum voltage
123	O,C	Throttle Position sensor above maximum voltage
124	C	Throttle Position Sensor voltage higher than expected
125	C	Throttle Position Sensor voltage lower than expected
126	O,C,R	MAP/BARO sensor higher than expected
128	C	MAP sensor vacuum hose damaged or disconnected
129	R	Insufficient Manifold Absolute Pressure/Mass Air Flow change during Dynamic Response Check

* O = Key On, Engine Off; C = Continuous Memory; R = Engine Running

3 Digit Trouble Codes (continued)

Code	Test Condition*	Probable Cause
136	R	Heated oxygen sensor indicates lean condition, left side
137	R	Heated oxygen sensor indicates rich condition, left side
139	C	No heated oxygen sensor switching detected, left side
144	C	No heated oxygen sensor switching detected, right side
157	R,C	Mass Air Flow Sensor below minimum voltage
158	O,R,C	Mass Air Flow Sensor above maximum voltage
159	O,R	Mass Air Flow Sensor out of self-test range
167	R	Insufficient Throttle Position Sensor change during Dynamic Response Check
171	C	Heated oxygen sensor unable to switch, right side
172	R,C	Heated oxygen sensor indicates lean condition, right side
173	R,C	Heated oxygen sensor indicates rich condition, right side
174	C	Heated oxygen sensor switching slow, right side
175	C	Heated oxygen sensor unable to switch, left side
176	C	Heated oxygen sensor indicates lean condition, left side
177	C	Heated oxygen sensor indicates rich condition, left side
178	C	Heated oxygen sensor switching slow, left side
179	C	Adaptive Fuel lean limit reached at part throttle, system rich, right side
181	C	Adaptive Fuel rich limit reached at part throttle, right side
182	C	Adaptive Fuel lean limit reached at idle, right side
183	C	Adaptive Fuel rich limit reached at idle, right side
184	C	Mass Air Flow higher than expected
185	C	Mass Air Flow lower than expected
186	C	Injector Pulse-width higher than expected
187	C	Injector Pulse-width lower than expected
188	C	Adaptive Fuel lean limit reached, left side
189	C	Adaptive Fuel rich limit reached, left side
191	C	Adaptive Fuel lean limit reached at idle, left side
192	C	Adaptive Fuel rich limit reached at idle, left side
193	O	Flexible Fuel (FF) sensor circuit failure
211	C	Profile Ignition Pick-up circuit fault
212	C	Ignition module circuit failure/SPOUT circuit grounded
213	R	SPOUT circuit open
214	C	Cylinder identification (CID) circuit failure
215	C	PCM detected coil 1 primary circuit failure
216	C	PCM detected coil 2 primary circuit failure
217	C	PCM detected coil 3 primary circuit failure
218	C	Loss of ignition diagnostic monitor (IDM) signal - left side (dual plug EI)
219	C	Spark timing defaulted to 10 degrees SPOUT circuit open (EI)
221	C	Spark timing error
222	C	Loss of ignition diagnostic monitor (IDM) signal - right side (dual plug)
223	C	Loss of dual plug Inhibit (DPI) control (dual plug)
224	C	PCM detected coil 1,2,3 or 4 primary circuit failure (dual plug EI)
225	C	Knock sensor not detected during dynamic response test KOER
226	O	Ignition Diagnostic Module (IDM) signal not received (EI)
232	C	PCM detected coil 1,2,3 or 4 primary circuit failure (EI)
238	C	PCM detected coil 4 primary circuit failure (EI)
241	C	ICM to PCM - IDM pulse width transmission error (EI)
244	R	CID circuit fault present when cylinder balance test requested
311	R	Thermactor Air System inoperative, right side
313	R	Thermactor Air not by-passed
314	R	Thermactor Air inoperative, left side
326	C,R	EGR circuit voltage lower than expected
327	O,C,R	EGR Valve Pressure Transducer/Position Sensor circuit below minimum voltage
328	O,C,R	EGR valve position sensor voltage below closed limit
332	C,R	EGR valve opening not detected

* O = Key On, Engine Off; C = Continuous Memory; R = Engine Running

3 Digit Trouble Codes (continued)

Code	Test Condition*	Probable Cause
334	O,C,R	EGR valve position sensor voltage above closed limit
335	O	EGR Sensor voltage out-of-range
336	R	EGR circuit higher than expected
337	O,C,R	EGR Valve Pressure Transducer/Position Sensor circuit above maximum voltage
341	O	Octane adjust service pin open
381	C	Frequent AIR CONDITIONING clutch cycling
411	R	Unable to control RPM during Low RPM Self-test
412	R	Unable to control RPM during High PRM Self-test
415	R	Idle Air Control (IAC) system at maximum adaptive lower limit
416	C	Idle Air Control (IAC) system at upper adaptive learning limit
452	C	No input from Vehicle Speed Sensor
453	R	Servo leaking down (KOER IVSC test)
454	R	Servo leaking up (KOER IVSC test)
455	R	Insufficient rpm increase (KOER IVSC test)
456	R	Insufficient rpm decrease (KOER IVSC test)
457	O	Speed control command switch(s) circuit not functioning (KOEO IVSC test)
458	O	Speed control command switch(s) stuck/circuit grounded (KOEO IVSC test)
459	O	Speed control ground circuit open (KOEO IVSC test)
511	O	Read Only Memory test failed - replace PCM
512	C	Keep Alive Memory test failed
513	O	Internal voltage failure in PCM
519	O	Power steering pressure switch (PSP) circuit open
521	R	Power steering pressure switch (PSP) circuit did not change states
522	O	Manual Lever Position (MLP) sensor circuit open/vehicle in gear
525	O	Indicates vehicle in gear, AIR CONDITIONING on
527	O	Manual Lever Position (MLP) sensor circuit open, AIR CONDITIONING on during KOEO
529	C	Data Communication link (DCL) or PCM circuit failure
532	C	Cluster Control Assembly (CCA) circuit failure
533	C	Data Communications Link (DCL) or Electronic Instrument Cluster (EIC) circuit failure
536	C,R	Brake ON/Off (BOO) circuit failure/not activated during the KOER
538	R	Insufficient change in RPM/operator error in Dynamic Response Check
539	O	Air conditioning on during Self-test
542	O,C	Fuel Pump circuit open; PCM to motor
543	O,C	Fuel Pump circuit open; Battery to PCM
551	O	Idle Air Control (IAC) circuit failure KOEO
552	O	Air Management 1 circuit failure
552	O	Secondary Air Injection Bypass (AIRB) circuit failure
553	O	Secondary Air Injection Diverter (AIRB) circuit failure
554	O	Fuel Pressure Regulator Control (FPRC) circuit failure
556	O,C	Primary Fuel Pump circuit failure
557	O,C	Low speed fuel pump primary circuit failure
558	O	EGR Vacuum Regulator circuit failure
559	O	Air Conditioning On (ACON) relay circuit failure
563	O	High fan control (HFC) circuit failure
564	O	Fan control (FC) circuit failure
565	O	Canister Purge circuit failure
567	O	Speed Control Vent (SCVNT) circuit failure (KOEO IVSC test)
568	O	Speed Control Vacuum (SCVAC) circuit failure (KOEO IVSC test)
569	O	Auxiliary Canister Purge (CANP2) circuit failure KOEO
571	O	EGRA solenoid circuit failure KOEO
572	O	EGRV solenoid circuit failure KOEO
578	C	A / C pressure sensor circuit shorted
579	C	Insufficient AIR CONDITIONING pressure change
581	C	Power to Fan circuit over current

* *O = Key On, Engine Off; C = Continuous Memory; R = Engine Running*

3 Digit Trouble Codes (continued)

Code	Test Condition*	Probable Cause
582	O	Fan circuit open
583	C	Power to Fuel pump over current
584	C	VCRM Power ground circuit open (VCRM Pin 1)
585	C	Power to A / C clutch over current
586	C	A / C clutch circuit open
587	O,C	Variable Control Relay Module (VCRM) communication failure
617	C	1-2 shift error
618	C	2-3 shift error
619	C	3-4 shift error
621	O,C	Shift Solenoid 1 (SS 1) circuit failure KOEO
622	O	Shift Solenoid 2 (SS2) circuit failure KOEO
623	O	Transmission Control Indicator Light (TCIL) circuit failure
624	O,C	Electronic Pressure Control (EPC) circuit failure
625	O,C	Electronic Pressure Control (EPC) driver open in PCM
626	O	Coast Clutch Solenoid (CCS) circuit failure KOEO
627	O	Torque Converter Clutch (TCC) solenoid circuit failure
628	C	Excessive converter clutch slippage
629	O,C	Torque Converter Clutch (TCC) solenoid circuit failure
631	O	Transmission Control Indicator Lamp (TCIL) circuit failure KOEO
632	R	Transmission Control Switch (TCS) circuit did not change states during KOER
634	O,C,R	Manual Lever Position (MLP) sensor voltage higher or lower than expected
636	O,R	Transmission Fluid Temp (TFT) higher or lower than expected
637	O,C	Transmission Fluid Temp (TFT) sensor circuit above maximum voltage/circuit open
638	O,C	Transmission Fluid Temp (TFT) sensor circuit below minimum voltage/circuit shorted
639	R,C	Insufficient input from Transmission Speed Sensor (TSS)
641	O,C	Shift Solenoid 3 (SS3) circuit failure
643	O,C	Torque Converter Clutch (TCC) circuit failure
645	C	Incorrect gear ratio obtained for first gear
646	C	Incorrect gear ratio obtained for second gear
647	C	Incorrect gear ratio obtained for third gear
648	C	Incorrect gear ratio obtained for fourth gear
649	C	Electronic Pressure Control (EPC) higher or lower than expected
651	C	Electronic Pressure Control (EPC)circuit failure
652	O	Torque Converter Clutch (TCC) solenoid circuit failure
653	R	Transmission Control Switch (TCS) did not change states during KOER
654	O	Transmission Range (TR) sensor not indicating PARK during KOEO
656	C	Torque Converter Clutch continuous slip error
657	C	Transmission over temperature condition occurred
659	C	High vehicle speed in park indicated
667	C	Transmission Range sensor circuit voltage below minimum voltage
668	C	Transmission Range circuit voltage above maximum voltage
675	C	Transmission Range sensor circuit voltage out of range
998	O	Hard fault present

* *O = Key On, Engine Off; C = Continuous Memory; R = Engine Running*

6   Powertrain Control Module (PCM)

Refer to illustrations 6.3, 6.4 and 6.5

Note: *The PCM (computer) is located in various places depending upon the year and model. On feedback carbureted models equipped with the 7200 VV carburetor, the computer is located in the engine compartment (see Chapter 4A). On CFI and SEFI, the computer is located inside the engine compartment under the dash.*

1   The Powertrain Control Module (PCM) on later models is located inside the passenger compartment under the driver's side dashboard, tucked into the corner. The retaining bracket and bolts must be removed from the engine compartment and the module must be removed inside the driver's compartment. The PCM is easily distinguishable by the aluminum casing surrounding the module.

2   Disconnect the negative battery cable from the battery. **Warning:** *Some models have airbags. Always disconnect the negative battery cable, then the positive cable and wait two minutes before working in the vicinity of the impact sensors, steering column or instrument panel to avoid the possibility of accidental deployment of the airbag, which could cause personal injury (see Chapter 12).*

3   Working in the engine compartment, remove the bolt that retains

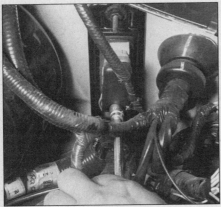

6.3 Working in the engine compartment, remove the bolt that retains the electrical connector to the PCM (4.6L engine shown)

6.4 Remove the nuts (arrows) from the PCM brackets

6.5 Remove the PCM from under the dash area on the driver's side

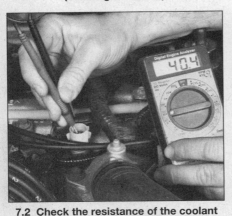

7.2 Check the resistance of the coolant temperature sensor with the engine completely cold and then with the engine at operating temperature. Resistance should decrease as temperature increases (4.6L engine shown)

7.3 Working on the harness side, check the voltage from the PCM to the coolant temperature sensor with the ignition key ON and the engine not running. It should be approximately 5.0 volts

7.4 To prevent leakage, wrap the threads of the coolant temperature sensor with Teflon tape before installing it

the electrical connector to the PCM (see illustration). Caution: The ignition switch must be turned OFF when pulling out or plugging in the electrical connectors to prevent damage to the PCM.

4   Remove the retaining nuts (see illustration) from the PCM studs.

5   Working inside the driver's compartment, carefully slide the PCM out far enough to clear the kick panel (see illustration). Note: Avoid any static electricity damage to the computer by using gloves and a special anti-static pad to store the PCM on once it is removed.

7   Information sensors

Engine coolant temperature sensor

Refer to illustrations 7.2, 7.3 and 7.4

General description

1   The coolant sensor is a thermistor (a resistor which varies the value of its voltage output in accordance with temperature changes). The change in the resistance values will directly affect the voltage signal from the coolant sensor. As the sensor temperature DECREASES, the resistance values will INCREASE. As the sensor temperature INCREASES, the resistance values will DECREASE. A failure in the coolant sensor circuit should set a Code 21, 51 or 61 for the two-digit code system or 116, 117 or 118 for the three digit code system. These codes indicate a failure in the coolant temperature

circuit, so in most cases the appropriate solution to the problem will be either repair of a wire or replacement of the sensor.

Check

2   Check the resistance value of the coolant temperature sensor while it is completely cold (50 to 65-degrees F = 58,750 to 40,500 ohms). Next, start the engine and warm it up until it reaches operating temperature (see illustration). The resistance should be lower (180 to 220-degrees F = 3,600 to 1,840 ohms). Note: Access to the coolant temperature sensor makes it difficult to position electrical probes on the terminals. If necessary, remove the sensor and perform the tests in a pan of heated water to simulate the conditions.

3   If the resistance values on the sensor are correct, check the signal voltage to the sensor from the PCM (see illustration). It should be approximately 5.0 volts.

Replacement

Warning: Wait until the engine is completely cool before beginning this procedure.

4   Before installing the new sensor, wrap the threads with Teflon sealing tape to prevent leakage and thread corrosion (see illustration).

5   To remove the sensor, unplug the electrical connector, unscrew the sensor and install the new one as quickly as possible to minimize coolant loss. Caution: Handle the coolant sensor with care. Damage to this sensor will affect the operation of the entire fuel injection system. Check the coolant level and add some, if necessary (see Chapter 1).

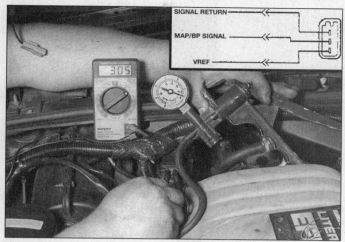

7.9 Using a tachometer set on the 6-cylinder scale, probe the backside of the MAP electrical sensor MAP/BP SIGNAL wire and SIGNAL RETURN (ground wire) and check for a frequency voltage. It should be between 300 and 320 "rpm" with no vacuum, depending on the altitude. Now apply a vacuum of 20 in-Hg. and confirm that the reading decreases to 200 to 230 "rpm". There should be a smooth transition between the readings

Manifold Absolute Pressure (MAP) sensor

Refer to illustration 7.9

General description

6   The Manifold Absolute Pressure (MAP) sensor monitors the intake manifold pressure changes resulting from changes in engine load and speed and converts the information into a voltage output. The PCM uses the MAP sensor to control fuel delivery and ignition timing. The PCM will receive information as a frequency generated voltage signal. This signal can be detected using a tachometer. The frequency will vary from 310 "rpm" at closed throttle (high vacuum) to 200 "rpm" at wide open throttle (low vacuum).

7   A failure in the MAP sensor circuit should set a Code 22 or 72 for the two digit code system or 126, 128 or 129 for the three digit code system.

Check

8   Disconnect the electrical connector from the MAP sensor. Using a voltmeter, check for reference voltage to the MAP sensor on the VREF wire **(see illustration 7.9)**. With the ignition key ON (engine not running), the reference voltage should be approximately 4.0 to 6.0 volts.

9   Connect the electrical connector to the MAP sensor and backprobe the harness with a tachometer set on the six-cylinder scale. With the ignition key ON (engine not running) check the signal from the MAP/BP Signal wire (middle terminal) to the signal return wire (ground) **(see illustration)**. Install a tachometer to the signal wire and set the meter to the six-cylinder scale.

10   Use a hand-held vacuum pump and apply 10 in-Hg of vacuum to the MAP sensor and observe the tachometer readings. Without vacuum, the tachometer should read approximately 310 "rpm". With 20 in-Hg of vacuum applied, the tachometer should read about 200 "rpm". Look for a smooth transition between these two readings.

11   If the test results are incorrect, replace the MAP sensor.

Oxygen sensor

Refer to illustrations 7.14 and 7.16

General description and check

12   The oxygen sensors (heated exhaust gas oxygen [HEGO] sensors on later models), which are located in the exhaust manifolds, monitor the oxygen content of the exhaust gas stream. The oxygen content in

7.14 The oxygen sensor creates a very small voltage signal when the sensor is warmed up. A quick oxygen sensor check is to immediately disconnect the sensor connector when it is warmed up and probe the signal wire (sensor side of connector) and check for a millivolt reading (4.6L engine shown).

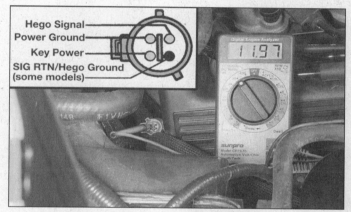

7.16 Working on the harness side, probe the electrical connector and check for reference voltage. It should be approximately 5.0 volts with the ignition key on and the engine not running

the exhaust reacts with the oxygen sensor to produce a voltage output which varies from 0.1-volt (high oxygen, lean mixture) to 0.9-volts (low oxygen, rich mixture). The PCM constantly monitors this variable voltage output to determine the ratio of oxygen to fuel in the mixture. The PCM alters the air/fuel mixture ratio by controlling the pulse width (open time) of the fuel injectors. A mixture ratio of 14.7 parts air to 1 part fuel is the ideal mixture ratio for minimizing exhaust emissions, thus allowing the catalytic converter to operate at maximum efficiency. It is this ratio of 14.7 to 1 which the PCM and the oxygen sensor attempt to maintain at all times.

13   The oxygen sensor produces no voltage when it is below its normal operating temperature of about 600-degrees F. During this initial period before warm-up, the PCM operates in open loop mode.

14   Allow the engine to reach normal operating temperature and check that the oxygen sensor is producing a steady signal voltage between 0.35 and 0.55-volts **(see illustration)**.

15   A delay of two minutes or more between engine start-up and normal operation of the sensor, followed by a low or a high voltage signal or a short in the sensor circuit, will cause the PCM to also set a code. Codes that indicate problems in the oxygen sensor system are 41, 42, 91 and 92 for the two digit code system and 136, 137, 139, 144 and 171 through 178 for the three digit code system.

16   Also check to make sure the oxygen sensor heater(s) is supplied with battery voltage **(see illustration)**.

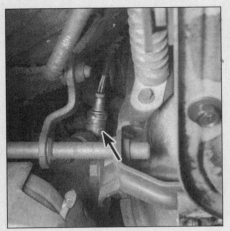

7.22 Typical oxygen sensor location (1988 Town Car with the 5.0L engine)

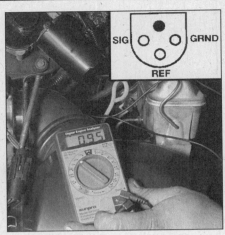

7.30a TPS voltage (SIG) with the throttle closed and the ignition key ON (engine not running) (5.0L engine with SEFI)

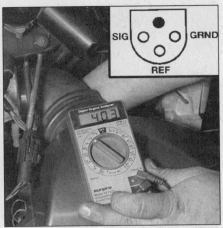

7.30b TPS voltage (SIG) with the throttle wide open (WOT). Watch for a smooth change from the closed position

17   When any of the above codes occur, the PCM operates in the open loop mode - that is, it controls fuel delivery in accordance with a programmed default value instead of feedback information from the oxygen sensor.

18   The proper operation of the oxygen sensor depends on four conditions:

a) *Electrical - The low voltages generated by the sensor depend upon good, clean connections which should be checked whenever a malfunction of the sensor is suspected or indicated.*

b) *Outside air supply - The sensor is designed to allow air circulation to the internal portion of the sensor. Whenever the sensor is removed and installed or replaced, make sure the air passages are not restricted.*

c) *Proper operating temperature - The PCM will not react to the sensor signal until the sensor reaches approximately 600-degrees F. This factor must be taken into consideration when evaluating the performance of the sensor.*

d) *Unleaded fuel - The use of unleaded fuel is essential for proper operation of the sensor. Make sure the fuel you are using is of this type.*

19   In addition to observing the above conditions, special care must be taken whenever the sensor is serviced.

a) *The oxygen sensor has a permanently attached pigtail and electrical connector which should not be removed from the sensor. Damage or removal of the pigtail or electrical connector can adversely affect operation of the sensor.*

b) *Grease, dirt and other contaminants should be kept away from the electrical connector and the louvered end of the sensor.*

c) *Do not use cleaning solvents of any kind on the oxygen sensor.*

d) *Do not drop or roughly handle the sensor.*

e) *The silicone boot must be installed in the correct position to prevent the boot from being melted and to allow the sensor to operate properly.*

Replacement

Refer to illustration 7.22

Note: *Because it is installed in the exhaust manifold or pipe, which contracts when cool, the oxygen sensor may be very difficult to loosen when the engine is cold. Rather than risk damage to the sensor (assuming you are planning to re-use it in another manifold or pipe), start and run the engine for a minute or two, then shut it off. Be careful not to burn yourself during the following procedure.*

20   Disconnect the cable from the negative terminal of the battery.

21   Raise the vehicle and place it securely on jackstands.

22   Carefully disconnect the electrical connector from the sensor **(see**

illustration).

23   Carefully unscrew the sensor from the exhaust manifold. **Caution:** *Excessive force may damage the threads.*

24   Anti-seize compound must be used on the threads of the sensor to facilitate future removal. The threads of new sensors will already be coated with this compound, but if an old sensor is removed and reinstalled, recoat the threads.

25   Install the sensor and tighten it securely.

26   Reconnect the electrical connector of the pigtail lead to the main engine wiring harness.

27   Lower the vehicle and reconnect the cable to the negative terminal of the battery.

Throttle Position Sensor (TPS)

General description

Refer to illustrations 7.30a, 7.30b, 7.31, 7.32 and 7.33

28   The Throttle Position Sensor (TPS) is located on the end of the throttle shaft on the throttle body. By monitoring the output voltage from the TPS, the PCM can determine fuel delivery based on throttle valve angle (driver demand). A broken or loose TPS can cause intermittent bursts of fuel from the injector and an unstable idle because the PCM thinks the throttle is moving. Any problems in the TPS or circuit will set a code 23 or 53 for the two digit code system or 121 through 125 for the three digit code system.

Check

29   To check the TPS, turn the ignition switch to ON (engine not running) and install the probes of the voltmeter into the ground wire and signal wire on the backside of the electrical connector. This test checks for the proper signal voltage from the TPS. **Note:** *Be careful when backprobing the electrical connector. Do not damage the wiring harness or pull on any connectors to make clean contact. Be sure the probes are placed in the correct position by referring to illustration 7.32.*

30   The sensor should read 0.50 to 1.0-volt at idle **(see illustration)**. Have an assistant depress the accelerator pedal to simulate full throttle and the sensor should increase voltage to 4.0 to 5.0-volts **(see illustration)**. If the TPS voltage readings are incorrect, replace it with a new unit.

31   Also, check the TPS reference voltage. With the ignition key ON (engine not running), install the positive (+) probe of the voltmeter **(see illustration)** onto the voltage reference wire. There should be approximately 5.0 volts sent from the PCM to the TPS.

32   Also, check the resistance of the potentiometer within the TPS. Disconnect the TPS electrical connector and working on the sensor side, connect the probes of the ohmmeter onto the ground wire and

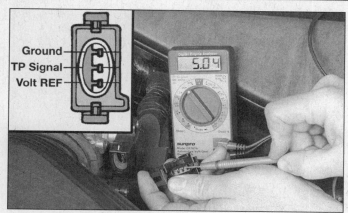

7.31 Check the reference voltage to the TPS with a voltmeter. Backprobe terminal VOLT REF with the positive (+) probe of the voltmeter and make sure the reference voltage is approximately 5.0 volts (4.6L engine)

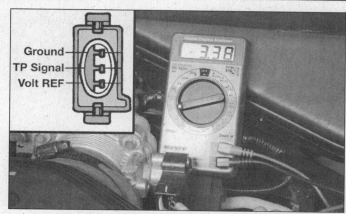

7.32 Use sharp-tipped electrical probes on TPS terminals GROUND and TP SIGNAL and, with the throttle completely closed, check the resistance of the sensor. It should be 3.0 to 4.0K ohms

7.33 The resistance should DECREASE to approximately 350 ohms with the throttle completely open

7.34 Remove the two screws (arrows) from the TPS and separate it from the throttle body

7.37 Probe the VPWR terminal on the harness side of the MAF sensor and check for battery voltage to the MAF sensor

the TPS signal wire. With the throttle valve fully closed, the TPS should read between 3.0 and 4.0K ohms (see illustration).

33 Now open the throttle with one hand (see illustration) and check the resistance again. Slowly advance the throttle until fully open. The resistance should be approximately 350 ohms. The potentiometer should exhibit a smooth change in resistance as it travels from fully closed to wide open throttle. Any deviations indicate a possible worn or damaged TPS.

Replacement

Refer to illustration 7.34

34 The TPS is a non-adjustable unit. Remove the two retaining screws (see illustration) and separate the TPS from the throttle body.
35 Installation is the reverse of removal.

Mass Air Flow (MAF) sensor (4.6L engines)

General Information

Refer to illustrations 7.37, 7.38a, 7.38b and 7.44

36 The Mass Air Flow (MAF) sensor is located on the air intake duct. This sensor uses a hot wire sensing element to measure the amount of air entering the engine. The air passing over the hot wire causes it to cool. Consequently, this change in temperature can be converted into an analog voltage signal to the PCM which in turn calculates the required fuel injector pulse width.

Check

37 Check for power to the MAF sensor. Disconnect the MAF sensor electrical connector, work on the harness side and probe the

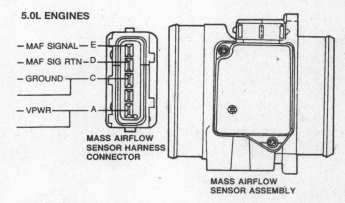

7.38a Use a voltmeter and probe MAF SIGNAL and MA1F SIG RTN for signal voltage (0.2 to 1.5 volts at idle) (5.0L engine shown)

connector to check for battery voltage (see illustration). Use the VPWR terminal indicated in illustrations 4.38a and 4.38b.
38 Reconnect the electrical connector and backprobe the MAF SIGNAL and MAF SIG RTN (see illustrations) with the voltmeter and check for the voltage. The voltage should be 0.2 to 1.5 volts at idle.
39 Raise the engine rpm. The signal voltage from the MAF sensor should increase to about 2.0 volts at 60 mph. It is impossible to simulate these conditions in the driveway at home but it is necessary

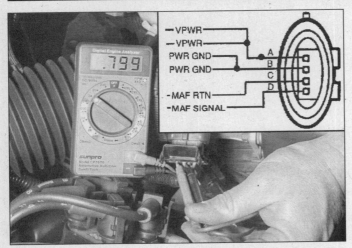

7.38b Use a voltmeter and probe MAF SIGNAL and MAF SIG RTN for signal voltage (0.2 to 1.5 volts at idle) (4.6L engine shown)

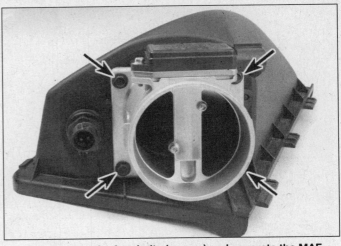

7.44 Remove the four bolts (arrows) and separate the MAF sensor from the air cleaner housing

to observe the voltmeter for a fluctuation in voltage as the engine speed is raised. The vehicle will not be under load conditions but it should manage to vary slightly.
40   Disconnect the MAF harness connector and use an ohmmeter and probe the terminals MAF SIGNAL and MAF SIG RTN. If the hot wire element inside the sensor has been damaged it will be indicated by an open circuit (infinite resistance).
41   If the voltage readings are correct, check the wiring harness for open circuits or a damaged harness (see Chapter 12).

Replacement

42   Disconnect the electrical connector from the MAF sensor.
43   Remove the upper section of the air cleaner assembly (see Chapter 4).
44   Remove the four bolts (see illustration) and lift the MAF sensor from the engine compartment.
45   Installation is the reverse of removal.

Manual Lever Position (MLP) sensor

Note: *The manual lever position (MLP) sensor has been renamed to the Transmission Range (TR) sensor on 1995 and later models. The TR sensor operates exactly the same as the MLP sensor - only the name has been changed.*

General description

Refer to illustrations 7.48a and 7.48b

46   The Manual Lever Position (MLP) sensor located on the transmission indicates to the PCM when the transmission is in Park, Neutral, Drive or Reverse. This information is used for starting, Transmission Converter Clutch (TCC), Exhaust Gas Recirculation (EGR) and Idle Speed Control (ISC) valve operation. For example, if the signal wire(s) become grounded, it may be difficult to start the engine in Park or Neutral. A problem with the Manual Lever Position (MLP) sensor will flash a code 67 (two digit code) or 522 (three digit code).
47   In the event there is a problem with the Manual Lever Position (MLP) sensor, first check the terminal connectors for proper attachment.
48   Use a voltmeter and with the ignition key ON (engine not running), check for power to each of the signal wires (see illustrations) of the

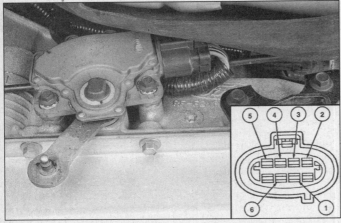

7.48a Manual Lever Position (MLP) sensor terminal designations (4.6L engine)

1 *PCM signal return*	4 *Accessory feed*
2 *Start*	5 *Start*
3 *Back-up lamps*	6 *Sensor signal to PCM*

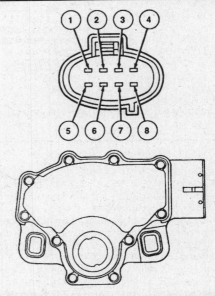

7.48b Transmission range sensor (1995 on models only)

1 *Starter control*	5 *(not used)*
2 *Accessory feed*	6 *Sensor signal-to-PCM*
3 *Back-up lamps*	7 *PCM signal return*
4 *Starter control-to-*	8 *(not used)*
interlock circuit	

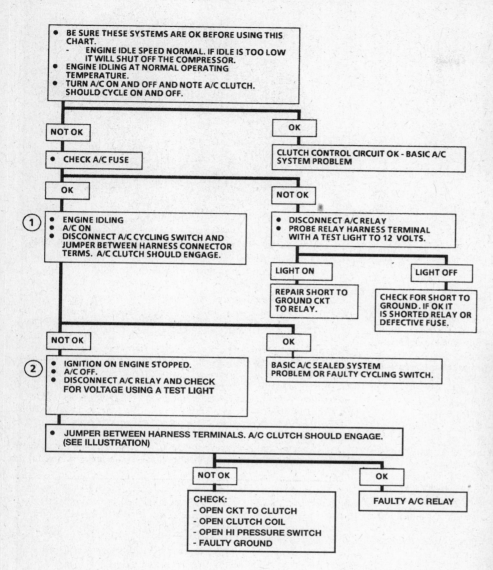

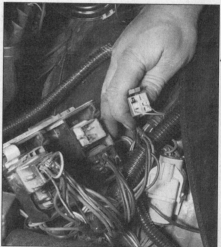

- BE SURE THESE SYSTEMS ARE OK BEFORE USING THIS CHART.
  - ENGINE IDLE SPEED NORMAL. IF IDLE IS TOO LOW IT WILL SHUT OFF THE COMPRESSOR.
- ENGINE IDLING AT NORMAL OPERATING TEMPERATURE.
- TURN A/C ON AND OFF AND NOTE A/C CLUTCH. SHOULD CYCLE ON AND OFF.

NOT OK | OK

- CHECK A/C FUSE | CLUTCH CONTROL CIRCUIT OK - BASIC A/C SYSTEM PROBLEM

OK | NOT OK

①
- ENGINE IDLING
- A/C ON
- DISCONNECT A/C CYCLING SWITCH AND JUMPER BETWEEN HARNESS CONNECTOR TERMS. A/C CLUTCH SHOULD ENGAGE.

- DISCONNECT A/C RELAY
- PROBE RELAY HARNESS TERMINAL WITH A TEST LIGHT TO 12 VOLTS.

LIGHT ON | LIGHT OFF

REPAIR SHORT TO GROUND CKT TO RELAY. | CHECK FOR SHORT TO GROUND. IF OK IT IS SHORTED RELAY OR DEFECTIVE FUSE.

NOT OK | OK

②
- IGNITION ON ENGINE STOPPED.
- A/C OFF.
- DISCONNECT A/C RELAY AND CHECK FOR VOLTAGE USING A TEST LIGHT

BASIC A/C SEALED SYSTEM PROBLEM OR FAULTY CYCLING SWITCH.

- JUMPER BETWEEN HARNESS TERMINALS. A/C CLUTCH SHOULD ENGAGE. (SEE ILLUSTRATION)

NOT OK | OK

CHECK:
- OPEN CKT TO CLUTCH
- OPEN CLUTCH COIL
- OPEN HI PRESSURE SWITCH
- FAULTY GROUND

FAULTY A/C RELAY

7.53a Diagnostic flow chart for checking the air conditioning clutch control system

7.53b An easy check to find out if the air conditioning compressor clutch is working is to remove the air conditioning relay (near fuel pump relay and power relay) and install a jumper wire from the battery (+) supply to the compressor clutch wire (4.6L engine shown)

7.53c Jumping the air conditioning clutch relay connector on 5.0L engines with SEFI

6

switch. There should be voltage present.

49 Check the adjustment of the switch (see Chapter 7). If the switch is out of adjustment, perform the procedure and clear the codes. Recheck the system for any other problems.

50 Any further diagnostics of the Manual Lever Position (MLP) sensor must be performed by a dealer service department or other repair shop because this system requires a special SCAN tool to access the working parameters from the PCM.

Adjustment

51 To adjust the Manual Lever Position (MLP) sensor or to replace the switch, refer to Chapter 7.

Air conditioning clutch control

Refer to illustrations 7.53a, 7.53b and 7.53c
Note: *Refer to Chapter 12, Section 6 for additional information on the location of the relays.*

52 During air conditioning operation, the PCM controls the application of the air conditioning compressor clutch. The PCM controls the air conditioning clutch control relay to delay clutch engagement after the air conditioning is turned ON to allow the BPA-ISC valve to adjust the idle speed of the engine to compensate for the additional load. The PCM also controls the relay to disengage the clutch in the event of an excessively high or low pressure within the system or an overheating problem.

53 The accompanying diagnostic chart outlines the testing procedures for the air conditioning clutch control **(see illustrations).**

54 In most cases, if the air conditioning does not function, the problem is probably related to the air conditioning system relays and switches and not the PCM.

55 If the air conditioning is operating properly and idle is too low when the air conditioning compressor turns on or is too high when the air conditioning compressor turns off, check for an open circuit between the air conditioning control relay and the PCM.

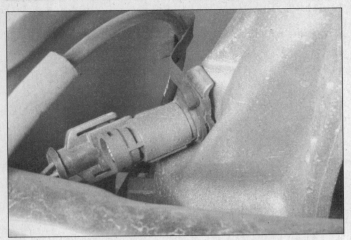

7.56 Location of the vehicle speed sensor on the transmission on 4.6L engines

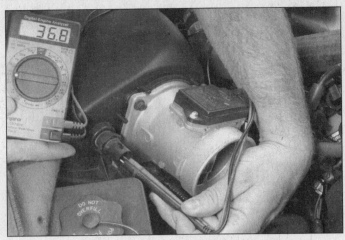

7.65 Remove the electrical connector from the IAT sensor (located in air cleaner housing), then check the resistance of the IAT sensor cold and warm. It may be necessary to use simulated conditions to obtain accurate results

Vehicle Speed Sensor (VSS)

Refer to illustration 7.56

General description

56   The Vehicle Speed Sensor (VSS) is located near the rear section of the transmission (see illustration). This sensor is a permanent magnetic variable reluctance sensor that produces a pulsing voltage whenever vehicle speed is over 3 mph. These pulses are translated by the PCM and provided for other systems for fuel and transmission shift control. The VSS is part of the Transmission Converter Clutch (TCC) system. Any problems with the VSS will usually set a Code 24.

Check

57   To check the vehicle speed sensor, remove the electrical connector in the wiring harness near the sensor. Using a voltmeter, check for signal voltage to the sensor. The signal wire should have 10 volts or more available. If there is no voltage available, have the PCM diagnosed by a dealer service department or other qualified repair shop.

Replacement

58   To replace the VSS, disconnect the electrical connector from the VSS.
59   Remove the retaining bolt and lift the VSS from the transmission.
60   Installation is the reverse of removal.

Intake Air Temperature (IAT) sensor

Refer to illustration 7.65

General description

61   The Intake Air Temperature (IAT) sensor is located inside the air intake duct. This sensor acts as a resistor which changes value according to the temperature of the air entering the engine. Low temperatures produce a high resistance value (for example, at 68 degrees F the resistance is 27.30K ohms) while high temperatures produce low resistance values (at 212-degrees F the resistance is 2.07K ohms). The PCM supplies approximately 5-volts (reference voltage) to the IAT sensor. The voltage will change according to the temperature of the incoming air. The voltage will be high when the air temperature is cold and low when the air temperature is warm. Any problems with the IAT sensor will usually set a code 54 on the two digit code system or 112, 113 or 114 on the three digit code system.

Check

62   To check the IAT sensor, disconnect the two prong electrical connector and turn the ignition key ON but do not start the engine.
63   Measure the voltage (reference voltage). The VOM should read

approximately 5-volts.
64   If the voltage signal is not correct, have the PCM diagnosed by a dealer service department or other repair shop.
65   Measure the resistance across the sensor terminals (see illustration). The resistance should be HIGH when the air temperature is LOW. Next, start the engine and let it idle (cold). Wait awhile and let the engine reach operating temperature. Turn the ignition OFF, disconnect the IAT sensor and measure the resistance across the terminals. The resistance should be LOW when the air temperature is HIGH. If the sensor does not exhibit this change in resistance, replace it with a new part.

Power steering pressure switch

Refer to illustration 7.66

66   Turning the steering wheel increases power steering fluid pressure and engine load. The pressure switch (see illustration) will close before the load can cause an idle problem. A problem in the power steering pressure switch circuit will set a code 52 (two digit code system only).
67   A pressure switch that will not open or an open circuit from the PCM will cause timing to retard at idle and this will affect idle quality.
68   A pressure switch that will not close or an open circuit may cause the engine to die when the power steering system is used heavily.
69   Any problems with the power steering pressure switch or circuit should be repaired by a dealer service department or other qualified repair shop.

Crankshaft position sensor

Refer to illustrations 7.70a and 7.70b

General information

70   The crankshaft position sensor (see illustrations) defines the engine position to the PCM. A crankshaft position pulse occurs at each TDC.

Check

71   Any problems with the crankshaft position sensor should be diagnosed by a dealer service department or other qualified repair shop.

Replacement

72   Remove the electrical connector and the retaining bolt and lift the assembly from the engine block.
73   Installation is the reverse of removal.

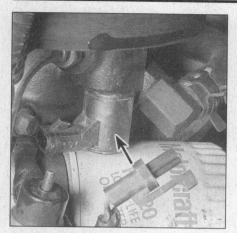

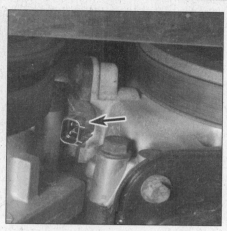

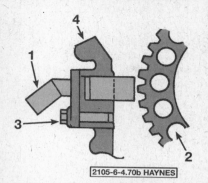

7.66 The power steering pressure switch (arrow) is located under the power steering pump

7.70a The crankshaft position sensor is located on the timing chain cover (4.6L engine)

2105-6-4.70b HAYNES

7.70b The crankshaft sensor detects crank position from the toothed pulse wheel

1 Crankshaft position sensor
2 Pulse wheel
3 Screw
4 Timing chain cover

Camshaft position sensor

General information

74   The camshaft position sensor is a variable reluctance sensor triggered by the high point mark on the camshaft sprocket. Any diagnostic work should be performed by a dealer service department or other repair shop.

Replacement

Refer to illustration 7.75

75   Remove the retaining screw and separate the camshaft sensor from the cylinder head (see illustration).
76   Installation is the reverse of removal.

Brake On/Off (BOO) switch

General Information

Refer to illustration 7.78

77   The brake On/Off switch (BOO) tells the PCM when the brakes are being applied. The switch closes when brakes are applied and opens when the brakes are released. The BOO switch is located on the brake pedal assembly.
78   The brake light circuit and bulbs are wired into the BOO circuit so

it is important in 1diagnosing any driveability problems to make sure all the brake light bulbs are working properly (not burned out) or the driver may feel poor idle quality (see illustration).

Check

79   Disconnect the electrical connector from the BOO switch and using a 12 volt test light, check for battery voltage to the BOO switch.
80   Also, check continuity from the BOO switch to the brake light bulbs. Change any burned out bulbs or damaged wire looms.

Replacement

81   Refer to Chapter 9, Section 15 for the replacement procedure.

8   Exhaust Gas Recirculation (EGR) system

General description

1   The EGR system is used to lower NOx (oxides of nitrogen) emission levels caused by high combustion temperatures. The EGR recirculates a small amount of exhaust gas into the intake manifold. The additional mixture lowers the temperature of combustion thereby reducing the formation of NOx compounds.

6

7.75 Remove the camshaft position sensor from the front of the left (driver's side) cylinder head

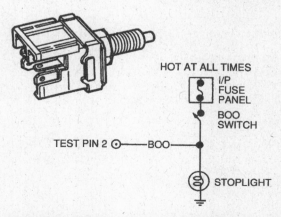

7.78 Since the brake light bulbs are wired into the BOO switch, double-check for any burned out bulbs that might cause the engine to idle poorly because of the open circuit (brake On signal)

Carbureted engines

Refer to illustrations 8.2a, 8.2b, 8.2c, 8.3a, 8.3b, 8.3c, 8.3d and 8.4

2   Early models are equipped with either a Ported Vacuum Control **(see illustration)** system or a Venturi Vacuum Control **(see illustrations)** system. The venturi vacuum system utilizes a vacuum tap at the throat of the carburetor venturi to provide the control signal. This signal is a low amplitude signal that requires a vacuum amplifier to increase the level of vacuum needed to operate the EGR valve. The ported vacuum control system uses a slot in the carburetor body

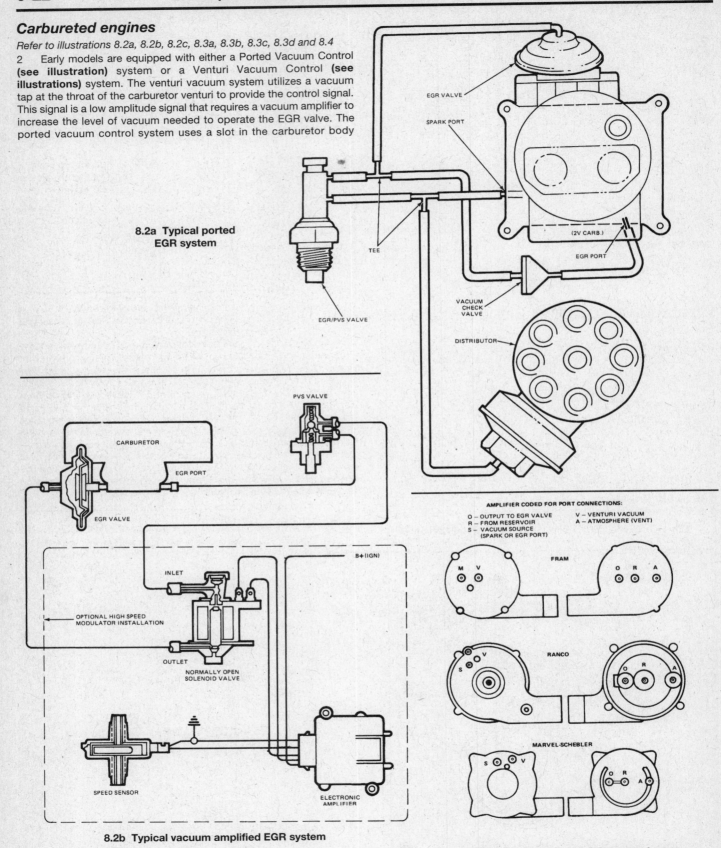

8.2a Typical ported EGR system

8.2b Typical vacuum amplified EGR system

8.2c Terminal designations for the venturi vacuum amplifier (dual connector type)

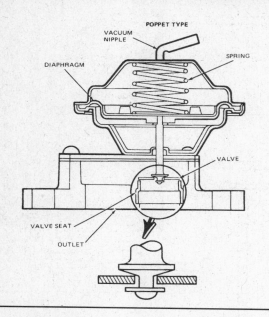

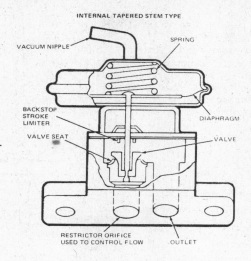

8.3a Poppet type and tapered stem type EGR valves

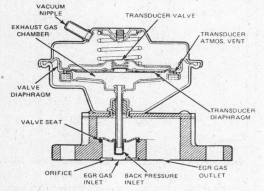

8.3b Typical integral backpressure transducer EGR valve

which is exposed to an increasing percentage of manifold vacuum as the throttle valve is opened up during acceleration. Ported systems do not require a vacuum amplifier.

3   Several different types of EGR valves are used on these models. The poppet type (**see illustration**) uses a strong spring pressure to retract the EGR valve quickly from its seat. The tapered stem type utilizes a pintle protruding through the valve seat to vary flow rates and flow curves. The integral backpressure EGR valve (**see illustration**) combines the exhaust backpressure transducer within the diaphragm housing of the older EGR valves. The exhaust back pressure regulates the flow by its pressure against the cavity between the orifice and the poppet or tapered stem. Some models are equipped with a back-pressure transducer connected to an adapter between the EGR valve and the intake manifold. The transducer modulates EGR flow by varying the EGR valve vacuum signal according to exhaust backpressure (**see illustration**).

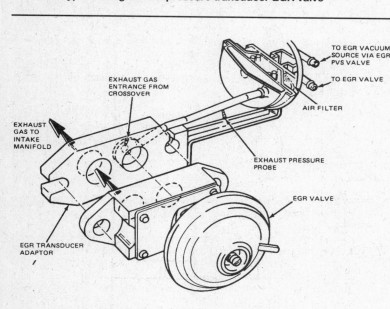

8.3c EGR valve exhaust backpressure transducer

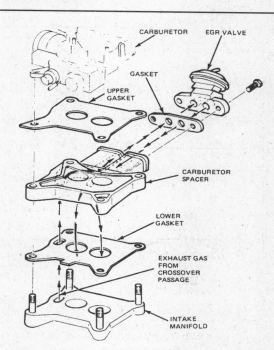

8.3d Exploded view of the spacer assembly on the EGR system

6

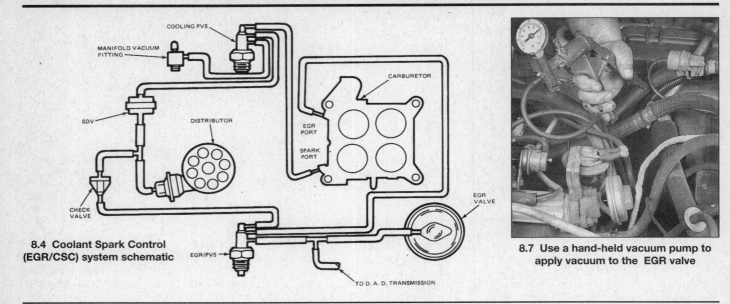

8.4 Coolant Spark Control (EGR/CSC) system schematic

8.7 Use a hand-held vacuum pump to apply vacuum to the EGR valve

8.18 EGR solenoid valve on CFI systems

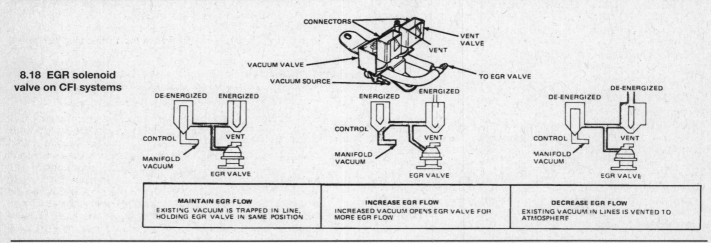

MAINTAIN EGR FLOW	INCREASE EGR FLOW	DECREASE EGR FLOW
EXISTING VACUUM IS TRAPPED IN LINE, HOLDING EGR VALVE IN SAME POSITION	INCREASED VACUUM OPENS EGR VALVE FOR MORE EGR FLOW	EXISTING VACUUM IN LINES IS VENTED TO ATMOSPHERE

4   Some models are equipped with a Coolant Spark Control (EGR/CSC) system that controls the timing and amount of the EGR signal by the use of a coolant temperature solenoid and check valves that work in conjunction with the distributor vacuum advance vacuum system (see illustration). At cold starting conditions, the EGR PVS connects vacuum from the carburetor (port) directly to the distributor through the check valve. As the engine temperature increases, the EGR PVS switches vacuum to the EGR valve. In warm running conditions, the vacuum signal is used to control the spark advance through the cooling PVS and the spark delay valve.

Check

Refer to illustration 8.7
5   Check all hoses for cracks, kinks, broken sections and proper connection. Inspect all system connections for damage, cracks and leaks.
6   To check the EGR system operation, bring the engine up to operating temperature and, with the transmission in Neutral (parking brake set and tires blocked to prevent movement), allow it to idle for 70 seconds. Open the throttle abruptly so the engine speed is between 2,000 and 3,000 rpm and then allow it to close. The EGR valve stem should move if the control system is working properly. The test should be repeated several times. Movement of the stem indicates the control system is functioning correctly.
7   If the EGR valve stem does not move, check all of the hose connections to make sure they are not leaking or clogged. Disconnect

the vacuum hose and apply ten inches of vacuum with a hand pump (see illustration). If the stem still does not move, replace the EGR valve with a new one. If the valve does open, measure the valve travel to make sure it is approximately 1/8-inch. Also, the engine should run roughly when the valve is open. If it doesn't, the passages are probably clogged.
8   Apply vacuum with the pump and then clamp the hose shut. The valve should stay open for 30 seconds or longer. If it does not, the diaphragm is leaking and the valve should be replaced with a new one.
9   If the EGR valve does not operate with the EGR/CSC bypassed, the carburetor must be removed to check and clean the slotted port in the throttle bore and the vacuum passages and orifices in the throttle body. Use solvent to remove deposits and check for flow with light air pressure.
10   If the engine idles roughly and it is suspected the EGR valve is not closing, remove the EGR valve and inspect the poppet and seat area for deposits.
11   If the deposits are more than a thin film of carbon, the valve should be cleaned. To clean the valve, apply solvent and allow it to penetrate and soften the deposits, making sure that none gets on the valve diaphragm, as it could be damaged.
12   Use a vacuum pump to hold the valve open and carefully scrape the deposits from the seat and poppet area with a tool. Inspect the poppet and stem for wear and replace the valve with a new one if wear is found.
13   Locate the vacuum amplifier (if equipped) and remove the rubber

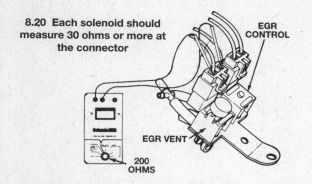

8.20 Each solenoid should measure 30 ohms or more at the connector

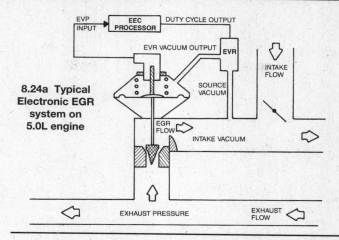

8.24a Typical Electronic EGR system on 5.0L engine

junction block along with the vacuum hoses.

14 With the engine running, check for a vacuum signal from the intake manifold. This test will determine if manifold vacuum is reaching the vacuum amplifier from the intake manifold.

15 Also apply vacuum to the port (vacuum hose) that is routed to the EGR valve. The gauge should hold vacuum. If not, check for broken hoses or ruptured diaphragms in the EGR valve.

16 Check the EGR solenoid (if equipped). Using a hand held vacuum pump apply vacuum and then apply battery voltage. The solenoid should activate and allow vacuum to pass through the solenoid.

17 Also remove the vacuum hose(s) from the solenoid and check for vacuum to the EGR valve.

CFI engines

General information

Refer to illustration 8.18

18 The dual EGR solenoid valve assembly consists of two solenoid valves (see illustration). One solenoid supplies vacuum to the sonic EGR valve while the other acts as a vent when de-energized. Both solenoid valves receive variable duty cycle signals from the computer in response to the necessary EGR flow requirements. A restrictor is added in the vacuum valve inlet port to reduce its flow compared to the vent valve. In case the vacuum valve sticks open, the vent valve will be capable of venting the flow without affecting the components being controlled by the computer.

Check

Refer to illustration 8.20

19 Check all hoses for cracks, kinks, broken sections and proper connection. Inspect all system connections for damage, cracks and leaks.

20 With the ignition key OFF, check the resistance of the EGR Control solenoid and the EGR Vent solenoid (see illustration). They should each read 30 ohms or more. If not, check the circuit for a short in the wiring harness.

21 Turn the ignition key to ON, and using a voltmeter make sure the EGR Control solenoid receives battery voltage.

22 Check the EVP sensor (see Steps 34 through 40).

23 If all the checks are correct, replace the component with a new part.

SEFI engines

Refer to illustrations 8.24a, 8.24b and 8.24c

24 These vehicles are equipped with two different systems:

a) *5.0L engines are equipped with the Electronic Exhaust Gas Recirculation (EEGR) system (see illustration). This system relies upon the PCM for EGR control. The control module (PCM) calculates the desired flow of exhaust gases into the combustion chamber and subsequently controls the EGR valve position with the EGR vacuum regulator. The EGR Valve Position (EVP) sensor detects the exact position of the EGR valve pintle and relays the information to the PCM. The PCM in turn, uses this information to regulate the duty cycle (On/Off time) of the EGR vacuum regulator. A duty cycle of 50-percent would hold the EGR valve half way open. The EEGR system uses "electronic" components to control the EGR valve.*

b) *4.6L engines are equipped with the Pressure Feedback EGR (PFE) system (see illustration). This system controls the EGR flow rate by monitoring the pressure drop across a remotely located sharp-edged orifice. This system uses a pressure transducer to receive*

6

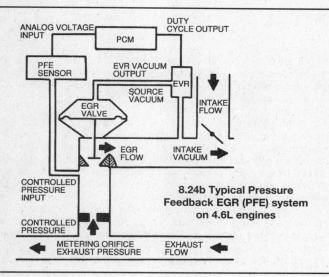

8.24b Typical Pressure Feedback EGR (PFE) system on 4.6L engines

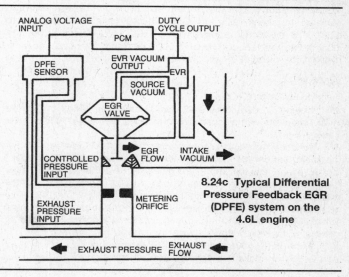

8.24c Typical Differential Pressure Feedback EGR (DPFE) system on the 4.6L engine

8.30 Apply vacuum to the EGR valve and check with the tip of your finger for movement of the diaphragm. It should move smoothly without any binding when vacuum is applied

8.36 Working on the harness side of the Electronic Vacuum Regulator electrical connector, check for battery voltage

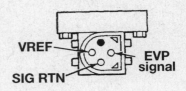

8.38 Terminal designations for the EVP sensor connector (5.0L engine)

pressure (feedback) and then vary the vacuum to the EGR vacuum regulator and consequently the EGR valve. This type of system serves only as a pressure regulator rather than a flow metering device. Some models are equipped with a Differential Pressure Feedback EGR (DPFE) system **(see illustration)**. *This operates in the same way as the PFE except it monitors the pressure drop across the orifice allowing for a more precise measurement of the exhaust gas pressures.*

Check

25   Too much EGR flow tends to weaken combustion, causing the engine to run rough or stall. When EGR flow is excessive, the engine can stop after a cold start or at idle after deceleration, the vehicle can surge at cruising speeds or the idle may be rough. If the EGR valve remains constantly open, the engine may not idle at all.

26   Too little or no EGR flow allows combustion temperatures to get too high during acceleration and load conditions. This can cause spark knock (detonation), engine overheating or emission test failure.

27   The following checks will help you pinpoint problems in the EGR system. Where the procedure says to lift up on the EGR valve diaphragm, it's a good idea to wear a heat-resistant glove to prevent burns.

EGR valve

Refer to illustration 8.30

28   The EGR valve is controlled by a normally open solenoid which allows vacuum to pass when energized. The PCM energizes the solenoid to turn on the EGR. The PCM controls the EGR when three conditions are present: engine coolant is above 113-degrees F, the TPS is at part throttle and the MAF sensor is in its mid-range. Code 31 through 35 on the two-digit code system or 328 through 337 on the three-digit code system will detect a problem with the EGR system.

29   Make sure the vacuum hoses are in good condition and hooked up correctly.

30   To perform a leakage test, hook up a vacuum pump to the EGR valve **(see illustration)**. Apply a vacuum of 5 to 6 in-Hg to the valve. The vacuum pump should hold vacuum.

31   If access is possible, position your finger tip under the vacuum diaphragm and apply vacuum to the EGR valve. You should feel movement of the EGR diaphragm. **Warning:** *The EGR valve becomes very hot during engine operation - it's a good idea to wear a glove when performing this check.*

32   Remove the EGR valve (see Step 41) and clean the inlet and outlet ports with a wire brush or scraper. Do not sandblast the valve or clean it with gasoline or solvents. These liquids will destroy the EGR valve diaphragm.

33   If the specified conditions are not met, replace the EGR valve.

EGR control system

Refer to illustrations 8.36 and 8.38

34   If a code is displayed there are several possibilities for EGR failure. Engine coolant temperature sensor, TPS, MAF sensor, TCC system and the engine rpm govern the parameters the EGR system use for distinguishing the correct ON time.

35   All systems use an Electronic Vacuum Regulator to control the amount of exhaust gas through the EGR valve. The valve is normally open (engine at operating temperature) and the vacuum source is a ported signal. The PCM uses a controlled "pulse width" or electronic signal to turn the EGR ON and OFF (the "duty cycle"). The duty cycle should be zero percent (no EGR) when in Park or Neutral, when the TPS input is below the specified value or when Wide Open Throttle (WOT) is indicated.

36   To check the EGR vacuum regulator, disconnect the electrical connector to the EGR vacuum regulator, turn the ignition key ON (engine not running) and check for battery voltage to the solenoid **(see illustration)**. Battery voltage should be present.

37   Next, use an ohmmeter and check the resistance of the EGR vacuum regulator. It should be between 30 and 70 ohms.

38   On 5.0L engines, also check the operation of the EGR valve position (EVP) sensor. This sensor is attached to the EGR valve to provide the PCM with the exact position of the EGR valve pintle. Disconnect the EVP electrical connector and working on the sensor side **(see illustration)** install the probes of an ohmmeter into EVP SIGNAL and VREF. Check the resistance of the sensor while applying vacuum to the EGR valve. It should fluctuate between 5,500 to 100 ohms as vacuum is slowly applied.

8.45 Unscrew the tube nut (arrow) to detach the EGR pipe from the manifold

8.46a Remove the two bolts (arrows) from the EGR valve (intake manifold removed for clarity) (4.6L engine shown)

8.46b Removing the EGR mounting bolts on an early system (1976 460 engine shown)

8.46c EGR valve removal on a 1988 SEFI 5.0L engine

39   Also, on 5.0L engines, check for reference voltage to the sensor. With the ignition key on (engine not running), check for voltage on the harness side of the EVP electrical connector **(see illustration 8.38)** on terminal VREF. It should be between 4.0 and 6.0 volts. If the test results are incorrect, replace the EVP sensor.

40   On 4.6L engines, check the operation of the Pressure Feedback EGR (PFE) sensor. **Note:** *The DPFE sensor on the Differential Pressure Feedback EGR systems have two exhaust lines hooked into the EGR tube.* Check for reference voltage to the sensor. With the ignition key on (engine not running), check for voltage on the harness side of the PFE electrical connector. It should be between 4.0 and 6.0 volts. If the test results are incorrect, replace the PFE sensor.

Component replacement

EGR valve

Refer to illustrations 8.45, 8.46a, 8.46b and 8.46c

41   When buying a new EGR valve, make sure that you have the right EGR valve. Use the stamped code located on the top of the EGR valve.

42   Detach the cable from the negative terminal of the battery.

43   Remove the air cleaner housing assembly (see Chapter 4).

44   Detach the vacuum line from the EGR valve.

45   Raise the vehicle and support it securely on jackstands. Remove the EGR pipe from the exhaust manifold **(see illustration)**. Lower the vehicle.

46   On 1996 4.6L engines, remove the mounting bolts securing the EGR valve to the throttle body spacer. On all other 4.6L engines and all 5.0L engines, remove the bolts securing the EGR valve to the intake manifold.

47   Remove the EGR valve and gasket from the manifold or throttle body spacer.

48   With a wire wheel, buff the exhaust deposits from the EGR valve mounting surface on the manifold and, if you plan to use the same valve, the mounting surface of the valve itself. Look for exhaust deposits in the valve outlet. Remove deposit build-up with a screwdriver. **Caution:** *Never wash the valve in solvents or degreaser - both agents will permanently damage the diaphragm. Sand blasting is also not recommended because it will affect the operation of the valve.*

49   If the EGR passage contains an excessive build-up of deposits, clean it out with a wire wheel. Make sure that all loose particles are completely removed to prevent them from clogging the EGR valve or from being ingested into the engine.

50   Installation is the reverse of removal.

EGR vacuum regulator

51   Detach the cable from the negative terminal of the battery.

52   Remove the air intake duct from the air cleaner assembly (see Chapter 4).

53   Unplug the electrical connector from the solenoid.

54   Clearly label and detach both vacuum hoses.

55   Remove the solenoid mounting screw and remove the solenoid.

56   Installation is the reverse of removal.

9   Evaporative Emissions Control System (EECS)

Refer to illustrations 9.2 and 9.14

General description

1   This system is designed to trap and store fuel vapors that evaporate from the fuel tank, throttle body and intake manifold.

2   The Evaporative Emission Control System (EECS) consists of a charcoal-filled canister and the lines connecting the canister to the fuel tank, ported vacuum and intake manifold vacuum **(see illustration)**.

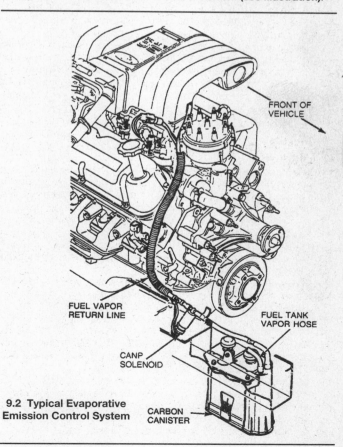

FRONT OF VEHICLE

FUEL VAPOR RETURN LINE

FUEL TANK VAPOR HOSE

CANP SOLENOID

CARBON CANISTER

9.2 Typical Evaporative Emission Control System

6

9.14 The charcoal canister is either mounted in the engine compartment or under the vehicle. This one, on a 1976 Continental, is secured to the right side frame rail with two mounting bolts (arrows)

3   Fuel vapors are transferred from the fuel tank, throttle body and intake manifold to a canister where they are stored when the engine is not operating. When the engine is running, the fuel vapors are purged from the canister by a purge control solenoid which is PCM controlled and consumed in the normal combustion process.

Check

4   Poor idle, stalling and poor driveability can be caused by an inoperative purge control solenoid, a damaged canister, split or cracked hoses or hoses connected to the wrong tubes.

5   Evidence of fuel loss or fuel odor can be caused by fuel leaking from fuel lines or the TBI, a cracked or damaged canister, an inoperative bowl vent valve, an inoperative purge valve, disconnected, misrouted, kinked, deteriorated or damaged vapor or control hoses or an improperly seated air cleaner or air cleaner gasket.

6   Inspect each hose attached to the canister for kinks, leaks and breaks along its entire length. Repair or replace as necessary.

7   Inspect the canister. If it is cracked or damaged, replace it.

8   Look for fuel leaking from the bottom of the canister. If fuel is leaking, replace the canister and check the hoses and hose routing.

9   Apply a short length of hose to the lower tube of the purge valve assembly and attempt to blow through it. Little or no air should pass into the canister (a small amount of air will pass because the canister has a constant purge hole).

10   With a hand-held vacuum pump, apply vacuum through the control vacuum signal tube near the throttle body to the purge control solenoid diaphragm.

11   If the purge control solenoid does not hold vacuum for at least 20 seconds, the purge control solenoid is leaking and must be replaced.

12   If the diaphragm holds vacuum, apply battery voltage to the purge control solenoid and observe that vacuum (vapors) are allowed to pass through to the intake system.

Component replacement

13   If the canister is mounted under the vehicle, raise the vehicle and support it securely on jackstands.

14   Clearly label, then detach, all vacuum lines from the canister. Loosen the canister mounting clamp bolt(s) **(see illustration)** and pull the canister out.

15   Installation is the reverse of removal.

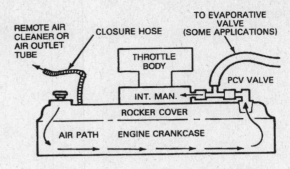

10.1 Gas flow in typical PCV system

10   Positive Crankcase Ventilation (PCV) system

Refer to illustration 10.1

1   The Positive Crankcase Ventilation (PCV) system reduces hydrocarbon emissions by scavenging crankcase vapors. It does this by circulating fresh air from the air cleaner through the crankcase, where it mixes with blow-by gases and is then rerouted through a PCV valve to the intake manifold **(see illustration)**.

2   The main components of the PCV system are the PCV valve, a fresh air filtered inlet and the vacuum hoses connecting these two components with the engine and the EECS system.

3   To maintain idle quality, the PCV valve restricts the flow when the intake manifold vacuum is high. If abnormal operating conditions arise, the system is designed to allow excessive amounts of blow-by gases to flow back through the crankcase vent tube into the air cleaner to be consumed by normal combustion.

4   Checking and replacement of the PCV valve and filter is covered in Chapter 1.

11   Catalytic converter

General description

1   The catalytic converter is an emission control device added to the exhaust system to reduce pollutants from the exhaust gas stream. A single-bed converter design is used in combination with a three-way (reduction) catalyst. The catalytic coating on the three-way catalyst contains platinum and rhodium, which lowers the levels of oxides of nitrogen (NOx) as well as hydrocarbons (HC) and carbon monoxide (CO).

Check

2   The test equipment for a catalytic converter is expensive and highly sophisticated. If you suspect that the converter on your vehicle is malfunctioning, take it to a dealer or authorized emissions inspection facility for diagnosis and repair.

3   Whenever the vehicle is raised for servicing of underbody components, check the converter for leaks, corrosion and other damage. If damage is discovered, the converter should be replaced.

Replacement

4   Because the converter is part of the exhaust system, converter replacement requires removal of the exhaust pipe assembly (see Chapter 4A). Take the vehicle, or the exhaust system, to a dealer or a muffler shop.

Chapter 7
Automatic transmission

Contents

Specifications

General

Transmission type	
1970 through 1979	C6 (3-speed)
1980 through 1982	C6 or AOD (4-speed overdrive)
1983 through 1991	AOD
1992	AOD or AODE (electronic 4-speed overdrive)
1993 and 1994	AODE
1995 on	4R70W (electronic 4-speed with overdrive and lockup torque converter)

Torque specifications

	Ft-lbs (unless otherwise specified)
Shift rod-to-manual lever nut (C6)	120 to 240 in-lbs
Shift cable-to-manual lever nut (C6)	120 to 180 in-lbs
Neutral start switch	96 to 132 in-lbs
Oil cooler line fittings at transmission	12 to 18
Transmission-to-engine bolts	40 to 50
Torque converter-to-driveplate nuts	20 to 34

1   General information

All vehicles covered in this manual come equipped with an automatic transmission, either a C6 (three-speed), an AOD (overdrive four-speed), an AODE (overdrive electronic four-speed) or a 4R70W (electronic four-speed with lock-up torque converter and electronic shifting).

Due to the complexity of the automatic transmissions covered in this manual and the need for specialized equipment to perform most service operations, this Chapter contains only general diagnosis, routine maintenance, adjustment and removal and installation procedures. For information regarding the diagnostic trouble codes for AODE transmissions, refer to Chapter 6 (the codes for the 4R70W, which are much more difficult for the home mechanic to access, are not included in Chapter 6).

If the transmission requires major repair work, it should be left to a dealer service department or an automotive or transmission repair shop. You can, however, remove and install the transmission yourself and save the expense, even if the repair work is done by a transmission shop.

2   Diagnosis - general

Note: *Automatic transmission malfunctions may be caused by five general conditions: poor engine performance, improper adjustments, hydraulic malfunctions, mechanical malfunctions or malfunctions in the computer or its signal network. Diagnosis of these problems should always begin with a check of the easily repaired items: fluid level and condition (see Chapter 1), shift linkage adjustment and throttle linkage adjustment. Next, perform a road test to determine if the problem has been corrected or if more diagnosis is necessary. If the problem persists after the preliminary tests and corrections are completed, additional diagnosis should be done by a dealer service department or transmission repair shop. Refer to the troubleshooting Section at the front of this manual for information on symptoms of transmission problems.*

Preliminary checks

1   Drive the vehicle to warm the transmission to normal operating temperature.

2   Check the fluid level as described in Chapter 1:

a) *If the fluid level is unusually low, add enough fluid to bring the level within the designated area of the dipstick, then check for external leaks (see below).*

b) *If the fluid level is abnormally high, drain off the excess, then check the drained fluid for contamination by coolant. The presence of engine coolant in the automatic transmission fluid indicates that a failure has occurred in the internal radiator walls that separate the coolant from the transmission fluid (see Chapter 3).*

c) *If the fluid is foaming, drain it and refill the transmission, then check for coolant in the fluid or a high fluid level.*

3   Check the engine idle speed. **Note:** *If the engine is malfunctioning, do not proceed with the preliminary checks until it has been repaired and runs normally.*

4   Check the throttle valve cable for freedom of movement. Adjust it if necessary (see Section 5). **Note:** *The throttle cable may function properly when the engine is shut off and cold, but it may malfunction once the engine is hot. Check it cold and at normal engine operating temperature.*

5   Inspect the shift control linkage (see Section 3). Make sure that it's properly adjusted and that the linkage operates smoothly.

Fluid leak diagnosis

6   Most fluid leaks are easy to locate visually. Repair usually consists of replacing a seal or gasket. If a leak is difficult to find, the following procedure may help.

7   Identify the fluid. Make sure it's transmission fluid and not engine oil or brake fluid (automatic transmission fluid is a deep red color).

8   Try to pinpoint the source of the leak. Drive the vehicle several miles, then park it over a large sheet of cardboard. After a minute or two, you should be able to locate the leak by determining the source of the fluid dripping onto the cardboard.

9   Make a careful visual inspection of the suspected component and the area immediately around it. Pay particular attention to gasket mating surfaces. A mirror is often helpful for finding leaks in areas that are hard to see.

10   If the leak still cannot be found, clean the suspected area thoroughly with a degreaser or solvent, then dry it.

11   Drive the vehicle for several miles at normal operating temperature and varying speeds. After driving the vehicle, visually inspect the suspected component again.

12   Once the leak has been located, the cause must be determined before it can be properly repaired. If a gasket is replaced but the sealing flange is bent, the new gasket will not stop the leak. The bent flange must be straightened.

13   Before attempting to repair a leak, check to make sure that the following conditions are corrected or they may cause another leak. **Note:** *Some of the following conditions cannot be fixed without highly*

specialized tools and expertise. Such problems must be referred to a transmission repair shop or a dealer service department.

Gasket leaks

14   Check the pan periodically. Make sure the bolts are tight, no bolts are missing, the gasket is in good condition and the pan is flat (dents in the pan may indicate damage to the valve body inside).

15   If the pan gasket is leaking, the fluid level or the fluid pressure may be too high, the vent may be plugged, the pan bolts may be too tight, the pan sealing flange may be warped, the sealing surface of the transmission housing may be damaged, the gasket may be damaged or the transmission casting may be cracked or porous. If sealant instead of gasket material has been used to form a seal between the pan and the transmission housing, it may be the wrong sealant.

Seal leaks

16   If a transmission seal is leaking, the fluid level or pressure may be too high, the vent may be plugged, the seal bore may be damaged, the seal itself may be damaged or improperly installed, the surface of the shaft protruding through the seal may be damaged or a loose bearing may be causing excessive shaft movement.

17   Make sure the dipstick tube seal is in good condition and the tube is properly seated. Periodically check the area around the speedometer gear or sensor for leakage. If transmission fluid is evident, check the O-ring for damage.

Case leaks

18   If the case itself appears to be leaking, the casting is porous and will have to be repaired or replaced.

19   Make sure the oil cooler hose fittings are tight and in good condition.

Fluid comes out vent pipe or fill tube

20   If this condition occurs, the transmission is overfilled, there is coolant in the fluid, the case is porous, the dipstick is incorrect, the vent is plugged or the drain-back holes are plugged.

Vehicles with AODE transmissions (some 1992 models, all 1993 and later models)

21   The Powertrain Control Modules in models with AODE (electronic) transmissions have special diagnostic trouble codes for the transmission. For information on these codes, refer to Chapter 6 (1995 models are equipped with the 4R70W, an all-electronic four-speed automatic which is controlled by the Powertrain Control Module; the diagnostic codes for this new transmission cannot be accessed by the home mechanic).

3   Shift linkage - check and adjustment

Check

1   Try to start the engine in each shift lever position; the starter should operate in Park and Neutral only. If the starter does not operate in Park or Neutral or operates in any position other than Park and Neutral, the shift linkage is in need of adjustment or the neutral start switch is defective (see Section 6).

Adjustment
Column-shift linkage or cable
C6 or AOD (1970 through 1992)
Refer to illustrations 3.3a, 3.3b, 3.3c and 3.3d

2   Push the shift lever tightly against the stop in the Drive or (on AOD) the Overdrive, position. To ensure that it stays against the stop during linkage adjustment, hang a weight from the shift lever (eight pounds for 1970 through 1990 models; three pounds for 1991 and 1992 models).

3   Loosen the shift rod or cable nut or bolt **(see illustrations)**. On

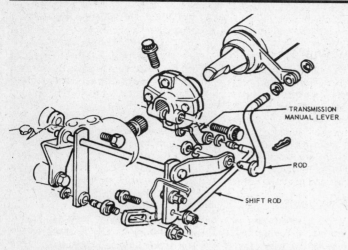

3.3a Typical shift linkage details (1970 Continental Mark III)

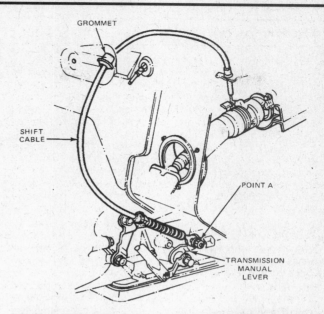

3.3b Typical shift linkage details (1972 through 1976 Continental Mark IV; 1977 through 1979 Continental Mark V)

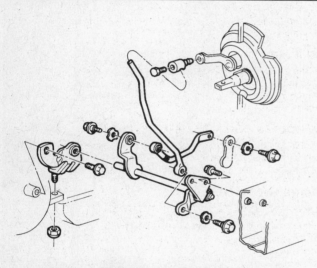

3.3c Typical shift linkage details (1980 and 1981 Lincoln Continental and Continental Mark VI with AOD - other models with AOD similar)

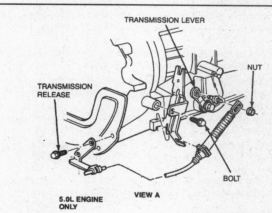

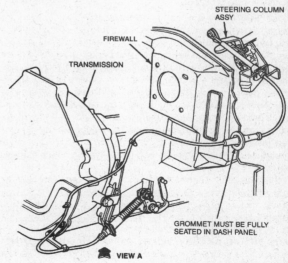

3.3d Typical shift linkage details(1990 and 1991 models and 1992 models with AOD)

models equipped with a cable, disengage the cable from the manual lever stud.

4   Shift the manual lever at the transmission into the Drive (C6) or Overdrive (AOD) position. The means by which this is achieved varies somewhat with the year and the model:

a) *1970 and 1971 models:* Third detent from the rear.

b) *1972 through 1979 models:* Second detent from the rear.

c) *1980 through 1985 models:* Push the column shift rod down to the lowest position and pull up two detents,

d) *1986 models:* Lincoln Town Car - Push the column shift rod down to the lowest position and pull up two detents; Continental - Second detent position from the full counterclockwise position.

e) *1987 through 1989 models:* Lincoln Town Car - Push the column shift rod down to the lowest position and pull up three detents; Continental - Third detent position from the full counterclockwise position.

f) *1990 and 1991 models:* - Rotate the manual lever clockwise and return it (counterclockwise) two detent positions to the Overdrive position.

7

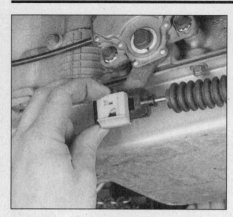

3.9a To open the shift linkage slide adjuster (the white plastic piece), push it down (1992 models with AODE transmission and 1993 and 1994 models)

3.9b The slide adjuster (the white part) must be in the released position before the linkage can be adjusted properly (adjuster removed from the transmission for clarity)

3.11 The slide adjuster must be in the locked position (pushed up all the way) after the linkage is adjusted

5   On models with a linkage *rod*, make sure that the slotted rod end has the flats aligned with the flats on the mounting stud. On models equipped with a shift *cable*, reattach the cable end to the transmission manual lever stud, using care to align the flats on the stud with the flats on the cable. Start the adjustment nut or bolt.

6   Make sure the shift lever hasn't moved from the D stop, then tighten the shift rod or cable adjusting nut or bolt to the torque listed in this Chapter's Specifications.

7   Check the operation of the transmission in all shift lever detent positions.

AODE (1992 through 1994)

Refer to illustrations 3.9a, 3.9b and 3.11

8   Have an assistant place the steering column shift lever in the Overdrive position and hold it there during the following procedure.

9   Open the slide adjuster **(see illustrations)**.

10   Move the transmission manual shift lever to the Overdrive position (the second detent from the most rearward position).

11   Push the slide adjuster closed **(see illustration)**.

12   Check the operation of the transmission in each selector lever position. Verify that the Park and Neutral start switch is functioning properly.

Console-shift cable

Refer to illustration 3.14

13   Put the transmission selector lever against the rearward Overdrive stop and hold it in this position during the following adjustment.

14   Raise the vehicle and loosen the manual lever shift cable retaining nut **(see illustration)**.

15   Move the transmission manual lever to the Overdrive position (third detent position from the full counterclockwise position).

16   With the transmission selector lever and manual lever in the Overdrive position, tighten the adjusting nut to the torque listed in this Chapter's Specifications.

17   Check the operation of the transmission in each selector lever position.

***

4   Downshift rod/throttle valve (TV) rod - adjustment

Downshift rod (1970 through 1979 and some 1980 through 1982 models)

Refer to illustration 4.1

1   Open the hood and locate the downshift rod **(see illustration)**.

2   Loosen the locknut on the rod and disconnect it from the ballstud on the bellcrank by sliding the spring clip off the end of the rod.

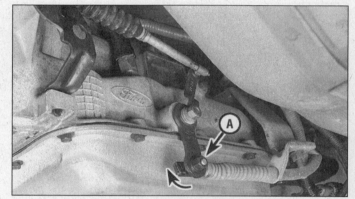

3.14 With the shift lever held in the Overdrive position (3rd detent from the full counterclockwise position), adjust the cable retaining nut (A)

3   Pull up on the rod and hold it tightly against the downshift rod against the internal slop. Adjust the length of the rod so that the hole in the link is aligned with the stud on the bellcrank assembly.

4   Lengthen the rod one turn, and position it on the bellcrank. Slide the spring clip over the end and tighten the locknut.

5   Be sure the outer bracket of the bellcrank is against the stop pin. If it isn't, lengthen the rod one more turn.

Throttle valve (some 1980 through 1985 vehicles)

6   The transmission throttle valve (TV) plays a role in keeping the engine in its best torque-producing rpm range (usually between 3000 to 5000 rpm) by making the transmission shift gears as needed. The TV opens or closes in accordance with throttle position, which is closely related to engine load. Depressing the accelerator pedal opens the throttle plate, which pulls or pushes the TV rod, which tries to open the throttle valve. As the throttle valve opens, it sends hydraulic pressure to a shift valve (it might be a 1-2 shift valve, a 2-3 shift valve or a downshift valve, depending on the conditions). Meanwhile, the governor valve opens or closes in accordance with road speed. The governor valve also sends hydraulic pressure to the shift valve. But governor pressure works in opposition to throttle pressure, trying to close the shift valve while throttle pressure tries to open it. The higher pressure at the shift valve - throttle or governor - determines when the shift occurs.

7   A TV rod that's adjusted too long will cause late shifting; a rod that's too short will cause early shifting. Correctly adjusting the TV rod

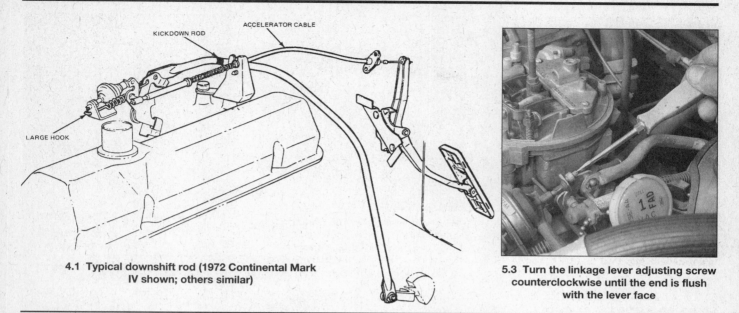

4.1 Typical downshift rod (1972 Continental Mark IV shown; others similar)

5.3 Turn the linkage lever adjusting screw counterclockwise until the end is flush with the lever face

can smooth out shifting that's too harsh, firm up shifting that's too soft, postpone shifting that's too early or speed up shifting that's too late.

8   Adjustments are possible at both ends - at the carburetor, or at the CFI or SEFI throttle body - and at the transmission. The range of adjustment under the hood is limited. If you can't lengthen or shorten the rod sufficiently by turning the adjustment screw, set it at midrange and close the hood. You need to make your adjustment at the transmission.

9   Raise the vehicle and place it securely on jackstands.

10   Loosen the sliding trunnion block on the rod. It's near exhaust components that might be hot, so be careful! Push the lower end of the rod firmly so that the other end of the rod makes contact with the throttle lever. Tighten the bolt on the trunnion block.

11   Lower the vehicle and verify that the rod has maintained contact with the throttle lever.

5   Throttle valve (TV) cable (AOD) - adjustment

1980 through 1986 models

Linkage adjustment at the carburetor

Refer to illustration 5.3

1   Remove the air cleaner.

2   Release the choke fast-idle cam so that the throttle lever is at the idle stop.

3   Turn the linkage lever adjusting screw counterclockwise until the end is flush with the lever face **(see illustration)**.

4   Turn the linkage lever adjusting screw clockwise to obtain 0.005-inch clearance between the end of the screw and the throttle lever.

5   Turn the linkage lever adjusting screw clockwise three full turns.

Note: *One turn is the minimum permissible if screw travel is limited. If one turn isn't possible, refer to the transmission linkage adjustment procedure.*

6   Adjust the idle speed (see Chapter 1).

7   With the throttle lever in the idle stop position, verify that the linkage lever and throttle lever contact one another.

Linkage adjustment at the transmission

Refer to illustrations 5.9, 5.10 and 5.11

8   If it's impossible to adjust the carburetor linkage adjustment screw, adjust instead the length of the TV control rod assembly (this adjustment is also required when a new TV control rod assembly is installed).

9   Loosen the 8mm bolt on the TV control rod sliding trunnion block. Remove dirt and corrosion from the control rod so that the trunnion block slides freely in the control rod **(see illustration)**.

10   Push up on the lower end of the TV control rod to insure that the carburetor linkage lever is held firmly against the throttle lever **(see**

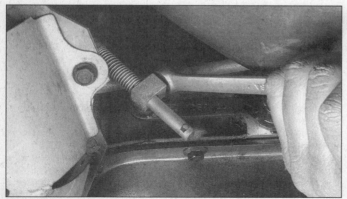

5.9 Loosen the 8mm bolt on the TV control rod sliding trunnion block. Remove dirt and corrosion from the control rod so that the trunnion block slides freely in the control rod

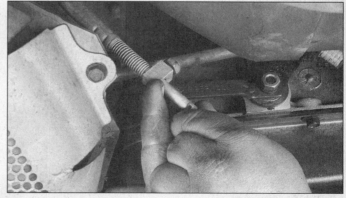

5.10 Push up on the lower end of the TV control rod to insure that the carburetor linkage lever is held firmly against the throttle lever; when the pressure is released, the control rod must stay in position

7

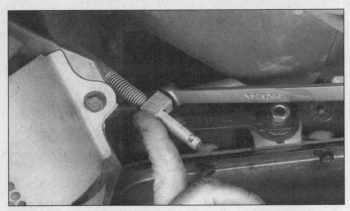

5.11 While maintaining pressure, tighten the trunnion block bolt; be sure to verify that the throttle lever is at the idle stop

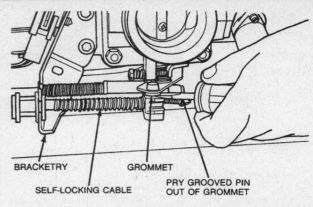

BRACKETRY   GROMMET

SELF-LOCKING CABLE   PRY GROOVED PIN
OUT OF GROMMET

5.15 Pry the grooved pin on the cable assembly out of the grommet on the throttle body lever with a wide-bladed screwdriver

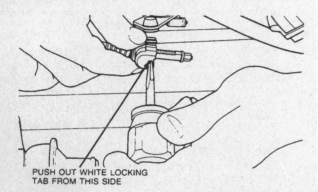

PUSH OUT WHITE LOCKING
TAB FROM THIS SIDE

5.16 Push the white locking tab out with a small screwdriver

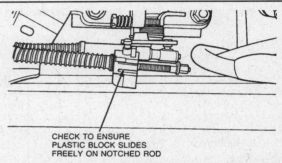

CHECK TO ENSURE
PLASTIC BLOCK SLIDES
FREELY ON NOTCHED ROD

5.17 Make sure the plastic block with the pin and tab slides freely on the notched rod; if it doesn't, the white tab may not be pushed out far enough

IMPORTANT: HOLD THE THROTTLE LEVER FIRMLY AGAINST IDLE STOP WHILE PUSHING GROUND PIN INTO GROMMET ENSURE THAT YOU DO NOT MOVE THROTTLE LEVER AWAY FROM IDLE STOP

GROOVED PIN-PUSH
GROOVED PIN INTO GROMMET

GROOVED PIN FULLY INSTALLED
WHILE HOLDING THROTTLE LEVER
FIRMLY AGAINST IDLE STOP

5.18 Hold the throttle lever firmly against the idle stop and push the grooved pin into the grommet on the throttle lever as far as it will go; make sure not to move the throttle lever away from the idle stop during this procedure

illustration). When the pressure is released, the control rod must stay in position.

11   Using firm pressure, force the TV control lever on the transmission against an internal stop. The control rod should not bind in the sliding trunnion block. While maintaining pressure, tighten the trunnion block bolt (see illustration). Be sure to verify that the throttle lever is at the idle stop.

1987 and later models

Refer to illustrations 5.15, 5.16, 5.17 and 5.18

12   The Throttle Valve (TV) cable and linkage controls transmission line pressure, shift points, shift feel, part throttle downshifts and detent downshifts. If the TV linkage is broken, sticky or misadjusted, the vehicle will experience a number of problems such as early and/or soft upshifts and no downshift or a harsh downshift function.

13   The engine should not be running and the shift lever must be in Neutral during this adjustment.

14   Remove the air cleaner assembly and inlet tube for access to the TV cable at the throttle lever.

15   Pry the grooved pin on the cable assembly out of the grommet on the throttle body lever with a wide-bladed screwdriver (see illustration).

16   Push the white locking tab out with a small screwdriver (see illustration).

17   Make sure the plastic block with the pin and tab slides freely on the notched rod (see illustration). If it doesn't, the white tab may not be pushed out far enough.

18   Hold the throttle lever firmly against the idle stop and push the grooved pin into the grommet on the throttle lever as far as it will go (see illustration). Don't move the throttle lever away from the idle stop during this procedure.

19   Install the air cleaner assembly.

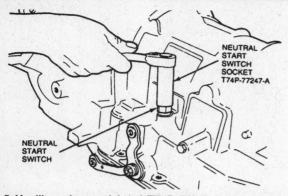

6.5 You'll need a special tool (T74P-77247-A, or equivalent) to remove the neutral start switch (arrow) on vehicles with an AOD transmission

6 Neutral start switch - check and replacement

AOD transmission

Check

1   To check the operation of the neutral start switch, apply the parking brake and try to start the engine in each position of the selector lever. The engine should start only in Park and Neutral. If it starts in any other position, adjust the shift linkage (see Section 3) and retest. If the engine still starts in any position other than Park or Neutral, replace the switch.

Replacement

Refer to illustration 6.5

2   Disconnect the cable from the negative battery terminal, place the shift lever in Low and apply the parking brake.
3   Raise the vehicle and place it securely on jackstands.
4   Unplug the electrical connector from the neutral start switch.
5   Carefully remove the switch and O-ring with Ford socket tool T74P-77247-A **(see illustration)**, or a suitable equivalent.
6   Install the switch and new O-ring and tighten it to the torque listed in this Chapter's Specifications. The Ford tool is designed to remove and install the switch without damaging it. If the tool is not available, be very careful to not overtighten the switch. Caution: *It is easy to crush or puncture the walls of the switch, so be careful.*
7   Install the electrical connector.
8   Connect the negative battery cable.
9   Verify that the engine starts only when the selector is in the Neutral and Park positions.

AODE transmission

10   The AODE transmission used on 1992 through 1994 models does not have a neutral start switch. That function has been incorporated into an information sensor known as the Manual Lever Position (MLP) sensor. And 1995 and later models, which are equipped with a 4R70W transmission, use a transmission range (TR) sensor; a similar device. For more information regarding the MLP and the TR sensors, refer to Chapter 6.

7 Transmission mount - check and replacement

Refer to illustration 7.1

1   Insert a large screwdriver or prybar into the space between the transmission extension housing and the crossmember and try to pry the transmission up slightly **(see illustration)**. The transmission should not move away from the mount much at all. If it does, replace the mount.
2   To replace the mount, remove the nuts attaching the mount to the

7.1 To check the transmission mount, pry between the crossmember and the mount - there should be very little movement; to replace a mount, remove the nuts (lower arrows) that attach the mount to the crossmember, then remove the bolts (upper arrows)

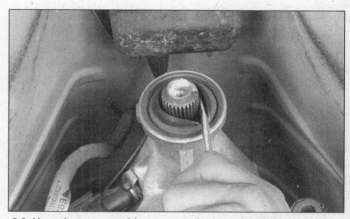

8.3 Use a large screwdriver or a seal removal tool to pry the seal out of the transmission extension housing

crossmember, then remove the bolts attaching the mount to the transmission extension housing.
3   Raise the transmission slightly with a jack and remove the mount.
4   Installation is the reverse of the removal procedure. Be sure to tighten the nuts/bolts securely.

8 Oil seal replacement

Extension housing seal

Refer to illustrations 8.3 and 8.5

1   Oil leaks frequently occur due to wear of the extension housing oil seal and bushing (if equipped), and/or the speedometer drive gear oil seal and O-ring. Replacement of these seals is relatively easy, since the repairs can usually be performed without removing the transmission from the vehicle.
2   The extension housing oil seal is located at the extreme rear of the transmission, where the driveshaft is attached. If leakage at the seal is suspected, raise the vehicle and support it securely on jackstands. If the seal is leaking, transmission lubricant will be built up on the front of the driveshaft and may be dripping from the rear of the transmission.
3   Using a screwdriver or pry bar, carefully pry the oil seal out of the rear of the transmission **(see illustration)**. Do not damage the splines on the transmission output shaft.

7

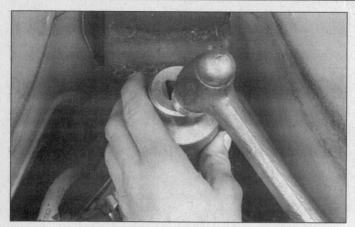

8.5 A large socket and hammer can be used to tap the new seal evenly into the bore

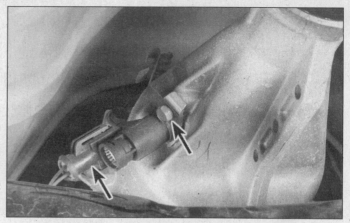

8.7 The speedometer driven gear housing, or vehicle speed sensor (shown), is located on the left side of the extension housing. To remove a driven gear housing or a speed sensor, simply remove the speedometer cable (speedometer driven gear only) or unplug the electrical connector (some electric speedometers and all vehicle speed sensors), then remove the hold-down bolt (all models)

4   If the oil seal cannot be removed with a screwdriver or pry bar, a special oil seal removal tool (available at auto parts stores) will be required.

5   Using a large section of pipe or a very large deep socket as a drift, install the new oil seal. Drive it into the bore squarely and make sure it's completely seated **(see illustration)**.

6   Lubricate the splines of the transmission output shaft and the outside of the driveshaft sleeve yoke with lightweight grease, then install the driveshaft. Be careful not to damage the lip of the new seal.

Speedometer driven gear housing/vehicle speed sensor O-ring

Refer to illustrations 8.7, 8.8 and 8.9

7   The speedometer cable and driven gear housing or the vehicle speed sensor AODE transmissions) is located on the side of the extension housing **(see illustration)**. Look for transmission oil around the cable housing to determine if the seal and O-ring are leaking.

8   Disconnect the speedometer cable or electrical connector **(see illustration)**.

9   Using a hook, remove the seal **(see illustration)**.

10   Install a new O-ring in the driven gear housing and reinstall the driven gear housing and cable assembly on the extension housing.

Vacuum modulator O-ring

Refer to illustrations 8.13 and 8.14

11   Raise the vehicle and place it securely on jackstands.

12   Drain the transmission (see Chapter 1), or be prepared for some

ATF to spill out when the modulator is removed.

13   Disconnect the vacuum line, remove the modulator hold-down bolt **(see illustration)** and remove the modulator.

14   Remove the old O-ring from the modulator **(see illustration)**.

15   Coat the new O-ring with clean ATF and install it.

16   Installation is the reverse of removal. Tighten the hold-down bolt securely. Refill the transmission (see Chapter 1).

Manual lever O-ring

Refer to illustration 8.17

Note: *The manual lever also has a seal, but in order to replace it, you must drop the pan and remove the valve body. Because the internal linkage connecting the manual lever shaft to the valve body is difficult to disconnect, and even more difficult to reattach correctly, we don't recommend attempting this procedure at home. If the manual lever seal is leaking, take the vehicle to a dealer service department or an other qualified repair shop.*

17   Disconnect the shift linkage from the manual lever **(see illustration)**.

18   Using a small hooked tool, pry out the old seal.

19   Using a deep socket and a hammer, place the new seal square to the bore and drive it into place.

20   Reconnect and adjust the shift linkage.

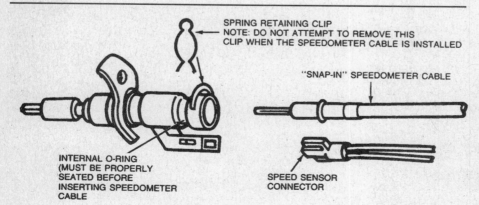

8.8 Typical speedometer driven gear assembly details (mechanical units have a speedometer cable; electric units have an electrical connector)

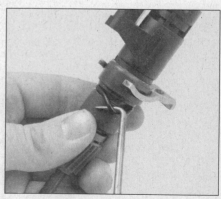

8.9 To replace the O-ring on a speedometer driven gear housing, or on a vehicle speed sensor (shown), simply pull it off with a hooked removal tool

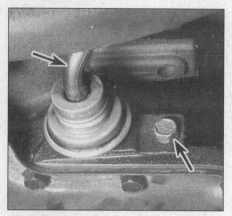

8.13 To remove the vacuum modulator, detach the vacuum line (arrow) and remove the hold-down bolt (arrow)

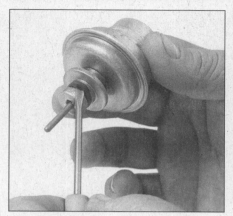

8.14 Remove the old modulator O-ring with a small screwdriver

8.17 To get to the old manual lever O-ring, remove this nut (arrow) and detach the linkage

21 Refill the transmission (see Chapter 1).
22 Remove the jackstands and lower the vehicle.

9 Automatic transmission - removal and installation

Removal

Refer to illustrations 9.3, 9.4, 9.5, 9.14a, 9.14b and 9.19

1 Disconnect the cable from the negative terminal of the battery.
2 Raise the vehicle and support it securely on jackstands.
3 Drain the transmission fluid (see Chapter 1), then reinstall the pan. Disconnect the oil cooler line fittings **(see illustration)** and plug the lines to prevent contamination.
4 Remove the torque converter cover **(see illustration)**.
5 Mark the relationship of the torque converter to one of the studs so they can be installed in the same position **(see illustration)**.
6 Remove the torque converter-to-driveplate nuts. Turn the crankshaft for access to each nut. Turn the crankshaft in a clockwise direction only (as viewed from the front).
7 Rotate the torque converter until the drain plug is at its lowest point. Place the pan under the torque converter, remove the drain plug and allow the fluid to drain. Install the drain plug and tighten it securely.
8 Remove the starter motor (see Chapter 5).
9 Remove the driveshaft (see Chapter 8).
10 Disconnect the speedometer cable or speed sensor electrical connector (see Section 8).

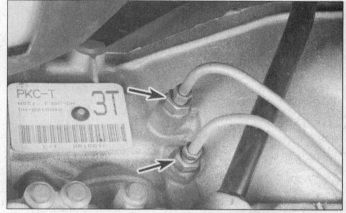

9.3 Unscrew the oil cooler line fittings (arrows), pull the lines away from the transmission and plug them to keep out dirt and moisture

11 Detach all electrical connectors from the transmission.
12 Remove any exhaust components which will interfere with transmission removal (see Chapter 4).
13 On C6 and earlier AOD units, disconnect the TV rod (see Section 4); on AOD units, disconnect the TV cable (see Section 5).

7

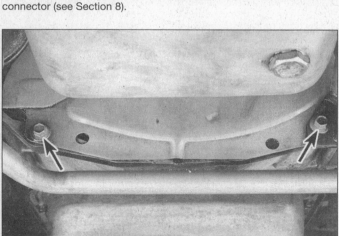

9.4 To remove the torque converter cover, remove these bolts (arrows)

9.5 Mark a torque converter stud to the driveplate to ensure that they're still in dynamic balance when reassembled

9.14a To disconnect the shift cable from the manual lever on newer vehicles, simply pop it loose with a screwdriver

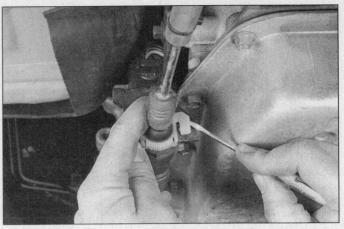

9.14b To disconnect the shift cable from this bracket on newer vehicles, pop the retainer clip positioning pin loose with a small screwdriver, then pry off the retainer clip

14   Disconnect the shift rod or cable from the manual lever and, on some vehicles, from the transmission cable bracket **(see illustrations)**.

15   Support the engine with a jack. Use a block of wood under the oil pan to spread the load.

16   Support the transmission with a jack - preferably a jack made for this purpose. Safety chains will help steady the transmission on the jack.

17   Remove the two mount-to-transmission extension housing bolts (see Section 7).

18   Raise the transmission, remove the crossmember-to-frame bolts, then lower the crossmember.

19   Lower the transmission. Remove the two upper transmission-to-engine bolts and the upper transmission-to-engine stud (to the right of the two upper bolts). Remove the bolts securing the lower part of the transmission bellhousing to the engine **(see illustration)**.

20   Disconnect and plug the transmission fluid cooler lines.

21   Remove the transmission dipstick tube.

22   Move the transmission to the rear to disengage it from the engine block dowel pins and make sure the torque converter is detached from the driveplate. Secure the torque converter to the transmission so it won't fall out during removal.

Installation

23   Prior to installation, make sure the torque converter hub is securely engaged in the pump. This can be done by turning the torque converter while pushing it in toward the transmission. If the converter was not fully engaged, it will "clunk" into place (it may even "clunk" more than once).

24   With the transmission secured to the jack, raise it into position. Be sure to keep it level so the torque converter does not slide forward.

25   Turn the torque converter to line up the studs with the holes in the driveplate. The mark on the torque converter and the stud made in Step 5 must line up.

26   Move the transmission forward carefully until the dowel pins and the torque converter are engaged.

27   Install the transmission-to-engine bolts. Tighten them to the torque listed in this Chapter's Specifications.

28   Install the torque converter-to-driveplate nuts. Tighten the nuts to the torque listed in this Chapter's Specifications.

29   Connect the transmission fluid cooler lines.

30   Install the transmission mount and crossmember through-bolts.

9.19 Left side lower transmission-to-engine bolts (arrows) (some vehicles may have only two bolts on this side)

Tighten the bolts and nuts securely.

31   Remove the jacks supporting the transmission and the engine.

32   Install the dipstick tube. Install the oil cooler line fittings and tighten them to the torque listed in this Chapter's Specifications.

33   Install the starter motor (see Chapter 5).

34   Connect the vacuum hose(s) (if equipped).

35   Connect the shift and TV linkage (see Sections 3 and 4).

36   Plug in the transmission wire harness connectors.

37   Install the torque converter cover.

38   Install the driveshaft (see Chapter 8).

39   Connect the speedometer cable or speed sensor connector.

40   Adjust the shift linkage (see Section 3).

41   Install any exhaust system components that were removed or disconnected (see Chapter 4).

42   Lower the vehicle.

43   Fill the transmission with the specified fluid (see Chapter 1), run the engine and check for fluid leaks.

Chapter 8 Driveline

Contents

Specifications

Torque specifications

	Ft-lbs (unless otherwise indicated)
Driveshaft companion flange bolts	71 to 95
Differential pinion shaft lock bolt	15 to 30
Differential cover bolts	
Metal cover	25 to 35
Plastic cover	15 to 20
Companion flange/pinion nut (minimum)	140
Pinion bearing preload	
Used bearings	8 to 14 in-lbs
New bearings	16 to 29 in-lbs

1   General information

The information in this Chapter deals with the components from the rear of the transmission to the rear wheels. For the purposes of this Chapter, these components are grouped into two categories: driveshaft and rear axle assembly. Separate Sections within this Chapter offer general descriptions and checking procedures for components in each of the two groups.

Since nearly all the procedures covered in this Chapter involve working under the vehicle, make sure it's securely supported on sturdy jackstands or on a hoist where the vehicle can be easily raised and lowered.

2   Driveshaft - inspection

1   Raise the rear of the vehicle and support it securely on jackstands.
2   Crawl under the vehicle and visually inspect the driveshaft. Look for any dents or cracks in the tubing. If any are found, the driveshaft must be replaced.
3   Check for any oil leakage at the front and rear of the driveshaft. Leakage where the driveshaft enters the transmission indicates a defective transmission rear seal. Leakage where the driveshaft enters the differential indicates a defective pinion seal.
4   While under the vehicle, have an assistant turn a rear wheel so the driveshaft will rotate. As it does, make sure the universal joints are operating properly without binding, noise or looseness.
5   The universal joints can also be checked with the driveshaft motionless, by gripping your hands on either side of the joint and attempting to twist the joint. Any movement at all in the joint is a sign of considerable wear. Lifting up on the shaft will also indicate movement

in the universal joints.
6   Finally, check the driveshaft mounting bolts at the ends to make sure they are tight.

3   Driveshaft - removal and installation

Refer to illustrations 3.2 and 3.3
1   Raise the rear of the vehicle an support it securely on jackstands.
2   Mark the relationship of the driveshaft to the differential companion flange **(see illustration)**.

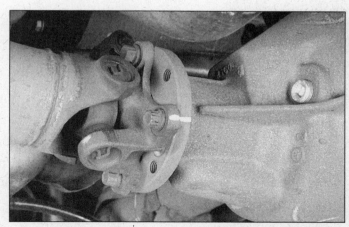

3.2 Mark the relationship of the driveshaft to the differential companion flange to ensure that the driveshaft retains its dynamic balance after reinstalling it

8

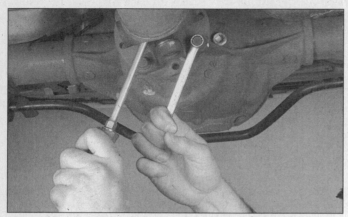

3.3 To remove the bolts that attach the driveshaft to the differential companion flange, insert a small prybar or large screwdriver through the rear U-joint and hold the driveshaft while you break loose the four flange bolts

3   Remove the bolts and separate the driveshaft from the differential companion flange (a 12-point socket or box end wrench will be necessary) **(see illustration)**. Pull the driveshaft toward the rear to remove it.

4   Wrap a plastic bag tightly around the extension housing of the transmission to prevent fluid loss.

5   Installation is the reverse of removal. Be sure to align the reference marks made during removal.

4   Universal joints - replacement

Single-cardan U-joints (some 1970 through 1988 models and all 1989 and later models)

Refer to illustrations 4.2a, 4.2b, 4.2c, 4.4 and 4.9

Note: *A press or large vise will be required for this procedure. It may be advisable to take the driveshaft to a local dealer service department, service station or machine shop where the universal joints can be replaced for you, normally at a reasonable charge.*

1   Remove the driveshaft as outlined in the previous Section.

2   Using a small pair of pliers, remove the snap-rings from the spider **(see illustrations)**.

3   Supporting the driveshaft, place it in position on a workbench equipped with a vise.

4   Place a piece of pipe or a large socket with the same inside diameter over one of the bearing caps. Position a socket which is of slightly smaller diameter than the cap on the opposite bearing cap **(see illustration)** and use the vise or press to force the cap out (inside the

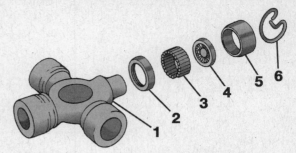

4.2a Exploded view of the universal joint components (thrust washers are not used before 1991)

1	*Spider*	*4*	*Thrust washer*
2	*Seal*	*5*	*Cap*
3	*Bearings*	*6*	*Snap-ring*

pipe or large socket), stopping just before it comes completely out of the yoke. Use the vise or large pliers to work the cap the rest of the way out.

5   Transfer the sockets to the other side and press the opposite bearing cap out in the same manner.

6   Pack the new universal joint bearings with grease. Ordinarily, specific instructions for lubrication will be included with the universal joint servicing kit and should be followed carefully.

7   Position the spider in the yoke and partially install one bearing cap in the yoke.

8   Start the spider into the bearing cap and then partially install the other cap. Align the spider and press the bearing caps into position, being careful not to damage the dust seals.

9   Install the snap-rings. If difficulty is encountered in seating the snap-rings, strike the driveshaft yoke sharply with a hammer. This will spring the yoke ears slightly and allow the snap-rings to seat in the groove **(see illustration)**.

10   Install the grease fitting and fill the joint with grease. Be careful not to overfill the joint, as this could blow out the grease seals.

11   Install the driveshaft, tightening the companion flange bolts to the torque listed in this Chapter's Specifications.

Double-cardan U-joints

Refer to illustrations 4.12a, 4.12b, 4.13, 4.14a, 4.14b, 4.15a, 4.15b, 4.16a, 4.16b, 4.17, 4.18, 4.19, 4.20a, 4.20b, 4.22a, 4.22b, 4.22c, 4.22d and 4.22e

Note: *The following overhaul procedure depicts a rear double-cardan U-joint, but the procedure for rebuilding the front U-joint is basically the same. The only difference is that, instead of a companion flange bolted to the drive flange (as used at the differential end of the driveshaft), the front end uses a centering socket bolted to the slip yoke. So, overhauling the front U-joint is actually a little easier than the rear unit*

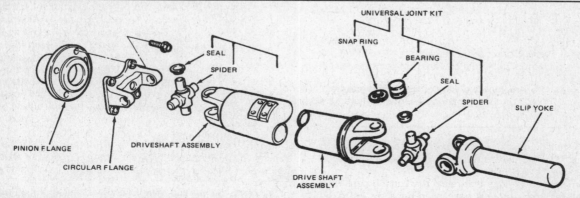

4.2b Exploded view of a typical driveshaft assembly (1991 and later models also have a thrust washer between the bearings and the cap)

4.2c A pair of needle-nose pliers can be used to remove the universal joint snap-rings

4.4 To press the universal joint out of the driveshaft yoke, set it up in a vise with the small socket pushing the joint and bearing cap into the large socket

4.9 If the snap-ring will not seat in the groove, strike the yoke with a brass hammer - this will relieve the tension that has set up in the yoke, and slightly spring the yoke ears (this should also be done if the joint feels tight when assembled)

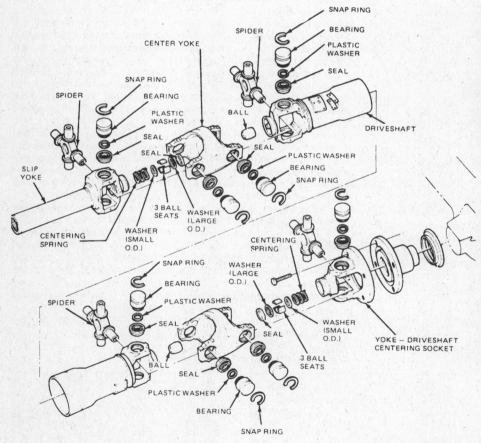

4.12a An exploded view of the double-cardan setup (1979 Lincoln Continental shown, others similar)

4.12b Remove all the old snap-rings

4.13 Marking the relationship of the parts to one another is essential, if you want to preserve dynamic balance and fit; if you're rebuilding the rear U-joint (the one depicted in these photos), mark the companion flange, the center yoke and the driveshaft yoke; if you're overhauling the front U-joint, mark the slip yoke, the centering socket yoke, the center yoke and the front driveshaft yoke.

8

depicted here, because you only have to press out two front spider bearing caps; the other two can be replaced by simply unbolting the centering socket from the slip yoke.

12   Remove the eight snap-rings that retain the bearing caps (see illustrations). Note: Some models have snap-rings on the outer surface of the bearing caps, while on other models the snap-rings are seated in a groove on the inner surface of the cap. Additionally, on

some models the bearing caps are retained by injected-plastic retaining rings - the plastic breaks as the joint is disassembled. Snap-rings will be installed during reassembly (they'll be included in the U-joint kit).

13   Mark the relationship of the companion flange, the center yoke and the driveshaft yoke (see illustration) or, if you're overhauling the front U-joint, the slip yoke, the centering socket yoke, the center yoke

4.14a Once you have pushed out a cap about 3/8-inch, twist it out with a pair of water pump pliers . . .

4.14b . . . and remove the cap

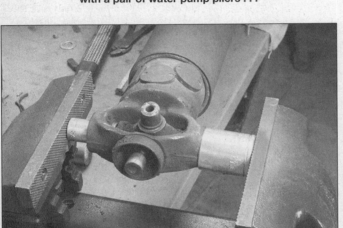

4.15a Once you have removed the center yoke, you can remove the two bearing caps from the driveshaft yoke in the same fashion: Place a large socket on one side and a smaller socket on the opposite side, then push the cap on the right into the larger socket until it protrudes about 3/8-inch as described above, twist the cap off with a pair of water pump pliers . . .

and the front driveshaft yoke. **Caution:** *The U-joints must be assembled with these pieces in their original positions to provide proper clearance.*

14   Starting with the two bearing caps in the companion flange end of the center yoke, position the U-joint in a bench vise as shown, with a smaller socket on one side, to push against the bearing cap and spider, and a larger socket on the other side, with an inside diameter large enough to allow the opposite bearing cap to protrude into it without interference **(see illustration 4.13)**. Tighten the jaws of the vise until the bearing protrudes about 3/8-inch out of the yoke. Loosen the vise jaws, rotate the U-joint 90-degrees so that you can get at the protruding bearing cap, work the cap out with a pair of water pump pliers **(see illustration)** and remove the cap **(see illustration)**. Then rotate the U-joint another 90-degrees, install the large and small socket again and press out and remove the opposite bearing cap (the one you just pushed in to drive out the first cap). Note that the companion flange spider bearings are being removed first. Then do the other two bearing caps for that spider. It's easier to start with the outermost spider, regardless of which U-joint you're overhauling. In other words, if you're rebuilding the rear U-joint, remove the spider and bearing caps that attach the companion flange to the rear end of the center yoke, then remove the spider and bearing caps that attach the forward end of the center yoke to the rear driveshaft yoke. If you're rebuilding the front U-joint, remove the spider and caps that attach the slip yoke and center yoke to the front of the center yoke, then do the spider and caps that attach the rear end of the center yoke to the forward

4.15b . . . and remove the cap; then flip the U-joint around and remove the other bearing cap the same way

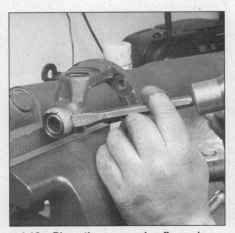

4.16a Place the companion flange in a bench vise as shown and remove the dust cover and centering ball: Since you're not going to reuse it, you can knock the old dust cover off with a hammer and chisel

4.16b Once you've got the dust cover off, rotate the centering ball as shown, grab it with the bench vise jaws and carefully tap off the companion flange

4.17 Carefully tap a new centering ball and dust cover onto the companion flange with a large socket; just make sure you don't damage the bearing surface of the centering ball (Dana units simply use a circular, flat seal, not a dust cover, to protect the centering ball)

4.18 Install a new spider bearing into the driveshaft yoke and secure it with a couple of new bearing caps (be sure to install a new seal with each new bearing cap unless, of course, the seals are integral with the caps, as they are in the Dana kit used in these photos)

4.19 Place the driveshaft yoke in the bench vise and press two opposite caps into the yoke until they're flush with the driveshaft yoke, then install a couple of sockets and press the caps into the yoke until they're fully seated (tops of caps flush with snap-ring grooves)

4.20a Install the center yoke on the other two legs of the new spider (make sure the marks you made on the center yoke and the driveshaft yoke are lined up) . . .

4.20b . . . and hold it in place with a couple more new bearing caps and seals place the driveshaft in the vise, press the two caps into the center yoke until they're flush with the yoke, install the two sockets, press the caps all the way in and install the snap-rings

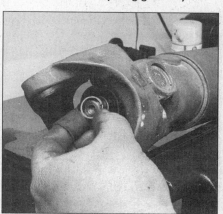

4.22a Install the centering spring and, if applicable, a new dust seal for the centering ball

driveshaft yoke.

15   After you've got the center yoke off, remove the two bearing caps from the driveshaft yoke in the same fashion as described above **(see illustrations)**.

16   Place the companion flange in a bench vise as shown and remove the dust cover and centering ball **(see illustrations)**.

17   Install a new centering ball and dust cover on the companion flange **(see illustration)**.

18   Install the new spider bearing in the driveshaft yoke and secure it with a couple of new bearing caps **(see illustration)**. Make sure the grease fitting on the spider faces *away* from the center yoke; if the spider is installed with the grease fitting facing toward the center yoke, it could create a clearance problem, and you won't be able to grease the spider. Don't forget to install a new seal with each new bearing cap **(see illustration 4.12a)**. Note: *The seals are integral with the caps on some rebuild kits.*

19   Place the driveshaft yoke in the bench vise and press the two caps into the yoke until they're flush with the driveshaft yoke **(see illustration)**.

20   Install the center yoke on the other two legs of the new spider and hold it in place with a couple more new bearing caps and seals **(see illustrations)**. Make sure the marks you made on the center yoke and the driveshaft yoke are lined up. Place the driveshaft in the vise and press the two caps into the center yoke until they're flush with the yoke.

21   Install a pair of sockets between each opposing pair of bearing caps and press in the caps until they're fully seated (the tops of the bearing caps must be flush with the lower edges of the snap-ring grooves in the driveshaft yoke, center yoke and companion flange (or the driveshaft yoke and center yoke, if you're rebuilding a front U-joint).

22   Install the centering spring **(see illustration)** and a new center seal on the centering stud and guide the centering stud into the centering ball. Connect the companion flange to the other end of the center yoke with a new spider **(see illustration)**. Make sure the grease fitting on the spider faces away from the center yoke **(see illustration)**; if the spider is installed with the grease fitting facing toward the center yoke, it could create a clearance problem, and you won't be able to grease the spider. Tap a couple of bearing caps into the center yoke to hold everything together **(see illustration)**, press in the caps so they're flush with the center yoke, press the other two caps into the companion flange until they're flush with the companion flange, then press in all four caps with a pair of sockets until they're fully seated.

8

4.22b Attach the companion flange to the center yoke with the other new spider

4.22c Make sure the grease fitting on the spider faces away from the center yoke (toward the companion flange) to avoid clearance problems, and to provide access to the fitting for lubrication

4.22d Tap the new bearing caps into place to hold the spider, then press in the caps the same way you did the caps for the other spider, with a pair of sockets

4.22e After the new bearing caps are fully seated (flush with the snap-ring grooves in the yokes), install new snap-rings

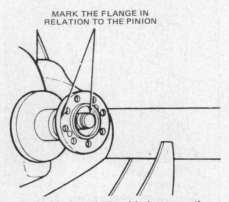

5.4 Mark the relationship between the pinion and flange as shown

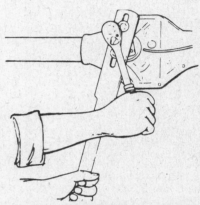

5.5 Hold the flange to keep it from turning while you're removing the pinion nut

Install new snap-rings **(see illustration)**. Note: *If difficulty is encountered in seating the snap-rings, strike the driveshaft yoke(s) sharply with a hammer. This will spring the yoke ears slightly and allow the snap-rings to seat in the groove* **(see illustration)**.
23   Disassembling and reassembling a front U-joint is a similar procedure, except that the front spider can be disconnected from the slip yoke by removing the centering socket.

5   Differential pinion oil seal - replacement

Refer to illustrations 5.4, 5.5, 5.6 and 5.8

1   Loosen the rear wheel lug nuts, raise the rear of the vehicle and place it securely on jackstands. Remove the rear wheels.
2   Remove the brake drums or calipers (see Chapter 9).
3   Mark the driveshaft and companion flange for ease of realignment during reassembly, then remove the driveshaft (see Section 3).
4   Mark the relationship between the pinion and companion flange **(see illustration)**.
5   Using an inch-pound torque wrench, measure and record the torque required to turn the pinion nut through several revolutions (pinion bearing preload). Using a suitable tool, hold the companion flange and remove the pinion nut **(see illustration)**. Using a suitable puller, remove the companion flange.
6   Pry out the old seal with a slide hammer and reversed jaws or other appropriate tool as shown **(see illustration)**. It may also be removed with a hammer and chisel.

7   Clean the oil seal mounting surface.
8   Tap the new seal into place, taking care to insert it squarely as shown **(see illustration)**.
9   Inspect the splines on the pinion shaft for burrs and nicks. Remove any rough areas with a crocus cloth. Wipe the splines clean.
10   Install the companion flange, aligning it with the marks made during removal. Gently tap the flange on with a soft-faced hammer until you can start the pinion nut on the pinion shaft.
11   Using a suitable tool, hold the companion flange while tightening the pinion nut to the minimum torque listed in this Chapter's Specifications. While tightening, take frequent rotational torque measurements, using the inch-pound torque wrench, until the measurement recorded in Step four is reached. **Caution:** *If the measurement recorded in Step four was less than the pinion bearing*

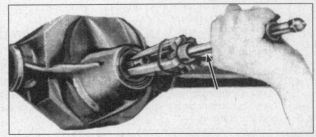

5.6 Pry out the old seal with a slide hammer and reversed jaws, or a similar setup

5.8 Tap the new pinion seal into place with the seal square to the bore

6.3a Position a large screwdriver between the rear axle case and a ring gear bolt to keep the differential case from turning when removing the pinion shaft lock bolt

6.3b Rotate the differential case 180-degrees and slide the pinion shaft out of the case until the stepped part of the shaft contacts the ring gear

6.4 Push in on the axle flange and remove the C-lock (arrow) from the inner end of the axleshaft

6.5 Pull the axle out of the housing, supporting it with one hand to prevent damage to the seal

7.2 Use a seal removal tool to remove the old seal from the axle housing

preload torque listed in this Chapter's Specifications, continue tightening until the specified preload is reached. If it was more than specified, stop when the specified preload is reached. Under no circumstances should the pinion nut be backed off to reduce pinion bearing preload. Increase the nut torque in small increments and check the preload after each increase.

12   Reinstall the driveshaft, brake drums and wheels.
13   Check the differential oil level and fill as necessary.
14   Lower the vehicle and take a test drive to check for leaks.

6   Axleshaft - removal and installation

Refer to illustrations 6.3a, 6.3b, 6.4 and 6.5

1   Loosen the wheel lug nuts, raise the rear of the vehicle, support it securely on jackstands and remove the wheel. Also remove the brake drum, or the caliper and disc (see Chapter 9).
2   Remove the cover from the differential carrier and allow the lubricant to drain into a container.
3   Remove the lock bolt from the differential pinion shaft. Slide the notched end of the pinion shaft out of the differential case as far as it will go **(see illustrations)**.
4   Push the outer (flanged) end of the axleshaft in and remove the C-lock from the inner end of the shaft **(see illustration)**.
5   Withdraw the axleshaft, taking care not to damage the oil seal in the end of the axle housing as the splined end of the axleshaft passes through it **(see illustration)**.
6   Installation is the reverse of removal. Tighten the differential pinion shaft lock bolt to the torque listed in this Chapter's Specifications.

7.3 Using a seal driver to install the new axleshaft oil seal

7   Install the differential cover (see Chapter 1).
8   Refill the axle with the correct quantity and grade of lubricant (see Chapter 1).

7   Axleshaft oil seal - replacement

Refer to illustrations 7.2 and 7.3

1   Remove the axleshaft as described in the preceding Section.
2   Pry the old oil seal out of the end of the axle housing, using a seal removal tool or the inner end of the axleshaft itself as a lever **(see illustration)**.
3   Using a seal driver or a large socket, tap the seal into position so

8

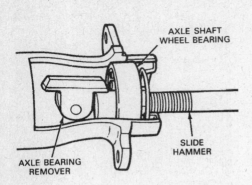

8.2 Use a bearing removal tool attached to a slide hammer to remove the axle bearing

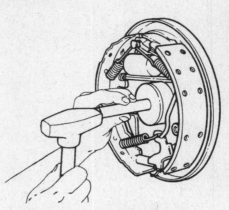

8.4 A correctly sized bearing driver must be used to drive the bearing into the housing

9.8 To remove the torque plate or brake backing plate from the axle assembly, remove these four bolts (arrows)

that the lips are facing in and the metal face is visible from the end of the axle housing **(see illustration)**. When correctly installed, the face of the oil seal should be flush with the end of the axle housing. Lubricate the lips of the seal with gear oil.

4   Install the axleshaft (see Section 6).

8   Axleshaft bearing - replacement

Refer to illustrations 8.2 and 8.4

1   Remove the axleshaft (see Section 6) and the oil seal (see Section 7).

2   A bearing puller will be required or a tool which will engage behind the bearing will have to be fabricated **(see illustration)**.

3   Attach a slide hammer and pull the bearing out of the axle housing.

4   Clean out the bearing recess and drive in the new bearing with a bearing driver **(see illustration)**. Lubricate the new bearing with gear lubricant. Make sure that the bearing is tapped into the full depth of its recess.

5   Discard the old oil seal and install a new one (see Section 7), then install the axleshaft.

9   Rear axle assembly - removal and installation

Removal

Refer to illustration 9.8

Caution: *If the vehicle is equipped with air suspension, be sure to turn the air suspension switch to Off before beginning this procedure.*

1   Disconnect the cable from the negative battery terminal.

2   Loosen, but do not remove the rear wheel lug nuts. Block the front wheels and raise the rear of the vehicle. Support it securely on jackstands placed under the frame. Remove the rear wheels.

3   Remove the brake drums, or the calipers and discs (see Chapter 9).

4   Remove the rear axle cover and allow the lubricant to drain (see Chapter 1).

5   If the vehicle is equipped with ABS, remove the sensors from the torque plates (see Chapter 9).

6   Remove both rear axleshafts (see Section 6).

7   Free the ABS sensor wires, parking brake cables and brake lines from their clips on the axle housing.

8   Remove the four bolts that attach the brake drum backing plates (drum brake models) or torque plates (disc brake models) to the axle

housing **(see illustration)**. Detach the brake backing plate or torque plate assemblies from the housing and wire them out of the way.

9   Unbolt the driveshaft from the differential companion flange (see Section 3) and wire it out of the way.

10   Place a floor jack under the differential and raise the rear axle slightly.

11   Place a safety chain through the coil springs or disconnect the air springs (see Chapter 10).

12   Remove the shock absorber lower mounting bolts (see Chapter 10).

13   Remove the upper suspension arm-to-rear axle housing nuts and bolts (see Chapter 10). If the vehicle is equipped with air suspension, disconnect the height sensor (see Chapter 10).

14   Lower the axle housing until the coil springs are fully extended, then remove them. Or remove the air springs, if equipped.

15   Remove the lower suspension arm-to-axle housing nuts and bolts (see Chapter 10).

16   Lower the axle housing and guide it out from underneath the vehicle.

Installation

17   Raise the rear axle assembly into place and install the upper suspension arm-to-axle housing bolts and nuts. Don't completely tighten the nuts at this time.

18   Install the coil springs or air springs (see Chapter 10) and connect the lower suspension arms to the rear axle assembly.

19   Raise the axle housing to simulate normal ride height and tighten the upper and lower suspension arm-to-axle housing nuts to the torque listed in the Chapter 10 Specifications. If the vehicle is equipped with air springs, attach the height sensor (see Chapter 10).

20   Connect the lower ends of the shock absorbers to the rear axle housing and tighten the bolts to the torque listed in the Chapter 10 Specifications.

21   Connect the driveshaft to the differential companion flange, align the matchmarks and tighten the companion flange bolts to the torque listed in this Chapter's Specifications.

22   Attach the brake backing plates or torque plates to the axle housing and tighten the bolts securely.

23   Connect the brake sensor wires, the brake lines and the parking brake cables to their clips on the axle housing.

24   Install the axleshafts (see Section 6).

25   Install the brake drums, or the disc and calipers (see Chapter 10).

26   Install the rear axle cover and fill the differential with the recommended oil (see Chapter 1).

27   Install the wheels and lug nuts. Lower the vehicle and tighten the lug nuts to the torque listed in the Chapter 1 Specifications.

Chapter 9 Brakes

Contents

Specifications

Brake fluid type .... See Chapter 1

Disc brakes

Minimum brake pad thickness	See Chapter 1
Front brake disc	
Standard thickness	
1970 through 1979	1.18 inches
1980 and later	1.03 inches
Minimum thickness*	
1970 through 1979	1.12 inches
1980 through 1991	0.972 inch
1992 and later	0.974 inch
Runout limit	0.003 inch
Thickness variation (parallelism)	
1970 and 1971	0.0007 inch
1972 and 1973	
Continental	0.0005 inch
Mark IV	0.00025 inch
1974 through 1979	0.00025 inch
1980 through 1991	0.0005 inch
1992 and later	0.00035 inch

9

Disc brakes

Rear brake disc

Standard thickness
    1975 through 1990.. 0.945 inch
    1991 and later
        Town Car .... 0.500 inch
        Mark VII .... 0.944 inch
Minimum thickness*
    1975 through 1990.. 0.895 inch
    1991 and later
        Town Car .... 0.440 inch
        Mark VII .... 0.890 inch
Runout limit
    1975 through 1990.. 0.004 inch
    1991 and later .... 0.003 inch
Thickness variation (parallelism)
    1975 through 1979.. 0.0004 inch
    1980 and later .... 0.0005 inch

Refer to marks stamped on the disc (they supersede information printed here)

Drum brakes

Drum diameter
    Standard
        1970
            Continental .... 11.090 inches
            Mark III .... 11.030 inches
        1971 through 1979.. 11.030 inches
        1980 and 1981
            5.8L (351 cid) .... 11.030 inches
            5.0L (302 cid) .... 10.000 inches
        1982 and later... 10.000 inches
    Maximum*
        1970
            Continental .... 11.130 inches
            Mark III .... 11.090 inches
        1971 through 1979.. 11.090 inches
        1980 and 1981
            5.8L (351 cid) .... 11.090 inches
            5.0L (302 cid) .... 10.060 inches
        1982 and later... 10.060 inches
Brake pedal height
    1970 .... 5-49/64 to 6-7/8 inches
    1971
        Mark III .... 6-35/64 to 7-9/16 inches
        Continental.. 7-15/32 to 8-15/64 inches
    1972
        Mark IV .... 6-23/64 to 7-1/8 inches
        Continental.. 7-37/64 to 8-23/64 inches
    1973
        Mark IV .... 6-7/8 to 7-1/2 inches
        Continental.. 7-1/2 to 8-1/4 inches
    1974
        Mark IV .... 6-3/4 to 7-1/2 inches
        Continental.. 8-1/8 to 8-7/8 inches
    1975 and 1976
        Mark IV .... 6-7/8 to 7-7/8 inches
        Continental.. 8-1/8 to 9 inches
    1977
        Mark V .... 6-29/32 to 7-51/64 inches
        Continental.. 8-3/32 to 8-29/32
    1978 and 1979
        Mark V .... 6-29/32 to 7-51/64 inches
        Continental.. 8-13/64 to 9-3/32 inches
    1980 and 1981 .... 7-13/32 to 8-13/64 inches
    1982 and 1983
        Mark VI/Town Car .... 7-13/32 to 8-13/64 inches
        Continental.. 6-13/32 to 7-19/64 inches

Brake pedal height
    1984 through 1988
        Town Car .... 7-13/32 to 8-13/64 inches
        Mark VII/Continental .... 6-13/32 to 7-19/64 inches
    1989 through 1992 .... 7-13/32 to 8-13/64 inches
    1993 and later .... 7-1/2 to 8-19/64 inches

Refer to marks cast into the drum (they supersede information printed here)

Torque specifications

	Ft-lbs (unless otherwise indicated)
Brake caliper bolts (front)	
1980 through 1988	40 to 60
1989 through 1991	45 to 64
1992 through 1994	45 to 65
1995 and later	18 to 26
Brake hose-to-front caliper banjo bolts	
1980 and 1981	17 to 25
1982 through 1985	
Town Car	17 to 25
Continental and Mark VII	20 to 30
1986 through 1991	20 to 30
1992	32 to 44
1993 through 1994	30 to 40
1995 and later	30 to 45
Brake caliper bolts (rear)	
1982 through 1988	29 to 37
1989 through 1994	
Town Car	19 to 26
Mark VII	23 to 36
1995 and later	22 to 30
Brake hose-to-rear caliper banjo bolts	
1982 through 1988	20 to 30
1991 through 1995	30 to 40
Brake hose-to-brake line fittings	
1982 through 1992	120 to 216 in-lbs
1993 and later	120 to 180 in-lbs
Master cylinder to-power brake booster mounting nuts	13 to 25
Power brake booster-to-firewall mounting nuts	13 to 25
Wheel cylinder-to-brake backing plate mounting bolts	120 to 240 in-lbs

1 General information

General description

Refer to illustration 1.3

    All models covered by this manual are equipped with hydraulically-operated, power-assisted brake systems. All front brake systems are disc type, while the rear brakes are either disc or drum type. Some models are equipped with an Anti-lock Brake System (ABS), which is described in Section 2.

    All brakes are self-adjusting. The front and rear disc brakes automatically compensate for pad wear, while the rear drum brakes incorporate an adjustment mechanism which is activated as the brakes are applied.

    The hydraulic system is a split design, meaning there are separate circuits for the front and rear brakes **(see illustration)**. If one circuit fails, the other circuit will remain functional and a warning indicator will light up on the dashboard, showing that a failure has occurred.

Master cylinder

    The master cylinder is located under the hood, mounted to the power brake booster or the Hydro-Boost unit. On older, cast-iron units, the reservoir is an integral part of the master cylinder body; on newer, aluminum units, a removable plastic reservoir is attached to the top of the master cylinder body. Both types of reservoirs are partitioned to

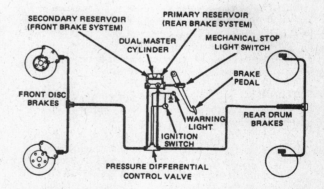

1.3 Typical dual master cylinder brake system (non-ABS)

prevent total fluid loss in the event of a front or rear brake hydraulic system failure.

    The master cylinder is designed for the "split system" mentioned earlier and has separate primary and secondary piston assemblies, the piston nearest the firewall being the primary piston, which applies hydraulic pressure to the front brakes.

9

Power brake booster

All 1970 through 1974 vehicles, and all 1980 and later vehicles use a vacuum-assist power brake booster to reduce driver effort when the brake pedal is depressed. This unit consists of a large diaphragm, operated by manifold vacuum, inside an airtight, cylindrical steel housing, a rubber hose between the intake manifold and the booster, and a one-way check valve which allows the intake manifold to pull down a vacuum inside the booster, but prevent the booster from causing an air leak to the manifold. Under deceleration, intake vacuum, which is high, pulls the diaphragm toward the master cylinder, depressing the pushrod.

All 1975 through 1979 vehicles use a hydraulically-operated unit known as "Hydro-Boost," which accomplishes the same thing as a vacuum-operated unit, but uses pressure generated by the power steering pump instead of intake vacuum. When the engine is running, the power steering pump supplies hydraulic pressure to a power flow regulator/accumulator. The regulator/accumulator stores and regulates the pressure to the hydraulic booster unit, which is mounted between the master cylinder and the firewall, just like a conventional vacuum brake booster. When the brake pedal is depressed, a pressure-regulating valve opens, admitting power steering fluid under pressure into a chamber. This pressure helps actuate the master cylinder, reducing pedal effort.

Brake pressure control valve

On non-ABS models, the brake pressure control valve is located in the master cylinder between the brake lines and the master cylinder body. On ABS models, the brake pressure control valve is on the underside of the ABS hydraulic control unit. Earlier non-ABS control-valve assemblies contain a proportioning valve and a pressure switch. On later non-ABS systems, pressure control is handled inside the master cylinder, but the proportioning valve is in a junction block on the frame.

The proportioning valve regulates the hydraulic pressure in the rear brake system. When the brake pedal is applied, the rear brake fluid pressure passes through the proportioning valve to the rear brake system until the valve's split point is reached. Above its split point, the proportioning valve begins to reduce the hydraulic pressure to the rear brakes thereby balancing the braking condition between the front and rear brakes. This condition will prevent the rear wheel from locking up and the vehicle from skidding out of control.

The brake pressure control valve is not serviceable - if a problem develops with the valve, it must be replaced as an assembly.

Parking brake

The parking brake mechanically operates the rear brakes only.

On drum brake models the parking brake cables pull on a lever attached to the brake shoe assembly, causing the shoes to expand against the drum. On models with rear disc brakes, the cables operate small parking brake shoes inside the brake disc hub, or operate a lever expanding the brake pads, depending on the model.

Precautions

There are some general cautions and warnings involving the brake system on this vehicle:

a) *Use only brake fluid conforming to DOT 3 specifications.*
b) *The brake pads and linings may contain asbestos fibers which are hazardous to your health if inhaled. Whenever you work on brake system components, clean all parts with brake system cleaner or denatured alcohol. Do not allow the fine dust to become airborne.*
c) *Safety should be paramount whenever any servicing of the brake components is performed. Do not use parts or fasteners which are not in perfect condition, and be sure that all clearances and torque specifications are adhered to. If you are at all unsure about a certain procedure, seek professional advice. Upon completion of any brake system work, test the brakes carefully in a controlled area before putting the vehicle into normal service.*

If a problem is suspected in the brake system, don't drive the vehicle until it's fixed.

2.2 The ABS hydraulic control unit is located on the left side of the engine compartment, under the air cleaner housing

2 Anti-lock Brake System (ABS) and Traction Assist (TA) - general information

Some 1990 and later models are equipped with an Anti-lock Brake System (ABS). The ABS system is designed to maintain vehicle steerability, directional stability and optimum deceleration under severe braking conditions and on most road surfaces. It does so by monitoring the rotational speed of each wheel and controlling the brake line pressure to each wheel during braking. This prevents the wheel from locking-up and provides maximum vehicle controllability. Some of these models are also equipped with an optional Traction Assist (TA) system which is designed to control wheel spin when accelerating on slippery or loose surfaces.

Anti-lock Brake System
Hydraulic control unit (HCU)
Refer to illustration 2.2

The hydraulic control unit is located in the left (driver's side) front corner of the engine compartment, below the air cleaner. It consists of a brake pressure control valve block, a pump motor and a hydraulic control unit reservoir with a fluid level indicator assembly **(see illustration)**.

During normal braking conditions, brake hydraulic fluid from the master cylinder enters the hydraulic control unit through two inlet ports and passes through four normally open inlet valves, one to each wheel.

When the anti-lock brake control module senses that a wheel is about to lock up, the anti-lock brake control module closes the appropriate inlet. This prevents any more fluid from entering the affected brake. If the module determines that the wheel is still decelerating, the module opens the outlet valve, which bleeds off pressure in the affected brake.

Wheel sensors
Refer to illustrations 2.6a and 2.6b

The ABS system uses four "variable-reluctance" sensors to monitor wheel speed ("reluctance" is a term used to indicate the amount of resistance to the passage of flux lines - lines of force in a magnetic field - through a given material). Each sensor contains a small inductive coil that generates an electromagnetic field. When paired with a toothed sensor ring which interrupts this field as the wheels turn, each sensor generates a low-voltage analog (continuous) signal. This voltage signal, which rises and falls in proportion to wheel rotation speed, is continuously sampled (monitored) by the control module, converted into digital data inside the module and processed (interpreted).

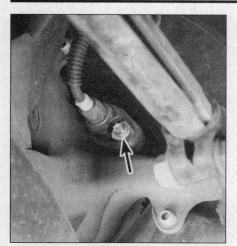

2.6a ABS front wheel sensor (arrow)

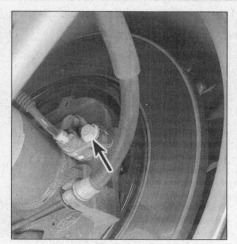

2.6b ABS rear wheel sensor (arrow)

2.7 The ABS brake control module is attached to the radiator support (plastic trim piece removed)

The front wheel sensors **(see illustration)** are mounted in the steering knuckle in close proximity to the toothed sensor rings, which are pressed onto the wheel hubs. The rear wheel sensors **(see illustration)** are mounted in the caliper torque plate and the sensor rings are pressed onto the axleshafts.

Brake control module

Refer to illustration 2.7

The brake control module **(see illustration)**, which is mounted in the engine compartment on a bracket attached to the radiator support, is the "brain" of the ABS system. The module (referred to as an Electronic Control Unit or ECU on 1992 models, ABS module on 1993 models and anti-lock brake control module on 1994 models) constantly monitors the incoming analog voltage signals from the four ABS wheel sensors, converts these signals to digital form, processes this digital data by comparing it to the map (program), makes decisions, converts these (digital) decisions to analog form and sends them to the hydraulic control unit, which opens and closes the front and/or rear circuits as necessary.

The module also has a self-diagnostic capability which operates during both normal driving as well as ABS system operation. If a malfunction occurs, a red "BRAKE" warning indicator or an amber "CHECK ANTI-LOCK BRAKES" warning indicator will light up on the dash.

a) If the red BRAKE light glows, the brake fluid level in the master cylinder reservoir has fallen below the level established by the fluid level switch. Top up the reservoir and verify that the light goes out.

b) If the amber CHECK ANTI-LOCK BRAKES light glows, the ABS and, if equipped, Traction Assist, have been turned off because of a symptom detected by the module. Normal power-assisted braking is still operational, but the wheels can now lock up if you're involved in a panic-stop situation. A diagnostic code is also stored in the module when a warning indicator light comes on; when retrieved by a service technician, the code indicates the area or component where the problem is located. Once the problem is fixed, the code is cleared. These procedures, however, are beyond the scope of this manual.

Diagnosis and repair

Warning: *If a dashboard warning light comes on and stays on while the vehicle is in operation, the ABS system requires immediate attention!*

Although a special electronic ABS diagnostic tester is necessary to properly diagnose the system, the home mechanic can perform a few preliminary checks before taking the vehicle to a dealer who is equipped with this tester.

a) Check the brake fluid level in the reservoir.
b) Verify that the control module electrical connector is securely connected.
c) Check the electrical connectors at the hydraulic control unit.
d) Check the fuses.
e) Follow the wiring harness to each wheel and check that all connections are secure and that the wiring is not damaged.

If the above preliminary checks do not rectify the problem, the vehicle should be diagnosed by a dealer service department or other qualified repair shop. Due to the rather complex nature of this system, all actual repair work must be done by the dealer service department or repair shop.

Traction Assist system

The traction assist (TA) system, which operates at speeds up to about 34 mph, operates as follows: During acceleration, if one or both of the rear wheels lose traction and begin to spin, the ABS pump motor rapidly applies and releases the appropriate rear brake(s). An isolation valve blocks hydraulic pressure to the front brakes, directing pressure to the rear brakes. The ABS brake control module monitors TA system cycling to prevent overheating of the rear brakes. If the TA system is used continually on slippery roads, the module may shut off the system to allow the rear brakes to cool. If the driver applies the brakes, the system is shut off.

---

3   Brake pads - replacement

Warning: *Disc brake pads must be replaced on both front wheels or both rear wheels at the same time - never replace the pads on only one wheel. Also, the dust created by the brake system may contain asbestos, which is harmful to your health. Never blow it out with compressed air and don't inhale any of it. An approved filtering mask should be worn when working on the brakes. Do not, under any circumstances, use petroleum-based solvents to clean brake parts. Use brake system cleaner only!*

1   Remove the cover from the brake fluid reservoir and siphon out about 1/2 of the brake fluid.

2   Loosen the wheel lug nuts, raise the vehicle and support it securely on jackstands.

3   Remove the wheels. Work on one brake assembly at a time, using the assembled brake for reference if necessary.

4   Inspect the brake disc carefully as outlined in Section 5.

5   If machining is necessary, follow the information in that Section to remove the disc, at which time the pads can be removed from the caliper as well.

9

3.7 An exploded view of the front disc brake assembly used on 1970 and 1971 models

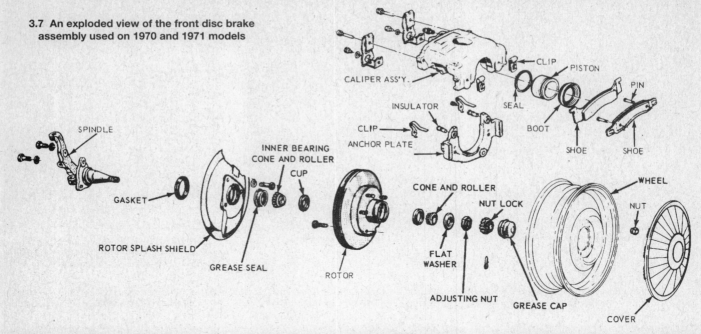

3.15a Remove the key retaining bolt

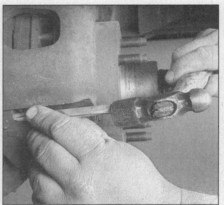

3.15b Tap out the key with a punch and hammer - make sure you don't damage the keyway or the key

3.15c Remove the key and the caliper support spring (the thin spring on top of the key)

1970 and 1971 models

Refer to illustration 3.7

6   Remove the master cylinder cap and check the fluid level in the primary reservoir (the larger of the two). Remove and discard about half of the fluid in the reservoir.

7   Remove the inner shoe hold-down clips **(see illustration).**

8   Insert a small screwdriver under the outer brake pad retaining clip tang, lift away from the pin groove and slide the clip from the pad retaining pin. Remove the other brake shoe retaining clip. Remove the outer brake pad.

9   Remove the caliper locating pins.

10   Remove the upper stabilizer-to-anchor plate attaching bolt and remove the upper stabilizer to avoid interference with the brake hose during caliper removal.

11   Lift the caliper assembly from the anchor plate and remove the outer pad and retaining pins from the caliper assembly.

12   Remove the caliper locating pin insulators, then hang the caliper from the upper control arm with a piece of wire hooked through the upper caliper locating pin hole.

13   Depress the piston into the caliper with a C-clamp **(see illustration 3.15g).**

14   Installation is the reverse of removal. Be sure to tighten all fasteners to the torque listed in this Chapter's Specifications.

1972 through 1979 models

Refer to illustrations 3.15a through 3.15n

15   If you're working on a 1972 through 1979 model, follow the accompanying photos, beginning with illustration 3.15a, for the front brake pad replacement procedure. Be sure to stay in order and read the caption under each illustration.

1980 and later models

Refer to illustrations 3.16a through 3.16q

Note: *On 1995 and later models, the front brake caliper and brake pads have been modified slightly. The brake pads are no longer held in place in the caliper assembly by retaining clips but by indexing the pads out of and into the caliper anchor plate.*

16   If you're working on a 1980 or later model, follow the accompanying photos, beginning with illustration 3.16a, for the front brake pad replacement procedure. Be sure to stay in order and read the caption under each illustration. If you're replacing the rear brake

3.15d Remove the caliper

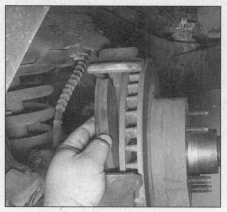

3.15e Remove the inner brake pad from the anchor plate

3.15f Remove the outer brake pad from the caliper

3.15g Depress the piston into the caliper with a large C-clamp

3.15h Install the anti-rattle clip on the new inner brake pad

3.15i Install the new inner brake pad on the anchor plate

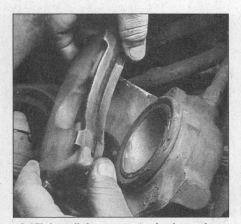

3.15j Install the new outer brake pad on the caliper

3.15k Coat the sliding surface of the caliper with high-temperature grease

3.15l Place the new inner brake pad in position against the inner side of the brake disc, install the new outer pad in the caliper and position the caliper and new outer pad over the disc and onto the anchor plate

pads, follow the photos beginning with illustration 3.16l.

17 When reinstalling the caliper, be sure to tighten the caliper bolts to the torque listed in this Chapter's Specifications. After the job has been completed, firmly depress the brake pedal a few times to bring the pads into contact with the disc.

18 Check the brake fluid level and add some, if necessary, to bring it to the appropriate level (see Chapter 1).

4 Brake caliper - removal, overhaul and installation

Warning 1: *Dust created by the brake system may contain asbestos, which is harmful to your health. Never blow it out with compressed air and don't inhale any of it. An approved filtering mask should be worn when working on the brakes. Do not, under any circumstances, use*

9

3.15m Tap the key and the caliper support spring into place with a small hammer

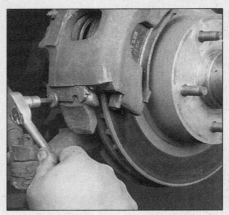

3.15n Install the key retaining bolt and tighten it to the torque listed in this Chapter's Specifications

3.16a Remove the caliper mounting bolts (arrows)

3.16b If the disc is worn down, it's impossible to pull the caliper and old pads off the disc without depressing the caliper piston into its bore far enough to allow the pads to clear the ridge around the circumference of the disc - insert a screwdriver into the cooling vanes of the disc, then pry the caliper out - this will move the caliper out (away from the vehicle), pushing on the inner brake pad and depressing the piston

3.16c Remove the caliper and brake pad assembly

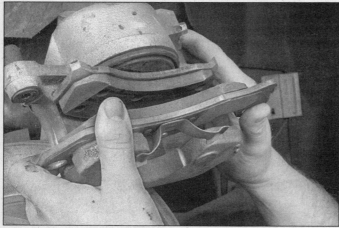

3.16d On 1988 through 1994 models, remove the outer brake pad. On 1995 and later models, slide the outer pad away from the outer leg of the anchor plate, disengage it from the anchor plate and remove the outer pad

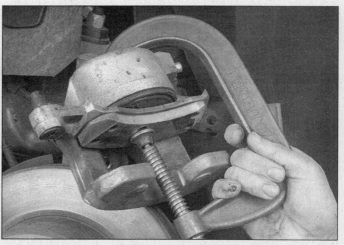

3.16e Before you can slide the caliper and two new brake pads over the disc, you'll need to depress the caliper piston all the way into its bore with a C-clamp (use the old brake pad); as the piston is depressed to the bottom of the bore, the fluid in the master cylinder will rise. Make sure it doesn't overflow. If necessary, siphon off some fluid.

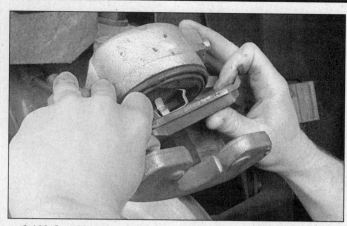

3.16f On 1988 through 1994 models, pull the inner brake pad retaining clips out of the piston and remove the inner pad. On 1995 and later models, slide the inner pad away from the piston, disengage it from the anchor plate and remove the inner pad

3.16g On 1988 through 1994 models, push the new inner brake pad into place - make sure it's fully seated. On 1995 and later models, make sure the anti-rattle spring is still in place in the caliper. First locate the new inner pad onto the caliper anchor plate, then push the inner pad up against the anti-rattle spring - make sure the pad is fully seated

3.16h On 1988 through 1994 models, to install the new outer pad, push it down until the clips snaps into place below those two bosses on the caliper housing; there are also a couple of locating pins on the pad backing plate that must engage a pair of matching holes in the caliper itself. On 1995 and later models, locate the new outer pad onto the caliper anchor plate, then push the inner pad up against the anti-rattle spring - make sure the pad is fully seated

3.16i Install the caliper

3.16j Apply a non-hardening thread locking compound to the caliper bolt threads

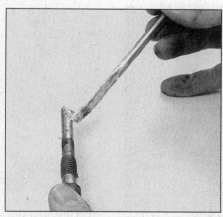

3.16k Apply high temperature grease to the sliding-surface portion of the caliper bolts

3.16l Remove the two rear caliper bolts (upper and lower arrows) with a Torx Drive bit - DO NOT remove the brake hose banjo bolt (middle arrow) unless you're planning to overhaul the caliper

9

3.16m Depress the caliper piston by squeezing the old pad with a pair of large water pump pliers (on 1991 and later Mark VII models, use a piston turning tool and rotate the piston clockwise until it's fully seated)

3.16n Pry off the old outer brake pad with a screwdriver

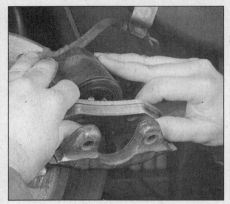

3.16o Remove the old inner brake pad by pulling the retaining clips out of the piston

petroleum-based solvents to clean brake parts. Use brake system cleaner only!

Warning 2: *If the vehicle is equipped with ABS, make sure you plug the brake hose immediately after disconnecting it from the brake caliper, to prevent the fluid from draining out of the line and air entering the HCU. The HCU on an ABS system cannot be bled without a very expensive tool.*

Note: *If an overhaul is indicated (usually because of fluid leakage) explore all options before beginning the job. New and factory-rebuilt calipers are available on an exchange basis, which makes this job quite easy. If it is decided to rebuild the calipers, make sure that a rebuild kit is available before proceeding. Always rebuild the calipers in pairs- never rebuild just one of them.*

All front calipers and 1989 and later Town Car rear calipers

Removal

Refer to illustration 4.2

1   Apply the parking brake and block the wheels opposite the end being worked on. Loosen the wheel lug nuts, raise the vehicle and support it securely on jackstands. Remove the wheel.

2   Unscrew the brake hose banjo bolt **(see illustration)** and detach the hose from the caliper - remove the sealing washer from each side

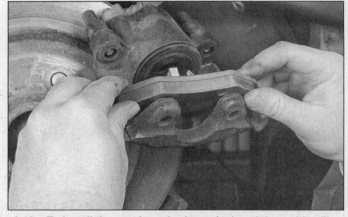

3.16p To install the new inner brake pad, place it in position like this, then push it all the way in until the retaining clips are fully seated

of the hose fitting and discard them. New sealing washers must be installed on reassembly. **Caution:** *On ABS-equipped models, plug the brake hose immediately to prevent air from getting into the hydraulic control unit (HCU). If air gets into the HCU, you will not be able to bleed the brakes properly at home.* On non-ABS models, wrap

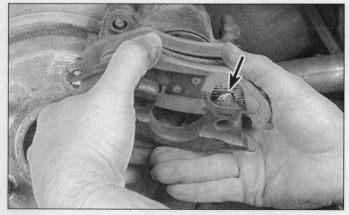

3.16q To install the new outer brake pad, slide it down like this until the locating pins (arrow) are fully engaged with the holes in the caliper housing; then install the caliper and pads over the disc, install the caliper bolts and tighten them to the torque listed in this Chapter's Specifications

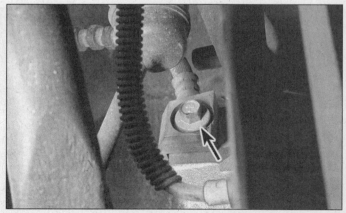

4.2 If you're removing the caliper for overhaul, remove this banjo bolt (arrow) and detach the banjo fitting - shove a piece of rubber hose through the banjo fitting to plug the hose (front caliper shown; rear caliper banjo bolt shown in illustration 3.6l)

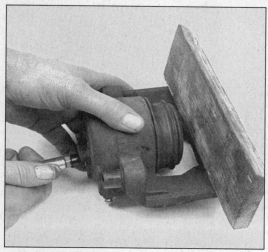

4.5 With the caliper padded to catch the piston, use compressed air to force the piston out of its bore - make sure your hands and fingers are not between the piston and the caliper!

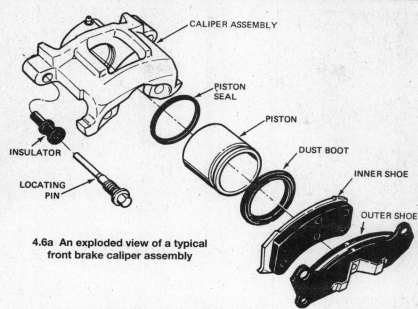

4.6a An exploded view of a typical front brake caliper assembly

4.6b Remove the dust boot from the caliper bore groove

4.7 To remove the seal from the caliper bore, use a plastic or wooden tool, such as a pencil

4.12 Grab the ends of the caliper bolt insulators and, using a twisting motion, push them through the caliper ears

a plastic bag around the end of the hose to prevent fluid loss and contamination.

3   Remove the brake calipers as described in Section 3.

Overhaul

Refer to illustrations 4.5, 4.6a, 4.6b, 4.7, 4.12, 4.14, 4.17, 4.18, 4.19a, 4.19b, 4.20 and 4.21

4   Clean the exterior of the caliper with brake system cleaner. Never use gasoline, kerosene or other petroleum-based cleaning solvents. Place the caliper on a clean workbench.

5   Position a wood block or rags in the center of the caliper as a cushion, then use compressed air to remove the piston from the caliper (see illustration). Use only enough air to ease the piston out of the bore. If the piston is blown out, even with the cushion in place, it may be damaged. Warning: *Never place your fingers in front of the piston in an attempt to catch or protect it when applying compressed air, as serious injury could occur.*

6   Pull the dust boot out of the caliper bore (see illustrations).

7   Using a wood or plastic tool, remove the piston seal from the caliper bore (see illustration). Metal tools may cause bore damage.

8   Carefully examine the piston for nicks, burrs, cracks, loss of plating, corrosion or any signs of damage. If surface defects are present, the parts must be replaced.

9   Check the caliper bore in a similar way. Light polishing with crocus cloth is permissible to remove light corrosion and stains.

10   Remove the bleeder valve and rubber cap.

11   Inspect the caliper bolts for corrosion and damage. Replace them with new ones if necessary.

12   Remove the caliper bolt insulators from the caliper ears (see illustration).

13   Use brake system cleaner to clean all the parts. **Warning:** *Do not, under any circumstances, use petroleum-based solvents to clean brake parts. Allow all parts to dry, preferably using compressed air to blow out all passages. Make sure the compressed air is filtered, as a harmful lubricant residue or moisture may be present in unfiltered systems.*

14   Push the new caliper bolt insulators into place (see illustration).

9

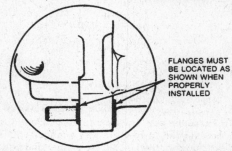

4.14 Push the new insulators through the holes in the caliper ears, making sure they're installed all the way

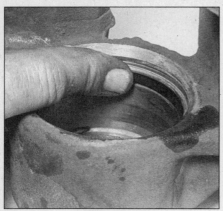

4.17 Push the new seal into the groove with your fingers, then check to see that it isn't twisted or kinked

4.18 Install the dust boot in the upper groove in the caliper bore, making sure it's completely seated

4.19a Lubricate the piston and bore with clean brake fluid, insert the piston into the dust boot (NOT the bore) at an angle, then, using a rotating motion, work the piston completely into the dust boot . . .

4.19b . . . and push it straight into the caliper as far as possible by hand

4.20 Use a C-clamp and a block of wood to bottom the piston in the caliper bore - make sure it goes in perfectly straight, or the sides of the piston may be damaged, rendering it useless

4.21 Install the lip of the dust boot in the groove on the caliper piston

15   Check the fit of the piston in the bore by sliding it into the caliper. The piston should move easily (don't install it yet).

16   Thread the bleeder valve into the caliper and tighten it securely. Install the rubber cap.

17   Lubricate the new piston seal and caliper bore with clean brake fluid. Position the seal in the caliper bore groove, making sure it doesn't twist **(see illustration)**.

18   Fit the new dust boot in the caliper bore upper groove, making sure it's seated **(see illustration)**.

19   Lubricate the caliper piston with clean brake fluid. Push the piston into the caliper, using a turning motion to roll the lip of the dust boot over the piston **(see illustrations)**. Push the piston into the caliper by hand as far as possible.

20   Using a C-clamp and a block of wood, push the piston all the way to the bottom of the bore. Work slowly, keeping an eye on the side of the piston, making sure it enters the bore perfectly straight with no resistance **(see illustration)**.

21   Seat the lip of the dust boot in the groove on the piston **(see illustration)**.

Installation

22   Refer to Section 4 for the caliper installation procedure, as it is part of the brake pad replacement procedure.

23   Connect the brake hose to the caliper, using new sealing washers. Tighten the banjo bolt to the torque listed in this Chapter's Specifications.

24   Bleed the brakes as outlined in Section 11. This is not necessary if the banjo bolt was not loosened or removed (if the caliper was removed for access to other components, for example).

25   Install the wheel and lower the vehicle. Tighten the lug nuts to the torque listed in the Chapter 1 Specifications. Pump the brake pedal several times to bring the pads into contact with the disc.

26   Test the operation of the brakes before placing the vehicle into normal service.

Rear calipers (1975 through 1990 Continental and Mark series and 1981 through 1988 Town Car)

Removal

27   Raise the vehicle and support it securely on jackstands.

28   Remove the rear wheels.

29   Disconnect the parking brake cable at the lever.

30   Disconnect the brake hose and plug the end to prevent the loss of fluid and entry of air into the system.

31   Remove the calipers as described in Section 3.

32   If the caliper cannot be removed easily, it will be necessary to

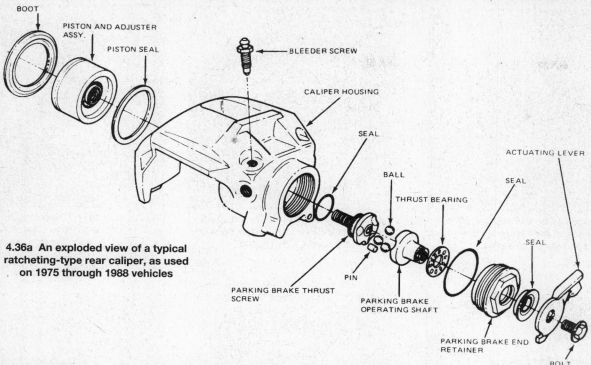

4.36a An exploded view of a typical ratcheting-type rear caliper, as used on 1975 through 1988 vehicles

4.36b Lift out the end retainer, then remove the thrust bearing and balls

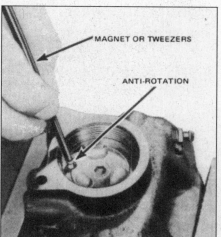

4.37 Remove the thrust-screw anti-rotation pin with a magnet or a pair of tweezers

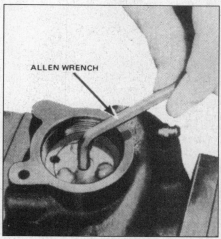

4.38 Remove the thrust screw from the caliper with an Allen wrench as shown, or, on older units. with a 1/4-inch drive socket

loosen the caliper and retainer 1/2-turn, which will allow the piston to be forced back into its bore. Before loosening the retainer remove the parking brake lever and scribe a line across the end retainer and caliper housing to make sure the retainer is not loosened more than 1/2-turn. If the retainer is moved more than 1/2-turn the thrust screw and retainer seal may be broken, allowing fluid leakage.

33 The piston can now be forced back into its bore and the caliper removed.

34 Remove the brake pads from the anchor plate. If the pads are to be reinstalled, mark them so that they can be installed in their original locations.

35 Clean and inspect the caliper, anchor plate and disc for corrosion, wear and fluid leakage. If the disc or pads are worn beyond specifications, they must be replaced with new ones. If the pads on one wheel require replacement, the pads on the other wheel must also be replaced to maintain equal braking action.

Overhaul

Refer to illustrations 4.36a, 4.36b, 4.37, 4.38, 4.39, 4.43 and 4.56

36 Remove the caliper end retainer (**see illustrations**) and lift out the operating shaft, thrust bearing and balls.

37 Use a magnet or tweezers to remove the thrust screw anti-rotation pin (**see illustration**). If the pins are difficult to remove, it will be necessary to use Ford tool T75P-2588-B or equivalent to push the piston back into the housing. Adjust the piston so that it protrudes about one inch. Push the piston back into the caliper housing and rotate the tool shaft counterclockwise until the thrust screw is clear of the anti-rotation pin.

38 Remove the thrust screw by turning it counterclockwise with a 1/4-inch Allen wrench (**see illustration**), or on earlier models, a 1/4-inch square socket drive.

39 Use Ford tool T75P-2588-A or equivalent to push the piston out as shown (**see illustration**).

9

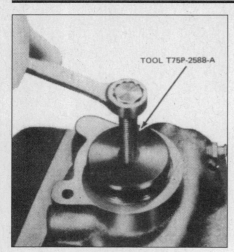

4.39 You'll need Ford's special tool (T75P-2588-A) or equivalent to push the piston out of the caliper

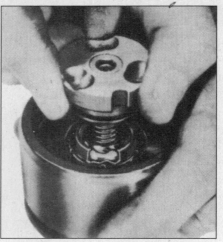

4.43 To check the operation of the adjuster, install the thrust screw and pull the adjuster and the screw apart about 1/4-inch; the brass drive ring must remain stationary during this operation, causing the nut to rotate. If this doesn't happen, replace the piston/adjuster assembly

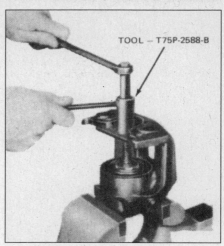

4.56 Again, using Ford's special tool (T75P-2588-B) or equivalent, bottom the piston as shown

40   Remove the piston seal, boot, thrust screw O-ring seal and end-ring lip seal.

41   Clean the metal parts with brake cleaner and dry with compressed air if possible.

42   Inspect the caliper for pitting, scoring or worn parts. If any of these conditions are found, or the chrome plating on the piston is worn, the components must be replaced with new parts.

43   Check the adjuster operation by assembling the thrust screw and pulling the two apart about 1/4-inch as shown **(see illustration)**. The brass drive ring must remain stationary during this operation, causing the nut to rotate. The piston/adjuster assembly must be replaced with a new one if this does not occur.

44   Inspect the parking brake lever for damage and replace if necessary.

45   Lubricate the new caliper piston seal with clean brake fluid and seat it fully into the cylinder bore, being careful not to twist it.

46   Install the new dust boot by seating it squarely in the caliper bore outer groove.

47   Lubricate the piston/adjuster assembly with clean brake fluid and install it in the cylinder bore, spreading the dust boot over the seal as it is installed. Make sure the dust boot is seated in the piston groove.

48   Place the caliper securely in a vise and fill the piston adjuster assembly to the bottom edge of the thrust screw with clean brake fluid.

49   Lubricate a new thrust screw O-ring seal with clean brake fluid and install it in the thrust screw groove.

50   Install the thrust screw into the piston adjuster assembly with a 1/4-inch Allen wrench (1/4-inch square socket on early models) until the screw tip surface is flush with the bottom of the threaded bore. Be careful not to cut the O-ring. Set the thrust screw so that the notches on the screw and caliper housing are aligned. Install the anti-rotation pin.

51   Place the three balls in their sockets in the thrust screw, apply liberal amounts of silicone grease on the parking brake mechanism components and install the operating shaft on the balls.

52   Cover the thrust bearing with a coat of silicone grease and install it.

53   Install a new O-ring and lip seal onto the end retainer.

54   Lightly lubricate the O-ring seal and lip seal with silicone grease and install the end retainer in the caliper. Hold the shaft firmly during installation to prevent the balls from being dislodged. Reseat the lip seal if necessary and tighten the end retainer.

55   Install the parking brake lever and tighten the retaining screw securely.

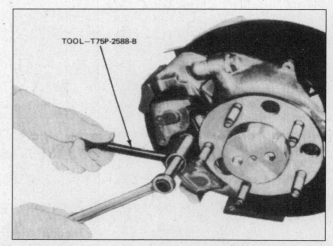

4.57 To adjust the rear disc brake piston depth, hold the shaft of Ford's special tool (T75P-2588-B) or equivalent, and turn the tool handle counterclockwise until the tool seats firmly against the piston

56   With the caliper in a vise, use Ford tool T75P-2588-B or equivalent to bottom the piston as shown **(see illustration)**.

Installation

Refer to illustration 4.57

57   Reinstall the brake pads. If installing new pads it will be necessary to screw the piston back into the caliper bore using Ford tool T75P-2588-B or equivalent to provide sufficient clearance. Remove the brake rotor. Install the caliper, without pads, using the key only. Referring to the accompanying figure, hold the shaft and turn the tool handle counterclockwise until the tool seats firmly against the piston **(see illustration)**. Loosen the handle 1/4 turn. Hold the handle and turn the tool shaft clockwise until the piston is fully bottomed in its bore. The piston will continue to turn even when bottomed, so check to make sure there is no further movement. Remove the caliper and reinstall the rotor.

58   With the anti-rattle clip in place in the lower inner pad support, position the inner pad on the anchor plate.

59   Install the outer pad so that the lower flange ends are against the

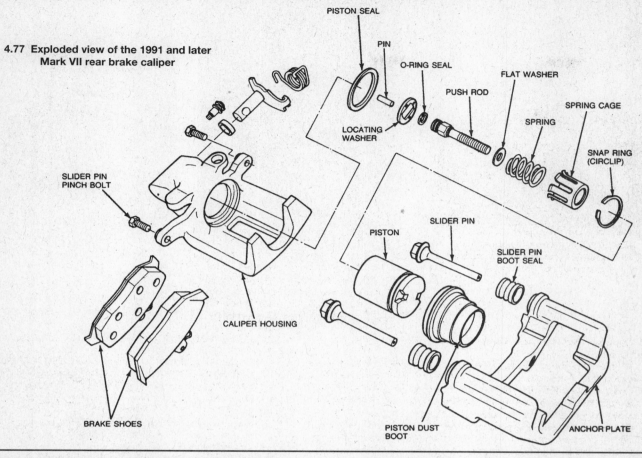

4.77 Exploded view of the 1991 and later Mark VII rear brake caliper

caliper leg abutments and the upper flanges are over the caliper leg shoulders.

60 Lightly lubricate the areas where the caliper and anchor plate will slide on one another.

61 Place the caliper housing lower V-groove on the anchor plate lower abutment surface.

62 Being careful not to damage the piston dust boot, rotate the caliper into position over the disc.

63 Seat the inner pad against the brake disc by pulling the caliper out. The clearance between the outer pad lining and the disc must be 1/16-inch or less.

64 If the gap is greater than 1/16-inch, remove the caliper and adjust the piston out following the procedure in Step 16.

65 Hold the caliper in place against the anchor plate and install the caliper support spring and key so that the key's semi-circular slot is over the retaining screw threaded hole in the anchor plate.

66 Install the key retaining screw and tighten it to the torque listed in this Chapter's Specifications.

67 If the brake hose has been disconnected, remove the plug and reinstall it. It will be necessary to bleed the brakes as described in Section 11.

68 Connect and adjust the parking brake cable.

69 Install the wheels, lower the vehicle, tighten the wheel lug nuts to the torque listed in the Chapter 1 Specifications and take the vehicle for a test drive to check for proper braking action.

Rear Calipers (1991 and 1992 Mark VII)

Removal

70 Raise the vehicle and support it securely on jackstands. Remove the rear wheels.

71 Remove the parking brake cable retaining clip and disconnect the cable from the parking brake lever.

72 Disconnect the brake hose from the caliper. Cap the open hose end.

73 Hold the slider pin on the hex head with an open-end wrench and remove the pinch bolts.

74 Remove the caliper from the anchor plate. Remove the slider pins and boots from the anchor plate.

Overhaul

Refer to illustration 4.77

75 Using a piston removal tool (Ford T87P-2588-A), or equivalent, remove the piston from the caliper. Remove the piston seal and dust boot.

76 Using a suitable pair of snap-ring pliers, remove the adjuster assembly retaining snap-ring. **Caution:** *The snap-ring and spring cage are under spring pressure, use caution when removing the snap-ring.*

77 Remove the spring cage, spring, push rod, washer and pin from the caliper bore **(see illustration)**. Remove the O-ring seal from the push rod.

78 Remove the parking brake lever return spring. Remove the parking brake lever stop bolt and remove the lever from the caliper housing. Pry out the lever shaft seal from the caliper housing.

79 Clean and dry the housing, piston and adjuster assembly parts with brake system cleaner. Clean the grooves and passages in the caliper bore.

80 Inspect the caliper bore and piston for damage, wear or excessive corrosion. Light amounts of corrosion can be removed with brake system cleaner and crocus cloth, but if the bore or piston are pitted or scored beyond repair, it will be necessary to replace the caliper assembly.

81 Press a new parking brake lever seal into the housing. Apply silicone grease to the lever shaft and install the parking brake lever. Install the parking brake lever stop bolt and install the return spring.

82 Install a new O-ring on the adjuster push rod and lubricate it with

5.5a To check disc runout, mount a dial indicator as shown and rotate the disc

5.5b Using a swirling motion, remove the glaze from the disc with sandpaper or emery cloth

5.6a The minimum thickness limit is cast into the inside of the disc

silicone grease.

83   Install the strut pin in the caliper housing. Install the locating washer and push rod, be sure the pin on the locating washer is properly positioned into the hole in the caliper housing.

84   Install the flat washer, spring and spring cage.

85   Place the snap-ring into the caliper bore and using a piston spring compressor tool (Ford T87P-2588-B) or equivalent, press the snap ring into the bore until it snaps into place. Do not over compress the spring.

86   Lubricate a new piston seal with clean brake fluid and install it into the groove in the caliper bore.

87   Coat the piston with clean brake fluid, spread a new dust boot over the piston and seat the dust boot in the groove. Install the piston and dust boot into the caliper bore. Rotate the piston clockwise with a brake piston turning tool until the piston is bottomed in the bore. Seat the dust boot into the caliper housing bore.

88   Position the slots on the piston face so one slot will engage the pin on the back of the brake pad when installed.

Installation

89   Apply silicone grease to the slider pins, install the slider pins and boots to the anchor plate.

90   Install the inner and outer brake pads and anti-rattle clips. Install the caliper to the anchor plate.

91   Clean the threads of the pinch bolts with a wire brush and apply thread-locking compound to the threads. Install the pinch bolts and tighten them to the torque listed in this Chapter's Specifications while holding the slider pins with an open-end wrench.

92   Install the brake hose using new washers, and tighten the retaining bolt to the torque listed in this Chapter's Specifications.

93   The remainder of installation is the reverse of removal. Bleed the brake system (see Section 11).

---

5   Brake disc - inspection, removal and installation

Inspection

Refer to illustrations 5.5a, 5.5b, 5.6a and 5.6b

Note: *This procedure applies to both front and rear disc brake assemblies.*

1   Loosen the wheel lug nuts, raise the vehicle and support it securely on jackstands. Remove the wheel.

2   Remove the brake caliper as described in Section 3. It's not necessary to disconnect the brake hose for this procedure. After removing the caliper bolts, suspend the caliper out of the way with a piece of wire. Don't let the caliper hang by the hose and don't stretch or twist the hose.

3   Reinstall three lug nuts (inverted) to hold the disc against the hub. It may be necessary to use washers as spacers between the disc and the lug nuts.

4   Visually check the disc surface for score marks and other damage. Light scratches and shallow grooves are normal after use and may not always be detrimental to brake operation, but deep score marks - over 0.015-inch - require disc removal and refinishing by an automotive machine shop. Be sure to check both sides of the disc. If pulsating has been noticed during application of the brakes, suspect disc runout.

5   To check disc runout, place a dial indicator at a point about 1/2-inch from the outer edge of the disc **(see illustration)**. Set the indicator to zero and turn the disc. The indicator reading should not exceed the specified allowable runout limit. If it does, the disc should be refinished by an automotive machine shop. **Note:** *Professionals recommend resurfacing of brake discs regardless of the dial indicator reading (to produce a smooth, flat surface that will eliminate brake pedal pulsations and other undesirable symptoms related to questionable discs). At the very least, if you elect not to have the discs resurfaced, deglaze the brake pad surface with emery cloth or sandpaper (use a swirling motion to ensure a non-directional finish)* **(see illustration)**.

6   The disc must not be machined to a thickness less than the specified minimum refinish thickness. The minimum wear (or discard) thickness is cast into the inside of the disc **(see illustration)**. The disc thickness can be checked with a micrometer **(see illustration)**.

Removal

Refer to illustration 5.7

7   On pre-1991 vehicles, the front brake disc is also the front hub; refer to the "Front wheel bearing check, repack and adjustment" Section in Chapter 1. On 1991 and later vehicles, remove the lug nuts that are temporarily holding the disc to the hub and lift off the disc **(see illustration)**. The rear brake discs on all vehicles are removed in the same manner as 1991 and later front discs.

Installation

8   Install the disc onto the hub assembly.

9   Install the brake pads and caliper assembly over the disc and position it on the steering knuckle (front), or on the torque plate (rear) (see Section 3). Install the caliper bolts and tighten them to the torque listed in this Chapter's Specifications.

10   Install the wheel, then lower the vehicle to the ground. Depress the brake pedal a few times to bring the brake pads into contact with the rotor. Bleeding of the system will not be necessary unless the brake hose was disconnected from the caliper. Check the operation of the brakes carefully before placing the vehicle into normal service.

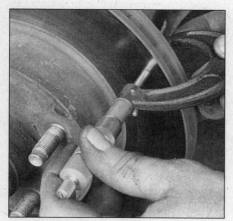

5.6b Use a micrometer to measure disc thickness at several points, about 1/2-inch from the edge

5.7 Lift the disc off the hub assembly

6.4a Remove the brake drum

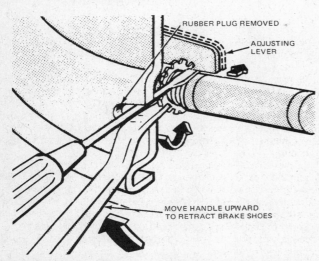

RUBBER PLUG REMOVED

ADJUSTING LEVER

MOVE HANDLE UPWARD TO RETRACT BRAKE SHOES

6.4b If the drum is difficult to remove, you may have to retract the brake shoes: Remove the rubber plug from the backing plate, insert a screwdriver through the hole, raise the adjusting lever off the star wheel and rotate the star adjuster with a brake adjustment tool or another screwdriver as shown

FRONT OF VEHICLE

ANCHOR PIN PLATE
ANCHOR PIN
BRAKE CYLINDER
RETRACTING SPRING
SECONDARY SHOE AND LINING
PARKING BRAKE LINK
RETRACTING SPRING
PARKING BRAKE LINK SPRING
CABLE GUIDE
BRAKE SHOE HOLD DOWN SPRING
SELF-ADJUSTER CABLE
PRIMARY SHOE AND LINING
PARKING BRAKE LEVER
ADJUSTER LEVER SPRING
PIVOT NUT
PIVOT HOOK
SOCKET
ADJUSTING LEVER
PARKING BRAKE CABLE
ADJUSTING SCREW

6.4c Details of a typical rear drum brake assembly

6   Brake shoes – replacement

Refer to illustrations 6.4a through 6.4v and 6.5

Warning: *Drum brake shoes must be replaced on both wheels at the same time - never replace the shoes on only one wheel. Also, the dust created by the brake system may contain asbestos, which is harmful to your health. Never blow it out with compressed air and don't inhale any of it. An approved filtering mask should be worn when working on the brakes. Do not, under any circumstances, use petroleum-based solvents to clean brake parts. Use brake system cleaner only!*

Caution: *Whenever the brake shoes are replaced, the retractor and hold-down springs should also be replaced. Due to the continuous heating/cooling cycle that the springs are subjected to, they lose their tension over a period of time and may allow the shoes to drag on the drum and wear at a much faster rate than normal.*

1   Loosen the wheel lug nuts, raise the rear of the vehicle and support it securely on jackstands. Block the front wheels to keep the vehicle from rolling.

2   Release the parking brake.

3   Remove the wheel. **Note:** *All four rear brake shoes must be replaced at the same time, but to avoid mixing up parts, work on only*

one brake assembly at a time.

4   Follow the accompanying photos **(illustrations 6.4a through 6.4v)** for the inspection and replacement of the brake shoes. Be sure to stay in order and read the caption under each illustration. **Note:** *If the brake drum cannot be easily pulled off, pry the rubber plug from the backing plate inspection hole and insert a screwdriver and a brake adjusting tool to lift the adjusting lever and rotate the adjusting screw. This will cause the brake shoes to pull together. Spray the assembly with penetrating oil and allow the oil to soak in if the mechanism is difficult to turn. The drum should now come off.*

5   Before reinstalling the drum it should be checked for cracks, score marks, deep scratches and hard spots, which will appear as small discolored areas. If the hard spots cannot be removed with fine emery cloth or if any of the other conditions listed above exist, the drum must be taken to an automotive machine shop to have it turned. **Note:** *Professionals recommend resurfacing the drums whenever a brake job is done. Resurfacing will eliminate the possibility of out-of-round drums. If the drums are worn so much that they can't be resurfaced without exceeding the maximum allowable diameter, which*

9

6.4d Remove the primary and secondary return springs with a spring removal tool

6.4e Unhook the adjusting cable eye from the anchor pin

6.4f Remove the shoe guide

6.4g Remove the shoe retaining springs and pins - this is done by pushing the retainer in, turning it 90-degrees, then pulling it off the pin

6.4h While separating the shoes, extract the adjusting screw and star wheel

6.4i Remove the primary shoe and the parking brake strut and spring assembly

6.4j Remove the adjusting lever . . .

6.4k . . . and remove the secondary shoe from the backing plate

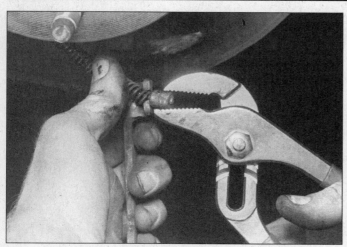

6.4l Separate the parking brake cable and spring from the actuating lever

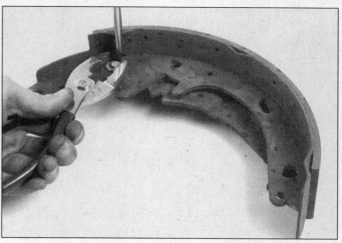

6.4m Remove the E-clip which attaches the parking brake lever to the shoe

6.4n Attach the parking brake lever to the new brake shoe, using a new E-clip

6.4o Disassemble, clean and lubricate the moving parts of the adjusting screw and wheel assembly

6.4p Lightly coat the shoe guide pads, wheel cylinder ends and anchor pin with high-temperature grease

6.4q Place the shoes in position and install the wheel cylinder assembly and the parking brake link; make sure the slots on the wheel cylinder links (A) and the parking brake link (B) are correctly engaged with the brake shoes

6.4r Install the hold-down springs; make sure the shoe retaining pins and springs are properly engaged

9

6.4s Install the adjusting screw - make sure the long end of the adjusting screw is pointing toward the front of the vehicle

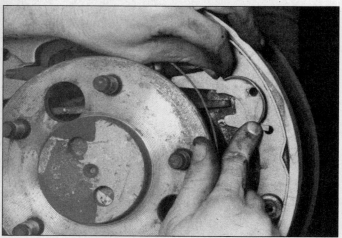

6.4u . . . then install the guide and adjuster cable

6.4v Connect the spring to the adjusting lever - now go back and compare your work to illustration 6.4c and make sure everything is installed correctly, then adjust the brake shoes so the drum just slips over them. Once the drum is in place, adjust the shoes out so they drag slightly as the drum is turned, then back off the adjustment a few clicks

6.4t Install the adjusting lever . . .

is stamped into the drum (**see illustration**), *then new ones will be required. At the very least, if you elect not to have the drums resurfaced, remove the glazing from the surface with medium-grit emery cloth using a swirling motion.*
6   Install the brake drum on the hub.
7   Mount the wheel, install the lug nuts, then lower the vehicle.
8   Make a number of forward and reverse stops to adjust the brakes until satisfactory pedal action is obtained.

---

7   Wheel cylinder - removal, overhaul and installation

Note: *If an overhaul is indicated (usually because of fluid leakage or sticky operation) explore all options before beginning the job. New wheel cylinders are available, which makes this job quite easy. If it's decided to rebuild the wheel cylinder, make sure that a rebuild kit is available before proceeding. Never overhaul only one wheel cylinder - always rebuild both of them at the same time.*

Removal

Refer to illustration 7.4
1   Raise the rear of the vehicle and support it securely on jackstands. Block the front wheels to keep the vehicle from rolling.
2   Remove the brake shoe assembly (see Section 6).

6.5 The maximum permissible diameter specification is cast into the brake drum

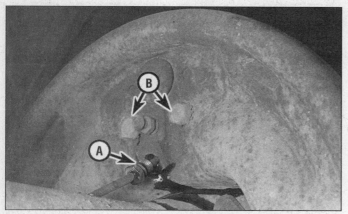

7.4 To remove the wheel cylinder, disconnect the brake line fitting (A) and remove the two mounting bolts (B)

3   Remove all dirt and foreign material from around the wheel cylinder.
4   Disconnect the brake line **(see illustration)**. Don't pull the brake line away from the wheel cylinder.
5   Remove the wheel cylinder mounting bolts.
6   Detach the wheel cylinder from the brake backing plate and place it on a clean workbench. Immediately plug the brake line to prevent fluid loss and contamination.

Overhaul

Refer to illustration 7.7
7   Remove the bleeder screw, cups, pistons, boots and spring assembly from the wheel cylinder body **(see illustration)**.
8   Clean the wheel cylinder with brake fluid, denatured alcohol or brake system cleaner. **Warning:** *Do not, under any circumstances, use petroleum-based solvents to clean brake parts!*
9   Use compressed air to remove excess fluid from the wheel cylinder and to blow out the passages. Make sure the compressed air is filtered and unlubricated.
10   Check the cylinder bore for corrosion and score marks. Crocus cloth can be used to remove light corrosion and stains, but the cylinder must be replaced with a new one if the defects cannot be removed easily, or if the bore is scored.
11   Lubricate the new cups with brake fluid.
12   Assemble the brake cylinder components. Make sure the cup lips face in.

Installation

13   Place the wheel cylinder in position, install the mounting bolts and tighten them to the torque listed in this Chapter's Specifications.
14   Connect the brake line and install the brake shoe assembly.
15   Bleed the brakes (see Section 11).

8   Master cylinder - removal, overhaul and installation

Warning: *If the vehicle is equipped with an Anti-lock Brake System (ABS), do not attempt to remove or overhaul the master cylinder. Have the master cylinder removed, rebuilt and installed at a dealer service department or other qualified repair shop. Removing a master cylinder from an ABS system can allow air to get into the ABS hydraulic control unit, which requires a special bleeding procedure impossible to perform at home. And overhauling a master cylinder used with ABS systems is beyond the scope of the average home mechanic because it requires special factory tools.*
Caution: *Although the master cylinders used on the vehicles covered in this manual are rebuildable, they will continue to leak even after an overhaul if they're assembled incorrectly or if the rebuild kit seals or cups are too small in diameter for the master cylinder bore. This can occur in either of two ways: If the wrong kit is purchased, it might be too small. Or, the bore may be too big for the rebuild kit, if any material is removed from the caliper bore in an attempt to remove corrosion or pitting by honing. For that reason, we don't recommend honing a master cylinder. If the bore of the master cylinder is seriously pitted or corroded, either replace it with a new or professionally rebuilt unit, or take it to an automotive machine shop for a professional opinion.*
Note: *Before deciding to overhaul the master cylinder, check on the availability and cost of a new or factory rebuilt unit and also the availability of a rebuild kit.*

Removal

1   Place rags under the brake line fittings and prepare caps or plastic bags to cover the ends of the lines once they are disconnected. **Caution:** *Brake fluid will damage paint. Cover all body parts and be careful not to spill fluid during this procedure.*
2   Unscrew the tube nuts at the ends of the brake lines where they enter the master cylinder. To prevent rounding off the flats on these nuts, a flare-nut wrench, which wraps around the fitting, should be used.
3   Pull the brake lines away from the master cylinder slightly and plug the ends to prevent contamination.
4   Unplug the electrical connector for the brake warning light, if equipped, remove the two master cylinder mounting nuts, and detach the master cylinder from the vacuum power brake booster or Hydro-Boost unit.
5   Remove the reservoir cap, then discard any fluid remaining in the reservoir.

Overhaul

Refer to illustrations 8.7a, 8.7b, 8.7c, 8.8, 8.9, 8.10, 8.14 and 8.19
6   Mount the master cylinder in a vise with the vise jaws clamping on the mounting flange.
7   Remove the pressure control valve, if equipped. Remove the stop bolt, if equipped **(see illustrations)**. Remove the primary piston snap-ring by depressing the piston and extracting the ring with a pair of

9

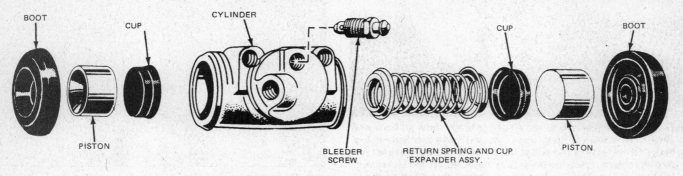

7.7 An exploded view of a typical wheel cylinder assembly

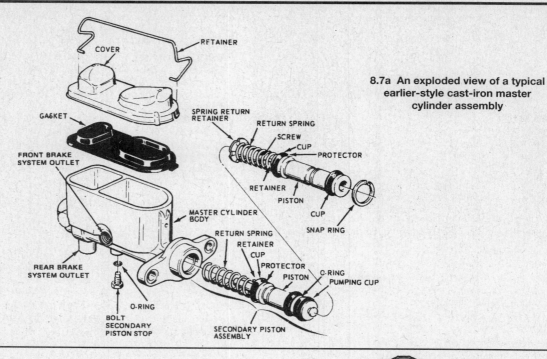

8.7a An exploded view of a typical earlier-style cast-iron master cylinder assembly

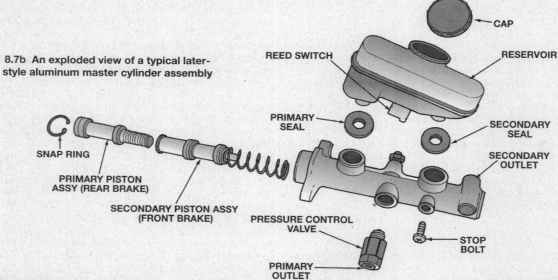

8.7b An exploded view of a typical later-style aluminum master cylinder assembly

8.7c Use a Phillips head screwdriver to push the primary piston into the cylinder, then remove the snap-ring

8.8 Remove the primary piston assembly from the cylinder

8.9 Tap the master cylinder against a block of wood to eject the secondary piston assembly

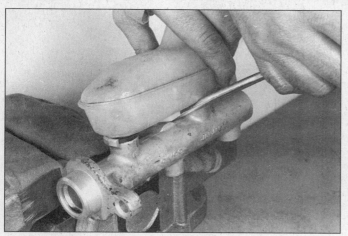

8.10 If you must remove the fluid reservoir to replace leaking seals or a broken reservoir, gently pry it off with a screwdriver or small prybar

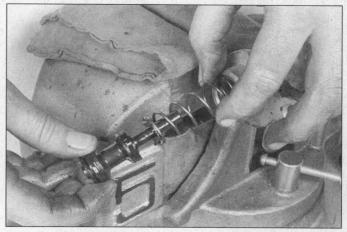

8.14 Coat the secondary piston with clean brake fluid and install it in the master cylinder, spring end first

snap-ring pliers. **(see illustration).**

8   Remove the primary piston assembly from the cylinder bore **(see illustration).**

9   Remove the secondary piston assembly from the cylinder bore. It may be necessary to remove the master cylinder from the vise and invert it, carefully tapping it against a block of wood to expel the piston **(see illustration).**

10   If fluid has been leaking past the reservoir grommets on a newer-style aluminum master cylinder, pry the reservoir from the cylinder body with a screwdriver **(see illustration).** Remove the grommets. Clean the master cylinder body and components with brake system cleaner. **Warning:** *DO NOT use petroleum-based solvents to clean brake parts - use brake system cleaner only.*

11   Inspect the cylinder bore for corrosion and damage. If any corrosion or damage is found, replace the master cylinder body with a new one, as abrasives cannot be used on the bore.

12   If the master cylinder has a removable reservoir, lubricate the new reservoir grommets with clean brake fluid and press them into the master cylinder body. Make sure they're properly seated.

13   If the master cylinder has a removable reservoir, lay the reservoir on a hard surface and press the master cylinder body onto the reservoir, using a rocking motion.

14   Lubricate the cylinder bore and primary and secondary piston assemblies with clean brake fluid. Insert the secondary piston assembly into the cylinder **(see illustration).**

15   Install the primary piston assembly in the cylinder bore, depress it and install the snap-ring. If equipped with a stop bolt, install it now, using a new sealing washer and tightening it securely.

16   On older master cylinder units, inspect the "gasket" (the rubber

liner between the cover and the master cylinder body) for cracks and tears. On newer units, inspect the reservoir cap and diaphragm for cracks and deformation before attaching the diaphragm to the cap. Replace any damaged parts with new ones.

17   **Note:** *Whenever the master cylinder is removed, the complete hydraulic system must be bled. The time required to bleed the system can be reduced if the master cylinder is filled with fluid and bench bled (refer to Steps 18 through 22) before the master cylinder is installed on the vehicle.*

18   Insert threaded plugs of the correct size into the cylinder outlet holes and fill the reservoirs with brake fluid. The master cylinder should be supported in such a manner that brake fluid will not spill during the bench bleeding procedure.

19   Loosen one plug at a time, starting with the secondary outlet port first, and push the piston assembly into the bore to force air from the master cylinder **(see illustration).** To prevent air from being drawn back into the cylinder, the appropriate plug must be replaced before allowing the piston to return to its original position.

20   Stroke the piston three or four times for each outlet to ensure that all air has been expelled.

21   Since high pressure is not involved in the bench bleeding procedure, an alternative to the removal and replacement of the plugs with each stroke of the piston assembly is available. Before pushing in on the piston assembly, remove one of the plugs completely. Before releasing the piston, however, instead of replacing the plug, simply put your finger tightly over the hole to keep air from being drawn back into the master cylinder. Wait several seconds for the brake fluid to be drawn from the reservoir to the piston bore, then repeat the procedure. When you push down on the piston it will force your finger off the hole, allowing the air inside to be expelled. When only brake fluid is being ejected from the hole, replace the plug and go on to the other port.

22   Refill the master cylinder reservoirs and install the diaphragm and cap assembly.

Installation

23   Carefully install the master cylinder by reversing the removal steps, then bleed the brakes (see Section 11).

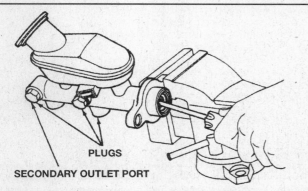

PLUGS

SECONDARY OUTLET PORT

8.19 When bench bleeding the master cylinder, start with the secondary outlet port

9   Pressure differential valve assembly - description, replacement and adjustment

Description

Refer to illustrations 9.1 and 9.2

1   The pressure differential valve **(see illustration)** senses an unbalanced hydraulic pressure condition existing between the front and rear brake systems. When there is a pressure loss in either system

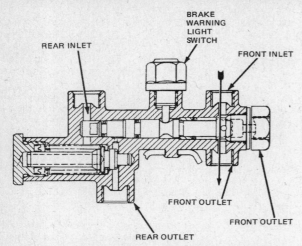

9.1 Typical pre-1984 pressure differential/control valve without metering valve

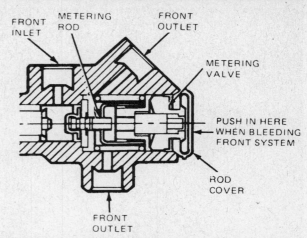

9.2 On vehicles equipped with a metering valve integral with the pressure differential/control valve body, press in on the metering rod cover as you bleed the front hydraulic system

during brake application, the piston will move off-center, causing the brake warning lamp to light. The warning lamp will shut off when the brake system is accurately serviced, properly bled and the brakes are applied to center the piston. The brake warning lamp switch is mounted on top of the control valve body. Under normal conditions, when the differential valve piston is centrally located, the spring-loaded warning switch plunger fits into the piston's tapered groove leaving the contacts of the warning switch open.

2   On 1984 and later vehicles, the metering valve is integrated into the differential valve assembly. This valve limits the pressure to the front brakes until a predetermined front hydraulic pressure has been reached. It is found in the forward end of the control valve central bore. The bleeder rod **(see illustration)** must be depressed manually when bleeding the front brakes.

Replacement

3   Unplug the electrical connector from the warning light switch.
4   Disconnect the hydraulic line fittings from the valve assembly. Plug the ends of the lines to prevent loss of hydraulic fluid.
5   Remove the nuts and bolts securing the valve bracket to the underside of the fender apron. Remove the assembly from the vehicle.
6   To install the assembly, position the valve on the fender apron holes and install the mounting nuts/bolts.
7   Reconnect all brake lines to the valve assembly.
8   Plug in the electrical connector to the brake warning light switch. Verify that the connection is good by turning the ignition switch to the Start position. The light should come on.
9   Bleed the brake system (see Section 11) and centralize the pressure differential valve.

Centralizing the valve

Note: *This procedure applies to pre-1990 vehicles. Later vehicles have a self-centering valve.*

10   After any repair or bleeding operations it is possible that the brake warning light will come on if the pressure differential valve remains in an off-center position.
11   To centralize the valve, turn the ignition switch to the ON position.
12   Depress the brake pedal several times and the piston will center itself, causing the warning light to go out.
13   Turn the ignition Off.
14   Test for a firm resistance at the brake pedal.

10   Brake hoses and lines - inspection and replacement

Caution: *If the vehicle is equipped with ABS, make sure you plug the brake line immediately after disconnecting it from the brake hose, to*

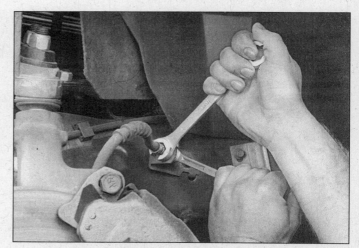

10.2 To disconnect the fitting that attaches the flexible brake hose to the metal brake line at the bracket in the wheel well, use a backup wrench on the hose fitting to ensure that the metal line doesn't get twisted

prevent the fluid from draining out of the line and air entering the HCU. The HCU on an ABS system cannot be bled without a very expensive tool.

Inspection

1   About every six months, raise the vehicle and support it securely on jackstands. Inspect the rubber hoses, which connect the steel brake lines with the front and rear brake assemblies for cracks, chafing of the outer cover, leaks, blisters and other damage. These are important and vulnerable parts of the brake system and inspection should be complete. A light and mirror will be helpful for a thorough check. If a hose exhibits any of the above conditions, replace it with a new one.

Replacement

Flexible hose

Refer to illustrations 10.2 and 10.3

2   Using a flare nut wrench, disconnect the brake line from the hose fitting, being careful not to bend the frame bracket or brake line. Hold the fitting on the hose with a wrench to prevent the metal line from twisting and the frame bracket from bending **(see illustration)**.
3   Remove the large retaining clip **(see illustration)** and detach the

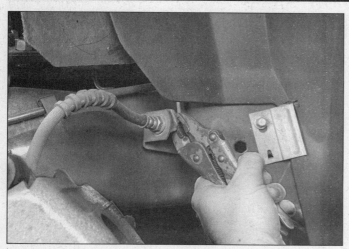

10.3   Once the fitting has been unscrewed, remove this large retainer clip and separate the hose from the bracket

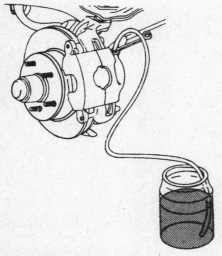

11.8   When bleeding the brakes, a hose is connected to the bleed screw at the caliper or wheel cylinder and then submerged in brake fluid - air will be seen as bubbles in the tube and container (all air must be expelled before moving to the next wheel)

hose from the bracket and the body. **Caution:** *Plug the metal brake line immediately to prevent air from getting into the system.*

4   Remove the banjo bolt from the caliper and discard the sealing washers.

5   Connect the hose to the caliper, using new sealing washers. Tighten the banjo bolt to the torque listed in this Chapter's Specifications.

6   Without twisting the hose, connect the other end of the line to the bracket on the chassis.

7   Connect the metal brake line to the hose fitting by hand, then, using a flare nut wrench, tighten the fitting securely. Be sure to use a wrench on the hose fitting to prevent the bracket from bending or the metal line from twisting.

8   When the brake hose installation is complete, there should be no kinks in the hose. Make sure the hose doesn't contact any part of the suspension. Check this by turning the wheels to the extreme left and right positions. If the hose makes contact, remove it and correct the installation as necessary.

Metal brake line

9   When replacing brake lines be sure to use the correct parts. Don't use copper tubing for any brake system components. Purchase steel

brake lines from a dealer or auto parts store.

10   Prefabricated brake line, with the tube ends already flared and fittings installed, is available at auto parts stores and dealers. These lines are also sometimes bent to the proper shapes.

11   When installing the new line make sure it's securely supported in the brackets and has plenty of clearance between moving or hot components.

12   After installation, check the master cylinder fluid level and add fluid as necessary. Bleed the brake system as outlined in the next Section and test the brakes carefully before driving the vehicle in traffic.

---

11   Brake hydraulic system - bleeding

Refer to illustration 11.8

Warning: *Wear eye protection when bleeding the brake system. If the fluid comes in contact with your eyes, immediately rinse them with water and seek medical attention.*

Note: *Bleeding the hydraulic system is necessary to remove any air that manages to find its way into the system when it's been opened during removal and installation of a hose, line, caliper or master cylinder.*

Conventional brakes (non-ABS)

1   It will probably be necessary to bleed the system at all four brakes if air has entered the system due to low fluid level, or if the brake lines have been disconnected at the master cylinder.

2   If a brake line was disconnected only at a wheel, then only that caliper or wheel cylinder must be bled.

3   If a brake line is disconnected at a fitting located between the master cylinder and any of the brakes, that part of the system served by the disconnected line must be bled.

4   Remove any residual vacuum from the brake power booster by applying the brake several times with the engine off.

5   Remove the master cylinder reservoir cover and fill the reservoir with brake fluid. Reinstall the cover. **Note:** *Check the fluid level often during the bleeding operation and add fluid as necessary to prevent the fluid level from falling low enough to allow air bubbles into the master cylinder.*

6   Have an assistant on hand, as well as a supply of new brake fluid, an empty clear plastic container, a length of 3/16-inch plastic, rubber or vinyl tubing to fit over the bleeder valve and a wrench to open and close the bleeder valve.

7   Beginning at the right rear wheel, loosen the bleeder valve slightly, then tighten it to a point where it is snug but can still be loosened quickly and easily.

8   Place one end of the tubing over the bleeder valve and submerge the other end in brake fluid in the container **(see illustration)**.

9   Have the assistant pump the brakes slowly a few times to get pressure in the system, then hold the pedal firmly depressed.

10   While the pedal is held depressed, open the bleeder valve just enough to allow a flow of fluid to leave the valve. Watch for air bubbles to exit the submerged end of the tube. When the fluid flow slows after a couple of seconds, close the valve and have your assistant release the pedal.

11   Repeat Steps 9 and 10 until no more air is seen leaving the tube, then tighten the bleeder valve and proceed to the left rear wheel, the right front wheel and the left front wheel, in that order, and perform the same procedure. Be sure to check the fluid in the master cylinder reservoir frequently.

12   Never use old brake fluid. It contains moisture which will deteriorate the brake system components.

13   Refill the master cylinder with fluid at the end of the operation.

14   Check the operation of the brakes. The pedal should feel solid when depressed, with no sponginess. If necessary, repeat the entire process. **Warning:** *Do not operate the vehicle if you are in doubt about the effectiveness of the brake system.*

9

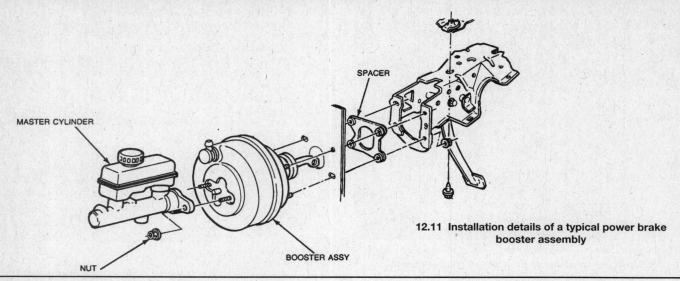

12.11 Installation details of a typical power brake booster assembly

Anti-lock brake system (ABS)

15   ABS-equipped models cannot be bled at home if air gets into the master cylinder and/or the hydraulic control unit (HCU). The first step in the bleeding procedure for these two components requires a special anti-lock test adapter which must be plugged into the control module. Any attempt to bleed the master cylinder and HCU without this special device will trap air in the HCU, which will result in a spongy brake pedal.

16   However, as long as no air has gotten into the master cylinder or the HCU, the brake lines and the calipers can be bled in the conventional manner. Refer to Steps 1 through 14 above.

12   Power brake booster - check, removal, installation and adjustment

Vacuum-operated boosters

1   The power brake booster unit requires no special maintenance apart from periodic inspection of the vacuum hose and the case.

2   Dismantling of the brake booster requires special tools and is not ordinarily done by the home mechanic. If a problem develops, install a new or factory rebuilt unit.

Check

3   Begin the power booster check by depressing the brake pedal several times with the engine off and make sure that there is no change in the pedal reserve distance. The reserve distance is the distance between the pedal and the floor when the pedal is fully depressed.

4   Now, depress the pedal and start the engine. If the pedal goes down slightly, operation is normal. Release the brake pedal and let the engine run for a couple of minutes.

5   Turn off the engine and depress the brake pedal several times slowly. If the pedal goes down farther the first time but gradually rises after the second or third depression, the booster is airtight.

6   Start the engine and depress the brake pedal, then stop the engine with the pedal still depressed. If there is no change in the reserve distance after holding the pedal for about 30-seconds, the booster is airtight.

7   If the pedal feels "hard" when the engine is running, the booster isn't operating properly or there is a vacuum leak in the hose to the booster.

Removal

Refer to illustration 12.11

8   Remove the nuts attaching the master cylinder to the booster (see Section 8) and carefully pull the master cylinder forward until it clears the mounting studs. Use caution so as not to bend or kink the brake lines.

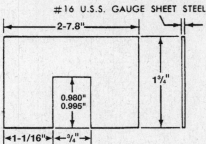

12.16a Power brake booster pushrod gauge template (1970 through 1974 vehicles)

9   Detach the manifold vacuum hose from the booster check valve.

10   Working in the passenger compartment under the steering column, unplug the electrical connector from the brake light switch **(see illustration 14.2)**, then remove the pushrod retaining clip and nylon washer from the brake pedal pin. Slide the pushrod off the pin.

11   Remove the nuts attaching the brake booster to the firewall **(see illustration)**.

12   Carefully detach the booster from the firewall and lift it out of the engine compartment.

Installation

13   Place the booster into position on the firewall and tighten the mounting nuts to the torque listed in this Chapter's Specifications. Connect the pushrod and brake light switch to the brake pedal. Install the retaining clip in the brake pedal pin.

14   Install the master cylinder to the booster, tightening the nuts to the torque listed in this Chapter's Specifications.

15   Carefully check the operation of the brakes before driving the vehicle in traffic.

Adjustment

Refer to illustrations 12.16a, 12.16b, 12.16c, 12.16d and 12.20

16   All *vacuum-operated* boosters feature an adjustable pushrod (Hydro-Boost units are not adjustable). They are matched to the booster at the factory and most likely will not require adjustment, but if a misadjusted pushrod is suspected, a gauge can be fabricated out of heavy gauge sheet metal using the accompanying template **(see illustrations)**.

17   Some common symptoms caused by a misadjusted pushrod include dragging brakes (if the pushrod is too long) or excessive brake pedal travel accompanied by a groaning sound from the brake booster (if the pushrod is too short).

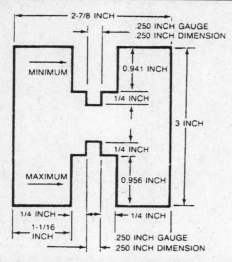

12.16b Power brake booster pushrod gauge template (1980 through 1986 vehicles)

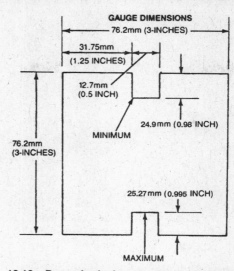

12.16c Power brake booster pushrod gauge template (1987 through 1989 vehicles)

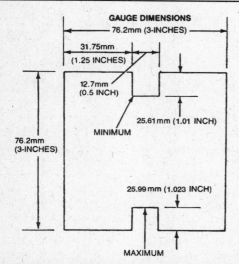

12.16d Power brake booster pushrod gauge template (1990 and later vehicles)

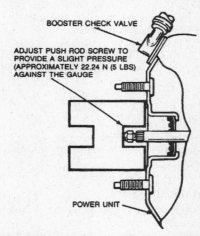

12.20 Check the pushrod length (the pushrod is preset at the factory and most likely will never need adjusting)

18   To check the pushrod length, unbolt the master cylinder from the booster and position it to one side. It isn't necessary to disconnect the hydraulic lines, but be careful not to bend them.

19   Block the front wheels, apply the parking brake and place the transmission in Park.

20   Start the engine and place the pushrod gauge against the end of the pushrod, exerting a force of approximately five pounds to seat the pushrod in the power unit **(see illustration)**. **Note:** *If you have a vacuum pump, you can simply apply vacuum to the booster instead of starting the engine.* The rod measurement should fall somewhere between the minimum and maximum cutouts on the gauge. If it doesn't, adjust it by holding the knurled portion of the pushrod with a pair of pliers and turning the end with a wrench.

21   When the adjustment is complete, reinstall the master cylinder and check for proper brake operation before driving the vehicle in traffic.

Hydraulically operated boosters (Hydro-Boost)
Check

22   Check the fluid in the master cylinder. If the fluid level isn't within 1/4-inch of the top of the master cylinder reservoirs, top it off with brake fluid (see Chapter 1).

23   Check the power steering pump fluid level with the engine off and the fluid at operating temperature (see Chapter 1).

24   Check the power steering pump belt tension and adjust it if necessary (see Chapter 1).

25   Inspect all power steering system hoses for leaks and kinks. If the fluid smells burned, check the hoses and cooler for restrictions.

26   Check the engine idle speed and adjust it to specifications (see Chapter 1).

27   Check the power steering hydraulic fluid for aeration (indicated by bubbles in the fluid). If there is any air in the system, bleed the power steering system (see Chapter 10).

28   If, after completing the above preliminary checks, you still can't find the cause of the condition, perform the following functional test of the Hydro-Boost system:

a) *Check the brake system for leaks or insufficient fluid in the master cylinder reservoir.*

b) *With the transmission in Neutral, stop the engine and apply the brake pedal several times to deplete all accumulator reserve.*

c) *Hold the pedal depressed and start the engine. If the Hydro Boost unit is operating correctly, the brake pedal will fall slightly, then it will push back against your foot. If you don't feel this "push-back" right after starting the engine, the Hydro Boost unit is not working correctly.*

9

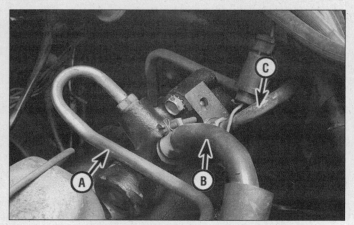

12.33 Hydro-Boost fluid pressure (A), return (B) and steering gear (C) hoses

12.34a To detach the Hydro-Boost unit from the firewall, remove these four locknuts (arrows)(two lower locknuts shown, upper locknuts not visible in this photo)

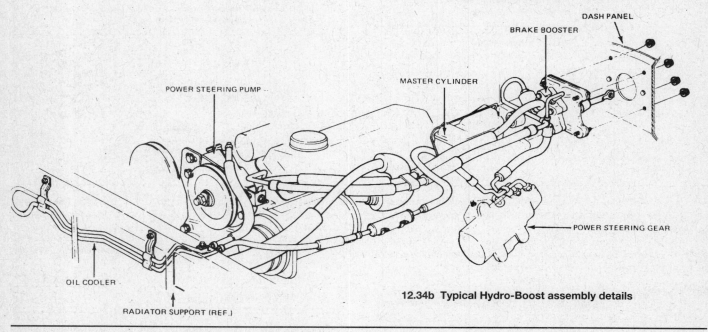

12.34b Typical Hydro-Boost assembly details

d) *Start the engine and operate it at idle speed. Turn the steering wheel to the stop. Hold for a maximum of five seconds. Return the steering wheel to center and turn off the engine.*

e) *Depress and release the brake pedal. Repeat this procedure until a "hard pedal" is obtained. There should be at least two power-assisted brake applications with pressure applied to the pedal.*

f) *Restart the engine and let it idle. Turn the steering wheel to the stop. There should be a light hissing sound as the accumulator is charged. Hold lightly against the stop for a maximum of five seconds. Return the steering wheel to center and turn off the engine.*

g) *Wait one hour and apply the brake pedal (do not restart the engine). There should still be at least two power-assisted brake applications when the pedal is depressed before you feel a "hard pedal."*

29   If the Hydro-Boost unit is working correctly, the problem lies somewhere in the brake system; if the Hydro-Boost unit is not working properly, verify that the power steering is operating normally. You'll have to take the vehicle to a dealer service department to have the power steering pump tested for flow and pressure.

30   If power steering operation is normal, and the Hydro-Boost unit is suspect, refer to the Troubleshooting section at the front of this manual

and check those items related to the Hydro-Boost system. If the Hydro-Boost unit itself is the problem, do not attempt to overhaul it; replace it with a new or rebuilt unit.

Removal

Refer to illustrations 12.33, 12.34a and 12.34b

31   Discharge the accumulator by making several brake applications until a "hard pedal" is obtained.

32   Remove the two nuts attaching the master cylinder to the Hydro-Boost unit (see Section 8), pull it off and secure it to one side, with the metal hydraulic lines still attached (make sure you don't kink or bend these lines, or they will have to be replaced).

33   Disconnect the pressure, steering gear and return lines from the booster **(see illustration)**. Plug the lines and the ports in the Hydro-Boost unit to prevent dirt from contaminating the system.

34   From under the dashboard, disconnect the Hydro-Boost pushrod from the brake pedal assembly as follows:

a) *Unplug the brake light switch connector (see Section 14).*

b) *Remove the hairpin retainer from the clevis pin.*

c) *Slide the brake light switch off the brake pedal pin just far enough for the switch outer hole to clear the pin, then remove the switch from the pin.*

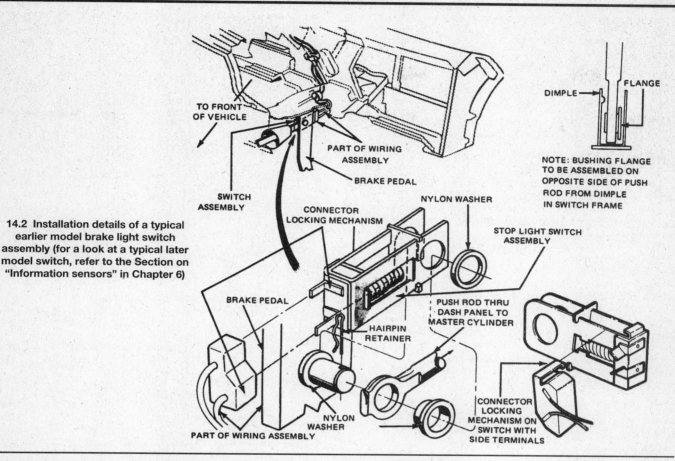

14.2 Installation details of a typical earlier model brake light switch assembly (for a look at a typical later model switch, refer to the Section on "Information sensors" in Chapter 6)

d) *Loosen the Hydro-Boost-to-firewall locknuts* **(see illustrations)**.
e) *Slide the Hydro-Boost pushrod and the nylon washers and bushing off the brake pedal pin.*

35 Remove the Hydro Boost-to-firewall locknuts and remove the Hydro-Boost unit , sliding the pushrod link out from the engine side of the hole in the firewall. Don't lose the rubber dust boot.

Installation

36 Place the Hydro-Boost assembly in position on the firewall and insert the pushrod and boot through the hole in the firewall. Loosely install the Hydro Boost-to-firewall locknuts.
37 Working under the dash, connect the Hydro-Boost pushrod to the brake pedal assembly as follows:

a) *Install the inner nylon washer, the Hydro-Boost pushrod and the bushing on the brake pedal pin.*
b) *Position the switch so that it straddles the pushrod with the switch slot on the pedal pin and the switch outer hole just clearing the pin. Slide the switch completely onto the pin and install the nylon washer. Be careful not to deform the switch.*
c) *Secure these parts to the pin with the hairpin retainer.*
d) *Plug in the brake light switch connector and install the wires in the retaining clip.*
e) *Tighten the Hydro Boost-to-firewall locknuts securely.*

38 Install the master cylinder on the Hydro Boost unit and tighten the master cylinder mounting nuts to the torque listed in this Chapter's Specifications.
39 Remove the plugs and connect the fluid pressure, steering gear and return hoses to the Hydro-Boost unit. Tighten the fittings securely.
40 Remove the coil wire to disable the engine. Fill the power steering pump reservoir and, while engaging the starter, apply the brakes with a pumping action. Do NOT turn the steering wheel lock-to-lock until all residual air has been purged from the Hydro-Boost.
41 Check the fluid level and add fluid as necessary.

42 Install the coil wire, start the engine and apply the brakes with a pumping action. Turn the steering wheel lock-to-lock several times. Check for leaks.
43 If you hear a whining noise after installing a Hydro-Boost unit, fluid aeration may be the problem. Bleed the power steering system (see Chapter 10).

13 Brake pedal height - check

1 With the engine running and the parking brake fully released, insert a slender, sharp-pointed prod through the carpet and sound deadener material until it contacts the firewall and measure the distance to the upper middle of the brake pedal.
2 If the position of the pedal isn't within the dimensions listed in this Chapter's Specifications, check the brake pedal linkage for missing, worn or damaged bushings and, if necessary, replace them.
3 If the pedal free height is still out of specification, check the pedal, booster and master cylinder and verify that the correct parts are installed. Replace any worn or damaged parts as necessary.

14 Brake light switch - removal and installation

Removal

Refer to illustrations 14.2 and 14.3
1 Remove the under dash panel.
2 Locate the brake light switch assembly **(see illustration)** near the top of the brake pedal and disconnect the switch from the brake pedal by removing the retaining clip.
3 Use a small screwdriver to unlock the electrical connector, then unplug the connector from the brake light switch **(see illustration)**.

9

Installation

4   Install the switch to the electrical connector by snapping the clip into place.
5   Reconnect the assembly to the brake pedal.
6   Install the under dash panel.
7   Check the brake lights for proper operation.

---

15   Parking brake - adjustment

1989 and earlier models

Refer to illustration 15.3

1   Place the transmission in Neutral and fully release the parking brake.
2   Raise the vehicle and support it securely on jackstands. Block the front wheels to prevent the vehicle from rolling.
3   On vehicles with rear drum brakes, tighten the adjusting nut against the cable equalizer or adjuster bracket until the rear shoes drag against the drums. Then loosen the adjusting nut until the rear brakes are fully released. There should be no brake drag. On vehicles with rear disc brakes, tighten the adjusting nut against the cable equalizer or adjuster bracket until the levers on the calipers just start to move **(see illustration)**. Then loosen the nut so that the levers on the calipers return to the "stop position," which is determined by inserting a 1/4-inch pin into the hole in each caliper housing. If the lever can be moved to the rear, it's too tight and must be readjusted.
4   If you've installed new cables, stroke the parking brake forcefully a few times (to stretch the cable), release it, then repeat the previous Step.
5   Lower the vehicle and check the operation of the parking brake.

1990 and later models

6   These models use a parking brake control assembly with an automatic tensioning device. No adjustment of the cable is necessary.

---

16   Parking brake cables - replacement

1989 and earlier models

Front cable

Refer to illustration 16.1

1   Raise the vehicle and support it securely on jackstands. Release the parking brake completely, then loosen the adjusting nut at the adjuster **(see illustration)**.
2   Disconnect the cable from the adjuster bracket and remove the clip retaining the cable to the body.
3   From inside the vehicle, disconnect the cable from the pedal assembly.

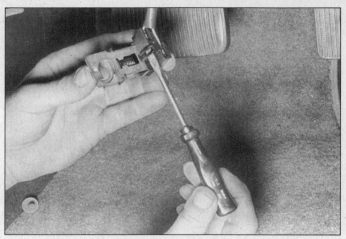

14.3 Use a small screwdriver to disengage the clip inside the electrical connector

4   Remove the cable down trough the floorpan.
5   To install, insert the cable through the floorpan holes and attach it to the control assembly inside the vehicle. Make sure the grommet is properly seated.
6   From underneath the vehicle, fasten the cable to the adjuster bracket.

Intermediate cable

7   From under the vehicle, remove the cable adjusting nut.
8   Disconnect the intermediate cable ends at the left rear and at the transverse cable.
9   Remove the cable and adjuster bracket assembly, keeping track of the order in which the cotter pin, washer and spring were removed for ease of reassembly.
10   Install the equalizer assembly onto the pin, holding it in place while installing the spring, washer and cotter pin.
11   Connect the cable ends to the left rear and the transverse cable.
12   Install the cable adjusting nut.

Transverse cable

13   Remove the cable adjusting nut.
14   Disconnect the cable ends at the right rear of the transverse cable and the intermediate cable.
15   Remove any retaining clips or brackets and remove the cable.
16   With the cable held in position, install the retaining clips or brackets holding the cable to the body.
17   Reconnect the cable ends.
18   Reinstall the adjusting nut.

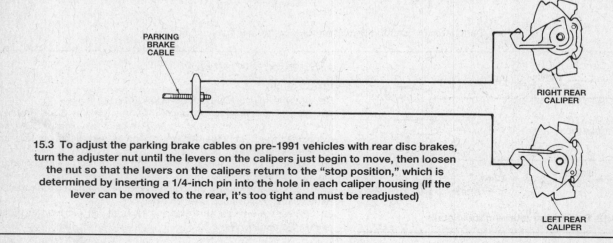

15.3 To adjust the parking brake cables on pre-1991 vehicles with rear disc brakes, turn the adjuster nut until the levers on the calipers just begin to move, then loosen the nut so that the levers on the calipers return to the "stop position," which is determined by inserting a 1/4-inch pin into the hole in each caliper housing (If the lever can be moved to the rear, it's too tight and must be readjusted)

LOWER SUSPENSION ARM REF.

FRAME REF.

ADJUSTER BRACKET

NOTE: L.H. CABLE TO GO OVER R.H. CABLE

VIEW Y

(MUST BE MOUNTED ON INBOARD SURFACE)

VIEW X
R.H. SHOWN — L.H. TYPICAL

VIEW R

VIEW W

MAXIMUM EFFECTIVE FORCE USED TO INSERT END FITTING IN BACKING PLATE 100 LBS. TO AVOID PERMANENT DAMAGE TO CONDUIT.

VIEW X

VIEW Y

VIEW U

VIEW T.B.D.

COWL REF.

VIEW T

VIEW V

VIEW Z

THIS SEAL MUST PASS THRU HOLE IN DASH.

VIEW U
CABLE WITHIN BRAKE DRUM
L.H. SHOWN — R.H. TYPICAL

PRONGS MUST BE SECURELY LOCKED IN PLACE

SOUND DEADENER REF.

BACK UP LIGHT SWITCH REF.

UPPER ARM

VIEW Z
MANUAL RELEASE

STEERING COLUMN REF.

VIEW Z
AUTOMATIC RELEASE

VIEW R

NO. 4 CROSSMEMBER

CABLE LOCATER SLEEVE

VIEW W

VIEW T.B.D.

SOUND DEADENER REF.

VIEW V

16.1 Installation details of a typical parking brake cable assembly

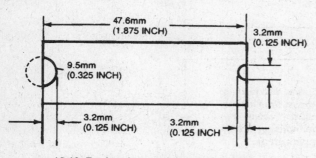

47.6mm (1.875 INCH)

3.2mm (0.125 INCH)

9.5mm (0.325 INCH)

3.2mm (0.125 INCH)

3.2mm (0.125 INCH)

16.19 Reel spring retaining tool details

1990 and later models
Front cable
Refer to illustrations 16.19, 16.23a and 6.23b

19   The front cable is connected to the parking brake control mechanism. You need to fabricate a special tool out of metal to disconnect the front cable from the spring-loaded automatic take-up reel **(see illustration)**.

20   Remove all the necessary trim panels to access the control mechanism (see Chapter 11).

21   Remove the Powertrain Control Module (PCM) (see Chapter 6). Remove the fuse box and position it aside.

22   Raise the vehicle and place it securely on jackstands. Fully release the parking brake.

9

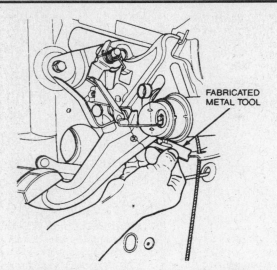

16.23a Pull the cable down and insert the fabricated reel spring retaining tool into the control mechanism . . .

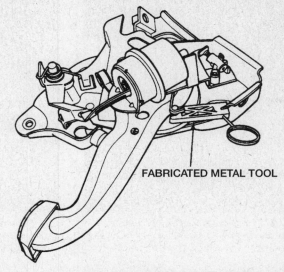

16.23b . . . between the stud on the take-up reel and the mounting bracket

23   With the help of an assistant, pull down on the intermediate cable and position the fabricated reel spring retaining tool between the take-up reel spring stud and the mounting bracket **(see illustrations)**. This will release the tension on the parking brake cable. **Warning:** *Keep your fingers away from the reel spring mechanism while the tool is in place.*

24   Disconnect the front cable from the rear cable at the connector **(see illustration 16.33)**. Disconnect the front cable from the take-up reel at the control mechanism.

25   Remove the screws retaining the left inner fender panel and pull it back exposing the point where the parking brake cable enters the frame. Depress the cable housing retaining tabs, pull the cable through the frame and let it hang down in the wheel well.

26   Depress the retaining tabs and remove the cable from the control mechanism. Push the cable down through the dash panel and remove it through the wheel well.

27   Install the new cable and connect it to the take-up reel and the rear cable. Pull the cable down and remove the reel spring retaining tool from the control mechanism. Apply and manually release the parking brake several times and check for proper operation.

28   The remainder of installation is the reverse of removal. Once the vehicle is sitting back on the ground, apply the parking brake and verify that it is holding the vehicle. Start the engine, apply the foot brake, shift to Drive and verify that the control releases the parking brake.

Intermediate and rear cables

Refer to illustrations 16.30a, 16.30b, 16.30c, 16.31, 16.32, 16.33 and 16.34

Note: *The following procedure applies to the intermediate cable (the short cable between the front cable and the two rear cables) and to either rear cable.*

29   Make sure the parking brake is released. Raise the rear of the vehicle and place it securely on jackstands.

30   Disconnect the rear cable. On models with rear drum brakes, you'll need to remove the brake drum and disassemble the brake (see Section 6) to disconnect the parking brake cable from the actuating lever **(see illustration 6.4l)**. On models with rear disc brakes, simply follow the accompanying procedure **(see illustrations)**

31   Disconnect the left rear cable from the intermediate cable **(see illustration)**.

32   Disconnect the right rear cable from the intermediate cable **(see illustration)**.

33   If you need to replace the intermediate cable, simply disconnect the front end of the intermediate cable from the connector at the rear end of the front cable **(see illustration)**.

34   Installation is the reverse of removal. When you reattach the two rear cables to the intermediate cable, make sure that the left cable is on top **(see illustration)**.

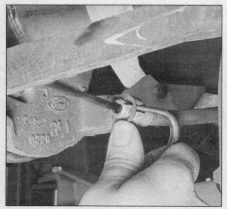

16.30a On models with rear disc brakes, remove this retaining clip from the bracket on the torque plate . . .

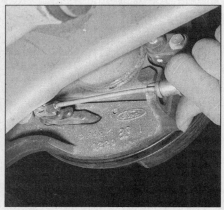

16.30b . . . pull the cable forward (toward the front of the vehicle) and guide it out of the bracket . . .

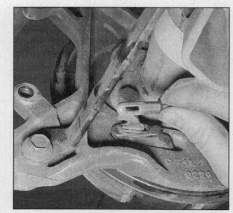

16.30c . . . then disconnect the cable from the parking brake lever

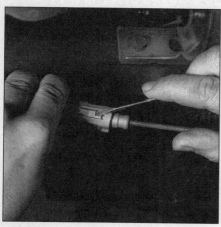

16.31 To disconnect the left rear cable from the intermediate cable, pry open this locking tang with a small screwdriver

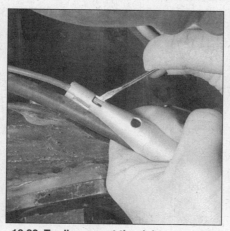

16.32 To disconnect the right rear cable from the intermediate cable, pry open this locking tang with a small screwdriver

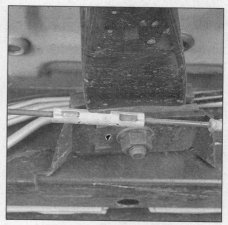

16.33 If you are replacing the intermediate cable, disconnect it from the front cable by prying it out of this connector with a small screwdriver (you'll find this connector under the crossmember for the transmission extension housing mount)

17 Parking brake shoes (1991 and later rear disc brakes) - inspection and replacement

Refer to illustrations 17.5a through 17.5i

Warning: *Dust created by the brake system may contain asbestos, which is hazardous to your health. Never blow it out with compressed air and don't inhale any of it. An approved filtering mask should be worn when working on the brakes. Do not, under any circumstances, use petroleum-based solvents to clean brake parts. Use brake system cleaner only!*

1   Loosen the rear wheel lug nuts. Raise the rear of the vehicle and place it securely on jackstands. Remove the rear wheels.

2   Remove the caliper (see Section 4) and the brake disc (see Section 5). It's not necessary to disconnect the brake hose from the caliper; but hang the caliper out of the way with a piece of wire to prevent damage to the hose.

3   Inspect the thickness of the lining material on the shoes. If the lining has worn down to 0.040 inch or less, the shoes must be replaced.

4   Disconnect the rear parking brake cable from the parking brake lever (see Section 16).

5   Follow the accompanying photos **(see illustrations 17.5a through 17.5i)** for the parking brake shoe replacement procedure. Be sure to stay in order and read the caption under each illustration.

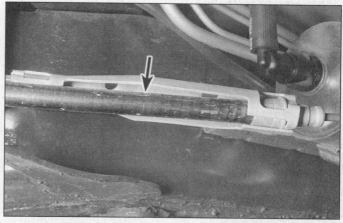

16.34 When you reattach the two rear parking brake cables to the intermediate cable, make sure the left rear cable (arrow) is on top, and attached to the forward end of the cable connector; the right rear cable should be under the left rear cable, and should be attached to the rear end of the connector

17.5a Remove the parking brake leading shoe hold-down spring with an Allen bit . . .

17.5b . . . and remove the trailing shoe hold-down spring

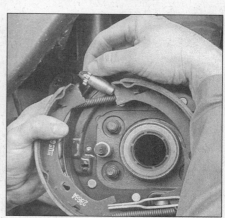

17.5c Rotate the star adjuster to its shortest length, then spread the parking brake shoes apart and remove the adjuster

9

17.5d Detach the upper return spring from the parking brake shoes (it's in the back)

17.5e Remove the parking brake shoes, the lower return springs and the parking brake lever as a single assembly; make sure you don't damage the rubber grommet that lines the hole in the backing plate for the parking brake lever

6   Install the brake disc. Temporarily thread three of the wheel lug nuts onto the studs to hold the disc in place.

7   Remove the rubber access plug from the backside of the brake torque plate. Adjust the parking brake shoe clearance by turning the adjuster star wheel with a brake adjusting tool or screwdriver until the shoes contact the disc and the disc can't be turned. Back-off the adjuster eight notches, then install the hole plug.

8   Install the brake caliper. Be sure to tighten the bolts to the torque listed in this Chapter's Specifications.

9   Install the wheel and tighten the lug nuts to the torque listed in the Chapter 1 Specifications.

10   To bed the shoes to the drum, drive the vehicle at approximately 30 mph on a dry, level road. Depress the parking brake pedal with about 20 pounds of force. **Note:** *The vacuum release mechanism will prevent the parking brake from setting, if it is operating properly. Be sure to check the function of the vacuum release before performing the bedding-in procedure.* Drive the vehicle for 1/4-mile with the parking brake applied like this.

11   Repeat this procedure two or three times, allowing the brakes to cool between applications.

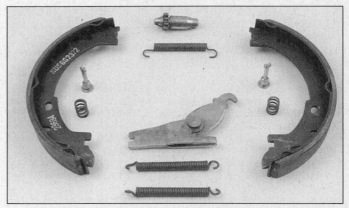

17.5f Finish disassembling the parking brake assembly on the bench: The two lower return springs (one in front of the shoes, one behind them) and the parking brake lever are shown bottom center

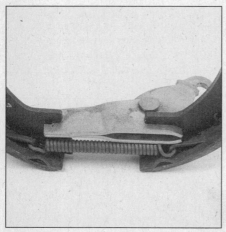

17.5g Here's a closeup of the correctly assembly parking brake lever and the lower return springs

17.5h A correctly assembled parking brake shoe assembly (on the bench)

17.5i A correctly assembled parking brake shoe assembly (on the vehicle)

Chapter 10
Suspension and steering systems

Contents

Specifications

Torque specifications
Ft-lbs (unless otherwise indicated)

Front suspension (except 1982 through 1987 Continental and 1984 through 1992 Mark VII)

Balljoint-to-(upper and lower) control arm nut (1970 through 1972)	24 to 28
Balljoint-to-steering knuckle nut	
1970 through 1972 (upper and lower)	60 to 90
1973 (upper and lower)	80 to 120
1974 through 1991	
Upper	75 to 90
Lower	105 to 120
1992 and later (lower)	80 to 119
Upper balljoint-to-steering knuckle pinch bolt	
1992	51 to 67
1993	76 to 104
1994	56 to 77
1995 and later	64 to 87

10

Torque specifications (continued)

Ft-lbs (unless otherwise indicated)

Front suspension (except 1982 through 1987 Continental and 1984 through 1992 Mark VII)

Lower balljoint-to-steering knuckle pinch bolt (1992 on)	80 to 119
Upper balljoint-to-upper arm retaining nuts (1992 on)	107 to 129
Hub and bearing assembly retaining nut (1992 on)	189 to 254
Lower arm-to-crossmember pivot bolt nut	
1970 through 1972	60 to 90
1973 and 1974	80 to 110
1975 through 1979	95 to 110
1980 on	120 to 140
Shock absorber	
Upper shock mounting nut	
1970	20 to 28
1971 through 1984	26 to 30
1985 and 1986	14 to 26
1987 through 1990	22 to 30
1991 and 1992	19 to 27
1993 on	25 to 34
Shock-to-lower control arm mounting bolts	
1970 through 1972	96 to 180 in-lbs
1973 through 1991	15 to 18
1992 through 1994	13 to 16
1995 and later	120 to 144 in-lbs
Stabilizer bar	
Stabilizer bar-to-frame clamp nuts	
1970	96 to 144 in-lbs
1971 through 1973	18 to 27
1974 through 1991	14 to 26
1992 on	44 to 59
Stabilizer bar-to-link nut/bolt	
1970 through 1974	72 to 144 in-lbs
1975 through 1979	180 to 216 in-lbs
1980 through 1991	108 to 144 in-lbs
1992 through 1994	30 to 40
1995 and later	19 to 26
Stabilizer link-to-lower arm nut (1988 through 1991)	108 to 180 in-lbs
Stabilizer link-to-steering knuckle nut	
1992	41 to 44
1993 and 1994	30 to 40
1995 and later	19 to 26
Strut bar	
Strut bar-to-frame	
1970 through 1972	60 to 90
1973 through 1979	95 to 105
Strut bar-to-lower arm	
1970	70 to 113
1971 and 1972	
Mark III	80 to 115
Continental	70 to 105
1973 through 1979	80 to 115
Upper control arm shaft retaining nuts	120 to 140

Front suspension (1982 through 1987 Continental and 1984 through 1992 Mark VII)

Lower arm-to-crossmember	
1982	215 to 260
1983 through 1985	150 to 180
1986 through 1992	110 to 150
Stabilizer bar mounting clamp-to-bracket	
1982 through 1986	20 to 25
1987	40 to 55
1988 on	37 to 50
Stabilizer bar-to-lower arm	72 to 144 in-lbs
Steering knuckle-to-strut bolts/nuts	150 to 180
Strut-to-upper mount nut	
1982	100 to 120
1983 through 1986	55 to 92
1987 on	50 to 75
Balljoint-to-steering knuckle	100 to 120
Strut upper mount-to-body nuts	62 to 75

Torque specifications (continued)

Ft-lbs (unless otherwise indicated)

Rear suspension (except 1982 through 1987 Continental and 1984 through 1992 Mark VII)

Lower suspension arm
  Lower arm-to-axle bolt (1970 through 1973) .... 90 to 120
  Lower arm-to-axle nut
    1970 through 1973 .... 70 to 90
    1974 on .... 120 to 130
  Lower arm-to-frame bolt
    1970 through 1973 .... 90 to 120
    1974 through 1979 .... 120 to 130
  Lower arm-to-frame nut
    1970 through 1973 .... 70 to 90
    1974 on .... 120 to 130
Shock absorber
  Shock absorber-to-lower arm (1970) .... 8 to 15
  Shock absorber-to-axle bracket nut
    1971 through 1991 .... 65 to 85
    1992 on .... 56 to 76
  Shock absorber-to-upper mount nut
    1970 .... 20 to 28
    1971 through 1991 .... 20 to 26
    1992 .... 16 to 21
    1993 on .... 25 to 34
Stabilizer bar
  Stabilizer bar bracket-to-frame nut
    1972 through 1979 .... 18 to 20
  Stabilizer bar-to-rear link nut (1972 through 1979) .... 16 to 20
  Stabilizer bar-to-lower arm nut
    1977 through 1979 .... 50 to 55
    1980 through 1991 .... 70 to 92
  Stabilizer bar link-to-frame nut (1992 on) .... 13 to 17
  Stabilizer bar bracket-to-axle bolts (1992 on) .... 16 to 21
Track bar (1970 through 1979)
  Track bar stud-to-axle
    1970 and 1971 .... 100 to 130
    1972 through 1973 .... 90 to 150
    1974 through 1979 .... 140 to 150
  Track bar-to-axle nut
    1970 and 1971 .... 85 to 110
    1972 through 1976 .... 85 to 100
    1977 through 1979 .... 75 to 85
  Track bar-to-frame
    1970 through 1973 (bolt) .... 70 to 90
    1974 through 1979 (nut) .... 50 to 70
Upper suspension arm
  Upper arm-to-frame nut/bolt
    1970 through 1972 .... 90 to 120
    1973 .... 100 to 130
    1974 through 1979 .... 120 to 130
    1980 and 1981 .... 103 to 133
    1982 on .... 120 to 150
  Upper arm-to-axle nut/bolt
    1970 .... 70 to 90
    1971 .... 95 to 130
    1972 and 1973 .... 65 to 85
    1974 .... 75 to 95
    1975 on .... 120 to 130

Rear suspension (1982 through 1987 Continental and 1984 through 1992 Mark VII)

Axle damper bolt and nut .... 55 to 70
Shock absorber-to-frame upper fastener
  1982 .... 24 to 26
  1983 through 1986 .... 17 to 27
  1987 on .... 12 to 20
Upper arm-to-frame bolt .... 100 to 105
Upper arm-to-axle bolt .... 90 to 100
Lower arm-to-frame bolt .... 100 to 105
Lower arm-to-axle nut .... 90 to 100

10

Torque specifications (continued)

Ft-lbs (unless otherwise indicated)

Rear suspension (1982 through 1987 Continental and 1984 through 1992 Mark VII)

Stabilizer bar-to-lower arm

1982	45 to 50
1983 through 1992	45 to 60

Shock absorber clevis bracket-to-axle bolt

1982	55 to 60
1983 through 1992	55 to 70

Steering (except 1982 through 1987 Continental and 1984 through 1992 Mark VII)

Tie-rods

Tie-rod-to-center link nuts	43 to 47
Tie-rod end-to-steering knuckle nuts	43 to 47

Tie-rod clamp-to-adjusting sleeve nuts

1970 through 1972

Continental Mark III	8 to 14
Lincoln Continental	9 to 15
1973 and 1974	15 to 20
1975 on	20 to 22
Center link-to-idler arm nut	60 to 67

Idler-arm bracket-to-frame nuts

1970	28 to 35
1971	30 to 40
1972 through 1979	45 to 50
1980 on	85 to 95

Pitman arm

Pitman arm-to-center link nut	43 to 47

Pitman arm-to-sector shaft nut

1970 through 1974	150 to 225
1975 on	236 to 250
Steering gear-to-frame bolts	60 to 65
Steering column flex coupling pinch bolt	22 to 33
Steering wheel retaining bolt	30 to 35

Steering (1982 through 1987 Continental and 1984 through 1992 Mark VII)

Steering gear-to-crossmember nuts	90 to 100
Tie-rod end-to-steering knuckle	35 to 47

1   General information

Refer to illustrations 1.1a, 1.1b, 1.4, 1.5a, 1.5b and 1.5c

On 1970 through 1979 models, the front suspension consists of upper and lower control arms, shock absorbers, coil springs and a stabilizer bar. These models also use a strut bar between the frame and the lower control arms **(see illustration)**. The front suspension of later models **(see illustration)** is similar, except for the lower control arm and strut bar. On all models, the inner ends of the control arms are attached to the frame; the outer ends are attached to the steering knuckles with balljoints.

On earlier models, the balljoints are riveted to the control arms; on these models, the rivets can be drilled out, the old balljoints pressed out and new balljoints pressed in. On later models, the balljoints are pressed into the control arms; on these models, it's not a good idea to install a new balljoint in a used control arm - instead, we recommend replacing the control arm and balljoint as an assembly. On 1992 and later models, the upper balljoints are bolted to forged upper arms; these balljoints *can* be removed from the arm and new balljoints installed.

The upper control arms pivot on a bushing-and-shaft assembly bolted to the frame. The lower control arms pivot on one (1979 and earlier models) or two (1980 and later models) bolts. The shocks and springs are mounted between the lower control arms and the frame. The stabilizer bar is attached to the frame with clamps. On pre-1992 models, the outer ends of the stabilizer bar are attached to the lower control arms with links; on 1992 and later models, the ends of the stabilizer bar are attached to the steering knuckles with links.

The front suspension on 1983 through 1987 Lincoln Continentals and 1984 through 1992 Continental Mark VIIs uses single lower arms and MacPherson struts with a stabilizer bar **(see illustration)**. These models do not have an upper control arm.

The rear suspension consists of shock absorbers, coil springs, and upper and lower suspension arms. All models have two lower arms. A single upper arm is used on 1970 through 1979 Lincoln Continentals and Town Cars **(see illustration)**; Continental Marks manufactured during this same period, and all 1980 and later models, have two upper arms **(see illustration)**. A track bar is used on 1970 through 1979 Lincoln Continentals and Town Cars. The upper end of the track bar is attached to the left (driver's side) frame rail and the lower end is attached to a bracket welded onto the right axle tube. A stabilizer bar is used on some 1972 through 1979 Continental Marks and on some 1980 and later models. The stabilizer bar is attached to the axle housing and to the lower arms. On all models except 1983 through 1987 Lincoln Continentals and 1984 through 1992 Continental Mark VIIs, the coil springs are mounted between the underside of the body and the axle housing. On 1983 through 1987 Lincoln Continentals and 1984 through 1992 Continental Mark VIIs, the coil springs are mounted between the underside of the body and the lower control arms **(see illustration)**. The shock absorbers are installed between the frame and brackets welded onto the underside of the axle assembly on all models.

All models except 1983 through 1987 Lincoln Continentals and 1984 through 1992 Continental Mark VIIs are equipped with power steering systems consisting of a power steering pump, a steering gearbox, the lines and hoses between the two components, and the steering linkage, which includes a Pitman arm, a center link, an idler arm, the inner and outer tie-rods and the threaded sleeves connecting them.

1.1a Typical front suspension and steering components (1970 through 1979 models)

1 Stabilizer bar	6 Lower control arm	10 Tie-rod
2 Stabilizer bar bracket	7 Lower control arm balljoint	11 Tie-rod adjuster
3 Stabilizer-to-control arm link	8 Center link	12 Tie-rod end
4 Strut bar	9 Idler arm	13 Shock absorber-to-control arm bolts
5 Coil spring		

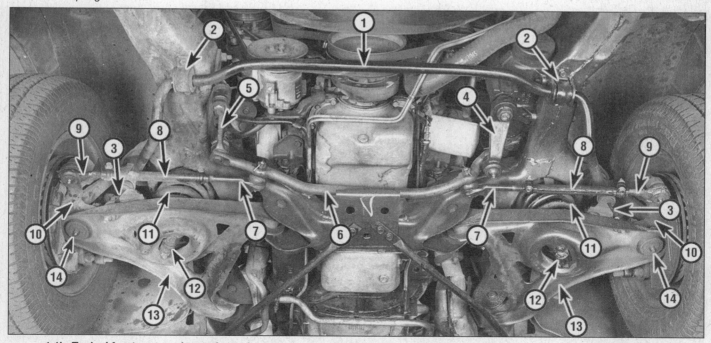

1.1b Typical front suspension and steering components (1980 and later models, except 1982 through 1987 Continental and 1984 through 1992 Mark VII)

1 Stabilizer bar	4 Pitman arm	8 Tie-rod adjuster	12 Shock absorber
2 Stabilizer bar bracket	5 Idler arm	9 Tie-rod end	13 Lower control arm
3 Stabilizer-to-control arm link	6 Center link	10 Steering knuckle	14 Lower control arm balljoint
	7 Tie-rod	11 Coil spring	

10

1.4 Typical front suspension and steering components (1982 through 1987 Continental and 1984 through 1992 Mark VII)

1	Stabilizer bar	5	Balljoint	9	Rack-and-pinion steering gear
2	Stabilizer bar bracket	6	Steering knuckle	10	Tie-rod
3	Stabilizer bar link and bushings	7	Coil spring	11	Tie-rod end
4	Strut assembly	8	Lower control arm	12	Steering gear boots

1.5a Typical rear suspension components (1970 through 1979 models)

1	Rear axle assembly	3	Coil spring	5	Lower suspension arm
2	Shock absorber	4	Track bar	6	Upper suspension arm

1.5b Typical rear suspension and steering components (1980 and later models, except 1982 through 1987 Continental and 1984 through 1992 Mark VII)

1   Rear axle assembly
2   Shock absorber-to-axle mounting bracket
3   Coil spring
4   Upper suspension arm
5   Lower suspension arm

1.5c Typical rear suspension (1982 through 1987 Continental and 1984 through 1992 Mark VII)

1   Rear axle assembly
2   Lower suspension arm
3   Upper suspension arm
4   Coil spring
5   Shock absorber
6   Driveshaft

10

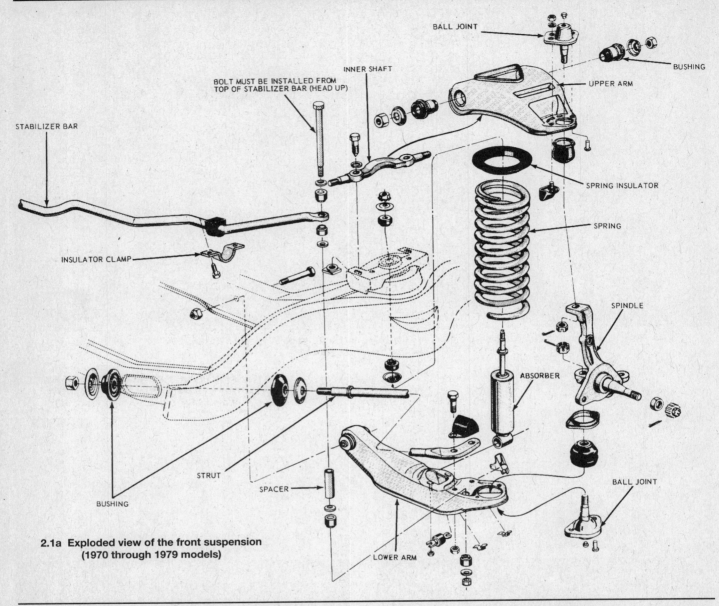

**2.1a Exploded view of the front suspension
(1970 through 1979 models)**

The power steering system on 1983 through 1987 Lincoln Continentals and 1984 through 1992 Continental Mark VIIs consists of a power steering pump, a power rack-and-pinion steering gearbox, the lines and hoses between the two components and a pair of tie-rods. **Warning:** *Some models are equipped with airbags. Always disconnect the negative battery cable, then the positive battery cable and wait two minutes before working in the vicinity of the impact sensors, steering column or instrument panel to avoid the possibility of accidental deployment of the airbag, which could cause personal injury (see Chapter 12).*

2   Shock absorber (front) - removal and installation

Refer to illustrations 2.1a, 2.1b, 2.1c and 2.3

1   Remove the shock absorber upper attaching nut, washer and bushing **(see illustrations)**.
2   Raise the vehicle and support it securely on jackstands.
3   Remove the two bolts which attach the lower end of the shock absorber to the lower control arm **(see illustrations)**.
4   Remove the shock absorber through the hole in the lower control arm. To ensure proper reassembly, note the order in which any bushings and grommets are installed both above and below the upper control arm. Inspect these parts for cracks, tears and deterioration, and replace as necessary.
5   Installation is the reverse of removal. But be sure you do the following:

a)   *Before installing a new hydraulic shock absorber, be sure to bleed the air from it. Hold the shock right side up and extend it fully. Turn the shock upside down and compress it all the way. Extend and compress the shock absorber in this manner at least three times.*
b)   *Install all bushings and grommets in the order in which you removed them. Also, it may be necessary to raise the lower control arm with a floor jack, after you've mounted the bottom of the shock to the lower control arm, to raise the shock rod high enough to install the upper mounting hardware.*
c)   *If the threads in the lower control arm are stripped or damaged, install 5/16-18 locknuts on the self-tapping bolts.*
d)   *Tighten all fasteners to the torque listed in this Chapter's Specifications. If you had to use locknuts on the self-tapping bolts, tighten them to the same torque specification as the bolts.*

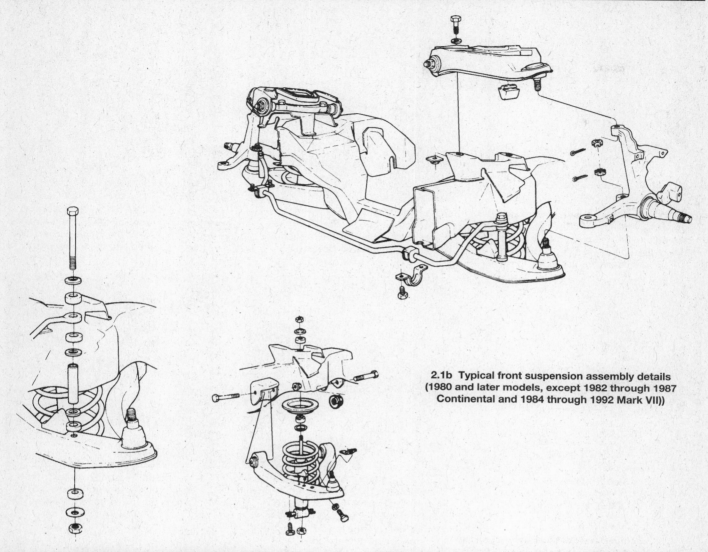

2.1b Typical front suspension assembly details (1980 and later models, except 1982 through 1987 Continental and 1984 through 1992 Mark VII))

2.1c To detach the upper end of the shock absorber from 1992 and later models, remove this nut (top arrow), then remove the large washer under it and the bushing under the washer. If you're replacing an upper balljoint on one of these models, be sure to mark the location of the alignment marks on the adjustment cams (middle and bottom arrows) before removing the two retaining nuts

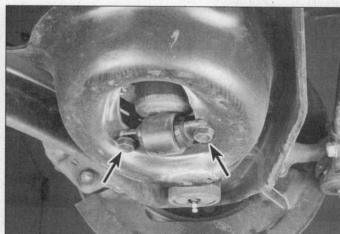

2.3 To detach the lower end of the shock absorber from the lower control arm, remove these two bolts (arrows), then pull the shock down through the hole in the arm (later model shown, early models similar)

10

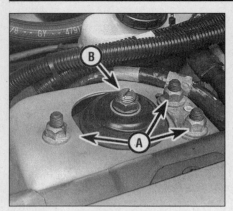

3.4 The strut upper mount is attached to the body by three nuts (A) - if the upper mount is to be removed from the strut assembly, loosen - but don't remove - the center nut (B) first

3.5 Remove the strut-to-steering knuckle nuts and bolts, separate the two components and lift the strut out of the wheel well (brake disc removed for clarity)

4.2a To prevent the link from turning while you're breaking loose the nut on top that attaches it to the stabilizer bar, hold the link with a pair of locking pliers

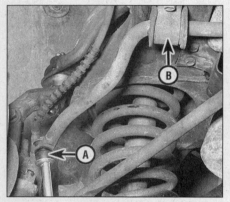

4.2b Typical stabilizer bar setup on pre-1992 models with the links attached to the lower control arms

    A   Link
    B   Stabilizer bar bracket

4.2c To disconnect the stabilizer bar from the links on a 1992 or later model (on which the links are attached to the steering knuckles instead of the lower arms), remove the nut (arrow) from each end (left nut shown)

4.3 To detach the stabilizer bar from the frame, remove the nuts (arrows) that attach the brackets to the frame

3 Strut (front) - removal and installation

Note: *This procedure applies to 1982 through 1987 Continentals and 1984 through 1992 Mark VIIs only. The struts on these models are not serviceable and must be replaced as complete assemblies.*

Removal

Refer to illustrations 3.4 and 3.5

1   Loosen the front wheel lug nuts, raise the vehicle and support it securely on jackstands. Remove the wheel.
2   Remove the disc brake caliper and hang it out of the way with a piece of wire (Chapter 9).
3   Place a floor jack under the lower control arm and raise it slightly. **Warning:** *The jack must remain in this position throughout the entire procedure.*
4   Unscrew the three upper mount-to-strut tower retaining nuts **(see illustration)**. If the upper mount is to be removed from the strut assembly, loosen (but do not remove) the center nut at this time.
5   Remove the strut-to-steering knuckle nuts and bolts **(see illustration)**.
6   Separate the strut assembly from the steering knuckle and remove it from the vehicle.
7   If the upper mount is to be replaced, remove the center retaining nut and slide off the mount.

Installation

8   If the upper mount was removed, place it over the top of the strut and install the nut.
9   Guide the strut assembly into position in the wheel well, pushing the upper mount studs through the holes in the shock tower. Install the three nuts and tighten them to the torque listed in this Chapter's Specifications. **Note:** *The Ford Motor Company recommends that the nuts not be re-used - replace them with new ones.*
10   Insert the steering knuckle into the lower mounting flange of the strut assembly and install the two bolts. Again, it is recommended that new bolts and nuts be used (genuine Ford parts or equivalent). Install the nuts and tighten them to the torque listed in this Chapter's Specifications.
11   Tighten the upper mount-to-strut assembly retaining nut to the torque listed in the Chapter 1 Specifications.
12   Remove the jack from under the control arm and install the disc brake caliper as outlined in Chapter 9.
13   Install the wheel, lower the vehicle and tighten the lug nuts to the torque listed in the Chapter 1 Specifications.

4 Stabilizer bar (front) - removal and installation

Refer to illustrations 4.2a, 4.2b, 4.2c and 4.3

1   Raise the vehicle and place it securely on jackstands.

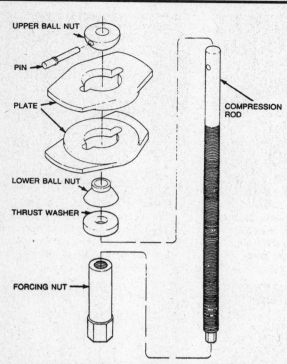

5.5a To compress the spring, you'll need either the factory tool (D78P-5310-A) or a suitable equivalent

5.6 To detach the inner end of the lower control arm from the frame, remove the pivot nuts and bolts (arrows)

2   Remove the nut at each end of the stabilizer bar and disconnect the bar from the links **(see illustration)**. On most models, the links attach the stabilizer bar to the lower control arms; on 1992 and later models, they attach it to the steering knuckles **(see illustrations)**.
3   Remove the stabilizer bar bracket nuts **(see illustration)** and remove the brackets.
4   Remove the stabilizer bar.
5   Installation is the reverse of removal. Be sure to tighten all fasteners to the torque listed in this Chapter's Specifications.

5   Coil spring (front) - removal and installation

Warning: *The following procedure is potentially dangerous if the proper safety precautions are not taken. A coil spring compressor of the type described below must be obtained and positioned properly to safely perform this procedure. Also, front coil springs should always be replaced in pairs.*

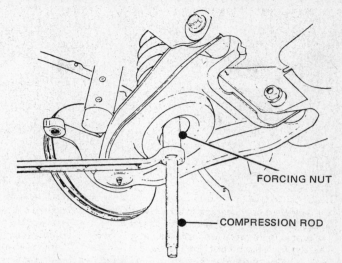

5.5b Once the spring compressor tool is installed in accordance with the manufacturer's instructions, simply turn the compression rod with a wrench until the spring no longer imposes a load on the lower control arm

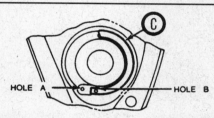

5.9 On 1988 through 1991 models, make sure the end of the spring coil (C) covers hole B, but not hole A

All models except 1982 through 1987 Continentals and 1984 through 1992 Mark VIIs
Removal
Refer to illustrations 5.5a, 5.5b and 5.6
1   Loosen the wheel lug nuts. Raise the vehicle and support it securely on jackstands. Remove the wheels.
2   On pre-1992 models, disconnect the stabilizer bar from the link (see Section 4).
3   Remove the shock absorber (see Section 2).
4   Disconnect the center link from the Pitman arm (see Section 21).
5   Install a suitable spring compressor, in accordance with the manufacturer's instructions, to relieve tension on the spring. Compress the spring **(see illustrations)**.
6   Remove the nuts and bolts that secure the inner end of the lower control arm to the frame **(see illustration)**.
7   Carefully and very slowly, lower the control arm. Remove the spring and compressor as a unit. Note how the upper insulator is installed between the upper end of the spring and the frame. If the spring is going to be replaced, loosen the spring compressor tool slowly, until all tension is removed from the spring, then remove the tool.

Installation
Refer to illustration 5.9
8   Place the spring upper insulator on the spring and secure it with tape. Install the spring compressor in accordance with the manufacturer's instructions, then compress the spring.
9   Position the spring on the lower control arm so that the lower end is properly engaged with the seat. On pre-1992 models, there are two holes in the lower control arm spring seat. The end of the spring must cover the first hole, but not the second hole **(see illustration)**.

10

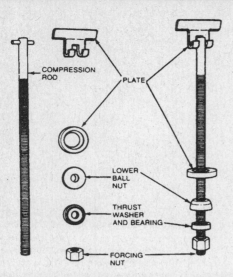

5.19a You'll need the special factory tool (T82P-5310-A), or a suitable equivalent, to compress the coil spring

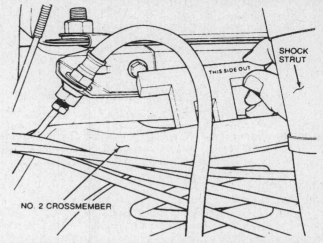

5.19b If you're using the factory tool, place the upper plate into the spring upper pocket in the crossmember, with the hooks facing up . . .

10   Raise the lower control arm carefully while guiding the inner end to align with the bolt holes in the frame. Install the pivot bolts into the control arm and the frame. Loosely attach the nuts on the bolts.
11   Attach the center link to the Pitman arm (see Section 21).
12   Attach the lower end of the shock absorber to the lower control arm (see Section 2).
13   On pre-1992 models, attach the stabilizer bar to the link (see Section 4).
14   Attach the upper end of the shock absorber to the vehicle (see Section 2).
15   Install the wheels. Remove the jackstands, lower the floor jack and lower the vehicle. Tighten the wheel lug nuts to the torque listed in the Chapter 1 Specifications.
16   After the vehicle has been lowered to the ground and is at curb height, tighten the lower control arm pivot bolt nuts to the torque listed in this Chapter's Specifications.

1982 through 1987 Continentals and 1984 through 1992 Mark VIIs

Removal
Refer to illustrations 5.19a, 5.19b, 5.19c and 5.21

17   Loosen the wheel lug nuts on the side to be dismantled. Raise the vehicle, support it securely on jackstands and remove the wheel.
18   Disconnect the stabilizer bar link from the lower control arm (see Section 4).
19   Using Ford spring compressor No. T82P-5310-A or an equivalent spring compressor, insert the upper plate of the tool through the spring upper pocket in the crossmember with the hooks on the plate pointing towards the center of the spring. Guide the compression rod up through the hole in the lower control arm and the coil spring, then insert the end of the compression rod into the upper plate **(see illustrations)**.
20   Install the lower plate, ball nut, thrust washer and bearing and the forcing nut on the compression rod. Tighten the forcing nut just enough to feel spring pressure.
21   Remove the lower control arm-to-crossmember nuts and pivot bolts **(see illustration)**. It may be necessary to remove the steering gear mounting bolts and reposition the gear to allow bolt removal. Loosen the forcing nut on the compressor tool until all of the spring pressure is relieved.
22   Remove the spring compressor compression rod then maneuver the coil spring out from between the lower control arm and crossmember.

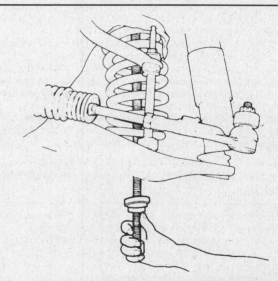

5.19c . . . then insert the compression rod up through the lower control arm and coil spring, hooking it to the upper plate

5.21 The lower control arm pivot bolts/nuts (arrows) can be removed AFTER the coil spring has been restrained with the special factory tool

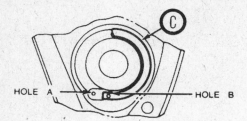

5.25 The bottom of the coil spring must be situated so that the end of the spring coil C covers hole B, but not hole A

Installation

Refer to illustration 5.25

23   Install the coil spring insulator on the top of the spring.

24   Install the spring in between the lower control arm and the spring upper pocket in the crossmember.

25   Position the bottom of the spring so that the pigtail covers only one of the drain holes, but leaves the other one open **(see illustration)**.

26   Locate the spring in the upper seat in the crossmember. Install the spring compressor tool as described in Steps 19 and 20, then tighten the forcing nut until the lower control arm bushing holes line up with the pivot bolt holes in the crossmember.

27   Install the pivot bolts and nuts in the direction shown in illustration 5.21, but don't tighten them completely at this time.

28   Remove the spring compressor tool. Position a floor jack under the outboard side of the lower control arm and raise it to simulate a normal ride position. Now tighten the pivot bolt nuts to the torque listed in this Chapter's Specifications.

29   Reconnect the stabilizer bar link to the lower control arm.

30   Install the wheel and lug nuts. Lower the vehicle and tighten the nuts to the torque listed in the Chapter 1 Specifications.

6   Strut bar (1970 through 1979 models) - removal and installation

1   Loosen the wheel lug nuts. Raise the front of the vehicle and support it securely on jackstands. Remove the front wheel.

2   Remove the nut from the strut bar at the frame **(see illustrations 1.1a and 2.1a)** and remove the washer and bushing from the strut bar.

3   Remove the nut, washer and bolt attaching the strut to the lower control arm and remove the rubber bumper.

4   Inspect all rubber bushings and the rubber bumper. If any rubber pieces are cracked, torn or deteriorated, replace them.

5   Installation is the reverse of removal. Be sure to tighten all fasteners to the torque listed in this Chapter's Specifications.

7   Lower control arm - removal, inspection and installation

All models except 1982 through 1987 Continentals and 1984 through 1992 Mark VIIs

Removal

Refer to illustration 7.5

1   Loosen the wheel lug nuts. Raise the front of the vehicle and support it securely on jackstands. Remove the front wheel.

2   Remove the shock absorber (see Section 2).

3   On pre-1992 models, disconnect the stabilizer bar (see Section 4).

4   Remove the front coil spring (see Section 5).

5   Remove and discard the cotter pin from the balljoint stud **(see illustration)**. Loosen the castle nut on the stud one or two turns. Rap the steering knuckle sharply in the immediate vicinity of the stud to relieve stud pressure and loosen the stud in the knuckle. If the stud won't come loose, you might have to resort to a "picklefork" type of

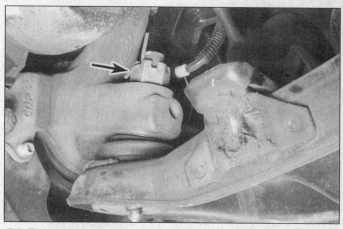

7.5 To separate the lower control arm from the steering knuckle, remove the cotter pin (arrow), loosen the castle nut one or two turns and give the steering knuckle a few sharp raps on the boss area adjacent to the balljoint stud to loosen the stud

balljoint stud separator. **Caution:** *The use of a picklefork balljoint separator usually results in balljoint boot damage.*

6   Remove the balljoint stud nut and remove the lower control arm.

Inspection

7   Inspect the bushings for cracks and tears. If they're damaged or worn, take the control arm to an automotive machine shop to have new bushings installed. This procedure requires a number of specialized tools, so it's not worth tackling at home.

Installation

8   Insert the balljoint stud into the steering knuckle, install the castle nut and tighten it to the torque listed in this Chapter's Specifications. Continue to tighten the nut, if necessary, until the hole in the stud is in line with the slot in the nut. Install a new cotter pin.

9   Install the spring compressor in accordance with the manufacturer's instructions and place the spring in position on its seat in the lower control arm. Make sure the spring is properly seated (see Section 5).

10   Place a floor jack under the lower control arm, raise the lower control arm and guide the upper end of the spring into position. Make sure the insulator is properly installed on top of the spring (see Section 5).

11   Install the lower control arm pivot bolts and nuts. Don't fully tighten the nuts at this time. Remove the floor jack.

12   On pre-1992 models, attach the stabilizer bar (see Section 4).

13   Install the shock absorber (see Section 2).

14   Install the wheel, remove the jackstands, lower the vehicle and tighten the wheel lug nuts to the torque listed in the Chapter 1 Specifications.

15   With the vehicle on the ground, tighten the lower control arm pivot bolt nuts to the torque listed in this Chapter's Specifications.

1982 through 1987 Continentals and 1984 through 1992 Mark VIIs

16   Loosen the wheel lug nuts, raise the vehicle and support it securely on jackstands. Remove the wheel.

17   Separate the lower control arm balljoint from the steering knuckle as described in Section 10. Do not remove the balljoint stud nut at this time.

18   Remove the coil spring as described in Section 5.

19   Unscrew the balljoint nut and remove the control arm from the vehicle.

20   Installation is the reverse of the removal procedure. Be sure to tighten all of the fasteners to the torque listed in this Chapter's Specifications.

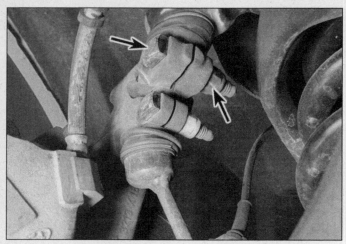

8.8 To detach the upper control arm balljoint stud from the steering knuckle, remove the nut and pinch bolt (arrows) (the lower pinch bolt and nut retain the stabilizer bar link balljoint stud on 1992 and later models - on earlier models, the upper arm is attached to the steering knuckle with a balljoint stud nut)

8   Upper control arm - removal, inspection and installation

Removal

1   Loosen the wheel lug nuts, raise the vehicle, support it securely on jackstands and remove the wheel.

1991 and earlier models

2   Remove the cotter pin from the upper balljoint stud and loosen the stud nut one or two turns **(see illustrations 2.1a and 2.1b)**.

3   Place a floor jack under the lower control arm and raise it slightly. **Warning:** *The jack must remain in this position during the entire operation.*

4   Rap on the steering knuckle near the upper balljoint stud with a hammer to loosen the stud in the steering knuckle. If the stud won't come loose, you might have to resort to a "picklefork" type of balljoint stud separator. **Caution:** *The use of a picklefork balljoint separator will usually result in balljoint boot damage.*

5   Remove the nut from the upper balljoint stud.

6   Remove the upper control arm pivot shaft attaching bolts. Remove the upper control arm and pivot shaft as an assembly.

1992 and later models

Refer to illustrations 8.8 and 8.10

7   Position a floor jack under the lower control arm.

8   Remove the pinch bolt and nut that retain the upper balljoint stud to the steering knuckle **(see illustration)**.

9   Using a prybar, spread the slot in the steering knuckle far enough apart to separate the balljoint stud from the knuckle.

10   Remove the upper control arm retaining bolts **(see illustration)** and remove the upper control arm assembly.

Inspection

11   Inspect the control arm bushings for cracks and tears. If they're damaged or worn, take the control arm to an automotive machine shop to have new bushings installed. This procedure requires a number of specialized tools, so it's not worth tackling at home.

Installation

12   Position the upper control arm pivot shaft on the frame and install the two attaching bolts and washers. Tighten the bolts to the torque listed in this Chapter's Specifications.

13   Insert the upper balljoint stud into the steering knuckle and install the ball stud nut or pinch bolt and nut. Tighten the nut to the torque

8.10 To disconnect the upper control arm from the frame on 1992 and later models, remove these two bolts (arrows)

listed in this Chapter's Specifications. On pre-1992 models, continue to tighten the nut, if necessary, until the cotter pin hole in the stud is in line with the nut slots, then install a new cotter pin.

14   Install the wheel and tighten the lug nuts to the torque listed in the Chapter 1 Specifications.

15   Remove the jackstands and lower the vehicle.

16   Drive the vehicle to an alignment shop and have the caster, camber and toe-in adjusted as required.

9   Hub and bearing assembly (1992 and later models) - removal and installation

Note: *Ford Motor Company recommends replacing the hub retaining nut anytime it is removed.*

1   Remove the wheel cover (if applicable). Remove the dust cap and break loose the hub and bearing assembly retaining nut with a 1/2-inch drive breaker bar and socket. Use a "cheater" bar or pipe if necessary. Don't remove the nut yet.

2   Loosen the wheel lug nuts. Raise the vehicle and place it securely on jackstands. Remove the wheel.

3   Remove the brake caliper and the disc (see Chapter 9).

4   Remove the hub and bearing assembly retaining nut and remove the hub and bearing assembly. If the assembly cannot be removed by hand, use a suitable hub puller.

5   Installation is the reverse of removal. After the vehicle is back on the ground, be sure to tighten the wheel lug nuts to the torque listed in the Chapter 1 Specifications and the hub and bearing assembly retaining nut to the torque listed in this Chapter's Specifications. **Warning:** *Do not attempt to tighten the hub retaining nut while the vehicle is on jackstands - do it with the vehicle on the ground, with the transmission in Park and the parking brake applied.*

10   Steering knuckle - removal and installation

All models except 1982 through 1987 Continentals and 1984 through 1992 Mark VIIs

1   On 1992 and later models, break loose the hub and bearing assembly retaining nut (see Section 9).

2   Loosen the wheel lug nuts. Raise the vehicle and support it securely on jackstands. Remove the wheel.

3   Remove the disc brake caliper (see Chapter 9). Wire the caliper to the underbody to prevent damage to the brake hose.

4   On pre-1992 models, remove the grease cap from the hub, then remove the cotter pin, nut lock, adjusting nut, washer and outer

10.19 Apply penetrating oil to the balljoint stud/steering knuckle area, then strike the steering knuckle boss sharply with a large hammer until the balljoint stud is freed (be sure the nut is loosened a couple of turns, but not removed) - this will probably take a few tries, because of the extremely tight fit between the two parts

bearing cone and roller assembly (see Chapter 1).
5   Remove the brake disc (see Chapter 9).
6   Remove the ABS sensor, if equipped, then remove the dust shield from the steering knuckle (see Chapter 9).
7   Disconnect the tie-rod end from the steering knuckle (see Section 21).
8   Place a jack under the lower arm of the balljoint area. Raise the jack until it supports the spring load on the lower arm. The jack must remain in this position throughout the remainder of this procedure. **Warning:** *Failure to perform this step could result in serious injury.*
9   Disconnect the lower and upper balljoint studs from the steering knuckle (see Sections 7 and 8).
10   On 1992 and later models, remove the pinch bolt and nut that retain the stabilizer bar link balljoint stud to the steering knuckle **(see illustration 8.8)**.
11   Remove the steering knuckle.
12   Installation is the reverse of removal. Be sure to tighten all fasteners to the torque values listed in this Chapter's Specifications.

1982 through 1987 Continentals and 1984 through 1992 Mark VIIs

Refer to illustrations 10.19 and 10.22

13   Loosen the wheel lug nuts, apply the parking brake and raise the vehicle. Support it securely on jackstands placed under the frame. Remove the wheel.
14   Remove the brake caliper and place it on top of the upper control arm (see Chapter 9).
15   Remove the brake disc (see Chapter 9) and hub assembly (see Chapter 1).
16   Remove the splash shield from the steering knuckle.
17   Separate the tie-rod end from the steering knuckle arm (see Section 22).
18   Remove the cotter pin from the lower control arm balljoint stud and back off the nut two turns.
19   Break the balljoint loose from the steering knuckle by rapping the steering knuckle boss sharply with a hammer **(see illustration)**. **Note:** *A picklefork type balljoint separator may damage the balljoint seals.*
20   Position a floor jack under the lower control arm and raise it slightly to take the spring pressure off the strut. **Warning:** *The jack must remain in this position throughout the entire procedure.*
21   Remove the two large nuts and bolts that attach the steering knuckle to the strut (see Section 3).
22   Remove the nut from the lower control arm balljoint stud,

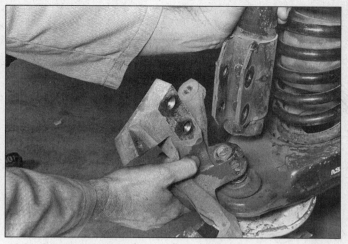

10.22 Separate the steering knuckle from the strut and remove it from the lower control arm

separate the steering knuckle from the strut and remove the steering knuckle from the vehicle **(see illustration)**.
23   Place the steering knuckle onto the lower control arm balljoint.
24   Insert the top of the steering knuckle into the opening in the strut and install the bolts. Tighten the nuts to the torque listed in this Chapter's Specifications. **Note:** *The Ford Motor Company recommends that these bolts (and nuts) be replaced, not reused.*
25   Tighten the lower control arm balljoint stud nut to the torque listed in this Chapter's Specifications.
26   Install the splash shield.
27   Connect the tie-rod end to the steering knuckle arm and tighten the nuts to the torque listed in this Chapter's Specifications. Be sure to use a new cotter pin.
28   Install the brake disc (see Chapter 9) and adjust the wheel bearings following the procedure outlined in Chapter 1.
29   Install the brake caliper (see Chapter 9).
30   Install the wheel and lug nuts. Lower the vehicle to the ground and tighten the nuts to the torque listed in the Chapter 1 Specifications.

11 Balljoint - check and replacement

Check

1970 through 1979 models

Upper balljoint

1   Raise the vehicle and place floor jacks under the lower arms.
2   Have an assistant grasp the lower edge of the tire and move the wheel in and out. As the wheel is being moved in and out, watch the upper end of the steering knuckle and the upper arm. If there's any movement between the upper end of the steering knuckle and the upper arm, replace the balljoint.

Lower balljoint

3   Raise the vehicle with a floor jack placed under the lower arm. This unloads the lower balljoints.
4   Adjust the wheel bearings (see Chapter 1).
5   Attach a dial indicator to the lower arm and position the indicator so that the plunder touches the inner side of the wheel rim directly under to the lower balljoint.
6   Grasp the top and bottom of the tire and slowly move the tire in and out. Note the reading on the dial indicator; if it's more than 1/4- inch, replace the balljoint.

1980 and later models

Refer to illustrations 11.8 and 11.10

7   On pre-1992 models, be sure to adjust the front wheel bearings (see Chapter 1) before checking the balljoints.

10

8   To do a quick visual inspection of the lower balljoints, wipe the grease fitting and checking surfaces so they're free of dirt and grease. The checking surface **(see illustration)** is the round boss into which the grease fitting is threaded. The checking surface should project outside the cover. If the checking surface is inside the cover, replace the lower control arm assembly (see Section 7).

9   Raise the vehicle and place floor jacks under the lower control arms.

10   Axial movement is up-and-down movement. Check axial movement by using a short prybar under the tire to move the wheel up and down **(see illustration)**. Replace the balljoints when axial movement exceeds 3/64-inch.

11   Radial movement is in-and-out play. Check for it by moving the tire toward and away from the vehicle by grasping the top and bottom of the wheel by hand. Replace the balljoints when radial movement exceeds 1/64-inch.

Replacement

Lower balljoints

1970 through 1972 models

Refer to illustration 11.16

12   Loosen the wheel lug nuts. Raise the vehicle and place it securely on jackstands. Make sure the lower control arms are free to drop as coil spring tension is released. Remove the wheels.

13   Drill a 1/8-inch pilot hole completely through each rivet, then drill off the rivet head by drilling through the pilot hole with a 3/8-inch drill bit and drive out both rivets.

14   Place a floorjack or safety stand under the lower control arm and lower the vehicle about six inches to relieve coil spring tension. **Warning:** *As a safety measure, always chain the coil spring to the control arm when releasing spring tension.*

15   Remove the cotter pin from the balljoint stud and remove the nut.

16   Install a special Factory tool (T57P-3006-A), or an equivalent tool, as shown **(see illustration)**. Make sure the tool is firmly seated against the ends of both studs, and not against the upper stud nut.

17   Turn the tool with a wrench until both studs are under tension, then tap the steering knuckle near the lower stud with a hammer to loosen the stud from the steering knuckle. In other words, don't loosen the stud with tool pressure alone. Remove the balljoint.

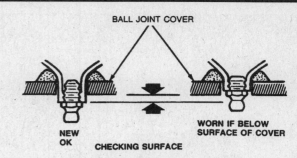

11.8 To do a quick visual inspection of the lower balljoints on 1980 and later models, look at the checking surface (the round boss into which the grease fitting is threaded) and note whether the checking surface projects outside the cover; if it doesn't, replace the lower control arm assembly

18   Clean the end of the control arm and remove all burrs from the hole edges. Check for cracks in the metal at the holes and replace the arm if it is cracked.

19   Insert the stud of the balljoint through the steering knuckle bore and install the stud nut finger-tight.

20   Attach the new balljoint to the lower arm with the bolts and nuts included in the kit. Do not rivet the new balljoint to the lower arm and do not use any other fasteners. Tighten the nuts to the torque listed in this Chapter's Specifications.

21   Tighten the balljoint stud nut to the torque listed in this Chapter's Specifications and install a new cotter pin.

22   Install the wheels. Remove the jack and lower the vehicle. Tighten the wheel lug nuts to the torque listed in the Chapter 1 Specifications.

23   Drive the vehicle to a dealer service department or to an alignment shop and have the camber, caster and toe-in checked and adjusted.

1973 and later models

24   The lower control arm balljoints on 1973 and later models are not removable or serviceable. If a lower balljoint is damaged or worn, replace the lower control arm (see Section 7).

11.10 To check axial movement, use a prybar under the tire to move the wheel up and down - if axial movement exceeds 3/64-inch, replace the balljoints

TOOL-T57P-3006-A

11.16 Install the special Factory tool (T57P-3006-A), or an equivalent tool, and position it as shown; the tool should be firmly seated against the end of both studs, and not against the upper stud nut

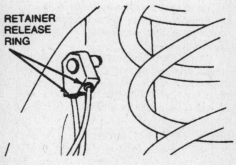

RETAINER RELEASE RING

12.2 To detach the air line(s) from the shock absorber, push the retainer release rings in, then pull the line(s) out

12.3 Locate the upper retaining nut (arrow) for the shock absorber on top of the frame. It may be necessary to prevent the piston rod from turning by holding it with a wrench or locking pliers while you break loose the nut

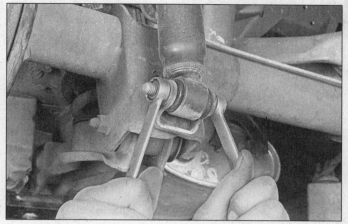

12.5 Remove the shock absorber lower mounting bolt and nut (some models only have a nut or a bolt)

Upper balljoints

1970 through 1972 models

Note: *You may wish to refer to illustration 2.1a*

25   Loosen the wheel lug nuts. Raise the vehicle and place it securely on jackstands. Remove the wheels.

26   Drill a 1/8-inch hole through each upper balljoint retaining rivet. Using a large chisel, cut off the rivets.

27   Remove the upper arm suspension bumper.

28   Remove the cotter pin and nut from the upper balljoint stud.

29   Install a balljoint removal tool (T57P-3006-A), or an equivalent tool, and position the tool as shown in illustration 11.16. Make sure the tool is firmly seated against the ends of both studs, and not against the lower stud nut.

30   Turn the tool with a wrench until both studs are under tension and then tap the steering knuckle near the upper stud with a hammer to loosen the stud from the steering knuckle. Do not loosen the stud with tool pressure alone. Remove the balljoint.

31   Clean the end of the upper control arm and remove all burrs from the hole edges. Check for cracks in the metal at the holes; replace the arm if there are signs of cracking anywhere.

32   Attach the new balljoint to the upper arm with the bolts and nuts provided in the kit. Do not rivet the new balljoint to the arm and do not use any other fasteners. Tighten the nuts to the torque listed in this Chapter's Specifications.

33   Install the upper arm suspension bumper. Tighten the nut securely.

34   Insert the stud of the new balljoint into the steering knuckle bore, install the stud nut and tighten it to the torque listed in this Chapter's Specifications.

35   Install the wheel, remove the jackstands and lower the vehicle. Tighten the wheel lug nuts to the torque listed in the Chapter 1 Specifications.

36   Drive the vehicle to a dealer service department or to an alignment shop and have the camber, caster and toe-in checked and adjusted.

1973 through 1991 models

37   The upper balljoints on these models are not removable or serviceable. If an upper balljoint is damaged or worn, replace the upper control arm (see Section 8).

1992 and later models

38   Loosen the wheel lug nuts. Raise the vehicle and place it securely on jackstands. Remove the wheel.

39   Position a floor jack under the lower control arm directly below the lower balljoint. Use a block of wood between the jack lifting pad and the balljoint to protect the balljoint. Raise the jack until it supports the spring load on the lower arm.

40   Remove the pinch bolt and nut from the upper balljoint stud **(see illustration 8.8)**.

41   Mark the position of the caster and camber adjustment cams **(see illustration 2.1c)**.

42   Remove the two nuts which attach the upper balljoint to the upper control arm **(see illustration 2.1c)**.

43   Remove the upper balljoint assembly.

44   Installation is the reverse of removal. Be sure to align the index marks on the adjustment cams with the reference marks you made before disassembly, then hold the cams in these positions as you tighten each balljoint retaining nut to the torque listed in this Chapter's Specifications. And be sure to tighten all other fasteners to the torque listed in this Chapter's Specifications.

12   Shock absorber (rear) - removal and installation

Removal

Refer to illustrations 12.2, 12.3 and 12.5

Caution: *On models with air suspension, turn the air suspension switch to Off before proceeding. Also, disconnect the height sensor connector link before allowing the rear suspension to hang past its normal point of full rebound.*

1   Raise the rear of the vehicle and support it securely on jackstands. If the vehicle is a pre-1992 model with automatic leveling rear suspension and *coil* springs (*not* air springs), allow the rear axle to hang free (be sure the ignition is in the Off position) until the shock absorbers are finished venting through the compressor (which will be evidenced by a hissing sound at the compressor).

2   Support the rear axle with a floor jack to prevent it from dropping when the shock absorber is disconnected. If you're removing an air-assisted shock absorber, detach the air line by depressing the retainer ring(s) and pulling the lines free **(see illustration)**.

3   On all models except 1982 through 1987 Continentals and 1984 through 1992 Mark VIIs, locate the upper retaining nut for the shock absorber on top of the frame **(see illustration)**. It may be necessary to prevent the piston rod from turning by holding it with a wrench or locking pliers while you break loose the nut. Remove the nut, washer and insulator from the stud on the upper side of the frame. Discard the nut. Compress the shock absorber to clear the hole in the frame and remove the inner insulator and washer from the upper retaining stud.

4   On 1982 through 1987 Continentals and 1984 through 1992 Mark VIIs, open the trunk, remove the side trim panel and remove the upper mounting nut from the shock absorber rod. It may be necessary to prevent the rod from turning by holding it with a wrench or locking pliers.

5   Remove the lower retaining nut **(see illustration)** and remove the shock absorber from the vehicle.

10

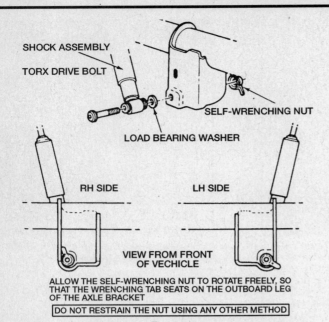

SHOCK ASSEMBLY

TORX DRIVE BOLT

SELF-WRENCHING NUT

LOAD BEARING WASHER

RH SIDE   LH SIDE

VIEW FROM FRONT
OF VECHICLE

ALLOW THE SELF-WRENCHING NUT TO ROTATE FREELY, SO
THAT THE WRENCHING TAB SEATS ON THE OUTBOARD LEG
OF THE AXLE BRACKET

DO NOT RESTRAIN THE NUT USING ANY OTHER METHOD

12.7 Installation details for models using Torx-head bolts

Installation

Refer to illustration 12.7
6   Before installing a new hydraulic shock absorber, expel all air. Hold the shock right side up and extend it fully. Turn the shock upside down and compress it all the way. Extend and compress the shock absorber in this manner at least three times.
7   Place the inner washer and rubber insulator on the shock piston rod and insert the rod through the upper mounting hole in the frame (all models except 1982 through 1987 Continentals and 1984 through 1992 Mark VIIs). Hold the shock in this position and install the outer insulator, washer and a new stud retaining nut on the upper side of the frame. Make sure the insulator "pilots" are properly engaged in the frame attaching holes. Tighten the nut to the torque listed in this Chapter's Specifications. **Note:** *Some models may use a Torx-head bolt and special locking nut. Refer to the accompanying illustration for information on this mount* **(see illustration)**.
8   On 1982 through 1987 Continentals and 1984 through 1992 Mark VIIs, place the inner washer and rubber insulator on the shock rod and insert the rod through the upper mounting hole. Push up on the shock absorber to align the lower shock eye in the mounting bracket and install the bolt and nut, tightening them securely. Then install the upper mounting rubber insulator and the dished washer on the shock rod. Install the nut and tighten it securely. Finally, install the side trim panel.
9   Extend the shock absorber, insert the lower shock stud through the hole in the bracket on the axle tube, install a new self-locking retaining nut and tighten it to the torque listed in this Chapter's Specifications.
10   Attach the air line(s), if equipped.
11   Remove the jackstands and lower the vehicle.
12   Before attempting to drive a vehicle equipped with air suspension, turn the air suspension switch to On, start the engine and allow the compressor to inflate the air suspension springs (they deflate automatically when the rear of the vehicle is raised).

13   Track bar (1970 through 1979 models) - removal and installation

1   Raise the vehicle and place it securely on jackstands. Support the axle housing with a floor jack; position the floor jack under the differential and put a block of wood between the jack head and the differential. Raise the jack just enough to take the weight of the axle off the track bar.
2   Remove the rubber cover at the axle end of the track bar.

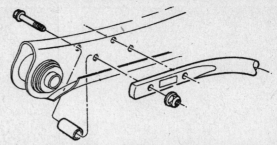

14.2 On pre-1992 models, the stabilizer bar is attached to the lower suspension arms with a pair of bolts on each arm

3   Remove the nut and washer attaching the lower end of the track bar to the upper arm bracket and disengage the track bar from the mounting stud.
4   Remove the nut and bolt attaching the upper end of the track bar to the frame side rail and remove the track bar.
5   Installation is the reverse of removal. Be sure to tighten all fasteners to the torque listed in this Chapter's Specifications.

14   Stabilizer bar (rear) - removal and installation

Refer to illustrations 14.2, 14.3 and 14.4
Caution: *On models with air suspension, turn the air suspension switch to Off before proceeding.*
1   Raise the rear of the vehicle and support it securely on jackstands. Place the jackstands under the frame, not under the axle housing. The axle housing must be free to hang down so that the shock absorbers are fully extended.
2   On pre-1992 models, remove the four (two on each arm) stabilizer bar-to-lower suspension arm bolts **(see illustration)** and remove the bar.
3   On 1992 and later models, remove the nuts that attach the stabilizer bar ends to their links **(see illustration)**.
4   On 1992 and later models, remove the bracket bolts that attach the stabilizer to the axle housing **(see illustration)**. **Note:** *Some pre-1992 stabilizer bars are also attached to the axle housing; others are only attached to the lower suspension arms.*
5   Installation is the reverse of the removal procedure. On pre-1992 models, be sure to install the bar with the paint mark on the right hand side of the vehicle. On all models, be sure to tighten all fasteners to the torque values listed in this Chapter's Specifications.
6   Before attempting to drive a vehicle equipped with air suspension, turn the air suspension switch to On, start the engine and allow the compressor to inflate the air suspension springs (they deflate automatically when the rear of the vehicle is raised).

15   Axle damper - removal and installation

Removal

Refer to illustration 15.2
Note: *This procedure applies only to 1982 through 1987 Continentals and 1984 through 1992 Mark VIIs.*
1   Loosen the wheel lug nuts, raise the vehicle and support it on jackstands. Remove the wheel and place a floor jack under the rear axle to support it, just in case it shifts when the axle damper is removed.
2   Remove the axle damper front attaching nut and bolt from the axle bracket **(see illustration)**.
3   Remove the rear attaching nut. Remove the bolts that hold the rear mounting bracket to the frame side member **(see illustration 15.2)** and remove the damper from the vehicle.

Installation

4   Place the rear bracket onto the axle damper and install the nut (don't tighten it yet).

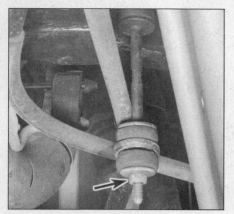

14.3 On 1992 and later models, remove this nut (arrow) that attaches the end of the stabilizer bar to the link (left link shown), then remove the other link nut

14.4 On 1992 and later models, remove this bracket bolt (arrow) which attaches the stabilizer to the axle housing (left clamp bolt shown), then remove the other bracket bolt

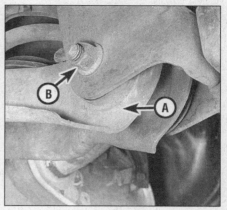

15.2 Axle damper mounting details (1982 through 1987 Continentals and 1984 through 1992 Mark VIIs)

5   Position the rear bracket on the frame side member and install the bolts, tightening them securely.

6   Swing the axle damper into the mount on the rear axle and install the pivot bolt and attaching nut, tightening them securely.

7   Tighten the rear retaining nut securely.

8   Install the wheel and lug nuts and lower the vehicle. Tighten the lug nuts to the torque listed in the Chapter 1 Specifications.

---

16   Coil spring (rear) - removal and installation

Warning: *Rear coil springs should always be replaced in pairs.*

All models except 1982 through 1987 Continentals and 1984 through 1992 Mark VIIs

Removal

Caution: *On models with air suspension, turn the air suspension switch to Off before proceeding.*

1   Loosen the wheel lug nuts, raise the rear of the vehicle and support it securely on jackstands placed under the frame. Remove the wheel and block the front wheels.

2   Remove the rear stabilizer bar (see Section 14).

3   Support the rear axle assembly with a jack placed under the axle housing. Position a safety chain through one of the spring coils and around a convenient frame member. This will prevent the spring from flying out after it's fully extended.

4   Unsnap the right parking brake cable clip from the right upper suspension arm.

5   Disconnect the lower studs of the two rear shock absorbers from their mounting brackets on the axle tube (see Section 12). Detach the height sensor connector link from the upper control arm.

6   Slowly lower the jack until the spring is fully extended. Remove the safety chain, coil spring and insulators from between the suspension arm and the spring upper seat.

Installation

7   Set the upper insulator on top of the spring, using tape to hold it in place, if necessary.

8   Place the spring between its seat on the axle tube and the frame seat, so that the pigtail (the lower end of the spring) is pointing toward the left side of the vehicle.

9   Raise the axle assembly with the floor jack and insert the studs on the lower ends of the shocks into their holes in the brackets on the axle tubes. Install the stud retaining nuts, but don't fully tighten them yet.

10   Snap the right parking brake cable into the upper suspension arm retainer.

11   Install the rear stabilizer bar (see Section 14). Connect the height

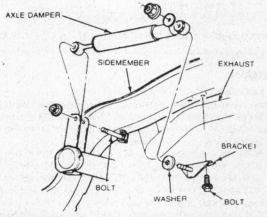

16.17 Support the rear suspension lower arm (A) with a jack placed under the pivot bolt, then remove the pivot bolt (B) and push the bolt through the bushing and axle bracket

sensor connector link to the upper control arm.

12   Install the wheels and lug nuts. Lower the vehicle and tighten the lug nuts to the torque listed in the Chapter 1 Specifications.

13   Before attempting to drive a vehicle equipped with air suspension, turn the air suspension switch to On, start the engine and allow the compressor to inflate the air suspension springs (they deflate automatically when the rear of the vehicle is raised).

1982 through 1987 Continentals and 1984 through 1992 Mark VIIs

Removal

Refer to illustration 16.17

14   Loosen the wheel lug nuts, raise the rear of the vehicle and support it securely on jackstands placed under the frame. Remove the wheel and block the front wheels.

15   Remove the rear stabilizer bar (see Section 14) if the vehicle is equipped with one.

16   Support the rear axle assembly with a jackstand placed under the axle tube on the side being dismantled. Position a safety chain through one of the spring coils and around a convenient frame member.

17   Place a floor jack under the lower suspension arm axle pivot bolt **(see illustration)**. Remove the nut and bolt.

18   Slowly lower the jack until the spring is fully extended.

19   Remove the safety chain, coil spring and insulators from between the suspension arm and the spring upper seat.

10

Installation

Refer to illustration 16.23

20   Set the upper insulator on top of the spring, using tape to hold it in place, if necessary.

21   Place the lower insulator on the lower suspension arm.

22   Install the internal damper in the spring.

23   Place the spring between the suspension arm and the frame, so that the pigtail (the end of the spring) on the lower suspension arm is pointing toward the left side of the vehicle **(see illustration)**.

24   Raise the lower suspension arm up into position and install the pivot bolt and nut, but don't fully tighten the nut yet.

25   Raise the axle to simulate a normal ride height and tighten the pivot bolt nut to the torque listed in this Chapter's Specifications.

26   If the vehicle is equipped with a rear stabilizer bar, install it, referring to Section 14 if necessary.

17   Suspension arms (rear) - removal and installation

All models except 1982 through 1987 Continentals and 1984 through 1992 Mark VIIs

Warning: *If you're going to remove both the upper and the lower arms at the same time, remove the coil springs first (see Section 16) or, if the vehicle has air suspension, deflate the air springs (see Section 19).*
Caution: *On models with air suspension, turn the air suspension switch to Off before proceeding.*

Upper arm

Note: *If one upper arm requires replacement, replace the other upper arm as well. The Ford Motor Company recommends installing new fasteners when reassembling the rear suspension components.*

Removal

Refer to illustrations 17.3 and 17.4

1   Loosen the rear wheel lug nuts. Raise the rear of the vehicle and support it securely on jackstands placed beneath the frame rails. Block the front wheels. Remove the rear wheels.

2   Position a jack under the differential and raise it slightly.

3   Unsnap the parking brake cable from its upper arm retainer. Remove the upper arm-to-rear axle pivot bolt and nut **(see illustration)**. If equipped, detach the height sensor connector link from the upper arm.

4   Remove the upper arm-to-frame pivot bolt and nut **(see illustration)** and remove the arm from the vehicle. Inspect the bushings at both ends of the arm. If either bushing is damaged or worn, have it replaced by an automotive machine shop.

Installation

5   Position the leading end of the suspension arm in the frame

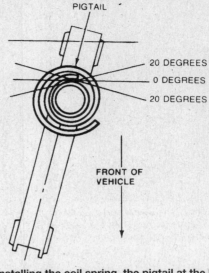

16.23 When installing the coil spring, the pigtail at the lower end of the spring must point to the left side of the vehicle (1982 through 1987 Continentals and 1984 through 1992 Mark VIIs)

bracket. Install a new pivot bolt and nut with the bolt facing forward. Don't fully tighten the nut at this time.

6   Attach the other end of the arm to the axle housing with a new pivot bolt and nut. Again, the bolt should be facing forward. It may be necessary to jack up the rear axle to align the holes. Don't fully tighten the nut yet. Attach the parking brake cable to its retainer on the upper arm.

7   Raise the axle to normal ride height and tighten the fasteners to the torque listed in this Chapter's Specifications.

Lower arm

Note: *If one lower arm requires replacement, replace the other lower arm as well. Also, the Ford Motor Company recommends installing new fasteners when reassembling the rear suspension components.*

Removal

Refer to illustrations 17.12 and 17.13

8   With the vehicle still on the ground, mark the rear suspension shock tube relative to the protective sleeve.

9   Remove the stabilizer bar, if equipped (see Section 14).

10   Loosen the rear wheel lug nuts. Raise the vehicle and place it securely on jackstands (do not place the jackstands under the axle itself; the axle must be free to allow the shocks to fully extend to relieve spring pressure). Remove the wheel.

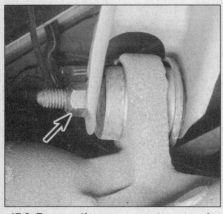

17.3 Remove the upper arm-to-rear axle pivot bolt and nut (arrow)

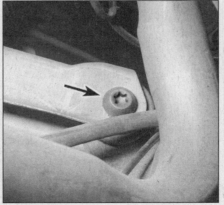

17.4 Remove the upper arm-to-frame pivot bolt (arrow) and nut and remove the arm from the vehicle; on some models, you'll need a Torx bit to hold the bolt

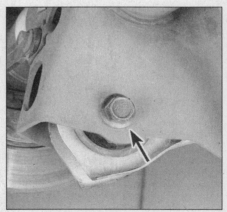

17.12 Remove the lower arm-to-axle pivot bolt (arrow) and nut

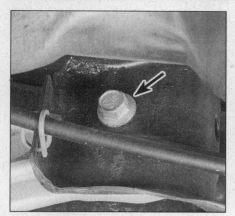

17.13 Remove the lower arm-to-frame pivot bolt (arrow) and nut, then remove the arm from the vehicle

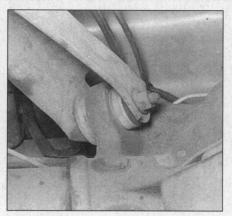

17.21 The upper suspension arm is held to the rear axle by a through bolt - the bushing in the axle housing is replaceable, but special tools are required for the operation

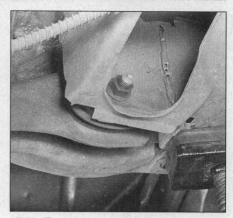

17.28 The lower suspension arm-to-frame pivot bolt/nut

11   Place a floorjack under the differential to support the axle.
12   Remove the lower arm-to-axle pivot bolt and nut **(see illustration)**.
13   Remove the lower arm-to-frame pivot bolt and nut **(see illustration)**, then remove the arm from the vehicle.

Installation

14   Position the lower arm in the frame mounting bracket and install a new pivot bolt and nut, with the nut facing out. Do not tighten the nut completely at this time.
15   Position the other end of the lower arm in the axle bracket and install a new bolt and nut. Do not tighten the nut at this time.
16   Raise the axle until the mark you made on the shock tube is aligned with the protective sleeve (this is the normal ride height), then tighten the pivot bolt nuts to the torque listed in this Chapter's Specifications.
17   Install the stabilizer bar, if equipped (see Section 14).
18   Install the wheel and lug nuts. Remove the jackstands and floor jack, lower the vehicle and tighten the lug nuts to the torque listed in the Chapter 1 Specifications.

1982 through 1987 Continentals and 1984 through 1992 Mark VIIs

Upper arm

Note: *If one upper arm requires replacement, replace the other upper arm as well. The Ford Motor Company recommends installing new fasteners when reassembling the rear suspension components.*

Removal

Refer to illustration 17.21
19   Raise the rear of the vehicle and support it securely on jackstands placed beneath the frame rails. Block the front wheels.
20   Position a jack under the differential and raise it slightly.
21   Remove the upper arm-to-rear axle pivot bolt and nut **(see illustration)**.
22   Remove the upper arm-to-frame pivot bolt and nut and remove the arm from the vehicle.

Installation

23   Position the leading end of the suspension arm in the frame bracket. Install a new pivot bolt and nut with the nut on the outboard side, but don't fully tighten the nut at this time.
24   Place the other end of the arm over the axle bushing ear. It may be necessary to jack up the rear axle to align the holes. Install a new pivot bolt and nut with the nut on the inboard side, but don't tighten it to the specified torque yet.
25   Raise the axle to normal ride height and tighten the fasteners to the torque listed in this Chapter's Specifications.

Lower arm

Note: *If one lower arm requires replacement, replace the other lower arm as well. Also, the Ford Motor Company recommends installing new fasteners when reassembling the rear suspension components.*

Removal

Refer to illustration 17.28
26   Loosen the wheel lug nuts, raise the rear of the vehicle and support it securely on jackstands placed under the frame rails. Block the front wheels and remove the rear wheel.
27   Remove the coil spring following the procedure outlined in Section 16.
28   Remove the lower arm-to-frame pivot bolt and nut **(see illustration)**, then remove the arm from the vehicle.

Installation

29   Position the lower arm in the frame mounting bracket and install a new pivot bolt and nut, with the nut facing out. Do not tighten the nut completely at this time.
30   Install the coil spring and connect the trailing end of the lower suspension arm to the rear axle bracket (Section 16). Raise the axle to simulate normal ride height, then tighten the pivot bolt nuts to the torque listed in this Chapter's Specifications.
31   Install the wheel and lug nuts. Lower the vehicle and tighten the lug nuts to the torque listed in the Chapter 1 Specifications.

18   Air suspension systems - general information

Automatic leveling suspension

Some models are equipped with an optional automatic leveling suspension system, which consists of an air compressor, a compressor relay, an air dryer, an exhaust solenoid, a control module, a height sensor, a pair of air adjustable rear shock absorbers and the air lines and fittings connecting the compressor to the shocks.

The adjustable air shocks used with this system are essentially conventional shock absorbers enclosed in air chambers. A rubber sleeve is attached to the dust tube and to the shock reservoir, creating a flexible chamber which can extend the shocks when air pressure is increased. When air pressure is reduced, the weight of the vehicle collapses the shocks.

As the vehicle is loaded, its weight increases, which lowers the vehicle and causes the height sensor's actuating arm to rotate up. This generates two sensor signals to the control module. After a continuous height sensor signal of 7 to 13 seconds, the control module activates the compressor through a relay. The compressor motor runs and air is sent through the system. As the shock absorbers inflate, the vehicle

10

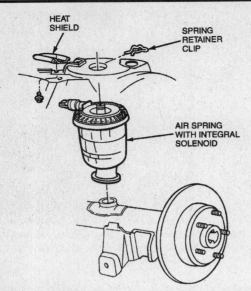

19.3 An exploded view of the air spring assembly on a model equipped with computer-controlled suspension

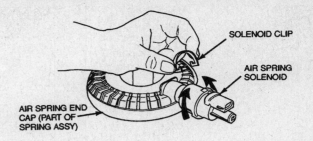

19.5 Before you can remove the air spring solenoid, you must remove this clip (arrow)

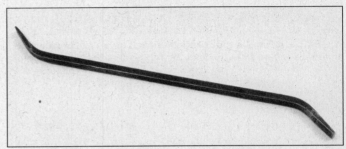

19.6a Using a Ford air spring removal tool (T90P-5310-A), or a suitable substitute (such as this small prybar) . . .

body moves up toward its former height and the height sensor actuating arm rotates down until the preset trim height is reached. When the body reaches the prescribed height, the control module stops the compressor.

As the vehicle is unloaded, its weight decreases, which raises the vehicle and rotates the height sensor actuating arm down. Again, this generates two sensor signals to the control module. 7 to 13 seconds later, the module activates the vent solenoid. As the body comes down, the height sensor actuating arm rotates up again until the preset trim height is reached. When the sensor arm reaches its original height above the ground, the module turns off the vent solenoid, preventing air from escaping.

Servicing this system is beyond the scope of the average home mechanic. If it malfunctions, take the vehicle to an authorized dealer to have the system serviced.

Computer-controlled suspension

Some models are equipped with an optional computer-controlled suspension system that automatically provides height control and soft spring rates to improve ride quality. This system automatically levels the rear of the vehicle and maintains the optimal vehicle attitude whether the vehicle is empty or fully loaded. The automatic air suspension system includes the following components: a compressor/air dryer assembly, a compressor relay, a pair of front air struts with integral height sensors, a pair of rear air springs, a pair of rear shocks, a control module, the air lines, a compressor, a rear height sensor (in the right rear shock absorber), a wiring harness assembly and a compressor cover.

The rear air springs, a pair of cylindrical inflatable bladders, are mounted in the same location as conventional coil springs (they even use the same upper and lower spring seats). Their main advantage over coil springs is that they allow a reduction in spring rate to soften vehicle ride quality. A pair of solenoid valves control air flow in and out of the air springs. Vehicle height is monitored and controlled by an electronic control module. A linear height sensor is located in front of the axle. The upper end of the sensor is attached to the frame crossmember and the lower end is attached to the left upper suspension arm. If vehicle height is too low (i.e. the vehicle is loaded down), the sensor gets shorter; when the ride height goes up (vehicle is unloaded), the sensor gets longer. Magnets in the lower sliding part of the sensor move up and down in relation to the sensor housing, generating a signal that is sent to the control module through two small Hall effect switches attached to the housing. The movement of these magnets determines whether the air suspension switch is open or closed. At trim (ride) height, the switches are both closed and the

control module receives a "trim" signal. If the magnets move up, they open one switch to indicate a "high" condition; if the magnets move down, they open another switch to indicate a "low" condition. When the control module receives a low signal, it energizes the solenoids and activates the compressor, which pumps up the air springs until the correct vehicle height is restored; if the control module receives a high signal (vehicle is emptied), the control module activates the solenoids, which vent air from the air springs until vehicle height is correct again.

Servicing this system is beyond the scope of the average home mechanic. If it malfunctions, take the vehicle to a dealer service department or other qualified repair shop to have the system serviced. To remove an air spring, see Section 19.

19 Air spring (rear) - removal and installation

Removal

Refer to illustrations 19.3, 19.5, 19.6a and 19.6b

Warning: *Never remove an air spring when there is still air pressure in the spring, and never remove any components supporting any air spring, or supported by it, without first either exhausting the air or providing support for the air spring.*

1   Turn the air suspension switch to Off.

2   Loosen the wheel lug nuts. Raise the rear of the vehicle and support it securely on jackstands. Remove the wheel.

3   Remove the heat shield **(see illustration)**.

4   Remove the spring retainer clip.

5   To remove the air spring solenoid:

a) *Unplug the electrical connector and disconnect the air line.*

b) *Remove the solenoid clip* **(see illustration)**.

c) *Rotate the solenoid counterclockwise to the first stop.*

d) *Slowly pull the solenoid straight out to the second stop to allow any residual air to bleed from the system.*

e) *After all air is bled from the system, rotate the solenoid counterclockwise to the third stop and remove the solenoid from the housing.*

6   Insert an air spring removal tool (T90P-5310-A) or a suitable equivalent tool between the axle tube and the spring seat **(see illustrations)**, and remove the spring.

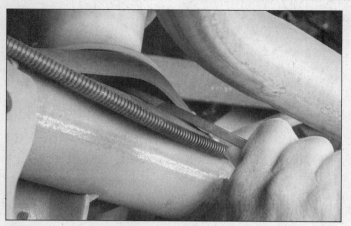

19.6b . . . insert the tool through the gap between the axle tube and the spring seat, position the tool so that the flat end rests on the piston knob, push down and force the piston and retainer clip off the axle spring seat

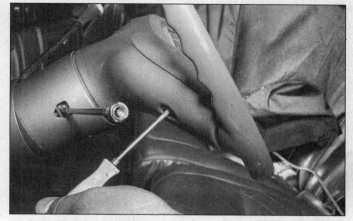

20.2a To remove the horn pad on early models, remove the screws from the side of the steering wheel facing toward the dash, . . .

Installation

7   Position the spring between the frame seat and the axle, then carefully pry it into place.

8   To install the air spring solenoid:

  a) *Inspect the solenoid O-rings for cracks and tears. Replace as necessary. Be sure to apply a light coat of silicone dielectric grease to the O-rings.*

  b) *Insert the solenoid into the air spring end cap and rotate it clockwise to the third stop, push it into the second stop, then rotate it clockwise to the first stop.*

  c) *Install the solenoid clip.*

9   Taking care to protect the open air and electrical connection at the solenoid, install the air spring into the frame (upper) seat.

10   From the upper side of the frame, install the push-on spring retainer clip.

11   Connect the air line and plug in the electrical connector.

12   Install the heat shield.

13   Align the lower end of the air spring piston with the axle (lower) seat. Squeezing the spring to increase pressure, push down on the piston, snapping the piston into the axle seat at rebound.

14   Install the wheel and lug nuts. Remove the jackstands and lower the vehicle until the wheels are on the ground. Then lower the jack a little further, but do not fully lower the vehicle until the air springs have been partially inflated.

15   Turn the air suspension switch to On. Turn the ignition key to On, but don't start the vehicle. Allow the air springs to partially inflate.

16   Lower the vehicle all the way and allow the springs to fully inflate.

17   Tighten the wheel lug nuts to the torque listed in the Chapter 1 specifications.

20   Steering wheel - removal and installation

Refer to illustrations 20.2a, 20.2b, 20.2c, 20.2d, 20.3a, 20.3b, 20.3c, 20.3d, 20.4 and 20.5

Warning 1: *To avoid the possibility of an accidental deployment of the airbag on models with a driver's side airbag - and the likelihood of personal injury, should such an event occur - disconnect the negative battery cable, then disconnect the positive cable, then wait two minutes before working in the vicinity of the impact sensors, steering column or instrument panel.*

Warning 2: *On models equipped with a driver's side airbag, put the wheels in the straight-ahead position and lock the steering column. The steering column must not be rotated while the steering wheel is removed.*

Removal

1   Disconnect the cable from the negative terminal of the battery. Position the front wheels in the straight-ahead position.

2   On some models without a driver's side airbag, you must remove a pair of screws from the front side of the steering wheel, pull off the horn pad and unplug the horn leads and, if equipped, the cruise control leads **(see illustrations)**. On later models, simply pull the horn pad straight off, then disconnect the horn leads and, if equipped, the cruise control leads **(see illustrations)**.

20.2b . . . remove the horn pad and disconnect the horn leads and, if equipped, the cruise control leads

20.2c On newer models, simply pull the horn pad straight off . . .

20.2d . . . and unplug the leads for the horn and, if equipped, the cruise control

3   On models equipped with a driver's side airbag, remove the four airbag module retaining nuts, lift the module off the steering wheel and unplug the module electrical connector **(see illustrations)**. Store the airbag in a safe place until needed. Also unplug the electrical connector for the cruise control, if equipped **(see illustration)**.

4   Remove the steering wheel retaining bolt **(see illustration)**. There should already be an alignment mark on the upper edge of the steering shaft and another mark on the steering wheel hub. If not, mark the relationship of the steering shaft to the hub (if marks don't already exist or don't line up) to simplify installation and ensure correct steering wheel alignment. **Warning:** *Discard the hub bolt. Use a new one during installation.*

5   Use a steering wheel puller to detach the steering wheel from the shaft **(see illustration)**. Don't use an impact puller and don't pound on the steering wheel or shaft. Route the contact assembly wire harness through the steering wheel as the wheel is lifted off the shaft.

6   If equipped with cruise control, make sure the slip ring grease is not contaminated. Check the slip ring contacts for wear or damage and make sure they are properly seated.

Installation

7   To install the wheel, align the mark on the steering wheel hub with the mark on the shaft and slip the wheel onto the shaft. Install a new bolt and tighten it to the torque listed in this Chapter's Specifications.

8   Plug in the cruise control connector, if equipped.

9   On models with a driver's side airbag, connect the airbag electrical connector and install the airbag module.

10   On models without a driver's side airbag, simply push the horn

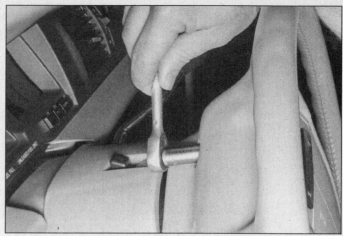

20.3a   To remove the airbag module on models equipped with a driver's side airbag, remove the four nuts (two on each side of the steering column) from the backside of the steering wheel

pad straight on to install it on the wheel. On models with a driver's side airbag, install the four airbag module retaining nuts.

11   Connect the positive battery cable (models with airbags), followed by the negative battery cable.

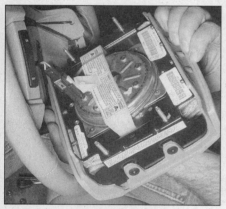

20.3b   Pull the airbag module straight off . . .

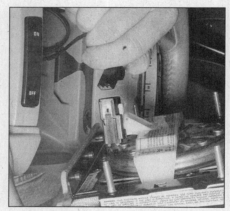

20.3c   . . . and unplug the electrical connector for the module

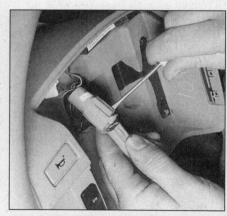

20.3d   Unplug the electrical connector for the cruise control system, if equipped

20.4   Remove the steering wheel retaining bolt (arrow) and make sure there are alignment marks on the upper edge of the steering shaft and on the steering wheel hub - if there aren't, make some

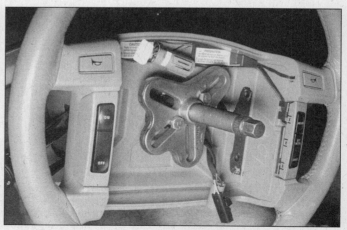

20.5   Install a steering wheel puller as shown to remove the steering wheel from the steering shaft

21.9 Use a two-jaw puller to separate the tie-rod end from the steering knuckle

21.10 Make sure you place a mark on the threaded sleeve in line with the end of the threaded portion of the tie-rod end; thus, when you install the tie-rod end and screw it in until the inner end is aligned with this mark, front toe-in will still be the same as before

21 Steering linkage - inspection, removal and installation

Note: *This procedure applies to all models except 1982 through 1987 Continentals and 1984 through 1992 Mark VIIs.*

1   The steering linkage connects the steering gear to the front wheels and keeps the wheels in proper relation to each other. The linkage consists of the Pitman (or steering gear) arm, the idler arm, the center link and two adjustable tie-rods **(see illustrations 1.1a and 1.1b)**. The Pitman arm, which is fastened to the steering gear shaft, moves the center link back-and-forth. The center link is supported on the other end by a frame-mounted idler arm. The back-and-forth motion of the center link is transmitted to the steering knuckles through a pair of tie-rod assemblies. Each tie-rod is made up of an inner and outer tie-rod end, a threaded adjuster tube and two clamps.

Inspection

2   Set the wheels in the straight ahead position and lock the steering wheel.
3   Raise one side of the vehicle until the tire is about one inch off the ground.
4   Grasp the front and rear of the tire and using light pressure,

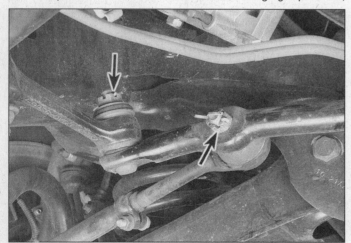

21.11 To disconnect an inner tie-rod from the center link, remove the cotter pin (lower arrow), loosen the castle nut and separate the tie-rod from the center link with a small two-jaw puller like the one used in Step 9; the idler arm balljoint stud (upper arrow) is separated from the center link the same way

wiggle the wheel back-and-forth. There should be no noticeable play. If the play in the steering system is noticeable, inspect each steering linkage pivot point and ballstud for looseness and replace parts if necessary.
5   Raise the front of the vehicle and support it on jackstands. Push up, then pull down on the center link end of the idler arm, exerting a force of approximately 25 pounds each way. If there is any looseness, replace the idler arm.
6   Check for frozen (extremely stiff) joints and bent or damaged linkage components.

Removal and installation

Tie-rod

Refer to illustrations 21.9, 21.10 and 21.11

7   Loosen the wheel lug nuts, raise the vehicle and support it securely on jackstands. Apply the parking brake. Remove the wheel.
8   Remove the cotter pin and loosen, but do not remove, the castle nut from the ballstud.
9   Using a two-jaw puller, separate the tie-rod end from the steering knuckle **(see illustration)**. Remove the nut and pull the tie-rod end from the knuckle.
10   If a tie-rod end must be replaced, mark the location of the threaded end of the outer tie-rod tube on the adjuster **(see illustration)**, so that when the new tie-rod is screwed into the adjuster, toe-in won't be affected. Loosen the adjuster tube clamp and unscrew the tie-rod end.
11   Remove the cotter pin and loosen the nut securing the inner tie-rod end to the center link **(see illustration)**. Separate the tie-rod from the center link in the same manner as in Step 9. Remove and discard the old nut.
12   Lubricate the threaded portion of the tie-rod with chassis grease. Screw the new tie-rod end into the adjuster sleeve until the threaded end reaches the mark you made on the adjuster sleeve. Don't tighten the clamp nut yet.
13   To install the tie-rod, connect the tie-rod end to the steering knuckle and install the castle nut. Tighten the nut to the torque listed in this Chapter's Specifications and install a new cotter pin. If the ballstud spins when attempting to tighten the nut, force it into the tapered hole with a large pair of pliers. If necessary, tighten the nut slightly to align a slot in the nut with the cotter pin hole in the ballstud. Install the cotter pin.
14   Insert the tie-rod ballstud into the center link until it's seated. Install a new nut and tighten it to the torque listed in this Chapter's Specifications. If the ballstud spins as the nut is tightened, force the tie-rod end into the center link with a pair of large pliers.
15   Tighten the clamp nuts. The center of the bolt should be nearly

10

21.20　To detach the idler arm assembly from the frame, simply remove these two nuts (arrows)

21.26　The Pitman arm balljoint stud (arrow) is separated from the center link the same way as shown in Step 9

21.33　Mark the Pitman arm and the threaded sector shaft to insure proper reassembly, then pull off the Pitman arm with a puller

horizontal and the adjuster tube slot must not line up with the gap in the clamps.

16　Install the wheel and lug nuts, lower the vehicle and tighten the lug nuts to the torque listed in the Chapter 1 Specifications. Drive the vehicle to an alignment shop to have the front end alignment checked and, if necessary, adjusted.

Idler arm

Refer to illustration 21.20

17　Raise the vehicle and support it securely on jackstands. Apply the parking brake.

18　Remove the cotter pin and loosen but do not remove the idler arm-to-center link nut **(see illustration 21.11)**.

19　Separate the idler arm from the center link with a two-jaw puller **(see illustration 21.9)**. Remove and discard the nut.

20　Remove the idler arm-to-frame bolts **(see illustration)**.

21　To install the idler arm assembly, position it on the frame and install the bolts, tightening them to the torque listed in this Chapter's Specifications.

22　Insert the idler arm ballstud into the center link and install a new nut. Tighten the nut to the torque listed in this Chapter's Specifications. If the ballstud spins when attempting to tighten the nut, force it into the tapered hole with a large pair of pliers.

Center link

Refer to illustration 21.26

23　Raise the vehicle and support it securely on jackstands. Apply the parking brake.

24　Separate the two tie-rods from the center link **(see illustration 21.11)**.

25　Separate the center link from the idler arm **(see illustration 21.11)**.

26　Separate the center link from the Pitman arm **(see illustration)**.

27　Installation is the reverse of the removal procedure. If the ballstuds spin when attempting to tighten the nuts, force them into the tapered holes with a large pair of pliers. Be sure to tighten all of the nuts to the torque listed in this Chapter's Specifications.

Pitman (steering box) arm

Refer to illustration 21.33

28　Raise the vehicle and place it securely on jackstands.

29　Remove the cotter pin and loosen the castle nut that attaches the Pitman arm ballstud to the center link.

30　Using a puller like the one in illustration 21.9, separate the center link from the Pitman arm ballstud. Discard the nut - don't reuse it.

31　Mark the Pitman arm and the steering gear shaft to ensure proper alignment at reassembly time.

32　Remove the Pitman arm nut and washer.

33　Remove the Pitman arm with a Pitman arm puller or a two-jaw puller **(see illustration)**.

34　Inspect the ballstud threads for damage. Inspect the ballstud seals for excessive wear. Clean the threads of the ballstud.

35　Installation is the reverse of removal. Make sure the marks you made on the Pitman arm and Pitman shaft are aligned. **Note:** *If a clamp type Pitman arm is used, spread the arm just enough, with a wedge, to slip the arm onto the Pitman shaft. Don't spread the arm more than necessary to slip it over the shaft with hand pressure. Do not hammer the arm onto the shaft or you may damage the steering gear.* Be sure to tighten the Pitman arm nut to the torque listed in this Chapter's Specifications.

22　Tie-rod ends - removal and installation

Note: *This procedure applies only to 1982 through 1987 Continentals and 1984 through 1992 Mark VIIs.*

Removal

Refer to illustrations 22.2a, 22.2b, 22.4 and 22.5

1　Loosen the wheel lug nuts. Block the rear wheels and set the parking brake. Raise the front of the vehicle and support it securely on jackstands. Remove the front wheel.

2　Hold the tie-rod end with a wrench and loosen the jam nut enough to mark the position of the tie-rod end in relation to the threads **(see illustrations)**.

3　Remove the cotter pin and loosen the nut on the tie-rod end stud.

4　Disconnect the tie-rod from the steering knuckle arm with a puller **(see illustration)**. Remove the nut and separate the tie-rod.

5　Unscrew the tie-rod end from the tie-rod **(see illustration)**.

22.2a　Hold the tie-rod end with a wrench and loosen the jam nut

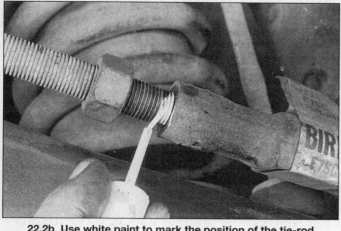

22.2b Use white paint to mark the position of the tie-rod end on the tie-rod

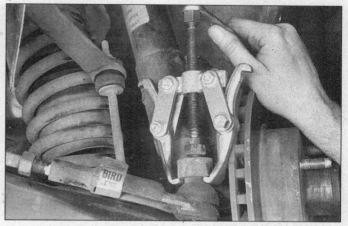

22.4 Use a two-jaw puller to detach the tie-rod end from the steering knuckle arm (note that the nut has been loosened, but not removed; this will prevent the tie-rod from popping violently out of the knuckle, which might result in injury or damage)

Installation

6   Thread the tie-rod end on to the marked position and insert the tie-rod stud into the spindle arm. Tighten the jam nut securely.

7   Install a new nut on the stud and tighten it to the torque listed in this Chapter's Specifications. Install a new cotter pin.

8   Install the wheel and lug nuts. Lower the vehicle and tighten the lug nuts to the torque listed in the Chapter 1 Specifications.

9   Have the alignment checked by a dealer service department or an alignment shop.

23   Steering gear boots - replacement

Refer to illustrations 23.3a and 23.3b

Note: *This procedure applies only to 1982 through 1987 Continentals and 1984 through 1992 Mark VIIs.*

1   Loosen the lug nuts, raise the vehicle and support it securely on jackstands. Remove the wheel.

2   Referring to Section 22, loosen the tie-rod end jam nut and separate the tie-rod end from the spindle arm.

3   Remove the steering gear boot clamps and slide the boot off **(see illustrations)**.

4   Before installing the new boot, wrap the threads and serrations on the end of the steering rod with a layer of tape so the small end of the new boot isn't damaged.

5   Slide the new boot into position on the steering gear until it seats in the groove in the steering rod and install new clamps.

6   Remove the tape and install the tie-rod end (see Section 22).

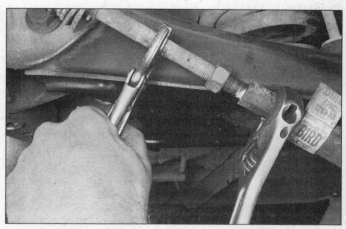

22.5 If the tie-rod end is difficult to unscrew, clamp a pair of locking pliers to the serrated area of the tie-rod (not the threaded portion) and use a wrench to remove the tie-rod end

7   Install the wheel and lug nuts. Lower the vehicle and tighten the lug nuts to the torque listed in the Chapter 1 Specifications.

8   Have the alignment checked by a dealer service department or an alignment shop.

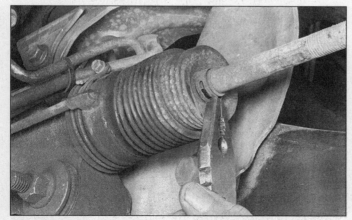

23.3a Remove the outer boot clamp with a pair of pliers

23.3b Loosen the inner boot clamp screw and slide the boot off the rack housing

10

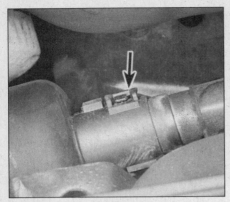

24.1 To remove the stone shield (if equipped) from the steering shaft coupling, unclip this lock tab (arrow); the shield then opens into two halves which can be separated and removed

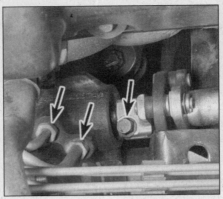

24.2 Before removing the steering gear, mark and disconnect the fluid line fittings (arrows) and remove the pinch bolt (arrow) that attaches the flex coupling clamp to the steering gear input shaft

24.6 To detach the steering gear from the frame, remove these four bolts (arrows) inside the left wheel housing (left front wheel removed for clarity)

24 Steering gear - removal and installation

All models except 1982 through 1987 Continentals and 1984 through 1992 Mark VIIs

Removal

Refer to illustrations 24.1, 24.2 and 24.6

1   Remove the stone shield **(see illustration)**.
2   Tag the pressure and return lines **(see illustration)** on the steering gear for future identification. Disconnect the lines from the steering gear. Plug the lines and ports in the gear to prevent contamination.
3   Remove the pinch bolt which secures the flexible coupling to the steering gear **(see illustration 24.2)**.
4   Raise the vehicle and remove the nut that attaches the Pitman arm to the sector shaft (see Section 21).
5   Remove the Pitman arm from the sector shaft **(see illustration 21.33)**.
6   Support the steering gear and remove the steering gear attaching bolts **(see illustration)**.
7   Work the gear free of the flex coupling and remove the gear. **Warning:** *On models equipped with airbags, make sure that the steering shaft is not turned while the steering gear is removed or you could damage the airbag system. One way to prevent the shaft from turning is to run the seat belt through the steering wheel and clip the seat belt into place.*

Installation

8   To install the steering gear, slide the flex coupling into place on the steering shaft assembly. Turn the steering wheel so that the spokes are in a horizontal position.
9   Center the steering gear input shaft and slide it into the flex coupling clamp and into place on the frame side rail. Install the steering gear mounting bolts and tighten them to the torque listed in this Chapter's Specifications.
10   Be sure the wheels are in the straight ahead position, then install the Pitman arm on the sector shaft (see Section 21). Install the Pitman arm nut and tighten it to the torque listed in this Chapter's Specifications.
11   Install the flex coupling-to-steering gear input shaft clamp bolt and tighten it to the torque listed in this Chapter's Specifications.
12   Connect the pressure and return lines to the steering gear. Tighten the line fittings securely. Fill the reservoir as described in Chapter 1. Turn the steering wheel from stop to stop to distribute the fluid.
13   Recheck the fluid level and add fluid if necessary.
14   Start the engine and turn the steering wheel from left to right and inspect for fluid leaks.
15   Bleed the power steering system as described in Section 26.

1982 through 1987 Continentals and 1984 through 1992 Mark VIIs

Removal

Refer to illustrations 24.18 and 24.20

16   Raise the front of the vehicle and support it securely on jackstands. Apply the parking brake.
17   Place a drain pan under the steering gear (power steering only). Remove the power steering pressure and return lines and cap the ends to prevent excessive fluid loss and contamination.
18   Mark the relationship of the intermediate shaft flexible coupling to the steering gear input shaft. Remove the pinch bolt **(see illustration)**.
19   Separate the tie-rod ends from the spindle arms (see Section 22).
20   Support the steering gear and remove the steering gear-to-frame mounting nuts and bolts **(see illustration)**. Lower the unit, separate the intermediate shaft from the steering gear input shaft and remove the steering gear from the vehicle.

Installation

21   Raise the steering gear into position and connect the intermediate shaft, aligning the marks.
22   Install the mounting bolts and washers and tighten the nuts to the torque listed in this Chapter's Specifications.
23   Connect the tie-rod ends to the steering knuckle arms (see Section 22)
24   Install the intermediate shaft pinch bolt and tighten it to the torque listed in this Chapter's Specifications.
25   Connect the power steering pressure and return hoses to the

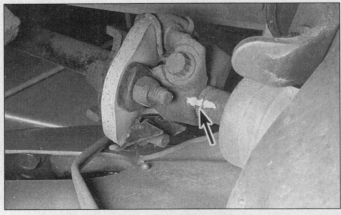

24.18 Mark the lower end of the intermediate shaft and the steering gear input shaft

24.20 Location of the steering gear mounting nuts (arrows)

25.3 Typical power steering pump fittings: When removing the power steering pressure line (arrow), a backup wrench should be used on the pump body fitting - the return hose is connected to the pump with a hose clamp

steering gear and fill the power steering pump reservoir with the recommended fluid (see Chapter 1).

26   Lower the vehicle and bleed the steering system as outlined in Section 26.

25 Power steering pump - removal and installation

Removal

Refer to illustrations 25.3, 25.4a and 25.4b

1   Relieve tension on the accessory drivebelt (see Chapter 1).

2   On some models, the pump can be accessed from above. On others, raise the front of the vehicle and place it securely on jackstands (the pump is more easily accessed from underneath the vehicle on these models).

3   Locate the pump on the left (driver's) side of the engine block **(see illustration)**. Disconnect the fluid return hose from the pump and drain the fluid from the pump reservoir. Disconnect the pressure hose from the pump (but do NOT unscrew the pressure fitting itself). Plug the lines to prevent contamination.

4   On some engines, the pump is mounted on a bracket bolted to the engine. You'll have to remove the pulley before you can remove the pump-to-bracket mounting bolts. A special puller for this purpose **(see illustrations)** is available at most auto parts stores. On other engines, the pump is mounted directly on the block, so the pulley doesn't cover up the mounting bolts. On these models, it's easier to remove the

pulley on the bench after you've removed the pump assembly.

5   Remove the pump mounting bolts and remove the pump.

Installation

Refer to illustration 25.6

6   Installation is the reverse of the above procedure. On some engines, you'll need a special pulley installer tool **(see illustration)**, available at most auto parts stores, to install the pulley once the pump is bolted to its mounting bracket.

7   Install the accessory drivebelt or the serpentine belt (see Chapter 1).

8   Install the pressure and return lines and fill the reservoir with an approved fluid. Start the engine and turn the steering wheel from lock to lock several times to distribute the fluid, then recheck the fluid level and top-off if necessary.

9   Bleed the power steering system as described in Section 26.

26 Power steering system - bleeding

1   Following any operation in which the power steering fluid lines have been disconnected, the power steering system must be bled to remove all air and obtain proper steering performance.

2   With the front wheels in the straight ahead position, check the power steering fluid level and, if low, add fluid until it reaches the Cold

25.4a If the power steering pump-to-bracket bolts are behind the pulley, you'll need a special puller to remove the pulley

25.4b Once the power steering pump pulley has been removed, the three mounting bolts are visible

25.6 If you had to remove the pulley to get at the pump-to-bracket bolts, you'll also need a special pulley installer tool to push the pulley onto the pump shaft; NEVER hammera pulley onto the shaft - you could damage the pump

10

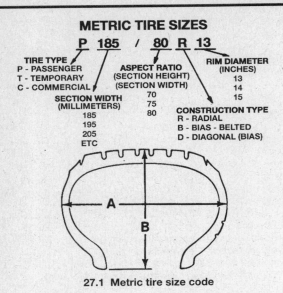

METRIC TIRE SIZES

P 185 / 80 R 13

TIRE TYPE
P - PASSENGER
T - TEMPORARY
C - COMMERCIAL

ASPECT RATIO
(SECTION HEIGHT)
(SECTION WIDTH)
70
75
80

RIM DIAMETER
(INCHES)
13
14
15

SECTION WIDTH
(MILLIMETERS)
185
195
205
ETC

CONSTRUCTION TYPE
R - RADIAL
B - BIAS - BELTED
D - DIAGONAL (BIAS)

27.1 Metric tire size code

A = Section width   B = Section height

mark on the dipstick.

3   Start the engine and allow it to run at fast idle. Recheck the fluid level and add more if necessary to reach the Cold mark on the dipstick.

4   Bleed the system by turning the wheels from side-to-side, without hitting the stops. This will work the air out of the system. Keep the reservoir full of fluid as this is done.

5   When the air is worked out of the system, return the wheels to the straight ahead position and leave the vehicle running for several more minutes before shutting it off.

6   Road test the vehicle to be sure the steering system is functioning normally and noise free.

7   Recheck the fluid level to be sure it is up to the Hot mark on the dipstick while the engine is at normal operating temperature. Add fluid if necessary (see Chapter 1).

27   Wheels and tires - general information

Refer to illustration 27.1

All models covered by this manual are equipped with metric-sized radial tires **(see illustration)**. Use of other size or type of tires may affect the ride and handling of the vehicle. Don't mix different types of tires, such as radials and bias belted, on the same vehicle as handling may be seriously affected. It's recommended that tires be replaced in pairs on the same axle, but if only one tire is being replaced, be sure it's the same size, structure and tread design as the other.

Because tire pressure has a substantial effect on handling and wear, the pressure on all tires should be checked at least once a month or before any extended trips (see Chapter 1).

Wheels must be replaced if they are bent, dented, leak air, have elongated bolt holes, are heavily rusted, out of vertical symmetry or if the lug nuts won't stay tight. Wheel repairs that use welding or peening are not recommended.

Tire and wheel balance is important to the overall handling, braking and performance of the vehicle. Unbalanced wheels can adversely affect handling and ride characteristics as well as tire life. Whenever a tire is installed on a wheel, the tire and wheel should be balanced by a shop with the proper equipment.

28   Front end alignment - general information

Refer to illustration 28.1

A front end alignment refers to the adjustments made to the front wheels so they are in proper angular relationship to the suspension

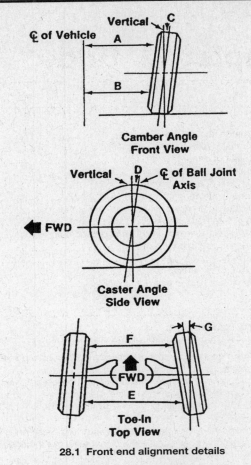

28.1 Front end alignment details

1   A minus B = C (degrees camber)
2   E minus F = toe-in (measured in inches)
3   G = toe-in (expressed in degrees)

and the ground. Front wheels that are out of proper alignment not only affect steering control, but also increase tire wear **(see illustration)**.

Getting the proper front wheel alignment is a very exacting process, one in which complicated and expensive machines are necessary to perform the job properly. Because of this, you should have a technician with the proper equipment perform these tasks. We will, however, use this space to give you a basic idea of what is involved with front end alignment so you can better understand the process and deal intelligently with the shop that does the work.

Toe-in is the turning in of the front wheels. The purpose of a toe specification is to ensure parallel rolling of the front wheels. In a vehicle with zero toe-in, the distance between the front edges of the wheels will be the same as the distance between the rear edges of the wheels. The actual amount of toe-in is normally only a fraction of an inch. Toe-in adjustment is controlled by the tie-rod end position on the tie-rod. Incorrect toe-in will cause the tires to wear improperly by making them scrub against the road surface.

Camber is the tilting of the front wheels from the vertical when viewed from the front of the vehicle. When the wheels tilt out at the top, the camber is said to be positive (+). When the wheels tilt in at the top the camber is negative (-). The amount of tilt is measured in degrees from the vertical and this measurement is called the camber angle. This angle affects the amount of tire tread which contacts the road and compensates for changes in the suspension geometry when the vehicle is cornering or traveling over an undulating surface.

Caster is the tilting of the top of the front steering axis from the vertical. A tilt toward the rear is positive caster and a tilt toward the front is negative caster. **Note:** *The caster cannot be adjusted on 1982 through 1987 Continentals and 1984 through 1992 Mark VIIs.*

Chapter 11 Body

Contents

1 General information

The models covered by this manual feature a separate frame and body construction.

Certain components are particularly vulnerable to accident damage and can be unbolted and repaired or replaced. Among these parts are the body moldings, bumpers, front fenders, the hood and trunk lids and all glass.

Only general body maintenance practices and body panel repair procedures within the scope of the do-it-yourselfer are included in this Chapter.

2 Body - maintenance

1   The condition of your vehicle's body is very important, because the resale value depends a great deal on it. It's much more difficult to repair a neglected or damaged body than it is to repair mechanical components. The hidden areas of the body, such as the wheel wells, the frame and the engine compartment, are equally important, although they don't require as frequent attention as the rest of the body.
2   Once a year, or every 12,000 miles, it's a good idea to have the underside of the body steam cleaned. All traces of dirt and oil will be removed and the area can then be inspected carefully for rust, damaged brake lines, frayed electrical wires, damaged cables and other problems. The front suspension components should be greased after completion of this job.
3   At the same time, clean the engine and the engine compartment with a steam cleaner or water soluble degreaser.
4   The wheel wells should be given close attention, since undercoating can peel away and stones and dirt thrown up by the tires can cause the paint to chip and flake, allowing rust to set in. If rust is found, clean down to the bare metal and apply an anti-rust paint.
5   The body should be washed about once a week. Wet the vehicle thoroughly to soften the dirt, then wash it down with a soft sponge and plenty of clean soapy water. If the surplus dirt is not washed off very carefully, it can wear down the paint.
6   Spots of tar or asphalt thrown up from the road should be removed with a cloth soaked in solvent.
7   Once every six months, wax the body and chrome trim. If a chrome cleaner is used to remove rust from any of the vehicle's plated parts, remember that the cleaner also removes part of the chrome, so use it sparingly.

3 Vinyl trim - maintenance

Don't clean vinyl trim with detergents, caustic soap or petroleum-based cleaners. Plain soap and water works just fine, with a soft brush to clean dirt that may be ingrained. Wash the vinyl as frequently as the rest of the vehicle.

After cleaning, application of a high quality rubber and vinyl protectant will help prevent oxidation and cracks. The protectant can also be applied to weatherstripping, vacuum lines and rubber hoses, which often fail as a result of chemical degradation, and to the tires.

4 Upholstery and carpets - maintenance

1   Every three months remove the carpets or mats and clean the interior of the vehicle (more frequently if necessary). Vacuum the upholstery and carpets to remove loose dirt and dust.
2   Leather upholstery requires special care. Stains should be removed with warm water and a very mild soap solution. Use a clean, damp cloth to remove the soap, then wipe again with a dry cloth. Never use alcohol, gasoline, nail polish remover or thinner to clean leather upholstery.
3   After cleaning, regularly treat leather upholstery with a leather wax. Never use car wax on leather upholstery.
4   In areas where the interior of the vehicle is subject to bright sunlight, cover leather seats with a sheet if the vehicle is to be left out for any length of time.

5 Body repair - minor damage

See photo sequence

Repair of minor scratches

1   If the scratch is superficial and does not penetrate to the metal of the body, repair is very simple. Lightly rub the scratched area with a fine rubbing compound to remove loose paint and built up wax. Rinse the area with clean water.
2   Apply touch-up paint to the scratch, using a small brush. Continue to apply thin layers of paint until the surface of the paint in the scratch is level with the surrounding paint. Allow the new paint at least two weeks to harden, then blend it into the surrounding paint by rubbing with a very fine rubbing compound. Finally, apply a coat of wax to the scratch area.

11

These photos illustrate a method of repairing simple dents. They are intended to supplement *Body repair - minor damage* in this Chapter and should not be used as the sole instructions for body repair on these vehicles.

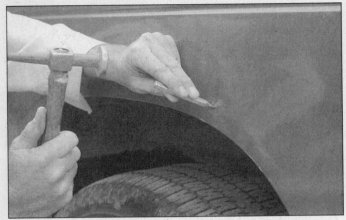

1   If you can't access the backside of the body panel to hammer out the dent, pull it out with a slide-hammer-type dent puller. In the deepest portion of the dent or along the crease line, drill or punch hole(s) at least one inch apart . . .

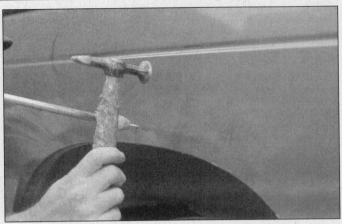

2   . . . then screw the slide-hammer into the hole and operate it. Tap with a hammer near the edge of the dent to help 'pop' the metal back to its original shape. When you're finished, the dent area should be close to its original contour and about 1/8-inch below the surface of the surrounding metal

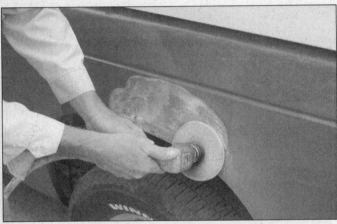

3   Using coarse-grit sandpaper, remove the paint down to the bare metal. Hand sanding works fine, but the disc sander shown here makes the job faster. Use finer (about 320-grit) sandpaper to feather-edge the paint at least one inch around the dent area

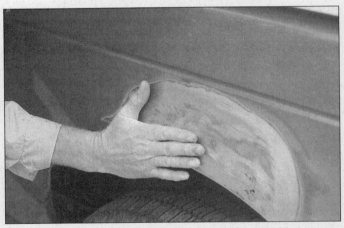

4   When the paint is removed, touch will probably be more helpful than sight for telling if the metal is straight. Hammer down the high spots or raise the low spots as necessary. Clean the repair area with wax/silicone remover

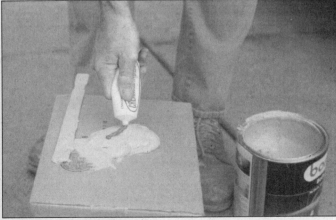

5   Following label instructions, mix up a batch of plastic filler and hardener. The ratio of filler to hardener is critical, and, if you mix it incorrectly, it will either not cure properly or cure too quickly (you won't have time to file and sand it into shape)

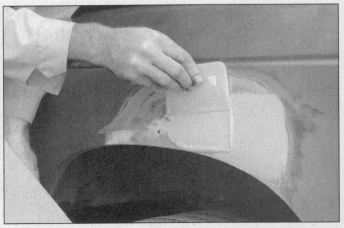

6   Working quickly so the filler doesn't harden, use a plastic applicator to press the body filler firmly into the metal, assuring it bonds completely. Work the filler until it matches the original contour and is slightly above the surrounding metal

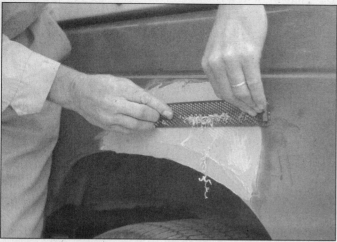

7   Let the filler harden until you can just dent it with your fingernail. Use a body file or Surform tool (shown here) to rough-shape the filler

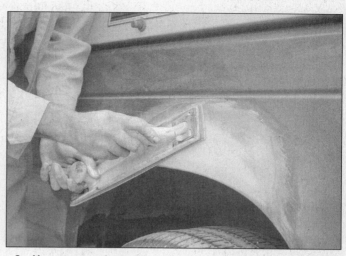

8   Use coarse-grit sandpaper and a sanding board or block to work the filler down until it's smooth and even. Work down to finer grits of sandpaper - always using a board or block - ending up with 360 or 400 grit

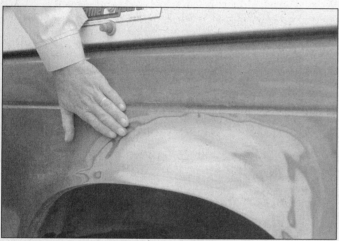

9   You shouldn't be able to feel any ridge at the transition from the filler to the bare metal or from the bare metal to the old paint. As soon as the repair is flat and uniform, remove the dust and mask off the adjacent panels or trim pieces

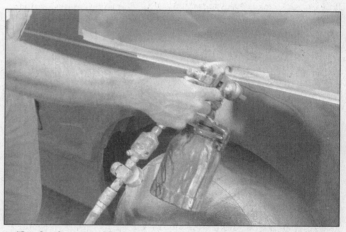

10   Apply several layers of primer to the area. Don't spray the primer on too heavy, so it sags or runs, and make sure each coat is dry before you spray on the next one. A professional-type spray gun is being used here, but aerosol spray primer is available inexpensively from auto parts stores

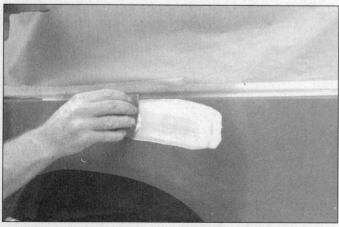

11   The primer will help reveal imperfections or scratches. Fill these with glazing compound. Follow the label instructions and sand it with 360 or 400-grit sandpaper until it's smooth. Repeat the glazing, sanding and respraying until the primer reveals a perfectly smooth surface

12   Finish sand the primer with very fine sandpaper (400 or 600-grit) to remove the primer overspray. Clean the area with water and allow it to dry. Use a tack rag to remove any dust, then apply the finish coat. Don't attempt to rub out or wax the repair area until the paint has dried completely (at least two weeks)

3   If the scratch has penetrated the paint and exposed the metal of the body, causing the metal to rust, a different repair technique is required. Remove all loose rust from the bottom of the scratch with a pocket knife, then apply rust inhibiting paint to prevent the formation of rust in the future. Using a rubber or nylon applicator, coat the scratched area with glaze-type filler. If required, the filler can be mixed with thinner to provide a very thin paste, which is ideal for filling narrow scratches. Before the glaze filler in the scratch hardens, wrap a piece of smooth cotton cloth around the tip of a finger. Dip the cloth in thinner and then quickly wipe it along the surface of the scratch. This will ensure that the surface of the filler is slightly hollow. The scratch can now be painted over as described earlier in this section.

Repair of dents

4   When repairing dents, the first job is to pull the dent out until the affected area is as close as possible to its original shape. There is no point in trying to restore the original shape completely as the metal in the damaged area will have stretched on impact and cannot be restored to its original contours. It is better to bring the level of the dent up to a point which is about 1/8-inch below the level of the surrounding metal. In cases where the dent is very shallow, it is not worth trying to pull it out at all.

5   If the back side of the dent is accessible, it can be hammered out gently from behind using a soft-face hammer. While doing this, hold a block of wood firmly against the opposite side of the metal to absorb the hammer blows and prevent the metal from being stretched.

6   If the dent is in a section of the body which has double layers, or some other factor makes it inaccessible from behind, a different technique is required. Drill several small holes through the metal inside the damaged area, particularly in the deeper sections. Screw long, self tapping screws into the holes just enough for them to get a good grip in the metal. Now the dent can be pulled out by pulling on the protruding heads of the screws with locking pliers.

7   The next stage of repair is the removal of paint from the damaged area and from an inch or so of the surrounding metal. This is easily done with a wire brush or sanding disk in a drill motor, although it can be done just as effectively by hand with sandpaper. To complete the preparation for filling, score the surface of the bare metal with a screwdriver or the tang of a file or drill small holes in the affected area. This will provide a good grip for the filler material. To complete the repair, see the Section on filling and painting.

Repair of rust holes or gashes

8   Remove all paint from the affected area and from an inch or so of the surrounding metal using a sanding disk or wire brush mounted in a drill motor. If these are not available, a few sheets of sandpaper will do the job just as effectively.

9   With the paint removed, you will be able to determine the severity of the corrosion and decide whether to replace the whole panel, if possible, or repair the affected area. New body panels are not as expensive as most people think and it is often quicker to install a new panel than to repair large areas of rust.

10   Remove all trim pieces from the affected area except those which will act as a guide to the original shape of the damaged body, such as headlight shells, etc. Using metal snips or a hacksaw blade, remove all loose metal and any other metal that is badly affected by rust. Hammer the edges of the hole in to create a slight depression for the filler material.

11   Wire brush the affected area to remove the powdery rust from the surface of the metal. If the back of the rusted area is accessible, treat it with rust inhibiting paint.

12   Before filling is done, block the hole in some way. This can be done with sheet metal riveted or screwed into place, or by stuffing the hole with wire mesh.

13   Once the hole is blocked off, the affected area can be filled and painted. See the following subsection on filling and painting.

Filling and painting

14   Many types of body fillers are available, but generally speaking, body repair kits which contain filler paste and a tube of resin hardener are best for this type of repair work. A wide, flexible plastic or nylon applicator will be necessary for imparting a smooth and contoured finish to the surface of the filler material. Mix a small amount of filler on a clean piece of wood or cardboard (use the hardener sparingly). Follow the manufacturer's instructions on the package, otherwise the filler will set incorrectly.

15   Using the applicator, apply the filler paste to the prepared area. Draw the applicator across the surface of the filler to achieve the desired contour and to level the filler surface. As soon as a contour that approximates the original one is achieved, stop working the paste. If you continue, the paste will begin to stick to the applicator. Continue to add thin layers of paste at 20-minute intervals until the level of the filler is just above the surrounding metal.

16   Once the filler has hardened, the excess can be removed with a body file. From then on, progressively finer grades of sandpaper should be used, starting with a 180-grit paper and finishing with 600-grit wet-or-dry paper. Always wrap the sandpaper around a flat rubber or wooden block, otherwise the surface of the filler will not be completely flat. During the sanding of the filler surface, the wet-or-dry paper should be periodically rinsed in water. This will ensure that a very smooth finish is produced in the final stage.

17   At this point, the repair area should be surrounded by a ring of bare metal, which in turn should be encircled by the finely feathered edge of good paint. Rinse the repair area with clean water until all of the dust produced by the sanding operation is washed away.

18   Spray the entire area with a light coat of primer. This will reveal any imperfections in the surface of the filler. Repair the imperfections with fresh filler paste or glaze filler and once more smooth the surface with sandpaper. Repeat this spray-and-sand procedure until you are satisfied that the surface of the filler and the feathered edge of the paint are perfect. Rinse the area with clean water and allow it to dry completely.

19   The repair area is now ready for painting. Spray painting must be carried out in a warm, dry, windless and dust free atmosphere. These conditions can be created if you have access to a large indoor work area, but if you are forced to work in the open, you will have to pick the day very carefully. If you are working indoors, dousing the floor in the work area with water will help settle the dust which would otherwise be in the air. If the repair area is confined to one body panel, mask off the surrounding panels. This will help minimize the effects of a slight mismatch in paint color. Trim pieces such as chrome strips, door handles, etc., will also need to be masked off or removed. Use masking tape and several thicknesses of newspaper for the masking operations.

20   Before spraying, shake the paint can thoroughly, then spray a test area until the spray painting technique is mastered. Cover the repair area with a thick coat of primer. The thickness should be built up using several thin layers of primer rather than one thick one. Using 600-grit wet-or-dry sandpaper, rub down the surface of the primer until it is very smooth. While doing this, the work area should be thoroughly rinsed with water and the wet-or-dry sandpaper periodically rinsed as well. Allow the primer to dry before spraying additional coats.

21   Spray on the top coat, again building up the thickness by using several thin layers of paint. Begin spraying in the center of the repair area and then, using a circular motion, work out until the whole repair area and about two inches of the surrounding original paint is covered. Remove all masking material 10 to 15 minutes after spraying on the final coat of paint. Allow the new paint at least two weeks to harden, then use a very fine rubbing compound to blend the edges of the new paint into the existing paint. Finally, apply a coat of wax.

6   Body repair - major damage

1   Major damage must be repaired by an auto body shop specifically equipped to perform frame and body repairs. These shops have the specialized equipment required to do the job properly.

2   If the damage is extensive, the frame must be checked for proper alignment or the vehicle's handling characteristics may be adversely affected and other components may wear at an accelerated rate.

3   Due to the fact that all of the major body components (hood, fenders, etc.) are separate and replaceable units, any seriously damaged components should be replaced rather than repaired. Sometimes the components can be found in a wrecking yard that specializes in used vehicle components, often at considerable savings over the cost of new parts.

7   Hinges and locks - maintenance

Once every 3000 miles, or every three months, the hinges and latch assemblies on the doors, hood and trunk should be given a few drops of light oil or lock lubricant. The door latch strikers should also be lubricated with a thin coat of grease to reduce wear and ensure free movement. Lubricate the door and trunk locks with spray-on graphite lubricant.

8   Windshield and fixed glass - replacement

Replacement of the windshield and fixed glass requires the use of special fast-setting adhesive/caulk materials and some specialized tools and techniques. These operations should be left to a dealer service department or a shop specializing in glass work.

9   Hood - removal, installation and adjustment

Refer to illustrations 9.3, 9.9 and 9.10
Note: *The hood is heavy and somewhat awkward to remove and install - at least two people should perform this procedure.*

Removal and installation

1   Use blankets or pads to cover the cowl area of the body and the fenders. This will protect the body and paint as the hood is lifted off.
2   Disconnect any cables or wire harnesses which will interfere with removal.
3   Scribe or draw alignment marks around the bolt washers to ensure proper alignment on reinstallation **(see illustration)**. Have an assistant support the weight of the hood. Remove the hinge bracket-to-hood bolts.
4   Lift off the hood.
5   Installation is the reverse of removal.

Adjustment

6   Fore-and-aft and side-to-side adjustment of the hood is done by moving the hinge plate in relation to the inner fender panel after loosening the bolts.

7   Scribe a line around the entire hinge plate so you can judge the amount of movement.
8   Loosen the bolts and move the hood into correct alignment. Move it only a little at a time. Tighten the hinge bolts or nuts and carefully lower the hood to check the alignment.
9   If necessary after installation, the entire hood latch assembly can be adjusted up-and-down as well as from side-to-side on the radiator support so the hood closes securely and is flush with the fenders. To do this, scribe a line around the hood latch mounting bolts to provide a reference point. Then loosen the bolts and reposition the latch assembly as necessary **(see illustration)**. Following adjustment, retighten the mounting bolts.
10   Finally, adjust the hood bumpers on the radiator support so the hood, when closed, is flush with the fenders **(see illustration)**.
11   The hood latch assembly, as well as the hinges, should be periodically lubricated with white lithium-based grease to prevent sticking and wear.

10   Front fender - removal and installation

Warning: *Some models have airbags. Always disconnect the negative battery cable, then the positive cable and wait 2 minutes before working in the vicinity of the impact sensors, steering column or instrument panel to avoid the possibility of accidental deployment of the airbag, which could cause personal injury (see Chapter 12).*
1   Raise the vehicle, support it securely on jackstands and remove the front wheel.
2   Remove the splash shield from the fender and body.
3   Disconnect the antenna (some models) and all light bulb electrical connectors and other components that would interfere with fender removal.
4   Remove the fender-mounting bolts/nuts.
5   Detach the fender. It is a good idea to have an assistant support the fender while it's being moved away from the vehicle to prevent damage to the surrounding body panels.
6   Installation is the reverse of removal.
7   Tighten all nuts, bolts and screws securely.

11   Radiator grille - removal and installation

Refer to illustrations 11.1 and 11.2
Warning: *Some models have airbags. Always disconnect the negative battery cable, then the positive cable and wait 2 minutes before working in the vicinity of the impact sensors, steering column or instrument panel to avoid the possibility of accidental deployment of the airbag, which could cause personal injury (see Chapter 12).*

9.9 Adjust the hood closed height by loosening the bolts (arrows) and moving the latch up or down

9.10 Thread the rubber bumper in or out to make fine adjustments to the hood closed height

9.3 Use a marking pen to draw a line around the hood bolts

11

11.1 On earlier models the retaining screws are accessible from the front and the grille tilted forward for removal

11.2 On later models, the grille is retained by nuts (arrows), accessible from under the hood

12.4 Bumper retaining nuts (arrows)

1   On early models the grille is retained by screws which can be reached from the accessible from the front. Remove the retaining screws and pull out the grille **(see illustration)**.

2   On later models, the grille is held in place by nuts which are accessible from the engine compartment **(see illustration)**. Remove the nuts and detach the grille from the front.

3   Installation is the reverse of removal.

12 Bumpers - removal and installation

Refer to illustration 12.4

Warning: *Some models have airbags. Always disconnect the negative battery cable, then the positive cable and wait 2 minutes before working in the vicinity of the impact sensors, steering column or instrument panel to avoid the possibility of accidental deployment of the airbag, which could cause personal injury (see Chapter 12).*

Removal

1   Detach the bumper covers (if equipped).

2   Disconnect any wiring or other components that would interfere with bumper removal.

3   Support the bumper with a floor jack.

4   Alternatively remove the retaining bolts/nuts and detach the bumper **(see illustration)**.

Installation

5   Installation is the reverse of removal.

6   Tighten the retaining bolts securely.

7   Install the bumper cover and any other components that were removed.

13 Door trim panel - removal and installation

Refer to illustrations 13.2a, 13.2b, 13.3a, 13.3b, 14.4a, 14.4b, 13.5, 13.7a and 13.7b

Removal

1   Disconnect the cable from the negative battery terminal.

2   Remove all door trim panel retaining screws and door pull/armrest assemblies **(see illustration)**. Remove any hidden retaining screws or bolts **(see illustration)**.

3   Remove the switch housing screw, pry out the housing and unplug the switch **(see illustrations)**.

4   Use a screwdriver or trim panel tool to dislodge the clips, grasp the trim panel and rotate the bottom edge out, then lift the panel up to detach it from the door **(see illustration)**. Unplug any electrical connectors and remove the trim panel from the vehicle **(see illustration)**.

5   For access to the inner door on later models, carefully peel back the plastic watershield **(see illustration)**.

Installation

6   Prior to installation of the door panel, be sure to reinstall any clips in the panel which may have come out during the removal procedure

13.2a Use a screwdriver to pry out the door trim panel screw covers

13.2b Some retaining bolts may be hidden inside the door panel

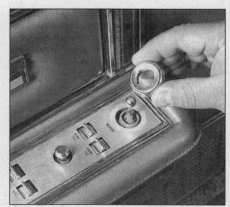

13.3a On some models it will be necessary to unscrew the mirror control collar so the switch housing can be removed

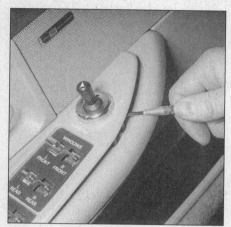

13.3b Pry up on the power window switch housing to detach

13.4a Use a screwdriver or similar tool to detach the retaining clips around the door panel

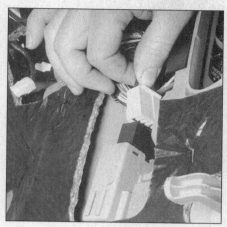

13.4b Pull the trim panel out and unplug the electrical connectors

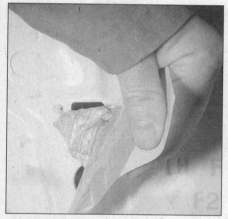

13.5 Peel the water deflector carefully away from the door, taking care not to tear or distort it

13.7a On earlier models, lower the door panel into place and insert the top edge into the door opening

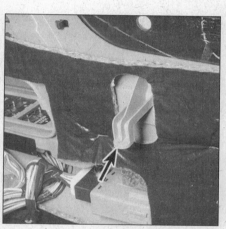

13.7b On later models, insert the molded plastic hooks (arrow) into the door and push down to lock the trim panel in the door

and remain in the door itself.

7   Plug in the wire harness connectors and place the panel in position in the window glass opening at the top of the door, then rotate it down into position and seat the clips (see illustration). On later models, insert the molded hooks into the door openings, then push straight down to seat them (see illustration). Install the armrest/door pulls. Install the power window switch housing assembly.

14 Door - removal, installation and adjustment

Refer to illustrations 14.4, 14.6a and 14.6b

Removal

1   Remove the door trim panel (see Section 13). Disconnect any electrical connectors and push them through the door opening so they won't interfere with door removal.
2   Place a floor jack under the door or have an assistant on hand to support the door when the hinge bolts are removed. Note: Place a rag between the jack and the door to protect the door's painted surfaces.
3   Scribe or draw alignment marks around the door hinges to ensure proper alignment on reinstallation.
4   Remove the hinge-to-door bolts and carefully lift off the door (see illustration).

Installation and adjustment

5   Installation is the reverse of removal.
6   Following installation of the door, check the alignment and adjust, if necessary, as follows:

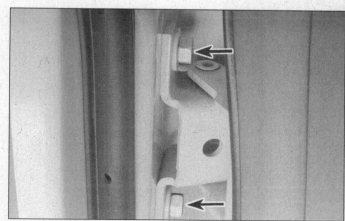

14.4 With the door supported, remove the door hinge bolts (arrows)

11

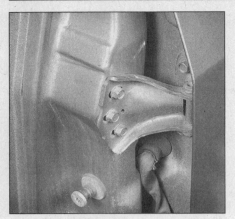

14.6a The door position can be adjusted by loosening the hinge bolts and moving the door slightly

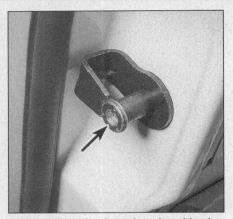

14.6b Adjust the door closed position by loosening the Torx head screw (arrow), then moving the striker by tapping it with a mallet

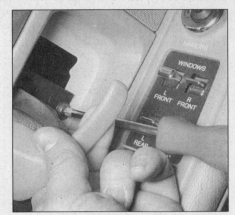

15.2a Remove the door remote control retaining screws

a) *Up-and-down and forward-and-backward adjustments are made by loosening the hinge-to-body bolts and moving the door as necessary (see illustration).*

b) *The door lock striker can also be adjusted both up-and-down and sideways to provide positive engagement with the lock mechanism. This is done by loosening the striker pin with a Torx-bit tool, moving the pin as necessary and retightening the striker (see illustration).*

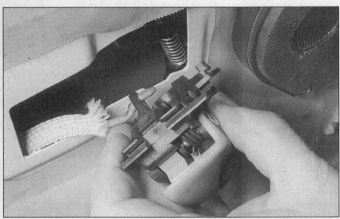

15.2b Pull the remote control out and disconnect it from the rod

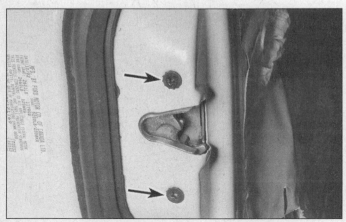

15.4 The latch is held in place by two screws in the end of the door (arrows)

15 Door latch and remote controls - removal and installation

Refer to illustrations 15.2a, 15.2b and 15.4

1   Remove the door trim panel and peel the watershield back (see Section 13).

2   Remove the remote control assembly and disconnect the rod at the control and the lock cylinder **(see illustrations)**.

3   Disconnect the push button or remote lock rod and handle from the latch.

4   Remove the screws located in the end of the door and detach the latch **(see illustration)**.

5   Installation is the reverse of removal.

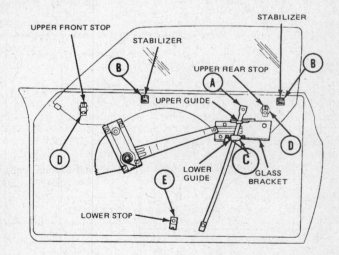

16.2 Typical tubular run-type door component layout and adjustment details

A   *Fore-and-aft adjustment is made at the upper tubular run screw and upper guide*

B   *Adjust the tightness of the glass against the beltline with the stabilizer screws loose - raise the glass fully, then tighten the screws*

C   *In-and-out adjustment is made at the lower guides*

D   *Adjust the upper limit of glass travel with the upper stops*

E   *The lower limit of the glass is adjusted at the lower stop*

16 Door window glass - removal, installation and adjustment

1   Remove the door trim panel and watershield (see Section 13).

Single tubular run type

Refer to illustration 16.2

Front door

Removal

2   Remove the screws and detach the glass stabilizers, then remove the upper front and rear stop brackets **(see illustration)**.
3   Use a punch to remove the centers from the rivets retaining the glass to the bracket. Drill out the rivets with a 1/4-inch drill bit. Be sure to use a block of wood to support the glass during the rivet removal process.
4   Remove the glass by aligning the stops with the notches in the door, then lifting it straight up.

Installation

5   Place the glass in position and install three 1/4-inch screws with washers and nuts. Tighten the nuts and screws securely.
6   Install the stop brackets and glass stabilizers. To adjust, refer to illustration 16.2.

Rear door

Removal

7   Use a punch to remove the centers from the rivets retaining the glass to the bracket. Drill out the rivets with a 1/4-inch drill bit. Be sure to use a block of wood to support the glass during the rivet removal process.
8   Loosen the screws and push the glass stabilizers out of the way.
9   Remove the glass support and lifting the glass out of the door.

Installation

10   Place the glass in position in the bracket and fasten it with two 1/4-inch screws with washers and nuts. Tighten the nuts and screws securely.
11   To adjust, refer to illustration 16.2.

Dropping vent-type front door glass

Refer to illustration 16.12

Vent window

12   Lower the glass until the two retaining rivets are accessible through the holes in the inner door panel **(see illustration)**. Use a punch to remove the centers from the rivets, then drill out the rivets with a 1/4-inch drill bit. Be sure to use a block of wood to support the glass during the rivet removal process.
13   Loosen the front glass run retainer and remove the vent glass and bracket assembly from the door.

Installation

14   Install the spacer and retainer securely into the retaining holes in the glass, then place the glass into position. Install the division bar and slide it up far enough to gain access to the retaining holes.
15   Position the window glass bracket over the vent window retaining holes and fasten it with two 1/4-inch screws with washers and nuts. Tighten the nuts and screws securely.

Adjustment

16   The door vent glass should always be adjusted at the same time as the door glass as described below (see Step 22).

Door glass

Removal

17   Loosen the vent glass run retainer screws and push the retainer forward, then loosen the division bar bolts and push it forward.
18   Lower the glass as necessary until the two retaining rivets are accessible through the holes in the inner door panel **(see illustration 16.12)**. Use a punch to remove the centers from the rivets, then drill out the rivets with a 1/4-inch drill bit. Be sure to use a block of wood to support the glass during the rivet removal process.
19   Remove the glass from the door by tipping it forward, then lifting it up and out of the opening at the top of the door, toward the outside.

Installation

20   Install the spacer and retainer assemblies into the retaining holes in the glass. Lower the glass assembly into the door and place it in position in the bracket, making sure the lower spacers are set securely into the channels.

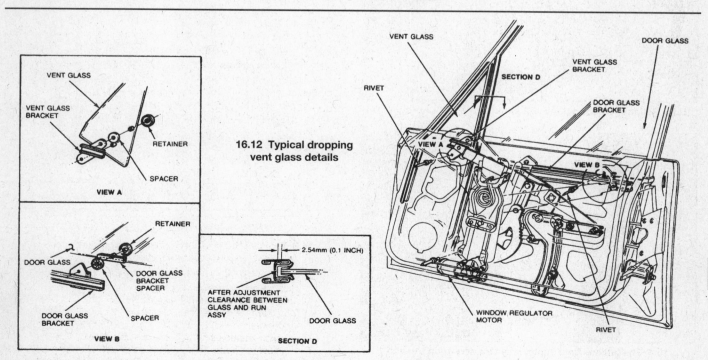

16.12 Typical dropping vent glass details

11

17.7a The trunk lid closed position can be adjusted by loosening the bolts (arrows) and moving the latch

17.7b Fine adjustments of the trunk lid can be made by threading the rubber bumpers in-or-out (later models)

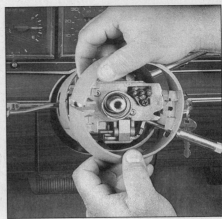

18.2a On earlier models, remove the collar from the top of the steering column

21   Attach the bracket to the glass with two 1/4 by 1-inch screws with washers and nuts. Tighten the nuts and screws securely.

Adjustment

22   Loosen the division bar nut and bolt and lock side screw and lower the glass to the bottom of the door.
23   Tighten the door glass lock side run retaining screw securely, then raise the glass three inches and move it to the rear, into the lock side run retainer.
24   Push the division bar into the front edge of the door glass.
25   Grasp the top edge of the glass and move it and the division bar forward 1/8-inch to provide enough clearance so it won't bind, then tighten the lower division bar nuts.
26   Raise the glass three quarters of the way up and make sure there is also 1/8-inch clearance at the division bar with no binding. If there is binding, adjust the bar position and tighten the attaching nut.
27   Raise and lower the vent glass several times to make sure it operates smoothly, then lower the vent glass 3-inches.
28   Loosen the front glass run retainer screws and nuts, then push the glass rearward and hold it. Tighten the screws and nuts.
29   Cycle the vent glass several times to make sure it doesn't bind.

Run and bracket-type

Removal

30   Raise or lower the glass as necessary until the two retaining rivets are accessible through the holes in the inner door panel. Use a punch to remove the centers from the rivets, then drill out the rivets with a 1/4-inch drill bit. Be sure to use a block of wood to support the glass during the rivet removal process.
31   Remove the glass from the door by tipping it forward, then lifting it up and out of the opening at the top of the door, toward the outside.

Installation

32   Lower the glass into the door, place it in position in the bracket and install two 1/4 by 1-inch screws with washers and nuts. Tighten the nuts and screws securely.

Adjustment

Front door

33   With the regulator run and bracket nuts and bolts loose, raise the glass to the top of the door.
34   Move the glass fore-and-aft as necessary until it is centered in the tracks, then tighten the bracket and run nut and bolt.

Rear door

35   Loosen the window division bar retaining screws and move the bar fore-or-aft as necessary to obtain smooth window operation. Tighten the screw securely.

Cable drive-type

Removal

36   Raise or lower the glass as necessary until the two retaining rivets are accessible through the holes in the inner door panel. Use a punch to remove the centers from the rivets, then drill out the rivets with a 1/4-inch drill bit. Be sure to use a block of wood to support the glass during the rivet removal process.
37   Remove the glass from the door by tipping it forward, then lifting it up and out of the opening at the top of the door, toward the outside.

Installation

38   Lower the glass into the door, place it in position in the bracket and install two 1/4 by 1-inch screws with washers and nuts. Tighten the nuts and screws securely.

Adjustment

1989 and earlier models

39   With the regulator run and bracket nut and bolt loose, raise the glass to the top of the door.
40   Move the glass fore-and-aft as necessary until it is centered in the tracks, then tighten the bracket and run nut and bolt.

1990 and later models

41   Loosen the upper window regulator nuts, raise the glass to the full up position, then tighten the nuts securely.
42   Loosen the front glass run bolt, lower the glass to the full down position and tighten the bolt securely.

All models

43   Cycle the glass several times to make sure it is properly adjusted.

---

17   Trunk lid - removal, installation and adjustment

Refer to illustrations 17.7a and 17.7b

Removal

1   Open the trunk lid and cover the edges of the trunk compartment with pads or cloths to protect the painted surfaces when the lid is removed.
2   Disconnect any cables or wire harness connectors attached to the trunk lid that would interfere with removal.
3   Scribe or draw alignment marks around the hinge bolt mounting flanges.
4   While an assistant supports the trunk lid, remove the hinge bolts from both sides and lift it off.

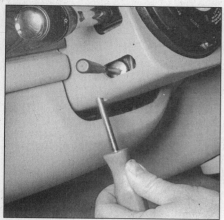
18.2b On later models, use a Phillips head screwdriver to remove the steering column cover screws

18.3 On earlier models, remove the screw and detach the steering column opening cover

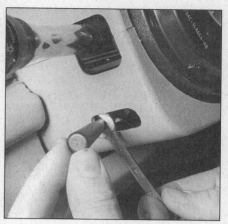
18.4 Remove the tilt lever with a small wrench (later models)

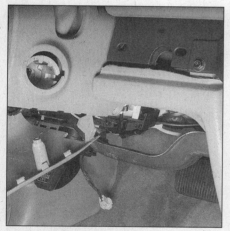
18.6a Detach the lower column cover

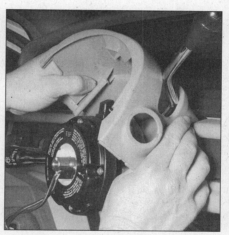
18.6b Lift the upper column cover up over the shift lever (later models)

19.1 Use a socket to remove the bolts from the lower edge of the knee protector

Installation and adjustment

5   Installation is the reverse of removal. **Note:** *When reinstalling the trunk lid, align the hinge bolt flanges with the marks made during removal.*
6   After installation, close the lid and check to verify if it's in proper alignment with the surrounding panels. Fore-and-aft and side-to-side adjustments of the lid are controlled by the position of the hinge bolts in the slots. To adjust, loosen the hinge bolts, reposition the lid and retighten the bolts.
7   The height of the lid in relation to the surrounding body panels when closed can be adjusted by loosening the striker bolts, repositioning the striker and retightening the bolts. The height can also be adjusted by loosening the latch bolts, repositioning the latch and retightening the bolts **(see illustration)**. On later models, finer adjustments of the trunk lid, when closed, can be made by threading the bumper/stops in-or-out **(see illustration)**.

18   Steering column cover - removal and installation

Refer to illustrations 18.2a, 18.2b, 18.3, 18.4, 18.6a and 18.6b
Warning: *Some models have airbags. Always disconnect the negative battery cable, then the positive cable and wait 2 minutes before working in the vicinity of the impact sensors, steering column or instrument panel to avoid the possibility of accidental deployment of the airbag, which could cause personal injury (see Chapter 12).*
1   Remove the steering wheel (see Chapter 10).
2   Remove the column cover retaining screws **(see illustrations)**.
3   Remove the steering column opening cover or knee protector (airbag-equipped models) **(see illustration)**.
4   On some tilt steering columns, a small wrench is necessary to unscrew the tilt lever **(see illustration)**.
5   On some models it will be necessary to remove the ignition lock cylinder to get the upper cover off (see Chapter 12).
6   Remove any remaining screws, then separate the halves and remove the covers **(see illustrations)**.
7   Installation is the reverse of the removal procedure.

19   Knee protector (airbag-equipped models) - removal and installation

Refer to illustrations 19.1 and 19.2
Warning: *Some models have airbags. Always disconnect the negative battery cable, then the positive cable and wait 2 minutes before working in the vicinity of the impact sensors, steering column or instrument panel to avoid the possibility of accidental deployment of the airbag, which could cause personal injury (see Chapter 12).*
1   Remove the retaining bolts at the lower edge of the knee protector **(see illustration)**.

11

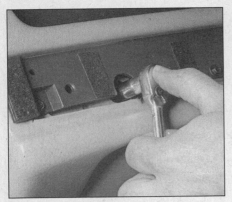

19.2 Remove the bolts from the upper edge of the knee protector

20.2a On earlier models the lower dash pad assembly will have to be removed for access to the bezel

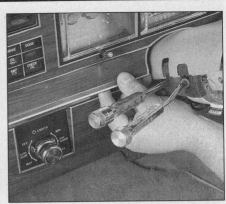

20.2b On later models, pry off the dash trim panels on the left . . .

20.2c . . . and right side for access to the bezel screws

20.3a Remove the upper cluster bezel screws (arrows) (later model shown)

2   Detach the instrument cluster trim panels, then remove the upper retaining bolts and lower the knee protector panel from the instrument panel **(see illustration)**.
3   Installation is the reverse of the removal procedure.

20 Instrument cluster bezel - removal and installation

Refer to illustrations 20.2a, 20.2b, 20.2c, 20.3a, 20.3b, 20.3c, 20.4a, 20.4b, 20.4c and 20.4d
Warning: *Some models have airbags. Always disconnect the negative*

battery cable, then the positive cable and wait 2 minutes before working in the vicinity of the impact sensors, steering column or instrument panel to avoid the possibility of accidental deployment of the airbag, which could cause personal injury (see Chapter 12).
1   Remove the steering column cover (see Section 18).
2   Detach the dash trim panels **(see illustrations)**.
3   Remove the bezel retaining screws **(see illustrations)**.
4   Detach the bezel and remove it from the vehicle **(see illustrations)**. On some later models, pry the left end of the bezel free and detach the retaining clips, working toward the right end until the bezel can be removed **(see illustrations)**.
5   Installation is the reverse of the removal procedure.

20.3b Remove the lower left edge cluster bezel screws (arrows)

20.3c Remove the right side bezel screws

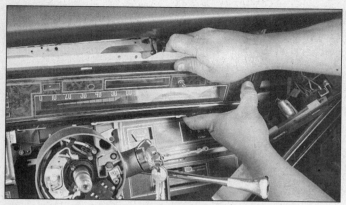

20.4a On early models, detach the bezel from the right side first, then rotate it out

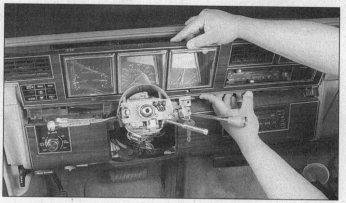

20.4b On later models, pull the bezel straight back and up off the steering column

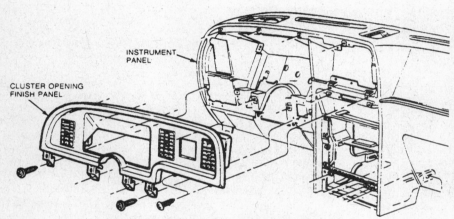

20.4c Typical Mark Series cluster bezel details

20.4d On some later models, detach the left side of the cluster bezel first, then work from left to right until it can be removed

21   Instrument panel - removal and installation

Refer to illustrations 21.2 and 21.8

Warning: *Some models have airbags. Always disconnect the negative battery cable, then the positive cable and wait 2 minutes before working in the vicinity of the impact sensors, steering column or instrument panel to avoid the possibility of accidental deployment of the airbag, which could cause personal injury (see Chapter 12).*

1   Remove the steering column cover (see Section 18).
2   Remove the dashboard finish panels **(see illustration).**

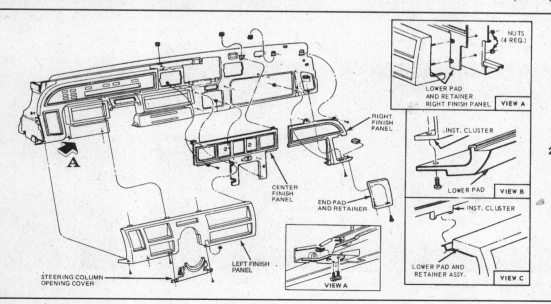

21.2 Typical early model dash panel details

11

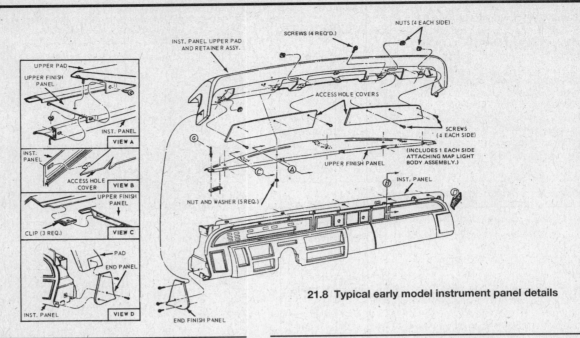

21.8 Typical early model instrument panel details

3   Remove the radio (see Chapter 12).
4   Remove the heater/air conditioner controls (see Chapter 3).
5   Remove the instrument cluster bezel (see Section 20) and cluster assembly (see Chapter 12).
6   Remove the retaining nuts and lower the steering column.
7   Remove the hood release handle.
8   Remove the attaching bolts and unplug the electrical connectors and disconnect any components that would interfere with removal **(see illustration)**. Pull the instrument panel back and lift it from the vehicle.
9   Installation is the reverse of removal. Make sure none of the wiring is crimped when the instrument panel is rotated back into position.

22 Console - removal and installation

Refer to illustration 22.1
Warning: *Some models have airbags. Always disconnect the negative battery cable, then the positive cable and wait 2 minutes before working in the vicinity of the impact sensors, steering column or instrument panel to avoid the possibility of accidental deployment of the airbag, which could cause personal injury (see Chapter 12).*
1   On models so equipped, remove the console glove box lock bezel **(see illustration)**.
2   Pull the rear of the front finish panel up and to the rear to detach it from the locating clips, then unplug the electrical connectors

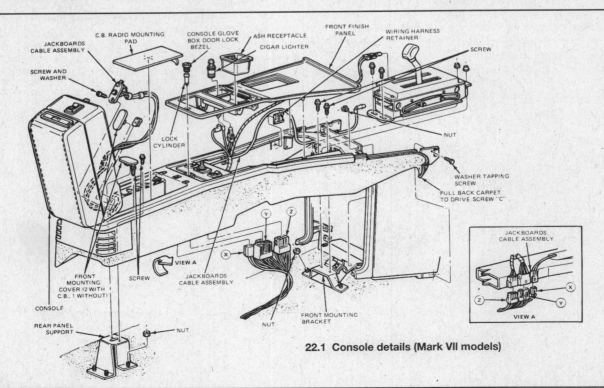

22.1 Console details (Mark VII models)

3   Remove the front console retaining nuts/screws.
4   Pull back the carpeting for access and remove the front console-to-instrument panel screws (later models).
5   Remove the switch mounting plate screws and unplug the electrical connectors.
6   Open the console lid for access, then remove the rear console attaching screws.
7   Remove the center bracket-to-crossmember screws.
8   Remove any remaining screws and pull the front edges of the console away from the instrument panel while sliding the console to the rear, then lifting up to remove it.
9   Installation is the reverse of removal.

23 Outside mirrors - removal and installation

Refer to illustrations 23.3 and 23.8
1   Remove the door trim panel and watershield (see Section 13).

Cable-operated mirrors

2   Working inside the vehicle, detach the control lever from the instrument panel or door and connect a string or thin wire to the end of the control cable, then detach any retaining clips.
3   Remove the attaching screws, detach the mirror and pull the control cable out of the door **(see illustration)**.
4   Attach the string or wire to the control end of the new cable/mirror assembly, pull it into position in the vehicle, then install the mirror and screws.
5   Secure the cable and connect it to the door or instrument panel.

Electric mirrors

6   Disconnect the cable from the negative battery terminal.
7   Pry off the mirror access hole cover.
8   Remove the nuts **(see illustration)**, detach the mirror from the door and unplug the electrical connector.
9   Installation is the reverse of removal.

24 Seats - removal and installation

Refer to illustrations 24.1, 24.3 and 24.5

Front

1   Remove the seat track retaining bolts/nuts, disconnect any electrical connectors and lift the seat and track assembly from the vehicle **(see illustration)**.
2   Installation is the reverse of removal.

23.3 On some models the mirror screws (arrow) are accessible from outside

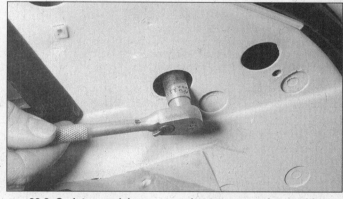

23.8 On later models, use a socket to remove the outside mirror nuts

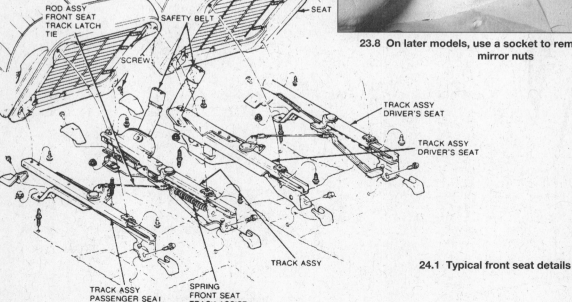

24.1 Typical front seat details

11

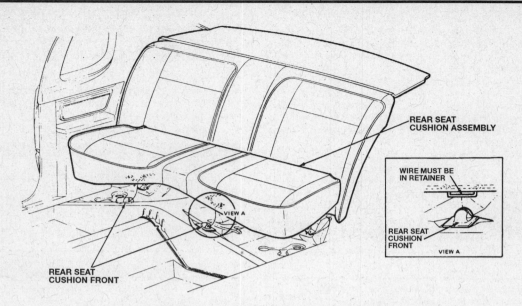

24.3 The rear seat cushion is retained by wire clips on most models

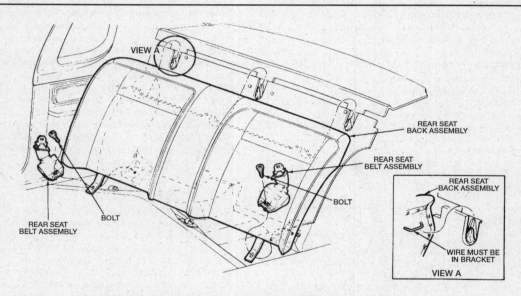

24.5 The rear seat back is held in place by the seat belt bolts

Rear

Removal

3   Apply knee pressure to the lower portion of the seat cushion and push toward the rear of the vehicle to disengage the cushion from the brackets, then remove the seat cushion **(see illustration)**.

4   If equipped, remove the rear armrests.

5   Remove the lower seat back bolts and the outer seat belt bolts **(see illustration)**.

6   Grasp the seat back securely at the bottom, lift up to disengage the hanger wire from the bracket, then remove the seat from the vehicle.

Installation

7   Lower the seat back into position so the hanger wires engage in the brackets, then install the seat belts and bolts.

8   Place the seat cushion in position, then push it down and back with your knee until it locks in place.

9   Install the rear quarter armrests and any other components that were removed.

Chapter 12
Chassis electrical system

Contents

1   General information

The electrical system is a 12-volt, negative ground type. Power for the lights and all electrical accessories is supplied by a lead/acid-type battery which is charged by the alternator.

This Chapter covers repair and service procedures for the various electrical components not associated with the engine.

Information on the battery, alternator, distributor and starter motor can be found in Chapter 5.

It should be noted that when portions of the electrical system are serviced, the negative battery cable should be disconnected from the battery to prevent electrical shorts and/or fires.

2   Electrical troubleshooting - general information

A typical electrical circuit consists of an electrical component, any switches, relays, motors, fuses, fusible links or circuit breakers related to that component and the wiring and connectors that link the component to both the battery and the chassis. To help you pinpoint an electrical circuit problem, wiring diagrams are included at the end of this Chapter.

Before tackling any troublesome electrical circuit, first study the appropriate wiring diagrams to get a complete understanding of what makes up that individual circuit. Trouble spots, for instance, can often be narrowed down by noting if other components related to the circuit are operating properly. If several components or circuits fail at one time, chances are the problem is in a fuse or ground connection, because several circuits are often routed through the same fuse and ground connections.

Electrical problems usually stem from simple causes, such as loose or corroded connections, a blown fuse, a melted fusible link or a failed relay. Visually inspect the condition of all fuses, wires and connections in a problem circuit before troubleshooting the circuit.

If test equipment and instruments are going to be utilized, use the diagrams to plan ahead of time where you will make the necessary connections in order to accurately pinpoint the trouble spot.

The basic tools needed for electrical troubleshooting include a circuit tester or voltmeter (a 12-volt bulb with a set of test leads can also be used), a continuity tester, which includes a bulb, battery and set of test leads, and a jumper wire, preferably with a circuit breaker incorporated, which can be used to bypass electrical components. Before attempting to locate a problem with test instruments, use the wiring diagram(s) to decide where to make the connections.

Voltage checks

Voltage checks should be performed if a circuit is not functioning properly. Connect one lead of a circuit tester to either the negative battery terminal or a known good ground. Connect the other lead to a connector in the circuit being tested, preferably nearest to the battery or fuse. If the bulb of the tester lights, voltage is present, which means that the part of the circuit between the connector and the battery is problem free. Continue checking the rest of the circuit in the same fashion. When you reach a point at which no voltage is present, the

3.1a On earlier models, the main fuse block is located on the left side of the interior bulkhead panel

3.1b On later models the main fuse block is under the driver's side of the dash

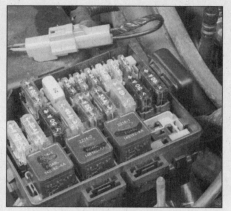

3.1c The later model auxiliary fuse block is located in the engine compartment near the battery

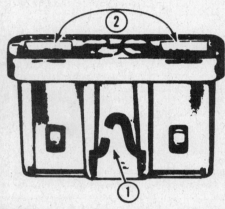

3.2 To test for a blown fuse, pull it out and inspect it for an open (1), then, with the circuit activated, use a test light across the terminals (2)

the circuit is passing current properly. If the light doesn't come on, there is a break somewhere in the circuit. The same procedure can be used to test a switch, by connecting the continuity tester to the switch terminals. With the switch turned On, the test light should come on.

Finding an open circuit

When diagnosing for possible open circuits, it is often difficult to locate them by sight because oxidation or terminal misalignment are hidden by the connectors. Merely wiggling a connector on a sensor or in the wiring harness may correct the open circuit condition. Remember this when an open circuit is indicated when troubleshooting a circuit. Intermittent problems may also be caused by oxidized or loose connections.

Electrical troubleshooting is simple if you keep in mind that all electrical circuits are basically electricity running from the battery, through the wires, switches, relays, fuses and fusible links to each electrical component (light bulb, motor, etc.) and to ground, from which it is passed back to the battery. Any electrical problem is an interruption in the flow of electricity to and from the battery.

problem lies between that point and the last test point with voltage. Most of the time the problem can be traced to a loose connection. **Note:** *Keep in mind that some circuits receive voltage only when the ignition key is in the Accessory or Run position.*

Finding a short

One method of finding shorts in a circuit is to remove the fuse and connect a test light or voltmeter in place of the fuse terminals. There should be no voltage present in the circuit. Move the wiring harness from side-to-side while watching the test light. If the bulb goes on, there is a short to ground somewhere in that area, probably where the insulation has rubbed through. The same test can be performed on each component in the circuit, even a switch.

Ground check

Perform a ground test to check whether a component is properly grounded. Disconnect the battery and connect one lead of a self-powered test light, known as a continuity tester, to a known good ground. Connect the other lead to the wire or ground connection being tested. If the bulb goes on, the ground is good. If the bulb does not go on, the ground is not good.

Continuity check

A continuity check is done to determine if there are any breaks in a circuit - if it is passing electricity properly. With the circuit off (no power in the circuit), a self-powered continuity tester can be used to check the circuit. Connect the test leads to both ends of the circuit (or to the "power" end and a good ground), and if the test light comes on

---

3   Fuses - general information

Refer to illustrations 3.1a, 3.1b, 3.1c and 3.2

The electrical circuits of the vehicle are protected by a combination of fuses, circuit breakers and fusible links. The fuse block is located below the left side of the dash. Later models have two fuse blocks, one for standard fuses located under the instrument panel on the left side of the dashboard and one for high current fuses in the engine compartment, adjacent to the battery **(see illustrations)**. Disconnect the cable to the negative battery terminal before replacing high current fuses.

On earlier models the fuses are tubular glass body types while on later models miniaturized fuses are employed. These compact fuses, with blade terminal design, allow fingertip removal and replacement. If an electrical component fails, always check the fuse first. A blown fuse is easily identified through the clear plastic body. Visually inspect the element for evidence of damage **(see illustration)**. If a continuity check is called for, the blade terminal tips are exposed in the fuse body.

Be sure to replace blown fuses with the correct type. Fuses of different ratings are physically interchangeable, but only fuses of the proper rating should be used. Replacing a fuse with one of a higher or lower value than specified is not recommended. Each electrical circuit needs a specific amount of protection. The amperage value of each fuse is molded into the fuse body.

If the replacement fuse immediately fails, don't replace it again until the cause of the problem is isolated and corrected. In most cases, the cause will be a short circuit in the wiring caused by a broken or deteriorated wire.

4   Fusible links - general information

Some circuits are protected by fusible links. The links are used in circuits which are not ordinarily fused, such as the ignition circuit.

In addition to the conventional type of fusible link described below (located in the wiring harness), cartridge fusible links, similar to a large fuses, are used on some models. Cartridge fusible links are located in the engine compartment fuse block and, after disconnecting the negative battery cable, are simply removed and replaced by a unit of the same amperage. Some cartridge fusible links are held in place by bolts which must be loosened before removing the link.

Fusible links cannot be repaired, a new link of the same size wire should be installed in its place. The procedure is as follows:

a) *Disconnect the cable from the negative battery terminal.*
b) *Disconnect the fusible link from the wiring harness.*
c) *Cut the damaged fusible link out of the wiring just behind the connector.*
d) *Strip the insulation back approximately 1/2-inch.*
e) *Position the connector on the new fusible link and crimp it into place.*
f) *Use rosin core solder at each end of the new link to obtain a good solder joint.*
g) *Use plenty of electrical tape around the soldered joint. No wires should be exposed.*
h) *Connect the battery ground cable. Test the circuit for proper operation.*

5   Circuit breakers - general information

Circuit breakers protect components such as power windows, power door locks and headlights. Some circuit breakers are located in the fuse box.

On some models the circuit breaker resets itself automatically, so an electrical overload in a circuit breaker protected system will cause the circuit to fail momentarily, then come back on. If the circuit does not come back on, check it immediately. Once the condition is corrected, the circuit breaker will resume its normal function.

6   Relays - general information

Several electrical accessories in the vehicle use relays to transmit the electrical signal to the component. If the relay is defective, that component will not operate properly.

The various relays are grouped together in several locations.

If a faulty relay is suspected, it can be removed and tested by a dealer service department or a repair shop. Defective relays must be replaced as a unit.

7   Turn signal/hazard flasher - check and replacement

Turn signal flasher

1   The turn signal flasher, a small canister-shaped unit located on or near the fuse block under the dash, flashes the turn signals.
2   When the flasher unit is functioning properly, an audible click can be heard during its operation. If the turn signals fail on one side or the other and the flasher unit does not make its characteristic clicking sound, a faulty turn signal bulb is indicated.
3   If both turn signals fail to blink, the problem may be due to a blown fuse, a faulty flasher unit, a broken switch or a loose or open connection. If a quick check of the fuse box indicates that the turn signal fuse has blown, check the wiring for a short before installing a new fuse.
4   To replace the flasher, simply pull it out of the fuse block or mount.
5   Make sure that the replacement unit is identical to the original. Compare the old one to the new one before installing it.
6   Installation is the reverse of removal.

8.9   Remove the retaining screws and disconnect the connector (arrows), then remove the multi-function switch

Hazard flasher

7   The hazard flasher, a small canister-shaped unit located on or near the fuse block under the dash, flashes all four turn signals simultaneously when activated.
8   The hazard flasher is checked in a fashion similar to the turn signal flasher (see Steps 2 and 3).
9   To replace the hazard flasher, pull it fuse block or mount.
10   Make sure the replacement unit is identical to the one it replaces. Compare the old one to the new one before installing it.
11   Installation is the reverse of removal.

8   Multi-function switch - removal and installation

Refer to illustration 8.9
Warning: *Some models have airbags. Always disconnect the negative battery cable, then the positive cable and wait 2 minutes before working in the vicinity of the impact sensors, steering column or instrument panel to avoid the possibility of accidental deployment of the airbag, which could cause personal injury (see Section 30).*
Note: *Not all models have multi-function switches.*
1   Disconnect the cable from the negative battery terminal.

1989 and earlier models

2   Grasp the switch lever securely and remove it by pulling straight out.
3   Remove the steering column covers (see Chapter 11).
4   Remove the switch cover, then disconnect the connector, remove the retaining screws and withdraw the switch assembly from the steering column.
5   Place the switch in position and install the screws, then connect the electrical connector.
6   Install the steering column covers.
7   Line up the tangs on the lever with the slot in the switch and install it by pushing straight in.

1990 and later models

8   Remove the steering column covers (see Chapter 11). Remove the ignition lock cylinder (see Section 11). If equipped with a tilt-column, tilt the column to the lowest position and remove the tilt lever.
9   Remove the two retaining screws, pull the switch out, disconnect the connector and detach the switch assembly from the steering column **(see illustration)**.
10   Connect the electrical connector, insert the switch into the steering column and install the screws.
11   Install the steering column covers, lock cylinder and tilt lever (if equipped).

12

9.5a   Remove the hazard switch retaining
screw (arrow)

9.5b   Lift the hazard switch out

10.6   To detach the ignition switch from
the lock cylinder housing, make notches
across the heads of the break-off bolts
(arrows) with a hammer and chisel, then
use a screwdriver to remove them

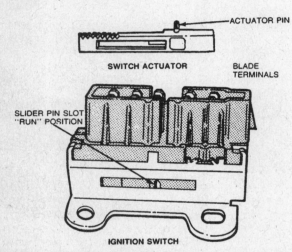

10.8   The ignition switch actuator pin slot must be in the Run
position when the switch is installed

All models

12   Connect the cable to the negative battery terminal.

9   Steering column switches - replacement

Refer to illustrations 9.5a and 9.5b
Note: *On earlier models the hazard and turn signal switches and wires
are integral parts of one assembly mounted in the steering column hub.*

Turn signal and hazard switch

1   Disconnect the negative battery cable.
2   Remove the steering wheel (see Chapter 10).
3   Remove the steering column lower cover.
4   Trace the wires from the switches down the steering column to
the harness connector and disconnect them.
5   Remove the retaining screw and lift the hazard switch out of the
hub **(see illustrations)**.
6   Unscrew the turn signal handle, remove the two retaining screws
and lift out the switch.
7   Remove the plastic cover from the column, pull the wires up
through the hub and remove the assembly.
8   Insert the new switch wires through the hub and route them down
the column to the connector and connect them.
9   Install the switches and screws in the hub.
10   The remainder of installation is the reverse of removal.

10   Ignition switch - removal and installation

Refer to illustrations 10.6 and 10.8
Warning: *Some models have airbags. Always disconnect the negative
battery cable, then the positive cable and wait 2 minutes before
working in the vicinity of the impact sensors, steering column or
instrument panel to avoid the possibility of accidental deployment of
the airbag, which could cause personal injury (see Section 30).*

Removal

1   Disconnect the cable from the negative battery terminal.
2   Remove the steering column covers and the lower insulator panel
(see Chapter 11).
3   On some models it will be necessary to remove the retaining nuts
and lower the steering column for access to the switch screws.
4   Disconnect the ignition switch electrical connector.
5   Turn the ignition key lock cylinder to the Run position.
6   Remove the two switch retaining screws **(see illustration)**.
7   Disengage the ignition switch from the actuator pin.

Installation

8   Make sure the actuator pin slot in the new ignition switch is in the
Run position **(see illustration)**. **Note:** *A new replacement switch
assembly will be set in this position.*
9   Place the new switch in position on the actuator pin and install the
retaining screws. It may be necessary to move the switch back and
forth to line up the screw holes.
10   Connect the electrical connector to the switch.
11   Install the upper steering column cover.
12   Raise the steering column into position and install the retaining
nuts. Tighten the nuts securely.
13   Install the steering lower column covers and lower insulator panel.
14   Connect the cable to the negative battery terminal.

11   Ignition lock cylinder - removal and installation

Refer to illustration 11.3
Warning: *Some models have airbags. Always disconnect the negative
battery cable, then the positive cable and wait 2 minutes before
working in the vicinity of the impact sensors, steering column or
instrument panel to avoid the possibility of accidental deployment of
the airbag, which could cause personal injury (see Section 30).*

Removal

1   Disconnect the cable from the negative battery terminal.
2   Turn the lock cylinder to the Run position.

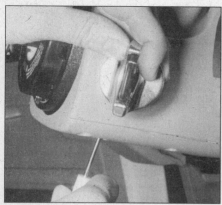

11.3 To remove the ignition lock cylinder, place the key in the "RUN" position, push in on the release tab with a screwdriver and pull the cylinder straight out

12.3 Use a Phillips head screwdriver to remove the headlight retainer screws

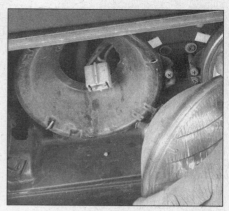

12.5 Pull the headlight out and disconnect the connector

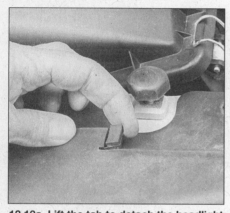

12.10a Lift the tab to detach the headlight bulb cover

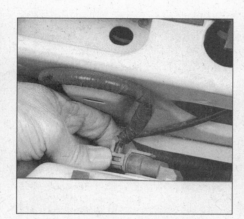

12.10b Rotate the bulb holder counterclockwise and pull it out of the housing

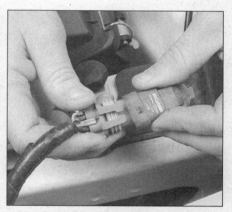

12.11 Detach the clip and disconnect the bulb assembly from the holder - when installing the new bulb, don't touch the glass surface, clean it with rubbing alcohol if you do

3   Insert an 1/8-inch punch into the hole at the bottom of the casting surrounding the lock cylinder. Depress the punch while pulling out on the lock cylinder to remove it from the column housing **(see illustration)**.

Installation

4   Install the lock cylinder by turning it to the Run position and depressing the retaining pin. Insert the lock cylinder into the lock cylinder housing. Make sure the cylinder is completely seated and aligned in the interlocking washer before turning the key to the Off position. This will permit the retaining pin to extend into the hole.
5   Turn the lock to ensure that operation is correct in all positions.
6   The remainder of installation is the reverse of removal.

12   Headlights - replacement

Refer to illustrations 12.3, 12.5, 12.10a, 12.10b and 12.11
Warning: *Some models have airbags. Always disconnect the negative battery cable, then the positive cable and wait 2 minutes before working in the vicinity of the impact sensors, steering column or instrument panel to avoid the possibility of accidental deployment of the airbag, which could cause personal injury (see Section 30).*

Sealed beam

1   Disconnect the cable from the negative battery terminal.
2   Remove the retaining screws and detach the headlight bezel.
3   Remove the headlight retainer screws, taking care not to disturb

the adjusting screws **(see illustration)**.
4   Remove the retainer and pull the headlight out enough to allow the electrical connector to be disconnected.
5   Remove the headlight **(see illustration)**.
6   To install the headlight, connect the electrical connector, place the headlight in position and install the retainer and screws. Tighten the screws securely.
7   Place the bezel in position and install the retaining screws.

Composite bulb-type

Warning: *Halogen gas filled bulbs are under pressure and may shatter if the surface is scratched or the bulb is dropped. Wear eye protection and handle the bulbs carefully, grasping only the base whenever possible. Do not touch the surface of the bulb with your fingers because the oil from your skin could cause it to overheat and fail prematurely. If you do touch the bulb surface, clean it with rubbing alcohol.*

8   Open the hood.
9   Disconnect the cable from the negative battery terminal.
10   Remove the cover (if equipped) and reach behind the headlight assembly, grasp the bulb holder and turn it counterclockwise to remove it **(see illustrations)**. Lift the holder assembly out for access to the bulb.
11   Release the clip and disconnect the bulb holder from the connector **(see illustration)**.
12   Insert the new bulb into the connector until it snaps into place.
13   Install the bulb holder in the headlight assembly.

12

13   Headlights - adjustment

Refer to illustrations 13.1a and 13.1b
Note: *The headlights must be aimed correctly. If adjusted incorrectly they could blind the driver of an oncoming vehicle and cause a serious accident or seriously reduce your ability to see the road. The headlights should be checked for proper aim every 12 months and any time a new headlight is installed or front end body work is performed. It should be emphasized that the following procedure is only an interim step which will provide temporary adjustment until the headlights can be adjusted by a properly equipped shop.*

1   Headlights have two spring loaded adjusting screws, one on the top controlling up-and-down movement and one on the side controlling left-and-right movement. On earlier models these screws are accessible from the front after removing the headlight bezel **(see illustration)**. On later models the adjusters are reached from the rear of the headlight assembly and are turned using a small wrench or pliers **(see illustration)**.

2   There are several methods of adjusting the headlights. The simplest method requires a blank wall and a level floor.

3   Position masking tape vertically on the wall in reference to the vehicle centerline and the centerlines of both headlights.

4   Position a horizontal tape line in reference to the centerline of all the headlights. **Note:** *It may be easier to position the tape on the wall with the vehicle parked only a few feet away.*

5   Adjustment should be made with the vehicle sitting level, the gas tank half-full, no unusually heavy load in the vehicle and the vehicle parked 25 feet away from the wall.

6   Starting with the low beam adjustment, position the high intensity zone so it is two inches below the horizontal line and two inches to the right of the headlight vertical line. Adjustment is made by turning the top adjusting screw clockwise to raise the beam and counterclockwise to lower the beam. The adjusting screw on the side should be used in the same manner to move the beam left or right.

7   With the high beams on, the high intensity zone should be vertically centered with the exact center just below the horizontal line. **Note:** *It may not be possible to position the headlight aim exactly for both high and low beams. If a compromise must be made, keep in mind that the low beams are the most used and have the greatest effect on safety.*

8   Have the headlights adjusted by a dealer service department or service station at the earliest opportunity.

14   Headlight housing (composite bulb-type models) - removal and installation

Refer to illustration 14.3
Warning: *Some models have airbags. Always disconnect the negative battery cable, then the positive cable and wait 2 minutes before working in the vicinity of the impact sensors, steering column or instrument panel to avoid the possibility of accidental deployment of the airbag, which could cause personal injury (see Section 30).*

1   Disconnect the cable from the negative battery terminal.

2   Remove the headlight bulb(s) (see Section 12).

3   Push forward on the headlight housing while using snap-ring pliers to spread the retainer clips, then detach the housing and remove it through the grille opening **(see illustration)**.

4   Insert the housing into the grille opening and press it into place until it seats securely in the retainers.

13.1a The adjustment screws on earlier models are located at the top and side of the headlight (arrows)

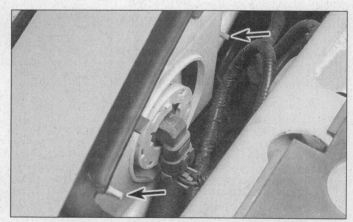

13.1b On later composite bulb-type headlights, the adjustment screws (arrows) are accessible from the back of the housing

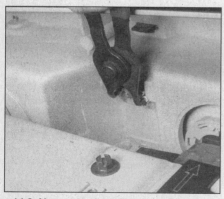

14.3 Use snap-ring pliers to spread the clips, then detach the headlight housing

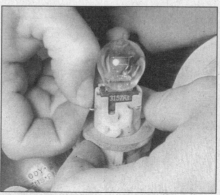

15.2a Pull out the retaining clip . . .

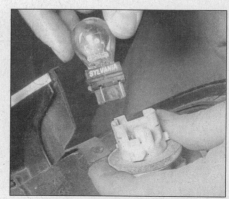

15.2b . . . then pull the bulb out of the holder

15 Bulb replacement

Refer to illustrations 15.2a, 15.2b, 15.3, 15.4 and 15.5
Warning: *Some models have airbags. Always disconnect the negative battery cable, then the positive cable and wait 2 minutes before working in the vicinity of the impact sensors, steering column or instrument panel to avoid the possibility of accidental deployment of the airbag, which could cause personal injury* (see Section 30).

1   The lenses of many lights are held in place by screws, which makes it a simple procedure to gain access to the bulbs.
2   On many lights the bulbs are held in place by clips. The bulb can be removed after detaching the clips **(see illustrations)**.
3   Some lights are mounted in a housing which must be removed for access to the bulb **(see illustration)**.
4   Several types of bulbs are used. Some are removed by pushing in and turning them counterclockwise **(see illustration)**. Others can simply be unclipped from the terminals or pulled straight out of the socket.
5   To gain access to the instrument panel lights, the instrument cluster will have to be removed first **(see illustration)**.

16 Radio/CD player and speakers - removal and installation

Refer to illustrations 16.4a, 16.4b, 16.4c, 16.7a, 16.7b and 16.10
Warning: *Some models have airbags. Always disconnect the negative battery cable, then the positive cable and wait 2 minutes before working in the vicinity of the impact sensors, steering column or instrument panel to avoid the possibility of accidental deployment of*

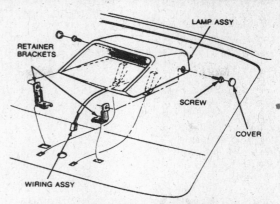

15.3 Typical high-mounted brake light details

the airbag, which could cause personal injury (see Section 30).
1   Disconnect the cable from the negative battery terminal.

Radio/CD player
Earlier models
2   Remove the screws and detach the bezel.
3   Remove the mounting screws.
4   Slide the radio/CD unit out and support it, disconnect the ground cable, antenna and electrical connectors, then remove the assembly from the instrument panel **(see illustrations)**.
5   Installation is the reverse of removal.

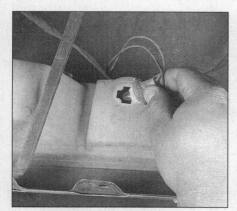

15.4 Rotate the bulb holder counterclockwise and withdraw it from the housing

15.5 After removing the instrument cluster, rotate the bulb holder counterclockwise and withdraw it

16.4a Remove the radio mounting bolts (arrows)

16.4b Pull the radio out of the dash

16.4c Disconnect the connectors from the back of the radio

12

16.7a Insert the tools until they seat, then flex them out to release the clips and withdraw the radio from the dash

16.7b Use a small screwdriver to detach the electrical connector clip

16.10 After removing the door trim panel, the speaker retaining screws (arrows) are easy to reach

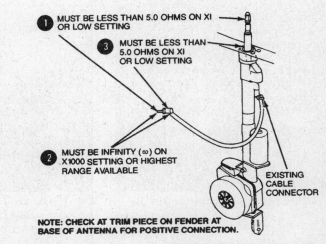

1 MUST BE LESS THAN 5.0 OHMS ON XI OR LOW SETTING

3 MUST BE LESS THAN 5.0 OHMS ON XI OR LOW SETTING

2 MUST BE INFINITY (∞) ON X1000 SETTING OR HIGHEST RANGE AVAILABLE

EXISTING CABLE CONNECTOR

NOTE: CHECK AT TRIM PIECE ON FENDER AT BASE OF ANTENNA FOR POSITIVE CONNECTION.

17.1 Check the antenna with an ohmmeter at the points shown

Later models

6   For theft protection, the radio receiver and CD player assemblies are retained in the instrument panel by special clips. Releasing these clips requires the use of two sets of Ford removal tool no. T87P-19061-A, or two short lengths of coathanger wire bent into U-shapes. Insert the tools into the holes at the corners of the radio/CD player assembly until you feel the internal clips release.

7   With the clips released, flex out simultaneously on both tools and pull the assembly out of the instrument panel, disconnect the antenna and electrical connectors and remove the unit from the vehicle **(see illustrations)**.

8   Install by connecting the electrical connectors, then sliding the radio or CD player along the track and into the instrument panel until the clips can be felt snapping in place.

Speakers

Door mounted

9   Remove the door trim panel (see Chapter 11).

10   Remove the mounting screws, withdraw the speaker, disconnect the electrical connector and remove the speaker from the vehicle **(see illustration)**.

11   Installation is the reverse of removal.

Rear quarter panel mounted

12   Remove the screws and pry off the speaker grille.

13   Remove the retaining screws, withdraw the speaker, disconnect

the electrical connector and remove the speaker from the vehicle.

14   Installation is the reverse of removal

Package shelf mounted

15   Open the trunk lid.

16   Working under the package tray, disconnect electrical connector, remove the retaining screws/nuts or detach the clips, then lower the speaker and remove it from the vehicle.

17   Installation is the reverse of removal

---

17   Radio antenna - check and replacement

Refer to illustrations 17.1, 17.5, 17.8, 17.9, 17.12a, 17.12b and 17.12c

Warning: *Some models have airbags. Always disconnect the negative battery cable, then the positive cable and wait 2 minutes before working in the vicinity of the impact sensors, steering column or instrument panel to avoid the possibility of accidental deployment of the airbag, which could cause personal injury (see Section 30).*

Resistance check

1   With the antenna cable installed on the vehicle and the cable disconnected from the radio, check the antenna with an ohmmeter at the points shown **(see illustration)**. If any readings are not as specified, replace the antenna and cable assembly.

17.5 Use needle nose pliers to unscrew the antenna stanchion nut

17.8 Remove the lower bolt (arrow) from the antenna

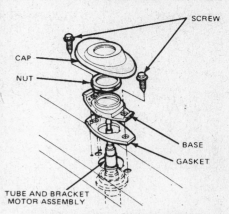

17.9 Antenna cap and base details

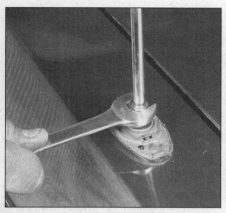

17.12a Remove the antenna mast nut

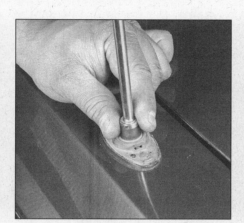

17.12b Slide the nut and retaining cap up off the mast

17.12c Pull the mast and drive cable up part way, note the direction the cable teeth face, then pull it out and remove it

Replacement

2　Disconnect the cable from the negative battery terminal.

Front mounted antenna

3　Lower the antenna.
4　Remove the rear screws from the right side front splash shield for access and remove the lower antenna bolt.
5　Remove the nut at the top of the antenna stanchion and remove the antenna by lowering it through the fender opening **(see illustration)**.
6　Installation is the reverse of removal.

Rear mounted antenna

7　Lower the antenna.
8　Open the trunk lid, remove the trim panel for access and remove the lower antenna bolt **(see illustration)**.
9　Remove the radio antenna base cap and remove the mounting screws **(see illustration)**. Disconnect the electrical connectors, lower the antenna assembly into the trunk and remove it from the vehicle.
10　Installation is the reverse of removal.

Antenna mast and drive cable

11　Sometimes the plastic antenna drive cable breaks off inside the power antenna housing. If the mast is bent or damaged or the mast doesn't move but the motor runs, replace the mast and cable. The antenna mast and plastic drive cable can be replaced without removing the motor assembly.
12　Remove the retaining nut and pull the mast part way out of the

motor, then activate the motor until the drive cable can be removed, noting the direction the drive teeth face **(see illustrations)**.
13　Use a hacksaw to cut off the old mast and slide the nut and tube off.
14　Insert the new cable into the drive mechanism of the motor. Run the motor while pushing on the cable until about 12-inches have been drawn in.
15　Lower the new antenna tube and nut into place, then tighten the nut securely.
16　Activate the antenna several times by turning the radio on and off to make sure it operates properly.

18 Horn check and replacement

Warning: *Some models have airbags. Always disconnect the negative battery cable, then the positive cable and wait 2 minutes before working in the vicinity of the impact sensors, steering column or instrument panel to avoid the possibility of accidental deployment of the airbag, which could cause personal injury (see Section 30).*

Check

Refer to illustrations 18.3 and 18.6
1　If the horn doesn't sound, first check the fuse and on later models, the relay.
2　If the fuse and relay are good, make sure the horn mounting bolts and ground wires are tight.
3　Connect one jumper wire from the mounting bracket bolt to the

12

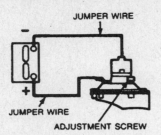

18.3 using jumper wires, connect the horn directly to the battery

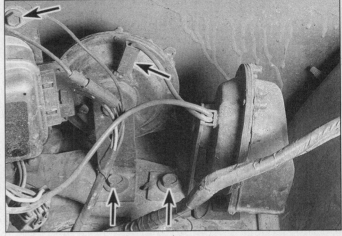

18.6 Disconnect the electrical connector, remove the bolt(s), then remove the horn (arrows)

negative battery terminal and another jumper wire from the horn terminal to the positive battery terminal **(see illustration)**.

4   If the horn does not sound and there is no sparking at the battery terminal, disconnect the jumper wires. Turn the adjusting screw counter-clockwise between 1/4 and 3/8 turn and use pliers to keep the screw from turning by squeezing the housing extrusions. If the horn still doesn't work when the wires are connected, replace it with a new one.

Replacement

5   Disconnect the negative battery cable.
6   Disconnect the horn electrical connector, remove the mounting bolts and lift the horn from the vehicle **(see illustration)**.
7   Installation is the reverse of removal.

19 Instrument cluster - removal and installation

Refer to illustration 19.3, 19.4, 19.5, 19.6a and 19.6b
Warning: *Some models have airbags. Always disconnect the negative battery cable, then the positive cable and wait 2 minutes before working in the vicinity of the impact sensors, steering column or instrument panel to avoid the possibility of accidental deployment of the airbag, which could cause personal injury* (see Section 30).
1   Disconnect the cable from the negative battery terminal.
2   Remove the instrument cluster bezel (see Chapter 11).
3   Detach the shift indicator assembly from the cluster **(see illustration)**.
4   Remove the instrument cluster retaining screws **(see illustration)**.
5   Reach behind the cluster housing and press on the release lever to disconnect the speedometer cable **(see illustration)** or disconnect the electronic speed sensor. Pull the cluster out and disconnect the electrical connectors.
6   Remove the cluster from the instrument panel **(see illustrations)**.
7   Installation is the reverse of removal.

20 Speedometer cable - removal and installation

Refer to illustrations 20.2 and 20.3
Warning: *Some models have airbags. Always disconnect the negative battery cable, then the positive cable and wait 2 minutes before working in the vicinity of the impact sensors, steering column or instrument panel to avoid the possibility of accidental deployment of the airbag, which could cause personal injury* (see Section 30).
1   Disconnect the cable from the negative battery terminal.
2   Disconnect the speedometer cable from the transmission or cruise control speed sensor adapter **(see illustration)**. Models with cruise control adapters have two speedometer cables: one between the transmission and the adapter and one leading from the adapter to the speedometer housing.
3   Detach the cable from the routing clips in the engine compartment and pull the cable up to provide enough slack to allow disconnection from the speedometer **(see illustration)**.
4   Remove the instrument cluster screws, pull the cluster out, then reach behind it and disconnect the speedometer cable from the back of the cluster by pressing on the cable release clip (see illustration 19.5).
5   Remove the cable from the vehicle.
6   Prior to installation, press a 3/16-inch ball of silicone or equivalent lubricant into the speedometer opening.
7   Installation is the reverse of removal.

19.3 Remove the screw and disconnect the wire loop from the pin on the column shift indicator

19.4 The instrument cluster is held in place by screws (arrows) at both sides of the housing (later electronic cluster shown)

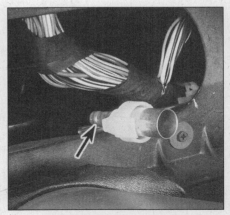

19.5 Reach behind the cluster and press the tab (arrow) to release the speedometer cable

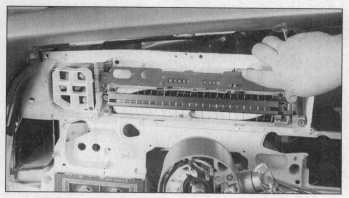

19.6a On early models, rotate the bezel out of the opening

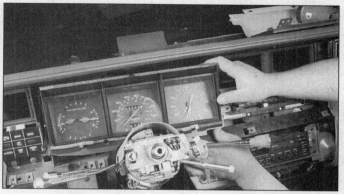

19.6b On later models, tilt the top of the bezel toward you, then pull it straight out

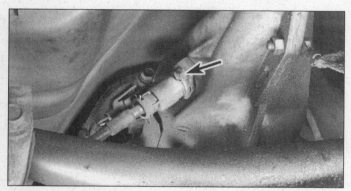

20.2 Typical speedometer cable connection - some later models may use a clip instead of a mounting bolt

21 Headlight switch - replacement

Refer to illustrations 21.2, 21.7a, 21.7b, 21.9 and 21.11

Warning: *Some models have airbags. Always disconnect the negative battery cable, then the positive cable and wait 2 minutes before working in the vicinity of the impact sensors, steering column or instrument panel to avoid the possibility of accidental deployment of the airbag, which could cause personal injury (see Section 30).*

1   Disconnect the cable from the negative battery terminal.

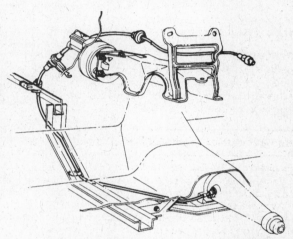

20.3 Typical speedometer cable routing details

Thumbwheel type

2   Pry up on the cluster and remove the switch lens **(see illustration)**.
3   Remove the lens retaining screws.
4   Disconnect the connector and remove the switch
5   Installation is the reverse of removal.

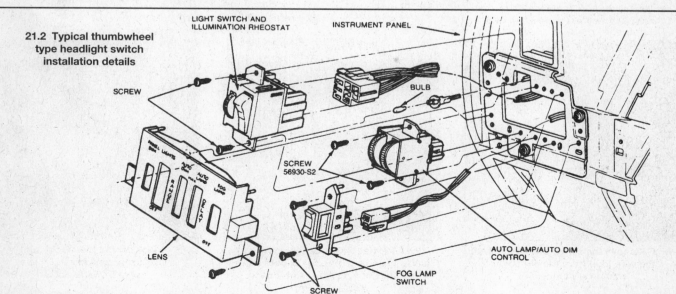

21.2 Typical thumbwheel type headlight switch installation details

LIGHT SWITCH AND ILLUMINATION RHEOSTAT

INSTRUMENT PANEL

SCREW

BULB

SCREW 56930-S2

LENS

AUTO LAMP/AUTO DIM CONTROL

FOG LAMP SWITCH

SCREW

12

21.7a Unscrew the retaining collar and push the switch back through the dash

21.7b Lower the switch, cut the tie strap then disconnect the electrical connector and separate the switch from the bracket

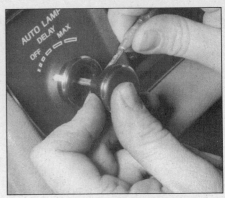

21.9 Use a pointed hooked tool to lift the retaining clip, the pull the knob off the shaft

Detachable shaft type

6   Reach under the dash and press the release button on the bottom of the switch, then withdraw the knob and shaft from the switch.

7   Remove the instrument cluster bezel (see Chapter 11). Remove retaining nut, then lower the switch and bracket, disconnect the electrical connector and separate the switch from the bracket **(see illustrations)**.

8   Place the new switch in position on the bracket and secure it with the nut. Insert the knob and shaft into the switch. The remainder of installation is the reverse of removal.

Detachable knob type

9   Detach the headlight switch knob by using a pointed tool to lift the release tab at it's base **(see illustration)**.

10   Remove the switch bezel.

11   Remove the retaining screws and withdraw the switch and bracket from the instrument panel **(see illustration)**.

12   Disconnect the connector, then remove the nut and separate the switch from the bracket.

13   Installation is the reverse of removal.

22 Windshield wiper/washer switch - removal and installation

Warning: *Some models have airbags. Always disconnect the negative battery cable, then the positive cable and wait 2 minutes before working in the vicinity of the impact sensors, steering column or instrument panel to avoid the possibility of accidental deployment of*

the airbag, which could cause personal injury (see Section 30).

1   Disconnect the cable from the negative battery terminal.

Dash mounted

2   Detach the headlight switch knob by using a pointed tool to lift the release tab at it's base **(see illustration 21.9)**.

3   Remove the switch bezel.

4   Remove the retaining screws and withdraw the switch and bracket from the instrument panel.

5   Disconnect the connector, then remove the nut and separate the switch from the bracket.

6   Installation is the reverse of removal.

Steering column mounted

Refer to illustration 22.8

7   Remove the screws and detach the steering column covers (see Chapter 11).

8   Remove the mounting screws and lift the wiper switch off the steering column **(see illustration)**. Disconnect the electrical connector and remove the switch.

9   Installation is the reverse of removal.

23 Windshield wiper motor - removal and installation

Refer to illustrations 23.5, 23.7a, 23.7b, 23.8 and 23.9

Warning: *Some models have airbags. Always disconnect the negative battery cable, then the positive cable and wait 2 minutes before working in the vicinity of the impact sensors, steering column or*

21.11 On the knob-type switch, remove the bracket bolts and withdraw the switch and bracket as an assembly

22.8 Remove the wiper switch bolts (arrows)

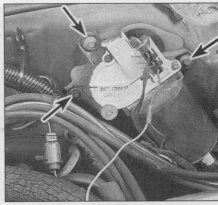

23.5 Wiper motor bolt locations (arrows)

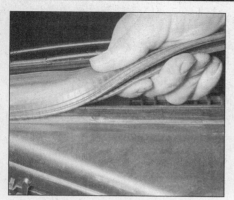
23.7a Pull off the rear hood seal weatherstripping

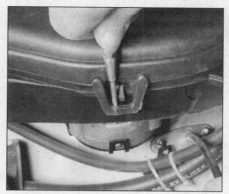
23.7b Use a small screwdriver to detach each of the wiper housing clips

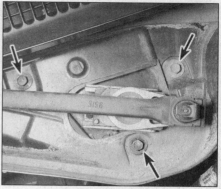
23.8 Remove the wiper motor bolts (arrows)

instrument panel to avoid the possibility of accidental deployment of the airbag, which could cause personal injury (see Section 30).

1   Disconnect the cable from the negative battery terminal.

1979 and earlier models

2   Detach the wiper arms from the pivot shafts.

3   Remove the left (driver's) side cowl screen for access to the motor drive arm linkage.

4   Remove the retaining clip and disconnect the drive arm from the wiper linkage.

5   Disconnect the electrical connectors, remove the retaining bolts and lift the motor out **(see illustration)**. Rotate the motor as you lift it out so the wiper drive arm will clear the firewall opening.

6   After making sure the wiper motor drive arm is in the parked position, installation is the reverse of removal.

1980 and later models

7   Remove the rear hood seal and the wiper motor housing cover **(see illustrations)**.

8   Remove the wiper motor retaining bolts **(see illustration)**.

9   Remove the clip from the wiper motor and disconnect the wiper linkage drive arm from the motor **(see illustration)**.

10   Disconnect the electrical connector and lift the wiper motor from the housing.

11   Installation is the reverse of removal.

24 Rear window defogger - check and repair

Refer to illustrations 24.9 and 24.19

Check

1   Use a strong light inside the vehicle. Visually inspect the wire grid from the outside. A broken grid wire will appear as a brown spot.

2   Run the engine at idle. Set the rear window defogger control switch to On. The indicator light should come on.

3   Working inside the vehicle with a voltmeter, contact the broad red/brown strips (the bus) on the sides of the rear window. The meter should read 10-to-13 volts. A lower voltage reading indicates a loose ground wire (pigtail) connection at the grounded side of the glass.

4   Contact a good ground point with the negative lead of the meter. The voltage reading should not change.

5   With the negative lead of the meter grounded, touch each grid line of the heated rear window at its midpoint with the positive lead:

a) A reading of approximately 6-volts indicates that the line is good.

b) A reading of 0-volts indicates that the line is broken between the mid-point and the positive side of the grid line.

c) A reading of 12-volts indicates that the circuit is broken between the mid-point of the grid and ground.

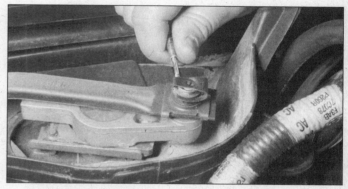
23.9 Use a small screwdriver to pry off the clip, then detach the wiper arm from the motor

Repair

Note: *Any break in the grid longer than one inch cannot be repaired. The rear window must be replaced. For breaks less than one inch in length, use the following procedure. You will need to obtain grid repair compound and brown touch-up paint from a Ford dealer.*

6   Bring the vehicle inside and allow it to reach room temperature, which should be 60-degrees F or above.

7   Clean the entire grid line repair area with glass cleaner or a suitable cleaning solvent. Remove all dirt, wax, grease, oil or other foreign matter. The repair area must be clean and dry.

8   Mark the location of the break on the outside of the window.

9   Using cellulose tape, mask off the area directly above and below the grid break. The break area should be at the center of the mask and the tape gap must be no wider than the existing grid line **(see illustration on following page)**.

10   If both the brown and silver layers of the grid are broken or missing, apply a coating of the brown touch-up paint across the break area first. Two coats may be necessary to obtain the proper color. Allow the touch-up paint to dry.

11   Apply three coats of the silver grid repair compound. Allow three to five minutes drying time between coats. The coating of the silver grid repair compound should extend at least 1/4-inch on both sides of the break.

Note: *If the brown layer of the grid is not broken or missing, apply only the silver grid repair compound to the break. Allow the compound to dry for five minutes, then remove the mask.*

12   After removing the mask, check the outside appearance of the grid repair. If the silver repair compound is visible above or below the grid, this excess should be removed. This can be done by placing a single edge razor blade on the glass parallel to the grid and scraping gently towards the grid. **Caution:** *Be careful not to damage the grid line with the razor blade.*

12

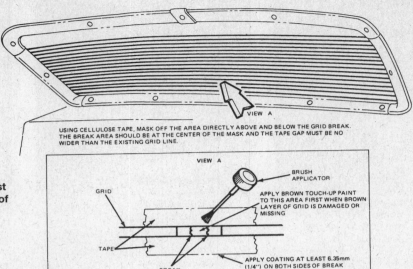

24.9 To repair the broken grid, first apply a strip of tape to either side of the grid to mask off the area

13   The repair coating will air dry in about one minute and can be energized within three to five minutes. Optimum hardness and adhesion occurs after approximately 24 hours. At that time, the repair area may be cleaned with a mild window cleaner.

Lead wire terminal service

14   Allow the rear window to warm up to room temperature for a half hour to an hour.

15   Clean the bus bar in the area to be repaired using fine steel wool (3/O to 4/O grade).

16   Restore the area where the bus bar terminal was originally attached by applying three coats of grid repair compound. Allow approximately ten minutes drying time between coats.

17   Working as quickly as possible to avoid overheating the glass, tin the bus bar with solder in the area where the terminal will be reattached.

18   Using a heat gun or heat lamp, pre-heat the glass in the solder area to between 120-degrees and 150-degrees F just prior to soldering the terminal on.

19   Position the terminal on the bus bar in the area that was tinned and hold it in place with an ice pick or screwdriver **(see illustration)**.

20   Apply soldering heat to the pad of the terminal until the solder flows. **Note:** *To avoid damaging the bus bar, remove the soldering gun or iron as soon as the solder flows.*

21   Start the vehicle, turn the heated rear window on and leave it on for five minutes.

25   Cruise control system - description and check

Refer to illustration 25.6

1   The cruise control system maintains vehicle speed with a vacuum actuated servo motor located in the engine compartment, which is connected to the throttle linkage by a cable. The system consists of the servo motor, brake switch, control switches, a relay and associated vacuum hoses. Cruise controls all work by the same basic principles; however, the hardware used varies considerably depending on model and year of manufacture. Some later systems require special testers and diagnostic procedures which are beyond the scope of the home mechanic. Listed below are some general procedures that may be used to locate common problems.

2   Locate and check the fuse (see Section 3).

3   Have an assistant operate the brake lights while you check their operation (voltage from the brake light switch deactivates the cruise control).

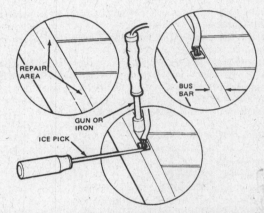

24.19 Rear window defogger bus bar repair details

4   If the brake lights don't come on or don't shut off, correct the problem and retest the cruise control.

5   Inspect the control linkage between the cruise control servo (or actuator) and the throttle linkage. This will consist of either a cable, chain or metal rod. The cruise control servo is usually fist-sized or slightly larger and is located near the carburetor or throttle body.

6   Visually inspect the vacuum hose(s) and wires connected to the cruise control servo and transducer (if equipped) and replace as necessary **(see illustration)**.

7   Cruise controls use a variety of speed sensing devices. On these models the speed sensor pick-up is located in the speedometer cable or at the transmission. Disconnect the speedometer cable, rotate the speed sensor and check it with a digital ohmmeter while it's rotating. If the resistance doesn't vary as the cable rotates, the sensor is defective.

8   Test drive the vehicle to determine if the cruise control is now working. If it isn't, take it to a dealer service department or an automotive electrical specialist for further diagnosis and repair.

26   Power window system - description and check

Refer to illustrations 26.10a, 26.10b, 26.12, 26.13a, 26.13b, 26.13c, and 26.13d

1   The power window system operates the electric motors mounted

25.6 The cruise control actuator on most models is connected to the throttle linkage with a small chain (A) and a vacuum source by a hose at the rear (B)

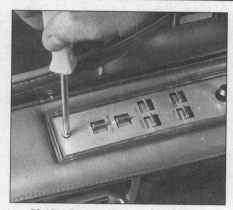

26.10a Remove the power window switch panel screws

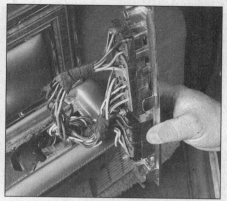

26.10b Lift the switch panel to access the wiring for continuity checks

in the doors which lower and raise the windows. The system consists of the control switches, the motors (regulators), glass mechanisms and associated wiring.

2 Power windows are wired so they can be lowered and raised from the master control switch by the driver or by remote switches located at the individual windows. Each window has a separate motor which is reversible. The position of the control switch determines the polarity and therefore the direction of operation. Some systems are equipped with relays that control current flow to the motors.

3 Some vehicles are equipped with a separate circuit breaker for each motor in addition to the fuse or circuit breaker protecting the whole circuit. This prevents one stuck window from disabling the whole system.

4 Most power window systems will only operate when the ignition switch is ON. In addition, many models have a window lockout switch at the master control switch which, when activated, disables the switches at the rear windows and, sometimes, the switch at the passenger's window also. Always check these items before troubleshooting a window problem.

5 These procedures are general in nature, so if you can't find the problem using them, take the vehicle to a dealer service department.

6 If the power windows don't work at all, check the fuse or circuit breaker.

7 If only the rear windows are inoperative, or if the windows only operate from the master control switch, check the rear window lockout switch for continuity in the unlocked position. Replace it if it doesn't have continuity.

8 Check the wiring between the switches and fuse panel for continuity. Repair the wiring, if necessary.

9 If only one window is inoperative from the master control switch, try the other control switch at the window. **Note:** *This doesn't apply to the drivers door window.*

10 If the same window works from one switch, but not the other, check the switch for continuity **(see illustrations)**.

11 If the switch tests OK, check for a short or open in the wiring between the affected switch and the window motor.

12 If one window is inoperative from both switches, remove the trim panel from the affected door and check for voltage at the motor while the switch is operated **(see illustration)**.

13 If voltage is reaching the motor, disconnect the glass from the regulator **(see illustration)**. Move the window up and down by hand while checking for binding and damage. Also check for binding and damage to the regulator. If the regulator is not damaged and the window moves up and down smoothly, replace the motor **(see illustrations)**. If there's binding or damage, lubricate, repair or replace parts, as necessary **(see illustrations)**.

14 If voltage isn't reaching the motor, check the wiring in the circuit for continuity between the switches and motors. You'll need to consult the wiring diagram for the vehicle. Some power window circuits are equipped with relays. If equipped, check that the relays are grounded properly and receiving voltage from the switches. Also check that each relay sends voltage to the motor when the switch is turned on. If it doesn't, replace the relay.

15 Test the windows after you are done to confirm proper repairs.

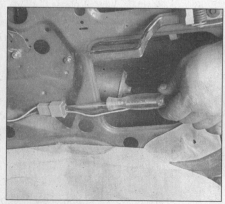

26.12 Use a test light to check for voltage going to the power window motor

26.13a Drill out the heads of these screws (arrows), detach the glass and make sure it moves freely in the channel

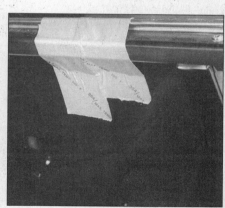

26.13b Hold the glass in place by taping it to the top of the door when replacing the motor - you will then have to drill out the heads of the rivets retaining the motor to the door

26.13c The motor is secured to the regulator by these
bolts (arrows)

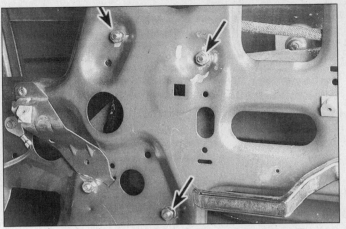

26.13d Use bolts and nuts (arrows) to reinstall the
regulator to the door

27 Power door lock system - description and check

The power door lock system operates the door lock actuators mounted in each door. The system consists of the switches, actuators and associated wiring. Diagnosis can usually be limited to simple checks of the wiring connections and actuators for minor faults which can be easily repaired.

Power door lock systems are operated by bi-directional solenoids located in the doors. The lock switches have two operating positions: Lock and Unlock. These switches activate a relay which in turn connects voltage to the door lock solenoids. Depending on which way the relay is activated, it reverses polarity, allowing the two sides of the circuit to be used alternately as the feed (positive) and ground side.

Some vehicles may have keyless entry, electronic control modules and anti-theft systems incorporated into the power locks. If you are unable to locate the trouble using the following general steps, consult your dealer service department. **Note:** *Some vehicles also have control switches connected to the key locks in the doors which unlock all the doors when one is unlocked.*

1   Always check the circuit protection first. Some vehicles use a combination of circuit breakers and fuses.
2   Operate the door lock switches in both directions (Lock and Unlock) with the engine off. Listen for the faint click of the relay operating.
3   If there's no click, check for voltage at the switches. If no voltage is present, check the wiring between the fuse panel and the switches for shorts and opens.
4   If voltage is present but no click is heard, test the switch for continuity. Replace it if there's not continuity in both switch positions.
5   If the switch has continuity but the relay doesn't click, check the wiring between the switch and relay for continuity. Repair the wiring if there's not continuity.
6   If the relay is receiving voltage from the switch but is not sending voltage to the solenoids, check for a bad ground at the relay case. If the relay case is grounding properly, replace the relay.
7   If all but one lock solenoids operate, remove the trim panel from the affected door (see Chapter 11). and check for voltage at the solenoid while the lock switch is operated. One of the wires should have voltage in the Lock position; the other should have voltage in the unlock position.
8   If the inoperative solenoid is receiving voltage, replace the solenoid.
9   If the inoperative solenoid isn't receiving voltage, check for an open or short in the wire between the lock solenoid and the relay.
Note: *It's common for wires to break in the portion of the harness between the body and door (opening and closing the door fatigues and eventually breaks the wires).*

28 Electric rear view mirrors - description and check

1   Most electric rear view mirrors use two motors to move the glass;

one for up and down adjustments and one for left-right adjustments. In addition, some mirrors have electrically heated glass defroster circuits, which are usually powered through the rear window defogger relay.
2   The control switch usually has a selector portion which sends voltage to the left or right side mirror. With the ignition ON but the engine OFF, roll down the windows and operate the mirror control switch through all functions (left-right and up-down) for both the left and right side mirrors.
3   Listen carefully for the sound of the electric motors running in the mirrors.
4   If the motors can be heard but the mirror glass doesn't move, there's probably a problem with the drive mechanism inside the mirror. Remove and disassemble the mirror to locate the problem.
5   If the mirrors don't operate and no sound comes from the mirrors, check the fuse (see Chapter 1).
6   If the fuse is OK, remove the mirror control switch from its mounting without disconnecting the wires attached to it. Turn the ignition ON and check for voltage at the switch. There should be voltage at one terminal. If there's no voltage at the switch, check for an open or short in the wiring between the fuse panel and the switch.
7   If there's voltage at the switch, disconnect it. Check the switch for continuity in all its operating positions. If the switch does not have continuity, replace it.
8   Re-connect the switch. Locate the wire going from the switch to ground. Leaving the switch connected, connect a jumper wire between this wire and ground. If the mirror works normally with this wire in place, repair the faulty ground connection.
9   If the mirror still doesn't work, remove the mirror and check the wires at the mirror for voltage. Check with the ignition ON and the mirror selector switch on the appropriate side. Operate the mirror switch in all its positions. There should be voltage at one of the switch-to-mirror wires in each switch position (except the neutral "off" position).
10   If there's not voltage in each switch position, check the wiring between the mirror and control switch for opens and shorts.
11   If there's voltage, remove the mirror and test it off the vehicle with jumper wires. Replace the mirror if it fails this test.

29 Power seats - description and check

1   Power seats allow you to adjust the position of the seat with little effort. Numerous configurations are available; however, most systems are four-way or six-way. A four-way seat goes forward and backward and up and down. In addition, a six-way seat tilts forward and backward.
2   Two basic methods of powering the seats are employed. Some manufacturers use one motor with a solenoid-shifted transmission for

all the seat functions. Others use a separate motor for each plane of travel (two motors for a four-way seat, three motors for a six-way seat). The control switch changes the direction of seat travel by reversing polarity to the drive motor.

3   Due to the complexity of seats with memory controls, side bolsters, lumbar supports and power head restraints, and also due to the special test equipment necessary to diagnose them, these components are beyond the scope of this manual. See your dealer service department or an automotive electrical specialist.

4   Look under the seat for any objects which may be preventing the seat from moving.

5   If the seat won't work at all, check the fuse or circuit breaker.

Note: *On some vehicles the ignition must be ON for the power seats to work.*

6   With the engine off to reduce the noise level, operate the seat controls in all directions and listen for sound coming from the seat motor(s).

7   If the motor runs or clicks but the seat doesn't move, check the seat drive mechanism for wear or damage and correct as necessary. If the motor runs freely on seats with a single motor and transmission, check the transmission shift mechanism for proper operation.

8   If the motor doesn't work or make noise, check for voltage at the motor while an assistant operates the switch.

9   If the motor is getting voltage but doesn't run, test it off the vehicle with jumper wires. If it still doesn't work, replace it.

10   If the motor isn't getting voltage, check for voltage at the switch. If there's no voltage at the switch, check the wiring between the fuse panel and the switch. If there's voltage at the switch, refer to the wiring diagrams for the vehicle and check the switch for continuity in all its operating positions. Replace the switch if there's no continuity.

11   If the switch is OK, check for a short or open in the wiring between the switch and motor. If there's a relay between the switch and motor, check that it's grounded properly and there's voltage to the relay. Also check that there's voltage going from the relay to the motor when the switch is operated. If there's not, and the relay is grounded properly, replace the relay.

12   Test the completed repairs.

30 Airbag - general information

Later models are equipped with a Supplemental Inflatable System (SIR), more commonly known as an airbag. This system is designed to protect the driver, and on some models, front seat passenger, from serious injury in the event of a head-on or frontal collision. It consists of an airbag module in the center of the steering wheel and the right side of the instrument panel, two crash sensors mounted at the front and the interior of the vehicle and a diagnostic monitor which also contains a backup power supply located in the passenger compartment.

Airbag module

Drivers-side airbag

The drivers-side airbag inflator module contains a housing incorporating the cushion (airbag) and inflator unit, mounted in the center of the steering wheel. The inflator assembly is mounted on the back of the housing over a hole through which gas is expelled, inflating the bag almost instantaneously when an electrical signal is sent from the system. A coil assembly on the steering column under the module carries this signal to the module.

This coil assembly can transmit an electrical signal regardless of steering wheel position. The igniter in the air bag converts the electrical signal to heat and ignites the sodium azide/copper oxide powder, producing nitrogen gas, which inflates the bag.

Passenger-side airbag

The passenger-side airbag is mounted above the glove compartment and designated by the letters SRS (Supplemental Restraint System). It consists of an inflator containing an igniter, a bag assembly, a reaction housing and a trim cover.

The air bag is considerably larger that the steering wheel-mounted unit and is supported by the steel reaction housing. The trim cover is textured and painted to match the instrument panel and has a molded seam which splits when the bag inflates. As with the steering-wheel-mounted air bag, the igniter electrical signal converts to heat, converting sodium azide/iron oxide powder to nitrogen gas, inflating the bag.

Sensors

The system has three sensors: two forward sensors at the front of the vehicle and a safing sensor on the left side of the cowl in the passenger compartment.

The forward and passenger compartment sensors are basically pressure sensitive switches that complete an electrical circuit during an impact of sufficient G force. The electrical signal from these sensors is sent to the electronic diagnostic monitor which then completes the circuit and inflates the airbag(s).

Electronic diagnostic monitor

The electronic diagnostic monitor supplies the current to the airbag system in the event of the collision, even if battery power is cut off. It checks this system every time the vehicle is started, causing the "AIR BAG" light to go on then off, if the system is operating properly. If there is a fault in the system, the light will go on and stay on, flash, or the dash will make a beeping sound. If this happens, the vehicle should be taken to your dealer immediately for service.

Disabling the system

Whenever working in the vicinity of the steering wheel, steering column or near other components of the airbag system, the system should be disarmed. To do this, perform the following steps:

a) *Turn the ignition switch to Off.*
b) *Detach the cable from the negative battery terminal, then the positive cable and wait 2 minutes for the electronic module backup power supply to be depleted.*

Enabling the system

a) *Turn the ignition switch to the Off position.*
b) *Connect the positive battery cable first, then the negative cable*

31 Wiring diagrams - general information

Refer to illustration 31.3

Since it isn't possible to include all wiring diagrams for every year covered by this manual, the following diagrams are those that are typical and most commonly needed.

Prior to troubleshooting any circuits, check the fuse and circuit breakers (if equipped) to make sure they're in good condition. Make sure the battery is properly charged and check the cable connections (see Chapter 1).

When checking a circuit, make sure that all connectors are clean, with no broken or loose terminals. When disconnecting a connector, do not pull on the wires. Pull only on the connector housings themselves **(see illustration)**.

BK	Black	O	Orange
BR	Brown	PK	Pink
DB	Dark Blue	P	Purple
DG	Dark Green	R	Red
GY	Gray	T	Tan
LB	Light Blue	W	White
LG	Light Green	Y	Yellow
N	Natural		

31.3 Wiring color codes

12

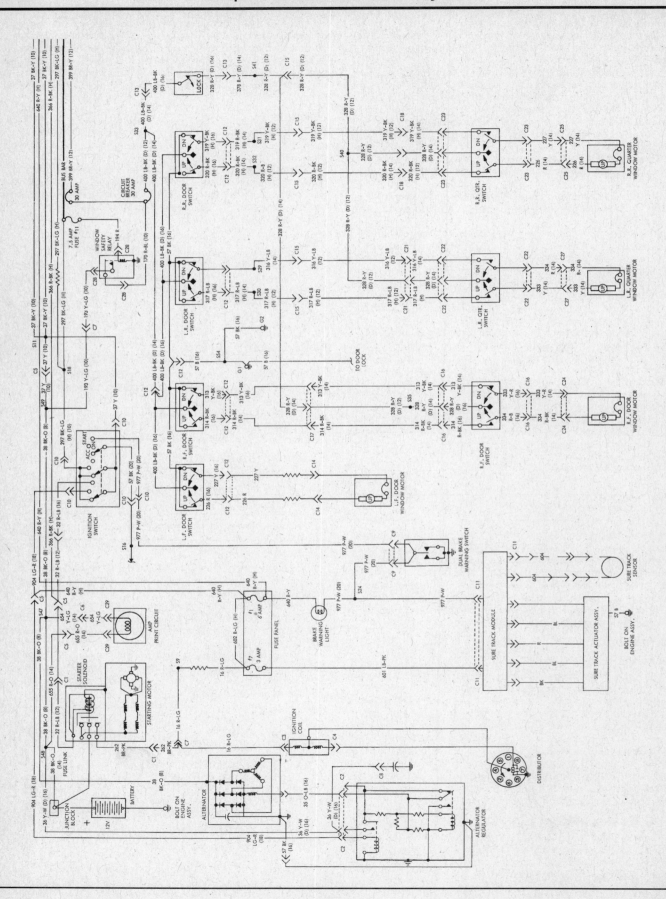

Typical 1976 and earlier wiring diagram (1 of 6)

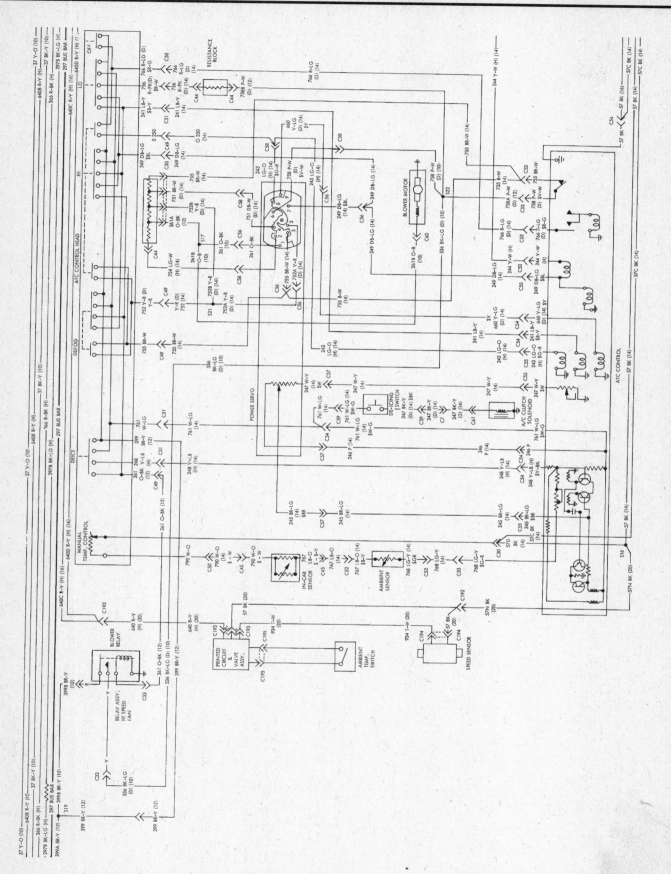

Typical 1976 and earlier wiring diagram (2 of 6)

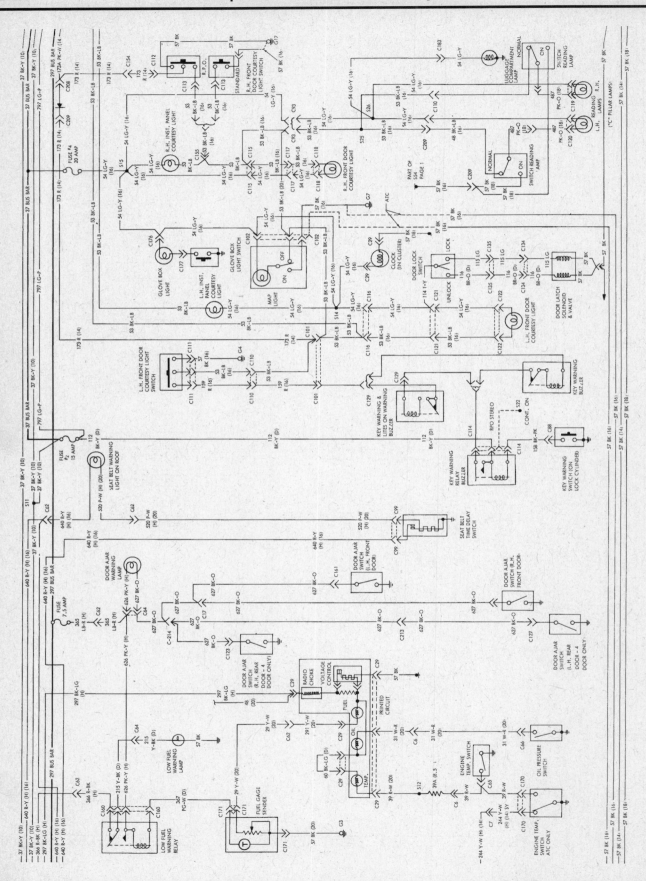

Typical 1976 and earlier wiring diagram (3 of 6)

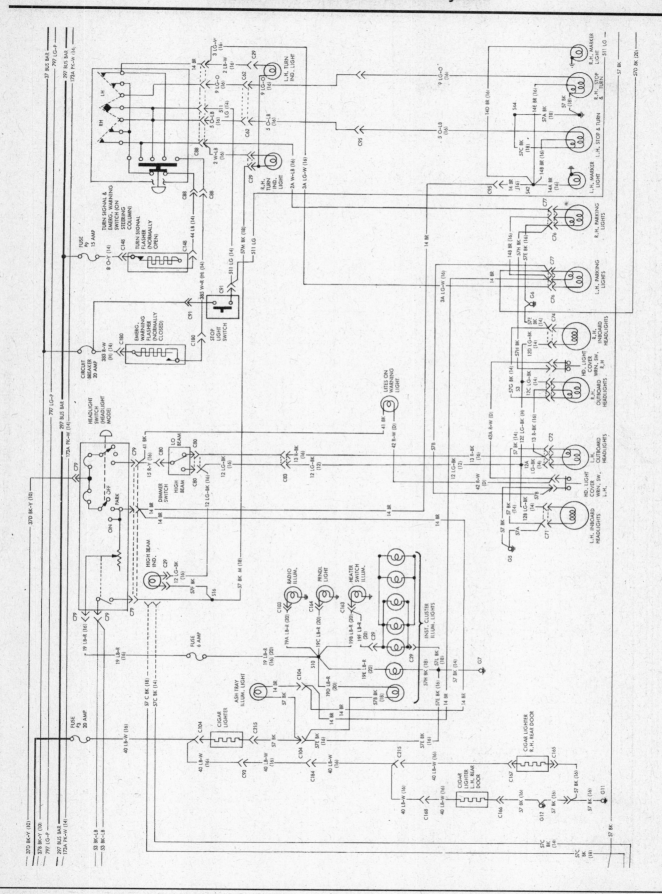

Typical 1976 and earlier wiring diagram (4 of 6)

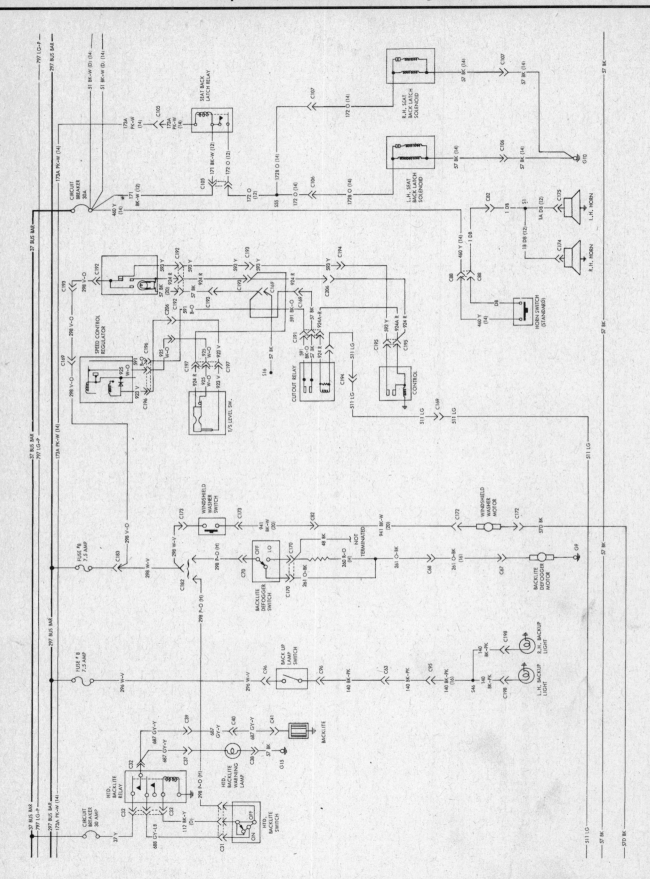

Typical 1976 and earlier wiring diagram (5 of 6)

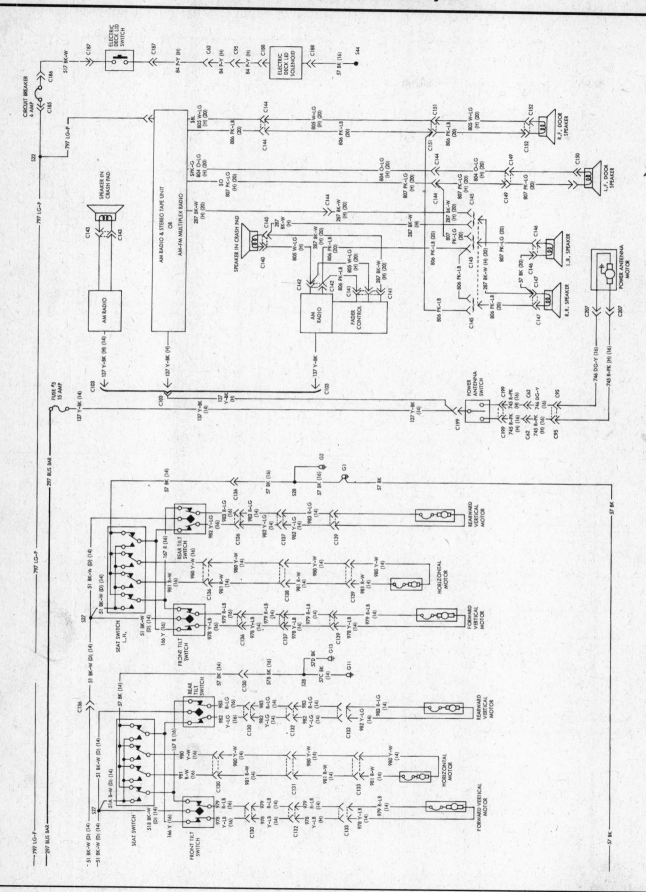

Typical 1976 and earlier wiring diagram (6 of 6)

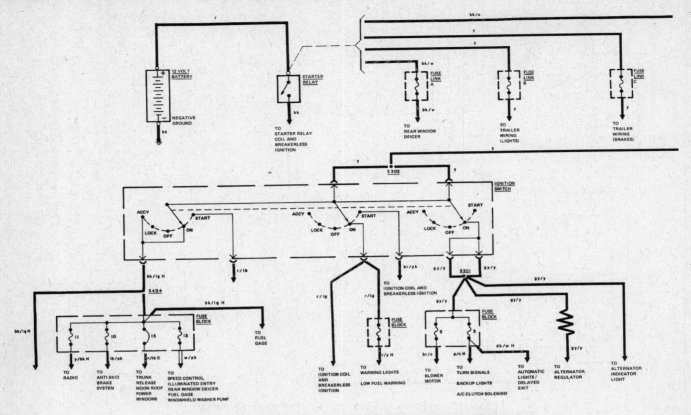

Typical power distribution wiring diagram (1977 through 1980) (1 of 2)

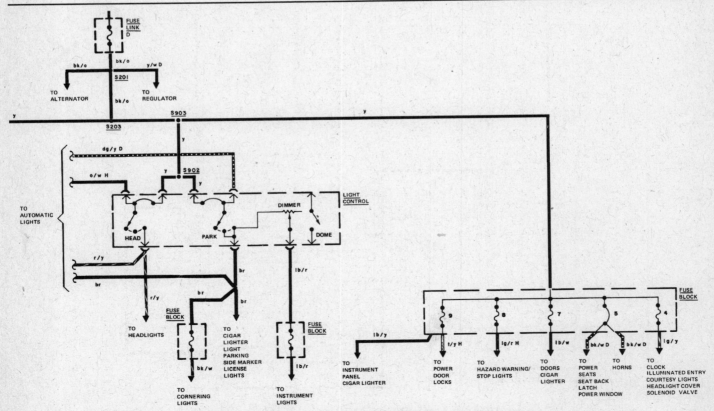

Typical power distribution wiring diagram (1977 through 1980) (2 of 2)

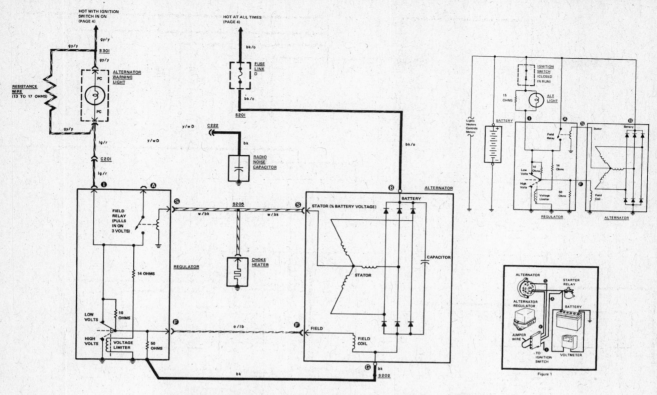

Typical charging system wiring diagram (1977 through 1980)

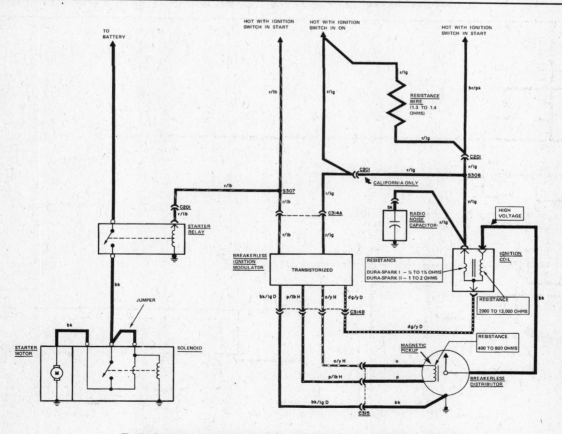

Typical starting and ignition system wiring diagram (1977 through 1980)

12

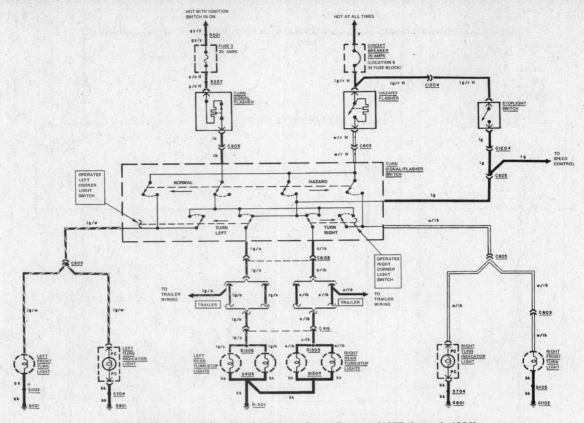

Typical turn signals and brake lights wiring diagram (1977 through 1980)

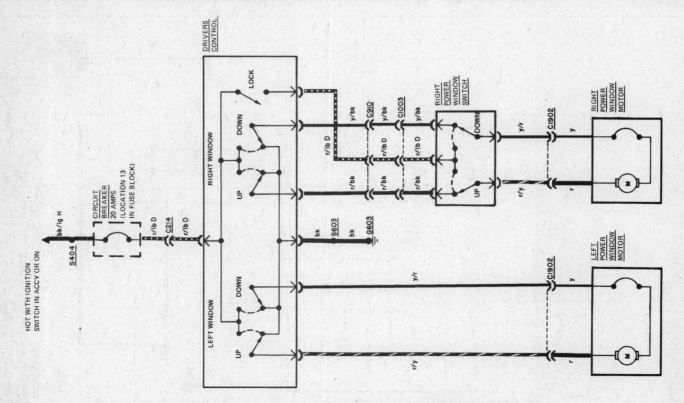

Typical power window system wiring diagram (1977 through 1980)

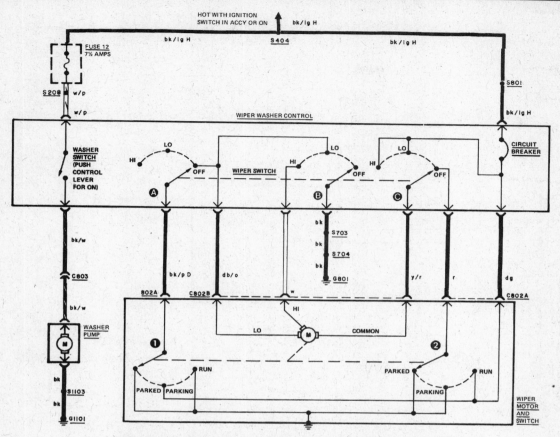

Typical windshield wiper and washer wiring diagram (1977 through 1980)

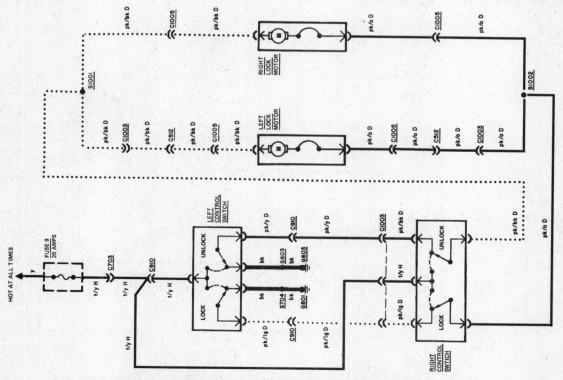

Typical power door lock system wiring diagram (1977 through 1980)

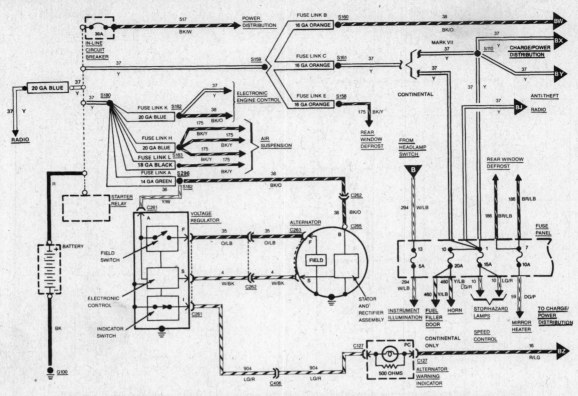

Typical charging system wiring diagram (1981 through 1988 Continental and Mark series)

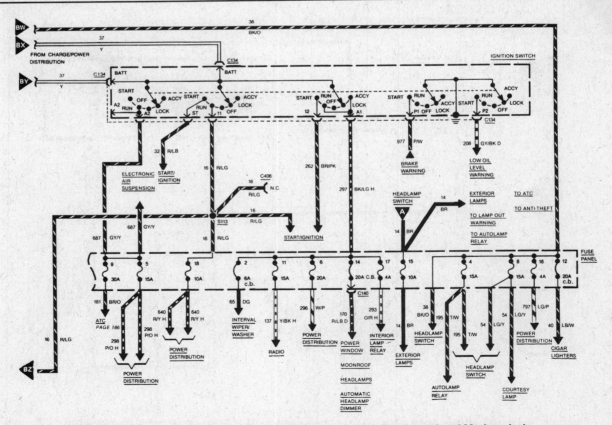

Typical power distribution wiring diagram (1981 through 1988 Continental and Mark series)

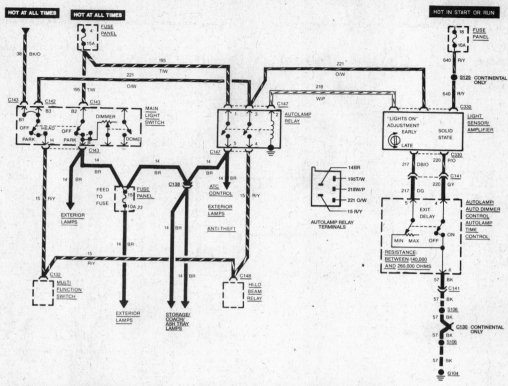

Typical headlight system wiring diagram (1981 through 1988 Continental and Mark series)

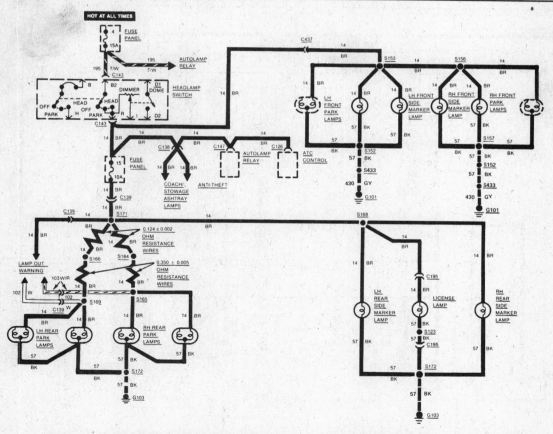

Typical exterior lighting system wiring diagram (1981 through 1988 Continental and Mark series)

12

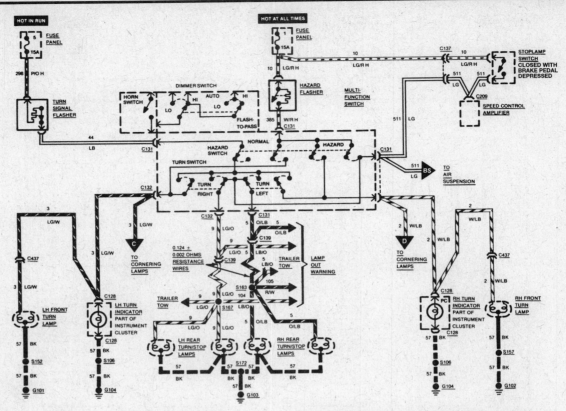

Typical turn signal/hazard lights wiring diagram (1981 through 1988 Continental and Mark series)

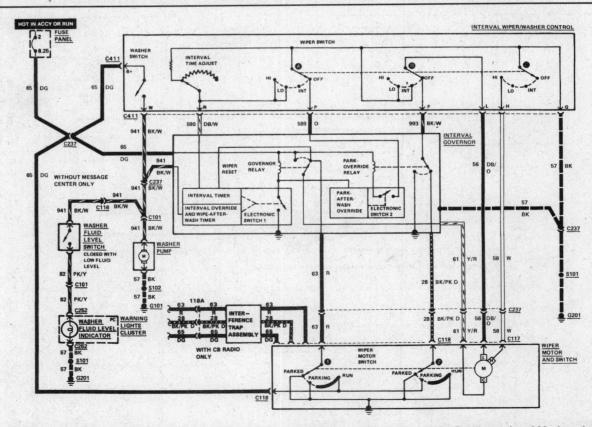

Typical interval windshield wiper and washer system wiring diagram (1981 through 1988 Continental and Mark series)

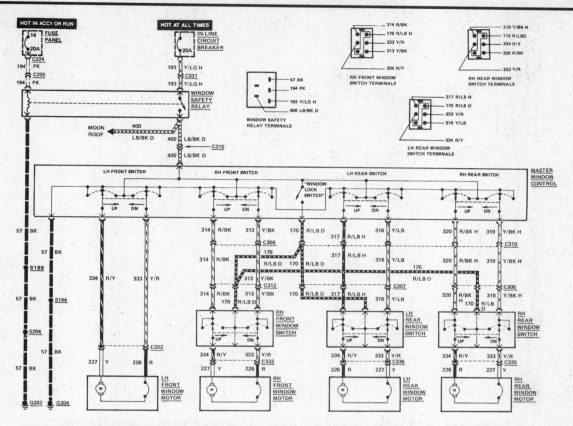

Typical power window system wiring diagram (1981 through 1988 Continental and Mark series)

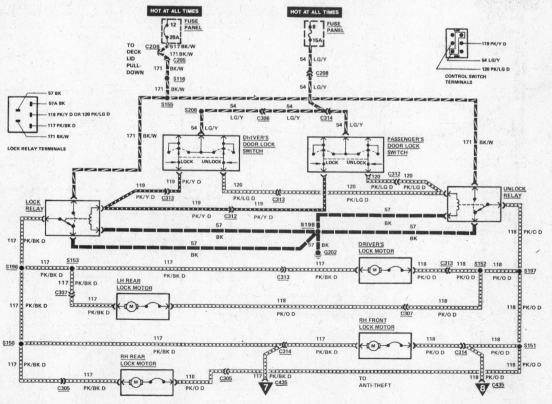

Typical power door lock system wiring diagram (1981 through 1988 Continental and Mark series)

12

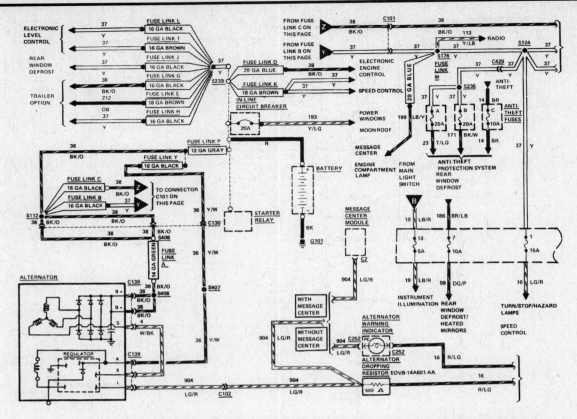

Typical charging system and power distribution wiring diagram (1987 through 1990 Town Car)

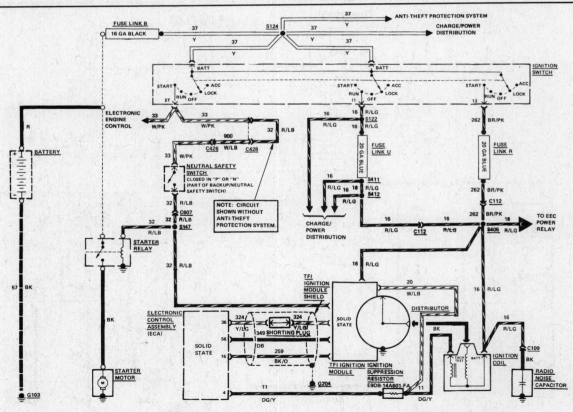

Typical starting and ignition system wiring diagram (1987 through 1990 Town Car)

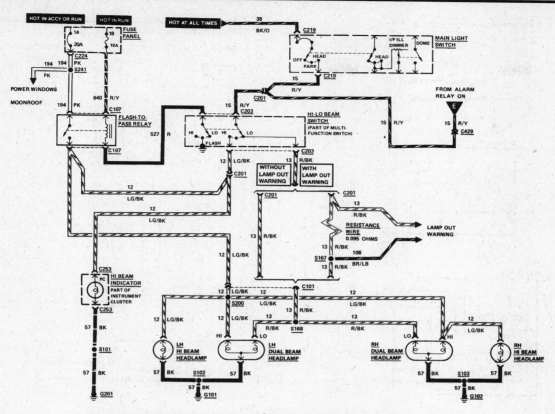

Typical headlight system wiring diagram (1987 through 1990 Town Car)

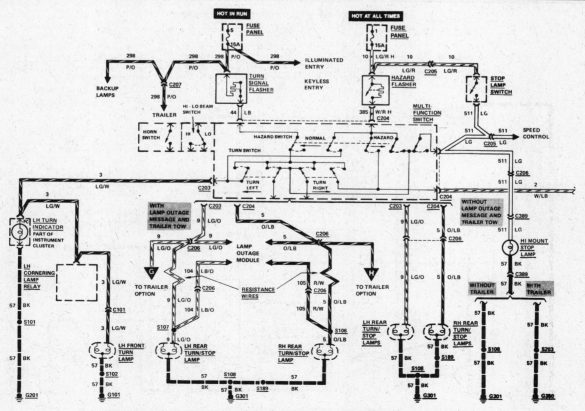

Typical turn signal and hazard lights wiring diagram (1987 through 1990 Town Car)

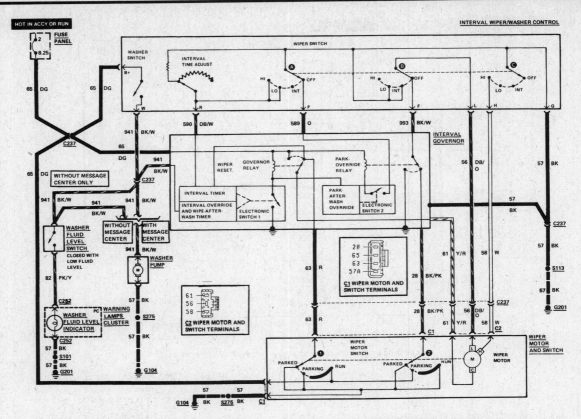

Typical windshield wiper and washer system wiring diagram (1987 through 1990 Town Car)

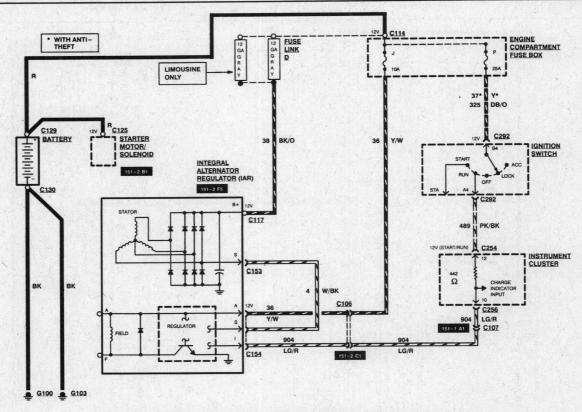

Typical charging system wiring diagram (1991 and later Town Car)

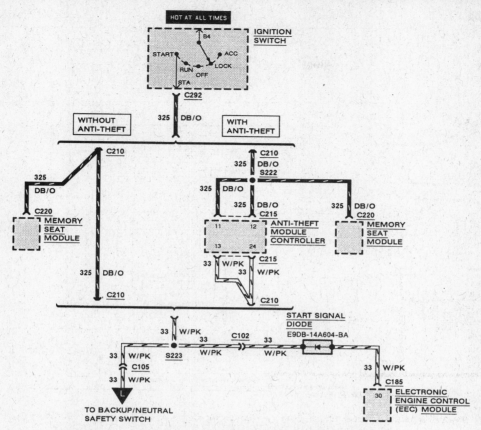

Typical starting system wiring diagram (1991 and later Town Car) (1 of 2)

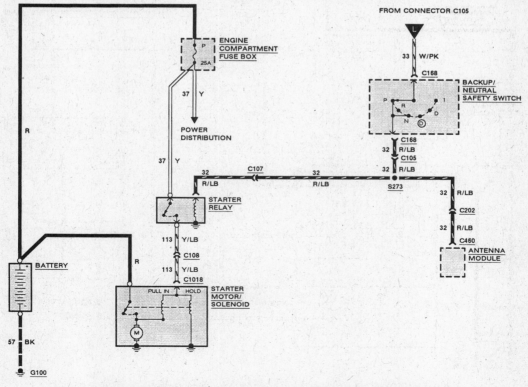

Typical starting system wiring diagram (1991 and later Town Car) (2 of 2)

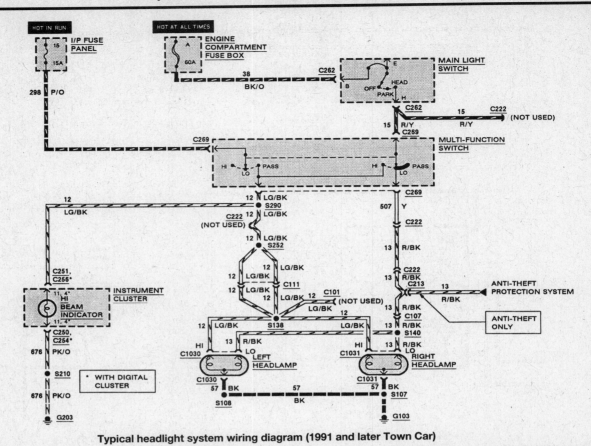

Typical headlight system wiring diagram (1991 and later Town Car)

Typical turn signal/hazard system wiring diagram (1991 and later Town Car) (1 of 2)

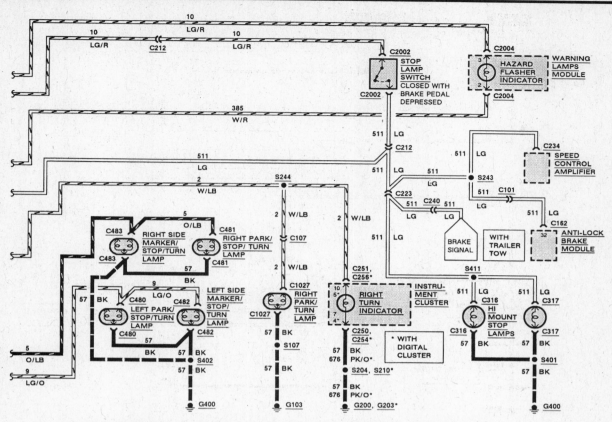

Typical turn signal/hazard system wiring diagram (1991 and later Town Car) (2 of 2)

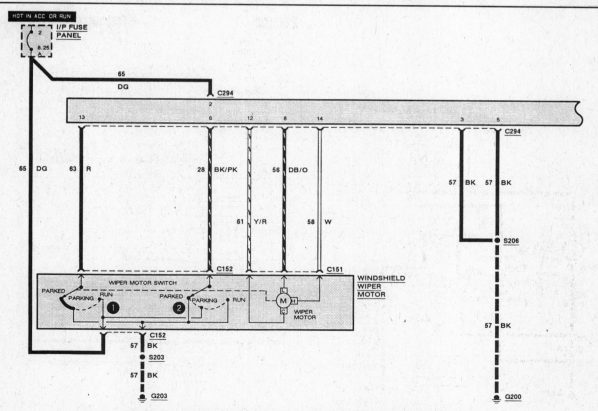

Typical windshield wiper system wiring diagram (1991 and later Town Car) (1 of 2)

12

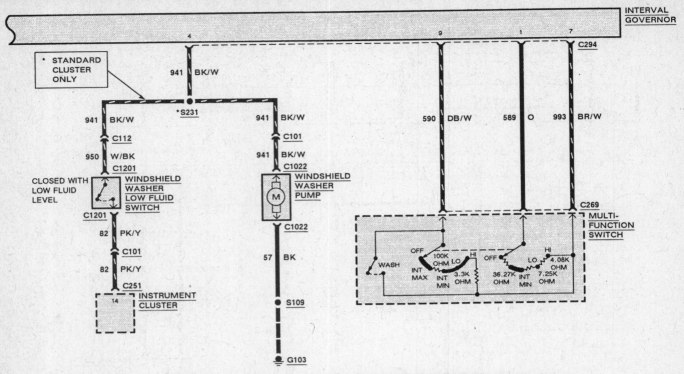

Typical windshield wiper system wiring diagram (1991 and later Town Car) (2 of 2)

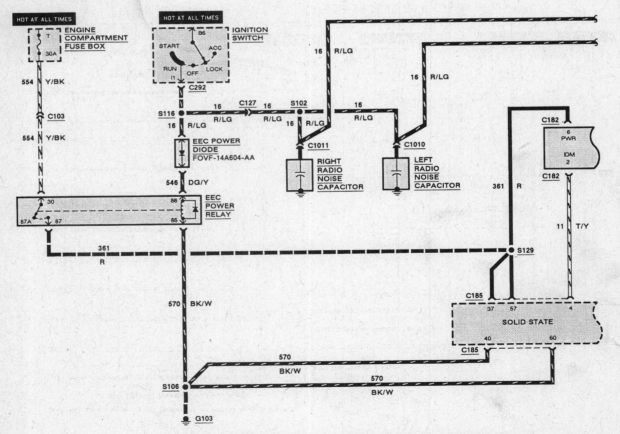

Typical ignition system wiring diagram (1991 and later Town Car) (1 of 2)

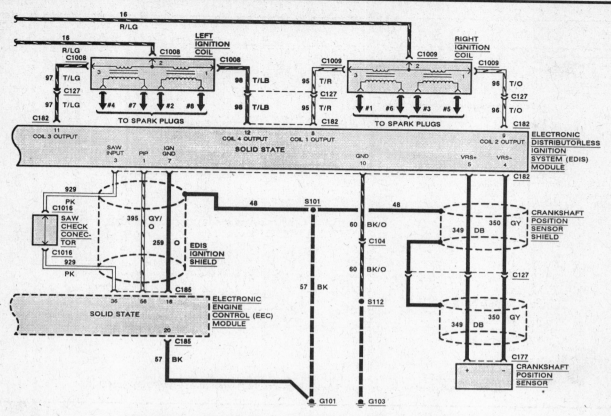

Typical ignition system wiring diagram (1991 and later Town Car) (2 of 2)

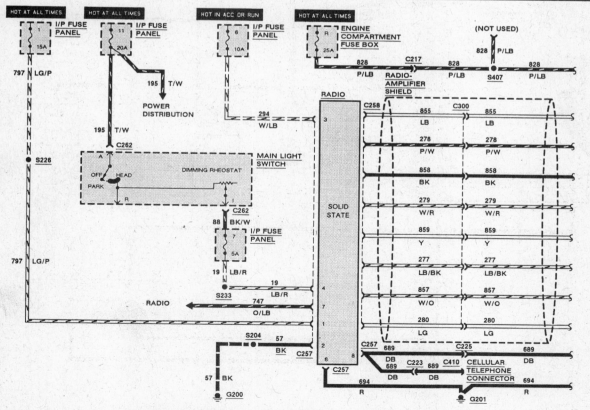

Typical radio system wiring diagram (1991 and later Town Car) (1 of 2)

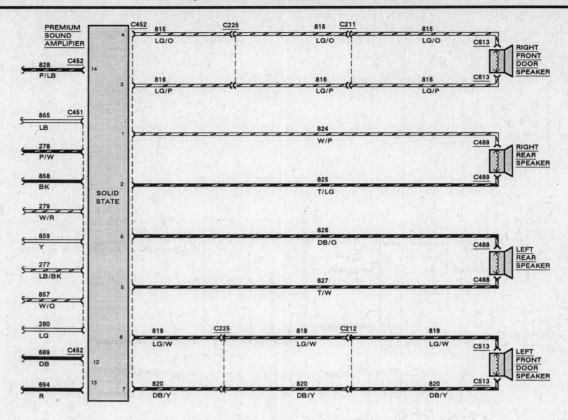

Typical radio system wiring diagram (1991 and later Town Car) (2 of 2)

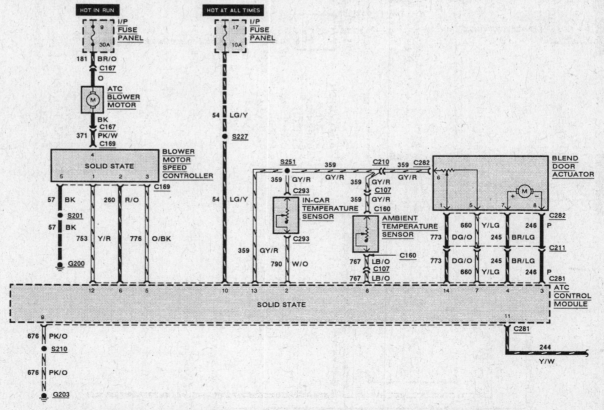

Typical heating and air conditioning system wiring diagram (1991 and later Town Car) (1 of 2)

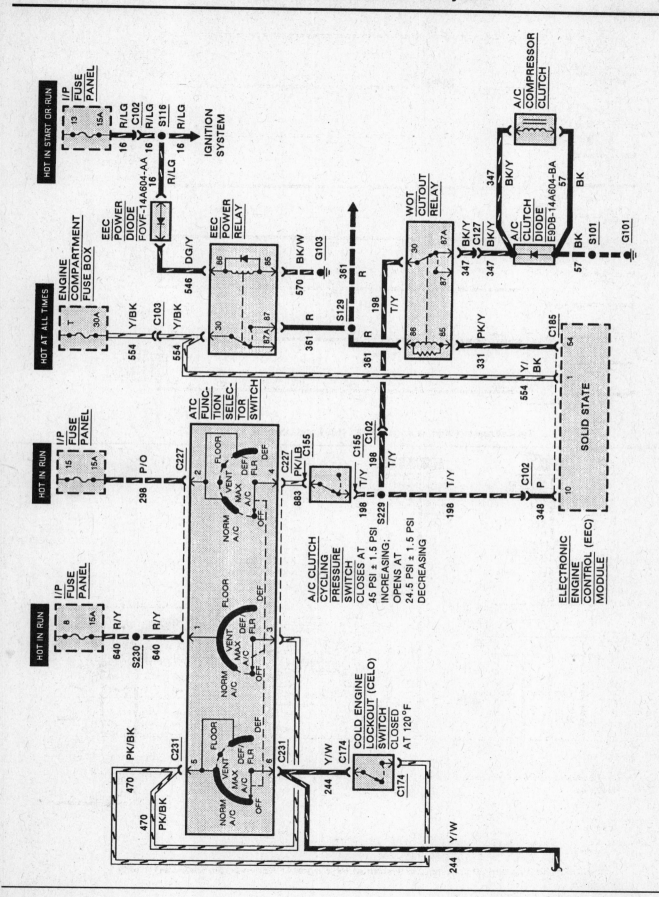

Typical heating and air conditioning system wiring diagram (1991 and later Town Car) (2 of 2)

12

Index

Haynes Automotive Manuals

NOTE: New manuals are added to this list on a periodic basis. If you do not see a listing for your vehicle, consult your local Haynes dealer for the latest product information.

ACURA
*1776	Integra & Legend '86 thru '90

AMC
	Jeep CJ - see JEEP (412)
694	Mid-size models, Concord, Hornet, Gremlin & Spirit '70 thru '83
934	(Renault) Alliance & Encore '83 thru '87

AUDI
615	4000 all models '80 thru '87
428	5000 all models '77 thru '83
1117	5000 all models '84 thru '88

AUSTIN
	Healey Sprite - see MG Midget (265)

BMW
*2020	3/5 Series not including diesel or all-wheel drive models '82 thru '92
276	320i all 4 cyl models '75 thru '83
632	528i & 530i all models '75 thru '80
240	1500 thru 2002 except Turbo '59 thru '77
348	2500, 2800, 3.0 & Bavaria '69 thru '76

BUICK
	Century (FWD) - see GM (829)
*1627	Buick, Oldsmobile & Pontiac Full-size (Front wheel drive) '85 thru '95 Buick Electra, LeSabre and Park Avenue; Oldsmobile Delta 88 Royale, Ninety Eight and Regency; Pontiac Bonneville
1551	Buick Oldsmobile & Pontiac Full-size (Rear wheel drive) Buick Estate '70 thru '90, Electra '70 thru '84, LeSabre '70 thru '85, Limited '74 thru '79 Oldsmobile Custom Cruiser '70 thru '90, Delta 88 '70 thru '85,Ninety-eight '70 thru '84 Pontiac Bonneville '70 thru '81, Catalina '70 thru '81, Grandville '70 thru '75, Parisienne '83 thru '86
627	Mid-size Regal & Century '74 thru '87 Regal - see GENERAL MOTORS (1671) Skyhawk - see GENERAL MOTORS (766) Skylark '80 thru '85 - see GM (38020) Skylark '86 on - see GM (1420) Somerset - see GENERAL MOTORS (1420)

CADILLAC
*751	Cadillac Rear Wheel Drive all gasoline models '70 thru '93 Cimarron - see GENERAL MOTORS (766)

CHEVROLET
*1477	Astro & GMC Safari Mini-vans '85 thru '93
554	Camaro V8 all models '70 thru '81
866	Camaro all models '82 thru '92 Cavalier - see GENERAL MOTORS (766) Celebrity - see GENERAL MOTORS (829)
625	Chevelle, Malibu, El Camino '69 thru '87
449	Chevette & Pontiac T1000 '76 thru '87 Citation - see GENERAL MOTORS (38020)
*1628	Corsica/Beretta all models '87 thru '95
274	Corvette all V8 models '68 thru '82
*1336	Corvette all models '84 thru '91
1762	Chevrolet Engine Overhaul Manual
704	Full-size Sedans Caprice, Impala, Biscayne, Bel Air & Wagons '69 thru '90 Lumina - see GENERAL MOTORS (1671) Lumina APV - see GM (2035)
319	Luv Pick-up all 2WD & 4WD '72 thru '82
626	Monte Carlo all models '70 thru '88
241	Nova all models '69 thru '79
*1642	Nova/Geo Prizm front wheel drive '85 thru '92
420	Pick-ups '67 thru '87 - Chevrolet & GMC, all V8 & in-line 6 cyl, 2WD & 4WD '67 thru '87; Suburbans, Blazers & Jimmys '67 thru '91
*1664	Pick-ups '88 thru '95 - Chevrolet & GMC, full-size models '88 thru '95; Blazer & Jimmy '92 thru '94; Suburban '92 thru '95; Tahoe & Yukon '95
*831	S-10 & GMC S-15 Pick-ups '82 thru '93
*1727	Sprint & Geo Metro '85 thru '94
*345	Vans - Chevrolet & GMC, V8 & in-line 6 cylinder models '68 thru '95

CHRYSLER
2114	Chrysler Engine Overhaul Manual
*2058	Full-size Front-Wheel Drive '88 thru '93 K-Cars - see DODGE Aries (723) Laser - see DODGE Daytona (1140)
*1337	Chrysler & Plymouth Mid-size front-wheel drive '82 thru '93; Rear-wheel drive - see DODGE Rear-wheel drive (2098)

DATSUN
402	200SX all models '77 thru '79
647	200SX all models '80 thru '83
228	B - 210 all models '73 thru '78
525	210 all models '78 thru '82
206	240Z, 260Z & 280Z Coupe '70 thru '78
563	280ZX Coupe & 2+2 '79 thru '83 300ZX - see NISSAN (1137)
679	310 all models '78 thru '82
123	510 & PL521 Pick-up '68 thru '73
430	510 all models '78 thru '81
372	610 all models '72 thru '76
277	620 Series Pick-up '73 thru '79 720 Series Pick-up - see NISSAN (771)
376	810/Maxima all gas models, '77 thru '84 Pulsar - see NISSAN (876)

DODGE
	400 & 600 - see CHRYSLER Mid-size (1337)
*723	Aries & Plymouth Reliant '81 thru '89
1231	Caravan & Plymouth Voyager Mini-Vans all models '84 thru '95
699	Challenger/Plymouth Saporro '78 thru '83
236	Challenger '67-'76 - see DODGE Dart (234)
610	Colt all models '71 thru '77
	Colt/Plymouth Champ (front wheel drive) all models '78 thru '87
*1668	Dakota Pick-ups all models '87 thru '93
234	Dart, Challenger/Plymouth Barracuda & Valiant 6 cyl models '67 thru '76
*1140	Daytona & Chrysler Laser '84 thru '89
*545	Omni & Plymouth Horizon '78 thru '90
*912	Pick-ups all full-size models '74 thru '91
*556	Ram 50/D50 Pick-ups & Raider and Plymouth Arrow Pick-ups '79 thru '93
2098	Dodge/Plymouth/Chrysler rear wheel drive '71 thru '89
*1726	Shadow/Plymouth Sundance '87 thru '93
*1779	Spirit & Plymouth Acclaim '89 thru '95
*349	Vans - Dodge & Plymouth '71 thru '91

EAGLE
	Talon - see Mitsubishi Eclipse (2097)

FIAT
094	124 Sport Coupe & Spider '68 thru '78
273	X1/9 all models '74 thru '80

FORD
*1476	Aerostar Mini-vans '86 thru '94
788	Bronco and Pick-ups '73 thru '79
*880	Bronco and Pick-ups '80 thru '95
268	Courier Pick-up all models '72 thru '82
2105	Crown Victoria & Mercury Grand Marquis '88 thru '94
1763	Ford Engine Overhaul Manual
789	Escort/Mercury Lynx '81 thru '90
*2046	Escort/Mercury Tracer '91 thru '95
*2021	Explorer & Mazda Navajo '91 thru '95
560	Fairmont & Mercury Zephyr '78 thru '83
334	Fiesta all models '77 thru '80
754	Ford & Mercury Full-size, Ford LTD & Mercury Marquis ('75 thru '82); Ford Custom 500,Country Squire, Crown Victoria & Mercury Colony Park ('75 thru '87); Ford LTD Crown Victoria & Mercury Gran Marquis ('83 thru '87)
359	Granada & Mercury Monarch '75 thru '80
773	Ford & Mercury Mid-size, Ford Thunderbird & Mercury Cougar ('75 thru '82); Ford LTD & Mercury Marquis ('83 thru '86); Ford Torino,Gran Torino, Elite, Ranchero pick-up, LTD II, Mercury Montego, Comet, XR-7 & Lincoln Versailles ('75 thru '86)
*654	Mustang & Mercury Capri incl. Turbo Mustang, '79 thru '93; Capri, '79 thru '86
357	Mustang V8 all models '64-1/2 thru '73
231	Mustang II 4 cyl, V6 & V8 '74 thru '78
649	Pinto & Mercury Bobcat '75 thru '80
1670	Probe all models '89 thru '92
*1026	Ranger/Bronco II gas models '83 thru '93
*1421	Taurus & Mercury Sable '86 thru '94
*1418	Tempo & Mercury Topaz '84 thru '94
1338	Thunderbird/Mercury Cougar '83 thru '88
*1725	Thunderbird/Mercury Cougar '89 and '93
344	Vans all V8 Econoline models '69 thru '91
*2119	Vans full size '92 thru '95

GENERAL MOTORS
*829	Buick Century, Chevrolet Celebrity, Olds Cutlass Ciera & Pontiac 6000 all models '82 thru '93
*1671	Buick Regal, Chevrolet Lumina, Oldsmobile Cutlass Supreme & Pontiac Grand Prix front wheel drive '88 thru '95
*766	Buick Skyhawk, Cadillac Cimarron, Chevrolet Cavalier, Oldsmobile Firenza Pontiac J-2000 & Sunbird '82 thru '94
38020	Buidk Skylar, Chevrolet Citation, Olds Omega, Pontiac Phoenix '80 thru '85
1420	Buick Skylark & Somerset, Olds Achieva, Calais & Pontiac Grand Am '85 thru '95
*2035	Chevrolet Lumina APV, Oldsmobile Silhouette & Pontiac Trans Sport '90 thru '94 General Motors Full-size Rear-wheel Drive - see BUICK (1551)

GEO
	Metro - see CHEVROLET Sprint (1727) Prizm - see CHEVROLET Nova (1642)
*2039	Storm all models '90 thru '93 Tracker - see SUZUKI Samurai (1626)

GMC
	Safari - see CHEVROLET ASTRO (1477) Vans & Pick-ups - see CHEVROLET (420, 831, 345, 1664)

HONDA
351	Accord CVCC all models '76 thru '83
1221	Accord all models '84 thru '89
2067	Accord all models '90 thru '93
*42013	Accord all models '94 thru '95
160	Civic 1200 all models '73 thru '79
633	Civic 1300 & 1500 CVCC '80 thru '83
297	Civic 1500 CVCC all models '75 thru '79
1227	Civic all models '84 thru '91
2118	Civic & del Sol '92 thru '95
*601	Prelude CVCC all models '79 thru '89

HYUNDAI
*1552	Excel all models '86 thru '94

ISUZU
*1641	Trooper & Pick-up, all gasoline models Pick-up, '81 thru '93; Trooper, '84 thru '91

JAGUAR
*242	XJ6 all 6 cyl models '68 thru '86
*478	XJ12 & XJS all 12 cyl models '72 thru '85

JEEP
*1553	Cherokee, Comanche & Wagoneer Limited all models '84 thru '93
412	CJ all models '49 thru '86
*50025	Grand Cherokee all models '93 thru '95
*1777	Wrangler all models '87 thru '94

LINCOLN
2117	Rear Wheel Drive all models '70 thru '95

MAZDA
648	626 (rear wheel drive) '79 thru '82
*1082	626 & MX-6 (front wheel drive) '83 thru '91
267	B Series Pick-ups '72 thru '93
370	GLC (rear wheel drive) '77 thru '83
757	GLC (front wheel drive) '81 thru '85
*2047	MPV all models '89 thru '94 Navajo - see FORD Explorer (2021)
460	RX-7 all models '79 thru '85
*1419	RX-7 all models '86 thru '91

MERCEDES-BENZ
*1643	190 Series 4-cyl gas models, '84 thru '88
346	230, 250 & 280 6 cyl sohc '68 thru '72
983	280 123 Series gas models '77 thru '81
698	350 & 450 all models '71 thru '80
697	Diesel 123 Series '76 thru '85

MERCURY
	See FORD Listing

MG
111	MGB Roadster & GT Coupe '62 thru '80
265	MG Midget & Austin Healey Sprite Roadster '58 thru '80

MITSUBISHI
*1669	Cordia, Tredia, Galant, Precis & Mirage '83 thru '93
2097	Eclipse, Eagle Talon & Plymouth Laser '90 thru '94
*2022	Pick-up & Montero '83 thru '95

NISSAN
1137	300ZX all models incl. Turbo '84 thru '89
*1341	Maxima all models '85 thru '91
*771	Pick-ups/Pathfinder gas models '80 thru '95
876	Pulsar all models '83 thru '86
*982	Sentra all models '82 thru '94
*981	Stanza all models '82 thru '90

OLDSMOBILE
	Bravada - see CHEVROLET S-10 (831) Calais - see GENERAL MOTORS (1420) Custom Cruiser - see BUICK (1551)
*658	Cutlass '74 thru '88 Cutlass Ciera - see GM (829) Cutlass Supreme - see GM (1671) Delta 88 - see BUICK Full-size RWD (1551) Delta 88 Brougham - see BUICK Full-size: FWD (1551), RWD (1551) Delta 88 Royale - see BUICK (1551) Firenza - see GENERAL MOTORS (766) Ninety-eight Regency - see BUICK Full-size RWD (1551), FWD (1627) Omega - see GENERAL MOTORS (38020) Silhouette - see GENERAL MOTORS (2035)

PEUGEOT
663	504 all diesel models '74 thru '83

PLYMOUTH
	Laser - see MITSUBISHI Eclipse (2097) Other PLYMOUTH titles, see DODGE

PONTIAC
	T1000 - see CHEVROLET Chevette (449) J-2000 - see GENERAL MOTORS (766) 6000 - see GM (829) Bonneville - see Buick Full-size FWD (1627), RWD (1551) Bonneville Brougham - see Buick (1551) Catalina - see Buick Full-size (1551)
1232	Fiero all models '84 thru '88
555	Firebird V8 models except Turbo '70 thru '81
867	Firebird all models '82 thru '92 Full-size Front Wheel Drive - see BUICK Oldsmobile, Pontiac Full-size FWD (1627) Full-size Rear Wheel Drive - see BUICK Oldsmobile, Pontiac Full-size RWD (1551) Grand Am - see GM (1420) Grand Prix - see GM (1671) Grandville - see BUICK (1551) Parisienne - see BUICK (1551) Phoenix - see GM (38020)

PORSCHE
	Sunbird - see GENERAL MOTORS (766) Trans Sport - see GM (2035)
*264	911 all Coupe & Targa models except Turbo & Carrera 4 '65 thru '89
239	914 all 4 cyl models '69 thru '76
397	924 all models incl. Turbo '76 thru '82
*1027	944 all models incl. Turbo '83 thru '89

RENAULT
141	5 Le Car all models '76 thru '83 Alliance & Encore - see AMC (934)

SAAB
247	99 all models including Turbo '69 thru '80
*980	900 including Turbo '79 thru '88

SATURN
*2083	Saturn all models '91 thru '94

SUBARU
237	1100, 1300, 1400 & 1600 '71 thru '79
*681	1600 & 1800 2WD & 4WD '80 thru '89

SUZUKI
*1626	Samurai/Sidekick/Geo Tracker '86 thru '95

TOYOTA
1023	Camry all models '83 thru '91
*92006	Camry all models '92 thru '95
935	Celica Rear Wheel Drive '71 thru '85
*2038	Celica Front Wheel Drive '86 thru '92
1139	Celica Supra all models '79 thru '92
361	Corolla all models '75 thru '79
961	Corolla rear wheel drive models '80 thru '87
*1025	Corolla front wheel drive models '84 thru '92
636	Corolla Tercel all models '80 thru '82
360	Corona all models '74 thru '82
532	Cressida all models '78 thru '82
313	Land Cruiser all models '68 thru '82
*1339	MR2 all models '85 thru '87
304	Pick-up all models '69 thru '78
*656	Pick-up all models '79 thru '95
*2048	Previa all models '91 thru '93
2106	Tercel all models '87 thru '94

TRIUMPH
113	Spitfire all models '62 thru '81
322	TR7 all models '75 thru '81

VW
159	Beetle & Karmann Ghia '54 thru '79
238	Dasher all models '74 thru '81
*884	Rabbit, Jetta, Scirocco, & Pick-up gas models '74 thru '91 & Convertible '80 thru '92
451	Rabbit, Jetta & Pick-up diesel models '77 thru '84
082	Transporter 1600 all models '68 thru '79
226	Transporter 1700, 1800, 2000 '72 thru '79
084	Type 3 1500 & 1600 '63 thru '73
1029	Vanagon air-cooled models '80 thru '83

VOLVO
203	120, 130 Series & 1800 Sports '61 thru '73
129	140 Series all models '66 thru '74
*270	240 Series all models '76 thru '93
400	260 Series all models '75 thru '82
*1550	740 & 760 Series all models '82 thru '88

TECHBOOK MANUALS
2108	Automotive Computer Codes
1667	Automotive Emissions Control Manual
482	Fuel Injection Manual, 1978 thru 1985
2111	Fuel Injection Manual, 1986 thru 1994
2069	Holley Carburetor Manual
2068	Rochester Carburetor Manual
10240	Weber/Zenith/Stromberg/SU Carburetor
1762	Chevrolet Engine Overhaul Manual
2114	Chrysler Engine Overhaul Manual
1763	Ford Engine Overhaul Manual
1736	GM and Ford Diesel Engine Repair
1666	Small Engine Repair Manual
10355	Ford Automatic Transmission Overhaul
10360	GM Automatic Transmission Overhaul
1479	Automotive Body Repair & Painting
2112	Automotive Brake Manual
2113	Automotive Detailing Manual
1654	Automotive Eelectrical Manual
1480	Automotive Heating & Air Conditioning
2109	Automotive Reference Manual & Illustrated Dictionary
2107	Automotive Tools Manual
10440	Used Car Buying Guide
2110	Welding Manual

SPANISH MANUALS
98905	Códigos Automotrices de la Computadora
98915	Inyección de Combustible 1986 al 1994
99040	Chevrolet & GMC Camionetas '67 al '87 Incluye Suburban, Blazer & Jimmy '67 al '91
99041	Chevrolet & GMC Camionetas '88 al '95 Incluye Suburban '92 al '95, Blazer & Jimmy '92 al '94, Tahoe y Yukon '95
99075	Ford Camionetas y Bronco '80 al '94
99125	Toyota Camionetas y 4-Runner '79 al '95

Listings shown with an asterisk (*) indicate model coverage as of this printing. These titles will be periodically updated to include later model years - consult your Haynes dealer for more information.

Nearly 100 Haynes motorcycle manuals also available

2-96

Haynes North America, Inc., 861 Lawrence Drive, Newbury Park, CA 91320 • (805) 498-6703